THE ISOLATIONIST IMPULSE
Its Twentieth-Century Reaction

SELIG ADLER
Professor of History, University of Buffalo

THE

ISOLATIONIST IMPULSE

Its Twentieth Century Reaction

COLLIER BOOKS
NEW YORK, N.Y.

This Collier Books edition is published by arrangement with Abelard-Schuman Limited.

Collier Books is a division of The Crowell-Collier Publishing Company.

First Collier Books Edition 1961

Library of Congress Catalog Card Number: 57-5629

Permissions

PERMISSIONS FOR THE USE of passages of copyrighted material from the following publishers and authors is gratefully acknowledged: Harper & Brothers, for *America's Rise to World Power, 1898-1954*, by Foster Rhea Dulles; Houghton Mifflin Company, for *Their Finest Hour* (*The Second World War*, Vol. II), by Winston S. Churchill; for *The Private Papers of Senator Vandenberg*, edited by Arthur H. Vandenberg, Jr. and Joe. A. Morris; Prentice-Hall, Inc., for *A History of United States Foreign Policy*, by Julius W. Pratt; The Macmillan Company, for *The Memoirs of Cordell Hull*; and *Time, Inc.*, for *Memoirs by Harry S. Truman*.

The author wishes to thank the Duke University Press for permission to use material from his article, "The Congressional Election of 1918," published in the October, 1937, issue of the *South Atlantic Quarterly*; and The University of Chicago Press for leave to draw on material from his article, "The War-Guilt Question and American Disillusionment, 1918-1928," published in the March, 1951, issue of *The Journal of Modern History*. He also wishes to thank *The American Scholar* for transferring to him the copyright on his article, "Isolationism Since 1914," originally published in the Summer, 1952, issue of that magazine.

Contents

TO

Janet, Ellen *and* Joseph Gary

Preface

ON FRIDAY, September 18, 1931, I arrived at the University of Illinois to pursue graduate study in the field of American History. The next day the newspaper headlines were black with the story of the Japanese invasion of Manchuria, an event destined to mark the dividing line between the temporary stability established by the 1919 Versailles settlement and the ruthless aggressions that were to culminate in another World War. The faculty was deeply stirred by the Japanese coup, the fumblings of the League of Nations, and the ominous threats of war in a world immobilized by economic depression.

The late Professor James W. Garner, Chairman of the Department of Political Science at Illinois, was especially moved by these tragic events. It was Professor Garner who first called my attention to the political, economic, and social forces that had undermined Woodrow Wilson's plan for collective security. I investigated the beginnings of the post-1918 reaction against international idealism in my master's thesis, but I later left the problem to write of a more remote period in our history.

My work at Illinois was completed just as the dictators of the 1930s were fulfilling Professor Garner's melancholy prophecies about the contagious nature of aggression. Once more I returned to foreign problems of the Wilson Era and became familiar with the available source material for the period. The 1941 collapse of neutrality, the new American war effort, and the renewed search for a durable peace stimulated my interest in isolationism as a persistent force in American history.

My original plan was for an intensive study of isolationism from the beginnings of the First World War to the onset of the Great Depression. I knew how embarrassingly rich the sources were for even so limited a period; I hoped to increase the intensity of my research by narrowing the time span and by focusing my attention primarily on the political ramifications of isolationism. From the beginning I wanted to do something more than merely tread the well-worn path blazed by competent scholars who had already explored the rejection by the Senate of the Treaty of Versailles, the abortive attempts of the United States to secure peace through disarmament and the outlawry of war, and the monotonous battles over the World Court. My object, therefore, was to blend diplomatic and intellectual history in such a way as to throw light on the first pendulum-like swings of public opinion in our century between the extremes of isolationism and internationalism. I did not attempt a study of diplomatic history in the traditional sense; I tried rather to weigh the impact of certain ideas and attitudes on contemporary American foreign policy and to trace the pattern of post-Wilsonian isolationist thought.

The major emphasis of my early research was on the causes and the manifold repercussions of these changes in mass opinion. To investigate the cause and effect of the resurgence of isolationism after 1918, I examined the writings of historians and other social scientists, the private correspondence, speeches, and published writings of politicians, the preachments of religious leaders, the speculations of philosophers, and the contemporary statements and memoirs of men of affairs. I tried to trace basic alterations in the assumptions and feelings of the average man as the notions of the molders of thought penetrated to the masses.

An analysis of modern American isolationism must begin with the composition of the weird coalition that frustrated Wilson's aims and halted the more limited objectives of his immediate successors. After explaining in detail the origin of this coalition, I found it essential to investigate the factors that intensified isolationism after 1920 and to evaluate the alternative plans to collective security. Ever since 1914 there have been, in addition to the uncompromising isolationists and the avid international cooperationists, a large number of people who strove for a policy of compromise between these opposite positions. A triple focus was therefore inevitable, for the three camps influenced each other in both theory and action.

In 1952, a grant-in-aid from the Social Science Research Council of Washington, D.C. made it possible for me to travel extensively in search of manuscript and other vital source materials. I owe this organization a special debt of gratitude, for its help made it possible for me to complete my original investigations.

At the suggestion of Mr. Lew Schwartz, president of Abelard-Schuman Limited, and his able editor, Mrs. Lillian L. McClintock, the scope of this work as first projected has been enlarged. In view of the popular nature of the subject it seemed best to write a book of general rather than specialized interest. My task in bringing the narrative beyond 1929 was greatly eased by a grant from the Committee on the Allocation of Research Funds of the University of Buffalo. The generosity of this committee made it possible for me to engage the services of competent research assistants, to do some additional research work outside of Buffalo, and to secure help in compiling the index.

In presenting a fuller analysis of isolationism, designed for the general reading public as well as for the guild of historians, it was necessary to include a brief examination of the historical roots of the tradition. In my introductory chapter, I have drawn heavily upon the findings of other writers who have already probed these origins. In order to carry the story forward through the past quarter century, I found it necessary to confine my reading to certain pertinent government documents, newspapers, periodicals, biographical material, highly specialized monographs, and general works on recent American history. More definitive conclusions on the recent course of isolationist thought must await the opening of primary sources now unavailable and the passage of time to lend clearer perspective to the complicated events of the past two and a half decades. Though phases of the isolationist theme have been fully developed by able scholars, no one, so far as I have been able to ascertain, has ever attempted as broad a treatment as the present undertaking with all its planned limitations.

In preparing this work for its present purpose I have found it necessary, in the main, to limit annotations to direct quotations, manuscript sources, and authors of secondary works to whom I was particularly indebted. The chapters dealing with the period subsequent to the outbreak of the Second World War are more fully documented because they deal with highly controversial matters and because here my conclusions have necessarily been more tentative.

In seven years of intensive reading on isolationism, I have absorbed, consciously and unconsciously, many ideas from the host of writers who have touched upon the subject. In view of the limited documentation possible, I have tried to acknowledge part of my intellectual debt by citing all fundamental sources and secondary works in the bibliography. Moreover, I hope that this extensive list of sources will prove useful to future investigators who may wish to study further the almost unmanageable mass of material relating to American isolationism.

Such merit as this book may have may be credited, in large measure, to a host of long-suffering friends and colleagues. Their sage advice resolved many doubts, their keen eyes detected mistakes of fact and reasoning, and their fine literary sense helped me prepare the manuscript in its present form. For the errors that, despite their diligence, have crept into my work, I alone am responsible.

I wish here to attest my obligations to the men and women to whom I am most heavily indebted. Professor Howard K. Beale, of the University of Wisconsin, read five chapters of the book in an early stage of its development and gave me the full benefit of his seasoned judgment and remarkable erudition. The final six chapters were carefully reviewed by Professor Glyndon G. Van Deusen, chairman of the Department of History at the University of Rochester. I am profoundly grateful to him for many cogent suggestions and illuminating criticisms.

Professors Thomas E. Connolly, Lyle E. Glazier, Henry Ten Eyck Perry, and Dr. Constantine N. Stavrou of the University of Buffalo's Department of English gave me many valuable suggestions about style and syntax.

It is a pleasure to express my appreciation to the fine team of co-workers who helped me so much in various stages of my endeavor. Mrs. John F. Reid, who enjoys the double advantage of professional training in both journalism and history, read and improved all of my chapters. She gave unstintingly of her time and remarkable literary ability. Mr. Robert F. Wesser, now pursuing graduate work at the University of Rochester, spent countless hours corroborating my facts, checking my footnotes, and preparing the manuscript for publication. My typist, Miss Dorothy E. Eells, gave me many services over and above the call of duty. It was my good fortune to secure the services of Miss Elizabeth R. Seymour, a graduate student in the University of Chicago's Department of History, for the preparation of the index.

In a special manner I wish to mention the generous help of Professor John T. Horton, chairman of my department, and Julius W. Pratt, Samuel P. Capen Distinguished Professor of American History at the University of Buffalo. With rare patience Professor Horton reviewed my problems, listened to my conclusions, and suggested changes in my reasoning and rhetoric. Professor Pratt gave me the benefit of his acute critical sense and masterful grasp of American diplomatic history by reading and criticizing many chapters in this book.

I also wish to acknowledge the tireless assistance of my

wife, Janet S. Adler. Her enduring cooperation made it possible for me to complete my work.

Selig Adler

October 15, 1956

Acknowledgments

IN MY ACADEMIC investigations I received invaluable aid and many helpful courtesies from librarians and archivists. I am especially grateful to Mrs. Margaret M. Mott, Mr. Paul E. Rooney, Miss Helen Cleland, and other staff members of the Grosvenor Reference Division of the Buffalo and Erie County Public Libraries, and to Mr. Edward F. Ellis, Reference Librarian at the Lockwood Memorial Library, University of Buffalo. In addition, my sincere appreciation is extended to the staffs of the New York Public Library, the Library of Congress, the Newberry Library, the Library of the Chicago *Tribune,* the Cornell Unversity Libraries, and the Rush Rhees Library of the University of Rochester.

I also wish to express my warmest thanks to the people who graciously granted me permission to read private manuscripts in the trusteeship of their families, and to the archivists who helped me use this material profitably. These include Mrs. William E. Borah; Mrs. Albert J. Beveridge; the family of the late Chief Justic Charles Evans Hughes; Mr. David C. Mearns, Chief, Manuscripts Division of the Library of Congress, as well as Miss Katharine E. Brand of this Division; Professor Paul W. Gates of Cornell University; Mrs. Edith M. Fox, Curator and University Archivist, Cornell University; Mr. William A. Jackson of The Houghton Library, Harvard University; Mr. Henry M. Fuller, Reference Librarian, Yale University Library; Dr. Stanley Pargellis, Librarian, The Newberry Library; Mr. Herman Kahn, Director, National Archives and Records Service, Franklin D. Roosevelt Library, Hyde Park, N. Y.; and Mr. Roland Baughman, Head of Special Collections, The Libraries of Columbia University.

I wish here to express my appreciation to the following colleagues and friends from other seats of learning who helped me in the gracious manner characteristic of American scholars: Dr. Moshe Davis, Provost of the Jewish Theological Seminary of America; Professor Frank Freidel of Harvard University; Mr. Milton Kessler, now a graduate student at the University of Washington; Mr. Joseph E. McGurn, formerly a graduate student at the University of Rochester; Professor Allan Nevins of Columbia University; Professors Richard W. Leopold and Arthur S. Link of Northwestern University; Professor Jacob R. Marcus of Hebrew Union College; Professor Dexter Perkins of Cornell University; and Dr. Norman Weaver of the State University of New York College for Teachers, Buffalo.

I owe special debts of gratitude to Dr. Abraham E. Millgram of the Jewish Theological Seminary of America for his sustained and friendly interest in my project, and to Messrs. Edward H. Kavinoky, Arnold B. Gardner, and Manus Roizen of Buffalo for intelligent lay criticism and cogent advice.

Because the subject of modern isolationism touched upon so many related disciplines, I asked many questions of specialists in various fields here at the University of Buffalo and my colleagues gave unselfishly of their time and knowledge. I wish to thank for particular favors: G. Lester Anderson, Vice-Chancellor for Educational Affairs; Mrs. Elwood G. Becker, Secretary of the Department of History and Government; Charles Jacques Beyer, Professor of Romance Languages; Harold A. Boner, Associate Professor of English; Willard H. Bonner, The James H. McNulty Professor of English; B. Richard Bugelski, Professor of Psychology; Edgar B. Cale, Professor of Political Science; Nathaniel Cantor, Professor of Sociology; Raymond Chambers, Professor of Economic History; Ronald H. Coase, Professor of Economics; Ralph C. Epstein, Professor of Economics; Marvin Farber, Distinguished Professor of Philosophy; Richard H. Heindel, Vice-Chancellor for Planning and Development and Professor of History and Government; Fritz L. Kaufmann, Associate Professor of Philosophy; Dr. Isaac Klein, Lecturer in Philosophy and Rabbi of Temple Emanu-El of Buffalo; Clinton M. Osborn, Professor of Biology; Julian Park, Professor of European History; Reginald H. Pegrum, Professor of Geology; J. Alan Pfeffer, Professor of German; Milton Plesur, Acting Director of the Division of General and Technical Studies; Dr. S. Mouchly Small, Professor of Psychiatry; Dr. Charles W. Stein, sometime Lecturer in History and Government; Robert H. Stern, Associate Professor of Government; Kurt P. Tauber, Assistant Professor of Government; and Dean Henry M. Woodburn of the Graduate School of Arts and Sciences.

To those men and women whose favors I inadvertently neglected to record or recall, I extend my apology and my appreciation.

Chapter 1

The Isolationist Glacier

THE HEARTBEAT of American isolationism continues to throb long after some over-eager historical coroners have completed their inquests. Why has this tradition shown such enduring vigor at a time when every school child knows that we live in one world? The answer to this strange paradox lies in the fact that the isolationist impulse has been woven into the warp and woof of the American epic.

Geographical factors led the earliest Americans to think in terms of a divided world. Such maps as were available to the colonists pictured the oceans in surrealistic proportions. From their own experience or that of their fathers they knew that the Atlantic was rough and hazardous to cross. They reasoned that God Himself had intended to divide the globe into separate spheres. America was the "New Zion" and Providence had severed this "American Israel" from a time-worn, corrupt, and warring continent. There seemed to be little sense in jeopardizing the peace of the New World with the ingrained rivalries of the Old. European wars could mean nothing but trouble for America.

Our colonial forefathers were the pawns of European diplomats. They had been repeatedly inconvenienced by conflicts that did not involve their immediate interest. The peace negotiated after each recurrent war for empire, so they thought, was concerned with European, not American welfare. Often forgetting that some of these wars had been necessary for their own protection from the encroachment of the Spanish, French, or Indians, these colonial pioneers remembered, instead, bickering with the mother country over British self-interest. Why not stay out of the European snare, be "free from Warre," live and let live, and do business as usual?[1] Eighteenth-century colonials were budding isolationists. For almost three centuries Americans have been mulling over the problem of confining conflicts to the Old World. They early acquired the habit of trying to shut out as much European turmoil as conditions would allow.

Such thoughts crystallized after the British victory in 1763 had exorcised the French menace in Canada. Thus, a spirit

15

of isolationism was rampant in the colonies before the first shot was fired at Lexington and Concord. John Adams summed it up well when, in 1775, he declared "we ought to lay it down, as a first principle and maxim never to be forgotten, to maintain an entire neutrality in all future European wars."[2]

The American Revolution was in itself an act of isolation, for it cut the umbilical cord with the mother country. Victory, to be sure, came because of an entangling alliance with the French king. This self-evident fact was soon obscured when American neutrality was endangered by the wars of the French Revolution. One can probe anywhere into the writings of the Founding Fathers and be certain to come upon the suggestion that the United States, alliance or no alliance, should stay out of Europe's wars. President George Washington disseminated this common point of view. His decision not to pay much attention to the literal terms of our pact with France added something new to the concept of isolation—we must be neutral in wars not impinging upon our vital interests. Henceforth, isolationism and neutrality would be studied together in the pages of our history books.

In 1796, Washington's Farewell Address was published in the newspapers. This valedictory was destined to be enshrined beside the Declaration of Independence and the Constitution as a national classic. The President warned against "permanent alliances," pointed up the perils of taking sides in Europe's chronic squabbles and invited his countrymen to capitalize upon their "detached and distant situation." With characteristic realism, however, he added that "we may safely trust to temporary alliances for extraordinary emergencies."

Washington's admonitions were taken to heart by a nation of hero-worshippers. Future generations, neglecting to consider his qualifying phrases, read new meaning into his words, added corollaries to his propositions, and tailored his doctrines to meet their own needs. In time, says Adlai E. Stevenson, men forgot that the first President's light was "a candle and his transportation a horse." Was Washington speaking only to his contemporaries or to generations yet unborn? No matter how one answers this debatable question, it is safe to say that the Father of our Country made neutrality and non-intervention national fixations. Thomas Jefferson, the spiritual polestar of every major American political party save the Federalists, further imbedded isolationism in the public mind. In his First Inaugural, Jefferson set forth our foreign policy in words that were to echo down through the ages: "Honest friendship with all nations, entangling alliances with none."

The isolationism of the Revolutionary Era possessed a dynamic quality that men of the future failed to perceive. The earliest PRESIDENTS guided the destiny of a weak and untried republic, striving to make its mark in a warring, unfriendly, and monarchical world. Independence, in the full sense of the term, had yet to be achieved. The United States was hemmed in on three sides by European colonialism. London, Paris, and Madrid tried to meddle in our domestic affairs and incite the Indians against us. Hence our statesmen regarded isolationism as a positive policy designed to insure American freedom of action, to prevent foreign subversion, and to enable us to take advantage of Europe's distress in order to round out our own boundaries. The Founding Fathers would have been startled to learn that later generations, speaking in their name, would use non-intervention and neutrality to escape the grim realities of *Machtpolitik*. Strategies formulated by the Fathers as the means of statecraft became in time the final goals of American diplomacy.

As long as war continued in Napoleonic Europe, American statesmen had to keep a close finger on the European pulse. Prior to 1815 it was clearly evident that the security of the United States was at the mercy of events beyond our borders. Our sailors were impressed by Britain, our commerce was despoiled by French and English ships, and political decisions reached in European council chambers governed the fortunes of American farmers and merchants. We blundered into the War of 1812 and, despite our ocean moats, a British fleet sailed up Chesapeake Bay to burn the Capitol and the White House. Through a series of fortunate circumstances the war was liquidated without American loss of territory or prestige. Napoleon was at St. Helena and glorious peace settled over an exhausted world. What now of isolationism? Oddly enough, it was to enjoy increased vitality during that interlude of comparative tranquillity between the downfall of Emperor Napoleon I and the war against Emperior William II of Germany.

There are many reasons for the growth of isolationism in the nineteenth century. By 1821 we had doubled our territory through the Louisiana Purchase, settled immediate differences with Great Britain, and freed ourselves of the Spanish stranglehold on Florida. Foreigners no longer supplied hostile Indian tribes with firewater and rifles. Americans could afford to relax their vigil on the Atlantic scene and turn their faces westward in the direction of the Pacific.

This welcome respite from world politics was briefly interrupted when, in the early 1820s, Russia pushed southward from Alaska and the European Quadruple Alliance seemed ready to help Spain regain her Latin American empire. The theory of isolationism was freshened and restated in the pronouncement of the Monroe Doctrine. Faced with possible European designs against the New World, President James Monroe said "Hands Off." In his celebrated message to Congress of December 2, 1823, Monroe emphasized once more the policy of non-involvement. He indicated that geography divided the world into two spheres and that the New World must insulate itself from the ambitions and disputes of the Old. The President thus joined the older policy of neutrality with a warning against European interference. In the course of time, the Monroe Doctrine became an object of exaggerated isolationist veneration.

It should be realized that men too young to remember 1812 all but forgot the facts of international life. These Americans were busy pioneering, building, trading, reforming, and talking politics and slavery. Their curiosity lay not in a Europe that they believed decadent, but in an America now united by railroad and telegraph, illuminated by gaslight, and photographed by the eye of the camera. The very size of the hinterland created an illusion of security. In time Americans were to measure the caliber of all hostile nations in terms of the Mexicans and Indians who impeded their way to the Pacific. With the passing of the years they forgot that peace in Europe had permitted them to spend their strength on the conquest of the western wilderness.

While speculations about the moral superiority of Americans over Europeans go back at least to Thomas Jefferson, such thoughts were not widely popularized until the eve of the Civil War. There was little hope, so the mid-century argument ran, for a continent addicted to dynastic rivalries, diplomatic intrigue, priestcraft, and class conflict. Europe had a score of bitter centuries to forget; America could fashion her own destiny free of the fetters of history. One is entitled to suspect that the tendency to portray the United States as an examplar for the rest of mankind rose, in part, as compensation for an innate deference to European culture. This deference became inverted and took the form of a moral braggadocio that early formed part of the isolationist line.

As the nineteenth century wore on, opinion divided sharply over the fulfillment of the American mission. In these years many subject peoples rose to overthrow their foreign or domestic oppressors. Americans, inclined to think of themselves as the moral renovators of the world, cheered on insurgents who sought to widen the area of liberty and democracy. A strongly ingrained belief that the future of our free institutions depended upon the universal triumph of democracy moderated the intensity of our isolationism.[3] European ethnic groups, streaming into America in ever greater numbers, pressed for active sympathy and aid for their struggling kinsmen beyond the waters. Vote-hungry politicians, anxious to build up their city machines, exploited these nationalist emotions. Thus a persistent problem arose: did the national interest demand active championship of all world groups fighting for freedom, or should the United States merely lend moral encouragement to such uprisings? The debates on this issue marked the first post-Napoleonic cleavage over the policy of non-entaglement.

For example, when, in the early 1820s, the valiant stand of the Greeks against their Turkish suzerain stirred American emotions to a high pitch, Secretary of State John Quincy Adams chilled the popular enthusiasm by severly limiting the range of our national interests. The United States, said the Secretary in a public address delivered July 4, 1821, would always view with kind sympathy any foreign group struggling against tyranny. "But," he added categorically, "she goes not abroad in search of monsters to destroy. She is the well-wisher to the freedom and independence of all. She is the champion and vindicator only of her own." Active intervention in behalf of foreign suppressed groups, he warned in words pregnant with future implications, would change "the fundamental maxim of her policy from liberty to force."[4] Significantly, it was also John Quincy Adams who first rebuffed a European suggestion that the United States assume a share of responsibility for world order. As Secretary of State he instructed our minister to Russia to decline, politely but firmly, the invitation from Czar Alexander I to join the Holy Alliance in its attempt to preserve the status quo established in 1815 at the Congress of Vienna. Ultimately, John Quincy Adams' precepts were incorporated into the isolationist creed: the United States would lend only moral support to the worthy cause of universal freedom, and would not deviate from non-entaglement even for the purpose of preserving world peace.

The vexing question, however, persisted: would a worldwide sweep of reaction jeopardize our own liberties? The argument was renewed at mid-century, when the contagious revolutionary spirit spread once again from France to Germany, Italy, and the Austrian Empire. Americans were particularly sympathetic to the Hungarian cause, widely advertised in this country by the Magyar patriot, Louis Kossuth. One group, exhilarated by the 1848 victory over Mexico and the unbridled expansionist spirit of the day, talked of helping Europe's subject nationalities. These champions of liberation dubbed their opponents "isolationists." An old word was thus endowed with a new meaning and eventually found its way into the American political vocabulary.

Kossuth, like many latter-day seekers of American aid, soon discovered our propensity for combining reckless diplomatic talk with cautious action. Secretary of State Daniel Webster, answering a protest from Vienna, boasted to the Austrian *chargé d'affaires* at Washington of the vastness of our territory and the richness of our resources. In comparison, he told the startled diplomat, "the possessions of the house of Hapsburg are but as a patch on the earth's surface." At a White House dinner, given for Kossuth by President Fillmore, Webster applauded "Hungarian independence, Hungarian self-government, Hungarian control of Hungarian destinies." But Webster told a friend pointedly that if Kossuth should ever suggest "intervention" to him, his words would fall on "ears more deaf than adders." When Kossuth sought out Henry Clay, the fast-failing Kentuckian mustered enough strength to give the Hungarian some gratuitous advice. The cause of world liberty, said Clay, would be better served by Americans keeping their "lamp burning brightly on this Western shore, as a light to all nations, than to hazard its utter extinction, amid the ruins of fallen or falling republics in Europe."[5]

The rigid interpretation of isolationism, conforming to the let-nature-take-its-course philosophy of the day, prevailed. Kossuth had to be satisfied with pious hope for supernatural intervention. As President Fillmore himself told the patriot, should Hungary never become free and Kossuth never be able to return home, the President would yet pray for him wherever his lot might be cast!

The isolationism of George Washington, voiced to promote independent action and freedom from foreign meddling, was lost amid overtones that emphasized American moral superiority and European decadence. If the informed minority retained part of the old-time colonial respect for European culture, vainglorious politicians and the uncritical majority spoke ever more enthusiastically of their countrymen as the elect of mankind. From their comfortable seats on their ocean-girt sidelines, Americans fell into the habit of cheering on foreign champions of national self-determination. This was a safe and innocuous pastime when the United States was a minor power in a relatively stable and placid world. It proved, however, a perilous one, once America became the prime democratic nation in the course of a restive and turbulent era.

In the middle decades of the nineteenth century the schism over slavery held the public interest. For thirty years, American energy was largely absorbed in trying to avoid fratricidal war, in fighting it, in binding up the nation's wounds, and in exploiting new economic opportunities unexpectedly revealed by the flash of gunfire. Curiously, American smugness grew apace during these hectic years.

Pristine isolationism reached its heyday in the decades that followed the Civil War. Ironically, the tradition was in full glory just as its foundations began to crumble. In retrospect, the original policy was both necessary and wise. There was no other sensible attitude to have taken toward Europe in the early days of the republic. We were weak, our national unity was beset by sectional rivalry, our population was small, and distrustful monarchs snarled at us from across the Atlantic. For many years after 1815 it would have been foolish to have disturbed the existing balance of power. We needed a "seed-time" to absorb our immigrants, to settle our domestic schism, and to subdue our thorny wasteland. Nineteenth-century isolationism was salutary even though it was hardly conducive to the diplomatic training of a people about to emerge as a world power.

Americans grew accustomed to tranquillity, failing to realize that there was peace here because there was peace elsewhere. And that peace, despite a widespread misconception, did not come just because we kept our noses clean. Our effortless security was the bounty of unusual circumstances. Capable Britons engineered a neat balance of power which kept Europe in equilibrium. Happily for American growth, no nation ran amuck and set out to reduce its neighbors to satellites. The local wars that were fought did not involve American interests. In the Far East, China and Japan were as yet dormant. Coexistence was practiced rather than mouthed. This unusual spell of fine weather continued so long that people came to regard it as the normal way of life. Americans equated Darwin's theory of survival through strife with biological evolution and business competition. It never seemed to occur to the men of those roseate years that nations, too, might regress to the law of the jungle.

Gradually, Americans began to reflect upon their complacency. History books of the day told of brave pilgrims who left a rotten continent to secure a new home for freedom. The children of these pioneers, so the epic went, fought that cruel and unusual tyrant, King George III, to establish their independence. For two generations after 1776, jealous monarchs sought to hamper and divide us, but we frustrated their plans. America was "God's last hope on earth."

Perhaps such statements were mere platitudes. The immigrants who came here, however, were lusty men and women filled with unpleasant memories of their shaky voyage across the endless miles of water that split the two worlds asunder. In many ways the Atlantic migration intensified the separationist spirit. The vast majority of the newcomers rejected European power politics and dynastic rivalries. They resented a system that forced young men into military service and disrupted the even tenor of family life. Moreover, the immigrants soon discovered that the easiest way to break down Yankee reserve and earn the label "American" was to indulge in the luxuriant nationalism of their adopted country. Most of these transplanted Europeans were willing to forsake their native culture for newer ways, but they never forgot that the poor man had suffered most in the wars of the Old World.

Political demagogues, looking for votes, found it profitable to keep ancient prejudices alive. Irishmen, for example, had their own reasons for joining in the old American sport of twisting the British lion's tail. Meanwhile, the older strains of Americans had taken a close look at the miserable and uprooted foreigners who were pouring into the country and paused to bless their own land.

Many other factors contributed to the feeling that the United States was the fair-haired child of history. Rural Americans, close to the soil, believed the world dependent upon our fertile wheat belt. This so-called "myth of the garden" enhanced the prevalent mood of complacency and self-sufficiency.[6] In the business-minded East, breathtaking advances in technology and industrial output fostered the illusion that Providence had exempted the United States from the ordinary vicissitudes of history. Why jeopardize this good fortune by international meddling? President Cleveland, in his 1885 inaugural, thus summed up the fully matured isolationist dogma:

> The genius of our institutions, the needs of our people in
> their home life, and the attention which is demanded for
> the settlement and development of the resources of our
> vast territory dictate the scrupulous avoidance of any
> departure from that foreign policy commended by the

history, the traditions, and the prosperity of our Republic. It is the policy of independence, favored by our position and defended by our known love of justice and by our power. It is the policy of peace suitable to our interests. It is the policy of neutrality, rejecting any share in foreign broils and ambitions upon other continents and repelling their intrusion here. It is the policy of Monroe and of Washington and Jefferson.[7]

Ironically, at the moment when the new President epitomized this truly bi-partisan foreign policy, powerful forces were already at work at the underpinnings of the isolationist structure.

In the 1880s American diplomacy began to pull out of the doldrums. Down deep one could already hear the rumblings destined to arouse the State Department from its lethargy. The captains of industry, having captured the domestic market, were about to broaden their horizons. Foreign trade doubled from 1870 to 1890 and American manufactured goods left the country in ever increasing volume. Still a debtor country in the sense that more capital was invested here than we were able to send abroad, the American dollar had already begun its Odyssey. All this meant competition and rivalry with other industrialized nations. In a relative sense the globe was shrinking. Express steamers made grand highways of the oceans while first the cable and later the wireless welded together a world business community. Modern science was rapidly bridging the barriers of the ages. Had human nature advanced along with technology all might have been well. A shrinking earth, however, seemed to tempt man's primitive aggressiveness.

Significantly, twentieth-century philosophers and theologians, in sharp contrast to their optimistic predecessors, emphasized once more the old concept of an inherently evil and self-centered human nature. The balance of power began to list as two land-hungry nations, Germany and Japan, edged their way into the closed corporation of imperialist powers. New rivalries threatened the peace just as America jumped into the economic maelstrom.

The international pace began to quicken as the United States participated in conferences called to solve common problems that could be more conveniently handled by collective action. Here and there came a grumble about nonentanglement, but the new departure was rationalized by the claim that isolationism meant only shying away from outright

23

political commitments. The Senate eased its conscience by consenting to international economic, humanitarian, and peace-preserving agreements with the explicit reservation that these were not to be construed as a departure from our cherished policy of isolationism.[8]

In the eighties we began building a steel navy. At first, it was assumed that the new battleships were for coastal defense, but a marked change came in 1890 when a Naval Policy Board frankly anticipated the end of isolationism and planned for a fleet capable of upholding the Monroe Doctrine and repelling possible invasion.[9] Our rapidly expanding commercial interests mandated adequate protection of all ocean highways, and before long the United States Navy was competing with Germany for second place to Britain. Meantime, however, we fought the war of 1898 with Spain. This spirited little bout made us, in many respects, a new nation. Quick and spectacular victories at Manila and Santiago begot a certain cockiness, self-buoyancy, and the desire to act the part of a great power. To play this role in the fashion of the day, we had to sport some colonies. The imperial years of American history lay just ahead.

Before the Spanish-American war the expansionist spirit had been confined mainly to navalists and their intellectual camp-followers. The conquest of the Philippines, however, opened the eyes of the American business man to the Far Eastern markets. With the acquisition of the Philippines our line of defense was thrust into the vicinity of China and Japan. Does this seem a strange lunge for a republic which vaunted its isolationism? If so, it can be explained by saying that our isolationist barricade had only one wall. We shut only our eastern door, for Americans marched out of their house in other directions. United States history is replete with exploits, successful and abortive, against the territories of our southern, western, and even northern neighbors. Isolationism accelerated rather than inhibited continental expansionism, for, in the beginning, we wanted to drive Europe out of North America. This impulse created a restlessness that drove Americans westward to San Francisco and in due course beyond the Golden Gate to Honolulu and Manila.

Long before Commodore Dewey's ships headed for the Philippines, some Americans began to display an interest in the retarded civilizations that lay beyond the wide Pacific. This curiosity was most marked among northeastern shipping magnates, New England reformers and clergymen, and a group of super-expansionists. Americans seemed far less afraid of entanglements in the Orient. Here we could spread the Gospel, extend trade, urge reform, and diffuse American ideas without danger of *immediate* political involvement. There was no fear of being contaminated by Asiatic ideas. Interestingly, Senator William H. Seward, later to become our first Republican Secretary of State, anticipated the declining influence of Europe and predicted that "the Pacific Ocean, its shores, its islands, and the vast regions beyond will become the chief theater of events in the world's great hereafter."[10]

On January 9, 1900, a spread-eagle Republican expansionist delivered his maiden speech to the Senate. "The power that rules the Pacific," said the thirty-seven-year-old Albert J. Beveridge, "is the power that rules the world. And, with the Philippines that power is and will forever be the American Republic."[11] In 1904, Halford MacKinder (later Sir Halford), a young British geographer, told the Royal Geographical Society that the combined land masses of Europe, Africa, and Asia constituted a huge World-Island destined to control the future history of mankind. He developed the thesis that eastern Europe was the key to the Heartland that commanded this dominant World-Island. The Americas, MacKinder maintained, were ancillary land bodies to the fulcrum of world power. It is no accident that a group of present-day isolationists, holding with Beveridge rather than with MacKinder, think of the Far East and not Europe as our primary line of defense against the Communist thrust. American isolationism and an exaggerated American concern for Asia bear a close historical relationship.

After 1898, thoughtful men reasoned that our Far Eastern démarche meant the scrapping of non-intervention and the Monroe Doctrine. Could we take some three thousand islands, situated so far from the United States, and still insist that land-hungry European powers should not indulge their appetites in Latin American adventures?

Germany and Japan had, along with the United States, become world powers. Our new position, economically and politically, was bound to collide with the interests of these countries. The balance of power, so long maintained by Great Britain, was tipping. Would we not have to step into power politics to counterweigh the tilt? These problems constituted the controversy of our time on foreign policy. Had they been met with sufficient realism and foresight, the entire course of recent history might well have been changed for the better.

Unfortunately, only a minority of the national-imperialists comprehended the changing pattern of world politics. Some of them even naively assumed that our new far-flung outposts would buttress our central defensive system and thus aid in preserving our non-involvement policy. Hence we posed as a world power without accepting the responsibility commensurate with our position. There was a widespread notion that American moral influence would act as a powerful agent for peace. In the event that this failed, then we could always depend on our oceans to quench the fires of war before they reached our shores. It was a dangerous illusion, and one fraught with dire consequences for the future.

Other national-imperialists wanted first to develop the American Empire and then maintain our world position by our own force of arms. These men founded a school of thought that, throughout the present century, has opposed both the pacifism of the isolationists and the multilateralism of the internationalists. A minority of imperialists were willing to scrap non-interventionism along with non-colonialism. Such adventurous unilateralists relished the game of power politics, for it afforded the country an opportunity to flex its national muscles.

The anti-imperialists, on the other hand, frequently quoted the isolationist advice of the Founding Fathers to support their stand. With the benefit of hindsight, however, it is apparent that they erred in believing that overseas expansionism would more likely lead to despotism at home than to entanglement abroad. Local anti-expansionist associations merged to form the Anti-Imperialist League, the first important national foreign policy pressure group of our propaganda-ridden century. Eventually, some members of this group became ardent international cooperationists. Prior to 1914, however, these utopian idealists were no more successful in weaning the country from isolationism than were their imperially minded opposites.

There was, then, no sharp reversal of non-intervention in the years following the war with Spain. Circumstances made it possible to abandon the practice of isolation and still cling tenaciously to the theory. Had we not wanted to act the part of a great power, we would not have taken the Philippines. In the years between this cardinal diplomatic decision and the opening of the First World War, the United States followed a grossly inconsistent policy. We cooperated with other major powers in the Far East, we used a big stick to insure our dominance over the New World, and to appease our stricken conscience, with some minor exceptions such as at Algeciras, we still shied away from European involvements. A world in equipoise permitted us, for a short span, to reconcile these conflicting aims.

Under the leadership of Secretary of State John Hay (1898-1905) we drew up a blueprint designed to stabilize the Far East, but characteristically failed to make good our program. On August 12, 1903, the learned Secretary boasted to President Theodore Roosevelt that the United States had accomplished much in the Orient "without the expense of a single commitment or promise."[12] Even the sophisticated Hay failed to comprehend that nations, like individuals, cannot have their cake and eat it too.

But the sands of time were fast running out on the United States. England's friendly attitude made it possible to take the Philippines and still enforce the Monroe Doctrine against Europe. The Royal Navy stood guard over the Atlantic and we were thus spared the necessity of a two-ocean fleet. There were no swollen military budgets to remind the people of their new responsibilities. Americans of this Progressive Era were busily engaged in curbing the power of their railroad-industrial moguls. Thus they gave little heed to the ominous sabre-rattling across the Atlantic. To be sure, there were humanitarians who apprehensively viewed the gathering war clouds, and pondered the foreign situation. Professor Merle Curti has demonstrated that on the eve of Sarajevo, American associations to promote peace proliferated and waxed strong. These societies made repeated inquests into the causes of war, and flooded the country with propaganda. Nevertheless, even the more prescient fell victim to the shallow optimism of their day. Despite recurrent and increasingly dangerous international crises, there was a deceiving notion that war had become anachronistic. Only a small minority of Americans thought in terms of world conflict and still fewer were willing to make substantial sacrifices to preserve peace. Even pessimists hastened to assure themselves that, come what might in Europe, America could isolate herself from war. Our mood of detachment had become part of the basic need known as security.

Some men, of course, correctly read the portents of the times and tried to arouse the country from its indifference. Despite much hard work and even occasional prophetic utterances, they failed. Denied the historian's hindsight, they were able to see only part of the problem. Hence their realism was all too often intermingled with militarism, navalism, imperialistic propaganda, or moral fulminations. Even had they couched their arguments in terms of the national interest, it is doubtful that they could have loosened isolationism's hold upon the American people. The world of 1910 appeared too peaceful, too secure, and too prosperous. Peace had been too long taken for granted. Only world-shaking events could destroy the popular belief in unilinear human progress. The spirit of the age contradicted pessimism and realism.

Who were these savants who demanded reassessment of the American placed in a changing world? First of all, there was Alfred Thayer Mahan. Dignified, patriarchal, and deeply religious, this naval officer had earned international fame by delineating the relationship in history between sea power and national greatness. Command of the sea, wrote Mahan, was necessary if the United States wished to become a great power and insure its future prosperity and security. A land-locked nation, he pointed out, must inevitably decay and collapse, for the simple fact that land "is almost all obstacle, the sea almost all open plain," will inevitably stunt its growth. In 1894 he urged the United States "to cast aside the policy of isolation which befitted her infancy" and to accept valiantly her "inevitable task and appointed lot in the work of upholding the common interest of civilization." In this bold stand, Mahan took a position far in advance of his fellow-imperialists who usually wished to work expansionism into the framework of isolationism.[13]

Mahan's thesis became the shibboleth of a coterie of intellectuals who wanted a big navy with bases and colonies to protect our vital interests. This school realized that the peace of the world was at the mercy of the have-not powers. Such countries, they declared, kept the peace only because of fear. If war ensued, they agreed with Mahan that the United States might be in serious danger, for salt water was a highway of attack as well as a barrier.

Captain Mahan's facile and prolific pen bore greater results abroad than at home. As a British writer later observed, his words were as "oil to the flames of colonial expansion everywhere leaping into life." In his own country, however, Mahan's warnings were frequently discounted as the trade-talk of a professional navalist. An obscure congressman spoke for everyday Americans when he said in 1910 that the likelihood of a war involving the United States was "as chimerical, and unlikely as a descent on our coasts of an army from the moon."[14] Idealists and visionaries, somewhat better informed, overrated current moves for disarmament and the peaceful settlement of international disputes.

The brilliant Albert J. Beveridge argued Mahan's case with

evangelical fervor. A nationalist, an imperialist, and later a Roosevelt PROGRESSIVE, the Indiana senator used his consummate oratory to tell the country that the Anglo-Saxon nations were, under God, "master organizers of the world." This mission, he argued, was paramount to "any question of the isolated policy of our country." Beveridge was to become, in time, a popular crusader against the internationalism of Woodrow Wilson. However, his later isolationism derived from rather than contradicted his zest for imperialism. Like his erudite Massachusetts colleague, Henry Cabot Lodge, Beveridge thought of an America made untouchable by the overseas defensive outposts that guarded her continental citadel. Both men were zealous nationalists, unwilling to barter away American freedom of action for a system of inadequate general security. Beveridge and Lodge overestimated the imperialist appetite of the American people. As it turned out, our experiment in colonialism proved short-lived and, until 1945, we were more inclined to contract our perimeter of defense than to widen it. The imperialist bombast of politicians of the McKinley-Roosevelt era served only to becloud the main issue. The wells of peace were running dry, and war sparks were to travel fast in a contracted world.

We have already argued that no words could convince the American people that peace was in danger. If Theodore Roosevelt, President for almost eight years after 1901 and one of Mahan's earliest disciples, could not persuade the American people to re-evaluate their foreign policy, who could have convinced them? Yet with all his magnetism and gift of expression, T. R. was unable to dispel the mood of self-complacency. Roosevelt's words, to be sure, often sounded like the affirmative case in a debate over the advantages of imperialism and strenuous national life. His realistic insights were generously larded with moral scoldings, for, in the Victorian manner, he judged nations by an ethical standard of conduct expected of gentlemen.

Roosevelt used his position as President to both act and preach. In his day the United States begun to strut the world like a first-class power. The Caribbean gradually became an American lake. We "took Panama" and built the canal. Roosevelt rattled the sabre, made secret agreements with other nations, and even dabbled in power politics. The President, far more discerning than most of his contemporaries, understood that changes in transportation, communication, and production had revolutionized the world of Rutherford B. Hayes. Although T. R.'s pronouncements on foreign policy had idealistic overtones, he was unwilling to leave the future to the mercies of blind faith or a smiling Providence.[15] Conditions, he insisted, required new diplomatic postulates that must be backed by *adequate* military and naval power. Responsibility tempered Roosevelt's impulsiveness and, realistically, he confined the country's foreign objectives to those national interests it was willing and able to protect. On August 16, 1905, Roosevelt confided to a friend that he was "trying to keep matters on an even keel in Europe."[16] In the event of a major clash between the European alliance systems, T. R. felt that our isolationist dykes would not prove watertight. Nor was his scope of vision limited to Europe, for he understood the world-wide ramifications of imperialism. If England could no longer balance global power, then the self-interest of the United States demanded that we help keep the scales in equilibrium. Without sufficient force at our command, Roosevelt argued, we would be helpless either to prevent a conflict or to protect our interests in a warring world.

Presidents, however, are limited by public opinion and constitutional prescription. The popular mind is not given to sensing nuances or to analyzing the subtly shifting drifts of power politics. People, including congressmen, are much more likely to cling to established policy than to approve a sharp about-face. Neither Theodore Roosevelt nor any other democratic leader, given the frame of reference in which he had to work, could have gone much further. The Founding Fathers had said "no meddling." What difference did it make if circumstances had changed? What good did it do to point out that the arch-isolationist Jefferson had once been willing to marry ourselves to "the British fleet and nation"? Only the acetylene torch of war could speed the thawing of the isolationist glacier. Even so, the melting was to be a slow process, destined to be frequently interrupted by new freezes.

During the course of the protracted twentieth-century debate over foreign policy, the word "isolationist" became a cliché. Through reckless use it acquired, like "appeaser" or even "liberal," a somewhat sinister meaning. Actually, the modern connotation of the word is much younger than the policy it is supposed to depict.

As we have already noted, Americans of the 1850s who wanted to promote Europe's democratic revolutions dubbed their opponents "isolationists." The political implication of the term was given new emphasis when, in 1896, Prime Minister Sir Wilfred Laurier of Canada referred to England's "splendid isolation." Sir Wilfred spoke just as England was about to jettison the policy to build an anti-German coalition.

America, separated from Europe by a wide ocean rather than a narrow channel, found it possible to steer clear of the European vortex for an additional period of grace. The Canadian's phrase, shortened to "isolationism," popularized an old American political idiom. It was a handy designation for our twin policies of neutrality and non-intervention.[17]

Although there have been decades when defenders of non-entanglement proudly confessed their isolationism, statesmen early formed the habit of disowning the epithet. In 1851, the Whig senator Charles Sumner, in what was possibly the first public utterance of the term in its modern usage, said: "I inculcate no frigid isolation. God forbid that we should ever close our ears to the cry of distress, or cease to swell with indignation at the steps of tyranny . . . [but] . . . I would uphold the peaceful neutrality of the country." Eleven years later, Secretary of State William H. Seward glorified our traditional policy, but explained that only "superficially viewed" could it be regarded as "a course of isolation and indifference."[18]

Americans have long and heatedly argued the contemporary import of the admonition of the Founding Fathers. Both sides have said and written so much about isolationism that it has come to mean anything from a proposal to build a Maginot Line from Bar Harbor to Miami to a suggestion that Christmast Island might lie out of our perimeter of defense. The present situation is so confused that people, who by all reasonable canons should be called isolationists, say that the word is a smear term "invented by globaloney addicts."[19] The semantic difficulty involved must be resolved by narrowing the definition of the word to the essential difference between the isolationists and their critics.

We can begin by saying that American isolationism has never meant total social, cultural, and economic self-sufficiency. Such a concept has had few rational advocates and the very idea is nullified by the history of the United States. Statesmen of the early republic were cosmopolites who realized that their fledgling country was not ready to be weaned from the breast of European culture. In the economic sphere, they tried to promote foreign trade so as to regain the commercial advantages that the colonies had enjoyed as part of the British Empire. They looked to a healthy interchange of products and ideas as a means of developing the country. (Upon occasion American isolationism has had economic implications, but a Yankee willingness to offer sacrifices of profitable business upon the altar of non-entanglement has been the exception rather than the rule.)

Hence, in contrast to the classic autarkial isolationism practiced by such erstwhile hermit nations as Japan, Korea and Siam, our government fostered rather than repelled commercial and intellectual intercourse with other countries. The American tradition has been distinctly one of political isolationism. While Britain, after 1870, tried to avoid advance commitments, nevertheless imperial considerations, physical proximity to the continent, and a long previous record of foreign entanglements thwarted the English attempt to maintain a splendid isolation. Thus the policy of the United States is the outstanding example of political isolation in modern history. Ironically, we set the pattern for the present-day neutralist states that now menace our foreign policy by remaining uncommitted.

To sum up, American isolationism coupled a determination to stay out of foreign wars with an unwavering refusal to enter into alliances. Until the Presidency of Harry S. Truman, we refused to put our weight into any peacetime balance of power designed to prevent any single nation or group of nations from gaining a preponderance. These generalizations, however, need serious qualifications. Uncle Sam was not unwilling to raise his head above his ocean ramparts to champion freedom and democracy for oppressed foreigners. Nor did the policy keep us from an early and earnest quest for peace on earth. Ardent isolationists have frequently advocated American leadership in the promotion of peace, provided always that we limit our efforts to moral suasion and scrupulously avoid commitments for coercive action to allay or punish aggression. Before 1914, it was possible to champion simultaneously non-entanglement, universal peace, and world liberty.

Herein lies the nub of the problem. Twentieth-century isolationists still believe that non-entanglement best serves the long-run interests of national security, business opportunities, and the universal triumph of liberty and democracy. They opposed our entry into both World Wars on the ground that our privileged continental position allowed us to risk the defeat of potential allies. Isolationists have persistently opposed prior commitments of American military aid to any league or association of nations designed to keep the peace by using force against recalcitrant nations. In other words, the isolationists have been willing to gamble on the destruction of friendly countries, preferring to fight only when confronted by immediate danger. An America grown to full strength, say the isolationists, can maintain her world position and best serve humanity by going-it-alone. They cling tenaciously to faith in the unchangeability of our changing world.

Men who have advocated the total abandonment or serious modification of isolationism have been loosely termed "internationalists." The name is misleading, for relatively few of them have ever wished to relinquish a jot of American sovereignty. They have long differed among themselves both in motive and purpose. Before the First World War, internationalism was an attitude rather than a movement. Each year, in the golden sunset of peace, an increasing number of American clergymen, teachers, writers, and industrialists crossed the Atlantic. Among these travelers could be found many members of the "better families"—genteel folk who liked to vary life in Newport or Palm Beach with some weeks in England and on the continent. Young Franklin D. Roosevelt, for instance, visited the Old World eight times before he reached adolescence. Such persons were apt to come back worldminded. They began to perceive the monolithic pattern of western civilization.

Democracy, after 1848, had made rapid strides in western Europe. The liberal-democratic ideal constituted a real link between America and the Atlantic fringe of Europe. To returning voyagers the old isolationist assumptions of European tyranny and class oppression were annoying. The internationalists began to write and speak and their influence left its mark, especially on the thought of the eastern seaboard.

Among the elite who understood Europe there were some clairvoyants. Unfortunately, however, their writings were not designed for the average reader. Henry Adams, scion of the presidential line, was a deep thinker who blended history, science, and philosophy. Disillusioned by the materialism of his own country and grief-stricken by personal tragedy, he roamed the world. Adams saw in 1906 that Germany was upsetting the balance of power, and thought that only a combine of the Atlantic powers, including the United States, could restore the equilibrium. His younger brother, Brooks Adams, feared Czar Nicholas more than Kaiser William, but he, too, reasoned that "the risk of isolation promises to be more serious than the risk of alliance."[20]

Then there was the editor, Herbert Croly. In the calm of 1909 this over-intellectualized, ungainly little man sketched a blueprint for the future called *The Promise of American Life*. He predicted that America would have to contribute to the maintenance of peace, for the road ahead might be piled mountain high with corpses. True peace, he reasoned, would come "only after a series of abortive and costly experiments." Prophetic words, but few Americans waded through the pages of this tortuous book. The Adamses, Croly, and others of their school were thinking in long-run terms. Most Americans had long since made up their minds that life is but a short-run affair. The egg-heads of the day failed to dent the hard crust of provincialism.

Old traditions, like old soldiers, do not die—they merely fade away. The stronger the tradition, the longer it lingers, even after its *raison d'être* has disappeared. Isolationism was deeply rooted in the geography of the New World. Time alone could adjust human minds to rapidly changing concepts of space. Few policies in American history were so fixed and so stable as non-intervention. It had been bequeathed from the Federalists to the Whigs, from the Jeffersonians to the Jacksonian Democrats, from Henry Clay to Abraham Lincoln and his Republicans. Isolationism could point to the greatest and most illustrious men in American history as its sponsors. The policy, moreover, was extraordinarily meaningful to the average man. He saw in it his own peace, convenience, prosperity, and even the safety of his household. It was associated with national pride and touched upon the same human emotions. Understandably, people would be reluctant to part with such a heritage.

Until 1914 the tradition had not withstood a real test. There were few, indeed, who grasped the implications of an American abstention from a balance of power. Arguments about isolation were mild and restrained for it seemed that only an abstraction was at stake. The American mind of those confident years, given to absolute decisions, thought of alliances as the only avenue leading to foreign turmoil. Kaleidoscopic events beyond the sea, however, revealed the unity of the closly knit industrialized world. More open-minded Americans soon perceived the overriding strength of these magnetic forces and realized that non-intervention was no longer able to resist their attraction. When war came in 1914, the great American debate on foreign policy began in earnest. It has not yet been resolved.

Chapter 2

A Shove from Mars

MILLIONS OF AMERICANS who have reached the age of thirty recall the creeping onset of the Second World War; the peaceful nations, so it seemed, were struggling to hold on and stay out of the morass. Considerably fewer millions remember 1914. Old-timers, who can still picture those hectic summer days, know that the storm broke suddenly, like a thunderstorm. The assassination of the heir to the Austro-Hungarian throne ignited a powder-keg that had been slowly stocked. For the moment, the neutral nations were too stunned to grasp the implications of the holocaust.

To the masses in the United States, the fighting seemed as remote as tales of an Indian scalping party. Our long kaleidoscopic course of education in foreign affairs was just beginning. Many learned for the first time that little Belgium had been supposedly neutralized and that Europe had been cloven by two hostile alliances. While the intelligentsia were better informed, they, too, were shocked at the blow against world stability. As the nation recovered its senses, two tendencies became apparent. A majority sided with England, France, Russia, and their allies. A far greater majority, in fact almost everyone, held that this was not our war and that the United States was secure behind the shield of neutrality and non-entanglement.

From President Woodrow Wilson down, men overlooked some salient facts in American history. National isolation had never before been subjected to a genuine test. The policy had not prospered in the wars of the French Revolution when we were a weak, agrarian power. How could it work now with American business burgeoning all over the world? Since 1815 we had been able to remain neutral in foreign wars because their outcome had borne no relation to long-range American interests. A World War was obviously different. What if the result should put Berlin instead of London in control of the lead-strings of the world? While these scales weighed in balance, could we afford just to sit back, guard our neutral rights, defend the western hemisphere, and let nature take its course?

The bulk of our economic, cultural, and political affinities was with the Allies. Imperial Germany, seen in the light of the communist menace of our time, looks benign in retrospect. To men of a previous generation, however, the Kaiser's vainglorious bombasts and iron deeds did not augur well for peaceful co-existence. It took, nevertheless, several years of war to convince a segment of public opinion that isolationism did not correspond to reality. American interests could not escape the scourge of global war.

President Wilson has suffered grievously at the hands of historians. One school has reproved him for adhering to neutrality in name rather than action, contending that the United States could have avoided war if the President had held England as well as Germany "strictly accountable" for violations of our neutrality. On the other hand, historians who think that we should have made war on Germany in defense of the national interest, chide Wilson for not evaluating and explaining the problem correctly. In truth, Wilson was deluded by the popular assumptions of his day. Perspective, at close-range, is not often given, even to as unusual a man as the President, Master teacher, historian, political scientist, administrator, and gifted writer and speaker, he nevertheless shared the naiveté of a provincial people. He apparently assumed, at least in the early stages of the conflict, that giants could struggle and that we could stand by. In 1914 he asked Americans to be impartial in both thought and actions. Had he forgotten that the United States had millions of first-generation immigrants bound by links of money, blood, and affection to the warring countries? And even among the older strains of Americans, "moral eunuchs" were rare.

We cannot follow in detail the vexatious course of almost three years of neutrality. Undoubtedly there were many reasons for our 1917 intervention and historians have not been able to agree upon their order of importance. The essential point for the future history of isolationism is that Wilson failed to explain the declaration of war in clear terms involving our own interests. He might have said that we could not risk letting the control of the Atlantic pass from the friendly supervision of the British navy. He could have argued also that an Allied defeat might mean fighting a victorious Germany in order to uphold the Monroe Doctrine. It is impossible to know whether Wilson ever thought in such concrete terms. We do know, however, that he chose to drift into war on legalistic grounds, defending an outmoded concept of neutral rights upon the seas. After our entry, Wilson had to search for a different rationale. He had to incite enthusiasm and quiet dissenters who said that we were fighting for Anglo-American capitalist interests. Here was another chance to turn to realism and enlightened self-interest. The President did not use it. Conditioned by heredity and evironment to the Presbyterian parson's point of view, he naturally looked at the war from a moral angle. He thus turned the fight into an ideological crusade—carrying a torch to make the world free from war and safe for democracy. Soon these aims mushroomed far beyond any possibility of fulfillment. A back-drop had been erected for the great disillusionment. Modern American isolationism was born in its shadow.

The *first* step, then, in creating a new isolationism, was the declaration of war. An impressive minority thought it foolish and unnecessary. Such persons were not only to cling to isolationism, but to revive and exalt it. They were later to be joined by those who consented to war but either never accepted, or later tired of, Wilson's idealism. The President had not realized that any permanent decision to make continuous sacrifices for world order would have to be based on the firm and materialistic foundation of self-interest.

In its attempt to awaken enthusiasm for war, the United States government erred in over-selling it. The eventual outcome was the *second* factor in the growth of neo-isolationism. We suffered from a clinical case of Walter Lippmann's "Democratic Malady." In an authoritarian government, the people are ordered to sacrifice. A democracy, however, must motivate the masses to sanguinary and economic offerings. To get this support, popular governments use hyperbole. They tend, therefore, to identify the enemy with the Devil, and they promise to clean out Hell. Exorcise this one evil, they promise, and all will be right in the world. Wilson ended up with perhaps the most gigantic propaganda campaign in all American history, far greater than the efforts of 1941-1945 when Hitler had really outmatched Satan. The overstatements of the earlier period exaggerated Hun atrocities, and promised too much for the future. The spell of unreal thinking led to the inexorable recoil against crusading.

One can readily understand how the barrage of words and pamphlets melted the reserve of ordinary folk. "The poor children of New York," wrote a doughboy of President Wilson, "go mad over his picture in the movies when it is on the screen . . . the poor people is with him and they got faith and believe in him."[1] The generators of this enthusiasm were college presidents and professors and men of affairs. Their customary constraint was loosened by the spirit of the age. Progress in human history was taken for granted, memories of the harsh side of war had been forgotten, and the current effort was interpreted as a short-cut to universal peace and reform.

The crusading motif was especially rampant on university campuses. Three hundred members of the University of Wisconsin faculty signed a round robin condemning the war record of Senator Robert M. La Follette who was using his constitutional rights to disagree with the majority about the war. Cornell University arranged a dinner, the menu for which included English biscuits, Russian rolls, Italian mayonnaise, "Belgium ice cream with aeronautic sauce," topped off with "U.S.A. and maple-leaf cake" and "patriotic mints."

The clergy, with some notable exceptions, supported the war enthusiastically and thundered bellicose sermons from the pulpit. The flag was draped around altars, and choirs sang national airs. Rabbi Joseph Silverman of New York City called upon other clergymen to follow his policy of declining to perform the marriage service for "shrinkers" or "slackers."

There were special reasons for all this excitement. This was the first time that America had waged total war. Everyone had to do his bit. Men, called from cloistered atmospheres to cheer or to sell Liberty bonds, frequently overshot the mark. They spoke of the "autocratic lawlessness" and "barbarous militarism" that would vanish, and the reign of right and justice that would arrive with victory. Even Herbert Hoover wrote that the German ruling class, mad with lust for booty, already was planning more rapine "upon the life blood of other peoples."[2] To Jacob Gould Schurman, Canadian-born philosopher and long-time president of Cornell, the "Kingdom of Heaven" was struggling with the "Kingdom of Hunland, which is force and frightfulness."

There was an academic flavor to the Wilson administration. Professors were called upon to write propaganda. Historians were specially favored, for who knew better the devious ways of absolute monarchs and the virtues of popular rule? The vice-chairman of the National Board for Historical Service advised his men to smite the Philistines "hip and thigh." They were, to be sure, cautioned against the extreme example of the German historians who had distorted the past for political purposes, but they were told to explain the war to the American people. Many of the drafted writers prided themselves upon being newer historians who believed in making the facts teach some lesson. They tackled their assignment with vim and vigor. Carl L. Becker of Cornell, one of the most acute thinkers of his generation, wrote a friend that he could not return to Ithaca, for having finished a job "on German deviltries in Belgium," he was ready to undertake another project.[3] Thus began the long association of the modern school of historians with current debates on foreign policy.

Even while the war was being oversold to the American people, preparation was under way to oversell the peace. Slowly the demand arose that this be more than just another peace treaty—it must hold in check the forces of Mars. Once more a complicated problem was oversimplified and one particular solution overvalued. Collective security, or, in other words, a league of nations designed to prevent the outbreak of war became the hope of millions. When it was found that this formula was no short-cut to utopia, men returned *en masse* to their isolationist point of departure. Unrealistic thinking concerning the nature of the peace, then, was the *third* factor in precipitating a new isolationism.

The background of collective security must be understood in terms of 1914 liberal thought in the United States, England, and other western European countries. Today, "liberalism" is a discredited and elusive word. Forty years ago, however, it connoted, in the main, a movement for the unfettered development of the individual.

Just prior to the war, the older nineteenth-century liberalism had been rejuvenated through a reconciliation with its ancient enemy, the state. This new coalition welcomed the use of national power, here and elsewhere, to bring about social and economic reforms. At a moment when liberalism looked forward to greater victories in all the democratic countries, its program was frustrated by war. The energy that had been used for domestic improvement was now deflected to bring a just peace to the world.

Liberalism, especially in the United States, was an attitude toward certain problems rather than a specific program. Its boundaries were fluid enough to include men who would appear in our eyes as economic reactionaries. This was particularly true after the liberals developed definite ideas toward the war and the peace. They were joined by many men who were conservative in domestic policy, but who had become internationally minded. For the time being, however, these two groups were able to bridge the deep schism that marked their outlook on life. In 1914, the liberal premise in international affairs was that the old peace machinery was bankrupt. Neither peace societies, nor treaties of arbitration or conciliation, nor

39

the Permanent Court of Arbitration at The Hague (a standing panel of jurists that could be called upon in an emergency) had been able to keep the peace. Power politics, alliances, secret treaties, all elements of the old European system, had been weighed and found wanting. The liberals reasoned that now these must go in favor of an idealistic and democratic system. Liberals, or, as they were then frequently called, progressives, believed in the efficacy of reason and the teachability of man. If the world were given the right kind of peace machinery, war would then be relegated to limbo. Blueprints for world organization were boldly sketched. The big question dividing the leaders of the movement was whether force or moral suasion should be used to guarantee the peace. The quandary was destined to vex the American peace movement for decades.

The earliest substantial result of this type of thinking was the formation of the League to Enforce Peace. Its pioneers were Hamilton Holt, prominent magazine editor, and Theodore Marburg, who had been Minister to Belgium. These men took others into their confidence, formed a "Plan of Action Committee," and secured the support of former President William Howard Taft. The League to Enforce Peace was founded in Independence Hall, Philadelphia, on June 17, 1915, and adopted a fire brigade scheme for peace, i.e., action only on an emergency basis. Essentially, it provided that disputes which could not be settled through ordinary diplomatic negotiations should go before either a judicial tribunal or a "Council of Conciliation." Force was to be used against a recalcitrant nation that refused to submit its dispute in the manner prescribed, and even when both disputants submitted to arbitration, room still remained for "legal war" if ultimately no decision could be reached. Although leaders of the movement were mostly Republicans and elected the genial Taft as president, the 1904 Democratic candidate, Judge Alton B. Parker, was chosen vice-president. Both men were economic conservatives who happened to have an internationalist outlook. Their very names were apt to arouse suspicion in progressive circles. Following the Philadelphia meeting, the League launched an extensive campaign of education. The new organization was soon a going concern with overwhelming press and popular support.[4]

All that was lacking was the President's approval. Wilson had long wanted a diplomacy that would seek the good of mankind above national selfish interests. He realized that the United States must play the part of a great power. Unlike

Theodore Roosevelt, who liked power politics, Wilson objected to our entry into the game as even more perilous than any possible alliance. Collective security, as a substitute for either power politics or alliances, then, fitted in neatly with Wilson's general outlook. Characteristically, he first thought of moral rather than physical coercion, but soon concluded that force alone would deter errant nations. May 27, 1916, was a notable day for the League to Enforce Peace. President Wilson addressed the assembled organization and shared the platform with the wiry little white-bearded Republican scholar in politics, Senator Henry Cabot Lodge of Massachusetts. Wilson thus became the first chief of state to endorse a plan for world organization. He had cast the die in favor of collective security. A few weeks later, on his insistence, the Democrats pledged a league of nations in their 1916 presidential platform. With Wilson's re-election and prominent Republicans leading the world organization parade, American participation in some kind of league seemed assured.

Following our own declaration of war, the demand for a peace organization grew rapidly. By June, 1918, Booth Tarkington thought that there was no one left to convince. "Such a league," he wrote, "is like a League to Enforce Not Kicking Your Grandmother."[5] Others, of course, were more skeptical, but the chorus of approval was a hearty one. Historians used the perspective of their guild and declared that the march of events had forever destroyed balances of power, neutrality, and isolation. In 1918, even the prolific historian Charles A. Beard, later to become the Nestor of the isolationists, thought that non-entanglement was incompatible with modern conditions.[6] From all sides came the injunction that the war must achieve something more meaningful than merely the defeat of Germany.

The prevalence of evolutionary thought contributed to the Utopian emphasis. Since the Civil War, Americans had applied Darwinian principles to everything from caterpillars and apes to architecture and economics. Had not the United States evolved from thirteen separate colonies to a weak union under the Articles of Confederation and then to the "more perfect union" of the Constitution? The next step in international evolution was obviously a league of nations.

The scientist-educator, David Starr Jordan, explained that even as feudalism had given place to nationalism, so nationalism must now yield to federation in the evolution from anarchy to law. A University of Michigan psychologist maintained that the idea of a league of nations had been slowly

41

developing through the centuries and that civilized men were now psychologically prepared for an "international or super-national" organization. Couching his language in the new Freudian jargon, the professor predicted that the league would subordinate "national assertiveness" and restrain "national egotism."[7] Kenneth S. Latourette, church historian, took his cue from the Gospels rather than from Darwin or Freud. In his book of daily readings, culled from the teachings of Jesus, he said that the Testaments did not mention a league of nations, but insisted that the fundamental principles of Jesus could throw light on the problem of establishing international order.

Meanwhile, the President had become the Allied spokesman and the revered leader of those who wanted a liberal peace. In his famous Fourteen Points speech of January 8, 1918, announcing the Allied war aims, he made it clear that he regarded the establishment of an association of nations, with guarantees of territorial integrity, paramount to all other goals. The mood of the country demanded a scheme for the future that would curb aggression and perpetuate the victory of the liberal-democratic ideals. Before long, however, men would see that fine words had covered deep-seated cleavages and strong under-surface drifts. There was still no basic agreement in the liberal camp. If, for the moment, the international-minded conservatives had been able to work with liberals of all varieties, their initial assumptions were miles apart. President Wilson had said that "politics is adjourned" but he might as well have emulated Joshua and ordered the sun to stand still in its course. The war itself acted like a flash of lightning to bring into focus the problem of world anarchy. When the light faded, people soon sank back into their national, partisan, and economic ruts. Overstimulated by propaganda, they were ready victims of disillusionment.

To understand the mustering of the opposition to a Wilsonian peace, it is necessary to turn from pious wishes to insidious historical forces. Dissenters to the collective security plan began to organize and work. In time they would grow strong enough to coalesce and defeat Wilson. The first on the scene were the nationalists. By an understandable paradox, the war spirit played up "red, white, and blue Americanism." The new chauvinism was thus the *fourth* factor which impeded the program of collective security.

Albert J. Beveridge was one of the first to utilize the quickened nationalist spirit. After his senatorial defeat in 1910, he directed his abundant energy to writing and lecturing. Five years later, he went to Europe as a war correspondent and began to argue the German case. His study of the plan of the League to Enforce Peace persuaded him that it bore earmarks of British propaganda. Beveridge did not change his opinion after his own country went to war. He found himself unpopular because he argued, with some caution, that we had put British and French imperial interests above our own proper ambitions. Sensing the growing popularity of the league idea, he decided to attack it. Beveridge had been one of the first men in the United States to call for the "outside look." Charles A. Beard, reflecting on American foreign policy in 1939, indicted Beveridge, Admiral Mahan, and Theodore Roosevelt for the whole policy of "lunging and plunging" which made embroilment in world politics inevitable. Beveridge and his fellows, however, had wanted to abandon isolationism in order to extend America's strategic interests and to strut forth as a great power. This was enhanced nationalism, and something very different from Wilson's idealistic concept of a league. There was, then, no basic inconsistency between Beveridge's older stand and his new nationalism. Still the frank and unabashed imperialist, he wanted in 1917 to march in and occupy Mexico.[8]

Beveridge advocated an all-out attack on Wilson for several personal reasons. He was hankering to return to the Senate chamber, but some past mistakes stood in his way. Fellow Republicans had not forgotten his "party treason" of 1912 when he had taken part in the Republican schism that had resulted in Wilson's election. The former senator's views on the war were heretical and highly unpopular. So he overcame his original doubts about the war and tried to become more patriotic than the President. Intense nationalism, he reasoned, would reunite the Republican party. Beveridge called for the unconditional surrender of Germany, dictated at the point of the American sword. His creed was simple: "We trust in God, we follow the flag, faltering not, nor doubting the way we march is the path of righteousness."[9] The next step was to say that any idea of an "association of nations" was contrary to the policy of the Founding Fathers. His intimates cheered him on in his effort to "puncture that balloon . . . inflated with poison gas."[10]

Beveridge's plan to keep America "out of a million wars" was sent to Chicago for use by the British-baiting demagogue, William Hale Thompson, in a local election. Meanwhile, Beveridge kept working on his former Republican senatorial colleagues, urging resistance to the President's "superstate" trap.

Because he earned his living writing and lecturing, Beveridge was in possession of a myriad of facts which could be used to predict the American economic future. He freely shared this information with his Washington friends and his Indianapolis study became the storehouse of isolationist ammunition.

Beveridge, of course, was only one of many voices calling for a re-baptized American nationalism. The newspaper Czar, William Randolph Hearst, also had some anti-war words to eat. He, too, chose the path of strident nationalism in order to prove his patriotism. The chief himself, in an editorial published in all his papers, demanded an end to this "hysterical . . . devotion to other nations." We must, he insisted, husband our resources for future fights of our own. Hearst reasoned that the main job ahead was to moderate the growth of "progressivism" and "radicalism" at home. About this time the National Security League, organized in 1914 to preach preparedness, added a new program of "Americanization." The war had touched off a chauvinist reaction that men like Beveridge and Hearst were eager to exploit.

Closely allied to the new nationalism was an enhanced concern for the Monroe Doctrine. Wilson had announced that he wanted to make President Monroe's principles "the doctrine of the world." He proposed that the new world organization guarantee the territorial integrity of all countries, thus merging the safety of the western hemisphere with security plans for all nations. Senator William E. Borah of Idaho, a capricious progressive, who was at one time an anti-imperialist and a strong nationalist, introduced a Senate resolution reaffirming the credos of the Monroe Doctrine and the Farewell Address. He was warmly supported by the arch-conservative Senator Henry Cabot Lodge. As long as the war continued, it was possible to say that the defeat of Germany was requisite for the preservation of the Monroe Doctrine. As the fighting waned, however, men began to charge Wilson with scrapping the twin ramparts of our security—isolation and the Monroe Doctrine. The President's opponents made excellent use of the peculiar hold of the Doctrine upon the American mind. Moderate opinion shied away from the thought of abandoning both the Monroe Doctrine and isolationism simultaneously. It was too abrupt a departure from American tradition.

Not all of Wilson's critics were ultraists. Many sincere friends of a better world order had never accepted the axiom that force alone could preserve peace. There was, for example, former Secretary of State Elihu Root who was widely respected for his wisdom and shrewd judgment. Root was anything but an isolationist, but he had refused to join the League to Enforce Peace. His legalistic mind was anchored to the old American belief that international disputes could be handled best through a world court applying a refurbished international law. Many others wanted the war to end with a plan for peace, but they also wanted to protect cherished American values.

The historian, Frederick Jackson Turner of frontier fame, was an old friend of the President. Turner wanted to organize the world, but he shared the American dread of diplomatic wiles. He urged Wilson to limit his organization to those nations who shared the American "passion for peace." At least, Turner urged, the new league ought to have some "checks and antidotes" in order to overcome regional jealousy and suspicion.[11] The President thus had to face not only implacable enemies, but also constructive critics who wanted to reconcile the new ideas with the older tradition. Time was to prove that Wilson was temperamentally unable to deal with the middle-of-the-roaders. Because he could not placate them, they eventually joined the rapidly coalescing opposition.

The First World War crystallized the phenomenon called mid-western isolationism which was to become the *fifth* factor in reviving isolationism. Geography played an important part in nurturing this sentiment. A certain inner security came from having thousands of miles of land, in addition to the oceans, act as a buffer to the outside world. In western communities, there were fewer people who had become aware of an Atlantic world united by trade, travel, and cultural contacts. War cries, so it seemed, always came from down east.

There were also strong economic reasons for mid-western isolationism. Prior to 1914, this section had been greatly influenced by movements which had either anti-eastern or antiforeign implications. Free coinage of silver, that panacea of the farmers, had been thwarted by British gold policy. The Populist crusade of the nineties had passed, but it had left feelings of frustration. The progressive movement followed hard in its wake. Unlike the eastern liberals who were often internationalists, their western counterparts had provincial ideas about foreign affairs. They oversimplified the complex causes of war by explaining them away as conspiracies of their old enemies—scheming British imperialists, international bankers, and eastern capitalists. The corollary followed naturally that the United States could stay out of war by resisting the call of the Pied Piper. The war of 1914, moreover, brought little direct profit to mid-westerners from the munitions trade or from bankers' loans to the Allies. The grain farmers felt no particular dependence upon the European market. Why fight to secure Wall Street's wagers and perpetuate British colonialism? Added to this, the way in which the Wilson administration conducted the war fanned the flames of this opposition. The mid-westerners resented a ceiling price on northwestern Republican wheat, while southern Democratic cotton was allowed to bring what the market would bear.

Geography and economics explain only part of the story. National and intellectual factors are at least equally important. The northern central states had been largely peopled by German or Scandinavian stocks. After 1914, the Swedes and Norwegians were quite as neutral as the German-speaking elements. Some of the Lutheran clergy were more than neutral; they were pro-German. Pastors of smaller denominations had brought with them, as part of their cultural baggage, a hatred of war and a belief that European conflicts were capitalist conspiracies. All elements of the population had been nourished on a mental diet that served generous quantities of American uniqueness and European depravity. The intellectual climate of the immigrants was congenial to an economic interpretation of the war. America fought because of bankers who had too much money to lend, munition-makers who wanted to vend their lethal wares, and greedy industrialists who were looking for new markets to conquer. This version was to become the watchword of the isolationist faith. It was to have a persisting influence on the course of American history.

Localized language groups, which flourished in the wheat belt, were suspected of disloyalty because they prayed in their native tongues. The governor of Iowa, by proclamation, forbade such services. The foreign press was repeatedly excluded from the mails. Since there was little outright disloyalty, these interferences were more resented than they would have been had there been more actual treason.

In North Dakota, the socialist-founded Non-Partisan League waxed strong and exploited war issues for its own advantages. It was in such an atmosphere that Gerald P. Nye, of future isolationist renown, served his political apprenticeship.

In Minnesota, the elder Charles A. Lindbergh wrote a book with a challenging title: *Why Is Your Country at War and What Happens to You After the War, and Related Subjects.*

46

Lindbergh, who waged an unsuccessful campaign for governor in 1918 on an isolationist platform, blamed the war on profiteers and international bankers. His sixteen-year-old son and namesake, the famous flier, stored up memories for use in a later crisis.

As Samuel Lubell has written, all of these factors acting in harmony produced a specific variety of isolationism. It would, of course, be highly misleading to think that all the people of the upper Mississippi valley shared these convictions. Some of the most notable isolationists came from the far west, New England, and the south. It does seem fair, however, to say that the region known as the mid-west was the focal point of progressive-isolationist thought. It fathered the idea that concern for the world would hamstring domestic reform. Strangely enough, men holding such views were to stand on common ground with reactionary Republicans who were fighting Wilson because they feared reform booby-traps in his global blueprint. Politics was to help bring these strange bedfellows together.

The *sixth* and perhaps the major obstacle in Wilson's path was the exigency of party politics. There were, in those days, more Republicans in the land than Democrats, and the G.O.P. leaders knew it. They regarded Wilson as a political accident. His peace plans were formulated just at a time when the "outs" were becoming extremely restive. Never before in their history had the Grand Old Party been exiled from the White House for eight years. It did not seem right to them that the inconstant Democrats should be in control while so many important things were happening. They were determined that the President should neither secure a third term nor found a political dynasty. Wilson happened to stand for collective security. Good politics demanded that they oppose his cardinal ideas. The Republican affinity for isolationism started almost by chance. Before 1914, the party had been more world-minded and less provincial than the Democrats. The attractive issues of nationalism and isolationism proved irresistible to a party anxious to return to power.

Quarrelling with the President, however, was more than expediency. Many Republicans genuinely hated the progressive reforms of Wilson's first term. Today they seem mild enough to reasonable folk. Then, however, business men had not yet become reconciled to effective curbs upon their activities. Many of them longed to turn the clock back to uninhibited free enterprise. Some of the more conservative of the group even feared that Wilson would use the war to lead the country into socialism. They disliked the Underwood tariff act of 1913 which had jeopardized the system of stout protection for American industry. During the war, American business had little to fear from European competition, but industrialists were anxious for the future. What if Wilson should incorporate world free trade into the conditions of the peace? Such fears were enhanced when the President announced his Fourteen Points. Point number three had called for the removal of international trade barriers. What of the war-born industries that would need protection from Europe during a perilous infancy? Obviously the time had come to restore the Republican party to health, and the panacea was to be opposition to the leader of the Democrats.

Fortunately for the G.O.P. cause, the party had a good nurse. National Chairman Will H. Hays, later famous as the Hollywood censor who "timed the kisses," tried to unite the Republican right and left wings before the 1918 congressional elections. To win, Hays needed issues, and Beveridge, who took upon himself the job of physician, prescribed massive doses of isolationism and nationalism. "I talked with three of the most important men in our party," he wrote to the editor of the Indianapolis *Star,* "and to my delight . . . they insist that Wilson's League of Nations must be attacked." If the Republicans refuse the plan, he added, then "we lose a great issue."[12] We should take advantage of the "sentimental influence of tradition," he suggested. Isolation, Beveridge pointed out, was the one policy that had been consistently followed since the days of Washington. Sounding out the president of the Detroit Republican Club, he was told that he was on the right track, for a European league would be certain to break down the American tariff wall.

The congressional elections were held just six days before the Armistice. To the surprise of the world, a Republican congress was elected. Actually the league question had not been a major issue in the campaign. Local and sectional irritations against the conduct of the war amply explain the narrow Republican margin of victory. President Wilson, moreover, had made the mistake of appealing for the return of a Democratic congress and his entreaty had back-fired. The Republicans were elated and set their sights for the coming presidential election. The war was now over and they could attack the President with impunity. Shortly thereafter, Wilson announced that he would go to Paris in person to make the peace. He failed to take with him any Republican congressional leader or any Republican high in the councils of the party. Senator Lodge watched the situation thoughtfully. He told Beveridge that if Wilson made a league that impinged upon domestic control of legislation, military policy, or the Monroe Doctrine, "then our issue is made up and we shall win."[13]

Lodge's friend, Theodore Roosevelt, in his last strut across the American stage, held aloft the banner of nationalism. The colonel had, in the course of his career, given some grudging support to world organization. Back in 1910, while accepting the Nobel Peace Prize, he had suggested "a League of Peace . . . to prevent by force if necessary" the outbreak of war. Some years later Roosevelt hesitatingly had endorsed the plan of the League to Enforce Peace. Following Wilson's 1916 re-election, however, Roosevelt had changed his mind. His hatred of the President bordered on the pathological. Wilson, he thought, was "exceedingly base," "his soul was rotten through and through," and he was possessed by "vindictiveness" and "malice." The President's pet idea of world organization became to the colonel a "mean and odious hypocrisy." John M. Blum has demonstrated that Roosevelt's reversal was not basically inconsistent, for he had always thought of collective security as a dream for the remote future. The colonel had never believed that international law had sufficient sanction to control major disputes between states. The only feasible deterrent to war, then, would be a new balance of power maintained by the victorious Allies. To play its part the United States must remain strong and help police the world. Roosevelt was probably entirely sincere in opposing any league sponsored by altruists and idealists of the Wilsonian stripe.

The defeat of the Democrats in 1920 became almost an obsession with Roosevelt. Beveridge congratulated him on giving the Republicans the issue of "straight Americanism . . . pure and exclusive nationalism versus mongrel and promiscuous internationalism." The colonel spent his ebbing strength arguing against a Wilsonian peace. Beveridge cheered him on, reminding him that the Republicans must have a free hand to clean up and straighten out Mexico. Roosevelt was more cautious. He was not ready to reject the league idea entirely, but preferred rather to think of it as a buttress to American military strength. When Beveridge reminded him that there might then be no issue for 1920, Roosevelt retracted. He said he was for nationalism, but wanted to keep the league as sort of a "platonic expression" to keep the Taft internationalists in the party. Such lip service, he admonished, was needed to prevent the charge "that we are ourselves merely Prussian militarists."[14]

Two months later, the "lion" was dead. He left posthumous messages to the American people that greatly aided the development of a T. R. cult based on "America First." The colonel's friend, William Rockhill Nelson, published the first of these legacies in his paper, the Kansas City *Star*. It was widely quoted because it had been written from Roosevelt's deathbed. He advised a stern peace with Germany and then a league of the victors, which might be gradually expanded. In this association, Europe and Asia would maintain their own police systems while the United States would preserve order south of the Rio Grande. We should, he warned, make it perfectly clear that we would not undertake any new European crusades unless for clear and urgent reasons. The *Metropolitan* of March, 1919, contained T. R.'s final message for the American people. In it, he warned once more against policing the Rhine or any place far removed from our immediate range of interests. In the New World, America would know instinctively what was right and our energies could be used to settle the Mexican question and to defend the approaches to the Panama Canal.

Roosevelt was certainly entitled to his views. Had they been implemented, they would have frozen the status quo, but they also might have brought peace. His ideas, unlike those of Wilson, did not outrun the possibilities of politics nor did they move too far from the thought habits of the American people. The colonel, however, put his worst foot forward in the evening of his life. He became impetuously vindictive and allowed his hatred of Wilson to rule his passions. It was unfortunate that at a critical moment in American history, a great man, who had appreciated our responsibility in the world, turned hysterical nationalist and demagogue. Almost unwittingly Theodore Roosevelt did much to create a climate of opinion congenial to the new parochialism.

Thus was the strident nationalism woven into a legend. Hatred of Wilson was made concomitant to belief in Roosevelt. On the day that the President returned from Europe, the colonel's daughter stood at the White House gate, crossed her fingers, made the sign of the evil eye, and wished a murrain upon him. William Roscoe Thayer, Roosevelt's friend and biographer, attacked Wilson in his presidential address before the American Historical Association. "The motto, 'America First,'" wrote Thayer, "should not only be on everyone's lips, but in everyone's heart."[15] The letterhead of the Roosevelt Memorial Association carried the message: "One flag, the American flag; one language, the language of the Declaration of Independence; one loyalty, loyalty to the American people." Such a creed, carrying with it a disavowal of our proper share in the world's burdens, did not convey the true import of Roosevelt's life.

The original enthusiasm for a strong league of nations was so great that possibly it could have withstood the opposition of war dissenters, fervid nationalists, and intense Republican partisans. What was certain to be fatal to the program, however, was the loss of liberal support. We have already seen that the word "liberal" meant many things to many men. In American political parlance, it had come to designate the political independents of both parties who were neither chronic partisans nor social revolutionaries. After the collapse of Theodore Roosevelt's 1912 Progressive party, many, if not most of the independents, had joined liberal Democrats in supporting the President. Wilson owed his close 1916 victory to this liberal support. A month after his second inauguration the country was at war. Many of the liberals had reluctantly consented to intervention. They could reconcile themselves to war only by thinking of it as an instrument to bring world democracy. Even so, liberal and leftist opinion divided on the issue.

John Dewey, Columbia philosopher and symbol of American humanitarianism, supported the war effort. His stand was savagely attacked by the young Greenwich Village pundit, Randolph Bourne. Speaking for those liberals who would not accept the use of force, Bourne denounced the internationalization of the world as a "palpable apocalyptic myth." He reasoned that while the world was crying for economic reform, Wilson was planning a league to freeze the status quo. Bourne was soon to die and become a symbol for the "Lost Generation" of the twenties. Dewey was to live on to become a fountainhead of leftist isolationist thought. The socialists, to the left of the liberals, also split during the war. They, too, were later to reunite in opposing the President. Thus, eventually, leftists who succumbed to the war fever and those who resisted it were to have similar influence.

Wilson had paid little attention to mending his liberal fences while the country was at war. He had taken their support for granted and had overlooked the fact that they were a testy group to hold in line. They had a tendency to picture a world full of hope threatened by sinister machinations. Even during the war they suspected that the President was hearkening to the wrong voices. Wilson's task was made more difficult when the new Soviet Russian government publicized secret treaties which showed how our Allies had planned to divide the spoils of war. This, of course, was not Wilson's fault, but domestic affairs were in his hands. Liberal editors never forgot the over-zealousness of Postmaster Albert J. Burleson in excluding certain periodicals from the mails. "The price of immunity," said one editor, "is undiluted servility."[16] Suppression of free speech was equally severe despite the warning of John Dewey that there must be no coercion of opinion. Why, asked the liberals, did the President sign the severe Espionage Acts? Why did his hand not stay the promiscuous arresting and censoring?

The war had followed hard upon a period that had glorified individualism and civil liberty in the name of liberalism. Independent thinkers, even before the Armistice, were beginning to turn in disgust from the war and Wilson. The President's failure to placate them, to prepare them for anything but a utopian peace, was to prove a fatal mistake. Growing liberal unrest thus formed the *seventh* factor in the creation of an anti-Wilson coalition. The group expected too much from the peace. If disappointed, they were ready to give up hope of reforming Europe and to return to their older task of cleaning house at home.

Some of the President's friends sensed the growing liberal unrest and the peril of the incipient revolt against Wilsonism. The trials and vexations of war had burned out illusions and ideals. Unshaken was the old belief in the isolated security of the United States. The masses did not share Wilson's basic convictions. The best hope of containing the opposition lay in a reassemblement of the liberal forces. In the summer of 1918 some sixty men and women began to meet in New York City to ponder the problem. The list of names grew until it became impressive. There were Charles and Mary Beard, Herbert Croly, John Dewey, Felix Frankfurter, and Hamilton Holt. They were later joined by the influential Judge Learned Hand, the philanthropist Dorothy Whitney Straight, Professor John R. Commons, labor economist from Wisconsin, the philosopher, Horace M. Kallen, and the president of Harvard, A. Lawrence Lowell. They were, on the whole, liberal rather than conservative internationalists. They formed themselves into the League of Free Nations Association. The older group, the League to Enforce Peace, scrapped its original plan, and with the new group published a Victory Program. The manifesto stated that a non-liberal league would be a menace to the world. It called for a bill of rights for all nations, freedom of the seas, and the removal of trade barriers. To accomplish these aims, so the prospectus said, it might be necessary to accept some limitation of national sovereignty. They warned Wilson against the European forces that would hamper a democratic peace, and the Senate against obstructionist tactics. The new program was made public just as Wilson was preparing to leave for Europe.

Could the President, or any man, achieve enough in Paris to satisfy the liberals? Wilson faced European diplomats hardened by greed, militarism, and vengeful spirits of war. How would the British, French, and Italians feel about surrendering immediate benefits to plant a sturdy league sapling? The President's aims, as Walter Lippmann has said, could not be achieved by the power he had at his disposal. The country that Wilson left behind him was growling in restlessness. He had more than the liberals to satisfy, for the isolationist combination was feeding upon other factors already enumerated. Wilson had rested his case for intervention on moral and legalistic grounds that did not explain to his countrymen the menace of a German victory. The campaign of propaganda that ensued was too vulnerable to outlast the fighting. The ground was prepared for the recoil and the wave of disenchantment. The ideals that it sought to popularize were disappearing among the masses and had been taken too literally by the liberal elite. People had been led to expect too much. There had been no preparation for the normal give-and-take of diplomacy that would be bound to pare down ideals at the peace table. Allies and enemies alike had been camouflaged in black and white colorations. Nationalism, sparked by war, was getting out of control. In the mid-west, an important and vocal group was already saying: "We told you so." And even more important, the political pendulum had swung to the Republican side and congress was controlled by the opposition.

The President, nevertheless, still held many trumps as his ship, the *George Washington*, ploughed the wintry seas eastward. He was the spokesman of the people in many countries who hoped for a new deal for mankind. His international prestige was at an all-time high as he set foot on European soil to acknowledge the plaudits of high and low. He would have to compromise on his program, for there could be no other way. Could he reconcile home opinion to the inevitable? There were, in retrospect, several chances. He might give ground to the nationalist opposition and so carry with him the moderate internationalists. Time was to demonstrate that Wilson would not do this. The opposition would have to take all of his settlement or none. The only hope, then, of winning was to hold the independents in line. He would have to prevent a liberal-conservative alliance against his proposals. With the liberals solidly behind him, he might muster enough public opinion to defy his enemies. The retention of liberal support was basic to American acceptance of a Wilsonian settlement.

Chapter 3

The Liberal Defection

EVERY THINKING PERSON who ponders recent history is tantalized by the question: would the subsequent years have been different if the United States had supported the League of Nations in 1919? Such speculation, however intriguing, provides no satisfactory conclusion, for the simple fact remains that we did not join. Why then, one might continue, did Woodrow Wilson succeed in fashioning a League of Nations at the Versailles Peace Conference only to fail to convince his own country of the necessity for collective security? After one hundred years of relative indifference to foreign affairs, a reaction against our first overseas venture was probably inevitable. Before Wilson had reached a single decision at Paris a stout opposition was brewing. To overcome his opponents, the President had to have support above and beyond his normal Democratic strength. He needed a coalition behind him. Instead of creating this bulwark, the Versailles treaty itself engendered three powerful counter movements. This chapter and the two following will describe the formation of that weird coalition which defeated the President's plan and pulled this country back to its isolationist moorings.

The defection of the liberals was the first great factor in the combination against Wilson. It provided the conservative-nationalists with the overwhelming argument that the President had been repudiated by his own followers. It destroyed a vocal source that hitherto had argued for a Wilsonian peace and shattered the alliance between the political independents and the Democrats which for so long had strengthened the Chief Executive's position.

To understand this defection it is necessary to explore the problems that Wilson met at Versailles, for it was his solutions to these questions that alienated men of liberal persuasion. When the peace conference opened on January 12, 1919, the President found himself at grips with stark reality. He faced David Lloyd George of Great Britain, Georges Clemenceau of France, Vittorio Orlando of Italy, and the Japanese diplomats. These men mirrored nationalist and imperialist aspirations, the wartime punitive spirit, and their peoples' hunger for repara-

55

tions. There were also secret treaty promises to be cashed in at the peace table. France and Italy insisted upon boundary adjustments for reasons of national security and ambition. Such demands ran counter to Wilson's formula of self-determination for subject peoples. All of the victorious powers, with the exception of the United States, cast greedy eyes on German and Turkish colonial possessions. Wilson had to compromise or else go home, because his opponents could not yield completely and still remain in office. Their flexibility was limited for they had fanned the hopes of their war-torn constituents by promises of "squeezing Germany till the pips squeaked," of boundary extensions, and of post-war security.

Wilson could not choose to leave. Bolshevism appeared to be spreading westward from a Russia that was capitalizing on fluid boundaries and internal disorder in new states. Wilson saw but one alternative. He would fight tenaciously for as much of his program as he could salvage. His prime objective was an organization to maintain peace. To achieve it he would make concessions on other stipulations. In the fullness of time, the President reasoned, an effective League would rectify the injustices engendered by the passions of the moment. To guarantee the birth of a living league, Wilson insisted that the Covenant of the League of Nations be incorporated into all the treaties of peace. As these agreements were ratified, nations would automatically become members of the new organization.

Wilson had decided that he would let the end justify the means. In taking this step he put himself in a vunerable position. Had his original program embraced merely American national interests, such demands could have been compromised without due loss of face. They would have been part of the usual international barter expected at peace conferences. As Hans J. Morgenthau has said, however, Wilson's program was studded with moral precepts. He found it impossible to compromise principles without abdicating his moral leadership. He had to pay a heavy price for having ignored European and Asiatic realities in proclaiming his peace program. Now there was nothing to do but to make the best of a bad situation.

As knowledge of Wilson's recession reached American shores, liberals were bewildered and dismayed. Compromise of principle did not fit into their tight frame of reference. Characteristically, these men were over-confident about big things—Utopia was a possibility, not a mere dream. They had had altogether too much faith that the European peoples, with the proper moral guidance, would sacrifice temporary benefits for enduring humanitarian gains. At the same time, they tended to be over-apprehensive about little things and equated concession to reality with wholesale betrayal.

The liberals had been reluctant to go to war. Simon-pure Darwinists, like Theodore Roosevelt, had believed war a natural part of the struggle for survival. Most of the liberals, however, were "reform" Darwinists who argued that it was man's duty to mitigate the harshness of nature by active steps. Some liberals had refused to follow Wilson to war. They had already prejudged the peace and were ready to enlighten fellow liberals who had decided to cast their lot with Wilson. None of them, moreover, had been happy warriors. They persuaded themselves that this was more than a war—it was the great opportunity for a new day for the world. Wilson, of course, had encouraged such unrealistic thinking. Taunted by pacifists for their acquiescence in the use of force, the Wilsonians took refuge in fond thoughts of peace. Eagerly they looked forward to the President's coming joust with the European reactionaries. When he was forced to compromise they were totally incapable of understanding his resort to expediency. He had destroyed their vision of a war-chastened world ready to turn over a brand new leaf. The President obviously was playing the ancient European game of diplomacy. This they could never forgive. To destroy him they were ready to make an unnatural alliance with his and their old enemies.

Of course not all of the liberals deserted. Some of them realized Wilson's predicament, accepted his solution, and fought valiantly for the League of Nations. It seems fair to say, however, that the majority of the politically independent liberals opposed both the treaty and its Siamese twin, the League. These independents were frequently theoretical internationalists. Their opposition to the treaty re-united them with liberals who had opposed the war and who were usually isolationists. This group in turn coalesced with the progressive-isolationists at the Borah-La Follette variety, who opposed any kind of international organization. The liberal front was considerably swollen by the influx of isolationist elements. The internationalists among them proclaimed loudly that they were not isolationists, but that they opposed this Covenant of the League of Nations. Such protests meant little for the net result was aid, comfort, and eventual victory for the great isolationist combine that was to frustrate Wilson's plans.

Why were the liberals so willing to go to such lengths to defeat the treaty? The Versailles settlement, they thought, was harsh, vindictive, permeated with greed, and, as William Allen

White put it, "purple with revenge." Wilson had proclaimed self-determination to the world and then had allowed the Saar to be detached from Germany and the Tyrol from Austria. Moreover, the Japanese imperialists had been assigned German economic rights in the Shantung Peninsula, subject only to oral promises to restore political sovereignty of the area to China. In addition, Wilson had agreed to reparations which contradicted his earlier promises that Germany would not be saddled with the costs of the war. Liberal critics harped on the points that the President had yielded and invariably overlooked the concessions he had wrested from his grasping opponents. Without Wilson's untiring determination and influence, the Paris settlement, in all probability, would have been even more vindictive.

The independents who had supported Wilson during the war did not fear that the League of Nations jeopardized American freedom of action. They had always wanted a world organization along liberal lines. They were certain, however, that no good could come from a league riveted to an unjust and war-breeding peace. There could be no compromise with this "Covenant of Death." Had not Wilson himself once said that only a "peace without victory" could last the years? These liberals would not accept new peace machinery superimposed upon the rotten hulk of European hatreds and rivalries. They felt that plans for economic and social betterment had been elcipsed by a political scheme to freeze the status quo.

Many of these same 1919 liberals had been veteran antiimperialists. They shared with many of their countrymen a deep distrust of colonialism. The Covenant, to them, provided for an organized division of the imperialist loot. If the United States had thrived on independence, why deny this boon to the inhabitants of Syria or of the German Pacific Islands? Wilson, to be sure, had prevented outright conquests by providing for a system of mandates to be supervised by the League of Nations. That such mandated colonies would ever become independent seemed an amusing suggestion. If the Allies had been sincere, Carl Becker suggested, they would have put all of their colonies under the League instead of leaving their older possessions subject to the "law of force."

Having equated the League with imperialist rapacity, the next step was to argue that the new association must lead to war rather than peace. Imperialism, it was contended, had helped precipitate the 1914 conflict because bankers and business men had insisted that colonial investments be backed by force. The way, then, to arrest war would be to harness predatory economic forces. Wilson, instead, had created a League with tap-roots for an expanded imperialism. Was this League, asked Professor Becker, the best possible "under the circumstances"? If so, he replied, then these very circumstances had been re-created by the same selfish men who had made the Covenant.[1]

Becker's argument was one of professional restraint and of discerning, if utopian, international insight. In New York City, however, the youthful Harold E. Stearns unabashedly pleaded for isolationism. Stearns, who had disdained the war, was a Greenwich Village writer for progressive journals. In his book, *Liberalism in America,* he disposed of the League as "an aggressive alliance to exploit the weak peoples of the world." Both isolationist and international liberals refused to accept Wilson's premise that the League was worth the concessions. They insisted that an organization born of such compromise would perpetuate, not alleviate, injustice. Here the issue was joined.

So much for the general reasons for the liberal revolt. The rupture did not come without clear warning. George L. Record, pioneer progressive from the President's own state of New Jersey, wrote a long letter to him in Paris. Record pointed out that Wilson was putting too much emphasis on the mere creation of a league of imperialistic governments. If such a league had any real power, he argued, it might be used as an international bulkark for privileged interests. The President, however, paid little heed to such advice. He wanted to complete his task in Europe and then state his case at home. By the time he was ready for this round, his liberal following had been split asunder.

The break between the President and the political left was personalized in the action of two editors who were the principal purveyors of liberal thought. These men were Oswald Garrison Villard and Herbert Croly. Villard, like his maternal grandfather of abolitionist fame, William Lloyd Garrison, was a severe and uncompromising idealist. Both as editor of the New York *Evening Post* and later of the *Nation,* Villard was a crusading perfectionist who would brook no compromise with the ideals that he had outlined for himself and the world. Throughout a long career he could never comprehend the Machiavellian truism that public responsibility frequently forced men to depart from both ethics and consistency. Villard was apt to clash with anyone who found it necessary to come to terms with an imperfect world. Even before 1917 he had written Wilson off as a man who would sacrifice both principle and belief for opportunity.[2] Villard, who was born in his father's homeland of Germany, had never been reconciled to American intervention. As the Armistice approached he announced that this was supposed to be a war for democracy and that he would judge it by its fruits. To evaluate the harvest, he sailed for Europe to cover the peace conference in person.

Upon arrival, Villard challenged the "secrecy at Versailles," as if it would have been feasible and wise to have shaped vital decisions within earshot of the world press. "No one knows tonight," he wrote just before the conference opened, "all that is happening except a few insiders. Much they may be putting through, the little group of men who rule the world."[3] Once in a while Villard would appreciate the sordid pressures which played on the President, but his charitable moods were infrequent and short-lived. He reserved final judgment, however, until February, 1919, when Wilson formally presented the League of Nations plan to the full session of the Peace Conference. His mind was then made up. Wilson, he concluded, had provided no far-reaching adjustments and had merely produced a league of governments tied together by archaic political and military devices. The *Nation* demanded that Wilson's league be defeated to frustrate a "calm, arrogant, and ruthless . . . plan" for Allied world domination. Villard's opposition was intensified when he read the terms of peace imposed on Germany. He assured the arch-isolationist Senator Robert M. La Follette that the treaty was "the most iniquitous peace document ever drawn," and that it reeked with bad faith, malice, and inhumanity.[4] Villard once had wished "sixty feet always" between himself and the Republican chairman of the Senate Foreign Relations Committee, Henry Cabot Lodge. Quite possibly the senator would have preferred even a greater distance, but Villard's *Nation* was doing yeoman work in the fight. This liberal flank attack on the President would prove invaluable to the Republican cause.

Herbert Croly's defection was shockingly unexpected and was welcome news to Lodge's ears. Since its founding in 1914, Croly's *New Republic* had been a prime source of liberal opinion. He had attracted a remarkable staff of writers whose gifted words had traveled far. This galaxy included the brilliant young publicist, Walter Lippmann, the trenchant literary editor, Francis Hackett, an astute observer of politics named Walter E. Weyl, and other men of talent. The very first issue of the *New Republic* had hailed the end of American isolationism. As the world was engulfed in war, the editors had argued that the United States must shed its tradition of non-meddling in order to participate in the making of a beneficent peace. We must, Croly insisted, use the great European upheaval to secure a better world.

Croly had looked to Theodore Roosevelt's leadership in the very early days of the *New Republic*. Before long, however, he broke with the colonel and backed Wilson's progressive program. The switch dramatized the realignment of independent liberals behind the President. Despite serious misgivings about the suppression of civil liberties after America declared war, the *New Republic* held tenaciously to the belief that Wilson would bring the Allies to see the advantages of a truly democratic peace. Unlike the suspicious Villard, Croly heralded Wilson's decision to fight the battle for liberalism on European ground. The dragons of reaction, he thought, would scatter before this modern St. George.

Croly sent Lippmann and Weyl to cover the Peace Conference. Before very long they concluded that liberalism had yielded to the better organized forces of reaction. Lippmann warned that if Europe insisted on maintaining peace by the bayonet, then there was nothing for America to do but leave the foreigners to their fate "and find our own security in this hemisphere."[5] He came home to supply, as he later admitted, "too much ammunition" to the Senate "Battalion of Death." In 1919, however, Lippmann told the country that there was no mystery at Versailles—it had all been plainly revealed in the acrid terms of the treaty.

Before Lippmann's companion, Walter Weyl, could bare his disillusionment to the world, Croly turned against Wilson. The *New Republic* had already noted the decline in the President's prestige. An editorial explained that Wilson had taken for his own the liberal precepts of the world only to abandon them in the house of the enemy. Croly took the final step the week that the text of the treaty reached the United States. He announced that "This is Not Peace" and demanded that America withdraw from all commitments under the proposed Covenant. This step, which the historian William E. Dodd called "one of the fatal blunders of history," cost Croly much soul-searching and many subscribers. His sensitive conscience, however, would permit no other course.

The *Dial*, another popular liberal organ of the day, had already deserted the President. The League of Free Nations Association reversed its endorsement of the League of Nations Covenant, Henceforth, the chief voices of liberal opinion demanded the defeat of the treaty. Without formal alliance, the liberals edged their way into the anti-Wilson coalition.

To the left of the liberals stood the Marxists and their sympathizers. Marxian socialism was not a new movement in the United States and it had shown considerable vigor before the war. Like the liberals, the American Socialists split over our entry into the war only to be reunited in a common effort to defeat the peace treaty. During the war all Socialists had been embittered by the severe treatment accorded dissenters. After 1917 there was the new factor of Soviet Russia. Its existence provided a chance to observe the principles of Marx, so long talked about in theory, actually put into practice by a great power. Would not something new, concrete, and challenging result from the experiment? Some American radicals were enthusiastic; others, borrowing a term coined by Wilson, decided upon a policy of "watchful waiting." All, however, resented Wilson's insistence that the Communist Revolution and the Bolshevist desertion of the Allies had made Russia a pariah among the nations.

The stirring events in Russia had a special appeal to certain Americans. They were men and women for whom, in Longfellow's words, "life was real, life was earnest." Downhearted at the liberal failure at Versailles, convinced that American progressivism had limited horizons, they veered leftward toward Russia. Light, thought many of the advanced liberals, seemed to come only from Moscow. Lincoln Steffens, gifted reporter and original muckraker, had covered Versailles. He returned home convinced that the liberal world was bankrupt and that Wilson and his coterie had surrendered their principles. What now would save the common people of central Europe from being thrown back into the old economic thraldom? Steffens winced at Bolshevist terror, but he was looking for men with principles. If Lenin seemed rough, Steffens explained that he was like the captain of a storm-tossed liner: "He can't bother about the weak stomachs of his passengers."[6] William C. Bullitt, who needed an ambassadorship to Russia to disillusion him, resigned in 1919 as attaché to the American Commission to Negotiate the Peace because he felt that Russia had been misunderstood and mistreated. Wilson's alarm over the spread of Bolshevism seemed unwarranted and narrow-minded. Was it not additional proof of his desire to abort economic and social progress? To some men the Russian experiment was worth a sympathetic observation.

While Wilson was at Versailles, the Third International was formed to organize communists outside of Russia. There ensued a three-way split among American Marxists. By the summer of 1919 there were the Communists, Communist Laborites and the old Socialist party which opposed the Soviet plan of revolution by force. Many of these radicals carried no party cards, but they were often interested in and friendly to the Russian experiment. In the hectic fever of 1919 it was difficult for ordinary Americans to differentiate between Socialists and Communists. For our purposes, however, it is safe to say that regardless of the shade of red, all of the radicals and their sympathizers were violently anti-League. There was a method to their madness. They regarded the League as a rival which had to be destroyed. The League was trying to organize the world along capitalist-nationalist lines, while the radical program called for world organization of all working men regardless of nationality. The League was, therefore, denounced as regressive and counter-revolutionary. The Communist argued that nationalism and imperialism were basic elements in the capitalist system. The League had enthroned both.

The "Berne International" of Socialists met during the Versailles Peace Conference and demanded a socialist league. If the United States joined the capitalist League of Nations, so the radicals argued, then Wall Street rather than Lombard Street or the French Bourse would dominate the world. Americans who demanded League membership, they explained, were out to enlarge the scope of American finance-imperialism. The radicals opposed the League for a reason opposite to that of nationalists like Albert J. Beveridge, who said that the League would hem in our expansion in the western hemisphere. Communists sometimes picked up the expansionist arguments of the nationalists, and in their jargon they equated "isolationism" with "imperialism."

It is impossible to estimate how much the radicals damaged Wilson's cause. In 1919 there were at least fifty Bolshevist papers published in the United States in twenty-six different languages. Half of these were printed in New York.[7] They reached, of course. only relatively small numbers. Any protest from a small minority, and from an "out" group of society at that, can have only limited effect on general public opinion. However, the protest of the Socialists, who had built up respect for their press outside of their party, did add some weight to the anti-League argument. This leftist press repeated, like the ceaseless call of the whippoorwill, that Woodrow Wilson, the servant of J. P. Morgan, took the country into war to save Wall Street's loans. The war in turn had produced the Versailles settlement which was created to stand guard over the swag of the victorious imperialists and to make certain that the common people would not revolt against this tyranny.

The activities of The New York Rand School of Social Science, which after 1906 had developed into a labor college, were especially important in spreading the gospel of the left. The college offered popular courses whose titles suggest that the instructors made snide remarks about Wilson and the League. The school, moreover, published its own material which was dispensed through the Rand Book Store located on the ground floor of the "People's House." One of their chief writers and lecturers was Dr. Scott Nearing, economist and sociologist, who had been indicted under the Espionage Act for anti-war activities. "Tomorrow," wrote the Harvard historian, Albert Bushnell Hart, to Senator Borah, "I try my hand against a very different kind of antagonist—Scott Nearing, the Socialist, whose objections to the League are as distant from your objections as your point of view is from mine."[8] A talented polemicist, Nearing wrote and spoke against this "League of Robber Nations." He explained in his Rand School publications that the League must be destroyed because it would prevent the economic emancipation of labor. To Marxists of all varieties, the League of Nations was the "cossack of Europe," designed to crush "all labor and revolutionary movements." Thus Senator Lodge found more unexpected allies. The new recruits were to prove embarrassing.

Neither the radicals nor the liberals could supply the senatorial leadership needed to prevent ratification of the Treaty of Versailles. There were no Marxists in the Senate, and only a relatively small group of liberals. Even the progressive-isolationists such as Senators Borah and George W. Norris of Nebraska had to look to the regular Republican partisans to organize the opposition. This task fell into the welcoming hands of Senator Lodge. Historians are not agreed on the gentleman's ultimate purposes. Many have argued that despite Lodge's insistence on the League with reservations that would safeguard American independence, his real intentions were to defeat the treaty, not to compromise with Wilson. Other authorities insist that Lodge wanted the treaty with strong reservations so that credit for joining a revamped League would go to the Republican party. One cannot say for certain. Whatever his true motives may have been, Lodge decided upon a flank attack. Because a direct assault might create too much popular reaction against the senators, the Republican leadership decided to recommend the treaty with strong modifications. If these amendments or reservations went through, well and good. If the treaty failed because Wilson would not agree to them, then blame for the failure could be placed on the Democrats.

Senator Lodge knew that he faced a stiff fight. He was ready to buttress his strength with support from groups outside of his own cabal of Republican conservative-nationalists. Socialists and Communists were too far removed for direct negotiations and they were of questionable value at best. Liberals and progressives, however, were milder heretics who, despite their profound errors, were still Americans. An informal working agreement was reached between liberals who felt that the League of Nations was a Machiavellian conspiracy with deceiving internationalist wrappings, and the nationalists who argued that Wilson's plan was an idealistic scheme that would undermine the foundations of American security. There was mutual suspicion. Villard wanted Senator Hiram W. Johnson of California, who had been the 1912 Progressive candidate for Vice-President, to lead the battle. Thus Villard would have preferred an outright Irreconcilable (one of the fifteen senators who were opposed to joining the League under any and all conditions), to Lodge who proclaimed himself a moderate internationalist. Villard, however, bowed to the inevitable, accepted the captaincy of the ultra-conservative Lodge, and even praised the "calm and clever way" in which the senator united his forces. The *Nation* and the *New Republic* wanted the treaty defeated as point number one on the liberal agenda.

During the critical year of 1919 Villard made a number of contacts with Republican senators. Beveridge, with whom the editor had long been friendly, served as a sort of liaison officer between the two groups. Despite his chauvinism, Beveridge was still remembered as a progressive. He had enjoyed the confidence of the regular Republicans and had unusual maneuverability because he currently was out of office. Villard's chief contact man, however, was his old newspaper associate, Lincoln Colcord, who was then in Washington. Dinners were arranged to bring together liberal and conservative leaders with Villard himself frequently coming from New York. Colcord advised the *Nation* to back not the reservationists but the Irreconcilables for there could be no compromise with "a peace of loot, a peace of hate, a peace of hunger and death and war."[9] Villard, like most of the liberals, was in a quandary. He agreed with the Irreconcilables that there could be no agreement with Wilson, but unlike them, he wanted a substitute plan. So he made the rounds among the senators to see if there was any possibility of a constructive program for international organization. He sounded out Senator Philander C. Knox of Pennsylvania, Taft's Secretary of State, who had become increasingly conservative with age. No help was forthcoming from this quarter, in spite of Villard's pathetic plea that he needed some alternative for his readers. He then turned to the progressive-isolationists who opposed the treaty on grounds similar to the liberals, but who, in contrast to them, opposed the whole league concept. Senator Borah, the leader of this group, was no more encouraging than Knox had been. He even rebuffed the suggestion of an immediate campaign for civil liberties which the editor thought might at least show the country that the liberals had not been won over by the conservatives. Borah insisted that Wilson's iniquitous scheme be dispatched first. Nor did Villard get any further with La Follette. The two men thought alike on domestic issues, but the publisher eventually realized that the Wisconsin senator was an incorrigible isolationist.

Like Villard, Croly wanted a league, but an entirely different one. Neither man wanted to defeat the treaty only to let the country drift back into isolationism. Meanwhile, in the Senate, the whole matter had bogged down in the morass of party politics, and the Republican leaders were thinking in terms of the election of 1920 and not about a liberalized Covenant. Villard and Croly might have joined a motley group who wanted the treaty with varying degrees of modification, but the two editors thought the Covenant beyond salvage. The reservations actually proposed by the Senate, moreover, were anything but liberal—they were distinctly nationalist in flavor. Croly thought the Lodge reservations were as selfish and as provincial as the ambitions of Clemenceau and Orlando. In his perplexity, he urged their adoption because they would make a "debating society" out of that League of "illiberal governments." Croly, then, was a reservationist only in the sense that if the treaty chanced to slip through, he wanted the League of Nations hamstrung. Actually, both men helped the Irreconcilables keep the United States out of the League. Stay out of "this bastard League of Nations," the *Nation* urged, and "free us from the hundred-fold entanglements which the present document carries with it."[10] In one year Villard's circulation quintupled. The new tack was paying dividends.

The liberals were clearly warned that the triumph of the Irreconcilables would mean isolationism, for the idea of a new league was obviously chimerical. Lord Robert Cecil, British statesman and one of the fathers of the League, told Villard that he was helping to destroy the only instrument, however imperfect, that could be contrived to unite the world. Professor Horace M. Kallen of the New School for Social Research, a pro-League liberal, bluntly pointed out to Villard and Croly that they were playing into the hands of reactionaries who would hold all the trumps when the fight was over. Both men, however, were visionaries who over-estimated the power of liberal opinion to implement their utopian hopes. Croly proclaimed endlessly that he and his associates were not isolationists and that they wanted only to destroy the treaty so that American generosity and helpfulness might yet save mankind. Meanwhile, liberals must return to their original role of local reformers. What such liberals did not seem to comprehend was that they were clearing the path to the White House for the Republican party. As time was to prove, a victorious G.O.P. would be congenial neither to a domestic housecleaning nor to a revived altruism abroad. The anti-League liberals helped inadvertently to create the Republican unity that made possible the victory of 1920. The country should have opened its eyes when La Follette and Lodge became "Bob" and "Cabot" to each other and when "Bob" rode down Pennsylvania Avenue with that high-priest of reaction, Senator Boies Penrose of Pennsylvania. Just as Beveridge had predicted, opposition to international organization proved a healing nostrum for the divided Republicans.

The liberals set out to reform the world in 1919 and retired in resentment, as Edgar Ansel Mowrer has put it, "as a jilted bride to a convent." John Dewey drifted off into peaceful Socialism wondering whether or not he had been wise in supporting the war. He blamed our "pious optimism" and "our evangelical hypocrisy" for our failure at Paris. Wilson, he thought, had not realized that ideals were not self-propelling and therefore had to be implemented by forceful action rather than words. In downtown New York, in the offices of the *New Republic,* Herbert Croly turned to the self-discipline of yoga, recognizing that without the impetus of religious truth, liberalism would always flinch away from meeting the critical questions raised by modern civilization. Liberals who were less sensitive than Croly railed and ridiculed, condemned the fatheaded complacency of American "boobocracy," and assumed airs of either superior irresponsibility or downright indifference.[11] Little constructive work was done to combat the isolationist spirit which the liberals had coincidentally helped to bring into existence.

Did the anti-League liberals, in the years after 1920, regret their steps? As the United States returned to continental know-nothingism, material self-interest, disillusion and reaction, did they think that they had erred in the hour of decision? Most of these liberals were men of paper-thin sensitivity and were thus given to soul-searching. One could hardly expect introspection from such a blatant nationalist as Hiram W. Johnson or from a self-sufficient homespun theorist like William E. Borah. The liberals, however, were different. Their hopes for the future had turned to apples of Sodom. Some, like Walter Lippmann, openly regretted their original anti-League stand. Three factors, nevertheless, that followed hard upon the treaty fight reinforced the liberals' belief that they had been right in their anti-Versailles stand. The first of these was the entry of John Maynard Keynes into the American intellectual scene.

Keynes was a young Cambridge economist, who after a wartime mission to the United States, represented the British Treasury at Versailles. Disillusioned, he resigned and hurriedly wrote *The Economic Consequences of the Peace* in the summer of 1919. It was promptly serialized in the *New Republic* and was destined to have far-reaching influence. Keynes' mastery of polemics, the fertile muckraking possibilities of Versailles, the intelligentsia's revolt against Wilson all played their part—the book became the bible of the liberals. Long to be remembered were Keynes' pen sketches of the Big Four at Versailles—Wilson, Lloyd George, Clemenceau, and Orlando. The European schemers, he explained, had "bamboozled" the provincial old Presbyterian President by clothing their vengeance in terms of freedom and international equality. The result was a new Europe, economically inefficient, torn by strife, and plagued by rivalries. Keynes closed with anguished words that solidified American opinion: the peace settlement lay like a dangerous derelict athwart the road to progress.

The major Keynesian arguments that the peace should have been magnanimous rather than harsh, that the drastic reparation settlements were economically impossible, and that the Allies had sacrificed economic realities to political vindictiveness were well received in the United States.[12] Especially impressed were the liberals who had so long contended that world economic reform was essential to peace. They were now doubly certain that Versailles, and its child, the League of Nations, were conspirators against the peace.

The Economic Consequences of the Peace came too late to influence the Senate's action in refusing consent to the treaty. Its importance lies in the fact that it became the thesaurus of the isolationists. Senator Borah read Keynes and stored up new arguments for use in future debates. Dr. Scott Nearing quoted the book to cinch his favorite proposition that capitalist nations must eat or be eaten. Herbert Hoover met Keynes and explained his break with Wilson partly on an exchange of thoughts with the British economist. Senator La Follette felt that Keynes, "being an Englishman," did not tell all that he knew, but that he had said enough to show that the allies had made another war inevitable by resorting to barbarism in the treatment of the conquered. Readers of the book took from it what they wished, and almost invariably overlooked the fact that Keynes hoped that world opinion might yet save the League of Nations.

Another factor in persuading the liberals that their disillusion with Wilson was justified was the Red Scare of 1919-1920, which occurred as men were regaling themselves on Keynes' words. The administration's attitude toward national hysteria seemed final proof that the President had turned reactionary. Strikes, reckless talk and action on the part of both labor and capital, some real bombs and much unreal fear, all seemed to threaten internal security. Highly placed federal officials became unduly alarmed and for a time there was great danger to American civil liberties. Wilson well understood the hatred of both foreign and domestic Bolshevists for his League of Nations and this knowledge did not soften his reaction. Actually, he was seriously ill during the worst part of the scare with the result that the official encouragement of the abnormal excitement often stemmed from his subordinates. The President, however, bore final responsibility for the arrests, raids, and suspension of usual court procedures for deported aliens.

Perhaps the most important effect of the Red Scare on the liberals was the way in which it cemented their relations with the progressive-isolationists. Both groups fought together once more, now in the name of individual freedom. The anti-League liberals were eager for battle. In addition to crusading for cherished convictions, they could cut the cord that had bound them to the nationalists during the treaty fight. They could run up their own standard of independence emblazoned with the shield of civil liberty. Their natural allies were progressive Irreconcilables like Borah, Norris, and La Follette. In the new camaraderie less and less was heard about the basic differences between the two groups. Soon the cleavage between the anti-League liberals and the progressive-isolationists would resolve itself into agreement for the present and polite arguments about the future.

Still another, and by all odds the most effective element in soothing the liberal conscience, was the spate of war-guilt revelations. As part of the "over-there" spirit of 1917-1918, the Allied case had been badly overstated and German responsibility for 1914 grossly exaggerated. As historical perspective returned, some reversal of the charges against Germany was both inevitable and also beneficial. Such revision of wartime history is common after every conflict, but this time it came prematurely. Bolshevist Russia had thrown open its archives in order to descredit the czar and his capitalist Allies. Russia's action was soon followed by the republican governments of Austria and Germany. They had everything to gain and nothing to lose by uncovering documents which showed the complex origins of the war. This evidence alone, printed and digested by American liberal journals, caused some reversal of opinion. In addition, there were Englishmen and Frenchmen, powerful with pen and tongue, who had dissented from the war. Americans had not known that a vocal Allied minority had always pinned the blame for the war on political opponents in their own countries. Here was the case of the man biting the dog and making headlines. Such disclosures were helped along by German historians, with whom the question of war-guilt had become an understandable fetish. By pursuing it they could vindicate their own country and undermine the reparations settlement of Versailles which had been based upon the premise of the German guilt.

The documents that came out of hiding were too choice to be buried in the cloistered pages of the *American Historical Review* or between the covers of heavily written and stoutly documented monographs. Journalists, good-intentioned amateurs, and debunkers often led in what should have been the work of historians, trained to digest and to interpret evidence. Much of the revisionism of the 1920s was unscientific and impressionistic. Along with psychological behaviorism, Freudianism, hedonism, and the new interpretive literature and art, it formed a revolt against the older values of society. There can be no general indictment of this revisionism, because much of it corrected judgments that needed reversal. Publicity-hungry journalists and politicians made reckless use of careful, scholarly war-guilt studies. From tenable conclusions of a divided guilt, amateurs created the reverse fallacy of 1918. They pictured the war as a Franco-Russian plot against Germany!

This literature was eagerly absorbed into the liberal mind. Men who had opposed intervention in 1917 felt vindicated.

Liberals, who turned against Wilson after Versailles, were happy that they had opposed a harsh treaty that punished a nation no more guilty than its vindictive enemies. George W. Norris did some reading and concluded that czarist Russia was the chief instigator of the war, aided and abetted by France. Senator La Follette reprinted serially in his own magazine Albert Jay Nock's *Myth of a Guilty Nation.* Nock, editor of the liberal magazine, *Freeman,* had used material pilfered from the Belgian archives by Junker propagandists. Charles A. Beard published his own findings based on the evidence. He was not willing merely to exchange German for Russian or French villains, but he was certain that henceforth we must "regard with cold blood all the quarrels of Europe."[13] The European war-guilt controversy formed another bond of union between the anti-League liberals and the progressive-isolationists. Both groups were intensely absorbed in the subject and derived similar conclusions from the evidence. Their basic differences were slowly obliterated by working together in common causes.

The argument about 1914 was certain to raise once more the question of American intervention. If the European war had been fought between rivals with equally soiled hands, why had we not been content to sit on the sidelines? The stock answer was that we had been beguiled by sinister forces— propaganda from without and bankers and munition-makers from within. Actually, this interpretation was an old one, harking back to the days of American neutrality. It was revived at the end of the war by Walter E. Weyl and Scott Nearing. For a time, such talk was hardly tolerated. A Republican congressman from Illinois was shouted down with cries of treason and scandal when he charged, on the floor of the House, that we had been seduced by an unscrupulous combination of wealth and its "kept literary harlots." The controversy over the European origins of the war, however, was bound to keep the argument over American motives alive. As Dexter Perkins has said, there has been a persisting tendency in American history to call all wars unnecessary after they were over and to display "bad conscience" toward them. Revision was the order of the day and it became increasingly common in progressive and liberal circles to say that American soldiers had died in Europe to save a Wall Street mortgage on the Allies.

Thus in the twenties "idealism" seemed always to mean "impractical," "sacrifice" was customarily modified with "useless," and "entanglements" seldom appeared unless accompanied by "foreign." "In war nobody wins" and "war never settles anything" became epigrammatic.[14] Few asked themselves whether or not an imperial German victory would have been compatible with American national interests. People seemed to take it for granted that wanting nothing from the war, we got nothing; that is, nothing of value, for a Socialist congressman explained that we got prohibition and the flu; while the Baltimore wit, Henry L. Mencken, said we got the pleasure of looking at American Legion parades and the creation of the Russian colossus. Inasmuch as we now had the ill will of the world, Oswald Garrison Villard reasoned that it would have been better to have sacrificed the lives of the soldiers "in cold blood on Broadway."[15] The Communists featured a cartoon showing twenty thousand veterans insane as a result of the war. Endlessly, people calculated how many hospitals could have been built, libraries opened, and colleges endowed with the money spent. The disillusionment was profound.

In sum, it is apparent that the defection of the liberals helped defeat Wilson's league and unwittingly aided the creation of a new isolationism. The liberals had not been content to stand by. They joined the reactionary enemies of the President and made common cause with the progressive-isolationists with whom they shared many points of view. Circumstances brought theoretical internationalists such as Villard and Croly together with obdurate isolationists of the Borah-La Follette variety. Having helped to defeat the League by joining in the anti-Wilson combination, their own hopes for a new league were caught up in the isolationist groundswell. Versailles had separated the President from his liberal flank. He then had to depend upon partisan Democratic strength and a few loyal internationalists to carry his program. The same treaty that alienated the liberals, however, destroyed the unity of the Democratic party by unequal treatment of European nations and minorities. This had serious repercussions in America, a nation of immigrants.

Chapter 4

Help from the Hyphenates

In 1919, William Roscoe Thayer, erudite historian, Republican nationalist, and Boston aristocrat paid his respects to the unassimilated immigrants. He called them "mongrels with a divided allegiance . . . hyphenates, whose hyphen, like the kiss of Judas, is a link for treachery."[1] As Thayer penned these pungent words his friend, Henry Cabot Lodge, who had long since descended from his Harvard ivory tower to the political cockpit, was developing a sudden cordiality for these newcomers. For decades the senator had argued in Congress that the United States must shut its doors to peasants and workers from the European heartland. Few men in public life had felt so ardently and preached so openly the Mayflower complex. Now, however, Senator Lodge was in the midst of the battle of his life against Woodrow Wilson and the Democratic party. Time and circumstances had put the immigrants in the Republican corner. Good politics demanded that this unexpected stroke of good fortune be exploited to the full. The senator found honeyed words to obliterate the prejudices of a lifetime.

The alienation of the hyphenates from Wilson and the Democratic party points up the importance of coincidence in history. The First World War marked the culmination of the great population shift from Europe to America. By this time there were millions of immigrants of the first and second generation in this country. The stirring events of the day revived ancient ties to European homelands and temporarily halted the weighty centripetal force of Americanization. The United States allied itself with one coalition of nations and made war upon another with the result of an accent upon hyphenization. There were now, as never before, Irish-Americans, German-Americans, Italian-Americans, and so on down the line. This emphasis increased as the European war stimulated the nationalist aspirations for independence of many subject peoples. Irishmen, Czechs, Poles, Latvians, Slavs, Hungarians, and other immigrant groups in America were stirred to action by the revolts of their parent nationalities. Each unit, incited by foreign agents, wanted the United States to stand godfather to the new states then in the making. But circumstances made it impossible for Wilson to deal equally with all these ambitions. He could, with equanimity, please the Poles whose reconstituted homeland had been wrested from the defeated nations and Bolshevist Russia. He could please the Jews by consenting to the Balfour Declaration for a Palestinian homeland because it happened to be sponsored by Britain. On the other hand, a strong stand for Irish self-determination would have meant a complete rupture with Lloyd George's government. Such a break the President could not risk.

The complete hostility of the German- and Austrian-Americans was also to be reckoned with. The war itself had already alienated most of them from Wilson and they became even more bitter when they learned of the harsh terms dealt to the vanquished in the treaties of peace. The President could afford no further nationalist defections. It was impossible, however, to please all of the splinter groups, for the good will of some could be bought only at the expense of displeasing others or, in some intances, by thwarting the territorial ambitions of land-hungry Allies.

There was more to the hyphenate revolt than resentment against the compromises on self-determination and the harsh terms of the peace. The second and third generations of immigrants were concerned more frequently with domestic rather than with foreign affairs. Until 1914, the cultural and intellectual leadership of the Old Americans had been taken for granted. Newcomers, to be sure, had found a place in the country, but they sat at the foot of the table. Their children had often been frustrated by social sneers and numerous obstacles which blocked the way up the ladder of success. Wartime prosperity had opened up new vistas to the "out" group of society, and as they pushed their way into bigger business, politics, and the professions, they demanded social equality. Some, at least, of the older stock Americans wanted to contest the challenge. Such people the immigrants identified with pro-British and pro-League groups because these movements were strong among the better people. Some of the hyphenates regarded the Scotch-Irish Wilson as one of their social enemies. The President did share the common conviction of the intellectual elite in regard to the superiority of Anglo-Saxon culture. He was also the leader of the pro-League Anglophiles, although he was less of a racist than Lodge or Beveridge. But the Republican opportunists had the best of the situation in spite of their previous records. As the "outs," they could wash their hands of direct responsibility for the war or for the peace. The emphasis of the G.O.P. on Americanism was welcome to immigrant ears despite its nativist overtones. For if nationality was something psychological rather than ethnic, it could be acquired. Newcomers saw a way of gaining increased status by capitalizing upon a fervid Americanism.

The Republicans grasped the situation. Circumstances had made it possible for them to split the internal unity of the Democrats, whose party had been nurtured on immigrant votes since the days of Jefferson. The hyphenate electorate, with some notable exceptions such as the Poles, was in their clutches. The next step was to amalgamate the new potential voters with the hard-core Republicans and the rabid nativists. Was there any other issue, besides hatred of Wilson and Versailles, that could unite the coalition and help close the yawning gap between reactionaries, hundred per cent Americans and fifty per cent hyphenates? By chance rather than design both the Republicans and the nascent isolationist coalition found a common denominator. All of the constituent groups were more or less anti-British. Twisting the lion's tail had long been standard political technique in the United States. It was time for a good hard wrench.

While the bulk of the Republicans did not hate England as did the German or Irish-Americans, they were nevertheless ready for a revolt against our partnership with the British in wartime. The Anglophiles had overreached themselves and now there was a Yankee rebound. This reaction came with sufficient force to congeal extraneous elements within the party. The pendulum was swinging back from the extreme pro-British position. On its return trip it was picked up by Republican isolationists and pushed farther in the opposite direction.

American feeling toward Britain before the war had been ambivalent. In the eyes of many, England was still "the hated redcoat of our school days" who begrudged us our success as a nation. This attitude was popular in Irish and German circles and among old Populists and other dissentients who feared and disliked London's policies. Running parallel to this ancient hatred was a newer pro-British sentiment, dominant among eastern Americans of Anglo-Saxon origin. This accord had been nurtured by half a dozen Anglo-American societies. Their mutual theme was the cultural affinities that united English-speaking peoples. Britain, as the mother of this civilization, deserved honor and filial respect. Such an attitude explains why so many Americans were pro-Ally at the very beginning of the First World War.

When the United States entered the war on the side of

England, the anti-British voices were temporarily silenced. Anglophiles took over and often let their enthusiasm outweigh their good judgment. School manuals were ordered revised, for the cry was: "Out with the old prejudices." Historians had long been champing at the bit, and the case for King George III was carried too far. Our boys were dying in France—so the new histories taught — to preserve the democracy and liberty which we had inherited from the mother country. Now, the time had come to pay our debt to the tight little isle. To cement the ties between the two nations, they urged that England and the United States work together in a common world organization.

Historians held no monopoly on pro-British prejudices. During the war a Federal judge enjoined film production of *The Spirit of '76* because the picture tended to slacken American loyalty to Great Britain. Robert Underwood Johnson's poem, *The Sword of Lafayette,* sang of how "we girded up to fight not England, but her Prussian king." The *Confederate Veteran* reminded the thinning gray ranks that one hundred and fifty thousand anti-British Irishmen had invaded the South clad in Union blue.

At the same time, the British worked assiduously to cultivate influential Americans. They did such a good job on Edward Price Bell, chief European correspondent of the Chicago *Daily News,* that he feared President Wilson was becoming subtly anti-British! They won a complete convert in Vice-Admiral William S. Sims, who commanded all naval forces of the United States in European waters. When Sims took occasion to blast American enemies of England he received so much fan mail that he was forced to resort to printed acknowledgments. John Strachey, editor of the London *Spectator,* was sufficiently impressed by the billing and cooing to confess his joy that Britain's war debt was to the United States, for he knew that America's sense of honor would not allow her to haggle over the money.

The reversal of this pro-British trend was not long in coming. The Anglophiles had gone too far and reaction was inevitable. While the war was still on, Sir Gilbert Parker, who had been in charge of British propaganda for America, revealed some secrets. Americans were not particularly pleased to learn that we had nothing to gain from the war except the enhancement of some of our spiritual, mental, and human qualities.[2] Parker's disclosures coincided with Beveridge's beating of the nationalist drums. As these sounds increased, the new chauvinism made blue-blooded Yankees suspicious of

Britons bearing gifts. Men of those years were very close to the nineteenth century and they could not envisage a decline in British power. Might not a victorious empire turn us into a nation of British sycophants? Beveridge thought the danger real and said that he feared reabsorption by England and the erection of a new Bunker Hill monument as a symbol of reunion.[3] William Randolph Hearst declared that his study of American history convinced him that a true patriot must frequently be anti-British. Other demagogues went even further. A minor politician in Nebraska called on all red-blooded Americans to help him organize a movement against accepting Lloyd George as premier of the Republic. The fear was openly voiced that if Herbert Hoover was elected President in 1920, the British would have their viceroy in the White House. To the nationalist right-wingers, atavistic fear of Britain became an obsession. It was part of the bitter fruits of a war-inspired nationalism. Certain groups of partisan nativists found it expedient to play up the recoil against England and to enlist the aid of immigrants. The hyphenate newcomers could join and, in bludgeoning the British vicariously, they could forgive the nationalists for their former attitude. Such a program was attractive to the inveterate Irish Democrats, the most important hyphenate defectionists.

The leadership of the hyphenate clusters fell naturally to the Sons of Erin. The princes of immigrants, the Irishmen had been here long enough to have acquired roots. They had established themselves in the professions and had a unique political leverage on urban politics. As a group the Irish had a real grievance against Wilson. They had watched the Emerald Isle's demand for home rule over generations, and the struggle reached its climax at the Versailles Peace Conference. It did not seem fair to have the President preach self-determination for everybody except the proud people under the British yoke. Thus a hatred that simmered for centuries became suddenly acute at a moment when Wilson was promising freedom to so many subject peoples.

The Irish were sufficiently well organized to stir up a storm of protest. The Clan-na-Gael, successor to the Fenians, was the American counterpart to the Irish Republican Brotherhood then in revolt. Shortly before America went to war, the Irish began to hold "Race Conventions" in the United States and organized a pressure group called The Friends of Irish Freedom. By the time of the Armistice the American-Irish were thoroughly aroused to action and were financing the republican revolt of the Sinn Fein (We Ourselves) movement.

As Wilson hammered out the Covenant of the League of Nations in Paris, the Irish parliament declared independence and promptly named Eamon De Valera, then in an English prison, as president. A delegation was dispatched to Versailles to join other nationalities in the search for self-determination.

In the United States, the Irish independence movement was studded with local politicians, the great majority of whom were Democrats. Perhaps the most important leader was the Tammany judge, Daniel F. Cohalan. He had been born in Middletown, New York, but both his first and second wives were natives of County Cork. Cohalan frequently spent summers in Ireland, and even educated his children there. By political opposition and caustic remarks about the war, he had earned Wilson's enmity. When the President counterattacked, Cohalan and other Irish leaders reciprocated with a vengeance. At the 1919 Philadelphia Race Convention Wilson was warned that the treaty would be killed unless it provided for Irish Independence.

Using Judge Cohalan's office as headquarters, the Irish formed a powerful and resourceful bloc. Headed by Dr. Patrick McCartan, the self-styled envoy of the new republic, Irish revolutionaries penetrated leading American cities. No effort was spared to make contact with other groups who were known to oppose the treaty. With the aid of some of the Catholic clergy, pressure groups began to bear down upon members of Congress. Late in February, 1918, Wilson came back to the United States for a few days in order to attend to domestic duties and was greeted by a delegation from the Irish Race Convention who presented their demands. While the President made promises that were beyond his power to fulfill, he refused to receive Cohalan with the rest of the group. The Irish had a new martyr.

Three delegates of the Irish Race Convention, called the American Commission on Irish Independence, followed Wilson back to Paris. The envoys included the prominent Kansas City attorney and former co-chairman of the War Labor Board, Frank P. Walsh; ex-governor Edward T. Dunne of Illinois; and Michael F. Ryan, recently of the Pennsylvania Public Service Commission. They were rebuffed by the harassed Wilson at Versailles, who told them that they had gone too far in their sojourn in Ireland enroute to France. The delegation then denounced the treaty and came home to say that no amendments could make it acceptable in their eyes. In the meantime, De Valera had been spirited out of an English jail and brought across the Atlantic to tour American cities. In

New York, Mayor John F. Hylan and the Board of Aldermen gave him the freedom of the city and launched the sale of Irish bonds. "Betrayed by Wilson and debarred from the League," wrote Patrick McCartan, "we had one last resort, the great-hearted American people."[4] One of the "great-hearted," Senator Henry Cabot Lodge, welcomed Irish testimony before hearings of the Senate Foreign Relations Committee. Impassioned speakers told the senators that the League of Nations was a super-state, that it infringed upon the sovereignty of the United States, and that in the proposed Assembly, Great Britain and her dominions would have six votes to our one. The Irish struck directly at Article X, which Wilson considered the heart of the Covenant. This item contained guarantees "as against external aggression" of the territorial integrity and political independence of all member states. The Irish used the familiar argument that the League might well muster a world force to suppress the revolts of subjugated peoples. They demanded the defeat of "that iniquity born of darkness and deceit . . . the 'league of nations.'"

The Irish sprang to battle all over the country and opened fire on many fronts. De Valera and McCartan, whose objective was independence rather than the mortification of Wilson, wanted to keep first things first. Cohalan, however, never lost sight of his personal feud and, to the consternation of the Irish-Irish, leveled his gunsights on the President. Big, shaggy Senator Borah served as a linchpin between the hyphenate group and the Irreconcilables. A man of lesser build and stamina would have broken under the strain, for he insisted on writing individual answers to all friends and foes. "If ever America wants to do anything for little Ireland," Borah wrote to a correspondent, "she had better do so before this League of Nations is clapped down upon the world."[5] Cohalan, with the Irish Victory Fund in his hands, was in almost daily contact with the senator. The judge converted The Friends of Irish Freedom into crusaders against the League. Copies of Frank Walsh's and Edward Dunne's testimony before the Senate Foreign Relations Committee were sent out under Borah's frank to all parts of the country. When Irreconcilable orators took to the hustings the Irish provided them with enthusiastic audiences. Judges Cohalan and Michael F. Ryan conducted their own tour to defeat the treaty. When the judge spoke in his home city of New York, Madison Square Garden was so packed that even the hostile press reluctantly admired the showing of strength. Cohalan's hatred of Britain eventually became an obsession. In due time he was to suggest that

Britain should either destroy her fleet or surrender it to America as hostage for good behavior.

Irish organizations were so numerous during the 1919-1920 treaty fight that it is almost impossible to keep track of all their activities. Eventually De Valera, who was interested in his cause rather than in American politics, formed his own group called The American Association for the Recognition of the Irish Republic. There were also, at one time or another, Knights of the Red Branch, Robert Emmett and Wolfe Tone associations, Friends of Ireland, and the Ancient Order of Hibernians. Every city of importance and innumerable small towns had either a Roger Casement Council or an Irish Self-Determination Club. Sometimes these local groups were part of larger organizations and sometimes they sprang up indigenously. In Portland, Oregon, the groups federated and demanded the defeat of the League under the motto: "Hold Ireland for the Irish." Portlanders reported to Senator Borah that they were pressuring Oregon's senators and boasted that "if we are not successful it will not be our fault."[6] Perhaps the most persistent propaganda issued from the Irish National Bureau in Washington which sent out daily clip sheets to senators. It is impossible to measure the effect of the combined Irish associations, because so many other factors were involved in the treaty's eventual defeat. A few instances, however, give some idea of the weight of Irish influence. At a critical moment in the struggle, England sent one of her greatest men, Viscount Grey, to America to hint that it would be better to modify the Covenant with severe reservations than to have America walk out on the League. The Friends of Irish Freedom helped frustrate even this last-minute effort. One can also see the strength of the pressure groups in the fifteenth reservation which was eventually attached to Lodge's fourteen. This final stipulation affirmed the Senate's interest in the Irish cause, and expressed the hope that after independence, the new state would be admitted to the League.

Because the Irish-American leaders detested Wilson, they avoided the moderate senators who were prone to compromise and cultivated instead the Irreconcilables. The white-mustached Senator Thomas J. Walsh of Montana tried to prevent the Irish uprising. An Irishman of Irishmen, despite his prohibitionist leanings, Walsh was loyal both to his party and to the land of his ancestors. He complained that the extremists in control of the Irish movement were so incensed that they wanted war, not peace, in the hope that in some future struggle the British Empire might go to smash. The Montana senator noted wryly that when the Hibernian "hundred per-centers" convoyed De Valera to Washington, they by-passed four Irish-American senators and took the "president" directly to Borah. This alliance between Sinn Fein and the Irreconcil-ables helped defeat the movement for compromise in the Democratic party spearheaded by men like Montana's Walsh. Had the Irish leaders and the President acted more charitably toward each other, it is possible that some agreement on the treaty might have been reached. A strong movement for reser-vations coming from the united Irish Democrats would have been difficult for even Wilson to refuse. By casting their lot with the Irreconcilables, the Irish leaders did their bit to make concessions impossible.

There had long been a marked affinity between the immi-grants and the liberals. In their ideal America, the latter en-visaged a cultural pluralism to which divergent European peo-ples would contribute the best aspects of their respective civili-zations. This, the great American sage, Ralph Waldo Emerson, had foreseen and felt would create a society different from anything that any one immigrant group had known in Europe. The liberals were distinctly unwilling to think of America as a mere outpost of English civilization. They jumped on the Irish bandwagon with considerable alacrity.

On the staff of Villard's New York *Evening Post* was Cap-tain William J. Maloney who, with the chief's blessings, voiced the Irish aspirations. "Playing the Irish" became a favorite sport. The crusading professor, Robert Morss Lovett, brought down the house at Irish meetings by reciting from Longfel-low's *Paul Revere's Ride*:

> You know the rest. In the book you have read,
> How the British Regulars fired and fled,
> How the farmers gave them ball for ball,
> From behind each fence and barnyard wall,
> Chasing the redcoats down the lane . . .

The *New Republic* thought that more important than the Irish cause itself was the clear revelation of British cruelty, injustice, and inflexibility. Long a home-ruler, William Ran-dolph Hearst made it a custom to "free Ireland once a month" in his newspapers. A prominent Des Moines editor noted that the Irish had won so many people to their side that only the courageous were willing to speak or write in defense of the British Empire.

There were, to be sure, many voices lifted in protest against

81

Irish activities. The *Unpartizan Review* asked if a century of differences between England and Ireland had not first corrupted our city politics and then kept us out of the League. Some said that home rule for Ireland meant "Rome rule" and such people tried to rouse the Protestant conscience in favor of their co-religionists in loyal Northern Ireland. To Admiral Sims the American-Irishmen were "asses" but he admitted that each jackass had one vote and that there were lots of them.[7] Senator John Sharp Williams of Mississippi, planter-politician, classical scholar, and friend of the League wanted to know whether any southerner had expected Irish help during the War Between the States. Some Americans withdrew their names from Irish organization lists because they felt that the public had been given only part of the story. The moderate and outright pro-British groups, however, were not well organized and they lacked the verve and zip of the fighting Irish. The fact that the treaty struggle coincided with the climacteric of Irish independence helped defeat the League of Nations in this country. The whole anti-British issue was used to pull together divergent isolationist forces. And the nationalists could not count on more allies, with hordes of Democrats amongst them.

As the oldest, most numerous and prosperous of the hyphenates, the Irish were the best organized and the most effective. They were, however, only one among many groups that battled against the League of Nations. The friends of the Indian nationalists were specially important. The war had ignited the fuse of Indian discontent. While the British recognized the power of the Irish vote in America, and found it expedient not to stop certain Irish-American activities that crossed their lines of power, there was no Hindu-American vote. Here the British felt free to flex their muscles. Thus John Bull offended the liberals who were particularly attracted to the Indian cause because it was free from clericalism and ward politics. Gandhi's "peaceful resistance" program had a special appeal for American pacifists and liberals who disliked Sinn Fein terrorism. They sympathized deeply with Indian refugees who were seized in the United States in defiance of the historic right of asylum for political offenders. Tarakanath Das, later a Columbia University historian, came out of Leavenworth (where, in 1917, he had been imprisoned for conspiring to ship arms to India) to help his friend Saliendranath Ghose muster recruits for the Hindu cause. The two men found that a group, many of whom belonged to the American Civil Liberties Union, had already organized The Friends of

Freedom for India. With an India News Service, mass meetings, India dinners, and Hindu bazaars, the group attracted attention. Frank P. Walsh took time from his professional and Irish activities to become legal adviser and was once vice-president of the pro-Indian organization. The movement spread and there was even a Pacific Coast Hindustan Association. All isolationist and anti-League elements lent assistance. The Communists found India more appealing than Catholic Ireland. Colonial peoples, they promised, will be helped "by truly internationalist Soviet Russia . . . [and] British world imperialism will soon be effaced from the earth."[8]

As usual, the Irreconcilables were anxious to be of help and Das and Ghose even made appeals on Senate stationery. Some of the charges bordered on the ridiculous. The British-controlled Indian National Congress, Ghose asserted, was backing Hoover's 1920 candidacy, in order to get the United States into the "unholy" League. The Friends of Freedom for India sent Frank Walsh "proof" that the British opium monopoly planned to drug the whole world. "We wish," wrote Ghose, "to send one of this memorandum to every Irish speaker in the country."[9]

Besides the Irish and the Indians, Far Eastern pressure groups were also important. Possibly no item in the Versailles treaty had been so severely criticized as the clause which left the Japanese in control of Shantung. There was a vigorous Chinese organization that argued against these provisions. Anti-Japanese feeling thus ran high in Washington and it was helped along by the League of the Friends of Korea. This group had been organized in Philadelphia to help Korea free itself from Japan. Dr. Syngman Rhee, who had been trained in American universities, was here building up a list of acquaintances for future reference. Offices were opened in Washington, and there was the usual Bureau of Information.

The Near Eastern pot was also boiling. The American Committee for the Independence of Armenia advertised the sufferings of that unhappy people. The Egyptian pressure group claimed that the treaty violated the rights of thirteen million inhabitants of the land of the Pharaohs. When Borah tried to get the Senate to recognize Irish independence, Senator Medill McCormick of Illinois, brother of the publisher of the Chicago *Tribune,* suggested that the resolution also include Egypt "just to show the British . . . they were in our thoughts"[10] Wilson also lost some of his Jewish support when, at Paris, he receded a bit from his original Palestinian stand and dispatched a commission to inquire into the Arab claims.

Such Arabs as were domiciled in the United States organized with the help of Near Eastern missionary interests to contest the Zionist position.

Concurrently, European groups were becoming restive. Wilson's determined resistance to Italy's demand for the city of Fiume and certain parts of the Dalmatian coast had partially turned Italian-American opinion against the treaty. The case for these cessions was pressed from the Italian propaganda headquarters in Washington. Close by this building Yoyslav M. Yovanovich directed the Jugoslavian counterattack. "You will appreciate," Senator Thomas J. Walsh wrote with some pathos, "how impossible it is for me here to inquire into the merits of the many contentions arising concerning the proper boundary lines in the reconstruction of the map of Europe."[11]

We have so far by-passed the efforts of the German-American groups. Their situation was peculiar and deserves individual scrutiny. Like the Irish, they were numerous and often well-to-do. Unlike the Irish, however, millions of German-Americans had lost their identity by wholesale assimilation into the American stream. No one religious attachment kept them together. Until 1914, the Fatherland had not needed their help and thus their earlier organizations had not been motivated by the need of liberating a subjugated nation. The Germans had been lulled into indifference because their homeland had fended for itself. Again, in contrast to the Irish, America's entry into the war had destroyed German organizations and attached the stigma of "Hun" to anything that smacked of the enemy. The vast majority of people of German descent accepted the war, and made many valuable contributions to the American effort. Only in the northwestern wheat belt was there any really questionable action and even here "disloyalty" was more agrarian socialism than treason. The Armistice found the German-Americans disorganized and discomfited. However, they were soon aroused from their apathy. Many of them, understandably, were deeply moved by the severity of the peace terms. They profoundly resented the Allied blockade against Germany which was continued after the actual fighting had ceased. As postal intercourse with the defeated countries was resumed, their relatives and friends complained of the food shortage and the suffering. The German-Americans, moreover, were anxious to remove the blot which had blighted their name and their culture. Under the circumstances, they resented a League of Nations that promised to perpetuate the power of the victors and to keep the yoke of bondage fastened on their Fatherland. Furthermore, the majority of them were Republicans and it was natural for them to oppose a Democratic peace. Thus they welcomed the isolationist resurgence for it expressed their convictions. A complete repudiation of Versailles might well remove the tarnish from the Teutonic name.

As the opposition to Wilson gathered, the German hyphenates anxiously watched and waited. They were prudent enough to realize that if they joined openly in the attack, the President might denounce the isolationists as "Hun sympathizers." Gradually, as the coalition gained momentum, Germans relaxed their caution. The New York City groups emerged from their cyclone cellars to welcome Jeremiah O'Leary, the much publicized critic of Wilson and war. The revival of German-American organized strength, however, had its real beginnings in May, 1919, when nine men met secretly in New York to form the nucleus of the Steuben Society. Its object was clearly stated in the very first number of the organization's mouthpiece, *Issues of To-Day*. It promised to "get" those who had "gotten" them during the war. As time passed, the Steubenites dropped their initial hesitation, began to speak out, and encouraged the formation of branches all over the country. The first step in their program was to oppose the Treaty of Versailles and the League of Nations.

Like the Irish, the German hyphenates found Senator Borah and his fellow Irreconcilables ready and willing to help and advise. The Idahoan had his contact men in the chief racial pockets. The German newspapers of La Crosse, Wisconsin, reported regularly to him. In Philadelphia, Luther S. Kaufmann of the True American League told the senator that he was using his organization to fight both the Catholic Church and the League of Nations. C. A. Sehlebrede of Corvallis, Oregon, distributed bundles of speeches for Borah. In St. Louis there was R. C. Schrader, while Walter B. Heineman, chairman of the Wisconsin Republican State Central Committee, did the Idaho senator's chores in the Badger State. Other isolationist senators, such as the Democrat, James A. Reed of Missouri, and the Republican mavericks, Norris and La Follette, received German support and encouragement. The treaty fight of 1919 began a long-lasting affinity between German racial voting blocks and isolationist senators.

The German efforts had far-reaching effects upon the crystallization of the isolationist sentiment. While, as we have seen, they helped indirectly to defeat the treaty, their position in the country was much too insecure to imitate the Irish plan of a direct assault. In time, however, German-American sentiment, along with persisting Irish efforts, was to create a distinct type of hyphenate-isolationist. The Germans specialized in the uncompromising form of war-guilt revisionism. The *Progressive,* an organ of the Steuben Society, became a clearing house for this type of literature. The Publicity Committee of this society promised "guerrilla warfare" on all "liars" until the German-Americans could meet them in open battle. The *Progressive* was later taken over by The National Historical Society of Chicago, which subsidized and dispensed the sale of isolationist and exaggerated revisionist books. Infiltrated, to say the least, by German-American influences, The National Historical Society waged a vigorous anti-British and isolationist campaign of formidable size. It is only fair to repeat that much of the revisionist work was careful, historical scholarship that served the country well by reversing a false portrayal of the war. Basically, the origins of the war had nothing to do with the question of whether we should return to isolationism or assume the burdens of a great nation in maintaining the peace. The findings of the revisionists were absorbed and used by strong adherents of the internationalist point of view. It is also fair to say, however, that the German societies purveyed a type of revisionism which tried to substitute one faulty hypothesis for another that was even more untenable. The Germans spread the views of writers who editorialized their history. Thus, they explained, Germany had been the artless victim of a Franco-Russian conspiracy. The obvious lesson was that we had intervened, to our own detriment, on the side of the guilty against the innocent. The League of Nations, then, had been designed to perpetuate a wrong. The least that we could do to atone for our own errors was to stay out of the League and work for a revision of Versailles in Germany's favor. Such judgments were eventually to influence the thinking of a large segment of the American people.

One of the lasting results of the strange alliance of hyphenates and nativists was the purgation of history textbooks. Nowhere does the isolationist spectrum show more revealing colors than in the united efforts to revise the school books. William Randolph Hearst, the Knights of Columbus, the Steuben Society, the Sons of the American Revolution, the Daughters of the American Revolution, the Ku Klux Klan, and ward politicians all wanted to "purify" American history.

An understanding of the motives behind the textbook wars sheds light upon the diverse elements that made up the isolationist forces. As the immigrant groups gained status they be-gan to resent the overemphasis placed by historians upon British factors in explaining American development. Non-English groups demanded their rightful place in American history. This meant a revision of the work of many authors, including Henry Cabot Lodge, who had overplayed the Anglo-Saxon theme to the exclusion of the contributions of other races. German and Irish hyphenates also wanted to remove the "mid-commercial" plugs in textbooks for the League of Nations. The patriotic societies and the "pure American" chauvinists felt that our history had become too pro-British in revising the standard interpretations of our old quarrels with the mother country. They wanted pupils to be stirred by vibrant nationalism rather than to be fed subtle arguments for world organization. "The heroic history of a nation," declared the Veterans of Foreign Wars, "is the drum-and-fife music to which it marches. It makes a mighty difference whether America continues to quick-step to *Yankee Doodle* or takes to marking time to *God Save the King*."[12] The organized pa-triots were not anxious to have historians play up the colonial Irish as the "tugs" who had pulled the country through the Revolution, nor did they want to incorporate new chapters on how Germans built *"Unser Amerika."* Despite this basic dif-ference, the groups joined to fight the historians of the Amer-ican Revolution. Together they would cleanse the pages of British idolatry and internationalist balderdash.

Charles Grant Miller's work reflected the hyphenate aspira-tions, the patriotic suspicions, and the wild charges of Hearst and Mayor William Hale Thompson of Chicago. Miller had been editor-in-chief of the Cleveland *Plain Dealer* and the *Christian Herald*. After the war he organized the Patriotic League for the Preservation of American History. On occa-sion he wrote for the Hearst syndicate and was possessed of an unusual ability to please all isolationist factions. Senator La Follette forgave him his Hearst connections and featured his articles in his magazine under such headlines as "Betsy Ross is Forgotten" or "John Paul Jones is Degraded." To Miller, conventional American history books were part of the "international mind" which, he hastened to add, "is always the British mind." The California Sons of the American Revo-lution published Miller's first larger work, *Treason to the American Tradition,* in which he charged that half a dozen leading writers of history were plotting with the British for an intellectual re-colonization of the United States. Later, Miller became an adviser to "Big Bill" Thompson in His Honor's attempt to run King George V out of Chicago. Some of Miller's later work was published by the German-controlled National Historical Society. He said in *The Poisoned Loving Cup* that while treason texts had been banned in five states, "the soul of Benedict Arnold still survives." Miller demanded a nationalist reinterpretation of American history which would give credit to German and Irish contributions, and at the same time would defeat the wily internationalist plans of churchmen, professors, and peace societies.

This war on textbooks forms a sordid chapter in our history. The weird combination of hyphenates and nationalists was powerful enough, in many instances, to force the capitulation of the law makers. Oregon and Wisconsin banned eight books while educators in Indiana and Ohio forestalled legal action by self-censorship. There were purges all over the country, highlighted by the New York City investigation by David Hirshfield, Commissioner of Accounts. Over the protest of the superintendent of education, Hirshfield's report, probably written by Charles Grant Miller, found evidence of a British conspiracy and advised the exclusion of eight books. As the Wisconsin historian and archivist, Joseph Schafer, noted, the country was judging textbooks largely by what they said about the late war and the League of Nations. The crusade against the history books forged a lasting link among the strange bedfellows of the isolationist coalition. The hyphenates had used a perverted nationalism to wedge their way into the group who shouted "America First."

Reflection shows that never before in American history had Congress, state legislatures, and public opinion been so disturbed by hyphenate and nativist claims and countercharges. There was a babel of voices and a confusion of tongues. It began when Wilson stirred to hope and action a score of subject races and their American sympathizers. When he was unable to please all of them, his senatorial enemies invited the hyphenates to ride the nationalist train. They climbed aboard with alacrity, and in their enthusiasm, they blew the whistle long and hard. With their fellow-passengers, the nativists, they shouted that the roadbed of American history had been twisted and torn by Anglophiles and internationalists. Concurrently, the larger group of everyday unhyphenated Americans was ready to say: "A plague on all houses." They had sickened of both the noise of the hyphenate-patriots, and the internationalist clamor to make the world a better place for Europeans and Asiatics. Why not return to normality, let the foreigner fry in his own fat, and enjoy prosperity? "Deal us out," men said, of the game of world politics. Such sentiments were part of the deeper but more unspectacular groundswell which pulled the American masses into the great isolationist undertow.

Chapter 5

The Disenchantment of the Masses

IN THE EXUBERANT and confident days of 1918 the spirit of internationalism had captured the American mind. Slowly the skeptics rallied to undermine this attitude. At first there were only special interest groups—unremitting Republicans, disheartened liberals, flag-waving hundred percenters, and indignant hyphenates. For some time this alliance constituted a distinct minority. A war-weary people demanded a design for peace to compensate the world for the agony of strife. As it became apparent that it was difficult to translate ideals into reality, the isolationist combine became a majority. The sublimity of Wilson was to give way to the aridity of Harding and Coolidge.

The conventional reasons given for the retreat to isolationism are often more shallow than profound. It is commonplace to read that a senatorial cabal forced Wilson to accept either serious restrictions upon the Covenant or else outright defeat. The President refused to compromise and staked his program on the outcome of the 1920 presidential election. The Republicans won, so the contention continues, and decided to abandon the League. The outline of the story is correct as far as it goes. Such a superficial interpretation, however, begs the question. Had the American people really been persuaded that their own security demanded a collective formula for the world, no party could have permanently thwarted their desires. Mere political triumph does not explain the rejuvenation of Washington's Farewell Address. The majority of Americans, Republicans and Democrats alike, spurned Wilson's premise that peace was a seamless fabric. Popular opinion swung back to the older concept that American self-interest demanded a return to insulation from Old World political entanglements. Let us analyze the factors that reversed the internationalist tide.

The regression can be comprehended only in the light of the post-war spirit. Americans had soon wearied of saving the world. The trials and tribulations of war and the frustration of peacemaking had dissipated the spell of idealism. Affairs in the wide world and at home seemed confused. The Bolshevist advance made the very word "international" suspect, and sent Americans scurrying to the shelter of traditional values. Unassimilated immigrants in city slums were blamed for economic heresies stemming from their European homelands. People came to feel that the only way to preserve order and property against the ideology of Lenin and Trotsky was to debar outside influences.

At the same time that men were drawing back from foreign contacts, they were enlarging their personal ambitions. Wartime prosperity had created a new and swollen middle class. Millions of people were anxious to relax their tensions and to enjoy their new status in old-fashioned tranquillity. Isolationism was part of the acute nostalgia for the good old days—for cigar store wooden Indians, for the *Police Gazette,* and for Casey who waltzed with a strawberry blonde. The impression was widespread that if we would shake off the responsibilities of the world, we could turn the clock back to a normality that had known no high costs of living, no income taxes, no small and oppressed nations, no grisly Reds, no thought of Article X or a League of Nations.

Americanism was the order of the day. Such sentiment was particularly strong among mature men who did so much of the talking and writing. Their impressionable years had been spent during the marvelous spurt of American economic power and prestige that came in the late nineteenth century. No other nation, certainly none in modern history, had achieved so much in such a short period of time. People gloried in the power of the United States and an innate selfishness made them reluctant to share our good fortune with other peoples. We should not, said one writer, trade the "Aladdin's lamp" of nationalism for "a newfangled contraption of a cheap, hastily constructed, foreign-made lamp of internationalism."[1] Why forsake a protective tariff or an isolated foreign policy that had made possible such abundance? More perspicacious thinkers knew that the pre-war Old World stability was gone and that our long-run interests demanded that we lend a stout hand to the restoration of order. However, the masses were attracted to the simplest expedience which was to divorce ourselves from the turmoil of other peoples and watch the ramparts of the western hemisphere.

To dispel this mirage, strong and plain words were needed. Pro-League arguments, however, were usually clad in shopworn idealistic and utopian garb. The war had thrust us into the vortex of world events so swiftly and so irrevocably that men had little time to digest the changes. What was needed

91

was a broader conception of enlightened self-interest. The point should have been hammered home that in a shrunken world we could not escape the effects of foreign war. Hence it was to the material interest of the United States to make real sacrifices to create machinery that would curb aggression and war. The question was all too seldom posed in this form. The country was on the brink of Professor Samuel F. Bemis's "Fool's Paradise of American History"—the shallow belief that we could be of the world and still not play the part of a major power in curbing the forces that might threaten the peace.

While the isolationists had the advantage of a well-defined program that was easy to grasp, Wilson had made no provisions for the inevitable sobering aftermath of war. As long as the nation was poised to send troops anywhere, the League idea sounded attractive. But with demobilization and the sigh of relief that it was "over, over there," Americans began to look at it in an entirely different light. The implications of Article X were too much for a provincial people to accept upon second thought. Hidebound isolationists were not the only ones shocked at the specter of a perpetual guarantee of the boundaries and independence of scores of states. Internationalists like Elihu Root, Herbert Hoover, and the 1916 Republican presidential candidate, Charles Evans Hughes, balked at the idea. Not only was it too radical a departure from the American past, but sober minds thought it impossible of long-run fulfillment in view of the vagaries of American politics. Lawyers, like Root for instance, believed in an association of nations whose foundation would be based on the enthronement of international law. Disputes that could not be settled by the conventional means of diplomacy, arbitration, or conciliation, would go before an international court. If war then threatened, it might be aborted by an extraordinary convocation of nations. Thus peace could be secured without surrender of sovereignty or the yielding of American freedom of action in any future dispute which might arise. There was a strong basis for this type of thinking in the evolution of American thought on the subject of peace machinery. Wilson made no attempt to blend his plan of assuring the sanctity of political frontiers with the strength of inbred tradition. He thus alienated the support of many sincere internationalists. Had the President given ground, in time he might have united various strains of internationalist thought under his own leadership. By not breaking so abruptly with the American past, he might have assuaged the fear of the masses against incessant involvement in European wrangles.

Isolationists were able to capitalize on more than the mere abandonment of non-entanglement. There was a widespread notion that the League would cripple or destroy the Monroe Doctrine. For a full half century, exclusive American control of the western hemisphere had been welded to the older policy of isolationism. Now, it was argued, both would go to the scrap heap at the same time. To become one of the world's policemen was enough of a deviation from tradition. Did the League Covenant also mean that henceforth foreign nations would be the guardians of New World order? The question had been raised from the moment Wilson began to talk of collective security. While at Paris the President had been informed by leading Republican internationalists that if the Monroe Doctrine could be properly safeguarded the treaty would be "promptly ratified." At considerable cost to his own bargaining power at Versailles, Wilson had reopened the finished Covenant and had persuaded the powers to agree to the new Article XXI. This stipulated that nothing in the proposed arrangement would affect the validity of such "regional understandings" as the Monroe Doctrine. The language was necessarily ambiguous because no precise definition of the Doctrine could have pleased both the Senate and the rest of the world. Despite the nebulous concession, Wilson's enemies still said that the twin bases of our foreign policy were both to be sacrificed in one fateful leap in the dark.

Article XXI disturbed many Americans. Ultraists were sure that it was a subtle British plot to do away with the Doctrine forever. Some also conjured up all kinds of hypothetical cases whereby Europe might thwart our hegemony in the western world. They and old-fashioned expansionists were certain that we were now hemmed in by a "scheme of stagnation." Judge Wesley O. Howard of the New York State bench promised that, League or no League, the American Army would soon cross the Rio Grande in emulation of Zachary Taylor. Senator Warren G. Harding said, with his customary grandiloquence, that he "would rather make Mexico safe and set it aglow with the light of new-world righteousness, than menace the health of the republic in old-world contagion."[2] The more temperate Elihu Root was seriously concerned about the future of the Monroe Doctrine. Moderate men were confirmed in their fears by the best authorities. The leading light in the country on international law was John Bassett Moore, who had spent most of his sixty years in teaching at Columbia, compiling profound treatises, working for the State Department, and representing the United States on important world tribunals. Moore's pronouncements had an *ex cathedra* acceptance. He said that to make the Doctrine part of world politics would sacrifice its unique and distinct meaning.

Linking the abandonment of the Monroe Doctrine to the end of non-entanglement posed a double-barreled threat to the foundations of American foreign policy. Many moderate internationalists hesitated to go that far, and while the moderates were reflecting, events played into the hands of the isolationists. The daily news from Europe made people shrink from further involvement at the expense of forsaking cherished policies. Time was on the side of the isolationists. A feeling of smugness, superiority, and safety behind our deep ocean moats was sweeping the country.

The new isolationism was floated in on a wave of resentment against our wartime associates, an unavoidable result of naive and unrealistic portrayal of our erstwhile European hosts. Familiarity bred the usual contempt. Walter Hines Page, Ambassador to the Court of St. James's, was an intimate friend of the President and perhaps the earliest advocate of American intervention. He wrote his son that except for the British and the French "there's no nation in Europe worth a tinker's damn. The whole continent is rotten, or tyrannical, or yellow dog."[3] Others were less discriminating and put all of the Allies in the same basket. Letters from Europe warned that the English and French were fair-weather friends who would turn against us at the drop of the hat. Such feelings greatly accelerated during the irksome days of the Peace Conference. Some of Wilson's most intimate advisers took umbrage at suggestions that America not only forgive the Allied war debt, but also reckon the possibility of sharing the pre-1917 obligations of England, France, and Italy.[4] Reporters and observers at Versailles usually came home completely dejected because of European cupidity. They told their countrymen that all of the Allies stood ready to wreck the conference for colonies, enlarged boundaries, seaports or reparations.

The anti-foreign feeling was augmented by the petty wars and turmoil that followed the formal end of the fighting. There was little in the American experience to make men realize that wars, unlike prize fights, do not stop at the sound of the gong. The new small states, often implemented by larger powers like France, tried to expand before boundaries would jell. Confusion was confounded by the Bolshevist menace and the appetite of the Soviet Union's small neighbors for the inviting Russian borderlands. Why, asked Albert J. Beveridge, send our boys back into this maelstrom of blood and death? Why join a League of Nations to "pacify" and "regulate" war-hungry, ungrateful, and greedy aliens? The most logical solution seemed to be to get out of Europe and to stay out. The chancellor of the University of Kansas said that the only insulation from all this pernicious strife was "the rediscovery of the American tradition." "We were a nice prosperous nation when we were just for ourselves," a constituent wrote Senator Sheldon P. Spencer of Missouri. "Now, if some blatherskite is not working up some sort of a 'drive' for money, old clothes or nighties for the 'down-trodden' . . . some other thimble-head is kicking and screaming for internationalism."[5]

Reports and dispatches from newsmen in Europe added weight to the anti-foreign sentiment. Hunting for headlines after the war, the press hawked extras telling of new intrigues. The Italian harbinger of fascism, Gabriel D'Annunzio, settled a battle of words with guns and seized Fiume. Roumanian soldiers marched into the Hungarian capital of Budapest for what promised to be a quick coup. Trusted correspondents wrote home that the treaty had been nullified before the Senate could vote. There was talk of another conflagration and on-the-spot observers doubted that any league could arrest the rapacious forces of revolution and aggression that made up the backwash of war. Even stalwart friends of the League were appalled at the way England, France, and Italy hungrily eyed potential colonies that were to be mandates held under the League. The American commanding officer at Coblentz wrote home that the late war had been just another round in a thousand-year battle between Germany and France. A thousand years of inbred hate and fears seemed to have poisoned the European bloodstream. To Philip Marshall Brown, professor of international law at Princeton, there was only one solution. We must recognize, he urged, that Europe's interests were different from our own and act accordingly. To this and similar pleas, came an ever swelling chorus of "Amens."

The returning doughboys swelled the isolationist chorus. They came back chauvinistic, anti-foreign, and determined to go on no more troop-ship cruises. Lustily they sang:

> We drove the Boche across the Rhine,
> The Kaiser from his throne,
> Oh, Lafayette, we've paid our debt,
> For Christ's sake, send us home.

One need not search long for the causes of their vexation. The soldiers of 1917 had marched off to the cheers of enraptured bystanders. In Europe they met Allies soured by four years of war. They saw the ruins and smelled the stenches of devastated northern France. Expecting a gratitude that was not forthcoming, the Yanks cursed the Frenchies from hell to breakfast and circulated stories of avaricious Parisian strumpets and dollar-hungry Gallic peasants. Few soldiers had ever seen a real Frenchman before the war, and they had mental images of an unreal stereotype with gay manners and waxed mustaches. The French *poilus* whom they saw made them homesick for the German grocer or butcher of their native towns. The Germans they encountered in their occupation duty seemed well scrubbed, submissive, hard-working and genuine. And the women of the Rhineland were so understanding of the Yankee willingness to fraternize! No matter where they were stationed, however, the doughboys dreamed of Hoboken and home. "Our work is done," an army captain wrote Senator Borah, "so let's get these peace terms signed and get to Hell out of here."[6] An official of the National War Work Council of the Y.M.C.A. interviewed hundreds of soldiers as they stepped off the transports. He found the soldiers anti-League almost to a man. They needed but one argument —never again.

After the veterans acknowledged the booming of the brass bands and the welcoming speeches of the local politicos, they doffed their uniforms and began to look for jobs. Their disillusionment grew apace. "Slackers" had grown rich, and the labor market was swamped by precipitated demobilization. There was no G.I. Bill of Rights or anything like it. Soldiers had to fend for themselves in a country torn by industrial strife, inflation, and temporary business recession. The government seemed concerned only about feeding the Armenians and clothing the Poles. The veterans had had enough. Where was the peace or any other tangible profit for the suffering and the lost years? The isolationists alone seemed to have an answer. If we get nothing else out of the war, soldiers concluded, let it at least serve as an expensive but necessary lesson for the future.

Despite this manifest swing back to isolationism, there were many friends of the League left in the country and they held certain great advantages. A majority of the people wanted an association of nations of one kind or another. It was going to be difficult to keep America out of Wilson's league or a revamped substitute. To defeat this end the isolationist elements would have to coalesce and plan their strategy. Action on the treaty must be postponed until the hosts could gather together. The more time that could be gained, the more avenues of public opinion that could be turned against the League. The leadership and cadence came from the United States Senate. Isolationists in that august body supplied the generalship for the country-wide coalition. Not only did they defeat the treaty, but they also brought together strands of the new isolationism and nourished it till it won the hearts of the people. The activities of the senators and their allies are of prime importance in understanding the popular reversal from collective organization back to the isolationist tradition.

While liberal and hyphenate isolationists were important, they were specially oriented groups with limited representation in the Senate. Thus the most effective leadership in marshalling public opinion came from the blatant nationalists. Their arguments were couched in the appealing terms of Americanism. These senators both created and in turn reflected the mood of the country. Return to the policy of the Fathers, demanded the nationalists. Become Americans once more, they urged, and limit political questions to local concerns that we can understand and handle. America—great, self-sufficient, and refreshingly different—had no need for a League of Nations. In joining a world political body we had everything to lose and nothing to gain. Perplexed by continental disorders? they queried. Solve the problem by minding our own business. To Main Streeters, far more interested in the coming Dempsey-Willard fight than in Fiume or Danzig, this made sense. Nationalism, the nostalgic appeal to tradition, and the exaggerated fears of possible entanglements were arguments that struck the fancy of the common people. Mr. and Mrs. John Doe were becoming rapidly bored with the whole League business. They were shrinking back to their old lack of interest in and indifference to foreign affairs. The First World War had not brought the enduring conviction that a peaceful Europe was essential to American well-being.

The senatorial conclave that steered the fight against the League was, of course, headed by Lodge. In spite of the fact that the Massachusetts senator claimed to be a strong reservationist, his polished oratory supplied the extreme nationalists with many arguments against Wilson's plan. Lodge and his fellow reservationists insisted that only if America's hands were untied in future emergencies could she be of service to world peace and the welfare of mankind. Because the battle in the Senate chamber took most of Lodge's time, mustering the support of the country was left mostly to the admitted isolationists. William Edgar Borah was the original Irreconcilable, the leader of his self-styled "Battalion of Death." This band of fifteen equated compromise on the League question with treason. Borah not only commanded the die-hards in Washington, but also took upon himself the job of coordinating the nation-wide isolationist coalition. His unique position in American politics made him precisely the right man for the job. Progressive in his own consistent way, he enjoyed the confidence of the liberals. At the same time he had not bolted to the Bull Moosers in 1912, and thus, in the eyes of the Old Guard, was innocent of that most heinous of American political crimes, party treachery. No other senator had such wide hyphenate connections. Yet despite his Irish and German associations, Borah's patriotic record was unassailable because, unlike so many of the other progressive-isolationist senators, he had voted for war. At that time he told Congress bluntly that he was joining no crusade nor sought any alliance but would fight only for his country and its rights. He called for the unconditional surrender of Germany dictated at the sword's point, and labeled all talk of world association "moral treason." Time and again Borah held Lodge and other reservationists from making any real concession to the pro-League forces. He insisted that the G.O.P. make no compromise with this "bolshevism" of world unity. Realizing the power of the press, Borah enlisted the invaluable aid of the magazine and newspaper tycoon, Frank A. Munsey, whose New York *Sun* was able to offset important pro-League papers in the big city. The senator told Munsey that if the people were informed of the real details of Wilson's proposal, the plan would be defeated by an avalanche of public indignation. Munsey did his best, supplied with plenty of information from Borah's office. The senator's indefatigable energy, wide connections, and enthusiasm wove together the various strands of isolationist thinking.

There can be little doubt of Borah's utter sincerity. His creed was simple and easy for the Philistines to grasp: return to the teachings of Washington and foster "a strong national spirit, a national mind and purpose." Any friend of the League, he insisted, must admit that he was no longer willing to see the American flag above the banners of other nations. Like so many other senators, Borah was essentially old-fashioned, for he considered it unthinkable to abandon a policy that had so long insulated the United States from the vicissitudes of world turmoil. He was utterly impervious to the fact that changing concepts of space and economic entanglements had pushed America much closer to the European world. He could not comprehend that some new plan to keep the peace would have to replace the old balance of power. Borah was convinced of America's singular capacity to handle matters arising from Old World instability when and if they impinged upon her own welfare. Hence the very idea of a League maintained by force looked like treachery designed only to betray the true interests of the country. The motives for this treason, to Borah's uncomplicated mind, seemed clear enough. Bankers, he thought, wanted the League in order to "gather their fruits from exploitation and investment." Desperately he wrote around the nation for documentary proof of this "sale of our country." When such evidence was not forthcoming, he interpreted the silence as meaning that the conspiracy was all the more subtle. Giving no ground to friend or foe, Borah carried the message of isolationism from Versailles to the Second World War.

While the Idahoan was running a one-man committee of correspondence to rouse the countryside, important Senate moves were planned by Frank B. Brandegee of Connecticut or Philander C. Knox of Pennsylvania. Brandegee was an aging bachelor who later ended his own life. Dependable sources credit him with planning the more adroit parliamentary maneuvers of the "Battalion." His motives were partisan and nationalist. One spring night in 1919, the Irreconcilables caucused in Brandegee's home. The chances of stopping the treaty seemed slim—as yet there was only some mid-western support, the disaffected liberals, and such sympathetic journalists as Hearst, Munsey, Nelson of the Kansas City *Star,* Colonel Robert R. McCormick of the Chicago *Tribune,* and James Thomas Williams, Jr., editor of the Boston *Evening Transcript.* Knox, who had already given the group some astute lessons in parliamentary manipulation, suggested that they go after big money in order to wage a national campaign. As it turned out, the isolationist sponsors were right in Knox's own Pittsburgh. Henry Clay Frick, Andrew Carnegie's old steel partner, and Andrew W. Mellon, Pennsylvania aluminum magnate, were heavy contributors. With an ample reserve of funds, senatorial orators were thus able to tour the country without charging local gatherings for traveling expenses. There was no need to economize on broadsides, pamphlets, letters and circulars.

The munificence of the Pittsburgh millionaires also helped to advertise Hiram W. Johnson to the American people. The Californian's nationalism was not marred by even an occasional flirtation with thoughts of world cooperation. Part of Johnson's ardor was undoubtedly sincere, but there was a method to his chauvinism. He had been badly stung by the presidential bee. A cynic once said of him that he found it difficult to serve God and William Randolph Hearst at one and the same time. Pretentious nationalism was a convenient screen for an ambitious and ambidextrous orator who tried to bridge this wide chasm. Johnson was untiring, flamboyant, and an effective speaker. If we enter the League, he once said, "I must abandon the lessons of my youth, which until this moment have been the creed of my manhood, of American ideals, American principles, and American patriotism." He demanded the immediate recall of the soldiers from Europe so that business could return to its normal channels and life could "be American again." Johnson was to remain in the Senate to harass all friends of international accord until the very eve of the Atomic Age.

Another soldier who fought with the "Battalion of Death" was George H. Moses, a freshman senator from New Hampshire, whose possibilities were immediately recognized by the Old Guard. They promptly elevated him to the Foreign Relations Committee. His caustic tongue and sardonic wit were freely used in the anti-Wilson cause. In contrast to the conservative Moses, Senator Joseph I. France of Maryland, a physician with decidedly unorthodox Republican domestic views, formed a valuable Irreconcilable link with the liberal isolationists because of his championship of civil liberty.

The only outright Democratic Irreconcilable was James A. Reed of Missouri, whose oratorical ability and legal acumen made him a pillar of strength. Reed made isolationism his crotchet, for he had gone to war most reluctantly. He then deserted his party's stand on foreign affairs and brought to the Irreconcilables the skill of an outstanding trial lawyer. For many years the senator was to plead eloquently and effectively for a return to unabashed isolationism.

In addition to Reed, two Democratic senators defected from the party to the strong reservationists. They were Thomas P. Gore of Oklahoma and John K. Shields of Tennessee. Shields's desertion was unexpected, for League sentiment had generally been very strong in the South. Even Reed's desperate argument that the prolific colored peoples of the world might gain control of the League failed to shake Dixie's internationalist stand. So it was both surprising and painful to the Democrats when the usually orthodox Shields joined the Lodge reservationists.

Coaching from the sidelines because of his exile from the Senate, Beveridge put incessant pressure upon wavering Republicans who wanted to save the League by compromise. Like Borah, he insisted that the party make no concessions to this "leech policy, sucking our subsistence and our strength."[7] In important speeches, widely read articles written in a popular vein, and innumerable private letters, the former senator insisted that the Covenant would rob Congress of the power to decide for war or peace. He, too, raised the race issue, saying that a hybrid group of white, brown, black, and yellow nations had conspired to make Uncle Sam the "paying teller" of the world. Then engaged in writing his monumental life of John Marshall, Beveridge hastened to devote full time to the alleged issue—the independence of the United States.

It is important to understand the difference between Americans and Europeans who were skeptical of the League as a total panacea. Clemenceau made room in his *Vive la France* psychology for a League of Nations. Buttressed with a good national army and some conventional alliances, it might be another weapon in the arsenal of French security. All too often Americans took the proposition of collective security without this kind of mental reservation. The Irreconcilables conjured up thoughts of a complete revolution in foreign policy which would make the United States subservient to a world political organization. In addition, men like Borah, Johnson, and Beveridge felt that our interests would be outweighed by the combined power of other nations, and would not concede for a moment that the League might be used as an instrument to enhance American aims. Implicitly then, there was also a lack of confidence in the good judgment and power of future American statesmen, who would have a permanent seat on the League Council, to protect our national safety and welfare. Finally, the isolationists looked at Article X with the most literal interpretation—every European sneeze would mean that America would contract pneumonia. Hence they hugged ever closer the isolationist policy initiated by Washington, blessed by Jefferson, and announced to the world by Monroe.

Nationalists throughout the country organized to support the Irreconcilable senators. The League for the Preservation of American Independence, for instance, was formed by men who wanted isolationism backed by military might. With a strong army and navy, they maintained, we could rely on ourselves alone to insure our security. The leaders of this movement were the colorful and contentious Kentucky editor,

"Marse" Henry Watterson, and Henry A. Wise Wood, a New York inventor and writer. With headquarters in New York and a Chief Field Division in Washington, the new organization demanded to know: "Is America so unable to care for herself that she needs must place herself under an international protectorate?" Publicity specialists were engaged to propagandize such sentiments among the people.

All over the country similar groups sprang up spontaneously. In Minneapolis, The American Club was formed to keep the country free from all alliances. Thirty-one prominent citizens of Buffalo, Republicans and Democrats, united to uphold the senators who insisted that America retain control of her own future decisions on peace and war. A Committee of American Business Men in New York, determined to fight to "Save the Republic," circulated an open letter from the Wall Street banker, Otto H. Kahn, pleading that the American eagle be not transformed "into an international nondescript."

Scholars, educators, and journalists helped present the isolationist cause to the people. They harped particularly on the danger of being drawn into war through uncontrolled machinations of foreign politicians. From Wilson's own Princeton, Professors Philip Marshall Brown and Edward S. Corwin lent scholarly reinforcements to the Irreconcilables. Brown thought the League too daring an experiment and was unwilling to gamble with the nation's destiny. Corwin maintained that the whole plan ran counter to the traditional framework of American constitutional government. The activities of David Jayne Hill are also especially worthy of notice. Hill, a former president of the University of Rochester and ambassador to Germany, was a prolific writer in a heavy sort of way. To him the League was a conspiracy of the victorious powers and their satellite countries to unite against the rest of mankind. The scheme, he argued, was absolutely contrary to the old American concept of settling international disputes by judicial means rather than by force. He predicted that the League would be unworkable because the members would not make the necessary sacrifices to enforce settlements that did not involve their own interests.

Standing at the head of the nationalist school of journalists, George Harvey worked, schemed, spoke, and wrote for the Irreconcilables. A tall, solemn, owl-like man with thick horn-rimmed glasses, Harvey was conducting a personal vendetta. One of the most prominent newspaper men in the country, he had been responsible for Wilson's debut in politics. The two men had early come to a parting of the ways, however, and Harvey became a vindictive and reckless opponent of all Wilson's policies. It was he, along with Theodore Roosevelt and Albert J. Beveridge, who had done most to urge that the Republicans embrace the cult of hyper-patriotism. Citing Daniel Webster's words "my country, and nothing but my country," Harvey said he would not sacrifice independence even for humanity. In New England, Editor James T. Williams, Jr., of the Boston *Evening Transcript* did such good work for the isolationist cause that Borah promised him that when the League was "buried in Hell, exceptional credit will be due to you."[8] Such zealousness began to bear results as the isolationist senators were flooded with fan mail from the humble and the great.

The Borah group won an immense victory when the Senate, on two separate occasions, voted down the treaty. The Republican leadership, under Lodge, had agreed upon fourteen reservations. Ten were of no great significance, because they merely clarified certain powers to be retained by the United States, that could hardly have been denied by ordinary interpretation of the Covenant. There were, however, four reservations that seriously imperiled Wilson's objectives. First of all, there was to be no obligation to act under the provisions of Article X without the specific approval of Congress in each question at issue. Thus any action by the League in preserving the peace was certain to be placed at the mercy of a congressional debate. Second, assent was withheld from the Shantung clause of the treaty, a step that would endanger Japanese support of the settlement. Third, the Monroe Doctrine was to be segregated from the League's scope of action, and the United States would refuse to arbitrate any dispute that impinged upon her traditional surveillance of New World security. Finally, we would not be obligated by a decision of the Council or Assembly where any one country (meaning the British Empire) had more than one vote, nor would we be bound by a decision to which we were a party if the nation pitted against us used more than one vote in obtaining the judgment.

The Irreconcilables played a masterful game of cards. They deliberately helped Lodge load these reservations on the treaty's back. Then when the treaty with addenda came before the Senate on November 19, 1919, Borah & Company voted with the Wilsonian Democrats against consent. On the question of the treaty as it stood, the Irreconcilables lined up with the Republican majority to vote nay. With four-fifths of the senators, puissant public opinion, and many organizations inclining toward the Covenant in one form or another, the issue was bound to rise once more. All attempts to reach a feasible compromise failed because the irresistible force of the President met the immovable object of the Republican high command. Thus, under virtually similar circumstances, the treaty failed once more in the Senate on March 19, 1920. More than a majority of the senators, but not the required two-thirds, voted for the League with reservations. Complete rejection of the League, even in the Senate, was not in 1920 the will of the majority. Time and events, however, were to play into the hands of the "Battalion of Death."

It is tempting to speculate what might have happened had a presidential election not been just around the corner. The internationalist spirit was still strong among cosmopolitan Republicans. Had Wilson's term not been at an end, it is conceivable that the Allied powers, anxious to launch the League with the United States a member, might have induced him to negotiate the entire matter. Had this occurred, the quickening of the League in Geneva might have revived waning American internationalism. All this, however, was not destined to be, for the isolationists were immensely strengthened by the campaign ballyhoo of the 1920 election. Wilson took the fatal step of asking the impossible—namely, that the election be "a great and solemn referendum" on the League. It would be difficult to imagine a more egregious error. The Republicans, who formed the ordinary majority, would be sure to pick up the President's gauntlet.

The merits of the League question aside, the Wilsonians would have had the odds heavily against them. Eight years of Democratic rule had built up the usual resentments against the party in power. To this must be added the jaded disillusionment against the war and its inconveniences which were bound to react against the "ins." Wilson, a competent political scientist, should have known that presidential elections are so intricate that it is impossible to fight them on any one issue. The League question could not be isolated and separated from the anti-Wilson political tide. As the President might well have anticipated had illness not blurred his foresight, the Republicans would not let the question be precipitated categorically. The G.O.P. could not afford to alienate their internationalist wing by an outright isolationist platform. Instead they straddled, compromised, overstated, and emotionalized the League issue. When the verdict was in, the Democrats had gone down to inglorious defeat. Thinking men knew that it was not a mandate to bury the League. In the excitement of the campaign, however, so much had been said against the Covenant that it would prove impossible for the League to live down the calumny. There was room for a superficial judgment that the Democrats had thrown the dice on the issue and had failed to make their point. In history often what people think happened is more important than what actually did happen. The isolationists could say that the question had been posed, voted upon, and downed. Thus the election of 1920 was recorded in the minds of the masses as a compulsive verdict against world organization.

The importance of the election of 1920 in the rebirth of isolationism merits detailed consideration. At the Republican national convention the first task of the politicos was to frame a meaningless plank that would unite their reservationist wing with the classic isolationists. Drafted by the sagacious Root, the platform avoided specific mention of the League or even of the reservations. "The first two paragraphs," as the historian Thomas A. Bailey has put it, "seemed to promise international cooperation, the next four paragraphs seemed to take it away, like the small print in a fraudulent contract." In essence, it was a victory for the Irreconcilables, for nothing had been promised that was tangible enough to implement. No action at all on world organization would be tantamount to a return to isolation.

After arguing over the platform there was brisk battle, for the nomination promised to be equivalent to election. The senatorial clique in control dictated the choice of the handsome and affable Warren G. Harding of Ohio, whose limited vision and less than mediocre ability they must have sensed from six years' association in that most exclusive of clubs, the upper house of Congress. The senators had had their fill of presidential leadership. They wanted to ride up Pennsylvania Avenue to give, not to take orders.

As the campaign pulled out of the mid-summer doldrums, Harding was under pressure from both the isolationists and the reservationists. The Borah-Johnson faction, remaining adamant, insisted that the party stand fast to the principle of no participation in any league, combine, alliance, or concert of powers. Thus would the country be saved from the "witches' cauldron of dragon teeth" which brewed nothing but international complications. There was, however, another side to the Republican coin. Men like William Howard Taft, Charles Evans Hughes, Elihu Root, and President Nicholas Murray Butler of Columbia had been acclimated to the twentieth century. They were entirely convinced that nineteenth-century isolationism was completely outdated. These men had pioneered the broader outlook in this country and it was difficult for them to swallow their words even had they so desired. It is essential to understand, however, that they were anti-Wilson Republicans, many of whom thought Article X defiant of American thought on international organization. Ex-President Taft had done splendid work for the League to Enforce Peace, but his hatred of Wilson had helped make him a reservationist. Taft then persuaded himself that Harding's election would assure America's participation in some sort of an international combine. Root, despite his world-wide vision, sincerely thought Article X dangerous, and was genuinely concerned about the future of the Monroe Doctrine. Above all, he feared the continuation of Democratic domestic policies. So Root gave the President's worst enemies the benefit of his peerless advice and beguiled himself into believing that a Republican "judicial" League would replace a Democratic "political" organization. Blessed with many years of life, Root was to live to ponder his 1920 optimism.

Nicholas Murray Butler was a moderate reservationist who insisted that the Republicans formulate a positive alternative to Wilson's proposal. Yet falling prey to the campaign fever, he called the treaty "sinister," "unpatriotic," "un-American," and even "half-conscious" socialism.[9] Butler, too, was to live on to work for an enlightened foreign policy only to find himself frustrated by the lasting results of the Harding landslide. A recent convert to Republicanism, Herbert Hoover had to tread carefully, for his alleged liberalism was suspect in orthodox circles. He favored the League, but like Root and Hughes, shrank from the mammoth implications of guarding foreign frontiers. Henry L. Stimson, whose name in history was to become a symbol for international cooperation, thought in 1920 that Wilson had promised something more than the American people would be willing to deliver.

Faced by these conflicting pressures within the party, the Republican candidate, or more properly the ghosts who did his thinking, made the conventional gyrations. As Harding steered in the direction of the isolationists, he alarmed the eastern intelligentsia. The latter group warned him that while they were good Republicans who could applaud criticisms of the League, they wanted him to sketch the outlines of the "association of nations" that he had in mind. Harding parried the suggestion, even when Root cabled from Europe that for American to abandon the League would invite chaos and disaster that would inevitably affect our fortunes. The candidate, however, went on with his bromidic speeches. In answer to a brutally frank letter from William Allen White, the sage Kansas editor, Harding promised an open mind on the League—"the rest of it you will have to take on trust."[10]

There were, in addition, a group of teachers, ministers, and men of affairs who also wanted something more tangible than what they were being offered. These people knew that all the political signs pointed to a G.O.P. victory, and they were anxious to have something on record for use after the election. They met the Republican National Chairman, Will H. Hays, in New York on September 9, 1920, and were promised action to hold what we would call today the "egghead" vote. Meanwhile, Harding wrote to Jacob Gould Schurman, describing in faint outlines a world association that would be inspired by ideals of justice and fair-dealing, and that would not demand surrender of our "supreme inheritance" of "national freedom." He confessed himself a progressive, adding that he nevertheless liked to arrange terminal facilities before starting on any journey.[11] But a Niagara-like flow of pompous clichés would not quiet the New York group who wanted to disengage the candidate from the Irreconcilable clutches. They met again on October 2 with Schurman acting as chairman of the subcommittee that included Lowell of Harvard and Hoover. Stimson had already told Hays bluntly that there was general alarm at Harding's Des Moines speech in which the candidate seemed ready to discard the League. The Republicans, Stimson insisted, must have a concrete plan which would modify rather than destroy the Covenant. Schurman presided at a full meeting of the group which considered and revised statements composed by two New York lawyers, Paul D. Cravath and George B. Wickersham. To Root went the assignment of putting the ideas together and phrasing the declaration which was to become famous as the manifesto of the Committee of 31. Essentially the views of conservative internationalists who wanted the League minus the entangling Article X, the statement was intended to hold the votes of the world-minded Republicans and to bind the candidate to some positive action.

The newly formed coterie told the country that Harding's election would mean entry into the League, for he could get the powers to agree to eliminate the objectionable Article X. A Republican victory, they insisted, would break the deadlock between the White House and Congress and so facilitate the acceptance of a revised Covenant by the American people. "When Republicans of distinction allow themselves so to mistake and misrepresent the facts," the New York *Times* commented, "what is to be expected of persons less scrupulous and more fanatically partisan?" But Harding lost none of his composure, and replied that he too, was utterly opposed to Article X, but was in favor of a full association of nations. He explained that if his speeches seemed inconsistent, it was because he had had to vary his language from time to time to answer the charges of his opponents. Some independents accepted the dodge, others held their noses and remained Republicans, while a few defected to the Pro-League Independents, organized to support the Democrats.

There was no clear issue before the voters on November 2, 1920. The Democratic platform sounded like an outright endorsement of the League, but also indicated that the party did not oppose reservations that would clarify or make more specific the obligations of the United States. The Democratic candidate, James M. Cox, was another Ohio newspaper man whose colorless liberalism aroused little enthusiasm. Facing almost certain defeat, late in the campaign he began to explain away his Wilsonian convictions. In the end, Cox took the moral obligation out of Article X, so that there was no absolute cleavage between the thirty-one Republicans who explained that a vote for Harding was a vote for the League, and Democrats who were willing to tone down the original proposition. Cox's running mate, the charming young Franklin D. Roosevelt, made gracious and simple speeches, sometimes talking out of turn. Even F.D.R.'s iron-bound optimism was shattered against the hopeless odds, and he conceded privately that the cause was lost. The people were weary of two years of debate over the League. They wanted a change and the unprecedented Republican landslide reflected this desire in unmistakable terms. Cox and Roosevelt went down to overwhelming defeat.

No informed or impartial observer in 1920 or since has thought that the election was an absolute repudiation of the League. An eccentric New York busybody named Samuel Colcord wrote a book to show that the results meant that a clear majority wanted to enter the League with reservations. In an exceptionally keen analysis of the vote, the New York *Evening Post* summed up the accumulated grievances against the Democrats and held that the verdict was "the chill that comes with the doctor's bills." Probably the voters of 1920 were more interested in chastening Democrats than in repudiating the concept of collective security. To men who were tired of living in a state of emergency, Harding had promised healing nostrums. He had made it seem that we could return to the Garden of Innocence, retain American aloofness, and still cooperate in the guardianship of peace. It was a large order and time was to prove that these incompatible pledges could not be reconciled. The fantastic promises evaporated with the smoke of the campaign.

Thus the election of 1920 is of prime importance in the history of isolationism—not because of the way the people voted, but because of the dangerously simple popular interpretation of the result. We have seen that millions of Americans had been given a promissory note by the Committee of 31 that a vote for Harding was a vote for the League with reservations. Would the note be made good? The President-elect gave the answer two days after the polls closed. He said that the question of joining was "now deceased," and in practice he was to regard the League issue as "dead as slavery." Thus blatantly ignoring the fact that he had beclouded the issue, and that there were many other more important factors involved, Harding chose to interpret his tremendous victory as a popular mandate against the League. As even his commonplace mind must have suspected, a new world association was out of the question. To abandon the League, then, meant a return to isolationism. The Irreconcilables had won once more by coincidental circumstances.

In the United States, where elections mean so much to so many, the returns are studied closely by professional politicians. Their analyses make no provisions for the intricate contributing factors that impress the political scientist. To the politicians the League was a liability. Harding had captured 60.35% of the popular vote—not to be surpassed even in the New Deal landslides of later years. The astounding results of 1920 gave the politicians pause. Never again would the Democratic party precipitate the League question in its unadulterated form. They had been beaten by a complex of factors, but the thumping licking was laid at the doorstep of the League. The severity of the defeat has been explained by the defection of normally stable Democratic voting blocs. The worst setbacks came in parts of the country where the hyphenate vote was most concentrated.[12] Politicians were duly impressed.

As the Democrats retired to their southern lairs to lick their wounds, the League of Nations issue loomed as an obstacle to party re-unification. They could not afford to alienate permanently important hyphenate voting blocs. To be sure, Republican strength was founded upon many factors, but the League remained to harass the Democrats. Thus the election of 1920 was important in forcing the Democrats away from the Wilsonian concept of collective security to gain the return of the

Irish and German defectionists. Their 1920 turn to internationalism had proven to be premature.

Tired of political harangues, Americans sank back after 1920 to enjoy, as Nicholas Murray Butler said, "the drowsy syrups of prosperity." Disdain for Europe was coupled with complacency. Novelist Sinclair Lewis's George Babbitt told the Zenith Real Estate Board that the real American was "the ideal type to which the entire world must tend if there's to be a decent, well-balanced Christian, go-ahead future for this little old planet!" Looking at the European complex of small wars, tyrant-cursed lands, ruinous inflation, and congenital hatreds, Main Streeters felt superior and smug. Frederick Lewis Allen termed the twenties the "Indian Summer" of the nineteenth century. A "back to McKinley" mood dominated the country and it was but natural that it should be complemented by a reactionary foreign policy.

An uncritical nationalism was part and parcel of the new climate of opinion. America, people said, had gotten ahead by hard work and free enterprise. Europeans, too, could be happy if they only saw the light. Pending that far off day but one creed was possible: "America for America, and let the rest of the world seek its safety and happiness by the methods its reason may dictate."[13] The vast majority of the nationalists wanted to go no further. The hundred percenters, however, carried the nationalist dogma to a point where they began to talk like home-grown fascists. A magazine entitled *America First* wanted to bring patriotism to homes and schools. Senator Borah thought the name "perfectly captivating." The True American Publishing Co. dedicated itself to fighting the atheists who kept the name of God out of the Treaty of Versailles. The League of Loyal Americans promised to fight for "One Tongue, One Ideal and One Flag." The biographer, Louis A. Coolidge of Boston, headed the Sentinels of the Republic, while an American Flag Movement aimed to put the national colors in each home in the land. Springing up indigenously all over the country, these organizations represented the stirrings of a revived nationalism. Whatever their immediate purpose or pet phobia, they all shared one thing in common: they looked back at an earlier America that had been shielded from the world and they demanded an end to European entanglements.

The resuscitated Ku Klux Klan, which rode to full power on the post-war wave of nationalism, was the most prominent organization of the semi-crackpot right. Klansmen were generally members of the lower middle class of old American stock. They were unusually resistant to change and suspicious of anything foreign or different. While the Klan was primarily interested in domestic affairs, it formed the extreme right wing of the isolationist front because their brand of know-nothingism put a curse on all foreigners.

Paradoxically enough, the war that was to save the world for democracy set in motion a nationalist reaction which was inimical to the concept of global collective security. By March 4, 1921, when the florid Harding rode up Pennsylvania Avenue with the peaked Wilson, the great isolationist front had been formed. The coalition contained many different types of active members. There were liberals who wanted no part of a League that had been fashioned by the turncoat Wilson. Communists gave active help to the isolationists because they regarded the League as a dangerous derelict lying in the path that led to the economic unity of mankind. Strangely enough, many immigrants were isolationists simply because of strong European attachments. Some of the victorious Republicans, especially those of the eastern seaboard, wanted an international organization, but opposed the League scheme in its existing form. Borah, Johnson, La Follette and their cohorts held tightly to a nineteenth-century form of nationalism, a concept which left no room for effective world organization. And there were the zealots who condemned everything foreign and who thought of our oceans as the Chinese had once thought of their wall. Important as all other factors were in evoking this mood of detachment, the nationalist creed was paramount. For that was a doctrine that immigrants and nativists, progressives and reactionaries, insular politicians and career diplomats had in common. Thus isolationism formed a common and seemingly solid ground amidst the drift of the twenties.

Chapter 6

The House Divided

"I SUPPOSE," wrote Elihu Root in 1922, "that the people of the United States have learned more about international relations within the past eight years than they had learned in the preceding eighty years. They are, however, only at the beginning of the task."[1] Root might have added that the war had taught many people how to rationalize their isolationist convictions. On the other hand, the years of strife had also reinforced internationalist thinking. Before 1914, the masses had been indifferent and only a few cosmopolites were aware that vital American interests had been projected far beyond the water's edge. Despite the vigor of the new isolationist coalition, the friends of international organization were more numerous, more vocal, and more potent in the 1920s than they had ever been in the quiet years before the holocaust. "The literature of 'Internationalism,'" complained the editor of the Grand Rapids *Herald,* Arthur H. Vandenberg, in 1925, "continues at flood-tide."[2]

Thus the postwar decline in internationalist zeal was relative rather than absolute. Educators, liberal clergymen, club women, idealistic journalists, public officials, and enlightened businessmen challenged the basic concepts of the renovated isolationism. After the war, crucial decisions in American foreign policy could be made only after both sides had had their say.

The isolationists were trying to hold back the integrating forces of the twentieth century. Once the United States had been initiated into the wiles of power politics, there was no turning back, for the lessons of the war had been too encompassing. At home and abroad horizons were steadily widening. Provincialism was lessened by trips in Model T Fords, by movies filmed in Hong Kong or Timbuktu, and by radio broadcasts tuned in through crystal sets from the capitals of the world. Foreign correspondents, books, and magazines all stressed European and Asiatic affairs. Although soldiers brought back stout prejudices, they also returned with a more cosmopolitan outlook. Isolationism now had to be defended, something quite unnecessary when the policy reflected genuine salt-water insulation. The philosophy no longer enjoyed a monopoly of thought, for it now had to contend with rival attitudes based upon more realistic foundations. As rapid transportation and communication brought the nations together, it became increasingly apparent that war could not be quarantined. The march of science had undermined the Irreconcilable position.

The isolationists, nevertheless, still held certain great advantages. Their gospel was simple, direct, and easy to comprehend. They followed in the footprints of what had once been a great and universally popular tradition. Isolationist rural areas were over-represented in Congress, thanks to the workings of the Constitution. Above all, the isolationists were better able to settle basic differences among themselves than were the internationalists. It is always easier to unite against something than to muster unity for so specific a cause as the League of Nations, and the internationalists were unable to do even that.

The array of internationally minded men and organizations of the twenties is large and impressive. Their effectiveness, however, was seriously hindered by failure to agree upon a program. The only feasible and tangible peace plan in the postwar years was the League. Yet many internationalists could not overcome their initial distaste for any organization that sanctioned the use of force. This was tantamount to spurning any program that held a reasonable expectation of success.

Some of the most stalwart opponents of the League were, in theory, internationalists rather than isolationists. Liberal and pacifist critics of the Covenant were often willing to sacrifice aspects of national sovereignty in the interests of peace. But in effect they were isolationists because they opposed all peace efforts related to the League. Nor were these theoretical internationalists able to agree among themselves on an alternate peace formula. Frequently, confirmed internationalists made common cause with the Irreconcilables in order to defeat some specific proposal. Circumstances had made the League the object of a tug of war, and there were strange partners on each end of the rope.

Many of the internationalists were only half-hearted converts to the cause. Deep down in their hearts they still clung to the old belief that the United States would always be safe and secure regardless of the outcome of their efforts. Therefore, many of their campaigns lacked a sense of urgency, for peace in Europe was not seriously threatened until the next decade. While a majority of the internationalists remained true to the League ideal, there were those who wanted the impossible—a maximum amount of world leadership with a minimum risk of foreign entanglements.

Another factor in the perplexity of the twenties was derived from the nature of our government. Congress and public opinion always had to be taken into consideration, and both were afflicted with "insular sclerosis." Shortsighted political bromides were found to yield more votes than candid disclosures of unpleasant facts to an electorate eager to enjoy the new affluence. (Perhaps there is something to Clement Attlee's observation that our Constitution was designed for an "isolationist state.") Yet despite all the smugness, men sought to influence the formation of foreign policy as never before. Secretary of States Charles Evans Hughes later complained of the telegrams that fell like snowflakes in a thick storm, clouding each issue with diverse opinions. He commented upon the great amount of knowledge needed to appraise even a single diplomatic decision.[3] This was a new dilemma for the modern democracies, for streamlined pressure techniques threatened to destroy the time-honored *in camera* habits of the statesmen. Diplomacy, too, was in danger of becoming socialized.

Elihu Root cautioned that if the masses insisted upon influencing foreign policy, they must learn the facts lest ignorance and error should govern our decisions. To be sure, international affairs were studied now as never before—in schools, colleges, service clubs, press columns, and institutes. Often, however, confusion was only intensified. Peace, rather than national security in the broadest sense, was made the goal. Headlines and digests oversimplified complex situations. Commentators seldom made allowance for the temper of less fortunate nations and cavalierly assumed that Americans had cornered the market on international morality. Only a minority recognized that the world's best chance for peace lay in an effective association that must necessarily include the United States. Hence the contradiction: as American political, economic, and moral influence penetrated to all parts of the globe, we withdrew into the cocoon of a rejuvenated isolationism and left the peace to the safekeeping of other nations.

Educators and liberal ministers rose to expose this inconsistency. Frederick Jackson Turner stated that a shrinking earth was compelled by irrepressible forces to exercise restraint, to associate, agree, and adjust, or to commit suicide. It was pointed out by Dean Frank Thilly of Cornell that whether the people would admit it or not, every disturbance in the economic, political, and social arrangements of other states would inevitably affect our national life. Former Harvard President Charles W. Eliot, long an internationalist crusader, spend his octogenarian years denouncing those senators who beguiled the masses with specious words.

Foundation lectures, designed to dispense information leading to a more enlightened world order, were the current fad. Edward W. Bok, the Dutch immigrant boy who became a famous editor, helped to launch the new Walter Hines Page School of International Relations at Johns Hopkins. In nearby Washington, Georgetown University had its School of Foreign Service, and the Jesuit Fathers sponsored popular lectures. Current events, and sometimes even American diplomatic history, were emphasized in high school classrooms.

International education, in the modern sense, dates from the establishment of the Rhodes Scholarships in 1904. At the end of the First World War, Nicholas Murray Butler, Elihu Root, and Professor Stephen P. Duggan of the City College of New York fostered the movement by establishing an Institute of International Education. Founded on a shoestring, the Institute acted as a clearing house for American students who wished to study abroad, and encouraged public and private groups to subsidize international cultural exchange. (The program of the Institute was given a tremendous fillip when, in 1946, Congress passed the Fulbright Act which authorized the Secretary of State to use funds from the sale of surplus war materials to finance American students studying abroad and to bring foreign students to our own universities. Later, Congress expanded the plan in order to facilitate the exchange of teaching personnel throughout the free world. In 1956, the Ford and Rockefeller Foundations and the Carnegie Corporation gave over five million dollars to the Institute of International Education. Between 1919 and 1955, 212,696 persons from some 151 countries and political areas left their homelands to further their education.)

Prior to the Second World War, however, if faculty and students on campuses throughout the world showed interest in the fitful progress of the League of Nations, their voices were smothered by the hordes of Babbitts who surrounded the cloistered walls of the universities.

In the religious world, while American Catholics tended to be anti-League because of Irish and sometimes German affinities, worldly Protestant clergymen were usually international cooperationists. Their motives were varied. In some cases the old missionary spirit called for a League of Nations to save the Armenians from the hands of the atrocious Turks. Modernists projected their evangelical impulses in a move to spread the benefits of American education, science and sanitation to far away countries. Such ministers were advocates of a social gospel that sublimated into humanitarian channels the energy that had once been used to fight the Devil. Religion's paramount duty, they said, was to conquer war by teaching the necessity for cooperation among nations. Unfortunately, there was no real coordination of effort or general agreement on program. Time and again disjointed action was to foil the efforts of the internationalists.

The Federal Council of Churches of Christ in America (now the National Council of the Churches of Christ in the United States of America) emerged from the war as the most powerful pressure group of its kind. Its Commission on International Justice and Goodwill flooded the country with propaganda. Originally the Federal Council blessed Geneva as an agent of Christian unity, but it retreated to preach internationalism while seldom mentioning the League by name. The World Alliance for International Friendship through the Churches, a wartime offshoot of Andrew Carnegie's Church Peace Union, followed a somewhat similar policy. Two groups, however, continued to call for American entry into the Covenant—the Methodist Episcopal Church, one of the two largest Protestant sects in the country, and the National Synod of the Reformed Presbyterian Church. Such a step was also urged by the nationally prominent Episcopal Bishop of Western New York, Charles H. Brent.

There was a marked tendency toward pacifism in some religious circles. In 1925, the Central Conference of American Rabbis (constituting the liberal wing of Jewish religious thinking) created a Commission on Justice and Peace. The Commission, which showed a penchant for pacifism, avoided the divisive League issue, and urged policies upon the Conference that would strike at war in other ways. The current movement to outlaw war made powerful inroads among all religious groups. Fundamentalist Christians proclaimed that this was God's world and the war system must go along with slavery and the saloon.

Additional pro-peace sentiment came from the distaff energy released when the women's suffrage movement terminated logically with the adoption of the Nineteenth Amendment. Limitation of families, urban apartments, prepared foods, and labor-saving household gadgets found increasing numbers of college-bred women with too much leisure time on their hands. While the League idea enjoyed great popularity among the silk-stocking women, it was by no means acceptable to all. The newly formed League of Women Voters discovered that disarmament held out a far better promise of rallying its membership behind a peace program. Why, asked *The Woman Citizen,* descend into the valley of the shadow of death to bear a son to be sacrificed to Mars in 1940? The *Ladies' Home Journal,* as well, campaigned for the scrapping of arms. While these forces were not necessarily anti-Geneva, it was another case of not pushing the one plan that *might* have worked. Some women were not satisfied with merely ignoring collective security, and Jeannette Rankin (the first woman who was elected to Congress and who voted against entry into both World Wars) helped organize the American Women Opposed to [the] League of Nations.[4]

The press reflected the quickened interest in foreign affairs. Three factors influenced newspaper treatment of international relations: completion of the pre-war trend of consolidation of independent dailies into huge chains; the increasing importance of the foreign correspondent; and the rising popularity of the columnist. All over the country newspapers were becoming standardized by using the same syndicated pieces. The consolidated press wielded a terrific influence on the dispensation of news and the consequent formation of public opinion.

Despite some important exceptions, most of the newspaper chains had strong isolationist leanings. Even among papers that remained independent, there was a large overturn in ownership. Frequently, affluent Republicans bought up tottering journals in order to nurse them back to health. They, or their editors, accepted the new isolationism as a tenet of G.O.P. orthodoxy. There was an increasing tendency toward a one-party press. "Democrats everywhere," complained a citizen of Iowa, "are compelled to read Republican daily newspapers. They have no choice."[5] In Coolidge's day, Minnesota and Iowa had hardly a single Democratic journal of any importance.[6] Even Chicago was said to be without a Democratic daily and, in the hinterland, the few remaining rural papers were being rapidly absorbed by owners with Republican leanings.

Among the press moguls were veteran enemies of the League of Nations. Frank A. Munsey had done yeoman work for the Irreconcilables. One of his Washington correspondents served as Borah's walking encyclopaedia, while another kept up a running correspondence with Beveridge. Munsey had regarded the whole League plan as a dangerous scheme to

117

gratify the whims "of the greatest autocrat of all time."[7] His newspaper empire grew rapidly after the war. By 1923 he controlled the *Sun, Telegram,* and *Herald* in New York alone, and was about to absorb the *Globe,* the *Evening Mail,* and the *Commercial Advertiser.* Obviously all of these papers could not pay, so Munsey merged a number of them and, in the journalistic world, his touch was held to be the kiss of death. To him, any traffic with the League was equivalent to a surrender of independence.

Munsey's counterpart was William Randolph Hearst, who, wrote William Allen White in a private letter, "is my idea of a rattlesnake crossed with the smallpox . . . I would not work for him for any money on earth."[8] Part of Hearst's exasperating chauvinism was a cover-up for his reluctance to fight Germany. As he expanded his empire in the twenties, there was no deviation from this narrow patriotism. His newspapers listed a circulation of 3,400,060 in 1923 and the chain was still growing! One American family in four, it was said, regularly read a Hearst publication. With his own morning and evening news service, and control of the King Features Syndicate, Hearst was almost invulnerable. Lloyd George was enticed into writing for him, and newspaper feature syndicators, who despised his methods, accepted his contracts. Unpredictable on many subjects, impossible to type as a conservative, liberal, racist, imperialist or anti-imperialist, Republican or Democrat, Hearst's only consistency was a vicious type of parochial isolationism. He even regarded naval disarmament as a British-Japanese plot to scuttle the American fleet. He was, however, willing to make an agreement among the English-speaking peoples to keep peace among themselves and to promote it in the world. Probably Hearst and Munsey reflected, rather than shaped, the opinions of many of their readers; yet both dabbled in politics to strengthen the isolationist congressional clique. They certainly nurtured the prevailing tendency with their editorials contrasting our own moral superiority with the congenital wickedness of other folk.

More middle-of-the-road was the Scripps-Howard (formerly Scripps-McRae) chain which controlled over two dozen dailies scattered from the Denver *Rocky Mountain News* to the Washington *News.* Edward W. Scripps was rough and somewhat ruthless, but unlike Heart or Munsey, he was restrained by unusually clear and shrewd insights. Much of Roy W. Howard's acerbity came only after the New Deal, and in the twenties, the Scripps-Howard papers favored international cooperation short of joining the League. Frank E. Gannett, who branched out of Elmira to acquire ten papers, was internationally minded in the twenties. (He later swung to the extreme Republican line in general repudiation of both the foreign and domestic policies of the second Roosevelt.) Cyrus H. K. Curtis, of *Saturday Evening Post and Ladies' Home Journal* fame, started with the Philadelphia *Public Ledger* and later picked up the venerable New York *Evening Post*. Curtis developed a widely syndicated foreign news service, which along with his papers held to a mildly pro-League point of view.

The stronger papers remained independent despite steadily rising costs of production. The Chicago *Tribune* and the Kansas City *Star,* two of the most important isolationist journals of the interior states, penetrated the countryside far from their home offices. Colonel Robert R. McCormick's *Tribune* could be found on every train, in every leading hotel, and on the Main Street newsstands of every town within hundreds of miles of Chicago. Like Hearst, McCormick had to live down a pro-German reputation. His cynicism, arrogance, militarism, and pretentious patriotism perhaps were affected in order to assure the world of his unadulterated Americanism.[9] The rest was that the *Tribune* carried the most erratic and inconsistent editorial column in the country. The Kansas City *Star,* on the other hand, commanded the respect of its competitors and critics. William Allen White, who disagreed with the *Star's* isolationism, called the paper "clean, brave and fair." Yet, as it was circulated in Kansas, Oklahoma, northern Texas, Colorado, and even New Mexico, it advocated no political ties with the League. William Rockhill Nelson, the owner and founder, believed that he was carrying out the last wishes of his friend, Theodore Roosevelt.

There were, of course, some strongly internationalist journals. No paper fought more vigorously for the League of Nations than Adolph Och's New York *Times*. Its editorial page reflected the views of the eastern business groups and intelligentsia who had both economic and cultural affinities beyond the sea. When Munsey sold the *Herald* to Ogden M. Reid, the newly combined *Herald Tribune* joined the *Times* in pleading for a broader world outlook.

In the midwest, Victor Fremont Lawson, owner of the Chicago *Daily News,* tried valiantly to neutralize the prejudice of the *Tribune*. Lawson, a successful journalist of the old school, had pioneered in foreign reporting since the days of the Russo-Japanese war. In 1914, he had a European service ready to take advantage of the big story. Headed by Edward Price Bell, such able men as Raymond Gram Swing and the two Mowrer brothers, Paul Scott and Edgar Ansel, worked for the *Daily News's* syndicated service. A few big scoops advertised the usefulness of these dispatches and increased the market for the releases. Lawson was genuinely interested in world organization, and at times the foreign service was run at a loss for the sake of creating enthusiasm for international organization. In order to combat Colonel McCormick's growing influence in the corn belt, Lawson sent Bell on a lecture tour. As part of this campaign, Bell used the radio and the subject of his first broadcast was "If Not a League—What?" The *News's* foreign service, avowedly dedicated to breaking down international misgivings, was at one time used by almost one hundred papers. After Lawson's death, his successors, first Walter A. Strong and then the redoubtable Colonel Frank Knox, continued to beard the *Tribune*. Other important world-minded papers in the Mississippi Valley were the Chicago *Evening Post,* the Wichita *Eagle,* White's Emporia *Gazette,* The St. Louis *Globe-Democrat,* and ex-Senator Gilbert M. Hitchcock's Omaha *World-Herald.*

Except for the Lawson correspondents and the European staff of the New York *Times,* the foreign news guild sent home chits which often bristled with prejudice. Denunciation of Europe made lively reading and, more often than not, conformed to local inclinations. Since those American newspapers that were opposed to the League were violently so, while those that supported it were often lukewarm, it paid correspondents who wanted to sell syndicated dispatches to write disparagingly. It became axiomatic among the journalists abroad that kind words for Geneva or its undertakings just did not help business. Generally speaking, then, American correspondents exaggerated the faults of the League and minimized its achievements. Reports on foreign convulsions were interlarded with prayers of thanks for the wise statesmanship that had spared American composure. Many lazy news gatherers took only enough time off from wine and song to make carbon copies of each other's communications. Such cribbers were dubbed the "black sheet gang."[10]

The rise of the newspaper columnist centered the interest of readers on foreign affairs. The old-time personal journalism, with its lively vituperative editorials, had given away to a deceivingly objective listing of facts. The reader was left adrift without a compass to guide his reflections on complicated problems. The answer to the confusion was the syndicated column, which has done so much to shape opinion in America. The first of these modern publicists were Arthur Brisbane,

Heywood Broun, and Walter Lippmann. Brisbane's "Today" began in 1917 and William Randolph Hearst pushed the column so that it eventually reached millions of Americans. Coating his views with a religious unction, Brisbane echoed Hearst's bumptiousness, militarism, and indubitable isolationism. What a far cry from his famous father, Albert Brisbane, who had returned from Europe in 1834 to spread utopian socialism! Lippmann and Broun were much more world-minded than Arthur Brisbane. They were, however, frequently censorious of Europe, and their readers remembered the barbs rather than the occasional reminders that other countries also might be honestly groping for the path to peace.

To sum up, it is apparent that the isolationists enjoyed most of the advantages of a good press. The pro-League papers, foreign correspondents, and urbane columnists were not commensurate with the Irreconcilable big chains, independently owned dailies that made a fetish of isolationism, and the multitude of conforming Republican editors. The internationalist papers were more often apologetic than scintillating. The press, that did so much to mold American opinion before the age of radio and television, helped on balance to argue the isolationist case.

Newspapers, nevertheless, did stimulate interest in foreign affairs. This concern was abetted by a new type of organization which came into being to provide neutral, non-partisan information to its constituents. Thus the Foreign Policy Association and the Council on Foreign Relations evolved from wartime groups. The former, the old League of Free Nations Association, adopted in 1921 the name by which we know it today. For about a year the revamped group pressed for naval disarmament and for joining the World Court, but then abandoned propaganda for purely educational activities. Branches were established in leading cities, a speakers' bureau was set up, and the organization grew. The F. P. A. published weekly bulletins, supported a research department, and opened a Washington bureau. In leading cities, luncheon, dinner and evening meetings were devoted to discussions of world affairs.[11]

Whereas the F. P. A. actively sought members, the Council on Foreign Relations limited its numbers. The dues were high, and membership came only on invitation from the Board of Directors. In 1920, the Council merged with the American Institute of International Affairs, which had been formed in Paris during the Peace Conference. The following year the group took over publication of an established journal, and changed its name to *Foreign Affairs*. The new editor was Hamilton Fish Armstrong, who had learned his way around Europe as a military attaché and foreign correspondent. The Council promoted an objective and non-partisan study of American foreign policy by publications, educational dinners, the formation of study groups, and the establishment of a library in New York. It is significant that neutrality on the League question did not make for complete unity. Apparently it was difficult for the internationalists to agree, even where the goal was enlightenment rather than action.

The Institute of Politics, which opened its first annual meeting in Williamstown, Massachusetts, on July 29, 1921, was of more ephemeral importance. Each summer brought leading European and American thinkers to the pleasant Berkshire town for round-table discussions and formal lectures. The Institute's Board of Advisors contained both friends and critics of the League as well as some whose position was difficult to define. All participants were supposedly thirsting for peace, but liberals were suspicious of the generals and admirals who came to lead the talks on disarmament. Frequently, these Williamstown round-tables stimulated isolationist talk when they made the news headlines. This was particularly true when the gray-beared Englishman, James Bryce, long beloved for his interest in American problems, called the Treaty of Versailles more wicked than the settlement which had ended the Napoleonic wars. Although able opponents of this view had ample opportunities to refute it, this singular assertion struck a responsive chord.

The World Peace Foundation, which had been established in 1910 by the textbook king, Edwin Ginn, found a certain amount of neutrality on vital issues necessary. The Foundation did, however, become the official distributor of League of Nations publications. The Carnegie Endowment for International Peace also leaned unofficially toward the League. The war had increased the value of Carnegie's initial gift of ten million dollars in United States Steel bonds, so now the Endowment had more money than ever with which to pursue its elusive goal. Thus *International Conciliation* was distributed at nominal rates, one thousand International Relations Clubs were sponsored, and the "International Mind" alcoves in small libraries were well stocked.[12] Both Nicholas Murray Butler, president of the Carnegie Endowment, and James T. Shotwell, director of its Division of Economics and History, were friends of international organization. Butler rued his 1920 stand because he realized that the progress of the League was retarded

122

by American abstention. Shotwell, Canadian-born Columbia specialist in intellectual history, worked quietly but incessantly to awaken the American international conscience. The Carnegie Endowment sent selected groups to Europe and Asia and generally arranged stop-overs at the League in Geneva and the World Court at The Hague. The Endowment's Division of International Law was headed by a friend of world organization, James Brown Scott, who had often served the State Department.

The National Civic Federation was more nearly neutral on the League issue. Its Committee of One Hundred on Foreign Relations merely sought to present non-controversial material to the American public. The very fact that institutions designed to promote international accord had to treat the League so gingerly is a pointed reflection of the spirit of the times. The front door to Geneva had been barred by politics, with the result that would-be American consociates had to search for a side entrance.

For a century the organized America peace movement had run a familiar course, gaining ground between wars that always managed to appear different and therefore justifiable. George Haven Putnam, the publisher who had fought his way from private to major in the Civil War, was re-elected a vice-president of the American Peace Society while clamoring for war against Germany.[13] The less bellicose officers and members of this venerable society opposed collective security of the League variety because they could not give approbation to any plan which rested upon coercion. They denounced the League as wrong in principle, contrary to the teachings of history, and dangerous to the peace of the world. Dr. Arthur Deerin Call, secretary of the organization, used the *Advocate of Peace* to attack the League and to broach impossible substitutes.

These castle-building American internationalists failed to realize that they were aiding the isolationists by attacking the one existing world organization potentially capable of settling major disputes. In Europe, the desolation of war had convinced realistic men of the necessity of the League. Hence peace organizations abroad invariably championed the tangible, while American peace groups, paradoxically larger and more powerful than those in Europe, were torn by divided counsels and fragmentary plans. Too little thought was given to the practical implementation of attractive but visionary proposals. It was naively supposed that the will for peace, like love, could conquer all things.

As American organizations pursued the dove of peace, reports, inquiries, and recommendations multiplied. What did all of this fact-finding accomplish? From the published data men usually selected parts which buttressed their own previous convictions. Frequently, societies interested in foreign relations prompted celebrated debates in which the internationalist contenders were more often apologetic than enthusiastic about the League. Yet some positive achievements are evident. By their very existence, the internationalist organizations kept the country from sinking even farther into a twentieth-century variant of know-nothingism. In the schools and among the intellectually curious they built attitudes that were later to pay dividends in hard-fought battles against invincible ignorance.

Thus organizations mushroomed with obtrusive names, gaudy stationery, voluble fund-raising campaigns, inane conventions, and annoying pressure techniques. These societies were studded with peace bureaucrats—men and women who ran the organizations while their constituents pursued happiness and prosperity. Frequently, hired personnel and fanatical volunteer staffs resisted concerted action that might threaten the autonomy of their own groups. And always they gave more thought to program than to ultimate ends.[14] Their leaders failed to comprehend that the primary task was to make a parochial people understand that modern science had changed our problem of defense in both space and time relationships.

There were many other schemes to bring about the golden age. Conservative religious leaders called for a revival that would span the boundaries of nations and by its impact would force the League to respect moral values. Some even argued that a universal grass roots reform movement would make peace machinery superfluous, for the newly inspired peoples would prevent their governments from going to war. Even so seasoned a thinker as the veteran correspondent, Frank H. Simonds, held that the pronouncements of righteous judgments would be more effective in keeping the peace than any form of compulsion.

The demand for the enthronement of international law came from experts rather than dilettantes. Deeply ingrained in the American mind was the belief that the codification of international law would eliminate war by substituting judicial settlement. Thus there were insistent requests for a new meeting at The Hague to continue the work started at the two prewar conferences in that city. This third Hague meeting, it was predicted, would systematize the law of nations and replace League power politics with international morality. (As a postscript one might add that when the United States, backed by the League, eventually did convoke a Third Hague Conference, the net result was a "Protocol Relating to Military Obligations in Certain Cases of Double Nationality.") Totalitarianism had not yet demonstrated that brutality, inhumanity, and fiendish ambitions could not be curbed by incantations, codification of international law, and wishful thinking. A persisting nineteenth-century optimism over-estimated the better side of human nature, and obscured the fact that only force could checkmate force. A curious mixture of idealism and irresponsibility was an intrinsic ingredient of American thought of the period.

The uncompromising pacifists formed a small but clangorous minority. Their solution to the problem of war was as simple as it was unrealistic: let the United States resolve never again to resort to armed strife. Frequently they made common cause with militaristic ultra-nationalists to denounce all rapport with the League and its agencies. The English pacifist, Arthur Ponsonby, helped the Women's Peace Union (affiliated with the War Resisters' International), in its effort to create enough conscientious objectors to frustrate any war effort. The quadrennial Convention of Student Volunteers, meeting at Indianapolis, took the pledge never to aid, directly or indirectly, in the prosecution of war. The pacifists celebrated "No More War Days," their handbills demanded "Disarm or Die," and they held endless discussions and prayer meetings.

The real issue of American help in the preservation of world order was thus obscured by a plethora of plans. There was a major split between those who wanted to enforce peace and those who eschewed coercion whether used by a nation, alliance, or international body. The former were usually outright leaguists, or men who hoped some day to rewrite the Covenant to suit American specifications. The opponents of the use of force were prone to cull ancient peace schemes from the tomes of history. The American Association for International Conciliation held that a sincere effort to build upon our treaties of arbitration and conciliation would solve the problem. To add to the confusion, the same Chicago *Tribune,* that so often championed the mailed fist, turned to twenty-eight existing pacification treaties as an American rather than an Old World remedy for war. Few took the trouble to point out that while these agreements had gathered dust in the State Department's files, bloody wars had rocked the world.

There was more general agreement on disarmament than on

any other specific program. In the early twenties the peace societies momentarily buried their differences and concentrated on the scrapping of arms. The new coalition contained some outright pacifists and a conservative element that wanted only such disarmament as was consistent with security. The front was broad enough to include both isolationists and those discouraged leaguists who preferred American leadership in disarmament to a seat on the sidelines. Joseph Pulitzer's New York *World* launched a sweeping crusade that made newspaper history. Even Hudson Maxim, of smokeless powder fame, lent his support to the *World's* "disarmament editor."

The movement was given terrific impetus in 1921 when President Harding convened the Washington Naval Arms Conference, details of which belong to an ensuing chapter. An analysis of the disarmament combine is pertinent here, however, for it will elucidate the workings of the American peace organizations. The most effective body was the National Council for the Limitation of Armament, a union of religious, farm, labor, and educational groups. Frederick J. Libby, a Congregationalist minister turned Quaker, was its executive secretary and presiding genius. Started as a temporary medium to facilitate the work of the 1921 conclave, it organized permanently as the National Council for Prevention of War, with headquarters in Washington. Guided by the pacifist Libby, it raised a good deal of money and, at the height of its power, sent out 430,000 pieces of anti-war material in a single month.[15] Libby's convictions made him an avowed enemy of the League of Nations, but he did urge American adherence to the World Court.

The NCPW's work was paralleled by two women's organizations which were founded in the belief that the new female voting power would make war politically impossible. Jane Addams, pioneer settlement worker, dominated the WILPF-US, the American branch of the Women's International League for Peace and Freedom. Like Libby, Miss Addams condemned the League of Nations because the Covenant approved of war to deter aggression. Interestingly enough, WILPF members attached to their income tax returns the following reservation: "That part of this income tax which is levied for preparation for War is paid only under Protest and Duress."[16]

Devotion to the cause of peace did not preserve tranquillity within the sanctum of the WILPF-US. Mrs. Carrie Chapman Catt's ambitions had been whetted by the triumph of the prohibition and suffrage movements and her personal success as a popular lecturer. She contested Miss Addams's leadership and walked out of the WILPF-US to federate nine women's groups into the National Council on the Cause and Cure of War. The new organization was far less inclined toward pacifism than the WILPF-US. At the very first meeting of the Council, the square-jawed and fiery Rabbi Stephen S. Wise denounced the enemies of collective security with every suitable adjective in the English language. Within a short time a pro-League faction captured control of the organization and proceeded to castigate the country's provincialism.

Neither the pacifists nor the more moderate disarmament leaders caused the isolationist rebound. Many in both camps were internationalists who were not in accord with the League bond of world union. Their organizations, however, incessantly scolded Europe for its standing armies, viewed unrealistically the problem of security, and erred in oversimplifying the complex causes of and remedies for world disorder. Their commotion and fanfare helped delay American acceptance of the responsibilities of a major power in an imperfect world.

The number of crackpot schemes for peace in the twenties was legion. They defy classification, but some common tendencies are apparent. Men of good will sought immortality by trying to solve the problem of peace that had daunted the best minds of generations. The belief persisted that heroic individual efforts would find the answer. Sincere but unsophisticated thinking led to romantic and utopian recipes for ending global turmoil. The new formulas often spliced together shopworn peace plans, forming a maze of contradictions and absurd suggestions.

One of the most persistent would-be architects of a new world order was Samuel Colcord of New York. He had enough money, septuagenarian energy, and contacts to promote his plans. After beginning as a League reservationist, he quickly gave ground in the face of Republican opposition. He then argued that we should police the western hemisphere for the League, freeing ourselves, at the same time, of all European pitfalls. Through a front organization called the Committee on Educational Publicity in the Interests of World Peace, with William Allen White as chairman and Henry L. Stimson on the board, Colcord worked to unite the various groups that favored the outlawry of war. His technique was to deluge prominent officials, from the President down, with personal appeals and circulars. Neither cold silence nor studied incivility was able to dampen his zeal.

The manuscript collections of the period are replete with the peace activities of fleeting organizations, unknown personages,

127

and public figures. The Michigan Council For Peace worked out a plan for world government. A Committee of One Hundred staged a demonstration in Washington "For Law Not War." One Benjamin Blumenthal drafted the outlines of a League of People's Peace. The socially prominent Mrs. Frank A. Vanderlip planned a Peace Pageant called the March of Mankind. William Jennings Bryan, with three unsuccessful tries for the White House and service as Secretary of State behind him, gave some thought to the peace problem. He urged the adoption of a constitutional amendment that would make the declaration of war, except in case of invasion, subject to a popular referendum. This was three years prior to his burial in the full regalia of a colonel of Nebraska Volunteers!

These grandiose schemes mirrored the American thought of the day—isolationist, unrealistic, peace-loving, and for all that unwilling to make genuine sacrifices to secure an ordered world. All groups, including the isolationists, wished to follow the arrow marked "To Peace." Because the country seemed secure, the more world-minded felt free to engage in a Donnybrook Fair among themselves. Despite their cosmopolitan talk, they did not realize the immediate need for American action to stabilize the world. They shared, perhaps far more than they themselves comprehended, the isolationist delusion of American invulnerability. It was in this fog of wistful thought that the Republican statesmen of the twenties were to grope their way in the post-Versailles world.

Chapter 7

The Republican Straddle

WARREN GAMALIEL HARDING faced some perplexing choices in the formation of the new Republican foreign policy. He had helped to create some of his own problems. During the 1920 campaign he had persuaded millions of his fellow citizens that membership in the existing League of Nations would constitute a standing invitation to the blood-baths of Europe. Prematurely he had interpreted his overwhelming victory as a popular mandate against the League. Thus he narrowed down the possible alternatives to the dilemmas which confronted his administration. The United States had emerged from the war as potentially the strongest power on earth. How could the country which refused to join the League still consider itself the world's exemplar of idealism? Could the ancient policy of non-entanglement be reconciled with the new interests and rivalries forced upon us by the march of events? Whether we liked it or not, the other victorious nations had decided to try the experiment of collective security. The League was now a condition rather than a theory, and the United States would have to adopt some attitude toward the new organization.

In retrospect, there seemed to be several options open to the restored Republicans. Most of these choices, however, were ruled out by circumstances. The President's own reading of the election barometer and the strength of isolationist sentiment eliminated the possibility of joining the League with reservations. It is probable that even if President Harding had chosen such a course, he could not have mustered the necessary two-thirds vote in the Senate to implement his decision. Another alternative was also infeasible. It might have been wise to join the Allies in creating a new balance of power that would keep the peace until the infant League could become truly effective. Not only was the necessary vision for such a step lacking, but it would never have been countenanced by public opinion. A third course, Harding's campaign oratory about a new "Association of Nations," had to be promptly jettisoned. There was no possibility of prompting a new organization to compete with a living rival at Geneva. Such a move would have been ridiculous, for Europe was not willing to tear up the Covenant and start all over again to please the whims of G.O.P. international theorists.

The Republicans were, therefore, compelled to reconcile non-entanglement, acceptance of the existence of the League, and the inescapable necessity of playing the part of a dominant power. This Herculean task was bound to lead to the inconsistencies of our foreign policy during the twenties and early thirties. In theory the United States still held to isolation, while in practice we were forced to depart from its hidebound tenets. This curious mixture of the old and the new has been called neo-isolationism.

The incongruities of the new policy were glossed over by pious over-statements concerning American moral superiority. The neo-isolationists argued that the motives of the United States were so pure and clean that it was best for the world to have our powerful hands unfettered so that we might use our own judgment as to when humanity was really deserving of help. This type of reasoning led to incalculable self-conceit. In our broad expanse of land, said the Wisconsin scholar and diplomat Paul S. Reinsch, secret plotting and underhanded transactions were "unnatural, inappropriate, and unnecessary."[1]

It is significant that the three Republican Presidents of the inter-war years were all strong adherents of this theory of American uniqueness. Harding boasted that the United States had made greater contributions to human welfare in a century and a half than had all the peoples of the world since the beginnings of civilization.[2] "America first," said Calvin Coolidge modestly, "is not selfishness; it is the righteous demand for strength to serve."[3] Long before Herbert Hoover became President, he already was persuaded that the American system was the great promise of the human race.[4] If our ways were both better than and different from those of other nations, we were then justified in abjuring the League system. We would bind ourselves to no outright advance commitments, but would rely on our own judgment to determine when to extend the hand of fellowship and when to withdraw once more into our isolationist shell. This superiority complex lay at the base of the new foreign policy that was destined to dominate American thought until the very eve of the Second World War.

Personalities and events were jointly responsible for the new departure, and must, therefore, be scrutinized. We must begin with Harding, for his blunted thinking colored the foreign policy of his administration. The new President had less originality than even the average run-of-the-mill politician. As a senator he had been a strong reservationist and not an Irreconcilable. After his election he laid down the debatable proposition that the League issue had been thoroughly ventilated and that a plebiscite had decided against foreign entanglements. Vacillations from this conviction must be attributed to a multiplicity of forces playing upon a weak personality. Even as President-elect he soon found himself the victim of his own party's contradictory promises. Nicholas Murray Butler went to Harding's home at Marion, Ohio to urge qualified League entry or, failing that, an alternate plan that would insure American leadership in the quest for world stability. A month before the inauguration William Allen White satisfied himself that, for the moment, Harding was listening to forward-looking people, but admitted that the situation could change overnight. The President-elect, White conceded, would find it impossible to honor both his personal promise to scrap the League and his contradictory pledge to go in with reservations. Yet so pervasive was the Ohioan's geniality, that White soon apologized to him for some "flippant and irrelevant" remarks, and told a friend that Harding had the tact of McKinley, the kind heart of Lincoln, and all the resoluteness that the perplexing situation would permit.[5]

White, however, had no direct knowledge of the amount of confidence that Harding had, or would have, in the isolationists' counsel. If railroad trains carried Hughes, Hoover, and Taft to Marion to urge a modified internationalism, the same roads also provided accommodations for the isolationist leaders. Beveridge, Mellon, Knox, Harvey and even the Democratic Senator Reed came to pay respect and give advice. Day by day news from Europe, they insisted, made it clear that the Senate alone had saved us from perpetual embroilment in foreign squabbles. Soon after the election, Senator Medill McCormick went abroad and Harding was swayed by reading the strongly isolationist dispatches of this fellow journalist and erstwhile senatorial colleague.

After Harding moved into the White House the isolationists did not relax their vigilance. The diplomat and later propagandist, Richard Washburn Child, and the Irreconcilable Senator George H. Moses, both of whom had the President's ear, wanted to bury the League and let us go it alone. No matter how tempting this advice might have sounded, there was another horn to the dilemma. It soon became apparent that if we could dispense with the League, Europe could not, for its interment would tip the delicate balance of European equilibrium. The riddle now posed was how much recognition of and association with a foreign League and its ancillary bodies should be accorded. It was obvious that the administration had no intention whatsoever of reopening the question of American entry, and yet every step that looked like innocent cooperation was followed by a quick visit to the President from his isolationist confidants.

Thus Harding was forced to move in the center of a party that was split between hard-shell isolationists and moderate internationalists who wanted cooperation and understanding rather than union with Geneva. Harding lacked world vision and a specific program. He was more interested in pursuing the small pleasures of life than in providing dynamic leadership to the nation. His pompous and platitudinous speeches eschewed consistency. From one side of his mouth he spoke the hackneyed phrases of primitive isolationism, while from the other came vague promises that we would accept our new world responsibilities. To great applause, Harding told Congress, on April 12, 1921, that we would have no part in the existing "world-governing" League endowed with "superpowers." This speech, however, was followed by one pledging America's help to humanity without alignment with other nations. In the same vein he said that we would aid in economic adjustment without encumbering ourselves with positive commitments. Yet, despite this proclivity for double talk, the presidency widened Harding's perspective. He admitted, in 1923, that we could no longer maintain an air of aloofness from world problems. Characteristically, he quickly added that nevertheless we must not abandon the "cherished policy to which we are long and strongly committed."[6] En route to the Pacific Coast on a trip that was to end in his death, Harding warmly urged American entry into the World Court that had been established by the League. Thus ultimately he rejected the doctrine of the Irreconcilables and pursued the middle course charted by his brilliant Secretary of State, Charles Evans Hughes.

That Harding and Hughes should have come to essential agreement on foreign policy is a pointed commentary on how peculiar forces, working in a given period, mold the course of history. Hughes belonged to the Atlantic seaboard intelligentsia who so often combined Republicanism with an international orientation. His legal, judicial, and political career had brought him in close contact with leading industrialists. The big corporate business interests looked toward Europe for markets. Importers and exporters did a two-way trade, while metropolitan bankers not only financed these transactions but also had a vested interest in global stabilization. The war had convinced many eastern business and professional men, including Hughes, of the necessity of world organization. Yet when Wilson's plans were put on paper, Hughes dissented from the far-reaching implications of Article X. Like Elihu Root, to whom he bore an intellectual resemblance, Hughes's legal mind inclined toward a judicial rather than a political settlement of international disputes. He originally thought that the Covenant could be saved by reservations, arguing that it was necessary to compromise between outright isolationism and inescapable advance commitments. He was a member of the Committee of 31 who had led the country to believe that Harding would take the United States into the League with reservations. The Irreconcilables, understandably, were dismayed at Hughes's appointment to the chief cabinet post. For four years he had to contend with a group of mistrusting senators. Geneva, like Moscow of a later day, was the *bête noire* of the State Department.

As he took up the reins of office, Hughes gave serious consideration to his own previous convictions that the United States ought to enter into a limited partnership with the League. His hand was stayed, however, when the President pledged the administration to a contrary course. Hughes quickly sensed the mounting wave of anti-European feeling in the country and persuaded himself that the day for United States entry had passed. The Secretary faithfully explored the possibilities of sponsoring a new world organization to redeem his party's campaign speeches, but his practical mind rejected a plan that would invite scorn in Europe and defiance in the Senate. A middle course alone seemed feasible, and so Hughes headed the ship for midstream. There would be scorn and jeers from the extremists on each of the opposite shores, but the Secretary clenched his determined jaw, masked by bristling whiskers, and set himself for the voyage.

An unfortunate incident first drew the fire of the internationalist batteries. On July 18, 1921, Edwin L. James, of the New York *Times,* began a series of sensational dispatches from Europe which charged the State Department with gross discourtesy to the Geneva authorities. The pro-League people, already organized in a half-dozen associations, fervently took up the cry. They clamored that Washington had not bothered to answer communications from the League. Hughes investigated and found that a bungling minor official had decided to put the League mail in the dead-letter file. He promptly rectified the mistake. Yet there is some truth in the statement that the Harding administration began by treating the League as an unwanted child. Hughes himself was overzealous (until 1924) in corresponding with the League as if it were some foreign institution which chanced to be domiciled in friendly Switzerland.[7] But whatever his initial reticence, he soon realized that the League was performing many indispensable functions. One might even go so far as to say that the League abetted the American return to isolationism, for Geneva liquidated many wartime residual problems that might otherwise have necessitated our interference. Such observations were not lost upon the astute Hughes. "Non-recognition" soon yielded to "unofficial cooperation" and the sending abroad of "unofficial observers." We had come to believe that the organization of less fortunate nations was at the least beneficent.

The internationalists, however, were far from satisfied. Like most zealots in the service of good causes they forgot that politics is the science of the possible. The unprecedented Republican victory had put a political premium upon isolationism and had made the Senate Irreconcilables more pert and confident. When the League began to function, Americans expected too much. It soon became apparent that cardinal decisions still were being made in London, Paris, and Rome. Such issues as were debated or resolved in Geneva appeared continental in nature and beyond the scope of our ordinary interests. Press reports emphasized national selfishness, for the major powers took the Covenant seriously only when it did not conflict with their vital interests. If Article X meant a guarantee of territorial integrity, queried the New York *Evening Post,* why did not the League nations help Poland when the Soviet forces sent her army reeling back to Warsaw? Paul S. Reinsch studied the effects of the League on the abolition of secret diplomacy only to conclude that "amphibology" and "falsiloquy" were still the ways of Europe.

To realists, however, the League was neither the millennium envisaged by the ardent Wilsonians, nor the dangerous Goliath so dreaded by the isolationists. The new organization was instead an infant trying to cut its milk-teeth on some necessary but non-momentous problems. To Hughes's logical mind the facts dictated but one policy—countenance without involvement. "We are not promising that we cannot perform," he wrote to a critic, "but . . . we have not been hesitant when we see an opportunity to accomplish something worth while."[8]

We know today that this straddle failed. Because the selfish diplomacy of all the Atlantic powers was unable to halt the fiendish aggression that precipitated a second war, it is commonplace to indict the men who could not insure peace in their time. As far as the United States is concerned, Hughes's policies must be judged in the world setting in which they were conceived. The dismal outlines of the grim future still remained veiled. Some of the best minds of the day insisted that America must remain uncontaminated by foreign ties until the world could learn the meaning of liberalism. Thus our most eminent philosopher, John Dewey, warned that we should confine our commitments to Europe to the "irreducible minimum" and spell out each engagement in specific terms.[9]

A mounting wave of anti-foreign feeling hindered creative international leadership. Daily events beyond the water intensified provincialism among both the informed and the ignorant. Anti-foreignism, as always, was the Siamese twin of isolationism. Distrust of Europe grew so rapidly that it is questionable if any leader could have successfuly broached a plan of collective security which called for outright American participation. John Foster Bass, a seasoned war correspondent, argued that if Europeans were bent on conquest and revenge they were entitled to be the arbiters of their own destiny. The best that America could do was to sit it out on the sidelines, helping and advising wherever possible. Herbert Hoover, becoming every day more nationalistic, was convinced that the European and American civilizations, separated by the gap of three hundred years of history, had clashed at the Versailles Peace Conference. The educator, David Starr Jordan, insisted that the war killed the best of the Europeans, so that the continent had fallen into the hands of unscrupulous adventurers. The Chicago *Tribune* preached the doctrine that Europe defined peace as a brief interval between wars. If America was isolated, said this paper, it was so because it was the only nation on earth that had a dollar for every outstretched hat.

Each summer men of affairs vacationed in Europe only to return with new tales of guile and iniquity. Senator Thaddeus H. Caraway of Arkansas reported that while all of our former allies detested each other, they were still united in their hatred of America. Medill McCormick made frequent Atlantic crossings and used his journalistic pen to describe a continent woefully lacking in Christian charity. "'Twas ever thus," said Senator Brandegee, "Europe has been . . . quarreling ever since the dawn of history and for thousands of years before it."[10] Beveridge was sure that the "Devil's orchestra" of war was being assembled once more and predicted that before fifteen years it would play again "the old and hideous tune." Will Rogers' homey humor reflected the general prejudice. "Why if they had Niagara Falls," he wryly commented, "they would have had 85 wars over it at various times to see who would be allowed to charge admission to see it." His position on war debts was a simple one—we never should have let them have the money in the first place.[11]

Thus we see that there was little realization of the intricate nature of the world disorder and much feeling that foreigners were, at best, a hopeless lot. The American people were not ready to accept chronic turbulence as endemic to their generation. Why then, they asked, should the American taxpayer be saddled with the costs of the war? Why be swindled by wily Europeans and slant-eyed Asiatics?

As Europe returned sneer for sneer, international good will was put to a serious strain. Cartoons depicted Yankees rifling the pockets of Europe sandbagged by Mars or the old stereotype Uncle Shylock demanding his pound of flesh. Foreign writers were prone to emphasize American materialism and greed. The French statesman, André Tardieu, thought the United States more difficult to deal with than any other nation because of our unconquerable assurance that we alone had the instinct for righteous conduct in a disconcerted world. On the other hand, Americans felt that to chaffer with Europeans meant to be hornswoggled. The arch-isolationist Kansas City *Star* observed that after the war our allies "took everything that was to be had, and we came home, picked up our load of taxes, and announced that virtue was its own reward."

Frequent misunderstandings with France made a Republican *rapprochement* with the League even more difficult. French influence in both Geneva and its Reparations Commission had been strengthened when the United States refused to join the new organization. It was difficult for Americans to reconcile French militarism with Gallic leadership in a peace organization. We failed to comprehend the French demand for a double-barreled security uniting a strong army with League protection. Americans did not realize the potential threat to France of a revived Germany and mistook apprehension for aggression. This misunderstanding was strengthened by both British and German publicists who seized every opportunity to bring home to America exaggerated accounts of French bellicosity. The result was that Woodrow Wilson, in quiet retirement in Washington, told a friend that France had scrapped the League and that we should not join until there was clear agreement on disarmament.[12] France had become the new bogeyman of Europe and it looked as if the war had substituted one militarism for another.

To men who believed that if we but kept clear of foreign quarrels the flames of war could not jump the ocean waves, our course was clear—Europe must work out its own salvation. As Professor Dexter Perkins has emphasized, every President and Secretary of State of the inter-war period had to abide by the dominant mood of withdrawal. This same spirit of isolationism even held Franklin Roosevelt captive until Hitler's fire melted the chains. Distrust of Europe had grown so rapidly that statesmen had to ponder the effect of the slightest overture in the direction of international cooperation. Working in such a climate of opinion, Charles Evans Hughes had to proceed cautiously in his attempt to help a sick continent.

The Secretary was hampered by more than the prevalent desire "to take the foreigner by the beard." Each time America has fought a major war, the President has gained power at the expense of Congress. Hughes's work came at a time when Capitol Hill was trying to redress the constitutional balance of power in its own favor. Hence every treaty or agreement that came from the executive was put under the microscope and weighed as if on an apothecary's scale. The Senate was studded with provincials who traditionally voted only those agreements which were overwhelmingly one-sided in the American direction. Each senator felt free to indulge at any length in obstructionary debate. A Senate minority persistently boasted that it alone mirrored the prevailing sentiments of the country. The senatorial cabal which had won the fight against the League in 1920 was determined to deny the internationalists a return engagement. A friend advised Borah to yield to the opposition on nonessentials because there is a "vague popular idea that we must 'do something'—even if it is only adopting resolutions, 'paying dues' and wearing ribbons in our buttonholes—to establish a basis of universal peace."[13] But the "Lion of Idaho" and his fellows looked at every move toward decent cooperation as a snare to entrap the country in foreign imbroglios. Thus they were apt to oppose any step directed toward shouldering our share of the residual responsibilities of a World War. It required all of Hughes's acumen to outflank the Irreconcilables on measures that now seem as innocuous as they were futile.

Before the Congressional elections of 1922, James M. Cox reminded the Democrats that the League fight was not over. Borah scoffed at the thought of a Democratic victory, but he expressed concern because he felt that Hughes was trying to lead the country into the League through a trapdoor. He demanded an open admission of intentions from the Republican internationalists. The senator feared that the administration was moving in slow but certain stages toward a full political alignment with other nations. Our concern with the German reparations tangle, he charged, was inveigling us gradually into the European morass.

The First World War had made the United States the world's creditor. Obviously, this new position mandated some concern about the ability of our debtors to collect reparations from Germany. As Hughes tried to hammer out a policy that fitted our new status, he was beset by inquisitorial senators. When we appointed an observer to the Reparations Commission established by the Treaty of Versailles, he had to render a full account to Senator Lodge. George Moses wrote that he raised enough Hell over Hughes's plan on reparations for the sound to reach Beveridge's Indianapolis study. A rhythmic cycle would be repeated endlessly. First, there would be a considered and limited attempt to share problems arising from the war. Then would come a thunderous revolt from Capitol Hill and the isolationist press, followed swiftly by a State Department denial that the action involved either moral or legal obligations. If almost all Americans took it for granted that we were the greatest power on earth, few of them were willing to assume the responsibilities that went with the position.

In addition to the senators, Hughes had to contend with the truculent George Harvey, who even promised to give up drinking for the sake of wearing knee breeches at the Court of St. James's. Ambassador Harvey promptly told the Pilgrim Society in London that we went to war merely to save our own skins, and promised that the Harding administration would ignore the League's committees and commissions. This speech elicited congratulations from Beveridge, for he regarded it as clear warning to the Europeans that the war debts would have to be paid.

The midwestern isolationist complex, nurtured by the war, was another factor which inhibited the State Department. When the postwar conditions threatened agricultural prosperity, senators and representatives from the heartland states united to protect the interests of their constituents. This farm bloc formed a convenient club where solons would discuss foreign policy as well as wheat prices. The long farm depression, which began in 1922, encouraged a hunt for foreign scapegoats. Some penetrating inquirers pointed out that our

138

high tariff walls made it impossible for Europeans to buy our foodstuffs. Such men argued that our nationalist economic policy, a concomitant of isolationism, made American farmers burn their corn while Europe starved. Even Frank Munsey's New York *Herald* wondered what was happening to our foreign markets when the price of wheat fell below one dollar a bushel. The general tendency, however, was to say that venality and militarism had ruined the European continent for the American farmer. The Kansas senator and journalist, Arthur Capper, declared that even if perpetual European disorder limited the demand for wheat and corn, the farmer preferred poverty to a renewed American attempt to pacify the Old World.

There was, however, another side to the coin. If certain forces stayed Secretary Hughes's hands, counter pressures pulled President Harding away from his innate provincialism. Those Republicans who wanted to salvage part of Wilson's program were often as articulate as the isolationists. They could count on strong Democratic support in their attempt to bait the Irreconcilables. Eastern bankers urged a foreign policy that would take full cognizance of American financial and industrial might, and a big business administration was prone to listen to their arguments. Men of the market places were anxious to shove off from the isolationist mooring in order to protect ever widening global interests. Simultaneously they usually added that they wanted to anchor American independence and other precious values. This was in harmony with pilot Hughes's intermediate course which ran the straits between Wilson and Borah.

The Bureau of Political Research, sponsored by the Democratic National Committee, kept a close watch on the Republicans. Where, they asked, was Harding's substitute for the League? What had become of the promises of the "Thirty-One" published over the signature of Hughes? The editor of the *Independent,* Hamilton Holt, called incessantly for the redemption of pledges given to the internationalists. The New York *Times* used its mighty resources to hammer home the shame of the 1921 separate treaty of peace with Germany, which accepted the evil parts of Versailles and squarely disavowed our obligations as a victor nation. Even the senators, said the *Times,* averted their faces as they voted consent to this Treaty of Berlin. Raymond B. Fosdick, an American who had served as Under Secretary-General of the League, reminded Hughes that even if we had no legal accountability to Geneva, we owed the world some common courtesy.

The business depression of 1921-1922, sharp if short, led to the assertion that our own prosperity would not return until we helped put Europe back on its feet. Continental turmoil was a two-edged argument, for after each new episode the internationalists charged that the League was hamstrung by American abstention. The Newark *Evening News* observed that while Hughes lamented the failure of a weak League to keep order, he would be the first to denounce any action that smacked of supernational power. All this talk of humanitarian cooperation was fine, said the New York *Times,* but after three and a half years of good will, common action against anthrax and the narcotic traffic sparkled as the "splendid jewels in the Republican crown."

Thus Hughes was railed at by both isolationist and internationalist ultraists as he forged his policy on the anvil of political reality. "Let us," he said, "not debate over formulas but do useful things." He felt that if we met each problem in a practical way, we could gradually reach out beyond our shores and help in the solution of world problems. In the meantime, he warned, we must be vigilant in the protection of our rights, maintain an honest and direct diplomacy, stay out of foreign entanglements, and cooperate when good sense dictated mutual action. But never, he insisted, would we write out blank checks to be cashed in future contingencies.[14]

The crowning achievement of Hughes's leadership was the Washington Naval Arms Conference of 1921-1922. The international situation and the domestic disarmament campaign provided the opportunity to champion peace while ignoring the League of Nations. Disarmament was a perfect solvent for Republican moderates, Wilsonian internationalists, and liberals who resented any scheme based ultimately upon coercion. The most ardent leaguist hardly could oppose lifting the armament burden, while at the same time the plan was consistent with isolationist thinking. It conformed to the theory that an insulated country needed a navy only for self-defense, and could, therefore, afford to defy the navalists, imperialists, and armament builders. Any move that would lead to reduction of the tax burden was bound to be welcome. There were few indeed who realized that real disarmament must come as a result of rather than as a prelude to the alleviation of world tensions. The move was almost universally popular, but the bitter-end isolationists were to resent the international understandings that had to be made before the big battle wagons could be sunk at sea.

A series of coincidences led the Harding administration to

call the conference. Strangely enough, the unpredictable Borah had favored a naval disarmament conference at a time when such a suggestion still annoyed President Harding. But now Washington began to take note of the mounting sentiment for disarmament. The anti-navy group in Congress, made up of veteran enemies of preparedness, mustered their full strength and demanded limitation of the weapons of war. As church and peace group pressure mounted, it became obvious that public opinion required something more than the withdrawal of Japanese soldiers from Siberia or the recognition of our cable rights on the island of Yap. *Collier's* thought in terms of a new peace conference. A meeting in the pure and bracing air of Washington might well improve upon those agreements made in the mysterious and immoral setting of Versailles.

The administration, however, was goaded to action by international events. Great Britain was anxious for an understanding that might both curb American naval expansion and provide an escape from an embarrassing Anglo-Japanese alliance that was up for renewal. On July 8, 1921, Hughes suddenly seized the initiative and called the conference. Beveridge speculated that we were about to sell our birthright, but took solace in Lodge's appointment as an American delegate. He felt certain, moreover, that Harding himself would resist involvement. Senator Brandegee was positive that our foreign guests would use every opportunity to ensnare us into world financial stabilization. Our men, he feared, would "go too far in complying with the desires of other nations to entangle us in their complications."[15]

The details of the meeting need not concern us here. The diplomats succeeded in limiting, for the time being, the capital-ship rivalry among the nations. The United States, which made the greatest sacrifices in tonnage, predicated its acceptance upon two agreements designed to stabilize the Far East. The Nine Power Pact pledged the signatories to respect the territorial integrity of China and reaffirmed the old American policy of the Open Door in that country. The Four Power Pact (among the United States, Great Britain, France, and Japan) abrogated the Anglo-Japanese alliance, and promised that the signatory powers would respect each other's Pacific possessions. The treaties were to run for ten years, and controversies arising from them were to be settled by conference in the event that regular diplomatic negotiations failed. There was no real opposition to the Nine Power acceptance of our old Chinese policy, but mutual consultation, with the ever present threat of entanglement was more than most isolationists could stomach. They opened fire in the Senate on these provisions. Was there not more to the Four Power Pact than appeared on the surface? Would Japan give up her English alliance just for a promise that the Pacific status quo would not be disturbed without consultation? In a decade where every molehill of a treaty looked like a mountain of entanglement, the Republican senatorial leaders were hard pressed to explain. To disconcert them even further, some of the Democrats charged that the whole scheme was but an ineffective substitute for the League. The shoe was on the other foot, and it was Lodge who was now on the defensive.

President Harding presented the treaties to the Senate with an absolute pledge that they included no Old World embroilments. "There is," he promised, "no commitment to armed force, no alliance, no written or moral obligation to join in defense."[16] Lodge then denied that the Four Power Pact carried with it even a moral obligation to help in the event of outright aggression. But the senators were not satisfied. The President had to give repeated guarantees of no secret clauses, while the Secretary of State found it necessary to say that we had told the powers even before the conference that we would make no alliance. The Senate Foreign Relations Committee, still apprehensive, recommended the treaty with a reservation which denied commitment to armed force, alliance, or obligation to help in case of aggression. As one wit has put it, in the 1920s the Senate would not have consented to the Ten Commandments without qualifications!

The ensuing debates on the Washington treaties are an interesting comment on the spirit of the times. Lodge was able to calm most of the Republican critics, but Hiram Johnson emerged as the most unqualified isolationist in the country. The Californian bluntly charged his party with reversing its role on internationalism. He refused to enter into any partnership with imperialist nations who ignored their pledged words. The Democratic isolationist, David I. Walsh of Massachusetts, asked with much logic: what good was the pact without the force to back it up? Some of the Democrats took particular delight in taunting those Republican Irreconcilables who yielded to the party whip and voted for the treaty.

The congressional propaganda for this toothless pact is even more revealing. "The advocates of the treaty," writes the contemporary historian J. Chal Vinson, "having 'proved' that it was not an alliance in name, now sought to prove that it was not one in fact." Thus they explained that while there were no obligations of any sort, this piece of paper would, nevertheless,

142

secure the safety of the Philippines. And it was, they claimed, a boon for a peace-hungry world. So the naval bill passed with one dissenting vote, the Nine Power Pact was approved unanimously, and the Four Power agreement squeezed through by a margin of four votes.

In the country at large, liberals regretted that disarmament had been limited to battleships and that Japanese imperialism had not been further curbed. Yet Franklin D. Roosevelt hailed the work as a harbinger of peace with Nippon. His former chief in the Navy Department, the rustic Tar Heel editor, Josephus Daniels, disagreed. He thought that we had surrendered the sea to Britain, the air to France, and the Far East to Japan. Hearst was sure that we were now tied, hand and foot, to the imperialist war machines. The real significance of the Washington treaties was generally overlooked. Actually Hughes and his colleagues had turned their backs upon the Wilsonian concept of collective safeguards. The treaties they had made relied for enforcement only on the good will and the continued power of the Japanese liberals. Today we know that this was a vain hope, but treaties are not made under the mantle of prophecy. Despite the fact that some recalcitrant Irreconcilables opposed the Four Power Pact, the Washington treaties reflected the pervading philosophy of the new isolationism.

The ephemeral success of naval disarmament plus the illusory quiescence in the Far East intensified isolationist self-complacency. In 1923, as smug Americans watched a kaleidoscopic series of coups, invasions, and war scares throughout the world, this sentiment became more profound. Within twelve months the tenuous peace in the Near East was threatened, Lithuanians drove French troops out of Memel, and France occupied the Ruhr region of Germany. The League reeled and sat back helplessly in the face of mounting disorder. Isolationists took gruesome satisfaction in the confusion and were now certain that they were true prophets. Their doctrine became more widespread as liberals and reactionaries, nationalists and erstwhile leaguists, Republicans and Democrats, the ignorant and the learned, became increasingly appreciative of our ocean-washed shores. The business recession was over, the sun of prosperity rose once more, and Americans were more determined than ever to dodge foreign war clouds.

Secretary Hughes, however, felt that the Ruhr problem was too grave for complete detchment. The German reparations situation had become so acute that the impending crisis threatened European stability. France, under the leadership of the energetic and chauvinistic Premier Raymond Poincaré, was determined to defy Britain and force payment by the occupation of the Ruhr, a highly concentrated German industrial area. Hughes took advantage of a scheduled speech before the New Haven convention of the American Historical Association to speak his mind. The Secretary warned that France's contemplated action would bring disaster rather than secure the desired payments. He then enunciated the nucleus of what was to become the Dawes plan, suggesting that a commission of financial experts, including some Americans, should judge the dispute on its merits. Our own interests were obviously involved, for we did not relish the possible consequence of an invasion of German territory. The settlement of the reparations problem might, moreover, facilitate the collection of war debts owed the United States by Germany's creditors.

The immediate results of Hughes's open and frank diplomacy were not encouraging. At home the Irreconcilables beat their war drums loudly, while the French became defiant and announced, on January 10, 1923, that their soldiers would march. At the behest of the Senate, President Harding promptly ordered American troops out of the Rhineland. Hiram Johnson demanded the recall of our own man from the Reparations Commission. Senator Robert L. Owen of Oklahoma, a faithful adherent of Wilson in 1919, accused the French of destroying the League's guarantee of territorial inviolability. Before the year 1923 was out, Owen studied the war-guilt question in Europe, and came home dedicated to a defense of Germany's 1914 actions. Americans, already disillusioned with France, now substituted Poincaré for Emperor William II as the mad militarist of Europe. Norman H. Davis, high in the counsels of the Democratic party, wanted to use the war debt as a lever to force France to respect German sovereignty. And even the moribund Woodrow Wilson said that he wished he could tell the French ambassador to his face that he would like to see Germany clean up France!

The French, of course, still had their friends, and the Ruhr debate formed anew the old battle lines. The intervening years since the war, however, had made significant changes in the alignment. Many former Wilsonians accused France of betraying the spirit of the League and were now openly pro-German. The powerful Anglophile internationalist phalanx repeated Lloyd George's question: "Against whom is France arming?" England had not only refused to sanction the French action, but law officers of the Crown also had declared the invasion illegal. The Ruhr occupation split the American Anglophiles from the Francophiles. Since both groups had been internationally oriented, the rupture threatened the unity of the American pro-League bloc. The friction still further dissipated internationalist ardor.

The old isolationist coalition was not entirely pro-German. Some of the nationalists, reared in the school of Theodore Roosevelt, understood Poincaré. This was especially true of men who had not dissented from Wilson's war but from his peace. The isolationist Kansas City *Star,* for instance, defended the French. On the other hand, the liberal isolationists defended Germany almost to a man. Senator Robert M. La Follette, with his namesake and heir, visited the Ruhr, and French rule reminded them of the Russian Cheka. The publicist Lewis Gannett took time off from fraternizing with French war-guilt revisionists to write some articles for the *Nation* about the watch of French colonial black troops along the Rhine. For the *Nation's* editor, Oswald Garrison Villard, the case against France was clinched when he had to pay 750 million marks for a copy of his own periodical in Berlin. Wandering through the old pre-war German book shops, Villard found pornographic specialties instead of the rare Goethe and Schiller volumes that he sought. He wished that Theodore Roosevelt were alive to see for himself the final results of the war. The hyphenate isolationists, with whom Villard was so closely associated, were bitterly anti-French. The New York group of German-Americans staged a huge protest meeting at Madison Square Garden and formed the Committee of One Hundred Against the Ruhr Invasion. The American Communists were glad to fish in these troubled waters. Germany had recently signed a treaty of accord with the Soviets, and the Communist contention of the moment was that the two nations would work together to check French rapacity.

For a short time the Ruhr tangle promised to rouse the country from its apathy. As the dispute lagged, however, Americans became bored with the whole business and turned once more to Mah Jong, the fortunes of Jack Dempsey and Babe Ruth, and the search for drinkable liquor. Current events could not disrupt for long the prevailing hedonism. The Ruhr crisis, moreover, began to wane in the languid summer days of 1923. Gustav Stresemann became chancellor of Germany and gave the word to stop passive resistance to the French intruders. Hughes, in the meantime, had been careful not to irritate the French, and on November 23, 1923, the Reparations Commission agreed to the substance of the American scheme. The Dawes Plan, with its two committees of experts, settled the problem for the time being. Germany was granted a substantial international loan to rehabilitate her economy, and in return promised to resume reparations payments in annually increasing amounts. In the United States the most abiding result of the Ruhr debacle was the realization that it had all happened under the very nose of the League of Nations. The concept of world organization appeared more chimerical than ever.

Slowly Hughes's philosophy of a golden mean between primitive isolationism and permanent foreign commitments was absorbed into the stream of American thought. The League in operation had proven to be neither the Hell of the Irreconcilables nor the Utopia of the Wilsonians. At best it now appeared a feeble but necessary step in the eventual evolution of an adequate peace formula. Elihu Root, who often waxed reflective in his later years, argued that the acceptance of nationalism lay at the basis of international law. Wilson, he reasoned, had erred in allowing the League to be made the agent for carrying out the punitive parts of the Treaty of Versailles. Because the victor powers refused to entrust Geneva with vital postwar decisions on new problems of peace, all that remained for the League was to execute the penalties upon the belligerents. Root thought that Harding and Hughes had no choice but to seek peace as reason might dictate and without resort to coercive machinery. Before long, however, Root was to indict the Republicans for their antipathy to the League.

Reflecting upon the 1920 turn in the course of American history, the University of Wisconsin historian, Carl Russell Fish, decided that the American people had had their chance to vote for the League. If they allowed extraneous issues to determine their choice of Harding, then this indifference in itself was a decision against Geneva. Fish sensed that the American people failed to understand the Covenant, and that their instinct had vetoed a scheme that they could not comprehend. The professor was wise enough to foresee that world conditions eventually might make collective security absolutely necessary. When the day came, Fish reasoned, the move would have overwhelming popular sanction. For the time being, however, the Washington authorities could only think in terms of an intermediate course that did not mortgage the future.

The clearest outline of the Republican postwar philosophy was sketched by George H. Blakeslee, professor of history and international relations at Clark University. A staunch admirer of Hughes, Blakeslee believed that American opinion was overwhelmingly opposed to involvement in European politics. Statesmen had to heed this temper, and yet it was also their duty to remember that a Balkan squabble in 1914 had thrown the world into turmoil. Blakeslee felt that the quandary could be solved by turning to Theodore Roosevelt's advice to stay out of ordinary European quarrels and to concern ourselves only with matters of transcendent importance. Could not the League Covenant be amended to permit groups of nations to maintain regional peace while Geneva woud confine itself to major international disputes? Blakeslee recognized that the American people were deeply torn between advocates of collective action and those who wanted only independent action. There must be, he insisted, a planned compromise between the two extreme points of view.

Hughes's démarche found favor among the masses and the non-doctrinaire thinkers. Irreconcilables and devoted Wilsonians, of course, reacted unfavorably. And apart from all others there were Marxists who spoke the language of economic determinism. But the vast majority were reconciled to abandoning in practice, if not in theory, the nineteenth-century type of circumscribed isolationism. Now the question was whether to have pre-arranged partnerships with other nations or unilateral action on each individual problem. The Democratic politician and renowned sportsman, Perry Belmont, wrote a book entitled *National Isolation: An Illusion.* Belmont was not enthusiastic about joining the impotent League, but he insisted that the day of genuine isolation had passed without recall. On this point, at least, all cosmopolites were agreed.

Politics had ruled out membership in the League, and the prime position of the United States precluded a return to aloofness. Hughes's intermedial policy was dictated by the logic of events but fraught with danger. The deft Secretary was able to make some progress through a maze of obstacles. His less able successors were too easily deflected by the senatorial barricade. Thus for many years American foreign policy oscillated between isolation and ineffective schemes of collective action. Major decisions were usually based on popular estimates of European conditions rather than on an accurate appraisal of the situation. In the affluent twenties there was little inclination to tackle remote but troublesome problems.

The naive masses still regarded our oceans as Heaven-built Maginot Lines. This national delusion fostered the attitude that, come what may, the United States had two unique reservoirs of security. Whenever we extended a helping hand it was interpreted as sacrifice rather than pursuance of our own long-range goals. Charity is usually dispensed with utopian hopes for the recipients, and a limit on the obligations of the giver. Thus high-sounding but non-binding schemes were the order of the day. The prevailing temper would tolerate only limited and specified digressions from the isolationist tenets. The most severe indictment against the Republican leadership or for that matter of Franklin D. Roosevelt's to 1937, is that their international deeds were invariably too little and almost always too late.

The weakest link in the Republican chain of thought was the economic one. Hughes and his successors made no serious attempt to coordinate the political aspects of the program with economic reality. They failed to develop a foreign policy broad enough to parallel the economic entanglements created by American credit and business expansion. At the base of this paradox lay the failure to comprehend twentieth-century complexities. Our shift from a debtor nation of two billions to a creditor one of fourteen billions came so rapidly that its import did not penetrate. The Harding administration was dominated by a desire to return to Republican orthodoxy. Hence they viewed many policies as purely domestic in a world where American decisions influenced the economies of other countries. It was impossible to sever the business ties of the Atlantic community. A nineteenth-century frame of reference made no allowance for the grim fact that in a closely knit world the chief victor must forgive the debts of his allies, and prevent the festering of malignant ulcers upon the body politic of the vanquished.

The cardinal American error was to try simultaneously to retain the immunities of isolationism and reap the benefits of a privileged position in the market places of the world. Thus the Republicans promptly rebuilt the high tariff walls, shutting off European exports and making it impossible for debtor nations to pay us through the sale of their goods. Even Hughes gave little attention to this absurdity. Had American business been willing to draw in its horns and pay the price of true isolationism, the policy might have worked. But as Washington washed its hands of responsibility for world economic recovery, business men pushed out into the far ends of the earth. American capital flowed into all continents, producers looked for markets and raw materials, while Wall Street loans converted bankrupt nations into customers. The war had demonstrated the potentialities of assembly-line production and the peacetime surplus poured forth into many lands. For the first time many Americans discovered the possibilities of foreign ventures. Big business created new entangling economic alliances, while the State Department was trying to cut the political cords. In a decade of alleged isolationism there was little objection to the economic explorers, the engineers and investors who enlarged the boundaries of our financial empire. There was an ever growing dichotomy between the restricted internationalist aims of the statesmen and the unlimited global ambitions of the industrialists.

The bankers also strained the confines of the new foreign policy. Today, with the United States acting as the world's counting house, at least some measure of foresight on foreign loans is possible. The government tries to make these subsidies serve the interests of the United States. In the twenties, however, it was the private bankers who buttressed foreign economies. (Hughes made no attempt to change Wilson's policy of letting *private banking,* rather than the government, bolster wobbling economies.) Despite some pleasant words, their goal was profits rather than global stability. Even had Wall Street had the best of intentions, its firms possessed neither the objectivity nor the necessary information to make proper use of the American dollar. The high-pressure technique developed to promote Liberty Loans was applied to the sale of foreign bonds. There was little consideration given to the overall consequences of such investments.

Some clairvoyants recognized the impossibility of reconciling economic selfishness and truncated internationalism with economic imperialism. "We get out of Europe," said the Chicago *Evening Post,* "but we enter the race for that thing for which Europe cares most—trade supremacy." John F. Bass and the young economist, Harold G. Moulton, bluntly warned that the plexus of economic forces would draw us right back into the European orbit. The next time our security is menaced, they predicted, we will not "call it a debt which our fellow in arms owes us."[17] The vice-chairman of the United States Tariff Commission, Dr. William S. Culbertson, warned that our economic position would have to be maintained either by force or by widespread cooperation. Even the Chicago *Tribune* realized that our commercial expansion would inevitably invite the resentment of other nations. If we insisted on eschewing force to maintain our stand, it advised that we level the tariff wall, open our doors to the surplus population of other countries, forgive our debtors, and stay out of foreign markets. The anomaly of the Republican attempt to combine neo-isolationism with finance imperialism was denounced by Benjamin H. Williams in his *Economic Foreign Policy of the United States*. Williams, a political scientist, held that the best hope of coordinating American foreign, economic, and financial policies lay in closer cooperation with the League machinery. But, admittedly, he spoke only for the future, for the diplomats were yet unaware of the danger of economic forces let loose a world unprepared to control their effects.

Today it is apparent that economic myopia destroyed the Republican straddle. Failure to take into account the postwar economic trends was one of the factors in the coming of the Great Depression. This calamity in turn prepared the way for fascist aggression. Thus the entire League structure and the Republican policy of independent cooperation were to tumble down together. Ultimate disaster from a policy based on intrinsic economic selfishness might have been averted by either of two means. Had we taken the course plotted by Wilson, a strong international association possibly could have ironed out the complications arising from our far-flung business ventures. Barring that, we could have protected our inimitable economic position by the time-honored method of unilateral military force. The Republicans, however, scrapped the League of Nations, weakened the navy, and restricted the army to farcical limits. Hughes's policy was to end in tragedy because it tried to maintain an impossible world economy without either adequate military protection or an effective peace organization. Only subsequent events were to point up these shortcomings. Meanwhile, the new isolationism was to share an ephemeral popularity with Calvin Coolidge and the great bull market.

Chapter 8

The Coolidge Conundrum

THE UNEXPECTED death of President Harding, in 1923, brought Calvin Coolidge to the White House. This dour, raw-boned Yankee, who someone has said looked like a holder of mortgages in a small county-seat, remained in office until 1929. American tradition has depicted Coolidge as a typical, narrow isolationist, but such a description is, at best, a half-truth. His original outlook on foreign affairs was broader than Harding's, and as President he was usually at loggerheads with the Irreconcilables. On the subject of diplomacy he shared the big business philosophy which tried to adjust the old isolationist reserve to the needs of global financial and commercial expansion. His concealed departures from isolationist tenets are often forgotten, while his laconic, provincial assertions are still remembered.

The new President was no bitter-end isolationist of the Borah or Johnson variety. He held a personal grudge against Lodge, which perhaps explains a sneaking sympathy for Wilson during the treaty fight. While Harding promptly called his election a verdict against the League, Coolidge astutely realized that the issues of 1920 had been too complex to permit a true plebiscite. As Vice-President, he had cautiously praised the League's noble aspirations. Yet, despite these fleeting internationalist sympathies, he was not the man to brave the waxing isolationist sentiment. Coolidge was a canny politician who made it a point not to declare himself on controversial issues until the scales of public opinion had tipped. By 1923, the balance showed clearly, and it was apparent that the majority wanted no advance contracts for collective action. His isolationist leanings, moreover, were entirely in character with his popular role as a Puritan relic in an age of jazz, flappers, and bootleg whiskey.

The President found Secretary Hughes's modified isolationism politically useful. It allowed him to hold the Irreconcilables at bay with platitudes about non-entanglement, and to appease the internationalists by supporting American entrance into the World Court. Our wartime debtors would have to pay their honest obligations, but our high tariff would protect American workers and producers from foreign competition. We would help unravel the reparations tangle, we would lend unofficial cooperation to the League, but we would never make political commitments that would limit our freedom of action. The essential contradictions of the neo-isolationist program explain why Elihu Root could say that Coolidge did not have an international hair in his head, while the Irreconcilables were shivering lest he be a Woodrow Wilson in Republican guise.

These policies were seldom boldly announced or widely publicized. Coolidge built upon what he found and was responsible for no major turn in the course of American foreign policy. He was handicapped by restricted vision and limited physical energy. An alert Secretary of State might have compensated for his shortcomings and might have implemented the more constructive aspects of the middle-of-the-road program, but when Hughes decided to retire in 1925, Coolidge showed no signs of dismay. Instead of filling this key post with another superior person, he chose a man who would be no threat to his own mental stature. The naming of Frank Billings Kellogg as Secretary of State was Coolidge's cardinal error in the diplomatic field. This appointment consigned foreign affairs to the doldrums. The Kellogg years were destined to mark the nadir of Republican postwar statesmanship.

The new Secretary's education had been limited to the reading of law in a Rochester, Minnesota, law office. After making his mark as a local trust-buster, Kellogg found it more advantageous to work for the corporations than against them. As a senator, he had wished the Treaty of Versailles in Hell rather than be forced to take a stand, but he ultimately followed his party and voted for the Lodge reservations.[1] Yet for all his deliberation, he lost his seat in 1922 to an ultra-isolationist Farmer-Labor candidate. While in the Senate, Kellogg had been kind to the shy and retiring Vice-President; this consideration brought its due reward when President Coolidge asked him to leave his London ambassadorship for the ranking cabinet post.

The Minnesotan stood out in glaring contrast to the austere and forceful Hughes. Unlike his resourceful predecessor, Kellogg made little effort to capitalize on new situations in order to augment the neo-isolationist approach. In his hands the policy grew stale and sterile. The new Secretary was a hard worker, but he was irascible and prone to shower profanity on those about him. He was oversolicitous of Westerners who had long accused him of being a Wall Street lackey. He was so worried, fretful, and apprehensive of senatorial power and rebuke that Washington reporters labeled him "Nervous Nellie." This fear of the Senate put him continually on the defensive. However, the suspicious attitude of the Irreconcilables toward the Secretary was unjustified, for Kellogg truly believed that Washington's advice on foreign relations was still as sound as on the day the Farewell Address had been penned.[2] As time passed, he became more and more chary of possible foreign entrapments. His timidity and air of futility left the impression that the isolationists had won all the rounds in the battles of the Coolidge era.

In fairness to Coolidge and Kellogg, it is necessary to concede that the spirit of the day had made constructive world leadership most difficult. Harding might possibly have reignited the fag-ends of wartime idealism. But by 1923, internationalist zeal had waned, while the isolationist front had broadened and deepened. The isolationist coalition now represented more than a pooling of groups who hated Wilson for diverse reasons. It had become a genuine groundswell of public opinion, formidable enough to give pause to even intrepid and far-sighted makers of foreign policy.

The isolationists still ran the economic gamut from dogmatic Communists to flinty reactionaries. On the extreme left of the coalition, the radicals were determined enemies of all existing peace machinery. The spell of Moscow had mesmerized many intellectuals who never carried a party card. These Marxists and their chamber-fellows believed that the promised world proletarian revolution would break down national and class barriers and bring true peace. The League, which they considered an instrument of capitalist power, blocked the road to this Marxist paradise. Thus Geneva had to be harassed, impeded, and eventually destroyed so that Soviet Russia could rescue mankind from the twin scourges of capitalism and war.

Communist claptrap added venom to the anti-League arguments. Like their intellectual opposites, the hyper-nationalists, the radicals tarred Wilsonian Democrats and Republican neo-isolationists with the same red-handled brush. The United States, said the Communists, was the fulcrum of a capitalist conspiracy that happened to have its headquarters at Geneva. America, it was explained, would formally join the League as soon as Wall Street was certain that it could rule the organization. Such a step was inevitable, for according to Communist logic, the United States had entered the imperialist capitalist stage and it would need the League to fulfill its ambitions. J. P. Morgan & Co., the American Federation of Labor, and the armed forces (truly a weird partnership) had their plans for world conquest in readiness and would soon be ready to strike. A party spokesman promised that the American Communists would turn this coming conflict into a civil war in order to establish a people's government of workers and farmers.[3]

Such palaver must have taxed the credulity of even the party hacks. Did the predominantly isolationist mood belie such bellicose ambitions? The incongruity was dispelled by saying that the Republicans scorned European entanglements so as to free their hands for the subjection of other continents. There were some true isolationists, it was conceded, who really wanted to keep America at home. Such men, however, were identified as small and uninfluential capitalists who had fallen victim to a foolish pacifism. But were not some industrial big-wigs also isolationists? Yes, because for the moment they were busy exploiting the home market, but they would soon be attracted to the greater profits which lay in a world-financed imperialism.[4] The *Worker's Monthly* predicted that Wall Street would override all remaining opposition to American global domination. President Coolidge was described as the tool of the industrialists who cunningly planned to get the country into the League by first having it join the World Court. On occasion the Communists were careless enough to fly in the face of the most obvious facts, and they demanded American withdrawal from a World Court which this country was never destined to join. The Communists thus snickered at the isolationists but were on the same side of the fence in throwing brickbats at the League.

Among the retinue of fellow-travelers was the so-called dean of the muckrakers, Lincoln Steffens. Like so many other reporters, he had returned from the Versailles Peace Conference with blighted hopes. Steffens, whose brilliant revelations had done so much to popularize the pre-war reform movement, had lost heart. He had realized that the Progressive movement had neither enlightened the people nor yielded basic and lasting reforms. He was further disappointed in the peace that had brought no peace. Travel and reflection persuaded him that only a revolutionary solution would relieve the misery of the European masses. He was stimulated by stories of the "simple, heroic, self-sacrificing people" of Russia who defined an honest man as one "who does not expect to get from society more than he tries to return." Ella Winter, the wife of his later years, was known as "Comrade Ella" to

154

party members.[5] While in all probability Steffens never formally became a Communist, he showed warm sympathy for the cause. His prominence and journalistic connections made it possible for him to purvey the radical point of view to the American middle class.

Steffens struck sledge-hammer blows at the Versailles peace mechanism. He once said that he would rather see the United States back in the British Empire than a member of the League of Nations. It seemed to him that conventional American internationalism merely reflected the desire of the big bankers to play a hand in world politics so as to insure their foreign investments. At home, the newly exposed Harding administration scandals offered a splendid opportunity for Steffens's pen, but the old zest was gone. The day had passed when he could believe that domestic reform might, in a Bessemer-like fashion, blow the impurities out of the social order. The war had internationalized his liberalism, and he no longer thought of even governmental corruption in national or local terms. The full facts about the Teapot Dome oil mess, he insisted, would explain why the war had come and why Versailles had failed to establish true peace. Steffens argued that a highly developed civilization needed such things as oil, and countries would get sufficient essential materials by fighting, conquering, bribing, and exploiting. He felt that the only remedy for war was to alert the people of the world to the real facts behind international bickering. Until this was done, he said, superficial peace agencies did more harm than good. Thus he pointed to the Carnegie Peace Endowment as a prime example of the "admirable American capacity to talk theory in the face of hard fact."[6]

The Socialist Marxists, who had parted company with the Communists in 1919, were somewhat more conventional and cautious. The family of America's premier Socialist, Eugene V. Debs, even celebrated Christmas as the fleeting moment when the capitalist world tries to be human. Although the Socialists denounced violent means, their ultimate goal was economic world unity in the Marxian sense. Hence they reasoned that the League and World Court, underwritten by the capitalists, would have to be fought to the finish for such organizations would use their power to impede the fulfillment of the Socialist dream. The Debs faction of the party, now in full control, had never accepted the war. They now vindicated their 1917 predictions by harping upon the evil consequences of American intervention. Norman M. Thomas, a Presbyterian minister who inherited the party from Debs, said that no peace plan was workable as long as the participating nations exploited their own workers and their subject peoples. Radical thought of the day infiltrated beyond Communist and Socialist boundaries and constituted a distinct left-wing challenge to conventional internationalism. The Marxists thought the League and World Court just as pernicious as did those conservative-nationalists who equated a free America with free enterprise.

The liberals and progressives stood to the right of the radicals in the isolationist formation. It is difficult to make an absolute distinction between liberals and progressives, for on many issues their lines crossed and merged imperceptibly. The most that may be said is that the former were usually more intellectualized, broader in general outlook, more apt to be found in urban industrialized areas, and less intimately associated with agrarian unrest. The liberals, moreover, were prone to be theoretical internationalists, while the progressives were ordinarily isolationists in both conviction and action. Eric F. Goldman has noted that after 1919, "liberal" was more commonly used in the reform vocabulary than "progressive." Nevertheless, Professor Goldman concedes that his observation is weakened by the fact that the political independents of 1924 organized a "Progressive" party.

The liberal-progressive ranks had been decimated by the war. The revolt against formalism and Victorianism, which had inspired American liberalism before 1914, had spent its force. In the intellectual derangement which followed the war, some liberals turned conservative, some became radicals, and those who remained loyal to their original tenets often indulged in bitter cynicism. Political thought had polarized at the right and left extremes so that a temperate liberalism was as dated as bric-a-brac. Some liberals, of course, remained ardent leaguists, but it seems safe to assert that the majority took a contrary position. Such men blamed the war for the wave of reaction which had swallowed up their domestic program, and the peace for the frustration of their internationalist aims. Surviving liberals were disillusioned about the past and suspicious that the League powers had nothing but reactionary plans for the future. In the name of progress they demanded the removal of all the Versailles ramifications.

Above all, the liberals were individualists and followed no single pattern of thought concerning foreign relations. There was no party line and each man listened to the dictates of his own conscience. Inspiring leaders, however, often set the example. John Haynes Holmes, celebrated lecturer and pastor of New York's Community Church, espoused the Quaker formula of complete pacifism. The Madrid-born philosopher, George Santayana, who long before had left Harvard for a more serene life abroad, was one of the prophets to whom some liberals paid special deference. He denounced the League enthusiasts as "the enemies of what is deepest and most primitive in everybody. They inspire undying hatred in every untamable people and every absolute soul."[7]

No issue was resolved for the liberals until the great pundit, John Dewey, had spoken his mind. The Columbia philosopher, true to his own maxim that theoreticians must speak out on current problems, had plenty of advice to offer on foreign policy. Dewey dismissed the League as an unregenerate coalition of governments whose selfishness had caused the war. Why, he asked, chide ourselves for non-cooperation when there was nothing truly international with which to cooperate? Why not make tolerance of Soviet Russia the test of our good will? Dewey even opposed American adherence to the World Court protocol because that tribunal was based on an international law that made war legitimate. The League powers, he warned, wanted us back in Europe "for the same reason that they wanted us during the war—to add power to *their* policies."[8]

The historical findings of Charles A. Beard, which stressed the economic dynamics of history, had also been incorporated into liberal thought. Beard, like Dewey, held that the scholar in a democratic society was duty-bound to voice his opinion on pressing problems. In the 1920s, he underwent a transition from internationalist to isolationist. But the change came slowly and Beard did not become an isolationist luminary until the New Deal era. Yet 1923 was a landmark for the famous historian. He went to Jugoslavia to try to make peace between the Slovaks and the Croats. In the midst of his efforts, the Croat leader killed his Slovak rival in open parliament. "Let Dorothy Thompson settle the problems of Europe," Beard later reflected, "I can't."[9]

The *Nation* and the *New Republic* continued to be the stewards of liberalism. Both journals had hard financial sledding in the post-war years and tried to increase their newsstand sales by brisk exposures. International muckraking had a wider appeal than the old domestic variety, for prosperity had dried up the fountains of middle class protests. To attract new readers these periodicals overemphasized the venality of American Caribbean imperialism, oversensationalized the vindication of Germany by revisionist historians, and overplayed

Wall Street's interest in the League of Nations. Villard and Croly spent so much time raking the international muck that they were sometimes hard-pressed for reporters and space to spell out the dangers of domestic reaction.

Some of the disenchanted liberals fled from prosaic America to the garrets of Paris's Latin Quarter, to sun-drenched Italian villas, and to quaint Spanish towns. Many of this "Lost Generation" had not served in the war, but they nevertheless believed that the blood-letting had stamped them with the mark of Cain. The émigrés reported regularly to friends in America, who, for one reason or another, still chose to endure Coolidge and prohibition. From the Pyreneean provinces, Francis Hackett, former *New Republic* literary critic, wrote Lincoln Steffens that America was a country of lies and that it was the duty of men who cherished the truth to teach the people the meaning of realism. The Idaho-born poet, Ezra Pound (later to be indicted for treason after the Second World War) observed that the British were putrified. As for the people back home, Pound wrote in his own matchless style: "Hell, if we don't start educating the bastards, who will? A hundred million people getting steadily less competent to govern themselves or be governed."[10] These voluntary expatriates seemed to take a nihilistic position in regard to everything except the refreshing nature of the little comforts they found in European byways.

Unlike the academic liberals, the progressive-isolationists were strongly represented in Congress. The election of an eastern liberal was largely a matter of chance, but the farming states of the West and Midwest elected men who usually reflected local bias. A highly trained scout for an eastern organization surveyed popular attitudes toward international questions in two mid-western states. He found that while the progressively inclined voters were isolationist almost to a man, the more orthodox urban Republicans were more tolerant of the League and World Court.[11] Corn-belt states, so largely peopled with German and Scandinavian stocks, sent men to Congress who championed agrarian relief and American insularity. Because each of these states had two senators, regardless of their population, extreme isolationist sentiment was more prevalent in the Senate than in the country at large.

Today it is a commonplace for isolationists to be hidebound economic reactionaries. Many of these people became so bitter against Franklin D. Roosevelt's New Deal reforms that they could not support anything he championed—including the United Nations. The farm prosperity of the early 1940s helped dissipate the progressive spirit, and Republican right-wingers took over the flickering torch of western isolationism. In the inter-war years, however, agrarian isolationists were usually economic reformers who were out to bring relief to their hard-pressed constituents. Many of these older isolationists, the heirs of the Populist-Progressive revolt, were either maverick Republicans or else members of splinter parties that had been formed to protest against G.O.P. favoritism to eastern capitalist interests. These marginal Republicans and party rebels formed a left-wing isolationist bloc in Congress. The basic premise of the group was that wars were conspiracies of bankers with too much money to lend, evil munitions-makers with lethal wares to vend, and greedy industrialists on the lookout for new markets. Hence the solution to war seemed simple enough. Congress could insure peace by insisting on disarmament, by outlawing the concept of war, and by arranging to settle future disputes through effective treaties of arbitration.[12] To checkmate future warmongers, some proposed that a constitutional amendment make the declaration of war, except to repel invasion, subject to a plebiscite. An over-simplification of the causes of war led to a credulous conviction that it could be controlled readily or eradicated entirely. Such notions were endemic among the progressive-isolationists. Like the Marxists, they had alternative plans to achieve collective security. Hence they were bitter against the leaguists who not only wanted to involve the country with a foreign agency, but who also scoffed at home remedies that seemed a far surer guarantee of peace.

During the Coolidge years the progressive-isolationists carried on the Irreconcilable tradition in the Senate. Natural causes and defeat at the polls (on issues usually unrelated to foreign policy) steadily depleted the ranks of the original "Battalion of Death." Eastern members were replaced by Republican conservatives who appreciated Coolidge's sterling business virtues and who seldom took serious issue with him on foreign policy. The veteran seaboard Irreconcilables who remained in the Senate found it increasingly difficult to work with westerners who badgered the President on farm prices, public utilities, and water-power control, as well as on American imperialism in Haiti and Nicaragua. The Progressive revolt of 1924 made relations especially bitter, and Senators Robert M. La Follette and Lynn J. Frazier were officially read out of the Republican party. It is significant that it was Senator George H. Moses, an original and inflexible Irreconcilable, who was to tag the western deviates with the name "sons of

159

the wild jackass." As the G.O.P. rebels took over the Irreconcilable leadership, the eastern isolationists separated themselves from these party heretics. Only in critical moments, such as during the World Court debates, was an eastern-western axis still possible. With the death of men like Knox and Brandegee from the East and McCormick and the elder La Follette from the Midwest, the bitter-enders had to turn to the more limited talents of Smith W. Brookhart of Iowa, Henrik Shipstead of Minnesota, and Magnus Johnson of North Dakota. Borah and Hiram Johnson, however, still remained to set examples for the new recruits.

In assessing responsibility for the nugatory diplomacy of Coolidge and Kellogg, it is necessary to remember the power of the indomitable Borah. The death of Henry Cabot Lodge in 1924 made the Idaho senator chairman of the Senate Foreign Relations Committee. This succession was unfortunate, for Borah lacked finesse, leadership ability, and the capacity for team work. He was a provincial orator, a showman, and a shallow thinker with supreme confidence in his own store of superficial answers to complicated problems. An expert at detecting the slightest flaw in an opponent's argument, Borah was singularly incapable of proposing workable plans of his own. In the Senate, as his party's spokesman on foreign policy, he often worked at cross purposes with the administration and, in some respects, even failed to give the uncompromising isolationists proper direction.

Senator Lodge, who had prompted the isolationists in his later years, had sufficient knowledge, ingenuity, and flexibility to give the cause intellectual respectability. Borah, however, sparkled only because of the magniloquent oratory he used to present his shop-worn arguments. He played a one-man game and was unable to provide the tatterdemalion Irreconcilable battalion with fresh ammunition. In the later Coolidge years, each revolt of the group aroused increasing public indignation. Under Borah's direction intransigent isolationism lost caste until it was revived by the stirring events of the 1930s.

While Borah could not find the proper answers to the country's problems, he succeeded in delineating the aims and accomplishments of the Republican neo-isolationist diplomacy. About all that party regularity meant to him was grudging support for the ticket in presidential years. Thus, Coolidge and Kellogg, despite G.O.P. control of the Senate, could not depend upon Borah for loyal partisan support of their foreign policy. The senator insisted on judging each situation in the light of his unique knowledge and insight. He boasted that he had his own sources of information, independent of official channels, but these newspaper and personal contacts were often spotty and inaccurate. Borah was sometimes called a radical, in spite of the fact that he believed that the Constitution had been written under the guiding hand of God. His views on foreign policy were bewildering and often grossly inconsistent. Though a blatant and unabashed nationalist he demanded recognition of the Soviet Union. He would sound the tocsin for American leadership on behalf of peace and disarmament, but just when his suggestions bore fruit he would usually argue that we were being entrapped by foreigners.

To say the least, the State Department found such a man difficult to work with and almost impossible to convince. Borah's periodic outbursts of eloquence were especially perturbing. He had the knack of choosing an embarrassing moment in which to make a speech on foreign policy that would be quoted, in and out of context, far beyond the water's edge. "Well, when Borah starts," observed the Kansas City *Star,* "it's just like a lion getting out on a circus ground, everybody hunts a high pole and holds their breath until they hear they got him back again." He seldom used these speeches to help the administration implement its policies. As chairman of the Senate Foreign Relations Committee, he thought of himself as a watchdog to keep tabs on the President and the State Department. In one respect the Senator was always undeviating—he was adamant against any peace plan that involved the use of force. He was utterly impervious to the fact that the wealth, power, and far-flung interests of the United States involved a responsibility for world peace over and above inflated words and good intentions.

Hiram Johnson, on the other hand, was a staunch isolationist who wanted very much to be President. To realize this ambition it was necessary for him to have the regular Republicans forget his brazen 1912 Bull Moose apostasy and still to remain on good terms with the Progressives. An intense isolationism was helpful to him in playing this double role, for it was a doctrine common to both extreme wings of his party. It was the main ingredient of Johnson's old-fashioned American program which, he insisted, would furnish all the answers to all our foreign, domestic, economic, and spiritual problems. Borah was at least solicitous of the needs of mankind, but Johnson thought that there was no such thing as *noblesse oblige* among nations.

After Johnson's 1922 denunciation of the Four Power Pact,

he emerged as the most intractable of all the isolationists, and was determined to maintain his position. Once again, he defied the moderates in his party and refused to accept any American responsibility for facilitating the collection of war reparations or promoting German recovery. His isolationism was entirely consistent and he called the Reparations Commission another plan for supergovernment. Harding's death whetted his White House ambitions, and he laid plans to capture the 1924 nomination from Coolidge. Johnson artfully dodged controversial domestic issues and preached a homespun isolationism that he hoped would attract political support. His attacks on the administration's foreign policy managed to keep his name on the front pages of the newspapers. The Senator was careful, however, to make it clear that he was preaching simon-pure Republicanism, lest he be confused with the progressive-isolationist rebels.

Coolidge's nomination thwarted Johnson's ambitions, but he still found stirring isolationist speeches a capital way of keeping in the public eye. "Responsibility," he once said scornfully, [is] "always on the tongue of the international statesman, always on the tongue of those who are looking abroad." He begged his colleagues, who were busying themselves with postmasterships in Grizzly Gulch and collectorships in Prairie Town, to think what would happen if our tampering with German reparations payments should pull us once more into the European quagmire.[13] Such statements were quoted far and wide. Thus Borah and Johnson actively fanned the isolationist flames.

Each year the gap widened between the White House and the extreme isolationists. The line was clearly drawn on the growing unofficial relations with Geneva, the World Court issue, the reparations question, and the administration's benevolence toward foreign banking and industrial investments. After the congressional elections of 1926, the two major parties were so closely balanced in the Senate that the farm bloc held the balance of power. This leverage still further impeded any forward-looking diplomatic moves. The liberal-progressive influence in the Coolidge years involves a brace of paradoxes: unable to arrest domestic Toryism, it had an undue effect upon foreign policy; unsuccessful in checking economic entanglements, it did its best to cripple plans designed to cope with problems certain to arise from this expansion.

The liberal-progressive brand of isolationism was somewhat more prevalent in Congress than in the country at large, where conservatism had triumphed. The hyphenates, with the exception of the German and Scandinavian mid-westerners, usually separated their isolationism from their economic thinking. Hyphenate-isolationism was based more on resentment of our former Allies than on fear of either economic or political entanglement. Some of the hyphenate organizations dissolved or grew quiescent once the excitement of the treaty fight had abated. The Irish still regarded the League as a British minion, but their fire-eating lessened after the Free State was proclaimed by King George V, December 6, 1922.

The German-American groups, particularly the Steuben Society, grew in strength and influence in the twenties. As the Weimar Republic of the new Germany gained prestige and respect, the American societies quickened their efforts to reverse the wartime indictment of the Fatherland. The United States, their spokesmen said, had fought for the side that had started the war. Senator Robert M. La Follette was a special favorite of the Steubenites because of both his anti-war record and his persistent attacks on the harsh peace terms. When La Follette campaigned for the presidency in 1924, the Society turned out 18,000 strong to greet and serenade him. Now more highly organized than ever before, the German hyphenates sponsored isolationist books, lectures, and pressure groups.

Interestingly enough, the most telling efforts in behalf of Germany came from old stock Americans rather than hyphenates. As the Reich once more enjoyed a decent respect, men began to suffer bad conscience toward their former enemy. Americans visited Germany in far greater numbers than before the war and they were impressed by the dynamic culture of this tidy, punctual people. Prominent tourists returned home to say that German cordiality to Americans stood out in sharp contrast to French derision and British contempt. Reports of atrocities committed by French colored colonial troops in the occupied portion of Germany fell upon sympathetic American ears. Alanson B. Houghton, United States Ambassador at Berlin, regarded Germany as a great dam holding back the dangerous flood waters of Bolshevism. Before Houghton left his post in 1925, he pronounced German militarism dead and declared that the Reich's ambitions were limited to economic rehabilitation.

The new cordiality was enhanced by Chancellor Gustav Stresemann's moderate policies and his friendly overtures to Germany's conquerors. Following a visit to his Mannheim birthplace, the New York banker, Otto H. Kahn, stated that the Germans were recovering because they had given up flag-waving for hard work and sacrifice. Pro-German feeling in the United States gained momentum rapidly when Stresemann's efforts led to the 1925 Locarno Pact, in which Germany accepted her shorn western boundaries as a definitive settlement, and entered into a series of engagements with other powers that promised the peaceful solution of future disputes. Germany and her chancellor gained much of the credit for the general relaxation of tension. The Reich was admitted into the League, and Americans applauded an announcement that the new member did not construe Article X to mean that German troops would ever be called upon to enforce the Covenant. To base security on coercion, said a German spokesman, was to build a house by laying the roof first. According to the veteran Hearst editor, Norman Hapgood, the annals of history did not record a more stable revolution than the German substitution of democracy for autocracy. The *New Republic* demanded that the League insist on the recall of foreign troops from the Rhineland, the return of the Saar and Danzig to Germany, and the obliteration of the war-guilt clause of the Treaty of Versailles. In the sunny prosperity of the late twenties, republican Germany gained the respect of the United States.

Weimar restraint and American self-reproach only partially explain the prevalent good will. The United States was acquiring a heavy monetary stake in German stability. The Dawes Plan, which floated a loan on the international money market to provide Germany with gold, invited further investments. Eventually, Americans ventured over two billion dollars in reparation plan loans, German state bonds, and private industries ranging from steel mills to chain stores. Some of this money even went to build public swimming pools.[14] The fountains of German prosperity had been refreshed, but how long would the flow continue? Too much had been borrowed, especially in short-term credits subject to recall at the whim of Wall Street. German recovery rested upon the shifting sands of the American bull market.

The most important implications of the German investment boom belonged to the future. Unable to pay her creditors in goods, Berlin met reparations in foreign credits, most of which came from American sources. The dollars made the full cycle —to Germany as loans, to Allied capitals as reparations, and back to Washington as payment on war debts. But perpetual motion was no more possible in the economic world than in the physical. In the days of Hitler these German securities dwindled to almost nothing, so the American investor eventually footed the bill for the two billion dollars of war debts that were paid to the United States from 1924 to 1931.[15] The round trip of the dollar was to leave its mark on isolationist thought.

Jacob Gould Schurman, United States Ambassador to Germany, fostered this financial bonanza by being overconfident in Germany's future. He had been born in Canada of Dutch loyalist ancestors who trekked northward after the American Revolution. For six years he was Professor of Philosophy and Ethics at Cornell, after which he served for almost three decades as president of that university. When President Harding appointed him minister to China, he had already filled several diplomatic posts. In 1925 he was sent to Berlin, just at a time when American capital began to flow into Germany. Schurman had done more than his share of Hun-baiting during the war, for he was a faddist by nature. Originally a moderate internationalist, he turned against the League and championed the cause of Versailles' chief victim, Germany.

Schurman was elated by his transfer from war-torn China to sophisticated Berlin society. Seldom troubled by doubts, he always completely identified himself with the project at hand. He was captivated by the Weimar spirit of moderation, and paid no attention to the Nazi sore festering under the skin-deep prosperity. A man of forceful speech, abundant energy, and great fervor, Schurman made it his mission to bring Germany back into moral and intellectual communion with the United States. The Weimar Republic could not have asked for a better advertising agent.

One of the ambassador's failings was his inability to recognize the artificial nature of the Reich's business boom. Nothing, he was certain, could go wrong in a land of honest, hardworking people who were accustomed to meeting their personal obligations. Such a country, he thought, would lead the way to European stabilization. The delightful hospitality of Direktor Krupp von Bohlen and other industrial tycoons quite overwhelmed him. He was deeply impressed by the ability and character of the banking wizard, Dr. Horace Greeley Hjalmar Schacht. "If you read in the newspapers that something radical is proposed in Germany," said Schurman, "you may be sure that it can never amount to anything."[16]

As long-time president of an Ivy League university, Schurman had excellent rapport with eastern men of wealth. On visits home he made charming after-dinner speeches which pointed up opportunities in Germany. He advised the members of the New York Chamber of Commerce to invest in German stocks, bonds, and mortgages. In Berlin, the ambassador entertained visiting industrialists and went out of his way to extend a personal welcome to Americans who came to establish factories in the Reich. The State Department began to worry about his excessive concern for Germany's welfare. Secretary Kellogg warned him pointedly not even to suggest that Germany might be unable to meet her financial obligations under the Dawes Plan. Such a default, said Kellogg, would not only endanger the peace, but might jeopardize the payment of Allied war debts to the United States. Yet, less than a year later, Schurman was once more reprimanded for indiscreet talk to newspaper correspondents.

As a philosopher and academician, Schurman found ready entrée into select German intellectual circles. He worked diligently to restore the time-honored contacts between American scholars and German universities that had been interrupted by the war. He arranged exchange professorships and procured help for German learned societies from American endowments. He also used his skill at loosening purse-strings to raise a half million dollars for Heidelberg University, associated in the American mind with beer mugs, duelling swords, and student princes. The French took umbrage when the ambassador, at Heidelberg, said that Americans and Germans had joined together to rebuild the old university in the interest of European civilization. Nor were the French pleased to read that Chancellor Stresemann, on the same occasion, said that Bismarck had known the right road to peace. The Nazi press sneered at the Jewish names among the Heidelberg donors, but what was to be expected of noisy political outcasts? Americans and Germans, said Schurman, would both abide by the words of Jefferson: "Peace, commerce, and honest friendship with all nations, entangling alliances with none."

The new amity between Germany and the United States was hailed by the internationalists who thought it a healthy development. Friendliness to Germany no longer connoted criticism of League policies, for the Reich had entered the Covenant. In a larger sense, however, the restoration of German respectability aided the isolationist argument. It was now easier than ever to say that our 1917 intervention had been a mistake. Visiting German business men and scholars never lost an opportunity to denounce the malevolence of the Treaty of Versailles. A disarmed and deceivingly tranquil Germany stood out in sharp contrast to the constant petty colonial warfare, naval rivalries, and military aims of the French, British and Italians.

A further analysis of the isolationist coalition reveals that the extreme right was made up of nationalists, foreign-baiters, and militarists. These right-wingers are to be differentiated from the senatorial Irreconcilables, who ordinarily were not chauvinists, racists, army or navy enthusiasts, or anti-foreign monomaniacs. A Borah or a Johnson wanted an America free of all ties that might possibly involve us in war, while the nationalist extremists feared foreign ideological encroachment rather than another conflict. In fact, some of them were perversely isolationist, for they relished the thought of a home-made fight. The desire for independent American military action, or unilateralism as it is often called, has long been found among more reactionary isolationists.

George H. Lorimer, whose *Saturday Evening Post* reached millions of American homes, was an arch-conservative who saw the specter of Karl Marx behind every move for closer international accord. Because Lorimer paid top prices for his articles, he commanded a choice array of talent to inveigh against his twin bugbears of Socialism and foreign entanglements. One of his feature writers was Albert J. Beveridge, who had turned more and more conservative with the passing years. The former senator thought that a Jeffersonian type of insulation was necessary to preserve the American way of rewarding ability and hard work. It is difficult to understand how one whose monumental biographical writings are critical, precise, and accurate could have so credulously accepted anti-foreign canards. His fear of subtle propaganda, supposedly planned by British and French master minds, at times bordered on the irrational. He despaired of the Atlantic seaboard, but hoped that the old frontier spirit of the West might yet preserve American values. At one time he went so far as to ask Borah for confirmation of the rumor that the United States had paid the French government rent for trenches used during the war!

The outstanding mouthpiece of the patrioteers was the Chicago *Tribune*. Europe, said its editorial page, had been suckled on American gold since the days of Columbus. When American independence ended colonial exploitation, unwanted hordes were dumped on our shores. As America matured and checked this foreign intrusion, the Old World found it necessary to restrict our sovereignty and get us back under the tent. Hence, according to the *Tribune,* arose the European desire to lure us into the League.

Such far-fetched conjectures were not the monopoly of the Midwest. Representative George H. Tinkham of Massachusetts, a formidable, white-bearded reactionary, explained that a minority was determined to get us into the World Court. The United States, he contended, would then be in great danger, for if Europe were to turn Bolshevist, we would catch the disease through fraternization at The Hague. While southern feeling was generally tolerant of world organization, there were important exceptions. Some sour old Populists, whose lives had been spent in championing losing causes, blamed foreign influence, at home and abroad, for the frustration of their youthful aims. Such men combined nationalism and isolationism with a bitter hatred of foreigners. For example, Senator Cole Blease of South Carolina, who began his career as an agrarian reformer, was a master of invective. America would not, he fumed, give allegiance to a "supergovernment, a flag three-balled, a pawn-lure flag, representing that imperialistic and militaristic state, the League of Nations."[17]

The conservative-nationalists made a fetish of the Monroe Doctrine and wanted to retain our Caribbean protectorates. Their great fear was that the League would destroy the American Empire, in direct contrast to the liberals who thought it the instrument of a still wider imperialism. There was a sharp cleavage between isolationists who wanted to keep the iron grip on smaller countries that guarded the approaches to the Panama Canal, and those who desired to get out of Europe, Nicaragua, Santo Domingo, and Haiti at one fell swoop. The former group represented the nineteenth-century spirit that shunned European involvements for expansionist adventures elsewhere. The left-wingers, reflecting a newer point of view, were more consistently isolationist for they also opposed Latin American and Far Eastern imperialist ventures. Hence, the latter challenged the traditional contention that the Monroe Doctrine was ours alone, to have, to hold, and to interpret as we pleased.

There could not have been many bumptious nationalists in the Coolidge years who actually feared a European or Japanese New World coup. The more rational among them knew perfectly well that the day had passed when any nation could risk the defiance of the United States to invade or coerce any Latin American country. What the conservatives did fear, however, was that a strong League or World Court might be used to settle Latin American disputes, thus jeopardizing our control of New World adjudication. Their real concern, then, was not so much for the Monroe Doctrine, as for the more recent policy of understanding and comity among the trans-Atlantic nations that we call Pan-Americanism.

The nationalists conjured up all sorts of hypothetical cases to demonstrate how the League machinery might undermine the dominant position of the United States in the New World. What would happen if Mexico invaded Guatemala and the League applied economic and military sanctions? Would Latin American states, which viewed the United States with envious suspicion, turn to Geneva or The Hague to settle their disputes? Was it not significant that as soon as the American marines left the Dominican Republic this little country was admitted into the Covenant? So far, it was conceded, Geneva had handled Latin American problems with circumspection. However, the Monroe Doctrine cultists refused to risk a League powerful enough to question America's unique position in the New World. The Senate was especially sensitive to the slightest possible impairment of the policy. This unreasoned fear helped circumscribe the neo-isolationist diplomacy.

On the question of adequate defense the nationalists were in general disagreement. The spiritual heirs of Theodore Roosevelt, in league with the generals and admirals, fought for large military budgets. Although this group often found it convenient to work with the isolationists, they actually thought of an expanded, rather than a contracted, American role in the world. They may be regarded as isolationists only in their distaste for concerted international action. On the other hand, nationalists of the Borah or La Follette variety believed that a truly insular state needed only a minimum of armed protection. Therefore, generally speaking, these isolationists were more interested in the navy than the army. A wall of ships guarding the shoreline would substantially add to the protective powers of the ocean breakers, and would guarantee an isolated security. This line of reasoning, however, did not convince the progressive-isolationists from the interior states who were against the big navy bills of the period. Nor did it appeal to those conservatives, who, like President Coolidge, placed thrift ahead of power.

The Navy League of the United States (dating from 1902) had made many converts during the war. Plans to equal or surpass the British navy were hailed by the German- and Irish-Americans. The professional militarists, often making common cause with the isolationists, disdained collective security because it rivalled their own program: peace secured by national power. Major-General Robert Lee Bullard scoffed at the very idea that vital decisions could be settled without fighting. A reporter, covering a collegiate institute on foreign affairs, found five admirals, a general, and a group of majors and captains arguing for "America first and only." The warrior's golden rule, said a retired admiral, must be "DO UNTO OTHERS AS THEY WOULD DO UNTO YOU, BUT DO IT FIRST." Such a perverted gospel, so abhorrent to the liberal isolationists, was common among the ultra-conservatives. Dominance through fear, advised Hearst's New York *American*, was the way of the world. The war, said the Chicago *Tribune,* had at least made one thing clear: "To be right, be victorious."

There were, then, many varieties of isolationists: militarists and pacifists, Bourbons and Marxists, hyphenates and jingoists, polished New England congressmen and rough-hewn solons from the South and West. This motley group was united by a common opposition to the League. An analysis of its fears yields a bundle of contradictions. The League was warlike, criticized some, while others were certain that joining it would destroy manly Americanism. The organization was created to pave the way for Socialism, said the conservatives, while the radicals saw it shackling the world in capitalist chains. The liberals denounced it as an agent of nationalist aggression, while patriots claimed it demanded allegiance to an anaemic internationalism. Though it was held certain to fetter American business, it apparently would also put the world at the mercy of Wall Street. These composite arguments are possibly more imposing in retrospect than they were at the time they were uttered or written. Everyday Americans, absorbed with the pursuit of business and pleasure, took little time for serious contemplation. Fortune smiled at home, there were no threats from abroad, and the future seemed well able to take care of itself.

The citizenry of Coolidge's day were tired of the reform ferment that preceded 1914 and the wartime perturbation that came after it. They wanted to be left alone to draw their pay and enjoy their leisure hours. This prevailing mood explains the apathy of the masses far better than do any logical arguments for or against the League. The time had not yet come when Americans associated their personal well-being with a parley of statesmen, the wiles of the Chinese Communists, or peace along the picket lines on far-off rivers. Coolidge, it has been said, will go down in history as the last American President able to afford the luxury of a daily siesta.

In such a setting neither the enthusiastic internationalists nor the apprehensive isolationists could rouse the country from its lethargy. That tart old Virginian, Senator Carter Glass, complained that even Democrats were too busy making

170

money to care any more about their country's honor. There was a comfortable feeling, shared by all except a few alarmists, that the United States was invulnerable, and that prosperity was here to stay. The fallacy of the hour was that minding our own business was the only prerequisite for continued blissful existence. And this ancient republican prudence seemed embodied in the person of that downeastern Yankee, Calvin Coolidge.

The President had sensed the temper of the country by the election of 1924, and the results of the three-cornered contest of that year indicated to him the prevailing unconcern for foreign policy. Significantly, the senatorial Old Guard that had bossed the 1920 Republican convention had lost its power over the party conclave. Coolidge's business-minded friends were in control, and the platform favored American entry into the World Court, with reservations, but assured the country that it would not be enticed into the League. The G.O.P. pointed with pride to its diplomatic record: we had been helpful to the world and yet had kept clear of commitments, and the Washington Conference had shown that not all paths to peace led to Geneva.

The Democrats did not take strong issue with the new isolationism. The Wilsonian bloc failed to carry the convention and had to accept a flaccid foreign policy plank that called for a referendum before joining the League. John W. Davis, an able corporation lawyer who was nominated after the historic deadlock between William G. McAdoo and Alfred E. Smith, reproved the Republicans for their provincialism, but made no startling suggestions for bolder action. Tied to Davis's coattails as candidate for Vice-President was the rustic Charles W. Bryan, brother to William Jennings Bryan, and hardly an apostle of vigorous world leadership.

The newly formed Progressive party, headed by Senators Robert M. La Follette and Burton K. Wheeler of Montana, denounced Coolidge's middle way and preached unadorned isolationism. Founders of this party had long insisted that the addiction of the New York money-changers to foreign investments and concessions was dangerous to the peace of the country. The Progressives could speak out on this subject, but they found it necessary to avoid an outright indictment of the League in their platform. La Follette's name appealed to men who hated the Democrats for the war and the Republicans for the alliance with big business. But the new party also wanted to attract liberal internationalists who might be willing to overlook La Follette's isolationism in order to avoid the horrors of a choice between Coolidge and Davis. So the platform avoided mention of the League by name, and denounced, instead, the Treaty of Versailles and the Republican encouragement of international banking and monopoly. All the non-coercive plans were bundled together in a shotgun prescription for peace—outlawry of war, drastic disarmament, and a public referendum on war. La Follette's official campaign book amplified the platform by explaining that he was no ordinary isolationist, for unlike other Irreconcilables, he had refused to accept the rapacious parts of the Treaty of Versailles as well as its entangling clauses.

The Senator's original plan was to minimize foreign questions and to pound away incessantly at the dangers of monopoly. Wheeler and Oswald Garrison Villard, however, insisted that he explain the Progressive views on foreign relations in order to divert attention from the issue of radicalism. La Follette acquiesced, and, at St. Louis on October 14, 1924, he repeated the familiar charge that the bankers and the munition-makers had forced the country into war. If elected, he promised to end secret intrigue and, barring armed invasion, never go to war without the sanction of a plebiscite. In the unlikely event of war, La Follette vowed that he would denude the venture of profit by conscripting wealth as well as men.

Foreign affairs played little, if any part in the outcome of the election. La Follette carried Wisconsin and received about one-sixth of the total popular vote, but such strength as he showed was more a protest against economic conservatism than a demand for still more isolationism. Davis carried only the Solid South, and Coolidge was swept back into office by a vote of landslide proportions. George Harvey, who had said that the nation had a choice between Coolidge or chaos, heaved a sigh of relief. "Prosperity is at the door," he wrote, "good will is on the way, happiness gleams through the clouds, the world over."[18] If Harvey overstated the case, the future did seem bright enough to warrant the continuation of the Republican foreign and domestic program.

In the light of the foregoing pages, it is possible to understand why Coolidge pleased neither the ardent internationalists nor the stringent isolationists. By its very nature any policy of compromise is vulnerable. The leaguists were annoyed at the President's terse isolationist platitudes. At different times he said that the League existed as a foreign agency; he advised America to stay American; and he dismissed the Allied war-debt question with the observation that they had "hired the money." With characteristic naiveté he once declared that if the European nations distrusted each other sufficiently, no alliance would feel secure enough to go to war. The President enjoyed scolding Europe, and he sometimes threatened that the United States would withdraw all help unless the nations demonstrated that they really wanted peace. In his second term he denied the basic premise of the Covenant of the League by stating that reason and law must supplant a collective security based on force. On two propositions the Chief Executive was in complete agreement with the isolationists: he was entirely convinced of American moral superiority; and he preferred the gamble on general war to the pooled risks of collective security. Because of these considerations, Coolidge has often been portrayed as "Mr. Isolationist" in person.

Such a characterization, however, runs counter to the facts, for some of the Irreconcilables thought Coolidge an internationalist. Unquestionably, the United States moved much closer to an unofficial understanding with the League during his years in office, and the isolationists tried in vain to halt this drift. To the extremists, Coolidge's actions belied his words, for he approved of American participation in the reparations tangle. There was no fear in the President's heart that foreign loans, investments, and business offshoots would tie us to Europe with chains of gold. (The diplomatic historian, Thomas A. Bailey, has remarked that a nation can withdraw from a league, or denounce an alliance, with greater ease than it can get its industrialists to dismantle a three-million-dollar plant in a foreign danger spot.) Coolidge neither prevented the growth of economic entanglements nor perceived that this expansion was incompatible with the retention of political isolationism.

However, the most important battle between the President and the Irreconcilables was not fought on the economic front but over the World Court issue. To understand this conflict in full perspective it is necessary to turn to the story of the unyielding internationalists who insisted upon another assault on the isolationist citadel.

Chapter 9

The Rally of the Wilsonians

PERIODS OF TIME, like men, bear the impress of both dominant and recessive characteristics. The credulous Middle Ages had its skeptics, the libertine England of George IV its prudes, and the insouciant United States of the 1920s its zealots. If the many were apathetic to our role in the council of the nations, the few were heartily concerned. Thus the unbending isolationists were opposed by iron-willed men and women who insisted that a durable peace without an effective world organization was inconceivable. Such people construed the postwar resurgence of isolationism as only a temporary counteraction, which could be reversed by faith in and good works for the League of Nations.

The internationalists sorely needed this enduring courage, for their cause had fallen upon hard times. The multitude had relegated the war to history books, where they hoped readers would learn the consequences of a nation's not minding its own business. Then, too, a new European balance of power seemed in the making that probably would preserve the peace without America's having to throw her weight on either side of the scales. If, perchance, the balance some day should tip dangerously enough to threaten our own security, future American statesmen always could be counted on to save the situation by timely intervention. Besides, the 1922 Washington treaties had allayed the Japanese threat, so why borrow trouble by planning for eventualities that might never come to pass? There was, in those blissful, strainless years, no inkling of total annihilation in the current sense of that fear. Atomic warfare, capable of crippling any country on earth overnight, was still in the fanciful stage. Hence to the unimaginative masses, membership in the League would only barter away our God-given ocean barriers for intimate concern with foreign anarchy.

There was, however, a nucleus of determined people who knew, even before modern science had made a veritable ribbon of the ocean, that the Atlantic Ocean had not insulated the New World from consequential wars. Such men realized that our business frontiers had been pushed to the uttermost parts of the earth. If the big guns boomed once more, there could be no retreat to a chimerical isolationism. The only hope of escaping future conflicts, they reasoned, lay in preventing the outbreak of foreign wars. To most, but by no means to all internationalists, the League seemed to offer the best promise of averting another catastrophe. They resolved to strengthen the beacon of light that flickered from Geneva.

The strenuous efforts of the hard-core leaguist minority bore few immediate results. It is almost superfluous to say that they would have accomplished much more had all the internationalists supported their program. After 1920, American entry into the League was never again seriously considered. Repeated attempts to bring the United States into the World Court also came to naught, and Wilson's program was jettisoned by his own party. Strange as it may seem, the internationalists met their soundest defeats in the 1930s, at a time when the Democrats were in complete control of the country's destiny. Internationalism thus made few tangible gains in the inter-war years.

Even Woodrow Wilson, crushed by illness and disappointment, came to realize that the country had not been sufficiently prepared for the abandonment of isolationism. He advised Democratic friends of the League to cultivate the moulders of public opinion—the professional classes, teachers, educated business men, leaders of social effort, and others in key positions. This patient work of the Wilsonians bore fruit when the children of the 1920s matured to face the crucial questions that the Second World War brought to the surface. At a time when the outlook for their cause appeared all but hopeless, the internationalists reached many younger Americans through their influence in the schools and churches. They helped rear a generation that, impelled by the totalitarian threat, accepted American leadership in world politics.[1] An ever increasing number of youngsters went to high school and college, where they were usually exposed to the non-isolationist point of view. Higher education aroused the intellectual curiosity of these graduates and, as time went on, there were more people to take advantage of the programs of the cultural agencies that bespoke a broad outlook on foreign affairs. Internationalism became intellectually fashionable, while isolationism lost caste among the informed.

What manner of men and women inspired this intellectual revolution? They were, for the most part, middle-aged people whose opinions had crystallized in the confident years that preceded 1914 and whose optimism had not been shattered by the war. As a class, the internationalists clung to a belief in the inevitable progress of human society. Hence they were free from the cynicism and callousness that so marked the generation that had matured during the years of strife and global trepidation. Frequently they were doctrinaires who were attracted by the moral appeal of an international society that would make humanitarian reform its chief concern. Some of them, especially the church people, were answering the venerable Protestant call of service to mankind. Many ardent leaguists were college graduates who had gained a broad world perspective in the course of their education or travels. They usually enjoyed a position in life that allowed time for intellectual speculation and communal interests. Hence, there was a high percentage of educators, lawyers, judges, theologians, philanthropists, and semi-retired business executives among them. More often than not, prominent internationalists were the descendants of old-stock, affluent families who felt no need to proclaim their Americanism from the housetops. Obviously, their position in life was secure enough to let them laugh off the charges that they had been seduced by foreign propaganda.

College-bred women, whose interest in public affairs had been stimulated by their recent political emancipation, did much tedious routine work for the internationalist organizations. In New York City, Mrs. Franklin D. Roosevelt and some of her socially prominent friends supplied verve and energy for the Women's Pro-League Council. The Chicago *Tribune* took note of the female enthusiasm for the cause and explained to its readers that women for so long had been shielded from the hard facts of life that they fell ready victims to the delusion that an international organization could control a wicked world of rivalries, sordid ambitions, and perpetual violence.

Although a goodly proportion of the internationally minded were also interested in domestic reform, the movement attracted the support of many arch-conservatives like bankers and industrial bigwigs who were inclined to favor the League. Because so many internationalists thought in terms of competition and the efficacy of monetary rewards, they delighted in stimulating interest in the cause by essay and other cash prize contests. Frequently, these men were internationalists because of a genuine cosmopolitan interest, but some did fear the effects of a derelict Europe upon their foreign investments and wanted a world organization strong enough to preserve stability. It is also likely that some capitalists, who had become sensitive to the charges hurled against them during the muckraking years, embraced a liberal internationalism as a sort of compensation for an antediluvian business philosophy.

While many Republicans did yeoman work in behalf of the League, only in rare instances did prominent men publicly renounce their party allegiance. Usually a conviction that the G.O.P. knew how to run the country, and that Democrats did not, overcame opposition to Republican neo-isolationism. Some, perhaps, reasoned that they could do internationalism more good by working inside of the majority party than by criticizing from within the ranks of the minority.

After the final defeat of the Treaty of Versailles there was not much cleavage on foreign policy between the two parties, for the Democrats were by no means united in support of the League. Wilson, to be sure, still cast his spell over many Democratic politicians and voters, and this group was the backbone of the pro-League movement. On the other hand, many Democrats regarded the League as an unhappy liability. Collective security, they argued, had been put to the supreme test at the polls and had been found wanting in political appeal. Some Democratic spokesmen were forthright isolationists, but a greater number were opportunists who were wondering how the party could quietly bury the League issue and still save face.

The leaguists, therefore, had to carry on their campaign of education without full support from the party of Woodrow Wilson. It is significant that they labored in the inter-war decades without any real expectation that a Democratic national victory would fulfill their hopes. One must admire the fervor and tenacity of these zealous men and women. They rationalized repeated frustrations by saying that it was unreasonable to expect a country, devoted to isolationism for over a century, to assume a commanding role in world affairs without a temporary reversion to provincialism. The heirs of the Wilsonian tradition believed that eventually they could convince the American people that effective world organization offered a far better chance for peace than reliance upon an antiquated geographical insulation.

Many of the internationalists had been indoctrinated with the maxims of Social Darwinism. Thus they believed that human institutions, as well as organic life, were constantly in a state of change as man tried to adjust his needs to his environment. Progress was not always invariable; indeed evolution was marked by plateaux and regressions, but the final result must be in the direction of higher development. The

Covenant of the League of Nations was but a step in the evolution of government from a pattern of nationalistic wrangling toward a workable concord of all the states. For centuries, it was argued, men had been struggling to find a substitute for unbridled force and violence, and the creation of the League was a landmark in this quest. In a forgotten book published in 1926, Franklin D. Roosevelt, for the moment talking theory rather than practical politics, summed up the evolutionary contention: "First [there was] the self-sufficient small community, then the grouping of several communities, then the small state, then the nation, then alliances between and now a permanent congress of nations."[2]

The advance of any movement depends upon the ability of its leaders and their willingness to make personal sacrifice of time and energy in the interest of the cause. Although Woodrow Wilson lived on until 1924, he was physically and temperamentally unable to lead the forces that were trying to perpetuate his ideals. The ex-President had grown querulous and dogmatic, and he virtually secluded himself from his most faithful lieutenants. The leaguists could still capitalize upon the enduring attraction of Wilson's name to millions of Americans, but active leaders had to be recruited to reorganize the shattered League forces. Perhaps the most effective of the new strategists was John Hessin Clarke, former Associate Justice of the United States Supreme Court. During the war, Clarke had resolved to devote his life to the cultivation of opinion favorable to world peace. In 1922, he resigned from the Supreme Court and dedicated over a score of his remaining years to the fulfillment of his pledge.

College and university faculties furnished the pro-League forces with many able leaders and workers. The same historical forces that had broadened Wilson's international outlook similarly shaped the thinking of many fellow academicians. Hence professors were especially apt to comprehend and sympathize with his precription for ending global anarchy. The Wilson administration deliberately had enlisted the services of historians, economists, and political scientists. There was, then, some justification for the isolationist contention that Wilson's ivory tower champions had vested interests in defending the way in which he waged the war and made the peace. There were few campuses, in the 1920s, that did not have at least one fervent Wilsonian to propagandize for the League. These men often wrote history and government textbooks, heavily documented monographs, and lighter pieces for the highbrow magazines. Some of their writings at least gained the coveted honor of a place on the night-tables of the more literate reading public.

Possibly no single individual worked more assiduously to uphold the Wilsonian thesis than the crisp and spruce Professor William E. Dodd. This University of Chicago master teacher and prolific historian was, like Wilson, a native Southerner who had spent many years in a northern university. The intimate exchange of opinion with Wilson, which Dodd had enjoyed, he now utilized in preparing a readable defense of the President's policies entitled, *Woodrow Wilson and His Work*. He enlarged upon the points made in this book in speeches around the country, in talks on the hustings, and in conversations and correspondence with colleagues and students.

Professor Charles Seymour of the Yale history department, one of the retinue of experts at Versailles, returned to hammer away at the isolationist contention that Wilson first had been decoyed by economic forces into a needless war, and then beguiled by crafty Europeans into fashioning an unworkable peace. At the University of Illinois there was the stately Mississippian, James W. Garner, who made his department of political science a national center for the study of international relations. Garner used his wide erudition and mastery of language to defend Wilson and the concept of collective security in his crowded classroom, on the lecture forum, and in many books and articles. The number of other professors of national or merely college-hill reputation who introduced their students to the internationalist approach is legion. One can only guess at the effects of their influence upon future teachers and other citizens, but it seems safe to assume that they helped break down the parochial prejudices of a rising generation. To be sure, there were many stout isolationists on university faculties, and some of them were just as effective teachers and gifted writers, but they were in the minority. The cataclysmic events of the Second World War changed the opinion of many of these academic dissenters, so that by 1945 professorial isolationism was confined to a few outstanding nonconformists.

The most celebrated of Wilson's historical defenders was the journalist, Ray Stannard Baker. Before going to Versailles in a key press position, Baker had won national recognition as a scholarly and accurate muckraker. Wilson was so impressed by Baker's defense of the treaty that he opened to him the historical secrets hidden in his personal correspondence. Extracts from a projected book soon oppeared in the New York

Times, and Baker eventually received the Pulitzer prize in biography for an eight-volume work which carried the Wilson story through the war years. Although Baker's writings freshened public interest in Wilson, his judgments were sometimes uncritical and he often failed to digest properly the rich sources at his disposal. Isolationists and other critics of the ex-President turned some of Baker's revelations into stinging indictments of Wilson's statesmanship.

In addition to this literary espousal, the leaguists always could rely on some devoted Democrats to plead their case in Congress. Capitol Hill's most effective Wilsonite (until his retirement in 1923) was John Sharp Williams. This Mississippi planter-statesman, with the conventional, dangling, black string-tie, was one of the most forceful and poignant debaters of his generation. Williams's racy but logical speeches, which reflected his masterful grasp of foreign affairs, aroused the admiration of even his most bitter senatorial opponents. He once told the Republicans that he believed that the Wilson whom they had crucified would surely be resurrected.[3]

Senator Morris R. Sheppard of Texas took special delight in badgering the opposition with detailed reports on the achievements of the Versailles peace mechanism. On one occasion, he spoke for six hours on the League's work without moving from his place or pausing for a drink of water. Virginia's two old-fashioned senators pursued similar tactics. Carter Glass predicted that time would vindicate the 1920 stand of his party. He claimed that a Republican partisan conspiracy had hindered a practicable plan to enforce world peace and scoffed at the half-way measures of the neo-isolationists that had made a riddle of American foreign policy. Virginia's senior senator, Claude A. Swanson, was the ranking minority member of the Senate Foreign Relations Committee. He accused the Republicans of clinging to a foreign policy predicated upon isolationism at a time when the ever widening grasp of American commercial tentacles made shambles of the concept.

A Far-Western Democrat, Thomas J. Walsh, was another severe critic of Republican diplomacy. Former President Wilson was so impressed with one of the Montana senator's speeches that he kept a copy handy on his reading table.[4] How, asked Walsh, could we, in good faith, force Germany to disarm and yet refuse to protect her by a guarantee of collective action in case of attack? Did we not in our separate treaty of peace with Germany (Treaty of Berlin, 1921) take out the balm of the League and leave only the galling punitive measures of Versailles? Walsh's words commanded attention, for here was a true-blue Irishman whose faith in the League overcame any aversion that he might have to a closer association with Britain.

In such wise, the Wilsonian rebound was spearheaded by dedicated internationalists, scholars who were determined to uproot provincialism, historians who defended American wartime diplomacy, and Democratic politicians who remained steadfast to their party's 1920 stand. The group constantly found it necessary to improvise new strategy and arguments to use against the isolationists. Minorities generally find it more expedient to criticize specific actions of the majority than to dwell on the details of an alternative program. Hence the internationalists tended not to press American entry into the League and emphasized instead collateral questions raised by Republican policies. Since an outright demand for affiliation with Geneva was doomed to certain defeat, the Wilsonians pared down their demands to bring them within the scope of possible fulfillment. They tried to make progress by sponsoring schemes and proposals whose immediate objectives did not involve formal League association. It was obvious that their only hope of eventual victory lay in turning the isolationist flank.

While the principal purpose of these strategic maneuvers was to outwit the isolationists, the new departure demonstrated that the Wilsonians had also tumbled from wartime idealistic heights. It soon became apparent to all but star-gazers that the League was run by conventional European diplomats rather than by ebullient reformers. Americans also came to see that while the Allies had not troubled to make formal reservations to the Covenant, in practice the nations made such informal modifications as suited their own interests. The League was obviously neither the total solution to world problems envisaged by its friends, nor the dangerous behemoth that had been portended by its enemies. It was, instead, said the Harvard historian Samuel Eliot Morison, an international body composed of nations who had made very sure to limit their liability in this experiment in collective action. A visit to Europe, nevertheless, convinced Professor Morison that Geneva's fortunes were in the hands of sane and earnest men who were trying to solve a number of small problems in a big way.[5] The international cooperationists tried to make capital of the League's non-utopian methods, asserting that this down-to-earth approach proved that the Covenant was functional rather than visionary. Here was an organization, they argued, badly crippled by American abstention, that was doing its level best to restore some semblance of order to a disordered world. They boldly advertised every ephemeral League success and promptly rationalized each defeat. The more hard-headed internationalists set out to destroy the 1919 fancy that the mere existence of the League would make radical changes in the tactics of the nations. The League, they now warned, was only a practical way of transacting international business—it was not the precursor of the millennium.

The Wilsonians leveled their heaviest salvos at the Republican obeisance to isolationism. Such a retreat on the part of a great nation, they said, bespoke cowardliness and national selfishness. It was, moreover, dangerous and futile, for, since the dawn of American history, we had never been able to escape involvement in general European wars. By not cooperating with the League, contended the lawyer and scholar, Hunter Miller, we connive with the evil forces rife in the world. "We haven't got the pep of Paraguay. We haven't got the guts of Guatemala," said the ardent leaguist Edward Price Bell, "and we are not going to permit half-baked . . . provincials to cheat us of our rightful opportunity to serve."[6] The neo-isolationist compromise of sending unofficial observers to the League was denounced as queer, ineffectual, and insulting to the dignity of the United States. "Instead of facing the world openly and courageously," declared Senator Swanson, "we have been tiptoeing, walking with faltering and hesitating steps, unofficially peeping through the keyholes."[7] The call was for bolder action, to free the country from its isolationist shackles, and for unhesitating and open participation in the League's efforts. All but the most intrepid avoided the suggestion that the United States reconsider its refusal to bind itself formally to the Covenant. Like the Israelites of old, the internationalists were to wander long in the by-ways of the wilderness, for the direct route to the Promised Land was beset by insurmountable obstacles.

So the leaguists sought to popularize their cause without calling direct attention to their ultimate goal. An exaltation of Wilson's name would keep his ideas alive and refute the calumnies of his isolationist detractors. This campaign had some grass roots origins. In the drearists days of the Democratic exile of the twenties there were flutterings of pro-Wilson sentiment deep down in the political soundings. Washington County, Mississippi, had a Woodrow Wilson Democratic Club. Professor Dodd invaded the heart of the enemy's country to speak to an interested group in Ramsay County, Minnesota. Admirers of the former President organized in

San Bernardino, California. There was "The Woodrow Wilson Democracy" of New York City, and the faculty and students at Harvard formed a Wilson club. Like all other movements in America, fatuous or sublime, the local units federated into a national council that promptly elected Woodrow Wilson as honorary president!

The national efforts to sustain interest in Wilson were carefully planned. Franklin Roosevelt, in semi-retirement trying to overcome his paralysis, had plenty of time to meditate. He queried friends and acquaintances on the possibility of some marked tribute to the former President. Wilson was told of the project and objected to the creation of a memorial because it sounded too funereal, but he did assent to the collection of funds for an endowment that would recognize his work among men "throughout the world who love liberty and who intend to promote peace by the means of justice." After a futile attempt to find a name for the tribute that would be acceptable to all parties, Roosevelt and his friends agreed to call it *The Woodrow Wilson Foundation*. Contributions from men of wealth plus campaigns in more than one hundred colleges yielded $700,000 of a two million dollar goal. Originally, the trustees thought in terms of an American version of the Nobel Prize, to be awarded periodically to persons who did most to promote the Wilsonian ideals. Although the first prize was actually presented to a statesman no less distinguished than Viscount Cecil, the experiment proved abortive. Eventually the Foundation turned to the promotion of essay contests with cash awards to the winners, and the establishment of the Woodrow Wilson Library in New York City. While the money might have been spent to better advantage in a country that was tiring of such contests, the competition was publicized in the schools, thus affording teachers an opportunity to lay special stress upon the Wilson story.

The development of a national pro-League organization also helped to idealize Wilson's name. Some of the local groups, formed to urge ratification of the Treaty of Versailles, survived the 1920 campaign. National federation of these pro-League units was purposely delayed in the fond hope that the Republicans might be more inclined to compromise with Geneva if they were not pressed. By 1923, however, it was clearly evident that the Republicans had no more intention of joining the League than of giving Texas back to Mexico. The time had come to unify those internationalists who clung to Wilson's plan. Some leaders of local groups, along with members from the Commission on International Good Will of the

Federal Council of Churches, sponsored the League of Nations Non-Partisan Association (now the American Association for the United Nations). John H. Clarke was elected president and served until 1930. He was succeeded by George W. Wickersham, a former Republican Attorney-General of the United States, who had worked on the codification of international law for the League.

The new union soon found that popular enthusiasm for global causes had chilled since the war. After an initial spurt of strength, the League of Nations Non-Partisan Association settled down to become a New York City outfit with its branches largely located in university centers. The leaders, however, did an excellent job in putting out the League of Nations *Herald*. In just nine months of 1925 they distributed almost a million pieces of various forms of propaganda. Yet it was difficult, frustrating work, for they were always swimming upstream against the prevailing current of opinion. Bowing to the widespread determination to avoid formal ties with the League, individual chapters called only for more active American participation in the League's endeavors. Eventually the national organization declared that it sought to promote American entry into the League "on such terms as . . . may seem wise, provided only, that they are consistent with the dignity and honor, the moral responsibility and power of our Republic." That the principal pro-League organization in the country had to hedge to this extent is proof positive of the pervasiveness of the isolationist spirit.

Perhaps the most interesting internationalist attempt to skirt the isolationist ramparts was the 1924 Bok Peace Award. Edward W. Bok, retired millionaire publisher whose autobiography had won the Pulitzer Prize, pondered our wavering foreign policy. While editor of the *Ladies' Home Journal* he never failed to promote what he thought was a worthwhile project, even to crusading to outlaw the lowly public drinking cup. Bok's practical Dutch mind now turned to the perplexing question of how best to secure a warless world. He was certain that real progress toward this goal was hopeless without the active participation of the United States. For a time he considered appealing directly to the Washington authorities, but soon concluded this would be a waste of time. A staunch conservative who appreciated the incentive of monetary rewards, he then decided to stimulate American idealism "by the golden spur of self-interest."[8]

The American Peace Award, with headquarters in New York City, was a gigantic national contest designed to produce a workable peace plan. Blueprints were limited to 5,000 words and the winner was to receive $50,000 immediately and a like amount when and if the scheme was put into operation. A quarter of a million inquiries were handled by Bok's agents, ninety-seven influential national organizations backed the project, the press gave it heavy coverage, and libraries throughout the country reported a run on books dealing with international affairs. When the closing date for entries arrived, the jury of award headed by the venerable Elihu Root had to sift through 22,165 different peace formulas. Drafts were submitted by public figures, erudite professors, peace enthusiasts, and money-hungry amateurs who regarded contest entries as a free bet on the Irish sweepstakes.

Franklin D. Roosevelt worked out a plan, but refused to submit it apparently because his wife had been appointed one of the judges. His ideas deserve special consideration, for two decades later he stated that this 1923 draft influenced some of his thoughts on the United Nations.[9] Of equal importance, however, is the amazing lengths to which the 1920 Democratic candidate for Vice-President was willing to go in order to placate the isolationists. F.D.R. was ready to scrap the much defamed League of Nations so that thousands of its detractors might "help put the United States into a new Society of Nations, saving face, honor, and all other fool things they think have to be saved."[10] To enlist the support of the 1920 League reservationists, Roosevelt made it clear in the preamble to his plan that the United States had no intention of becoming involved in matters that did not concern the New World, nor would it invest a world organization with any control over its armed forces. Although Roosevelt retained some collective security guarantees, he carefully watered down the provisions of the much criticized Article X, which protected League members against external aggression.

On January 7, 1924, Mr. Bok broadcast over station WEAF the news that the winner was the elderly Charles E. Levermore, former president of Adelphi College, who, as secretary of the New York Peace Society, had been associated with League and World Court pressure groups. His plan, No. 1469, advocated immediate American entry into the Permanent Court of International Justice with the reservations recommended by the Coolidge administration. For the time being, without becoming a member of the League, the United States would cooperate fully in its work subject to the following stipulations: moral force and public opinion were to be substituted for military and economic sanctions; the Monroe Doctrine was to be held inviolate; we were to assume no obligations under the Treaty of Versailles without the consent of Congress; the Covenant was to be open for all nations to join; and the League was to champion the development of international law. In other words, Levermore brushed aside the thorny question of formal association, and tempered his suggestions for cooperation so as to make allowance for important American prejudices against the League.

There was a special reason for the exasperated reaction of the isolationists to Levermore's proposals. Bok announced the winning plan just as Coolidge was prodding the Senate to consider his World Court proposal, and the opposition smelled collusion. Isolationist tempers mounted even higher when the Bok organization promised an informal national referendum on the merits of their peace proposition. Newspapers, periodicals, colleges, women's clubs, and churches were to aid in the distribution of ballots and copies of the plan. Was this anything, asked the die-hards, but a dark conspiracy to put ballots in the hands of carefully selected groups so that the country could be told that an overwhelming majority favored going into the World Court?

Most of the newspapers and even the *New Republic* praised Levermore's restraint, but the ultra-isolationists outdid themselves in maliciousness. The Chicago *Tribune* said that the foreign-born Bok was ready to spend his last dollar to entice us into the League. The Irreconcilables thundered against the "bogus referendum" from the Senate floor, and vowed never to yield to pressure. They persuaded the Senate to investigate Bok's use of money, propaganda, and advertising in staging his "Peace Award Trick."[11] When the inquest was shelved after much vituperation, both the accusers and the accused claimed victory. Bok promptly offered to sponsor another contest with senators forming the jury of award, but his proposal fell flat. Thus Levermore had to content himself with the initial $50,000 inasmuch as his plan was never tried. The Peace Award, now re-christened The American Foundation, became the liveliest World Court pressure group in the country. Unfortunately, perhaps the most noteworthy effect of Bok's contest was a stiffening senatorial opposition to the World Court. The proposed referendum lent color to the charge that a band of conspirators planned to make the Court a back door passageway into the League. The Senate isolationists increased their vigil to seal any possible leaks in the isolationist dykes.

The World Court battle, which vexed American politics for

a dozen years, involved the heaviest internationalist counter-attack of the period. By 1925, the pro-League forces were once more in full panoply and anxious for a return bout with the isolationists, even if the consolation prize was only entry into the Court. As the infirmities of age crept upon Charles W. Eliot, he told his son that the World Court interested him more than Heaven. "When a good cause has been defeated," he said, "the only question that its advocates need ask is when do we fight again."[12] To say that the Wilsonians tried to use the Court as a Trojan horse to break throught the isolationist barriers into the outer League ramifications is substantially correct. It is also true, however, that only the interest of the Republican high command in the Court made it possible for the leaguists to try the ruse.

The concern of the moderate Republicans for the Court experiment was rooted in the party's foreign policy record. Secretary of State John Hay (1898-1905) and his successor, Elihu Root (1905-1909), had both urged the nations to create a court of law that would make possible the judicial settlement of international disputes. This proposal was a cardinal plank in the platform of the League to Enforce Peace, an organization in which Republicans had predominated.

Charles Evans Hughes had supported the court plan as the 1916 G.O.P. presidential candidate. There was more enthusiasm for international adjudication in the United States than in any other country, for there was a widespread conviction that law must be substituted for force as the ultimate arbiter in human affairs. American thinkers had shown far more interest in the enthronement of law in the world than in any scheme of collective security that rested upon physical coercion. Thus the World Court front was broad and bipartisan, consisting of leaguists, Republican 1920 reservationists, and pacifist internationalists who would accept the Court but could not, in good conscience, subscribe to the Covenant.

Acting under the auspices of the League, an Advisory Committee of Jurists drew up a statute for the Permanent Court of International Justice and the Court convened for its first session early in 1922. Elihu Root had been one of the chief architects of the plan, and the Court bore the imprint of his handiwork. Although the new body was the godchild and ward of the League, it was possible to join the Court without entering into the Covenant.

Secretary of State Hughes, a friend and admirer of Root, made American assent to the World Court protocol a major goal of his program. When the political decks were clear of other pressing matters, he revealed his plans to the country in a speech at Boston on October 30, 1922. To allay senatorial anxiety about possible entanglements, Hughes formulated reservations to the protocol which President Harding accepted and sent to the Senate with his approval. The United States, Hughes proposed, would adhere to the protocol subject to the following four explicit conditions: (1) There were to be no legal relations with the League or assumptions of any obligations under the Covenant; (2) The United States was to participate on an equal basis with League members to elect the judges; (3) Congress was to determine a fair share of the Court's expenses that would be paid by the United States; (4) No amendments were to be made to the statute of the Court without our consent.[18] When the Irreconcilables insisted that the Court was a bait for the League trap, Hughes spoke sharply. He warned the Wilsonians that their hopes of using the protocol as a wedge to reopen the question were as preposterous as the isolationist fears that joining the Court would lead to American acceptance of the Covenant.

The Secretary, however, was unable to prevent the gathering storm of protest. A revolt was brewing on Capitol Hill, engineered by Republican members of the Senate Foreign Relations Committee who took offense because they had not been consulted in drawing up the reservations. The League, said these isolationists, elected the Court's judges, and our participation would be tantamount to a recognition of Geneva without an adequate protection of American interests. Faced with growing party discord, Harding began to retreat. Shortly before his death he promised that the United States would not join until we were certain that we were dealing with a *World* and not a *League* Court. He further stipulated that we must be guaranteed full equality in participating with the Geneva nations in the disposition of Court matters.

One of Coolidge's first important decisions as President was whether to accept Harding's partial surrender or to stand firmly behind Hughes's original conditions. The President weighed the matter carefully and then announced his support of the Secretary of State's reservations which, he said, clearly indicated our determination not to adhere to the League. The disappointed isolationist senators then pulled out of the hat all their tried and proven tricks—they stalled for time, held tedious public hearings, and contrived alternate schemes to confuse the Court issue. This type of sparring between the White House and the Senate went on for over two years, despite mounting evidence that a popular majority approved of the Court. Eventually, the isolationists tried to substitute for the Hughes reservations the Pepper Plan. The author of this stratagem was Senator George Wharton Pepper, a prominent Philadelphia practitioner and professor of law. He wanted the Senate to insist that the Court be entirely divorced from the League without otherwise altering its identity. There was so much Republican support in the Senate Foreign Relations Committee for such a separation that a Virginia Democrat had to plead Coolidge's case, while Republican New Hampshire's George Moses grumbled privately that the President was uninformed and devoid of a spark of altruism. The 1924 platforms of both major parties endorsed the Court, and the Republican victory should have insured prompt action, but Borah clung stubbornly to the Pepper Plan. After another year of procrastination, the Court matter was placed high on the Senate agenda for the session that began in December, 1925.

By this time, both sides were arrayed for the greatest foreign policy battle since the defeat of the Treaty of Versailles. For the third time in seven years, the church groups, the club women, and the peace and uplift societies launched an all-out campaign. First there had been the 1919 League drive, then the 1921 disarmament crusade, and now the same people were sure that the World Court was the panacea. The more zealous among them exaggerated the benefits of joining, just as the Irreconcilables dolefully magnified the possible evil consequences of signing the protocol. Three cities procured stamp-cancelling machines which marked letters with the slogan "World Peace, Law Not War." Pro-League forces in New York City sponsored a World Court Ball. Bok's American Foundation perfected a standard technique and sent it around the country for local use. An avalanche of petitions fell upon Congress—from the Omaha branch of the American Legion, the Osteopathic Association and Smelterman's Union of Montana, the Society of the Genesee, dozens of state legislatures, scores of women's clubs and countless citizens assembled in mass meetings. Possibly eight per cent of the press (with the Hearst and Munsey chains as principal exceptions) supported Coolidge against the obdurates. Elihu Root, detecting the annoyance of some Westerners at eastern pressure, refused to go to Washington to lobby. The cause might have gained if some of the more indefatigable had practiced a similar restraint.

The unbridled eagerness and militant air of the Court propagandists alarmed the administration. Coolidge refused to acknowledge the support of organizations formed to press his own proposal because he disliked the measures of the extremists. Some of the leaguists candidly and foolishly stated that victory in the Court campaign would only mark a step toward the realization of their ambitions. The very size of the World Court movement was sufficiently formidable to make the isolationists fear that any compromise would lead to further demands. They were intent upon standing pat.

The anti-Court senators did not have the backing of a well-organized national group. Perhaps the Marxists, Klansmen, hyphenates, and inveterate isolationists who wanted no association with the Court relied too heavily on an Irreconcilable filibuster to block Senate action. As a showdown on the issue neared, however, these groups became apprehensive and tried to rouse the countryside to support the Irreconcilables. Senators took to the road to make anti-Court speeches, and the extreme isolationist press intensified its campaign. Theodore Roosevelt's daughter, Alice R. Longworth, organized her own private lobby in Washington. Beveridge thought that the League fight had to be won anew for the same old internationalist organizations were still claiming to speak for all the women, all the teachers, and all the preachers. He blamed the Wall Street bankers for the renewal of the agitation, and predicted that as soon as America joined the Court their initial financial swag would amount to at least five hundred million dollars. Were the Republicans willing, asked the Washington correspondent William Hard, to relinquish their one real claim to virtue and reverse their policy of non-entanglement by leading the country into this new foreign trap?

The extremists were not restrained by the dictates of good taste. The Chicago *Tribune* listed the judges who sat at The Hague, defied its readers to pronounce Didrik Galtrup, Gjedde Nyholm, Wang Ch'ung-hui, and asked: "HOW MANY FRIENDS CAN UNCLE SAM COUNT ON IF HE SUBMITS HIS AFFAIRS TO THE WORLD COURT?" "Rafael Altamira, of Spain," asked the Democratic Irreconcilable, James A. Reed, "now, just what does Rafael stand for? . . . Yorozu Oda, of Japan—just how does this gentleman regard the policies of America?"[14] Southern pro-Court senators should be warned, said the Boston *Post,* that European countries might sue us at The Hague for debts long since repudiated by the states that they represented. Members of the Republican National Committee and G.O.P. state politicians bluntly warned Coolidge that he was "courting" party disaster. For the time being, however, the President stood his ground and his senatorial spokesmen insisted on pushing the Court issue.

Despite the fact that the House of Representatives had gratuitously approved Coolidge's stand, 301 to 28, a coterie of senators was ready to filibuster, if necessary, to prevent favorable action. The Irreconcilables, with Borah in charge, charted their strategy. The Idaho senator, acting in character, was heartily in favor of a world tribunal, but he promised a fight to the finish against this particular Court. When his attempts to load the Court bill with impossible conditions failed, and when his suggestion to table the matter pending the codification of international law fell flat, Borah said that the resolution would be carried in twenty minutes if the reservations were made sufficiently stringent. George H. Moses, who was even more intransigent, distrusted Borah's leadership and conducted his own back-stairs campaign to whip the opposition into line. Recalling Lodge's 1919 tactics against the League, Moses wanted to stall for time until Beveridge's speeches could turn public sentiment against the bill. The mood of the country, however, was too relaxed for any sudden electrification.

By the time the Senate was ready to vote, the Irreconcilables found themselves opposing an altered version of the original Hughes reservations. Strangely enough, Senator Pepper had found an unexpected ally in the person of John Bassett Moore, who had sat on the bench of the permanent Court of International Justice since its inception. Judge Moore told the senators that there was some hazard to the United States in the power of the Court to give advisory opinions (an opinion given as to the right or wrong of a dispute before litigation). To be sure, in 1923, the judges had refused to give such an opinion, but Moore thought that it would be well to guard against the possibility of a future reversal. His suggestion aroused a number of latent fears. How could the United States request an advisory opinion, if it so desired, since the petition must come from the League's Council or Assembly? Might not such opinions, although not legally binding, embarrass us in preserving the Monroe Doctrine or in maintaining our tight immigration laws? Thus the Foreign Relations Committee added to the resolution of adherence a fifth reservation that Moore helped to frame. This new condition, which was to prove the actual stumbling block to American entry, stated that the Court should not render an advisory opinion unless it was publicly done after due notice and hearing, nor was it to render one in which the United States had or claimed an interest, without prior consent. American adherence to the protocol, moreover, was not to become effective until the forty-eight member nations indicated their acceptance of the five reservations through an exchange of notes. Here was a demand for special treatment that the other nations surely would be reluctant to grant. As if this were not enough, the Foreign Relations Committee added two other reservations before bringing in a favorable report on the resolution. Cases to which the United States was a party could come before the Court only through the provision of general or special treaties. This was equivalent to saying that the Senate reserved the power to veto any referral. Then came the oft-repeated denial that we were departing from the principles of President Monroe or surrendering our "traditional attitude toward purely American questions." The more responsible isolationists were now satisfied, but the thoroughgoing Irreconcilables still refused to yield.

Senator Reed argued that the severity of the reservations confirmed the dangers that the Court presented. He claimed that there was no difference in principle between the Bolshevist type of internationalism and the variety originally taught by the late Andrew Carnegie and perpetuated by his endowed societies. At a critical moment in the debate, Robert M. La Follette, Jr., heir to his father's seat, delivered his maiden Senate speech. The Court should be opposed, he said, because it was the agent of the League in enforcing the Treaty of Versailles. In joining we would ally ourselves, once more, with the greedy victors of the war who were intent upon controlling the world's oil, coal, rubber, iron, money, and trade routes. The contrast between Reed and La Follette illustrates the strange bed-fellowship among the isolationists. While the Missouri senator was an old, cross-grained conservative, his youthful Wisconsin colleague was the flag bearer of the insurgent Progressives.

As the party whip cracked in the Senate to muster support for the resolution, outside pressure tried to save the marooned band of ultraists. The New York *Sun* raised Munsey's ghost to remind the country that he had warned that the dice would be loaded against us at The Hague. From Washington, William Hard wrote a series of articles denouncing the Court as a gigantic war-trap. The country, however, refused to withdraw its attention from the enjoyment of the loaves and fishes of prosperity. The mercurial atmosphere of 1919 had long since vanished, and with the exception of extremists on both sides, people were indifferent to the outcome of the debate. Oswald Garrison Villard said that even the *Nation's* selected clientele was bored with the Court and out of patience with overstatements. The Senate, goaded by the administration, took the rare step of resorting to closure, thus limiting debate and preventing a filibuster. On January 27, 1926, the Senate by a vote of 76 to 17, passed the resolution with the reservations recommended by its Foreign Relations Committee. The new isolationism had apparently triumphed over the old.

This dubious victory provided only faint cheer for the internationalists. Even so, the Court reservationists had taken only one round, for the ultimate victory was to go to the Irreconcilables. Coolidge was told that the Republicans, generally, were either hostile or indifferent to the Court, and that many senators had voted for the resolution out of party loyalty rather than conviction. In spite of the fact that the congressional elections of 1926 were at hand, the isolationists refused to bury the Court issue in the interest of G.O.P. harmony. They hailed the results of the primary elections as a rebuke to the administration. In both Illinois and Wisconsin, Republican senators who had voted for the Court bill were defeated for re-nomination by unconditional isolationists. The situation was reversed in the November elections because fifteen pro-Court men (of both parties) were elected to the Senate while only ten such candidates were downed by anti-Court opponents. Five of the senators who had voted against the Court, moreover, were defeated for re-election and only two were returned to their seats.

One can only speculate on the part played by the Court in these victories and defeats, for all of the contests were complicated by national and local factors that were of far more intimate concern to the voter. Politicians, nevertheless, became chary of even a tepid internationalism, for the results in the primaries had been striking. They were impressed, too, by the defeat in Massachusetts of Coolidge's favorite, William M. Butler, who lost his seat to the veteran Democratic isolationist, David I. Walsh. Republican control of the newly elected Senate was so precarious that the Old Guard had to swallow its pride and take four western mavericks back into the party. The anti-Court bloc in the Republican caucus was now more influential than ever.

Meanwhile, no progress had been made in getting the other nations to agree to the Senate reservations to the protocol, and Secretary Kellogg showed little interest in cutting the Gordian knot. He declined an invitation from the Council of the League for the United States to meet with other members of the Court to find a solution to the problem. Although twenty-two of the signatory powers convened to end the impasse, the best that they would offer was a compromise on the Senate's demands in regard to advisory opinions. One week after the 1926 elections, Coolidge yielded to the isolationists. In an Armistice Day talk in Kansas City he declared that he would not ask the Senate to change its stipulations and that he saw no prospect of America joining the Court unless the other member nations agreed to our terms.

The isolationists now seized the initiative. Why, they asked, negotiate with the League just to risk the loss of American sovereignty? Why not encourage the codification of international law instead of perpetuating the League's own law as dispensed at The Hague? Friends of the Court tried to press Coolidge to break the deadlock, but he was impervious to their appeals. So complete was the Irreconcilable victory that neither party mentioned the Court in its 1928 platform. The issue, Franklin Roosevelt told a disappointed friend, had raised too much of a row to be safe political ammunition. (Roosevelt, of course, could not foresee that seven years later he would be President and a top-heavy Democratic Senate would defy him to to give the World Court movement in America the *coup de grâce*.) The internationalists, backed by the moderate Republicans, had used the Court as a battering-ram against the outer defenses of the Irreconcilables. They had bent the line slightly, only to be hurled back.

The proposal to cancel the Allied War Debts was not, in its earlier stages, a salient policy of the internationalists. Any suggestion to forgive foreign debts necessarily must have only limited appeal, and this was especially true during the twenties when the Allies were still making regular payments to the United States Treasury. The leaguists, moreover, were by no means all cancellationists, for Wilson himself had consistently regarded these debts as loans that had been tendered with the understanding that they would be repaid. There was, in addition, a prevalent feeling that the lenient interest rates granted by the United States to its debtors (in thirteen different debt settlements made between 1923 and 1926) were equivalent to the forgiving of a susbtantial part of the ten and one-third billion dollars that had been advanced. Politicians had promised their constituents that foreign repayments would make possible the magic of paying bonuses to veterans while Congress progressively reduced taxes. The question was neatly posed: should the American or European taxpayer be saddled with these debts?

Like so many other vital issues of those dulcet years, the debt problem had been dangerously oversimplified. Heavy private American loans to European countries plus investments in their securities and industries, which added to their war debt burden, resulted in staggering obligations. Inasmuch as a world currency did not exist, payments on these debts had to be made in goods, services, or gold. Older countries that previously had been world creditors had learned from experience that, to be paid, they had to buy the products of their debtors. The United States, however, rendered the European task of repayment almost impossible by virtually shutting out foreign commodities by a high protective tariff. Only a limited circle of men realized that we would have to purchase more foreign goods or relax our insistence on a full payment of war debts. Hence the pioneer cancellationists were either theoreticians or else bankers and investors who wanted to make private obligations more secure by urging Washington to show leniency to its debtors. Economists who suggested cancellation either were derided as classroom visionaries or denounced as kept hirelings of Wall Street. Even Herbert Hoover charged the international bankers with creating the delusion that payment of these debts would injure the United States more than it would the foreigners.

Such being the case, those internationalists who understood the problem usually thought it useless to urge cancellation. John H. Clarke hoped that the Washington authorities would show every consideration to our former Allies but admitted that the country stood unshaken in the demand that Europe pay its debts. The Democrats toyed with the possibility of challenging the Republican stand on the debts, but promptly dropped the issue as a hot potato. Adolph Ochs of the New York *Times* advised the Democratic leaders that only after a long, intensive campaign of education would it be possible to suggest that as a cold-blooded business proposition, the United States ultimately would get more money out of Europe by outright cancellation.

While the Wilsonians held their tongues in their cheeks, the isolationists added the war debt question to their arsenal of arguments. American money, they charged, had been used for foreign propaganda rather than for relief, and for building up armaments rather than for economic reconstruction. "Dog Borah," as the French liked to dub him, accused France of using American funds to promote aggressive militarism and to subsidize her eastern European satellites. The senator reminded his colleagues of the strong language of President Andrew Jackson when France unnecessarily delayed payment on American claims that she had promised to pay in an 1831 settlement. To the Buffalo newspaper columnist, Barnet Nover, the debt question was like a cat with nine lives, and each resuscitation of the issue deepened American resentment against an impenitent Europe.

The greatest blow to the loyal Wilsonians was neither the checkmating of their moves to outflank the isolationists, nor their inability to arouse the country from its dream-world reliance on seagirt security. All might have been well if they could have maintained control of the Democratic party, for the next political revolution would result in a change in our foreign policy. This hope, however, appeared doomed when the internationalists lost their ascendancy in the party of Woodrow Wilson. By 1928 Republican neo-isolationism had won tacit acceptance from the Democratic opposition. Strangely enough, this victory came at a time when the League's prestige was so high that most Americans hailed it as a capital device for keeping the peace among unruly outlanders. But the country was determined that our relationship with Geneva should continue to be of the common law variety, without blessing of a sealed agreement. The Republicans had won their point, and substantial difference in our foreign policy between the parties all but disappeared. The best that the leaguists could hope for from a Democratic triumph was a slightly more charitable appreciation of the League's problems and an increased amount of informal cooperation.

The internal history of the Democratic party in the 1920s affords a convenient rod for measuring the extent of the retreat from Wilsonian idealism. To be sure, the Democrats were glad to give aid and comfort to the pro-League people, for custom demanded help for any group that flayed the policies of the majority. The inner core of hard-headed politicians who dictated strategy, however, insisted on mending the party's seams even if such action meant appeasing the isolationists. When the 1920 debacle left the Democrats with only the Solid South intact, future victories depended upon winning back the northern and mid-western isolationist defectionists. The question was posed: had any member of Congress ever successfully appealed for votes on an outright pro-League platform? The answer was no, followed by the observation that countless local elections had been won by a contrary stand. That astute analyst of political trends, Samuel Lubell, has pointed out that the groundwork for the Democratic landslides of the Roosevelt era was laid by Alfred E. Smith when he attracted the support of newer immigrant groups that were heavily concentrated in vital urban voting areas. It would have been politically foolhardy for the party to have alienated some of these potential allies and to have rebuffed the old Irish and German Democrats by a straightforward League plank. The Democratic Bureau of Publicity denounced the timidity of the Republican foreign policy, but failed to spell out details of any proposed changes.

These facts were crystal-clear to the wizened Louis Mc-Henry Howe, Franklin Roosevelt's personal secretary and good genius, as he carefully planned his chief's political future. Howe discounted the popular appeal of internationalism, and insisted that the party cling only to issues that would bring victory at the polls. Always the political realist, Roosevelt early warned that the party must accept the fact that the United States was not in the League. In 1921, that trim product of the rough Tennessee country, Cordell Hull, took over the chairmanship of the Democratic National Committee. Although he shared Wilson's broad outlook on foreign affairs, he felt that insistence on American participation in the League would retard the party's recovery.

The Democratic National convention, which met in New York in 1924, revealed a three-way split on foreign policy. There was a small Irreconcilable faction led by James A. Reed, a much larger group of Wilsonians headed by former Secretary of War Newton D. Baker, and the great majority of delegates who were much more concerned with throwing the Republicans out of Washington than with putting the United States into the League. Baker made an impassioned appeal for the party to remain steadfast to Wilsonian principles, but he was beaten, two to one, in favor of a promise of American association with the League, contingent upon a national advisory referendum. The ensuing campaign clearly demonstrated that the Democrats offered no genuine alternative to G.O.P. neo-isolationism.

The resounding defeat of November, 1924 convinced the Democratic steersmen that it was necessary to free the party even more from the League encumbrance. Roosevelt, still in leisurely convalescence at Hyde Park, decided upon a personal inquest into the causes of the Election Day fiasco. He inquired of local politicos all over the country as to the causes of the overwhelming defeat and asked for their suggestions for the future. Some pro-League men blamed the party's gumshoe foreign policy plank, but more replies proposed that the rural nativist and urban Catholic segments of the party should be united under a Democratic isolationist banner. The farm vote, said a Mississippi correspondent, was entirely anti-League, and he added that "it would be well for our party hereafter to forget that proposition if we want to win."[15] It is significant that while many of the letters called for a return to Wilson's prewar domestic progressivism, relatively few replies advised retention of emphasis upon his contributions to foreign policy.

Roosevelt and Howe analyzed these letters with eyes fixed upon the party's future. They concluded that it would be best to avoid issues that were apt to promote serious discord. Howe advised that any new program must conform to the ancient Democratic insistence upon states' rights, for that would give local leaders greater leeway in explaining the issues to their own constituents. Both men privately conceded that Democratic prospects for a national victory were dim as long as the Republicans could claim prosperity. Looking ahead, however, they thought it salutary for the party to drop the kind of internationalist stand that had estranged farmers, hyphen groups, and blocs of urban immigrant voters. Even the stouthearted John H. Clarke admitted, in 1927, that the American people had no stomach for world leadership, and that his leaguist followers would have to be satisfied with something much more unpretentious than their original goal.

In the election year of 1928, Roosevelt tried to fashion a foreign policy plank upon which all Democrats could stand in comfort. He recognized that his party had been plagued by persisting antagonism between southern rural Protestants and northern urban Catholics. There was, moreover, the lingering aversion of the old Grover Cleveland conservatives for the progressives who had followed first William Jennings Bryan and later Woodrow Wilson. So deep was the cleavage between these segments on domestic issues that F.D.R. reasoned that foreign policy offered the best chance for any general agreement. His opportunity came when Hamilton Fish Armstrong invited him to write an article for *Foreign Affairs* as a companion piece to Under-Secretary of the Treasury Ogden L. Mills's defense of the Republican diplomatic record. As was to become his habit in his presidential years, Roosevelt drew on other minds for suggestions that he, in turn, weighed and wove together. He sent a preliminary draft of his work to Norman H. Davis. The critical comments of this Democratic strategist and former president of the Woodrow Wilson Foundation are most revealing. He advised that it was politically necessary for the Democrats to renounce any scheme of collective security backed by the use of force, or one that committed the United States to action in future unknown contingencies. This was stealing the G.O.P. thunder with a vengeance! Davis added rather weakly that the Republicans ought to be assailed for not acknowledging the League's many accomplishments and for cooperating with it only in a secretive and unconstitutional way.

The internationalists sensed the importance of the forthcoming article and tried to influence F.D.R. through Mrs. Roosevelt's friend Esther Lape. Walter Lippmann, then editor of the New York *World,* was doing penance for his 1919 anti-Wilson stand, and he tried to spur Roosevelt to boldness by pointed editorial remarks. But the squire of Hyde Park thought it time for bread and butter politics rather than heroics. He was certain that Smith would be the Democratic nominee and he knew that the New York governor had never given more than perfunctory obeisance to either Wilson or the League. The seaboard intelligentsia thought Smith a Bowery provincial, and Roosevelt was anxious to hold the internationalists among them in the party. He therefore wanted to say enough in the article to make the Democrats the lesser evil to the Wilsonians, and yet write nothing that would displease the Irish or any thirsty Germans who shared the governor's hatred of prohibition. To execute this sleight of hand, Roosevelt had to quibble about the League and the World Court. It would be beside the point, he declared, to agitate the question of formal American association. He did caution, however, that the belated Republican move to outlaw war might serve only to satisfy noble aspirations with something fanciful and unreal. Roosevelt saved his most stinging barbs for an attack on Republican Latin American imperialism. (He contradicted his own former enthusiasm for brass knuckle methods in the Caribbean, but he had already come to regard New World imperialism in a way that foreshadowed the Good Neighbor approach of the future.) Thus as an alternative to Republican neo-isolationism, all that he had to propose was American leadership in disarmament, official and wholehearted cooperation with the League, and an abstention from arbitrary intervention in the affairs of weaker nations.

Although the Smith forces were able to nominate their man without difficulty, the runner-up at the Democratic convention was Senator Reed, who based his candidacy on his struggle to keep American boys out of foreign graves. Every state in the union was represented on the Resolutions Committee; yet only Newton D. Baker, Carter Glass, and Josephus Daniels (F.D.R.'s superior in Wilson's Navy Department) urged a positive stand on either the League or the Court. The platform consequently ignored all mention of the Versailles peace mechanism, but it pledged the party to outlaw war while maintaining "freedom from entangling alliances with foreign nations." Baker lamented that Henry Cabot Lodge could have run on the Democratic foreign policy plank, and William McKinley on the party's domestic platform. Roosevelt, however, explained that it was far more important to elect friends of the World Court to Congress than to burden the platform with detrimental statements. "Glittering generalities would, on the whole," he explained, "lose fewer votes."[16] The most that the temper of the country would allow, he told a disheartened Wilsonian, would be to turn Coolidge's furtive League dealings into public and open cooperation. The Democrats appeared so safely isolationist, that the Kansas City *Star* happily relegated the League issue to the limbo of lost causes.

Starting from the contrary premises of 1920, it took the major parties eight years to arrive at a substantial agreement on foreign policy. One might even say that in 1928, the Republican aspirant, Herbert Hoover, was more internationally minded than his Democratic rival, Alfred E. Smith. All the propaganda, money, bustle, and devotion of the leaguists had failed to safeguard Wilson's ideals even in the house of the master. The internationalists had scattered many seeds in the schools and churches, on the lecture forum, and through the printed page, but these kernels were not to sprout until favored by a different climate of opinion. Their growth was retarded by the serene skies of the late twenties that gave small indication of the coming deluge.

Chapter 10

The Calm Before the Storm

TEN YEARS after the 1918 Armistice the new balance of power seemed in equipoise. The moderating attitudes of the French Foreign Minister, Aristide Briand, and the German Chancellor, Gustav Stresemann, had brought a welcome lull along the Rhine frontier. Mussolini's bellicose fulminations, so it was argued, were designed only to heighten the national consciousness of his easy-going Italians, and to assure the accuracy of train arrivals and departures. Comrade Stalin, who had just consolidated his power, had shelved plans to make the world safe for Communism in favor of an intensive program to make Soviet Russia economically self-sufficient. In the Far East, the victory of Chiang Kai-shek's Nationalist government gave birth to new hopes for Chinese stabilization. Few, if any, foresaw that China was soon to become the cockpit in the struggle between rival imperialisms and ideologies. To be sure, the Japanese warlords had already given the world a preview of their intentions, but the moderates soon regained control and were expected to abide by the terms of the Washington treaties.

Tolerance, a luxury of the new abundance, pervaded the atmosphere. It was an age of faith in paper—paper treaties, paper profits and paper stock certificates. In those roseate years of the late 1920s, most Americans agreed that the League of Nations was a superb idea for the rest of mankind. As for us, we ought to lend it every assistance, always provided that our patronage did not involve us in political wrangles or commit us to economic or military enforcement measures. This philosophy persisted until the depression and the onslaught of the dictators precipitated a new and even profounder isolationism.

There is an interesting contrast between the way the League won general acceptance in the United States and in Europe. On this side of the water, the collapse of the initial League fervor left only a hard-core minority loyal to the collective security cause. Europeans, however, knew the horrors of war from first-hand experience rather than from newspapers, and they clung to Geneva as the only hope of preventing another clash of arms. At first the life of the League hung by a thread, for the American rejection of the Covenant had been a severe blow. This initial crisis was passed, however, and the organs of the League began to function under the skillful guidance of Secretary-General Sir James Eric Drummond, who had learned the art of diplomacy in the British Foreign Office.

Drummond and his associates had to make a place for the League in a war-scarred, unstable, and rancorous world. They found it difficult to steer their frail vessel between the hazards of international hatreds and rivalries. In 1923 the League was tested and found wanting, when Mussolini, defying the Covenant, bombarded and landed troops on the Greek island of Corfu. The French occupation of the Ruhr, which occurred in the same year, also showed that the League could only stand by helplessly in a dispute that involved a major power.

Despite these defaults of the League's peace-preserving machinery, responsible European statesmen remained convinced of the necessity of international organization. In 1924, they tried to repair defects in the Covenant by a proposed Draft Treaty of Mutual Assistance that vested the Council with more power and made additional provisions for identifying and punishing an aggressor nation. In formulating the new plan, League statesmen tried to meet an American objection to the Covenant when they stipulated that member states were obliged to help execute sanctions only if the operations took place upon their own continent.

When this scheme proved unsuccessful, the League again tried to remedy its own defects by drawing up the 1924 Geneva Protocol for the Pacific Settlement of International Disputes. Henceforth, it was proposed, member nations would be forced to submit all disputes to pacific means of settlement before resorting to war. The Protocol also provided that any nation that refused to abide by its terms would, by that very fact, be branded an aggressor and restrained by the collective force of the other League countries. The Geneva Protocol received the unanimous endorsement of the League's Fifth Assembly and was submitted for international approval amidst considerable enthusiasm. Then a series of set-backs vitiated the project. The MacDonald Labour government that had favored the plan fell, the British Dominions were suspicious of the innovation, and the United States refused to show the slightest interest in any refinement of the Covenant's terms. Isolationism was not an exclusively American state of mind, for neither the new Tory ministry in London, nor the dominion governments wished to increase their international liabilities. The League's status was lowered considerably when the Protocol was rejected.

Help, however, now came from an unexpected quarter. On February 9, 1925, Chancellor Stresemann began the diplomatic maneuvers that were to culminate in the Peace of Locarno. In some respects this pact took the place of the ill-fated Protocol, for instead of committing themselves to act against would-be aggressors, the men of Locarno sought to preserve the territorial status quo in the West by specific guarantees, and tried to secure peace in eastern Europe by arbitration treaties between Germany and her neighboring states, Poland and Czechoslovakia. The pact was to become binding when Germany was admitted to the League, and was to remain in effect until the League Council decided that it was no longer necessary. Locarno was the high-water mark of the movement for collective security in the years between the wars.

In 1926, the prestige of the League soared, for Germany entered the Covenant and was assigned a permanent seat on the Council in recognition of its status as a first-class power. League enthusiasts had a double reason for rejoicing, for the Council had just averted hostilities between Greece and Bulgaria by settling an ugly border quarrel. Geneva began to assume the trappings of a world capital, and Assembly meetings at the Palace of Nations sparkled with the presence of illustrious statesmen. These were indeed the halcyon days of the League. It had proved to the world that it could handle small disputes between large states and large disputes between small states. Skeptics suspended judgment, pending the ultimate proof that Geneva could settle vital differences between major powers, but optimists believed with Nicholas Murray Butler "that, come what will, the old order shall not be restored."[1]

As the League began to prove its worth, it became apparent that while the United States was willing to support Geneva's auxiliary work, the Washington authorities would spurn all appeals to help the League perfect and tighten provisions for collective security. We approved of the sideshows, but were cool to the performance in the main tent. Thus Secretary Hughes made it clear that the neo-isolationist démarche confined the interests of the United States to those League actions unrelated to the Covenant's avowed purpose—the preservation of peace through collective action. It was to take the Republicans some years to realize that Wilson's scheme might serve American interests by keeping the peace in other hemispheres.

Hence all League overtures to the United States relating to

the paramount problem of collective security were rebuffed. We bluntly refused to consider a proposal to strengthen international control over the private production of and trade in armaments. When the State Department was told of the proposed 1923 Draft Treaty of Mutual Assistance, Hughes allowed five months to elapse before he replied that inasmuch as we were not members of the League, constitutional limitations forbade assent. In drawing up the 1924 Geneva Protocol, the League authorities tried to invite the interest of the United States by limiting the responsibility of each state for the enforcement of sanctions in the light of its particular geography and armament situation. Yet when the British ambassador broached the matter to Hughes, he got more than a flat refusal. The Secretary told him coldly that the proposed agreement might jeopardize the neutrality of the United States if the League ever applied economic coercion against a state with which we enjoyed friendly trade relations. It is entirely possible that all of these plans would have come to naught even had the United States viewed them with favor, but its unbending hostility to the use of force in curbing aggression helped to frustrate the League's main purpose.

Meanwhile, private organizations and American citizens were lending valuable assistance to many of Geneva's projects. By 1924, the Rockefeller Foundation had already given $500,-000 to the League's Health Service, while other American funds helped support the publication of treaties, Albanian and Near Eastern Relief, and the work of the White Slave Inquiry. Americans, after getting a nod of approval from the State Department, furnished expert advice on straightening out boundary tangles and clearing up financial muddles. Legal experts worked on the codification of international law under League auspices, and eminent American jurists (Hughes was later to be included among them) sat in succession on the World Court bench. All of these activities were useful and important, but a humanitarian program would be of only ephemeral value unless the League could prevent aggression. To this major task the United States gave no assistance and, for a while, it even disparaged the effort. Because this country failed to support repeated League undertakings to prevent national onslaughts, it helped create those world conditions that made possible the Fascist attack.

The prevalent American contention that the collective use of force could not insure peace was so strong that it even permeated the thinking of the Wilsonians. Prominent leaguists who tried for the 1924 Bok Award either played down or carefully camouflaged security provisions in their peace blueprints. Professor Manley O. Hudson of Harvard (ardent internationalist who was later to become a World Court judge) submitted a draft which guaranteed that the United States would never have to send troops abroad to maintain peace.[2] The winning essay of Charles H. Levermore conceded that practical experience had proved the force provisions of the Covenant unworkable. The concept of peace through coercion, he argued, must give way in favor of an international interdependence that would be sanctioned by moral suasion and world public opinion.

Examining the workings of the Covenant from a ringside seat at the University of Geneva in 1925, Professor William E. Rappard pointed out that there were, so to speak, three leagues: A League to Enforce Peace, a League to Execute the Peace Treaties, and a League to Promote International Cooperation. The Republican statesmen had discerned this separation of functions even before Rappard, and determined that the United States would participate only in the League's work to further joint action in humanitarian endeavors. Thus we accepted practically all invitations to take part in conferences that discussed economic and technical matters or social reform, while we carefully refrained from any association that might involve political decisions. Such cooperation, favored by all but the ultraists, denied Wilson's major premise that the League's *raison d'être* was the enforcement of peace. By viewing the League's functions in the light of their own philosophy, the neo-isolationists could participate in some of its work, and yet remain true to President Washington's admonition to keep clear of Europe's quarrels and power combinations. If the other nations still insisted upon experimenting with collective security, well and good, but the United States would continue to rely upon ordinary diplomacy, treaties of arbitration and conciliation, neutrality and its ocean insulators to fend off war. It was a delicate compromise, but it was to be a highly popular one until the international equilibrium was upset by the cataclysmic events of the 1930s.

A benign and patronizing attitude toward Geneva prevailed in the years immediately preceding the Great Depression. To the new, placid Europe the League seemed indigenous, and it proved so useful to Washington that some men on Capitol Hill grumbled that we were members in all but name. But the Irreconcilables had cried wolf too often for their warnings to be taken seriously. After all, back in 1919 a majority of the people, including senators, had favored going into the

League with qualifications which would safeguard American freedom of action. The great majority of these one-time reservationists now hailed the working agreement with the League. Some isolationists of the nationalist stripe had become less parochial, thanks to the boom in world trade that had increased their opportunities for foreign contracts. Liberal opposition to Geneva declined sharply after a German representative was seated on the Council, for reasonable men could no longer maintain that the League was merely a surrogate for the Allies, commissioned to execute judgment upon the vanquished.

Striking evidence of American willingness to give the League belated endorsement is to be found in the volte-face of some of Wilson's leading critics. The die-hards, of course, were never won over, but an impressive group of former critics veered around to hail Geneva's accomplishments. Among them was Elihu Root, who had coached the original Irreconcilables on the defects of the Convenant. Later Root drafted the statement of the Thirty-One which called for the election of Harding and entry into the League with the objectionable Article X struck from the Covenant. Root, unlike most of his thirty associates, refused to accept Republican neo-isolationism as adequate fulfillment of the party's 1920 pledges on foreign policy. He bluntly told President Coolidge that it was bad enough for the United States to have handicapped the League by rejecting the Covenant, but that it was absolutely hideous for us now "to hate it and condemn it and try to injure it."[3] In 1926 the Woodrow Wilson Foundation honored this elder statesman by recognizing his services in establishing the World Court. Root took the occasion to speak some sharp words to the country. Geneva and The Hague, he said, were the foremost contributions ever made to the cause of peace, and yet the United States had stubbornly refused to show the slightest sympathy or friendship for these organizations as they groped with the greatest problem that beset mankind. The American people, he charged, were so blinded by unreasoned prejudice that they had kept the government from its proper obligations to the rest of the world. Abundance and prosperity, he warned, would not save the soul of a nation that sat back and mocked while others taught the world to think in terms of peace rather than war.

During the debate over the Versailles treaty, Nicholas Murray Butler had been a harsh critic of Wilson and had acted as counselor to the Republican strategists. For a short while he seemed to have had the ear of President Harding to whom he sent confidential reports from Europe. As president of the Carnegie Endowment, however, Butler became the country's most indefatigable internationalist. While authentic Wilsonians lost faith in collective security, Butler was persuaded that only an international organization, wielding a big stick, could pacify the world. Like Root, he indicted the Republicans for abandoning the League without providing an adequate substitute. Butler asked himself whence sprang this isolationist taboo? A small, inner voice must have answered that one President Butler of Columbia University had helped revive this ancient prejudice in the year of decision after the Armistice. In 1927, he lamented that any chance for full American participation in the world's peace experiment had passed beyond recall. It therefore behooved us all the more, he declared, to support the League's program, strengthen its hands, and applaud its mounting successes.[4]

Charles A. Beard joined in this re-evaluation of the League's worth. In 1928, he thought that Geneva's fortunes had taken a sharp turn for the better. "If the devastations of war are to be prevented," he wrote, "then nations must associate themselves in understandings and guarantees. No doubt, the magnitude and difficulties of this undertaking are immense, but the League of Nations and treaties of renunciation [of war] already indicate what the strategy of peace may be."[5] He summarily dismissed isolationism as a myth rather than a fact and declared the United States a member of the League even without the benefit of "parchment and seals."[6] The temporary brightening of the international picture restored some of Beard's former faith in the possibility of uniting the nations. However, when the depression intensified the need for far-reaching home reforms, and dictators made a travesty of the Covenant, Beard championed a rigorous continental solution for America's domestic and foreign policies. He was to become the chief oracle of the incorrigible isolationists.

In the imperturbable years of the later twenties even Villard and Croly relented. The Versailles peace mechanism, the *Nation* acknowledged, had chastened the conduct of diplomatic affairs. The *New Republic* became even more reconciled to the League, and Croly turned to Geneva in the hope that it would ease the remaining world tensions. Edson L. Whitney, president of the century-old American Peace Society, admitted that his organization had been remiss in paying tribute to the more constructive aspects of President Wilson's handiwork. And, singularly enough, Professor Edwin M. Borchard of Yale, already on his way to fame as the foremost legalistic vindicator of isolationism, mellowed to the point where he hoped that the League would survive and prosper.[7] Unfortunately, all of this benevolence was to prove as fleeting as the prosperity and calm that generated it.

For many years now we have taken Herbert Hoover's irrevocable isolationism for granted. When he became President in 1929, however, his foreign policy statements reflected the dominant principles of the more restrained internationalists. Thus he urged full participation in the League's efforts to control the narcotics trade, to devise uniform regulations for international sea and air traffic and radio communication, to abolish the vestiges of human slavery, and to protect the world's esthetic treasures. Hoover admitted that the United States had shirked its responsibility in securing global peace, and he was eager to further all non-coercive designs to prevent war. But there the Quaker President insisted on calling a halt. He felt that Europe was a meshwork of ingrained hatreds, rival imperialisms, hostile alliances, and volatile armament build-ups. Thus he insisted that we refrain from any League associations that could conceivably commit us to the use of force in the event that these foreign powder-kegs exploded.[8]

Even in those flush years there were many people outside of the Irreconcilable ranks who continued to question the League's practicability. The meetings at the Geneva Palace of the Nations indeed had become brilliant affairs, but the absence of those strange isolationist partners, the United States and Russia, served as a pointed reminder to many that the organization was not catholic in nature. The Eighth Assembly's 1927 gathering was darkened by a threatening Balkan crisis. As was their wont, American lampooners of the League's pacification machinery now demanded miracles from the Council at the first rumblings of war thunder. The minor crisis passed and the skies again cleared. But the Foreign Policy Association warned, on the occasion of its tenth anniversary in 1929, that four years after the Locarno truce Europe remained armed to the teeth and that Big Navy talk in the United States was more rampant than ever.

Some scholars and general writers, perhaps realizing the growing confidence in the League's ability to restrict war, made a point of reemphasizing our isolationist advantages. Professor Samuel F. Bemis, the future dean of American diplomatic historians, explored the origins of our foreign policy and thought it wise to stress the words of John Adams that "it ought to be our rule not to meddle."[9] The veteran historian,

William MacDonald, advised Americans to keep on minding their own business and to be on guard against the wiles of a "sublimated League" and its "glorified Secretariat."[10] John Carter, a much traveled journalist who also had some practical diplomatic experience, said that the United States had, after all, gained one real victory from the war—an enhanced appreciation of our deep ocean moats. He thought that we ought to keep our unofficial observers at Geneva, for this periscopic view of European chicanery was necessary as a perpetual warning to maintain our own separate existence.

In spite of these misgivings, however, America had become increasingly hopeful about the future of world stability. The earlier distrust in collective security had given way to a feeling that it was salutary for foreigners to have some method of curbing their own turbulence. Americans, generally speaking, had re-evaluated the League and reached the following conclusions: all but one potential trouble maker, Russia, were now bound by the terms of the Covenant; in the fullness of time, Geneva would be able to localize all European disputes, and while such questions would be of no immediate concern to us, we would benefit from a diminution of the possibility of general war; hemispheric problems could be handled on this side of the water without any help from outside; the terms of the Washington treaties would prevent eruptions in the Far East.

By an irony of history the spirit of Theodore Roosevelt rather than Woodrow Wilson hovered over this American *rapprochement* with the League. For Roosevelt's suggestion that the world be divided into regions with different security provisions for each part had replaced Wilson's concept of a central clearing-house for all international complications.

The country had stumbled upon this Rooseveltian formula by accident rather than design, for most men had long since forgotten the Rough Rider's parting advice. Rediscovery of his plan resulted from the desire to be of the League and yet not in it. America insisted that it could best serve the world by keeping its hands unfettered and using its own good judgment as to when humanity needed saving. This presumption of moral superiority placed definite limitations on our cooperation with the League. Time was to prove that mass opinion, to which democratic statesmen must yield, would not sanction preventive measures, until the future of civilization itself hung in the balance. Had Americans of the 1930s believed in the collective enforcement of peace, we might have been in a shooting war long before Pearl Harbor. In retrospect, timely, limited action might have proven far less costly than our tremendous sacrifices during the Second World War.

Nevertheless, long before the Axis threat developed, the American conscience showed signs of uneasiness. How could the country that considered itself a paragon for the rest of the world reject membership in the most promising experiment ever devised to prevent war? We tried to resolve this quandary by busying ourselves with substitutes for the collective security that we had abjured. Thus, in the early 1920s we promoted disarmament with ephemeral success, and, at the end of the decade, we blundered into a pact to outlaw war that had been carefully pared beforehand of positive commitments.

Three months to a day before the stock market collapse ushered in the long depression, President Hoover proclaimed the Kellogg-Briand Pact. This over-advertised panacea was dispensed to the world just as the twin bubbles of prosperity and international *bonhomie* were about to burst. The outlawry of war, one of many American peace nostrums of the 1920s, had the good fortune to be launched by tenacious sponsors, and to be saved from oblivion by fortuitous circumstances. Certain inherent features of the plan made it agreeable to many different groups. It permitted Americans to reconcile, simultaneously, two incompatible longings—the preservation of the tradition of non-entanglement, and the desire to seize the initiative in the move for peace. The simplicity of the proposition made it intelligible to the masses, while its anti-war overtones appealed to those who were searching for a peace plan devoid of coercion. It was unique in that it was attractive to both isolationists and internationalists. This explains why the outlawry movement triumphed over its rivals and was eventually presented to the world for endorsement.

Salmon O. Levinson, a Chicago attorney who was expert in restoring ailing corporations to health, first enunciated the theory contained in the Kellogg-Briand Pact. Reflecting upon the current devastation, Levinson was amazed to find, in 1918, that international law did not forbid war. He therefore assumed that the law of nations sanctioned the right of countries to resort to armed force. Levinson failed to grasp that war was neither legal nor illegal, but a non-legal state of affairs the effects of which international law had tried to ameliorate.[11] In characteristically American fashion, he sought to root out an evil institution by legislative action. He coined the captivating slogan "outlawry of war," and popularized the idea by drawing upon his abundant store of energy and his well-filled pocketbook.

At the outset, Levinson tried to interest pro- and anti-League groups then locked in contest over the Treaty of Versailles. Both sides thought that they could use the Chicago attorney's brainchild to their advantage. The Wilsonians reasoned that if the nations renounced war, the sole right to use coercion must devolve upon the League. Some of the isolationists, on the other hand, welcomed the plan as still another possible substitute for Wilson's Covenant. This dichotomy among the outlawry enthusiasts was to hamper the movement for many years. Meanwhile, the American Committee for the Outlawry of War was organized just in time to present its views to the 1100 members of the 1921-1922 Washington Naval Conference.

During the early twenties, the movement divided into an anti-League Chicago branch led by Levinson and a New York offshoot headed by a staunch Wilsonian, Professor James T. Shotwell of the Columbia history department. The Levinson wing received the blessing of outstanding isolationists. Senator Borah agreed to press the plan in Congress only after he concluded that the outlawry of war could be enforced by universal public opinion and without recourse to the use of force against refractory states. John Haynes Holmes and Charles Clayton Morrison labored in the vineyard of the Lord, while John Dewey did missionary work among the secularists. "If the moral conviction of the world will not restrain a nation from resort to war," said the philosopher, "the world will not get rid of war under any system."[12] In an era when it was customary for liberals to suspend judgment on moot questions until John Dewey had spoken, his endorsement gave a fillip to any cause. Colonel Raymond Robins, a veteran of the Yukon diggings with a flair for evangelical oratory, spread the outlawry gospel in reform and uplift circles. The advocates of Levinson's doctrine now formed one of the most ebullient and persevering pressure groups in the country.

Time and again, the unity of the coalition was threatened by the exasperating question of whether it wanted to buttress the League peace machinery or to replace it. This split was clearly revealed in the protracted debates over the World Court. While Borah tried to shun The Hague proposal for the outlawry plan, Shotwell roused popular support for joining the Court. During the impasse that followed the Senate adherence to the Protocol, Borah again broached the Levinson plan in Congress. His efforts failed, and the movement was languishing badly when James T. Shotwell saved it by a master stroke.

On March 22, 1927, Shotwell and Albert Thomas, director of the International Labor Organization, were received by the French Foreign Minister, Aristide Briand. The Columbia historian promptly suggested that the first step toward a general renunciation of war ought to be a bilateral treaty between France and the United States. Shotwell not only urged Briand to act, but himself drafted a proposed message to America. On April 6, 1927 (the tenth anniversary of American intervention) Briand transmitted his proposal to the United States through the Associated Press, suggesting that war between the two countries should be declared unlawful. The battle for the acceptance of Levinson's proposal now entered its final stage.

President Coolidge and Secretary Kellogg read Briand's offer with scant enthusiasm and many misgivings. They disliked the way in which the Frenchman had by-passed official channels to appeal to the people. Besides they were in an unreceptive mood, for they were smarting over a recent French refusal to attend a disarmament meeting, and irked at Paris's cavalier attitude toward the American war debt. In addition, Briand's proposal might restrict freedom of action in a future war, for the world would know that America could intervene only on the side of France and not against her. (There is presumptive, but not conclusive evidence, that Briand was seeking to bind the United States, even in this indirect way, to the network of alliances that France had built up with five minor powers.) Kellogg was inclined to pigeon-hole the invitation.

The outlawry bandwagon, however, had picked up too much momentum to be so summarily halted. In the New York *Times,* Nicholas Murray Butler drew up a scathing bill of indictment against the State Department. Levinson sent frantic cables from Paris, and Colonel Robins used his personal influence with the President. Under pressure from all sides, Kellogg reluctantly agreed to discuss the matter. Then fate intervened once more, for Lindbergh's epoch-making flight to Paris (May 20-21, 1927) engendered a new cordiality between the United States and France. Briand acted promptly and, on June 20, handed the United States Ambassador the draft of a suggested treaty, the wording of which was to be used later in the celebrated Pact of Paris.

The Washington authorities, however, were still hesitant, and it took them over six months to answer Briand. But the public had been aroused and demanded action. Kellogg, after consultation with the Senate Foreign Relations Committee, found that there was a way out of the dilemma that might be created by a bilateral no-war treaty. Why not negotiate a multilateral treaty that would extend the benefits of outlawry to the whole world? "That's the best way to get rid of the damn thing," said George Moses cheerily. "France would never consent to outlaw war with Germany," he added.[13] But he was wrong, for Kellogg was now enthusiastic, and was pushing the treaty vigorously. Briand did not like this expanded proposal, but he gave it provisional acceptance, and the other major powers were taken into the discussions. On August 27, 1928, the Pact of Paris, which renounced war as an instrument of national policy, was signed with éclat by the representatives of fifteen countries gathered in the French capital. Ultimately, the pact was ratified by almost the entire roster of nations, including those powers which so soon were to perfect the art of aggression.

As it became obvious that Kellogg was in dead earnest, peace organizations that had hitherto derided the outlawry motion were anxious to join in a winning cause. The pro-League groups, thinking that the isolationist guard was down, tried to thrust forward, using outlawry as a spear. If the use of force were renounced by individual nations, the Wilsonians reasoned, then the world would have to provide another way of settling crucial disputes. And what was more logical than to use the existing peace machinery for this purpose? If the outlawry of war was to be more than an empty phrase, at the very least, the United States would have to cooperate with Geneva in sanctions leveled against a branded aggressor.

The leaguists were reading far too much into the administration's intentions. Secretary Kellogg explained that all that was necessary was a fresh series of arbitration treaties to supersede war as a method of handling serious disagreements. The Wilsonians insisted, nevertheless, that only an international body could distinguish between an illegitimate attack and the kind of defensive action which would still be permissible. Newton D. Baker pointed out that if the Pact were to be of any value, the signatory nations must abandon a policy of neutrality, for in any future war one side would be publicly denounced as the assailant. Given the proposition that war was illegal, the corollary seemed to follow that war-making nations must be halted and punished. At this time, the League was at the height of its prestige and it seemed reasonable to suppose that its constituent members would insist that Geneva be designated to name and chastise aggressors. With the decision of the Coolidge administration to press for the renunciation of war, the internationalists thought they saw a splendid opportunity to rid themselves of isolationism. Their idealistic minds refused to comprehend that the powers, under American leadership, were merely subscribing to a pious statement, without any intention of making the material commitments necessary to enforce so radical a prescript.

While the internationalists were beguiling themselves with dreams of a new world order, the isolationists were repeatedly promised that the treaty meant something considerably less than the words of the text seemed to imply. During the course of the negotiations, Kellogg made certain that the United States would assume no obligations arising from the Locarno treaty or other existing agreements. The Secretary warned buoyant members of the Council on Foreign Relations against millennial thinking, for, he said, the Pact was merely a long stride in the direction of ultimate peace. He pledged that force would never be used to carry out its terms, for its use would convert the Pact into a dangerous military alliance. Nor would he agree to define aggression in the treaty, for this, he insisted, would qualify and weaken its words. It should have been clear to his audience that the Secretary contemplated no departure whatsoever from the American tradition of non-entanglement.

To Kellogg's credit it must be said that he did not try to overstate the case for outlawry, and he did his best to keep the proposal from being bandied around in the 1928 presidential campaign. But he expected too much from his own party, for the Republicans were in need of an exhibit to offset Democratic charges leveled against their unimaginative diplomacy. So the Pact was proudly incorporated into the party's platform, and to use a *bon mot* of Professor Bemis, the Republicans could now feel that they had "outcovenanted" Woodrow Wilson. There was little to argue about, however, for the Democrats quickly followed suit and also promised to outlaw war. President Coolidge overcame his initial aversion to the scheme and praised it in a speech urging Hoover's election. By December, Coolidge was sufficiently enthusiastic to tell Congress that the "observance of this Covenant . . . promises more for the peace of the world than any other agreement ever negotiated among the nations."[14] The President was anxious to come in for at least part of the credit for this popular bid for peace.

After Kellogg had digested the replies of the foreign ministers to his proposal to renounce war, it became apparent to him that they were not willing to take the principle at face value. The Secretary consented to France's qualification that the Pact should be so construed as to permit wars in self-defense and military action taken to honor obligations arising

214

from the Covenant, the Locarno guarantees, or her postwar treaties of alliance. A violation of the Pact by one party, said the French, must free the hands of the others. Nor did Kellogg demur when the British not only said that they must live up to their existing obligations, but added that His Majesty's Government found it necessary to insist on full freedom of action in "certain regions of the world the welfare and integrity of which constitute the special and vital interest for our peace and safety." As a quipster later put it, the outlawry treaty became the most comprehensive agreement ever enacted to legalize certain categories of war!

Kellogg still had to answer to the inquisitorial Senate Foreign Relations Committee. Chairman Borah was duly assured that the United States would not be embarrassed in defending its special Caribbean interests. Despite the fact that he had long championed the renunciation of war, Borah demanded additional guarantees that, come what may, there could be no moral obligation on the part of the United States to help any victimized country. Kellogg assented once more, reminding the senator that "this is the only kind of a treaty, as you have always said, that we can possibly sign."[15] International good will alone was to sanction the fiat against war.

Realism is not an exclusive endowment of our own cynical generation. It would be highly misleading to wrench a few fine words out of context and thus infer that either many senators or any considerable number of their constituents believed that a piece of parchment adorned with imposing seals would bring a universal "Truce of God." There were men who kept their tongues in their cheeks, there were others who favored the treaty solely for political or diplomatic reasons, and there were some who tried to sneer down the proposal. Among the isolationists, David Jayne Hill said that outlawry was not only preposterous, but also unconstitutional. Professor Borchard demanded to know which nation had ever acknowledged war as an instrument of its national policy. He said that the Wilsonians were perfectly correct in saying that if the United States meant the Pact to be enforced, we would have to marry ourselves to the League. If, on the other hand, we had no intention of backing our words with action then we were inviting misunderstanding and recrimination. John Carter dismissed the Pact as an epitome of national selfishness. Even Borah confessed he thought the plan essentially part of a campaign of education for peace. The agreement, he admitted, might fail to prevent battles, but henceforth war would at least be a criminal action, prohibited by international law.

The internationalists made little effort to conceal their chagrin as the Pact was emasculated by understandings, qualifications, and interpretations. "Does anyone believe," asked Kirby Page, who described himself as a social evangelist, "that the aggressive designs of Mussolini could be checked merely by the good faith of the Italian people and the power of public opinion?"[16] The pages of history books are replete with accounts of treaties promising everlasting peace between the contracting parties, observed Professor Manley O. Hudson, Harvard luminary on international law. In spite of all these shortcomings, there was an overriding popular demand that the Senate approve this well-meant peace experiment that might possibly do some good and, at worst, little harm. Nicholas Murray Butler had long scoffed at Levinson, but he now crusaded for outlawry with all the zeal of a convert. He wanted to define an aggressor nation as one that began hostilities in defiance of promises to submit its disputes to pacific means of settlement.

By the time the Pact of Paris reached the Senate floor in December, 1928, Kellogg's reassurances had limited the opposition to the Big Navy men, some Irreconcilables more uncompromising than Borah, and a handful of outspoken realists. The Secretary had done his utmost to placate even the remaining dissenters. The navalists were promised that the Pact did not bear upon disarmament, and that its approval would not impede the passage of the cruiser bill then up for debate. But even a vis à vis talk between Kellogg and Colonel Robert McCormick was of no avail. The Chicago *Tribune* lamented that in signing the Pact, the United States was like Samson "walking into the barber shop." Our burgeoning world trade and unmatched economic position, it argued, could be maintained only by strength of arms. To renounce war publicly was thus equivalent to telling our debtors that they could tear up their notes with equanimity. Britain and France, the *Tribune* predicted, would be wise enough in the ways of the world to keep their military forces unimpaired, but the American pacifist lobby would use the Pact as still another pretext for disarmament.

The die-hard Irreconcilables fought doggedly. According to Senator John J. Blaine of Wisconsin, our assent to the British qualification put the American stamp of approval upon His Majesty's imperialist designs. The only real road to peace, said Tennessee's old-fogyish Kenneth McKellar, lay in building up a navy to match the British fleet.[17] Representative George Holden Tinkham, a New England old-timer, said that it was all very simple: the international bankers were once again trying to unlock the back door to the League. Senators Moses and Reed resorted to the old isolationist stratagem of insisting on precise reservations to the Pact that would insure American separation from European politics.

This opposition was effectively quelled by last-minute concessions and White House influence. Kellogg had testified at hearings of the Committee on Foreign Relations before the bill was reported. He revealed that the other nations had been warned that the United States refused to assume any obligations of enforcement or to promise help to any nations that might be attacked. Senator Walsh of Montana asked: "Supposing some other nation does break this treaty; why should we interest ourselves in it?" "There is not a bit of reason," Kellogg snapped back.[18]

The Foreign Relations Committee reported the Pact favorably to the Senate, with the following understandings in lieu of formal reservations: 1—There was no impairment of the right to self-defense, and each nation was to judge the necessity for such action; 2—The enforcement of the Monroe Doctrine was a component part of American self-defense; 3—The United States would assume no obligations to enforce the Pact against would-be violators. These were now to be added to the European qualifications that had already divested the agreement of much of its vitality.

Ironically enough, Borah had to argue for a place for the Pact on the Senate calendar with proponents of a bill calling for the construction of fifteen 10,000-ton cruisers. Borah won his point to get on with the outlawry of war before building up the navy, but he ended by supporting both measures. He carefully explained his committee's recommendation and gave his pledge that the country was not committed in any way in event of a breach of the Pact. The resistant forces, however, still clamored for reservations and, for a while, it looked as if they would carry the Senate. Then Coolidge appealed to Vice-President Charles G. Dawes for help. With a straight face, "Hell and Maria" Dawes told the senators that the outlawry of war and the cruiser bill formed an integrated American policy and that he considered formal reservations to the Pact superfluous.

Meantime, an avalanche of petitions fell upon the senators, and the opposition yielded. It was agreed that the Senate, besides consenting to the Pact, would formally adopt the report of the Foreign Relations Committee so as to place additional emphasis upon the understandings. "I am not willing," said

Senator Carter Glass who must have voiced the sentiments of many a less presumptuous colleague, "that anybody in Virginia shall think that I am simple enough to suppose that it is worth a postage stamp in the direction of accomplishing permanent peace. . . . But I am going to be simple enough, along with the balance of you, to vote for the ratification of this worthless, but perfectly harmless peace treaty."[19] And so the Senate consented to the Pact, 85 to 1 (Senator Blaine voting nay) and took up the next item on the calendar—a bill to appropriate $270,000,000 to build fifteen cruisers that were destined to sail the most war-plagued seas in human history.

The Kellogg-Briand Pact has often been depicted as a supreme isolationist achievement. Laden with interpretations and qualifications, the treaty itself was little more than a scrap of paper, while the Senate's publicized declaration of its understandings summarized the tenets of isolationism. Certainly a majority of the senators voted for the Pact in the belief that it was in accord with their contention that the United States could enjoy the blessings of peace without assuming any obligations for world order. The 1928 Democratic candidate for Vice-President, Senator Joseph T. Robinson of Arkansas told a London audience that the American espousal of outlawry was motivated by the twin desires to keep clear of foreign involvements and to assume no burdens in enforcing the peace. It was widely assumed that the Pact supplanted that part of the League Covenant that sought to maintain peace by police methods.

Viewed in perspective, however, the Pact of Paris marked a parting of the ways. Henceforth aggression was outlawed, and future events were to demonstrate how difficult it would be to maintain neutrality when one side was a law-breaking attacker and the other his innocent victim. Despite the forethought of Kellogg, Borah, and other protagonists of the scheme, the international renunciation of war did establish a close affinity between the United States and the Versailles peace mechanism. No amount of advance protestations could absolve the country from some degree of moral obligation to support the League in its attempts to halt aggression.[20]

The Kellogg-Briand Pact was a manifestation of the current American conviction that the presence of world opinion could keep the peace. We were willing to test this quixotic hypothesis because we believed that whether or not it proved valid, our own boundaries were inviolable. Perhaps it was fortunate that the experiment was tried, for its stupendous failure helped make us aware of the kind of world in which we really live.

Chapter 11

The Isolationist Tornado

ON SEPTEMBER 3, 1929, the great bull market reached its apex. It was Tuesday, the day after Labor Day, and all over the country Americans were basking in the serene fall atmosphere. If some among them were tempted to speculate about the future of United States foreign policy, they were justified in anticipating a gradual ebbing of the isolationist tide. America's booming economy had multiplied its business ties with other nations. Trade and finance had made the world our partner in the new prosperity. It seemed reasonable to suppose that, in time, our political aloofness would vanish, for a predominantly commercial power could not overlook the necessity of peace for itself and its customers.

The bursting of the stock market bubble (October, 1929) set in motion a chain of events that destroyed the international community of interests and engendered an exacerbated isolationism. American statesmen of the 1930s were confronted by an isolationist tornado. Like its physical counterpart, this whirlwind of sentiment was preceded by calm weather. The first warning was the heavy, oppressive antiforeign air that came with the business slump. When the big wind hit with terrific force, all but the most rash internationalists crawled into their cyclone cellars where they found the good company of Franklin D. Roosevelt and Cordell Hull. Here they remained until they were crowded out by the menacing flood-waters of aggression. They emerged to brave the isolationist storm, and to rouse the country to the totalitarian peril. The going was hard, but they made steady progress until the counter-blast of the bombs dropped over Pearl Harbor abated with the winds of domestic opposition.

The isolationism of the 1930s was much more profound than the rather superficial detachment of the preceding decade. There were greater numbers of isolationists in 1935 than in 1925, and they were more intense in their convictions, evincing less tolerance of dissent. Human beings react to immediate danger more violently than to conjectural threats; the localized fighting of the 1920s never implied the necessity for American intervention. Thus the only issue at stake was whether to join a system of collective security that some day might conceivably call for armed help. After 1931, however, the emergency was at hand and a decision in favor of internationalism might well have meant the disruption of family life in order to maintain world peace. This made the debates significant to the anonymous masses who were prone to think in short-run terms and were understandably anxious to postpone unpleasant decisions. Isolationism always becomes virulent when armed intervention is imminent, for the policy promises a reprieve from the horrors of war. While isolationism in time of acute international crisis becomes a mass movement, it is then that it is most vulnerable, for it is far easier to isolate a country from a League of Nations than from the repercussions of modern war.

From Wilson to Hoover the isolationists successfully defended their position against the proposals of the extreme internationalists. In the 1930s, with the primary reverberations of a new war under way, the isolationists took the offensive. "Keep out of war" now superseded "Keep out of the League." The newly activated isolationism differed in many ways from the older, relaxed variety. It embraced more than political separation when it succeeded in writing a species of economic isolationism into law. The later isolationists were usually hemispherists rather than continentalists, thinking in terms of a voluntary cooperation of all New World nations desirous of keeping clear of European and Asiatic wars. (It was Franklin Roosevelt, fresh from the success of his Good Neighbor policy toward Latin America, who was chiefly responsible for this tendency to think in hemispheric terms.) Although the pre-Pearl Harbor non-interventionists opposed a military build-up designed for foreign crusades, they conceded the necessity of standing vigilant guard over our two oceans. The quixotic belief had vanished that a smiling Providence, geographical remoteness, and an innocuous foreign policy would be enough to keep the country out of war. The new isolationism, like the New Deal economy of the same years, was planned, dynamic, positive, experimental, and highly debatable. All the old smoldering prejudices were fanned anew by the ill winds blowing across the seas. Little more was said of Columbia's mission to stand with hands unfettered, free to help suffering humanity. Every country was for itself in the harsh, brutal, hungry years of the thirties.

Two preponderant factors brought about this glorified isolationism. *First,* there was the impact of the Great Depression. Oddly enough, this world panic that did so much to intensify economic isolationism was partly caused by the reverse policy of American business expansionism. Ever since the Armistice, foreign economic pumps had been primed by American capital. When the New York money market tightened, putting an end to easy lending, foreign nations could no longer borrow dollars to buy American goods and pay their war debt installments to Washington. The golden chain of prosperity snapped at its weakest link—the constant flow of American money abroad. As our first great venture in foreign lending came to an end, a business paralysis spread throughout the world.

Soon Americans had new and very convincing material reasons to confirm their innate suspicions of foreign depravity. The two and a quarter billions of dollars gambled on the future of German stability, dwindled to almost nothing.[1] As the pall of depression covered the earth, each country tried to save its own economy at the expense of its neighbors. Tariff walls were raised, currencies were manipulated, and national recovery programs were launched. The head-long action of one nation forced the other to reciprocate in kind. International action to speed recovery proved as futile as international cooperation to guarantee peace. In almost every country, and especially in the United States, foreigners were blamed for their narrow self-regard. The pot could not see that it was as black as the kettle.

The depression was less than a year old when Congress raised the tariff rates to new heights. Over one thousand economists petitioned President Hoover to veto the Hawley-Smoot Act, correctly foretelling that it would further depress international trade, impede payments on the war debts, and invite retaliation against our own products. Hoover, however, yielded to the combined pressure of farm labor, and industrial organizations and signed the bill into law on June 17, 1930. International trade, which in former depressions had aided recovery, now offered no outlet for swollen factory and farm surpluses. There was a marked tendency to view foreign trade as undependable, risky, and not essential to the return of prosperity. Economic nationalism was a concomitant of the isolationism of depression.

The full force of the world-wide collapse was not felt in the United States until 1931. Then a series of disasters, crowded into a few months, made Americans more distrustful than ever of European guile. France precipitated the crisis by demanding payment of some three hundred millions of dollars of short-term credit loans from German and Austrian banks. The latter country's largest private bank was saved only by government action. At the same time, fear and panic gripped Germany and the Weimar Republic once again faced bankruptcy. England formed a national coalition government which suspended the gold standard in order to lower the price of British manufacturers in foreign markets. (This action shocked American conservatives, many of whom were old enough to remember the inflationary scare of the 1890s.) Then Britain, the pioneer free trade country, reversed her ancient policy and a protective tariff all but closed the English market to American goods. The British dominions, in turn, raised their tariff barriers a few notches in order to place themselves in a better bargaining position with the mother country. To meet the new crisis, European nations withdrew their gold deposits from American banks and unloaded securities on the swamped New York Stock Exchange. Pessimism, hunger, international cannabalism, and debt repudiation lurked around that proverbial corner that the Hoover administration was so anxious to turn.

Perhaps no other single result of the depression bred more isolationists than the repudiation of the war debts. Sensing the danger of a German economic collapse, President Hoover (June 20, 1931) proposed that for one year all payments be deferred on both reparations and war debts. The French demurred for three weeks, and, in the meantime, nearly all the banks in Germany and Austria closed their doors.

The Hoover Moratorium proved to be but a palliative. The President would have liked to reopen the whole debt question, but Congress was in no mood for compromise. After the moratorium expired, Germany met with her creditors at Lausanne, Switzerland, and made a settlement that freed her from nine-tenths of her remaining reparations. Ratification of this Lausanne agreement was made subject to the action of the United States in granting relief to its debtors. In other words, the United States was invited, and expected, to bear the chief burden of cancellation, for the Allies were to be compensated for their leniency to Germany by the final creditor's absorbing the loss. In December, 1932, many of the debtors paid their installments but, thereafter, only Finland paid in full while the rest sent merely token payments. (Even these bagatelles ceased when our debtors were told that they would still be held in default.) For all intents and purposes, the war debts had been repudiated, and our wartime allies were denounced as "welchers" and "fair-weather friends." The waxing isolationist sentiment had been given a gigantic fillip.

The *second* precipitating agent of the new dynamic isolationism was the wave of aggressions that undermined and then destroyed the Versailles peace settlement. Baffled and embittered by economic chaos, the so-called "have-not" countries revived the law of the jungle and preyed upon their weaker neighbors. The race for spoils was camouflaged by the trappings of the ideological warfare, then going on between the rival totalitarian systems of Fascism and Communism. The ephemeral prosperity of the later twenties had obscured the danger of the growth of anti-democratic and anti-liberal movements. When conventional governments could not solve problems arising from the depression by conventional means, they were overthrown by unscrupulous demagogues ready to revert to barbarism to achieve their goals.

During the ensuing melee Americans had to reconcile themselves to some unpleasant facts. If scientific and technological advances had brought great gains to mankind, such progress had also put a premium upon the use of modernized force. Smaller nations could be subdued almost overnight, and their peoples held captive by streamlined methods of physical and psychological coercion. Slowly, men of good will were to learn that peace in their time would be that strange interlude which separates one chain of wars from another. Perhaps it all could have been stopped if the peace-loving nations had been willing to make the immediate sacrifices necessary for collective security. Americans soon learned, however, that they held no monopoly on isolationism; the western European countries were also unwilling to resist until their vital interests were directly menaced. Like depression and aggression, isolationism was contagious.

Japan was the first major power to break the truce. The country's foreign trade had suffered badly during the depression, and its Manchurian holdings were threatened by the northward movement of the Chinese nationalists under Chiang Kai-shek. The militarists gained control of the government and correctly divined that a perplexed, depression-weary world would not unite against them. The Japanese blow came in the fall of 1931, at a time when the European economic situation was critical. On September 19, 1931, the news was wired that Japanese soldiers were pouring into the Chinese province of Manchuria. One League member had invaded the territory of another under the flimsiest of pretexts. Credulous Americans believed that Article X of the Covenant would now be invoked, for surely the League had to protect China against external aggression.

The United States had more at stake than the breach of a

Covenant to which it had not adhered. Japan had flagrantly violated the Nine Power Treaty (of the 1921-1922 Washington settlement) in which she had pledged respect for the territorial integrity of China. Our legitimate rights and interests in the Far East were seriously threatened. The Nipponese, in addition, had made a grim joke of the Kellogg-Briand Pact, for while they did not take the trouble to declare war, it was self-evident that they had *adopted* war as an instrument of national policy. Both the League experiment in collective security and the American postwar attempt to secure peace by independent treaties faced the acid test. "Civilization," writes the noted diplomatic historian, Julius W. Pratt "had reached a turning point."[2]

American devotees of the League derived but small comfort from the way in which Geneva met the Japanese defiance. The United States was under no legal obligation to enforce its treaties, for it had stipulated that it would rely on no coercive sanctions. We would, however, have liked to see the League restore the status quo in the eastern Pacific for its disruption was injurious to us. By any ordinary interpretation of Japan's actions, the League was obligated to come to the help of China. But Europe seemed to have become indifferent to collective action just at a time when the Japanese blow stimulated American interest in international unity. We were less willing to isolate ourselves from remote Asia than from Europe. The Hoover administration set an all-time record for close cooperation with the League in the Manchurian crisis, but the President refused to countenance any American actions that might risk war. In the end, the League did enough to make Japan quit the organization, while doing nothing to save Manchuria. The whole affair destroyed much of the remaining American faith in collective action. The League bungled a splendid opportunity to halt an onslaught by a main power against another large member state, and other plotters against the peace watched the default with interest.

By the time Japanese war planes soared over Manchuria, the European skies had already darkened. Gustav Stresemann was dead, and the sun of Locarno set over his grave. Thanks to borrowed American capital and assembly-line techniques, German production had increased rapidly. But the glutted and protected markets of the world could not absorb the surpluses that flowed from her factories. A favorable balance of trade, necessary if the Reich was to meet her reparations and other debts, was more chimerical than ever. After a year of street brawls, assassinations, despair over business, inconclusive elections, synthetic and real Communist threats, President Paul von Hindenburg, in January, 1933, invited Hitler to become chancellor, and in nine months Germany withdrew her delegation from the League of Nations. By the middle of the following year *Der Führer* had liquidated his domestic enemies, substituted absolute regimentation for civil liberties, and made himself supreme. Another first-class power had hoisted the Jolly Roger and was feverishly preparing to remake the map of Europe.

While Hitler was as yet only fulminating, Mussolini unhurriedly and openly planned the invasion of Ethiopia. *Il Duce* had watched the League's handling of Japan, and he decided to take a chance on collective security. In the fall of 1935, he was ready for the gamble and his black-shirted legions marched. This time the League Council acted more vigorously. Italy was denounced as an aggressor and sanctions were imposed. It was quite obvious, however, that oil, iron, steel, coal, and coke (all of which could be purchased from non-League countries), were omitted from the list of embargoed goods. American onlookers were disgusted when they learned of the attempt of Britain's Sir Samuel Hoare and France's Pierre Laval to satiate Mussolini's appetite with a large slice of Ethiopian land. This appeasement plan miscarried, but the League's efforts did not seriously impede Mussolini's celebration of a Roman triumph in the streets of Addis Ababa. Italy now followed the example of Japan and Germany and left the League in order to be able to operate more freely. The two European dictators, hitherto viewing one another with suspicion, made a *rapprochement. Il Duce* shouted that he held out an olive branch to the world—an olive branch that sprang "from an immense force of 8,000,000 bayonets well sharpened and thrust from intrepid young hearts."[3]

The peace barometer began to fall even before Mussolini's final cleanup campaign in Ethiopia and the British and French soon discovered that their fumbling was to cost them something besides guilt feelings about the luckless Abyssinians. Hitler took full advantage of the muddle by sending his troops goose-stepping into the demilitarized Rhineland (March, 1936). He thus tossed the Locarno Pact into a wastebasket already filled with scraps of paper treaties. We now know that his generals had orders to retreat if they met resistance, for Germany as yet had not completed its *Westwall* to keep out the French army. But London and Paris did not act, and Germany scored a major triumph.

Four months later, in July, 1936, the Spanish Civil War

broke out. Once again an intelligent schoolboy could have seen through the folly of the western democracies. Paralyzed by fear of war and Communist influence in the Loyalist government at Madrid, they allowed themselves to be duped into allowing the Fascist dictators to underwrite a Franco victory. This meant that France was to be surrounded by hostile dictatorships menacing her German, Italian, and Spanish borders. Although the United States followed the French and English example and refused to differentiate between the loyalist defenders and the insurgent attackers, the course of the Spanish Civil War disgusted many liberal Americans with Europe.

Meanwhile, the aggressor nations changed a sympathetic understanding into a formal alliance. The German Nazis and the Italian Fascists reached an agreement on October 25, 1936. A month later Germany and Japan signed the Anti-Comintern pact (supposedly aimed at the Communist International) and in 1937 the Berlin-Tokyo Axis became a triumvirate when Rome entered the combination. The predatory nations had teamed up against those peace-loving nations that wanted to preserve what was left of the 1919 Versailles settlement. The defense was so slow in forming that the challengers made steady progress toward their goal of destroying the status quo, overcoming the feeble interference as they tackled country after country that stood in their way. The aggressors were on the verge of success before they met effective resistance.

Some important questions must now be posed and answered. Why did the United States stand by and allow the situation to deteriorate to the point where only unlimited sacrifices could salvage those kindred countries who shared our own moral values? How did the delusion arise that Americans could preserve their heritage if totalitarianism destroyed Judeo-Christian ethics, decency, human freedom, and democracy in the rest of the world? Why did we not take the preventive measures that, viewed in perspective, seem to have been so logical? The answers to these questions are complex. Basically, however, American foreign policy in the 1930s is a pointed commentary on how slowly the creaking machinery of democracy responds to world upheaval.

The 1931 rupture of the peace came just as the government and its citizens were preoccupied with the deepening depression. Although the United States was under no legal obligations to stop the Japanese, the Manchurian coup proved the oft-asserted truth that our far-flung interests would be jeopardized by any significant aggression anywhere. The Hoover administration met the challenge by broadening, but not abandoning, the neo-isolationist point of view. An American representative sat with the Council of the League of Nations (while it was discussing matters involving the breach of the Kellogg-Briand Pact), and later General Frank R. McCoy served on the five-man Lytton Commission that tried in vain to settle the dispute. But moral suasion was as far as the Quaker President was willing to go, and he made it clear that he would not risk war by putting economic pressure on Japan.

Secretary of State Henry L. Stimson, growing bolder as the Japanese showed they were in dead earnest, would have liked more vigorous action. The differences between the President and his Secretary were partially reconciled by that policy known as the Stimson Doctrine. It was probably Hoover who first suggested that the United States proclaim that it would not recognize territorial changes in eastern Asia which either violated existing treaty engagements or were brought about by use of force.[4] The Stimson Doctrine points up the great American dilemma. Japanese rapacity shocked public opinion and people demanded that Nippon be castigated. The non-recognition policy helped quiet the American conscience, and although it gave moral support to China it did not settle the problem. Eventually we were faced with the choice of either acquiescing in the Japanese control of China or in precipitating war with Japan. There was no easy way out. "The generalization seems sound," writes Professor Pratt, "that to oppose international aggression with weapons that are irritating but ineffectual is worse than not to oppose it at all."[5]

The European danger to our security developed so gradually that Americans were able to build up a psychological immunity to its real implications. For several years after 1933, Hitler violated only the rights of his own countrymen—German Jews, radical and liberal dissenters, and other groups whom the Nazis chose to persecute. We now know that Washington had been warned of Hitler's warlike intentions at least as early as 1934, but the information was of the kind that could not be made public. These diplomatic dispatches were, moreover, only shrewd conjectures and the authorities awaited overt acts. When these came quickly and furiously it was readily apparent that the balance of world power was shifting rapidly in favor of the outlaw nations. But by then the great isolationistic bloc had been formed and its existence made bold executive action politically impossible.

The American mind of the 1930s was perversely obtuse to the all-important question of whether our national friends or our avowed enemies controlled the preponderance of power.

227

Because the military build-ups did not directly menace American interests, we did not perceive their true significance. The notion was widespread that it made no essential difference to an isolated America which combination of powers would police the seas, control the raw materials of war or be in control of strategic spots that guarded the gateways of the continents. In 1918, Americans had been led to believe that war would settle everything, but in their disillusionment they fell into the reverse fallacy of believing that war settles nothing. As the dictators played leap-frog over the countries that blocked their way to the control of Europe and Asia, Americans did not enjoy watching the game; albeit they concluded that the best way of dealing with the new turbulence was to ignore it.

The United States faced the possibility of deviating in another way from former foreign policy. Neo-isolationism, designed for a relatively stable world, would neither put out the new fires by collective action, nor keep the country sufficiently far from the flames. Either we had to join the western democracies and take immediate risks to halt aggression, or we had to prepare to sit out the coming war behind reinforced isolationist walls. The decision was not a difficult one for most Americans to make. It seemed hazardous and futile to rehabilitate a faltering League that had proved itself incapable of protecting its weaker members against their stronger brothers. Once Japan, Germany, and Italy had united for aggressive action, the balance of power shifted dangerously. It could have been restored in favor of the peaceful nations only if the United States had been willing to commit its powerful resources. This step the American people were unwilling to take; pending the great upheaval of war, they clung to the ingrained belief that the New World had a destiny all its own.

With this detailed background in mind, it is easy to understand why isolationist sentiment snowballed. The first indication of its entrenchment was a more profound disgust with the results of World War I. Beset by the personal anxieties of the depression years, men began to ponder the basic cause of their troubles. The war boom, they reasoned, had inflated the prosperity balloon, and this in turn had burst in their faces. The upshot of our 1917 intervention, said Senator George W. Norris, was starvation in the midst of plenty. As sheriffs, armed with writs of ejectment, drove farmers from their homes in the fertile Midwest, the people blamed their plight on "the tragic heritage that has come down to us from this so-called war to end wars."[6] Debts, taxations, the foreclosing

228

of mortgages, wholesale bankruptcies, bank failures, plummeting farm prices, and the fruitless hunt for jobs occupied the American mind. Why, men asked, should we concern ourselves with foreign matters when so much needed to be done at home? Why trouble ourselves with debt-defaulters and ingrates?

Hence there was an unprecedented recoil from the very thought of war. Veteran anti-Wilson men and erstwhile leaguists began to speak the same pacifist language. William Randolph Hearst claimed vindication for his wartime heresies. He predicted that American free enterprise would survive the domestic panic, but insisted that the next Armageddon would end with the bolshevization of the world. In 1931, a questionnaire was sent out to a large group of Christian ministers. Over fifty percent of those who replied said that it was their present intention never again to sanction any kind of armed conflict. The following year, Stephen S. Wise celebrated his twenty-fifth anniversary as rabbi of New York's Free Synagogue. He used the occasion to apologize to the country for his wartime fervor and pledged "without reservation or equivocation" never again to repeat the mistake. But Adolf Hitler had already formulated some plans that would make the rabbi change his mind.

The new tidal wave of isolationism had gathered so much momentum by the election year of 1932 that internationally minded politicians had to yield to its force. Newton D. Baker, one of the most loyal of Wilson's disciples, aspired to the Democratic presidential nomination. He retreated from his former inflexible position by saying that the United States ought not to enter the League until the day came when its people were really convinced of the necessity for world organization. A few days later, the leading Democratic candidate, Franklin D. Roosevelt, announced his surrender to the isolationists. F.D.R.'s keen political nose smelled Democratic victory in the air, and he wanted to make certain of the nomination. As Governor of New York, Roosevelt had carefully dodged comment on foreign affairs. His internationalist orientation, however, made him suspect among the isolationists. Hearst told the country in a radio broadcast that he would do his utmost to keep the Democrats from nominating any man who did not hoist the ensign of "America first." The Governor took the hint.

On February 2, 1932, Roosevelt spoke to members of the New York State Grange. The League, he explained disarmingly, was no longer the League of Woodrow Wilson, and

America had no place in it. But Hearst was still not satisfied and Roosevelt had to send him additional assurances through a mutual friend. When the Democratic national convention met in Chicago, Hearst and his fellow Californian, William G. McAdoo, were in a powerful position to influence the making of the platform and the choice of candidates. Thus the party declared itself opposed to the cancellation of the war debts. At a critical moment in the balloting, McAdoo helped arrange the deal whereby the California and Texas delegations switched from John N. Garner to Roosevelt, thus assuring his victory over Alfred E. Smith. Not much was said about foreign affairs in the ensuing campaign, for domestic problems were far too pressing. Roosevelt, however, came to the White House after having reached a proper understanding with the isolationists in his own party.

The new President was not tempted to break the truce in the early New Deal years. Although a theoretical internationalist, F.D.R. had always been willing to temporize with Democrats of contrary convictions. Roosevelt, moreover, was impervious to the economic implications of the internationalist approach and not disposed to quarrel with the demand of the isolationists that he look first to American prosperity. His primary concern, in 1933, was to extricate the country from the economic quagmire into which it had sunk. To achieve the New Deal goals of relief, recovery, and reform, the President needed the goodwill of those isolationist lodestars—William E. Borah, Robert M. La Follette, Jr., Gerald P. Nye, and Burton K. Wheeler. He had no intention of alienating the support of these progressives by raising the ghost of collective security. Although Hitler was already in power when Roosevelt was inaugurated, the Nazis at first seemed only a localized menace. The President was concerned about the unhappy course of events abroad, but he was a realist, and a proposal for concerted international action against any or all of the aggressors would have jeopardized the New Deal and might well have courted party disaster. He was not the man to tempt political fate for such a shopworn and discredited idea as collective security. In a democratic country, even so forceful a leader as Roosevelt had to defer to the isolationist temper of the people.

Perhaps one more striking example of the American mood of 1933 is in order. When Roosevelt came to the White House, a General Disarmament Conference, summoned by the League, had been deadlocked for over a year. In the hope of quieting French fears of a resurgent Germany, Roosevelt said that if the Conference really adopted a thoroughgoing disarmament plan, the United States would then make certain promises. We would, our delegate told the Conference, consult with other powers if the peace were threatened, and we would not interfere with the League's sanctions against an aggressor nation if we felt the condemnation deserved. This proposal did not save the Geneva Conference. It was wrecked by Germany's withdrawal from the League. Interestingly enough, however, America's outstanding authority on international law, John Bassett Moore, denounced Roosevelt's limited offer of cooperation as "the gravest danger to which the country had ever been exposed, a danger involving our very independence."[7] And this from the first American to sit on the bench of the World Court!

Less than two months after Roosevelt's unsuccessful attempt to salvage the Geneva Disarmament Conference, he decided in favor of the kind of nationalist recovery program strongly favored by the isolationists. There were, in 1933, two principal theories for combatting the depression. The economic internationalists, including the new Secretary of State, Cordell Hull, believed that permanent recovery could best be achieved by stimulating foreign trade through lowering tariff barriers and by a harmonious working agreement between the nations on currency stabilization. The World Economic Conference, called to plan a united attack on a globe-wide depression, met in London on June 12, 1933.

Besides tariff and currency matters, its sponsors hoped to solve the war debt muddle and to ease the paralysis on foreign lending. After Hull sailed for England, Roosevelt apparently made up his mind that we ought not to agree to any international currency stabilization which would prevent us from manipulating our own money by way of raising the price level. Unaware of this, the Conference worked out a program that pledged the United States to little more than an eventual promise to return to the gold standard and, pending that return, to discourage speculative fluctuation in currencies. Roosevelt boldly rejected this proposed declaration, with a message that destroyed the CONFERENCE and its hope of concerted action in alleviating the depression. The President thus identified himself with the economic isolationists who refused to give up a controlled currency for the sake of relieving the plight of foreign debtor nations.

For the next four years, Roosevelt deviated very little from the neo-isolationist policies formulated by his Republican predecessors. He told the members of the Woodrow Wilson

Foundation that the United States was not in the League and did not contemplate joining. January after January the President charmed Congress with delightfully spoken annual messages that stressed exclusively the economic welfare of the United States. The most fanatical nationalists in the audience must have applauded his more telling suggestions and promises. The obligations of our former Allies, said the President on one occasion, were sacred "debts of honor." Sometimes, in the manner of Calvin Coolidge, he would offer the foreigners gratuitous advice on how to pare down their expenses in order to square themselves with their creditor.

There is good reason to believe that F.D.R. was far from blind to the gathering war clouds on the foreign horizon. Personally, he well may have agreed with the persistent leaguists that the United States ought to join in collective action to cauterize the pullulating totalitarian infection before it got out of hand. But he did not say so publicly, and he made no real effort to brake the rolling isolationist bandwagon. On the contrary, he let Congress build the most formidable isolationist dykes since the days of Thomas Jefferson's Embargo Act. He did not want the new walls, but they were set up under laws that carried his signature.

The field day of the ultra-isolationists came during Roosevelt's first term. In 1934, Congress passed the Johnson Act (over the objections of the State and Treasury Departments) which forbade American citizens from lending money to, or buying the securities of, foreign governments in default to the United States. The net result was that the British stopped token payments, no nation was induced to resume its installments, and "Uncle Shylock" was more derided abroad than ever. Nor did Roosevelt follow Hoover's example and ask Congress to reconstitute the War Debts Commission in order to negotiate a compromise settlement. F.D.R. had blithely said that the war debts were "not his baby," and he showed no intention of adopting it.

The President became even more chary of the isolationists after their unexpected show of strength in a 1935 tilt. Nine years before, the Senate had created an impasse on American adherence to the World Court protocol by imposing reservations unacceptable to the other powers. In 1929, the eighty-four-year-old Elihu Root went to Geneva and, sitting with a commission of jurists, worked out a compromise. This "Root Formula" tried to solve the nettling question of advisory opinions. It was proposed that the United States be given equal opportunity with League members to object to the rendering of such opinions, and, if our refusal were not sustained, we could then withdraw from the Court without any imputations of ill will. Both parties had urged adherence to the Court under these conditions in 1932, and the proposal was presented to the Senate for favorable action by Presidents Hoover and Roosevelt.

The proposition languished in the Senate for four years while the isolationists used the time-tested tactics of delay and obstruction. By the time the question came to a vote, the issue had become stale and distasteful. The Court had lost a good deal of prestige in the United States when it ruled a proposed customs union between Austria and Germany to be in violation of existing treaties. To many Americans this decision was the ultimate proof that the Court's guiding star was politics rather than law. For this, and many other reasons, the Democratic majority leadership, in 1935, argued their case for the Court in a half-hearted fashion. Even so, without outside interference, they might have withstood the isolationist attack spearheaded by that triumvirate of veterans—Borah, Johnson, and Norris. Hearst, however, was determined not to lose the last round of this prolonged fight. He told Americans to mind their own business at a time when it most needed minding.

At the shrine of the Little Flower, near Detroit, Father Charles E. Coughlin was the radio charmer of the hour. He urged millions of listeners to tell their senators to "keep America safe for Americans . . . and not the hunting ground for international plutocrats." Two hundred thousand telegrams are said to have fallen upon the fidgety legislators. When the votes were tallied, the resolution for adherence was shy the required two-thirds majority by seven votes. And this in a Senate with sixty-eight Democratic members! It was a remarkable demonstration of the juxtaposition of the parties on the question of isolationism.

The President had urged the Court resolution upon the Senate in a special message. He had not, however, used an emergency executive squeeze play upon the senators, nor did he try to mesmerize the country by fireside chats. In letters to internationally minded friends he promised not to forget the Court defeat, but he said the time was inopportune for bold action. What he probably meant was that he needed isolationist support for another round of reforms that historians have called the "Second New Deal." It is exceedingly doubtful that even if the United States had joined the Court in 1935 with such severe reservations, it would have made any difference in the European situation. The Senate's action, however, made the League powers more certain than ever that America was utterly indifferent to what happened to the Versailles peace mechanism. England and France, under the circumstances, became even more loath to police the world through the League. They, too, would try their own variety of isolationism. In the United States, the defeat of the Court made the isolationists distrustful of the President. While he had not tried too hard to have his way, he had said enough to indicate to them that his hands needed to be tied to the isolationist steering gear.

The time was ripe for the supreme triumph of the isolationist concept—the neutrality legislation of 1935-1937. Six years of depression and cumulative aggression had stimulated introversive thinking. The particular frame of reference in which these laws were enacted can, however, be understood only by exploring several additional strains of thought that dominated the American mind of the mid-thirties.

In 1925, *The Big Parade* had begun a series of cinema lessons in pacifism. On the very eve of the Great Depression, Erich Maria Remarque's *All Quiet on the Western Front* was translated into English. Millions read this tale of horror, and still greater numbers sat agape in 1939 as the wretched misery of war was portrayed upon the silver screen. A spate of books and popular movies aroused the American people against war just as *Uncle Tom's Cabin* had once turned the people of the free states against Negro slavery. Stuart Chase, a popularizer of social and economic trends, warned of a two-hour war in which "not even a rat, not even an ant, not even a roach can survive . . . there is no defense."[8] Mr. Chase was a generation ahead of his time, but the outlook was grim enough even when the atom bomb was only a glint in a physicist's eye.

War, as General William Tecumseh Sherman said and proved long ago, was Hell. Having been persuaded of this fact, Americans began to search for the devils who fanned the flames of this Gehenna and found they were largely the same villainous crew of industrialists who were presently being accused of having caused the depression. The theory that Wall Street and its allies had beguiled the country into war was, of course, not a new one. It was popularized, however, at a time when big business stood indicted at the bar of public opinion for that most heinous of American crimes—the ruin of prosperity. In 1934, a liberal journalist, Helmuth C. Englebrecht, edited a book bearing the catchy title, *Merchants of Death*. Like "Arms and Men," an article in *Fortune* that appeared about the same time, it was a devastating exposure of the world's munition tycoons. It was time for Congress to investigate.

The House had already begun to hold hearings even before this latest publicity, but now the Senate took over. The new committee that began to sit in the fall of 1934 was destined to leave a strong imprint upon the course of American history. Vice-President John N. Garner made the egregious error of naming Gerald P. Nye chairman. The senator, a rough-hewn Solon from the North Dakota back country, had the advantages of a high school education, journalistic experience as editor of the Griggs County *Sentinel-Courier,* and nine years of give-and-take on the floor of the Senate. He was hardly equipped to winnow the mass of evidence, nor was he aware of the dangers of over-simplified interpretations of the complex workings of history. Nye, moreover, was a biased judge for he had long been certain that this country had been lured into war against Germany by grasping money-changers and unprincipled dealers in weapons.

The Nye Committee's report, made public in 1935, was some 1,400 pages long. It is a safe guess that only those inured to cruel and unusual punishment read it in its raw form; the rest absorbed the message after it had been pre-digested and garnished. Much of the information that the committee had unearthed was unquestionably true and shocking. The armament men had an international cartel, their agents had lobbied in Congress as well as at international conferences, and they undoubtedly had profited far too much from the war. They had, moreover, welcomed world disarmament as much as the cigarette manufacturers welcome investigations on the toxic effects of tobacco. But it did not necessarily follow that the munitions people and the Wall Street bankers, who made it possible for the Allies to buy the stuff of war, had inveigled the United States into intervening in favor of the side that owed a few of its citizens so much money. As the most competent historians have repeatedly demonstrated, the events of 1914-1917 were too complex for any monolithic interpretation. What of the German actions on land and sea that had incited the American people and their government? What of the inherent fear that an Imperial German victory would create a world antagonistic to American interests? How can one explain the absence of any convincing evidence that economic factors influenced Wilson's decision for war? Finally, the munitions-bankers thesis ran directly counter to the fact that the effective cause of America's intervention was Germany's deliberate gamble on the renewal of unrestricted submarine warfare.

In 1935, however, the country was in a mood to give credence to the Nye theory. Prejudice against all species of economic royalists was at its height. Another European war was in the offing, and these revelations seemed a lucid commentary on current events. Senator Nye was in incessant demand as a speaker and, larding his talks with hyperbole and occasional distortion, he traveled the church, synagogue, and service-club lecture circuit. The war-guilt subject was a welcome distraction from the tedium of the depression, and historians, publicists, and journalists exploited it with gusto.

The disillusionist interpretation of the war had long antedated the Nye Committee's findings, but it had not yet been made ready for mass consumption. Walter Millis of the New York *Herald Tribune* (who had already debunked our 1898 brush with Spain) wrote *The Road to War* in a clear and fascinating style that was almost bewitching. The dust-jacket of the book promised that it would recall to life "the Frenzied Years of 1914-1917 when . . . a peace-loving democracy, muddled but excited, misinformed and whipped to frenzy, embarked upon its greatest foreign war . . . Read it and blush! Read it and beware!" Millis's work, and that of his less able or more penetrating competitors, was picked up hungrily by old Wilson haters, Anglophobes, friends of the Third Reich, victims of the depression, and Marxists consecrated to the theory that capitalism breeds wars. It is almost superfluous to add that these new books made new converts to the isolationist cause.

By 1939, the disillusionist theory of the war had become part of conventional American thinking. It found its way into high school and college classrooms via textbooks and teachers anxious to purvey the newest point of view. Historians who refused to follow the intellectual fad were derided as obscurantists. The stoutest legalistic arguments against any departure —past, present or future—from the strict tenets of neutrality were presented by Edwin M. Borchard and William P. Lage in their *Neutrality for the United States*. Many of their indictments against Wilson's pro-Ally bias are unanswerable, but the authors ignored reality by assuming that it would have made no difference to the United States which side had won. They insisted that Wilson could have avoided war by adhering strictly to international law. The lesson had clear implications for the coming war—let the government maintain a genuine neutrality. The learned authors seemed oblivious to the fact that an international law, blatantly defied by the totalitarian powers, had lost its sanctions in the modern world.

Shortly after the appearance of the Borchard and Lage book, Professor Charles C. Tansill published *America Goes to War*, a study that was for many years the most comprehensive account of the 1917 collapse of neutrality. Tansill showed a restraint and fairness in judging Wilson's actions that he was to abandon in his later inquiries about the Pearl Harbor disaster. His earlier work, nevertheless, leaves the reader with the distinct impression that he believed that the victory of Hohenzollern Germany would have been preferable to an Allied triumph at the expense of American participation in the war.

The most assiduous and thought-provoking elaborations of the Nye Committee's findings came from the facile pen of Charles A. Beard. This sensitive and dauntless scholar had been deeply moved by the blight of the depression and the specter of a new war. He spelled out his program for an indestructible isolationism in a series of books and articles written during the morose years of the late thirties. Fundamentally, Beard built on two premises. First, he assumed that our 1917 aberration resulted from supplying the Allies with goods and money to the point where we had to insure the military victory of our debtors. Second, he held that the New Deal type of national planning could be widened in such a way as to free the United States from entangling foreign economic ties. He took the New Deal revolution seriously enough to think the country could start all over again and perfect an economic system able to withstand the shock of any overseas cataclysm.

Beard reasoned that the time had come to plan in the national interest. World trade, he insisted, was not indispensable for the prosperity of a continental country. Therefore he urged that the temptations of war be lessened by public control of foreign trade. If this were accompanied by the kind of thoroughgoing reform that would make the American masses contented and prosperous, we could peacefully continue to "till our own garden" regardless of what happened abroad.

Oddly enough, Beard, whose ears were so closely attuned to news of technological advances, took an old-fashioned view of an ocean-girt defense system. It is strange that such a gifted man insisted on dwelling so heavily upon past diplomatic mistakes while he overlooked the folly of allowing Hitler to prepare at leisure for war. Beard deplored the triumph of barbarism abroad, but he insisted that it was the duty of the United States to stay clear of foreign hates and loves, and to make certain only that the New World was safe. Like so many other liberals of the day, he put the future of domestic reform above the fate of freedom in the world. He remembered the reaction of the 1920s too vividly to want a repeat performance.

The publicist, C. Hartley Grattan, one of the pioneer writers of the disillusionist school, took much the same position. In *The Deadly Parallel*, written just before the actual outbreak of the Second World War, Grattan warned that another American intervention would put an end to plans for "social control of the economic position." Thus concern for the backwash of war was added to the fear of the devastations of war itself.

From all quarters there came cries of "get the profits out of war" and "let Congress keep us out." Overemphasis upon the events of 1914-1917, to the exclusion of other pre-war periods in our history, led to the fallacious notion that congressmen were always guardian angels of peace, and Presidents were invariably heady warmongers. A little history is a dangerous thing, for it fails to teach dilettantes that, while history may appear to repeat itself, it never actually does. The world of the 1930s was governed by a different set of forces from those that had set the earlier conflict in motion. The resulting war, therefore, was to prove very different, and involvement in it could not have been avoided by means that might have worked twenty-odd years before. So strong, however, was the popular belief that Wilson had been entrapped by a plexus of economic forces that his own Democratic party in 1936 pledged to avoid "being drawn by political commitments, international banking, or private trading, into any war which may develop anywhere." Despite the personal popularity of F.D.R., attested to in 1936 by his sweeping reelection, Congress had already fettered his hands with two Neutrality Laws. The immediate cause of this action had been the impending Italo-Ethiopian war. We have already considered the bearing of this conflict upon the creation of a new powder-keg of isolationist thought. Italy's wanton attack set off the fuse of the barrel and a new brand of isolationism came out of the explosion.

Mussolini had made it perfectly clear, in the summer of 1935, that he soon intended to march against Ethiopia. Emperor Haile Selassie was going to resist the Italians, and there would be war. The time had arrived when the United States would either have to join the other nations in an attempt to stop Mussolini, or else make certain that if the League's actions brought general war, we would do our legal best to stay out of it. There was a little vacillation over the course to follow. For five years the nations had tried in vain to cooperate in fighting the depression, in halting the armaments race, and in staying aggression. The American people were bored with futile international conferences and most of them had no faith left in collective action. It was quite evident that to make collective security work, we would have to bear the major share of the burden, for the European democracies had shown no willingness to make sufficient sacrifices to put down the law-breakers. Under the circumstances, it seemed much more practical to meet the crisis by riveting our neutrality to law. In the light of modern war conditions, so vividly brought home by Wilson's experiences, a successful neutrality seemed to demand the surrender of economic advantages and neutral rights upon which we had hitherto insisted. The militant isolationists of the 1930s revived a concept of neutrality that dated back to the presidency of Thomas Jefferson: that the main objective of foreign policy in wartime should be to stay out of the conflict rather than maintain arbitrary rights. This line of reasoning, upheld by Secretary of State William Jennings Bryan in 1914-1915 and extolled in recent writings, had captured the popular imagination. As a matter of fact, twenty different neutrality bills had been presented to Congress before that body acted.

In the debates that preceded the passage of the First Neutrality Law (August 31, 1935), the internationalist minority argued that the President ought to be free to use the new provisions in favor of the peace-loving nations. If he were empowered to distinguish between the assailants and their victims, he might then implement the League's efforts to punish aggressors. Presidents Hoover and Roosevelt had urged Congress to give them such discretionary power, and Hull's State Department had drafted a bill providing for it. The congressional isolationists, however, were more interested in subduing domestic war pressures than in deterring adventurous foreign dictators. In addition, they sought to prevent the possibility of the President's ranging the United States on the side of one set of belligerents. There is little question that mass opinion favored this check on Roosevelt's power.

As the Italian divisions prepared to storm the Ethiopian frontier, Congress passed a joint resolution that required the President, in event of a foreign war, to proclaim its existence and to withhold the shipment of arms to or for *all* belligerents. American vessels were prohibited from carrying such goods for the warring nations. The President might, if he thought wise, warn American citizens that they could travel on ships flying belligerent flags only at their own risk. The law also provided for a National Munitions Board to bring the armament industry under federal control. Roosevelt signed this joint resolution with a reluctance that he did not make public at the time. It is entirely possible that a veto would have been overridden by Congress.

The President promptly proclaimed the undeclared Italo-Ethiopian war. In this case, the neutrality provisions hindered the guilty party more than the innocent, for Ethiopia was in no position to have benefited from the free shipment of American arms. While the war was still in progress, the law expired. The Second Neutrality Law (February 29, 1936), besides extending the original provisions for fourteen months, forbade loans to belligerent powers made through the purchase of their securities or through any other way. Thus Congress bowed to the Nye Committee's contention that banking loans had been a lure to war in 1917.

Far more important, this Second Neutrality Law showed the League that the United States was not only unwilling to help halt aggression, but that it would not refrain from pursuing policies that would embarrass collective security efforts. Congress's refusal to empower the President to embargo oil and other commodities essential to the Italian war effort meant that Roosevelt had to rely on such moral pressure as he could bring to bear upon exporters in order to keep Mussolini's American purchases within normal limits. The League has been criticized for not levying effective economic sanctions against Italy, but the American attitude certainly did not encourage drastic action. For in the neutrality law of 1936, Congress went further than non-cooperation. The old law had provided that, if an existing war spread, the President was authorized to extend the arms embargo to the new belligerents. Now, however, Congress *directed* him to extend the provisions of the law to all nations which entered an existing conflict. This meant that if the League took actions stern enough to make Mussolini declare war, the United States would clap an arms embargo against the countries trying to stop the epidemic of lawlessness. If the League wanted to stop Mussolini, well and good, but, if the measures it chose to adopt led to general war, Congress was going to take no chances.

In the spring of 1937, Congress formulated a permanent neutrality policy. The Third Neutrality Act (May 1, 1937) indefinitely extended the arms embargo and the prohibition against loans. American citizens were now to be actually forbidden to take passage on the vessels of belligerent countries.

Recognizing the conditions created by the Spanish Civil War, Congress permitted the President to apply the act to foreign civil wars if he thought it necessary. (Congress had, on January 6, 1937, extended the arms embargo to preclude shipment to either Franco or the Spanish Loyalists.) For a period of two years, moreover, the President might, at his own discretion, prohibit the export of certain non-military goods to belligerents except if those commodities were paid for in advance and shipped out of the country in foreign bottoms. This much debated "cash and carry" provision was never put into effect because it expired before the outbreak of general war. Its inclusion in the law, however, is very revealing of the isolationist thinking of the day. Congress wanted to avoid, in the next war, the kind of maritime incidents that had so often jeopardized American neutrality. But, with few exceptions, the isolationists were not willing to follow their theory to its logical conclusion and embargo *all* goods to warring nations, thus crippling the economy. They devised a compromise that would preserve most of the war profits, but would place the risks on those belligerents having the money to buy our wares and the ships with which to fetch them.

Significantly, seasoned isolationists of the old nationalist stripe were not swept away by this "cash over the barrel-head" craze. "We seek," said Senator Borah, "to avoid all risks, all danger, but we make certain to get all the profits."[9] Senator Hiram Johnson argued cogently against an experiment that would jeopardize our neutrality by favoring those nations that had ready money and control of the seas. Both men would have preferred a strict and impartial neutrality of a more orthodox variety.

President Roosevelt watched the gathering war clouds with much foreboding. He wanted Congress to give him the power to distinguish between the nations that breathed fire and brimstone and those that wanted to preserve peace. If the law had to be applied impartially, it would be an incentive to aggression, for Hitler would know beforehand that the United States would not send arms to England and France. The President, however, was in a particularly poor bargaining position at the time, for his ill-fated proposal to enlarge the membership of the Supreme Court had weakened his influence in Congress. Roosevelt's personal popularity was waning momentarily, and Congress was in revolt against executive dictatorship. When the Neutrality Law of 1937 passed by considerable majorities (376 to 16 in the House, 63 to 6 in the Senate), Roosevelt bowed once more to expediency and signed it.

241

The vulnerability of this 1937 Maginot Line of neutrality, as it has sometimes been called, was apparent at the time it was enacted. The law was only seven months old when it was the subject of formal debate between rival high school teams in Buffalo, New York. A sixteen-year-old girl, urging its repeal, said:

> This act is based on the very false assumption that all wars are caused by trade disputes and credit investments. What of the other multitudinous causes of war—aggressions, encroachments on sovereignty, national insults and outrages, and shifts in the balance of power that no country can ignore with impunity? What does this law do to counteract these malevolent forces of our time except to lull the United States into a security that is as false as it is dangerous?[10]

More sophisticated observers realized that Congress had prepared to stay out of a 1914 war when it was obvious that the next one would be very different. Its outcome, moreover, would be far more pertinent to the United States than that of the earlier conflict. The New York *Herald Tribune* corrected the enacting clause of the 1937 law to read: "An Act to Preserve the United States from Intervention in the War of 1917-1918."

The Neutrality Laws, taken together, were much more than harmless errors in judgment, for they helped make war all the more inevitable. The Axis leaders, rash and imprudent men, found it easy to persuade themselves that the United States would stand by as they tore up the maps of Europe and Asia. We had served notice that, in the event of war, we would relinquish our unquestioned legal right to sell arms to the kindred democratic nations which needed them far more than their well-panoplied totalitarian challengers. Congress, in addition, insisted on binding the hands of the Chief Executive at a time when kaleidoscopic shifts of power necessitated instant maneuverability of the Ship of State. The congressional isolationists, so anxious to keep out of war, actually helped invite a foreign catastrophe of such immense proportions that no nation could have escaped its consequences.

Less than six months after President Roosevelt signed the Third Neutrality Law, he dramatically ended his truce with the isolationists. He and his Secretary of State felt that the outward thrust of Fascism could no longer be ignored with impunity. On October 5, 1937, Roosevelt took the offensive in what was to prove a long and bitter campaign to align America with the countries opposed to the Axis.

The President reached his decision slowly and hesitantly. His private correspondence and the published memoirs of his close associates reveal that he grasped the perils of the world situation long before he was either willing to throw down the gauntlet to the isolationists entrenched on Capitol Hill or to formulate a positive foreign policy. During 1935 and 1936, he needed liberal isolationist support to complete the Second New Deal reform program of labor legislation, the Social Security Act, tightening of federal control of public utilities, and agricultural rehabilitation. His speeches prior to 1937 sought to reassure suspicious isolationists. On October 2, 1935 he said that "the American people can speak but one sentiment — despite what happens in continents overseas, the United States shall and must remain, as long ago the Father of our Country prayed it might remain, unentangled and free." In his annual message of January, 1936 (written during the Italo-Ethiopian war), Roosevelt warned that he could no longer confine his remarks on foreign affairs to a few sentences and that the country would have to take notice of the impending threat from abroad. But he pledged, once again, America's determination to adhere to the ancient policies of neutrality and non-entanglement. Such comments as he made on foreign affairs in the heat of the presidential campaign of 1936 were much in the same vein. At Chautauqua, August, 1936, the President lauded the positive achievements of the neutrality program. Not only did he pledge once more devotion to our long-established policy of political non-entanglement but, mindful of the Nye Committee's findings, he declared that, if the nation were ever forced to choose between profits and war, it "will answer — must answer — 'we choose peace.'" A few weeks after his triumphant re-election, F.D.R. chose to make no mention of the deteriorating international situation. Before 1937 was out, however, he was to cross the Rubicon to battle the isolationist hosts.

The immediate cause of Roosevelt's decision to speak his mind was the outbreak of an undeclared, but sanguinary war between Japan and China in July, 1937. The Jaapnese militarists had begun the succession of major Axis aggressions which was to lead directly to the Second World War. Certain facts now became crystal clear to the Washington authorities. The newly formed Berlin-Tokyo Axis (soon to be joined by Rome) meant an organized assault against the peace. If the European theater was quiet but for the Spanish sideshow, it merely signified that the Nazis were setting the stage for the next act while the spotlight played upon their Japanese fellow-actors. America's stake in halting this chain reaction was rapidly increasing. Perhaps it would be possible for the United States to avoid war by abandoning its neutral rights in the Atlantic and renouncing its interests in the western Pacific. But could America allow Europe and Asia to be engulfed by nations dedicated to a militantly anti-democratic way of life? How safe would the United States be in a world governed by unreason? Professor Foster Rhea Dulles, in commenting upon the Axis threat, reminds us that the promotion of universal freedom was as much a part of the American tradition as the devotion to peace. Our historic concern for a democratic world, temporarily displaced by a desire for peace at all costs, was about to be renewed. President Roosevelt sounded the clarion call for its revival in his 1937 Chicago speech.

Secretary Hull had urged the démarche upon the President, and the State Department sent him a draft of the scheduled talk. Roosevelt, more impetuous than the cautious Hull, decided not to pull any punches. He spoke of the rampant "reign of terror and lawlessness" and declared that neither isolation nor neutrality would shield the United States from its effects. "When an epidemic of physical disease starts to spread," he counseled, "the community approves and joins in a quarantine of the patients in order to protect the health of the community against the spread of the disease." We are not privy to just what measures Roosevelt had in mind for he never elaborated upon his original suggestion. For some time after the speech he was kept busy fighting off the hornets that he had stirred from their nest.

Many years later, Hull wrote that Roosevelt's rash suggestion to quarantine the aggressors served only to retard the campaign to awaken the country to its peril. The assertion would be difficult to prove, but it is true that the President had spoken at a peculiarly inopportune moment. The country was irked by a severe business recession, skeptical of the New Deal's ability to bring lasting recovery, and angry over F.D.R.'s recent Supreme Court fiasco. Now, said the Republicans, *that* man was resorting to the time-honored ruse of all dictators—he was rattling the sabre in order to divert attention from failures on the home front. Roosevelt told Colonel Edward M. House (Wilson's closest adviser until 1919) that he was not at all surprised at the popular reaction to his speech. It would take time, he said, to "make people realize that war will be a greater danger to us if we close all doors and windows than if we go out in the street and use our influence to curb the riot."[11]

Almost two years elapsed between the "Quarantine Speech" and the outbreak of general war. During this perturbed period, public opinion on foreign affairs, engulfed for a time by the isolationist tidal wave, returned once more to its normal bifurcated streams. The restoration of a vigorous internationalist spirit was due to many factors. Communists and their intellectual camp followers were told by Moscow to stop maligning the New Deal and, for the duration of the orders, to form a popular front with the bourgeois liberals against Fascism. (Russia had been admitted to the League in 1934, given a permanent seat on the Council, and Stalin had become a belated convert to collective security.) Moreover, American Fascist organizations, some of which were European off-shoots and others homemade imitations, made men aware of the ideological implications of world events.

But, more than any other single factor, German ruthlessness reawakened the American conscience. For a dozen years after the Armistice, women's groups, cosmopolitan business leaders, educators, and liberal ministers had argued that the limited risks of collective security were preferable to the hideous uncertainties of another war. After 1933, the cries of certain groups more particularly affected by Nazi totalitarianism than other Americans intensified their call for action. The internationalist phalanx was re-enforced by recruits from Jewish ranks, labor organizations, devotees of civil rights, and others kindred to those German groups upon whom Hitler had laid hands. Defense of freedom and democracy, more than joining the League, became the chief internationalist objective.

The way in which one of these threatened groups turned from pacifism to militant internationalism is well illustrated in the annals of the Central Conference of American Rabbis. As late as 1935, the C.C.A.R.'s Committee on International Peace recommended that the Conference declare that "henceforth it stand opposed to all war, and that it recommend to all Jews that, for the sake of conscience, and in the Name of God, they refuse to participate in the bearing of arms." The plenary session of the Conference laid the suggestion aside for further study. When they met again in 1936, Hitler had rearmed the Rhineland and was becoming daily more truculent. No motions were made at this meeting to abjure war; instead, the Conference talked about nationalizing the munitions industry. When they assembled in 1939, the Axis was in full operation. The rabbis demanded that Congress amend the recently passed permanent Neutrality Law so that, in case of war, the President would not have to treat the attackers and the attacked alike. At the first Conference following Hitler's 1939 invasion of Poland, the Committee on International Peace reported that the Conference must recognize the possibility of the United States becoming "an active and aggressive champion of the principles of freedom."[12]

Although all Americans were not equally disturbed by Hitler's Austrian coup (March, 1938) or the way in which he blackmailed England and France into betraying Czechoslovakia a half year later, they could hardly shut their ears to the blow-by-blow descriptions of these events. As *putsches,* invasions, threats, surrenders, dramatic airplane flights of prime ministers followed one another *seriatim,* the dispensation of foreign news became increasingly efficient. Gifted on-the-spot radio correspondents broadcast round-ups that could be heard from four countries in one program. Never before had the Old World seemed so close as in those news-packed days when people sat hushed in their living rooms to listen as crisp summaries of the tribute demanded by Berlin, Rome, and Tokyo were followed by shrewd guesses from London, Paris, and Prague as to whether the price would be paid or the bombs would fall. Hitler's hysterical rantings, translated phrase by phrase as he spoke, were heard by millions in this country. It slowly began to dawn on more and more Americans that modern technology had made space disappear. Such men began to fear the spread of the totalitarian cancer more than the surgeon's knife of war. By the middle of 1939, public opinion polls indicated that the people were less isolationist than their representatives on Capitol Hill. The politicians woke up at last.

Public opinion in a democracy is almost invariably divided and confused on the eve of a crisis involving peace or war. Virtual unity comes only after the electrifying shock of a Fort Sumter or a Pearl Harbor. In a large country such as the United States the same happenings usually create opposite blocs of opinion, both of which can be massive at one time. Some men and women listened to the foreign news and thanked God for the oceans and the Neutrality Law. Thus, while the new internationalist movement was gaining momentum, isolationism was becoming even more intense and meaningful to the many millions who still gave it allegiance. Brazen-faced young men, who called themselves "Veterans of Future Wars," demanded government benefits *before* death. Men spoke and wrote of "The First World War" in a mixed vein of cynicism and prophecy.

246

The mass strength of this ultra-isolationist feeling was dramatically revealed in January, 1938. It took an extraordinary appeal from President Roosevelt to keep the House of Representatives from passing a proposed constitutional amendment to make war, except in event of actual invasion, subject to a national referendum. This attempt to put Congress's constitutional power to declare war in the hands of the people had been mulled over for some fifteen years. The proposition, supported by a pacifist-isolationist alliance, was pushed in the House by Representative Louis Ludlow, an Indiana Democrat. While its defeat marked a victory for the administration, the strength that so foolhardy a scheme was able to muster was a clear warning to Roosevelt and Hull to proceed with caution. They had to move with great circumspection as Hitler devoured Austria and browbeat the western democracies into the ill-fated settlement of Munich.

Cordell Hull talked a great deal in this critical year of 1938 about international morality. Eighteen years of congressional experience had made him chary of inciting a revolt on Capitol Hill. So the Secretary measured his words, and gave repeated assurances that the administration contemplated no alliance or action that would create a new balance of power to checkmate the Axis. He warned the country, however, that "isolation is not a means to security; it is a fruitful source of insecurity." The United States, he promised, would steer a middle course between internationalism and isolationism, using the sterling rule of reason to meet each new turn in the wheel of fortune.[13]

While the reserved and prudent Secretary of State was trying to educate the people to face grim reality, the President was feeling his way through the maze of isolationist obstacles. Early in 1938, he urged upon Congress a program of military and naval expansion. There was a good deal of opposition, especially from the pacificists, but Congress did pass the Vinson Naval Expansion Act which authorized the spending of one billion dollars over a period of ten years. Although this increase in naval power has been looked upon as preparation for taking the offensive in far-distant waters, the passage of the bill also indicated the desire of some isolationists to free the country of dependence upon Britain for defense of the New World. The anti-preparedness strain in isolationist thinking was on the wane. And, next, the President was authorized to accumulate stockpiles of raw materials essential for the country's defense. There is little doubt that F.D.R., at least,

247

was already thinking of how he might best help the English and French gird themselves for the coming war.

When Congress met in January, 1939, the European situation had taken a decided turn for the worse. For a few weeks after Hitler's appetite had been assuaged at Munich (September 29, 1938) by devouring a part of Czechoslovakia, men breathed easier. In November, however, *Der Führer* despoiled the German Jews by a series of acts that outraged the civilized world. Obviously, appeasement had incited rather than tamed Hitler. In a surprising move, Roosevelt summoned the American ambassador at Berlin to Washington for a report on the new brutality. As quipsters of the day put it, the democracies could not buy peace from the Axis—they could only rent it for short intervals at an ever-increasing rate.

Roosevelt spoke some sober truths to the newly elected Congress, now controlled by a coalition of conservative southern Democrats and anti-New Deal Republicans. To gain support for the administration's foreign policy he made it clear that he was willing to call a truce on domestic questions. No nation was safe, said the President, in a world in which three major powers would not sit down and reason at the council table. Although he admitted that the country was not prepared to insure peace by pledging the use of its armed forces, "there are many methods, short of war, but stronger and more effective than mere words, of bringing home to aggressor governments the aggregate sentiments of our own people." The President did not say what he meant by measures "short of war," but he made it clear that the existing neutrality legislation ought to be revised, for it "may operate unevenly and unfairly—and may actually give aid to the aggressor and deny it to the victim." The members of Congress who heard his words knew that he meant that the Neutrality Law of 1937 had not been invoked in the current Sino-Japanese conflict because it would have been harmful to Chiang Kai-shek. Would Congress act before a *declared* European war would compel the President to proclaim the arms embargo in force regardless of the consequences?

While Congress was thinking it over, the Axis partners began their perennial spring raids. Hitler seized the rest of truncated Czechoslovakia in March, and, on Good Friday, the Italians marched against Albania. The fall of Prague marked a turning point in British and French diplomacy. Appeasement had been predicated upon the assumption that Hitler's aims were limited, for he had said repeatedly that he wanted only to unite all German-speaking peoples. But now it was evident that Europe faced a would-be conqueror far more sinister than Napoleon. The British and French would have to resist the next step before the entire continent fell victim to Germany's lust for *Lebensraum*. Men (certain members of Congress excepted) no longer asked *if* there would be war but *when* it would begin.

During the portentous spring months of 1939, the President tried to reach a backstairs agreement with congressional leaders for the repeal of the arms embargo. When informal negotiations failed, he tried a direct approach, but neither house would go along with the administration's proposed changes. By a vote of 12 to 11, the Senate Foreign Relations Committee postponed consideration of the question. On July 18, 1939, at a White House Conference, the President made a final attempt to convince the obdurate senators. It seemed so reasonable to repeal a mandatory arms embargo that would injure friendly powers and aid potential enemies. Why not do it now, rather than wait until the fighting began and we would be changing the rules in the midst of the game? Why not serve this final warning upon the dictators that they could not expect the United States to stand calmly by while the lights of civilization were being systematically extinguished? But old Senator Borah had his own sources of information and he was sure there was no immediate danger of war. Vice-President Garner turned his weatherbeaten face to Roosevelt and said: "Well, Captain, we may as well face the facts. You haven't got the votes and that's all there is to it."[14] But this was the last major triumph of the isolationists.

As congressmen repaired to their summer haunts, leaving the Neutrality Act intact, the world stood on the brink of the greatest disaster of modern times. In the event of war, the President would have to deny the sale of munitions to all the belligerents. While the British and French were leisurely parleying for Soviet Russia's help, Stalin and Hitler agreed to the non-aggression pact of August 23, 1939. Secretly, these false friends agreed to divide up the territory of six independent states of central Europe. Hitler's eastern flank was safe, and, in the early hours of September 1, his armies crashed across the Polish border. Two days later England and France declared war on Germany. President Roosevelt promptly announced the neutrality of the United States and, out of necessity rather than choice, proclaimed the Neutrality Law of 1937 in effect. For the second time in twenty-five years, American isolationism faced the supreme test.

Chapter 12

The Repudiation of a Tradition: Poland to Pearl Harbor

SIX GHASTLY years intervened between the September day in 1939 when the Germans goose-stepped into Poland, and the September day in 1945 when the last Axis partner, Japan, made her formal surrender aboard the *Missouri*, lying at anchor in Tokyo Bay. In the course of this global upheaval, American thinking about foreign policy, military strategy, and world organization was transformed.

Our foreign policy, in those momentous years, shifted from formal nuerality to material help for the Allies and then to the creation of a grand alliance designed to win the war. On September 1, 1939, the Neutrality Law of 1937, that consummate triumph of the isolationists, still stood unchanged; a half dozen years later, the fondest dreams of the Wilsonians had been fulfilled on paper, and collective security had become the touchstone of our policy. The war began with a wave of bitterness against the Communists for coming to terms with Hitler; by the time it ended, the United Nations Charter had been fashioned, based on the supposition that the United States and Russia could be congenial senior partners.

Military thinking was even more drastically revolutionized. From a nation whose strong navy and ludicrously small army mirrored the current belief that we should confine long-range plans to defending the western hemisphere, we advanced to the point where our fighting ships were scattered in every sea, our airplanes were based on all the continents, and our civilian army had penetrated enemy lines in Africa, Europe, and Asia. At the very end of the war our perfection and use of the atomic bomb ended one cycle in the annals of mankind and began another. It was soon to become apparent that this new thermonuclear war would consume the winner as well as the vanquished. The atom bomb had destroyed the assumptions of Washington, Jefferson, Wilson, and even Franklin D. Roosevelt that, either by minding our own affairs as the first two men advocated, or by helping other nations to resist aggression as the latter two wished, we could keep the theater of war away from our homeland. To meet one totalitarian threat,

President Roosevelt had spoken of making America the "arsenal of democracy"; to ward off a later menace, Secretary of State John Foster Dulles was to speak of an "arsenal of retaliation." The Atomic Age, ushered in by the Second World War, explains the difference between the two concepts.

The implications of atomic warfare took some time to filter down to the level of popular thinking. Before the masses could adjust themselves to this new state of affairs, they had already been converted from isolationists to internationalists. The policies of the two major parties illustrate the abyss that was to separate the spirit of 1939 from that of 1945. Before the war, both Republican and Democratic platforms vied with each other in promising the maintenance of neutrality and isolationism; by 1944, their respective presidential candidates outdid each other in promising a new world based on collective security. In 1940, Senator Arthur H. Vandenberg was the favorite candidate of the Republican isolationists for President; by 1945, the senator was a leading exponent of the new internationalism. The government, Vandenburg, and the majority of the people had repudiated neutrality, non-entanglement, a reliance on ocean defenses, and the old policy of taking no responsibility for the policing of the world. To understand this about-face, it is necessary to survey briefly the impact of these war years upon the American mind.

A prolonged and bitter encounter between the isolationists and their opponents was inevitable in the twenty-seven months that elapsed between the onset of the European war and the Japanese attack on Pearl Harbor. This great debate was the logical result of a twenty-year schism over the feasibility of American neutrality in any war that might reverse the balance of world power. Circumstances made that struggle bitter, for the stakes were exceedingly high on both sides. This time, for the so-called interventionists, it was not a case of preserving the freedom of the seas, avoiding possible effects of a Hohenzollern-dominated Europe, or protecting loans to the Allies. It was a matter of watching western civilization, as they knew it, destroyed by powers whose barbarism was made all the more hideous by a perverted use of modern science and technology. To many, the risk of war seemed far preferable to the horrors of co-existence with a victorious Hitler. At the same time, to the isolationists, it meant the ultimate test of their theory that America had a destiny all its own. If they lost, it meant more than a war which most of them genuinely dreaded and thought unnecessary. If the United States intervened once more to settle a world conflict, it could never again withdraw from the arena of power politics. This much was taken for granted by both sides as they prepared for a fight to the finish.

At the beginning, the isolationists held many advantages. They were flushed with victory, for in the pre-war years they had won every round in Congress. They had able and experienced leaders, adequate financial resources with which to advertise their cause, and, in time, they were to perfect a national organization. Their promise to keep the boys out of the trenches was to find responsive chords in millions of American homes in which 1917 was recalled with a shudder. The mood of the country, when the war began, was expressed in the current saying: "We'll sit this one out." The isolationists could tax their opponents with warmongering, thus putting them on the defensive. In addition, they could rely on powerful support from many Republicans, at a time when the political pendulum was beginning to swing back in the G.O.P. direction. The Republican appetite for victory, whetted by successive defeats, would naturally tempt the party to exploit the congenial issues of neutrality and isolationism.

How could American fathers, mothers, wives, sweethearts, and men of draft age fail to show their appreciation at the polls? Isolationism was especially strong in Congress, where, in addition to the large group who held ingrained convictions on the subject, there were many battle-scarred veterans of the New Deal legislative contests ready to oppose any policy that Roosevelt might approve. The isolationists, moreover, could count on some valuable Democratic support as well as that of many liberals who, for the time being, disagreed with the administration's foreign policy. The anti-war coalition was to be powerful, well organized, and resolute in purpose.

Despite these great advantages, time was to reveal that the isolationists had already shot their bolt, for Hitler's deeds spoke louder than any words they could muster. In the first year of the war, *Der Führer* yanked the strongest props from under the isolationists by subduing the friendly nations which fringed the western Atlantic, thus making the ocean a pathway to our eastern door. When, in June, 1940, Hitler stood poised at the French Channel ports, he jolted Americans out of their false sense of security. In turning the Maginot Line, he uncovered not only France, but also the nearest approaches to the New World by way of the French African colonies. Just one rapidly shrinking ocean between ourselves and the Nazi demon was not enough for most Americans. The isolationists were, therefore, unable to stop any measure "short of war" to help the enemies of Hitler. Although they were still arguing vociferously when Japanese bombs at Pearl Harbor signaled the end of the debate, their cause had been steadily losing ground.

Once in motion, the rapidity of the Second World War made American abstention more difficult and hazardous than in the period immediately preceding 1917. The earlier conflict had been a war of position, with a stabilized western front that blocked the German army from its chief objectives. At that time, the German threat to America was based upon two probabilities which never occurred: the Kaiser would crush the entrenched Allied armies, and after decisive victory pursue policies detrimental to our interests. Imperial Germany never destroyed French independence, nor did she conquer Holland, Denmark, and Norway. She never seized the African littoral of the Mediterranean, threatened to invade Britain, made an alliance with Japan aimed at the United States, stationed fifth columns in Latin America, or demonstrated by open action her rapacity and avarice. Hitler's blitzkrieg conquests and world-wide ideological penetrations made the question of American intervention much more imperative than it had been in the more leisurely days of the First World War. Neutral rights upon the sea played little part in our decisions, for Hitler's warped thinking led him to avoid maritime incidents in the naive belief that we might thus overlook the destruction of friendly nations which so long had buttressed the Atlantic moat. Thus the United States was confronted with an unprecedented challenge. Could we afford the risk of facing alone a victorious Axis whose ambitions seemed to know no bounds? Was not material help for potential allies, while they still existed, preferable to waiting until our own turn came in the timetable of conquest? But, in addition to challenging future security, Hitler roused a wave of moral indignation. His outrages against public decency violated every principle that Americans had so long held sacred. The noninterventionists argued that we must blind ourselves to actions that did not directly concern us, but men are governed by their emotions as well as their reason. Hitler reactivated the American tradition of concern for a free and democratic world to the point where it outstripped in strength the rival heritage of isolationism.

Woodrow Wilson had foreseen the outcome should these traditions ever clash again. On September 4, 1919, he had predicted that, whether we were in the League or not, we would come to the help of the free world if Germany ran amuck once more. "We do not," he declared, "stand off and

253

see murder done. We do not profess to be the champions of liberty and then consent to see liberty destroyed. We are not the friends and advocates of free government and then willing to stand by and see free government die before our eyes."[1] Wilson, thoroughly familiar with American history, knew that isolationism had long run counter to another tradition, epitomized by the philosopher, Ralph Waldo Emerson, who once declared that "the office of America is to liberate."

Thus in order to succeed in their purpose, the isolationists of 1939-1941 had to quell the fears for American safety and material interests in the likely event of a Hitlerian victory. They also had to repress the strong sense of national mission that impelled Americans to aid the defenders of human dignity in resisting the totalitarian juggernaut. Moreover, the country had a President who knew how to mobilize public opinion in support of his contention that to risk war was better than to chance an Allied defeat.

The isolationists soon discovered that the Chief Executive had lost none of his cunning. Opposed to them was a master leader of men—experienced, sure-handed, eloquent; he would not be trapped into revealing any ultimate plans which might endanger his immediate objectives. Roosevelt's repeated victories over them came, of course, because Hitler's actions demonstrated the logic of the administration's policies. But the outcome of the closely fought legislative battles of 1939-1941 was also determined by the President's ingenious exploitation of recent technological advances in public communications. To win support for his foreign policy, he used the media of mass communications that had served him so well in promoting the New Deal. A sixth sense seemed to tell the President just when the country was in the mood for another folksy fireside chat. He was the greatest radio performer in the country—cool, relaxed, casual, understandable, and frequently delightfully humorous. Yet none of the millions of Americans whom he held spellbound could ever mistake the fact that he spoke in deadly earnest and that his words were designed to shape the course of history.[2]

Roosevelt persistently refused to formulate policies that might outrun the possibilities of majority support. If in doubt, he sent up a trial balloon and closely observed the way it was tossed about by the winds of opinion. He had certain new instruments at his command and he knew how to use them. The public opinion surveys of Elmo Roper and Dr. George Gallup (of the American Institute of Public Opinion), both dating from 1935, were carefully evaluated. No President ever made better use of the press conference, and F.D.R. employed his lively banter with the Washington correspondents to keep in touch with grass-roots sentiment. In Roosevelt's day, says Professor Daniel J. Boorstin, Washington developed the art of political public relations, and began to treat its citizens as a large corporation does its customers. The administration thus designed new blueprints for foreign policy changes, and advertised their advantages and promoted their acceptance. Always, however, the pace of the evolution was regulated by public reaction. When opinion was found unfavorable, the administration tempered its program or put it into secret operation. Roosevelt's caution was dictated by his determination to avoid an irrevocable act that might fail in Congress and thus dishearten the nations who were fighting the Axis. The very nature of his strategy in meeting the isolationist opposition led him to equivocation and questionable procedures. It is far easier for the moralist to defend F.D.R.'s ends than the means he employed to achieve them.

If the President's policy, then, appears at some junctures vacillating and at others deceitful, it does not follow that he held no deep-seated beliefs about America's role in the war. On the contrary, his over-all aims were based upon bedrock convictions. He believed, from the outset, that if Hitler won the battle of Europe, war between the United States and a victorious Axis was inevitable. If one grants him his original assumption, which seems to have been a reasonable one, it follows that his best hope of averting war lay in aiding Hitler's enemies. Such actions, of course, involved the risk of war, but F.D.R. was willing to take it. In all probability he was entirely sincere in saying that he wanted to keep the United States at peace. But, when it became apparent that Hitler could be defeated only by active American intervention, Roosevelt preferred that the United States fight while the English fleet and nation still remained intact.

Because Roosevelt did not present the issue to the American people as he himself saw it, he laid himself open to charges of prevarication and guile. Instead of taking the country into his confidence, he larded his proposals with promises of peace while he planned to insure the victory of one side even at the cost of a shooting war. It is not difficult to explain this dissimulation. Roosevelt faced a well-led, highly organized, and vocal opposition in Congress which was ready to use any candid statement against him. The country was badly divided, and he felt that national unity, so necessary in time of crisis, would be hampered by a frank disclosure of his ultimate objectives.

The powerful isolationist minority in Congress did not share his convictions that Britain, and later Russia, were defending American interests as well as their own. Had Roosevelt discarded subterfuge, his opponents would not have hesitated to seize the advantage to defeat him in Congress, with repercussions that might have destroyed the fighting will of those nations still resisting the Axis. The President refused to accept this dangerous challenge. He knew that the majority of the American people were non-interventionists rather than old-fashioned isolationists. They hoped for a miracle—a miracle that would insure Hitler's defeat without spilling American blood. Roosevelt encouraged this wishful thinking by continually playing down the risks inherent in a program of all-out aid for one side against the other. He simulated the technique of the kindly family doctor who purposely misleads an apprehensive patient in order to avoid an emotional upset that might endanger eventual recovery.

The President knew, long before the people were prepared to face the unpleasant reality, that the battle against the Axis could not be won entirely on the assembly lines of American factories. But he did not change his tactics even after he determined upon active intervention. If he had broached the question of peace or war in its absolute form at any time previous to Pearl Harbor, he might have risked grave consequences. Probably, he would have embarrassed his Republican congressional allies by forcing a complete split in the G.O.P. ranks. This, by itself, was less dangerous than another possible result. Isolationist strength in Congress, amounting to roughly one-third of the votes in both houses, never diminished until the Japanese bombed Oahu. He dared not hand them an out-and-out challenge which might reverse the administration's narrow margin of strength by alienating marginal supporters.

Unquestionably the President's circumspect actions helped him to keep the isolationists at bay, thus allowing him to place the material resources of the United States at the disposal of those countries resisting Germany. His decision against candor, however, created the fodder upon which a new school of revisionist historians was to feed. If one believes that the defeat of Hitler was necessary to save western civilization, Roosevelt's actions become comprehensible, even if they cannot be reconciled with a code of ethics ordinarily expected from a gentleman in private life. Reasons of state especially in time of crises, force even democratic statesmen to resort to Machiavellian conduct.

In retrospect, it is apparent that Hitler's crushing of the western European democratic barricade to the Atlantic, together with Roosevelt's skillful campaign of popular education, convinced a majority of the American people, even before Pearl Harbor, that neutrality and isolationism were no longer feasible. Isolationism, however, remained persistently stronger among congressmen than among their constituents. This was owing in part to the fact that rural inland areas were over-represented in Congress, and also because so many men on Capitol Hill were old-timers whose views on foreign policy had crystallized in a bygone age. Taken for what they are worth, the public opinion polls of 1940 and 1941 show a far sharper decline of isolationist sentiment among the people than among their representatives. In May 1940, 64 percent of those interviewed felt that the maintenance of peace was more important than the downfall of the Axis. The final pre-Pearl Harbor poll, taken in the first days of December, 1941, indicates that the verdict had been reversed to the point where only 32 percent were willing to buy peace at the expense of a Hitlerian triumph.[3] It is important to note, however, that Roosevelt had to appeal to Congress rather than directly to the people for the implementation of his program. This meant a long and protracted struggle, the final outcome of which was determined by the course of world events.

In order to understand how the United States abandoned neutrality for that twilight status between peace and war, now called non-belligerency, it is necessary to return to the events of September, 1939. The initial brush between the President and the isolationists came over the proposed repeal of the arms embargo for the purpose of allowing the United States to sell munitions to the Allies. The special session of Congress that convened September 21, debated hotly for six weeks. The net result, true to the spirit of American politics, was a compromise measure usually termed the Fourth Neutrality Law. Despite the fact that Roosevelt won his chief point, the repeal of the arms embargo, the new law had some isolationist overtones, for it was passed at a time when the Maginot Line still buttressed the security of the United States by confining Hitler to Central Europe. It provided that arms, ammunition, and implements of war could be purchased by all belligerents on a cash-and-carry basis. Inasmuch as only the British and French were in a position to buy these American wares and carry them across the sea, the repeal of the arms embargo changed the existing law in favor of the Allies. On the other hand, the isolationists could derive some comfort, for the new law empowered the President to mark out "combat zones" that were to be closed to American ships and travelers.

This first encounter revealed the pattern of the cleavage in the country. Newspaper opinion was overwhelmingly in favor of lifting the arms embargo. The opposition, insisting upon no traffic in arms even if this prohibition played into Hitler's hands, consisted mainly of the old isolationists, farm and labor organizations, and a hodgepodge of liberals who still feared involvement in war more than the totalitarian advance. Senator Borah spoke for all isolationists when he warned that a revision of the 1937 Neutrality Law in favor of England and France would mean that America had taken sides in the conflict. "You will," he predicted, "send munitions without pay and you will send your boys back to the slaughter pens of Europe."[4] Borah was as correct in guessing the result as he was mistaken in believing why it would happen. The American war spirit was not whipped up by the sale of munitions, propaganda, or financial investments; such militancy as existed prior to Pearl Harbor rose in response to Hitler's fierce lunges toward the nations bordering the Atlantic Ocean.

As long as France stood between the Nazi power and the Channel ports, Americans still regarded the war with a certain amount of detachment. While almost all of them wanted the Allies to win, an equally large number wanted no part in the fighting. At the outset, some even deluded themselves into believing that Hitler had fallen into a trap. French soldiers along the Maginot Line faced the Boche entrenched a few miles away along the equally impregnable Siegfried Line. In which direction could Hitler move after he had divided the carcass of Poland with his new comrade, Joseph Stalin? The Germans, so optimists argued, faced another 1914-1918 stalemate in the West, where they would be slowly choked to death as the Allies marshalled their potential resources and tightened their control of the seas. But Hitler soon showed the world that the tempo of war had increased tremendously since the days of the Kaiser. The Germans had perfected their blitzkrieg techniques to the point where major countries could be conquered in weeks while small neighbors could be overrun in days or even hours. It was in the tempestuous spring of 1940 that these revolutionary changes in warfare upset America's conventional reliance upon insulated security.

The "phony war" or the "sitzkrieg," as others called it,

ended unexpectedly when Hitler occupied tranquil Denmark and his planes swooped down upon neutral Norway. Americans, glued to their radios, found it difficult to realize that these proverbially neutral Scandinavian countries had fallen prey to the Nazis.

Men had hardly recovered their sense of balance before the scourge struck once more. It was Friday, May 10, 1940 when the Nazi sledgehammer felled Holland, Luxembourg, and Belgium in record time. The French were retreating everywhere. Who would stop these swarming Germans with their fifth columns undermining the foundations of ancient realms, with their Luftwaffe pouring down death from the skies, and with their panzer divisions racing toward the English Channel and scattering the frightened peasants before them like so much chaff in the wind? As far as France was concerned it was shortly over. Soon after June 22, Americans saw newsreels of an elated *Führer,* clicking his heels in unrestricted ecstasy as he forced the French to surrender in the same wagon-lit, in the same forest of Compiègne, where the Germans had signed the 1918 Armistice.

A shocked America anxiously watched the recently appointed British Prime Minister, Winston Churchill, rally his people. A new voice now commanded the attention of the war-swollen radio audiences in the free countries. Can any American who heard Churchill's address to Parliament (June 4, 1940) after the evacuation of the British troops from Dunkirk ever forget his majestic words? His peroration, designed for American ears, promised that Britain would not only remain an obstacle in Hitler's path, but would gird herself and turn the war against the enemy. The isolationists now had the two greatest radio speakers in the free world pitted against them—Franklin D. Roosevelt and Winston S. Churchill.

The fall of France and the ensuing German air assault on Britain underscored anew the question of American security. England was in the gravest peril, for there was no certainty that Hitler was not ready to invade the island, and there was serious doubt that the Royal Air Force could keep the Luftwaffe from reducing the country to rubble. Gamblers, willing to bet on the future of humanity, offered odds that the swastika would fly over Trafalgar Square before winter whipped up the waves of the Channel. What now of the Atlantic moat if the British fleet were destroyed, or if Churchill should be replaced by a prime minister ready to advise the King to surrender the Royal Navy? What now of the Monroe Doctrine if the well-oiled Nazi propaganda machine in Latin America were to make malignant the dictatorships that flanked our southern border?

The possible fall of Britain posed a three-fold threat to the United States—strategic, economic, and political. It was generally conceded that the military threat demanded an overhauling of the American defense system. Russia seemed to have a cordial understanding, perhaps even an alliance, with Germany. In the worst hours of the Nazi air attack on England, Japan signed a tripartite pact with Germany and Italy which promised that all the Axis powers would fight together if the United States intervened in either the Chinese or European war. Britain, of course, stood alone, and her survival was a matter of conjecture. Hitler had already exposed the Atlantic islands that formed the air bridges to the New World. Men scanned their maps and measured the short blue ocean space between Dakar where French West Africa bulged out into the Atlantic and the eastern hump of Brazil that projected eastward toward it. The arguments for arming for defense of the western hemisphere were irrefutable. It was on this point that the isolationists locked horns with the administration. Whereas they wanted merely to build up our own fortifications, F.D.R. wished to keep Hitler away by making certain that Britain would not fall. And although some of the non-isolationist military men close to him felt that Britain was doomed in any event, he did not despair. As it turned out, it was he who gauged the situation more correctly.

The specter of an Axis victory also posed a perplexing economic question. What would be the future of American business in a totalitarian world? Our economy was linked with the British and French systems; it was not geared to mesh with the Axis economies. Not only would it be inconvenient to substitute Berlin for London as our chief foreign trading post, but it was questionable whether we could really do business with Hitler. Some of the isolationists said yes, but the Nazi concept of foreign trade was just as totalitarian as their notion of government. They regarded trade not as a mutually beneficial exchange of goods but as another tool to be used to achieve their diplomatic aims. The triumph of a nation dedicated to such perverted business methods boded nothing but evil for the future of our own variety of free enterprise philosophy.

Granted, for the moment, that we could defend ourselves without Britain, and that a victorious *Führer* would heed his business-minded industrialists and make a satisfactory commercial treaty with us, there still remained the threat to our most cherished political beliefs. Did we want to try a hermit existence in a totalitarian world where England would be reduced to Vichy-like vassalage and the congenial little European democracies would be converted into German satrapies? The problem was thus set before the American people by Winston Churchill on the day that France decided to capitulate:

> If we can stand up to . . . [Hitler] all Europe may be free and the life of the world may move forward into broad, sunlit uplands. But if we fail, then the whole world, including the United States . . . will sink into the abyss of a new Dark Age, made more sinister, and perhaps more protracted, by the lights of a perverted science.[5]

In meeting the triple threat caused by the Allied disasters of 1940, President Roosevelt had little difficulty with the first part of his program—the proposal to expand and strengthen American military and naval power. By and large, the isolationists agreed to Roosevelt's blueprint for a two-ocean navy, for the first peacetime draft in American history, and for military and naval appropriations that reached a total of $17 billion before the year 1940 was over.[6] The administration made arrangements with other American republics for joint preservation of the Monroe Doctrine in the event Hitler decided to claim the New World colonies of his victims. A special agreement with Canada provided for the joint defense of that country and the United States. Had Roosevelt stopped there, he would have been reasonably certain of almost united Congressional support. But he did not. And over the issue of whether or not to lend material aid to Hitler's enemies, Roosevelt and the isolationists were to clash for eighteen critical months.

A week before France decided upon surrender, F.D.R. told the country that he would defend the New World by aiding the countries willing to stand up to Hitler. The day was June 10, 1940; the place was the old university town of Charlottesville, Virginia. The President was angry, for he had just learned that Mussolini, lying in wait like a vulture, had fallen upon prostrate France. Roosevelt declared that the United States would extend material aid to countries resisting aggression and simultaneously make itself strong enough to meet any threat to its own immediate interests. "All roads," he said, "leading to the accomplishment of these objectives must be kept clear of obstructions. We will not slow down or detour. Signs and signals call for speed—full speed ahead."[7]

The President had thrown down the gauntlet to the isolationists. They picked up the challenge and retorted that we must preserve our resources for the defense of Fortress America rather than to dissipate them in Europe, and thereby increase our danger by inviting Hitler's retaliation. The issue, however, was not always to be so sharply drawn. Some of the more moderate isolationists, such as former President Hoover and Senator Robert A. Taft, wanted to give Britain a limited amount of help that might enable her to negotiate a better peace with Germany. Had Roosevelt conceded, he might have split the isolationist coalition. But the President was determined to settle for nothing short of British victory. Hence, he consolidated the opposition and precipitated an argument that was to rival the slavery dispute in bitterness and invective. It was inevitable that both sides would organize on a national scale, for Americans were accustomed to resolving major differences of opinion by a joust between rival pressure groups.

The President's auxiliaries organized first. The most active members of these groups, willing to devote money and time to the cause, were generally veteran internationalists, educators, Protestant or Jewish clergymen, cosmopolitan business men, and journalists. Usually the national and community leaders were old-stock Americans who, because of racial descent or cultural affinity, were specially sympathetic to the fighting Britons. These men organized relief associations to bolster English civilian morale, and pressure groups to rally Congress and public opinion behind the President's proposals. The British American Ambulance Corps worked out of New York with branches all over the country. In addition to raising money for ambulances that would help the British bear their ordeal by fire, advertisements brought the blitz home to the American people. Similar functions were performed by the Allied Relief Fund and an organization that collected "Bundles For Britain." By 1940 it was difficult for Americans to shut their eyes or ears to the agony of Hitler's victims, for it was illustrated on billboards and in newspaper advertisements, it was brought to their doors by the mailman, it was flashed on movie screens, and it took the place of mid-commercial plugs in many broadcasts. America sang, "There will be bluebirds over the white cliffs of Dover."

The most important of the political pressure groups was promoted by the nationally famous editor of the Emporia (Kansas) *Gazette*, William Allen White. Known (after April, 1940) as the Committee to Defend America by Aiding the Allies, its original purpose was to support Hitler's enemies by means "short of war." Although the group obviously was non-isolationist, it eventually split into two factions. Some, like White himself, wanted to draw the line at material aid and to champion no steps that might lead directly to American belligerency. A growing faction in the organization, however, argued that the survival of Great Britain was more important to the United States than the preservation of the peace. Early in 1941 White resigned the chairmanship, and the bolder elements, under the leadership of Senator Carter Glass of Virginia and the Right Reverend Henry W. Hobson, bishop of the Episcopal diocese of Southern Ohio, formed the Fight For Freedom Committee.

The records of the pro-ally group in Buffalo, New York, have been preserved and therefore form a convenient peephole into the more localized activities of the White Committee and its successor. Conditions undoubtedly varied from place to place. The success of each local pro-British effort depended upon the ethnic make-up of the community, its religious divisions, its exposed or insulated geographical situation, the mood of its intellectual and business spokesmen, and such chance factors as the availability of talented leaders. While some allowance must be made for all of these factors, which tended to make the great debate over isolationism different in each city, the Buffalo story is characteristic enough to use as a case in point. Here was a large, industrialized metropolitan area, originally settled by westward-bound Yankees, long since outnumbered by the German and Irish strains of the old immigration together with Polish, Ukrainian, and Italian migrants who came after 1880. The Catholics formed a clear majority of the population. Because Buffalo lay just across the Niagara River from Canada, which was already at war, the conflict seemed nearer home than in some cities removed from the frontier. The situation made for a sharp division between the old-stock Americans and anti-Hitler immigrant groups on one side, and a German, Irish, and ultra-nativist isolationist coalition on the other.

On July 4, 1940, in the anxious days following the prostration of France, the Buffalo Niagara Frontier Defense Committee was organized "to aid in the defense of America at home and abroad." It was formed to cooperate with the national work of the White Committee and to keep an eye on subversive German ultraist elements that openly paraded their pro-Nazi sympathies. The original chairman was Mr. Chauncey J. Hamlin, a wealthy scion of one of the older families of the region. A man who lived in the *grand seigneur* fashion of the nineteenth-century American elite, Mr. Hamlin did not allow his staunch Republican conservatism to prejudice him against the Democratic President's foreign policy. On the contrary, he led the local movement to win popular support for the administration's policy of benevolent neutrality toward the Allies.

When it became apparent in December, 1940, that British pluck and grit might ward off, but not subdue, the Nazi terror, Mr. Hamlin's committee sent up a trial balloon suggesting a discussion of whether or not the United States ought to enter the war. The excited reaction of the city provides valuable insight into the popular feeling of the day. "Our sympathies for Great Britain are strong and our desire to be of assistance is great," responded the Buffalo *Courier-Express*, "but our recollections of experiences of a quarter of a century ago are stronger . . . we have too many white crosses in the cemeteries of France now." The Committee's feeler led to some resignations. The group, however, was reformed as the Niagara Frontier Committee to Defend America by Aiding the British Commonwealth and their Allies. It still had 445 members (few paying supporters had resigned) and Mr. Hamlin strengthened the organization by replacing the members of the Executive Committee who withdrew with men of equal, if not greater, prominence.

The records of the Committee for 1941 reveal that it had a downtown headquarters, paid secretarial help, had efficient intellectual leadership to keep its propaganda current with changing conditions, and that it was financed by contributing members who paid anything from fifty cents to ten dollars a month. Its roster shows that its chief backers were members of Buffalo's older families, administrators and professors associated with the local university, some anti-fascist Italians, leading business executives, and Poles aggrieved at the destruction of their homeland.[8] Because of the anti-Semitic overtones of some of the isolationist propaganda, Buffalo's Jewish leaders refrained from taking a very active part in the Committee's work in the fear that their help would do more harm than good.

In May, 1941, the group (now called the Niagara Frontier Committee for the Defense of America) affiliated with the Fight for Freedom Committee. By the autumn of 1941, there was a strong feeling in the Buffalo branch that the United States ought to go to war against Germany. This move was spearheaded by fourteen members of the University of Buffalo faculty, who felt that American intervention would hasten the defeat of Hitler and thus prove the swiftest road to world peace.

The formation of a national pro-Ally pressure group made it imperative for the isolationists to create a parallel organization. Before recounting the details of this new movement, it is necessary to understand how the events of the day revolutionized the pre-war isolationist coalition. The war had altered the isolationist bloc, wedging out some elements while at the same time attracting new components.

The core of the revamped isolationists was still the "hemispherist" group who insisted that this was not "our war." Some of the veteran Irreconcilables recognized the danger of the Hitlerian threat and rallied behind the President, but men of the stripe of William E. Borah or Hiram W. Johnson remained isolationists to the last. These old-line isolationists had many well-wishers in the country, including some prominent industrialists, many small business men, and a few outstanding leaders of organized labor.

The hyphenate variety of isolationism had become, by 1939, less widespread but potentially very dangerous. Hyphenate isolationism had been developed by certain non-English stocks who used it to prevent help for or association with Allies that happened to be enemies of their own mother countries. This sentiment was usually strongest among first-generation immigrants, and declined rapidly as their children and grandchildren were drawn into the mainstream of American life. After the First World War, when the great folk migration was checked by American immigration laws, the intensity of feeling on the part of the hyphenates declined. Nevertheless, several factors, peculiar to the Second World War, created a new type of divided loyalty particularly perilous to American democracy. The well-financed Nazi propaganda machine created a subversive kind of hyphenate whose activities were inimical to the welfare and security of the United States. Because the later conflict chanced to come after a decade of depression and economic experimentation, the Germans found allies among discontented native American groups who were attracted to the fascist program. Many of these malcontents had always been ultra-isolationists and they were desperate enough to accept any aid in fighting a losing cause.

An older and respectable hyphenate isolationism persisted alongside the newer variety. It was especially strong among the Irish-Americans—less intensely anti-British than in Wilson's day, but still prone to remember the old grievances. Eire, virtually independent for fourteen years, in 1939 still belonged to the British Commonwealth of Nations. But the republic refused to join in the war, and Irish-Americans were fond of pointing out that a small country, nestled in one corner of the British Isles, had found neutrality workable. Was this not an example for the United States, separated by 3,000 miles of water from the blood baths of Europe? This was a favorite argument of such groups as the Irish Foundation and the Ancient Order of Hibernians. An official of the Erie County (New York) division of the latter society stated that, even if the Axis won, Ireland could not be worse off than she had been under the long centuries of British tyranny. "The Irish have always been credited with a keen sense of humor," he added, "and they fully realize the joke of referring to England as a democracy."[9]

There can be little question that the great majority of the Irish-Americans were pre-Pearl Harbor isolationists. Some of them were strongly influenced by the doctrines of Father Charles E. Coughlin, who was then at the height of his power. While in 1932 Coughlin, in a characteristic overstatement, had said the issue of the election was "Roosevelt or Ruin," he later turned violently against the New Deal. In 1936 he founded the magazine *Social Justice* and, in its pages and on the radio, he mixed isolationism with anti-Semitic innuendos that were refined versions of the malicious statements of the Nazi minister of propaganda, Dr. Joseph Paul Goebbels. Coughlin's rantings, decried by liberal Catholics and Protestants alike, appealed to narrow-minded and ignorant groups, who thought of the radio priest as a St. George out to slay the twin dragons of atheism and Communism. Dyed-in-the-wool Anglophobes, who rejoiced at the thought of Britain's long-awaited downfall, found his words congenial. The Coughlinite movement was particularly strong in Brooklyn, New York, where the older Irish settlers resented the newer immigrants. Here Father Edward L. Curran and the Brooklyn *Tablet* imitated Coughlin's technique of compounding isolationism with racial prejudice. Inasmuch as the German-American leaders made anti-Semitism the touchstone of all their propaganda and nostrums, there seemed to be an issue on which the two groups could join.

The Mussolini brand of fascism had relatively little appeal to the millions of Americans of Italian birth or descent and had no deep or permanent effect upon them. Nazi propaganda, on the other hand, for a time seemed very formidable in the United States. Justice to the bulk of the descendants of the nineteenth-century German immigrants demands the recognition that, if many of them were vociferously anti-war before

Pearl Harbor, their isolationism stemmed from a long-standing prejudice rather than from an affinity for the Third Reich.

The Nazi appeal in the United States was limited to recent German immigrants and to a clump of American pseudo-fascists. Hitler's American agents realized that the country was overwhelmingly opposed to the cause they represented. They therefore sought to win allies among the fanatical isolationists, the racists, and the rabid anti-New Dealers. Their aim was to split American public opinion, and, in so doing, to immobilize help for Germany's enemies. As their patron saint they paraded not *Der Führer*, but—God save the mark—George Washington! Hence their texts were more often taken from the Farewell Address than from *Mein Kampf*.

The most notorious Nazi organization was the German-American Bund that tried, for a while, to parade in storm trooper fashion. It and other pro-German groups were financed in part by the Third Reich. There was a German Library of Information in New York, which circulated a *White Book* filled with crude forgeries allegedly found in the archives of the Polish Foreign Office. Inasmuch as these efforts impressed few outside the small circle who needed no further indoctrination, the Germans tried to work through native American fronts.

They found some sympathizers. There were frustrated men who imagined themselves the victims of the "British-Jewish-Communist conspiracy" that other people called the New Deal. Some unscrupulous opportunists were ready to take advantage of the confusion of the times to gain power or fortune. It has been variously estimated that there were from 400 to 700 fanatically isolationist agencies in the first years of the Second World War. One of the most widely known was the American Fellowship Forum, organized in 1939 to spread Nazi racist theories and to halt the move toward military preparedness. The Forum published *Today's Challenge* and counted among its contributors some of the more rash Congressional isolationists. William Dudley Pelley organized the Silver Shirt Legion and, through the pages of *The Galilean*, advocated a Nazi-like purge of the Jews. Verne Marshall, who headed the No Foreign Wars Committee, was another example of the prevalent unreason. Gerald B. Winrod edited *The Defender* while James True and Robert E. Edmondson tried to organize super-patriot groups along semi-fascist lines. George Deathrage was secretary of the Knights of the White Camelia and president of the American Nationalist Confederation. (In 1938 Deatherage had attended an international anti-Semitic conference held in Erfurt, Germany.) Especially active in New York and its environs were Joseph E. McWilliams' Christian Mobilizers and a group called the Christian Front. The latter organization, which pledged allegiance to the teachings of Father Coughlin, was divided into platoons and claimed to have 200,000 members willing to use force to launch its program.

All of these organizations and many not here mentioned pursued similar tactics. They tried to introduce German anti-Semitism to America; their propaganda often bore the earmarks of Dr. Goebbels; they cited statements torn out of contexts; they revived nineteenth-century forgeries about Jewish-Masonic plots for world domination; and they made prevarication the hallmark of their trade.[10] Perhaps the uttermost limit of credibility was reached when it was charged that Churchill's famous "V" sign for victory had its origin in Solomon's temple at Jerusalem where the priests had divided their fingers as they stretched out their hands to bless the people! These groups were composed of men and women who blamed their own failures in life on immigrant competition; of desperate isolationists obsessed by the fear of British domination; and of ignorant and gullible folk ready to believe the most far-fetched fabrications.

A good many of their leaders ran afoul of the laws. Some followed the example of the Ku Klux Klan leaders of the 1920s and robbed their own organizations. Fritz Kuhn of the German-American Bund was sentenced to twenty-one months in Sing Sing for embezzlement. In 1940, seventeen members of the Christian Front were tried for, but not convicted of, sedition. Heinz Spanknoebel had to flee the country because he failed, according to law, to register as a German agent. George Sylvester Viereck, whose questionable pro-German activities dated back to Wilson's day, went to jail when he was compelled to admit that his American chauvinism was a masquerade and that he had violated the foreign agents' registration act. These proto-fascist organizations broke the laws of the State of New York by creating riots, turning over gravestones in Jewish cemeteries, desecrating synagogues, and breaking up tolerance and goodwill meetings. On December 22, 1939, Mayor Fiorello H. LaGuardia of New York stated that of 238 members of such societies who had been arrested for street disorders, 112 had been convicted within a period of six months!

The great majority of the Congressional isolationists allowed their good sense to moderate their emotions and avoided association with these disorderly fanatics. The extremists, nevertheless, had some friends on Capitol Hill. Representative Hamilton Fish of New York and Senator Ernest Lundeen of Minnesota wrote for *Today's Challenge*. Jacob Thorkelson, Republican representative from Montana, spoke before the Christian Mobilizers, while John E. Rankin, Mississippi Democrat, told the House of Representatives that it was "Wall Street and a little group of our international Jewish brethren" that planned together to plunge the country into war.[11] It is a matter of record that over twenty isolationist congressmen, wittingly or unwittingly, misused their franking privilege in mailing out propaganda designed to impede American military preparedness.[12]

Ultimately the Nazi sympathizers and their cohorts did a great deal of damage to the isolationist cause. Their vicious actions convinced many people that Hitler was undermining American internal security as well as threatening the country's international well-being. The crackpot isolationists brought the moral issue into sharper focus, and aroused liberal interdenominational societies to action against them. Without the deadly embrace of these subversive elements, the legitimate isolationist groups could have fought a much more effective campaign.

An analysis of the grand isolationist coalition that battled Roosevelt discloses that, from 1939 to 1941, it was purged of its non-conservative elements. The 1939 intrusion of the Communists into the isolationist ranks and their 1941 departure came with startling suddenness. For several years prior to the outbreak of the war, the American radicals had ardently advocated a "popular front" of all non-fascist groups against the Axis. But the ink of the Moscow-Berlin agreement of August 23, 1939 had hardly dried when the *Daily Worker* announced the new creed of the true believers. This was an "imperialist war," according to the revised party plan, and all the capitalist belligerents were equally guilty of starting the bloodshed. Comrade Stalin, it was explained, had been unable to keep the rival imperialists from jumping at each other's throats, and therefore had moved into the eastern half of Poland to spare at least part of that unhappy country. The bewildered isolationists tried to keep the Communists out of their movement, but they were dealing with men who made an art of infiltration. One of the most publicized isolationist tracts of the day, a pamphlet entitled *The Yanks Are Not Coming*, stemmed from radical sources.[13] In those hectic years, its

269

origin was overlooked and its catchy title became a favorite isolationist slogan.

No segment of the isolationist coalition ever became enthusiastic internationalists with greater speed than the Communists. In the early morning hours of Sunday, June 22, 1941, the Nazis and their allies attacked the Soviet Union along a 1,600-mile front. Within a few days the by-word of the American Communists was significantly altered to "The Yanks Are Not Coming—Too Late." They were now the most rash interventionists in the country, for the life of Russia hung in the balance. The plague of the Communist touch was now once more upon the Rooseveltians.

The divided and perplexed liberals gradually changed their minds as Hitler's grand design unfolded. Many of these men and women were badly torn by inner personal conflict. They subscribed to a creed that held that wars solve no problems, that nations invariably fight at the fiat of selfish economic forces, and that, when a democracy resorts to armed conflict, it crushes civil liberties at home and delivers itself into the hands of its reactionaries. At first, the liberals tried to persuade themselves that no real moral question was involved, arguing that one side was as bad, or almost as bad, as the other. The "have-not" nations had been denied their rightful share of colonies and natural resources so long that a group of madmen were able to mesmerize their people into seeking justice through immoral means. If England and France appeared on the surface to be law-abiding and peaceful, they were like a pair of retired bank robbers who were anxious to secure legal protection for their plunder. What, they asked, was liberal or forward-looking about the British government of Neville Chamberlain or the French Cabinet of Edouard Daladier?[14]

In the fall of 1939 most of the liberals demanded that the United States sit the war out. Their position was well stated by Bruce Bliven of the *New Republic*: "I remember when a country that did not want to go to war was tricked and bullied and persuaded into doing so . . . and so I feel, as I watch the motion picture of events unreeling on the screen of time, that I have seen it all before. This is where I came in."[15] Let us not, Charles A. Beard implored, take up the "Atlas load" once more. He urged that the United States develop its continental resources and allay the desire for foreign adventures by a wider distribution of domestic wealth. If we would but surrender our "moneylending and huckstering abroad," he counseled, we could develop in peace a civilization that would be "more just, more stable, and more beautiful than anything yet realized."[16]

As long as Hitler was caged behind the Maginot Line, the Beardian approach dominated the liberal mind. Even some of the old crusaders for internationalism, tired by twenty years of futile efforts, demanded in 1939 a course of impartial neutrality for the United States. Thinking in terms of the long haul, such men insisted that the cause of true internationalism would be best served by such action. At least one country, so the saying went, ought to be left to pick up the pieces after the war was over. If the Age of Reason had ended in Europe, they contended, there was all the more reason for the United States to preserve the values of the Enlightenment for the New World.

The most vulnerable point in the liberal argument was its insistence that American security was independent of any possible shift in the balance of power. The United States, said the aging Oswald Garrison Villard, would be safer than ever after the European nations had spent their strength destroying one another. This type of wishful thinking was markedly prevalent among the liberal pacifists, many of whom had vowed never again to support a war fought for any cause whatsoever. The liberals failed to realize that a conquering country usually gathers rather than loses strength in the course of a major war. If the victor is ruled by an irresponsible tyrant with an insatiable lust for power, then his triumph imperils every remaining free country in the world.

Most of the liberals saw the point after Hitler's legions turned Europe inside out in the spring of 1940. Significantly, the *New Republic* dropped its most dogmatic isolationist columnist, John T. Flynn. Soon this journal was demanding redoubled aid to Britain and full panoply at home so that the United States could stand up to the Axis.[17] The Liberals, who had largely deserted Roosevelt after 1937, now returned to their natural leader. Faced with the cruel dilemma of risking loathsome war or allowing an abhorrent fascism to envelop the world, they made the choice of the lesser evil. Paradoxically, those men, who had so long censured the use of force, now hoped that force would save what was left of the old liberal ideals. When the liberals moved out of the isolationist camp, they left the bitter right in almost complete control. The progressive strain, so significant in the older generation of American isolationists, all but disappeared. Old-time progressives, like Senators Gerald P. Nye and Burton K. Wheeler, who remained intransigent isolationists, became more conservative in

271

domestic policy, while the liberal Senator George W. Norris overcame the prejudices of a lifetime and veered to support the President. Henceforth isolationism was to become the seminal power of the reaction against twentieth-century changes in American life. Resistant forces were to blame intervention in foreign wars for changes in the social and economic pattern. The conservative isolationists would remember and utilize the isolationist conclusions of Charles A. Beard, while they would jettison his plans for making isolationism work by expanding the New Deal at home.

The conservative revolution in the isolationist movement was completed by anti-New Deal leadership. Big business was divided in its attitude toward the European war. Many of the industrialists overcame their dislike of Roosevelt and acclaimed his foreign policy. Others, especially in the Midwest, refused to distinguish between the President's domestic and international objectives. It was easy for such men to rationalize their inherent isolationism. The national debt, swollen by New Deal expenditures, looked dangerously high. They had become tax-conscious, and they had an uneasy feeling that F.D.R. would make the rich bear the burden of building the "arsenal of democracy." But for the 1917 intervention, they reasoned, there would have been no 1929 depression and no 1933 New Deal. One war was enough—at least until the country was once again safely Republican.

By mid-summer 1940 the conservatives controlled the isolationist coalition, although their leadership was often embarrassed by unwelcome fascist and (until June 22, 1941) Communist side-partners. The word "isolationist" was henceforth to be associated with "reactionary" rather than with "progressive."

When the threat of declared war became more and more imminent, the isolationist ranks, as had so often occurred in the past, were temporarily swollen by certain men of military age, their parents, wives, sweethearts, brothers, and sisters. The natural reluctance of some Americans to don khaki uniforms was evinced in many ways. Marriage license bureaus did a land-office business, and the birth rate soared. Certain young men planned ahead for any turn for the worse in the foreign situation. Meanwhile, their mothers formed organizations that bore such names as "Our Sons for Defense Only— No Foreign Wars" or the "National Committee to Keep America out of Foreign Wars." Peace mobilization rallies were the order of the day. Eventually these ephemeral groups were to be combined into a national isolationist organization designed to coordinate local efforts.

The distaste for army service partly explains the strength of isolationist sentiment in the ranks of organized labor. The workers and their leaders were not fascist-minded, for they knew only too well what Hitler and Mussolini had done to the unions in their own countries and in their conquered provinces. But the laborers had special reasons for wanting the United States to stay out of the war. Many of them were young, male and able-bodied—which meant that they would be called upon to do the fighting. Some of the labor tycoons were isolationists for still other reasons. They realized their cause had made, since 1933, the most phenomenal gains in all of American history. War would bring regimentation, and they feared what might happen to the government's benevolent labor policy if the corporation managers moved into Washington to take charge of the mobilization.

The old isolationist coalition, dating back to First World War days, had been reshaped in the crucible of war. Some of its elements were drawn off, and other new ingredients were added, thus changing the texture of the new combination. This transformed isolationist group became a national front called America First. Led by the conservatives, it was organized formally in September, 1940, just at a time when the United States began to aid England in a way that completely repudiated the concept of neutrality. The founder was a wealthy Yale student, R. Douglas Stuart, Jr. (son of the First Vice-President of the Quaker Oats Company) who was helped by General Robert E. Wood, Chairman of the Board of Sears, Roebuck and Company. America First was supported by prominent leaders in many fields: the writers, Kathleen Norris and Irvin S. Cobb; the aviator, Charles A. Lindbergh, and the aviatrix, Laura Ingalls; Henry Ford; General Hugh S. Johnson of N.R.A. fame; William R. Castle, former State Department policy-maker; Chester Bowles, a prominent Connecticut business executive; Theodore Roosevelt's energetic daughter, Mrs. Nicholas Longworth; and the perennial crusader, Amos R. E. Pinchot. Its most prominent Senatorial allies were Wheeler, Nye, and Rush Holt of West Virginia. The National Committee flooded the country with pamphlets, letters, buttons, and stickers, while Lindbergh, Nye, and Wheeler made innumerable speeches in behalf of its cause. There was plenty of money with which to campaign. Much of this came from sympathetic business sources.

The new organization paralleled the nationwide network of

the White Committee. The Buffalo unit of America First made its appearance on December 19, 1940. "We are not," said a local spokesman, "anti-British, not anti-anybody, merely anti-war."[18] This branch, at least in the early days of its existence, received help from the Erie County and the New York State Women's Christian Temperance Union, the Disabled Veterans of the World War, the Women's International League for Peace and Freedom, and some of the labor unions. Feeling ran high in 1941 between America Firsters and members of the Niagara Frontier Committee, with each group impugning the patriotism of the other. It is impossible to gauge accurately either the local or national strength of America First at the noon-day of its influence. Reliable historical investigators, however, are inclined to think that the din of its propaganda led contemporary observers to overestimate its hold upon the country.

The founders of America First, isolationists but not subversives, had to guard themselves quite as much from their would-be friends as from their avowed enemies. For nine months after September, 1940 until Hitler swung eastward against Russia, they had to rebuff the Communists, who would have liked to have taken over the organization. This peril was removed on June 22, 1941, when the Communists suddenly perceived that they had been trying to infiltrate an America First which the new party line said was made up of quislings, traitors, anti-Semites, fascists, and dangerous reactionaries!

It was far more difficult for America First to avoid guilt-by-association with totalitarian elements of the right-wing variety. As Wayne S. Cole has pointed out in his able study of the movement, the original leaders were loyal Americans who wanted to shield their organization from the touch of disloyal pro-Nazis or nativist fanatics who specialized in dealing blows beneath the belt. America First had been founded to promote a three-fold program based upon chaste isolationist principles: 1 - To build up home defenses to the point where the United States would be militarily impregnable; 2 - To convince the public that American democracy could be best preserved by staying out of war and that intervention would jeopardize domestic liberties; 3 - To purvey the idea that the President's program of "aid short of war" would weaken American defense and lead to involvement in the war.[19] General Wood, as head of the organization, stressed the broad middle ground upon which all Americans (except outright interventionists and rabid anti-British fanatics) could meet.

General Wood discovered, however, that organizations

fighting for the same immediate purpose are drawn together by a magnetic force generated in the heat of the struggle. It was not always easy, in those agitated years, to be certain if the wearer of an America First button was a simon-pure isolationist, a man who believed that F.D.R. was planning the destruction of the republic with malice aforethought, a fifth-column Bundist, a member of a lunatic-fringe hate-group, or a devout Coughlinite.

By the middle of 1941 the high command of America First had split over the question of purging the organization. Large blocks of tickets for an important peace rally would often find their way into the hands of unwanted confederates who would fill half the hall with their noisy followers. When the meeting was over, detailed explanations and apologies to the general public would be in order. Senator Nye spoke under questionable auspices, while former Governor Philip La Follette of Wisconsin shared the platform with the notorious Coughlinite, Father Edward L. Curran. John T. Flynn, chairman of the New York City chapter, thought that the cause of isolationism would be best served by an open denunciation of America First's undesirable allies, but Wheeler and Lindbergh, who did much of the national speaking for the organization, refused to rebuff any help that came their way.[20]

The isolationists weakened their cause by keeping bad company. In the end, says Professor Cole, the revelations about these associations attracted more public attention than did the America First propaganda. The New York *Herald Tribune* scooped the story that part of the organization's money came from the German-American Bund and other pro-Nazi sources.[21] The country also learned that isolationist members of Congress had sent out pamphlets, under their franking privilege, with arguments in them that could have been credited to Dr. Goebbels. Some of this literature, containing words that smacked of treason, found their way into army camps. America First had fallen into wide disrepute before the organization sank from sight with the battleships that were destroyed at Pearl Harbor.

An analysis of the isolationist arguments reveals that they were closely attuned to an international situation made fluid by the shifting fortunes of war. Until the fall of France the isolationists assumed that the war was a limited one and would soon end, leaving the balance of power virtually intact. It followed, therefore, that America needed only to play 'possum to remain neutral and safe. Herbert Hoover and his friend, Senator Robert A. Taft, called for an old-fashioned reliance upon

275

ocean security. The Allies, said Hoover, would win without American help. To Senator Borah and the Communists, the new war was just another round in an endless European struggle between rival systems of imperialism. The United States, advised the isolationists, should pursue "wallflower diplomacy" and sit out this dance of death.

By mid-summer 1940, the threatened invasion of Britain put the isolationists on the defensive. Men began to tremble for the security of their country in a way unknown to people of the northern states since General Lee retreated from Gettysburg. To allay popular fears of the consequences of an Axis victory, the isolationists stressed the "Fortress America" concept, namely, that an adequately defended New World would be impregnable to any possible combination of foes. If one accepted this theorem, the corollary would follow that the United States could safely risk any upset in the world balance of power. Therefore, the isolationists argued, the strength of the country ought not to be dissipated by sending much-needed defense materials to beleaguered Britain nor ought its task of shielding the western hemisphere be magnified by including in its periphery such outposts as Greenland or Iceland.

Oddly enough, in view of what modern aerial warfare did to outmode our old defense system, the outstanding champion of the ocean-security theory was the man who made the first solo flight across the Atlantic—Charles Augustus Lindbergh. It is easier to account for this famous flier's original isolationist orientation than to explain his two major wartime errors of judgment, namely, that there was no possibility of a successful Axis air attack against us, and that we were powerless to carry the offensive overseas against their citadels.

Lindbergh, born in 1902, had been exposed in his formative years to the preachments and writings of his Swedish-born Congressman father, a prominent leader of the mid-western agrarian revolt against Wilson's alleged pro-Wall Street foreign policy. The younger Lindbergh had early become aviation-minded, and was graduated from the old army air corps flying school at Kelly Field, Texas. His epoch-making 33-hour flight from New York to Paris catapulted him, at the age of twenty-five, from obscurity into world fame.

After 1927, Lindbergh became interested in commercial aviation, and, as consultant for two leading transport companies, helped create the modern American network of domestic and overseas air lines. Paradoxically, the man who did so much to conquer space, became, through a series of circumstances, the leading spokesman for the argument that the classic

American security concept had not been doomed by the air lanes between the continents.

The first of a series of related events in Lindbergh's life came with the brutal murder of his infant son, for which a German immigrant paid the supreme penalty. In December, 1935, irritated by high-pressure American news-gatherers, and annoyed at some New Dealers who probed into his relations with commercial aviation companies receiving government subsidies, Lindbergh sought refuge in more restrained Britain. Here he was living in quiet retirement in the Weald, near Sevenoaks, when fate intervened once more. Quite suddenly he was to emerge as the leading American authority on the air-power potential of foreign nations.

One day in 1936 Lindbergh received a letter from Major Truman Smith, military attaché of the American Embassy in Hitler's Berlin. He was invited to come to Germany to help assess the international implications of Hermann Wilhelm Goering's burgeoning Luftwaffe. American diplomatic officials at Berlin had correctly divined that the vainglorious Goering would be sufficiently flattered by Lindbergh's visit to reveal some German air secrets to him. The plan worked better than expected. Lindbergh was fêted, allowed to fly the newest German planes, to visit the squadrons, to talk to the Nazi fliers, and to inspect the airplane assembly lines. He then helped Major Smith prepare one of the finest pieces of pre-war intelligence information, for which service Lindbergh received the Distinguished Service Medal.

After a short visit to the United States, Lindbergh did similar scouting missions for the government in France, England, and Russia. At the request of Hugh Wilson, United States Ambassador at Berlin, Lindbergh returned to Germany to take another look at the Luftwaffe and to try his hand at helping the perplexed diplomats establish closer rapport with the unruly Nazis. Just after the infamous Hitlerian blackmail coup of Munich in October, 1938, Goering decorated Lindbergh with the Service Cross of the Order of the German Eagle. Americans read their papers, listened to their radios, and began to wonder.

In the critical year of 1939, Lindbergh came back to his native land and spent four months in active military duty. Two days after he returned to the inactive list, at the very opening of the European war, he made the first of what was destined to be a long series of isolationist speeches. The next two years were to mark a strange and controversial interlude in the life of a man who, despite a great personal tragedy, had been singularly rewarded for his enterprise by fame and fortune. A naturally shy, retiring, and reserved man, he re-entered the limelight during the most heated controversy of his generation.

Putting the cards together, it is possible to understand Lindbergh's isolationism. While he undoubtedly remembered many of the arguments heard in his boyhood, his isolationism was of a very different stripe from his father's. The elder Lindbergh was of the classic, midwestern, liberal school; his writings and speeches show the concern of a socially minded Scandinavian-American for what war might do to fasten the hold of the "House of Morgan" upon the country, thereby increasing the maldistribution of wealth, and forcing the wheat farmer into further colonial subservience to Wall Street. Lindbergh *fils* had no such fears. On the contrary, he seems to have dreaded the effect of war upon the vested interests. Wealthy in his own right and married to a Wall Street heiress, Colonel Lindbergh was a prime example of the prevailing conservative isolationism of Second World War days. He thus let his fears of an ultimate Communist victory outweigh any concern for the more immediate Nazi menace and any moral revulsion that he might have had against Hitler's anti-humanitarianism. At Chicago in August, 1940, Lindbergh spoke of American co-operation with post-war Germany which, he said, would not be impossible if it were to the advantage of both countries. He clearly showed his preference for fascist rather than communist totalitarianism by demanding that the non-Marxist countries resolve their differences in order to "maintain the supremacy of our Western Civilization."

Men's motives, however, are always complex, and Lindbergh was influenced by other considerations. He was resentful because neither the British nor the French pre-war governments had heeded his warnings about German power. Of a mechanical frame of mind, with little insight into or understanding of non-scientific matters, Lindbergh over-valued Nazi technological efficiency and underestimated the resilience of the democracies. He joined America First and became one of its leading spokesmen. Sensitive by nature, unused to the rough game of politics, he became rash, bitter, and even vindictive. When the President returned blow for blow, and insinuated that Lindbergh was a modern-day "Copperhead," the Colonel, on April 28, 1941, resigned his commission in the air force reserve. His subsequent speeches, especially those made after the Nazis turned eastward against the Communists, show clearly that he lost his sense of balance.[22]

Lindbergh appeared to be a prize find for America First, for

278

he was a nationally advertised hero and an authority on the question of the hour—the feasibility of an air assault on the United States. With little previous experience in speech-making or radio broadcasting, he developed a style of his own that mirrored his calm, undemonstrative, phlegmatic, and reserved personality. He said, after the fall of France, that he wanted neither side to win so that the western powers could negotiate a peace. According to Lindbergh's considered judgment the oceans still protected us from an Axis attack, and at the same time made it impossible for the United States to carry the war to the opposite shores. Who, thought men as they listened to his strong words in crowded America First rallies, or tuned into his radio speeches in the quiet of their homes, was in a better position to know? Like almost all the latter-day isolationists, he insisted upon full defense of the New World. Here we could, he promised, keep the lamps of civilization trimmed and bright to serve as shining beacons amidst the gloom of the surrounding darkness. To fight for the English way of life, or the Chinese way of life would be as foolish as it would be futile. We could not, he warned, rescue any potential allies from destruction, for it was already to late. The Axis triumph was irreversible even if America went to war. One hundred million Americans were opposed to fighting for an England that was already doomed. It was therefore, he concluded, the duty of the overwhelming majority to checkmate a minority of warmongers who did not believe in an "independent American destiny."[23]

Lindbergh would have proved a far greater asset to America First had he not adumbrated these isolationist arguments with Nazi-like racial slurs. For example, at Des Moines, on September 11, 1941 he said: "The three most important groups which have been pressing this country toward war are the British, the Jewish, and the Roosevelt administration." "Their greatest danger to this country," he remarked of the Jews, "lies in their large ownership and influence in our motion pictures, our press, our radio, and our government."[24] Following this speech, the prestige of America First took a sharp decline. Lindbergh had unwittingly pointed up the affinity that existed between the current variety of isolationism and a dangerous foreign ideology. After Lindbergh's Des Moines performance, Senator Nye had to digress from his anti-Roosevelt philippics in order to deny that America First had embraced Nazi anti-Semitism. Privately, the North Dakota Senator admitted that Lindbergh had blundered, but he equivocated when the Jewish leadership in Cincinnati requested him to see to it that henceforth the isolationists drop their racial innuendos and handle the matter solely as a choice between intervention and non-intervention in the war.[25]

America First had conducted a strenuous and stirring campaign to check the growing conviction that, whatever the costs, the Axis must not be allowed to win. Although its followers lost every pitched battle against the President, they constituted an influential minority in both Congress and the country until the very Sunday afternoon of Pearl Harbor. Undoubtedly, America First had many sympathizers among many reticent people who made it a habit not to attend mass meetings, wear badges, or join pressure groups. But despite this great strength, the isolationist cause had been lost before the Japanese bombed Hawaii. Regardless of the type of case America First would have formulated, they probably could not have relieved the fear of the majority that an Axis victory would prove detrimental to the security, to the business interests, and to the political creed of the United States.

The existence of America First, however, deterred the President from placing his cards on the table. Roosevelt's decision to renounce conventional neutrality and at the same time to assure the country that such action would not lead to actual shooting, had been made long before the isolationists consolidated their ranks. But if America First was not responsible for F.D.R.'s original determination, its campaign was a factor in keeping him from precipitating the question of peace or war in its undistorted form. With so powerful a pressure group promoting an anti-war spirit, the President refused the ultimate gamble. Convinced that he was acting in the interest of the country and humanity itself, Roosevelt camouflaged his actions until the Japanese warlords settled his problem. Thus, in retrospect, America First not only fought the last rear guard action of the old isolationism, but it also helped make certain that out of Roosevelt's maneuvers would come eventually the rationale for a new brand of isolationism.

The critical decisions that ranged the United States squarely behind the British war efforts came in the fall and winter seasons of 1940-1941. The first radical departure from neutrality was the destroyer-bases deal of September 2, 1940. The hard-pressed Royal Navy was in desperate need of additional swift vessels in order to convoy war materials through the tangles of the German submarine net. Roosevelt came to its help by handing the British fifty over-age destroyers in return for the right to set up American bases (for a 99-year period) on eight English possessions scattered from Newfoundland to the mainland of South America. In taking what Winston Churchill later called this "decidely unneutral act," Roosevelt did not ask the consent of Congress. His Attorney-General managed to justify the deal by finding the necessary loopholes in existing domestic and international law. It was the first indication of how far F.D.R. was prepared to go to make sure that Britain would fight on to victory.

Roosevelt had acted in the midst of a presidential campaign in which he found himself pitted against the magnetic and forceful Republican aspirant, Wendell L. Willkie. The latter's surprise nomination over three leading isolationist or semi-isolationist rivals is a pointed commentary on the way world events sometimes influence domestic politics. In the excitement that followed the fall of France, the Wall Street non-isolationist Republican leaders, using steamroller methods to overwhelm the opposition, were able to smash through to victory.

Willkie's nomination was an unexpected boon for Roosevelt, for, although the public utilities lawyer proved to be a tough opponent, his candidacy diminished the danger of a sharp division over foreign policy in the most critical months of the war. But the issue was subdued rather than exorcised. Willkie took isolationism out of the campaign, only to put it back in modified form when the professional politicians insisted that he capitalize upon the anti-war sentiment. The Democratic politicians were frightened, and told the President that Willkie would hold the bedrock G.O.P. strength, would cut into the independent liberal vote, and would appeal to isolationists of both parties as the choice of the lesser evil. Roosevelt began to reiterate his no-war promises and found it expedient to say in the Irish stronghold of Boston: "I have said this before, but I shall say it again and again and again. Your boys are not going to be sent into any foreign wars."[26] Because political leaders—Republican and Democratic—felt the anti-war sentiment to be dominant in the country in the fall of 1940, both candidates ended up by saying that the chances of war would be greater if the other man won. Roosevelt was soon to regret his more rash promises and, after the election, Willkie called his own anti-war speeches just so much "campaign oratory."

The supreme crisis in the long debate over help to England came a few months after the American electorate returned F.D.R. to the White House for an unprecedented third term. Prime Minister Churchill now spoke boldly and made it clear to Roosevelt that any reasonable expectation of British victory would depend upon a ten-fold increase in American aid. England was in no position to pay for this help, and Roosevelt had no desire to start a fresh round of war debts. Mulling the matter over while relaxing aboard the cruiser *Tuscaloosa,* the President conceived the idea of lending goods rather than money. He told the country in a fireside chat that the United States would become the "arsenal of Democracy," and a few days later he laid his lend-lease proposal before the newly elected Congress that assembled in January, 1941.

It would be difficult to imagine a more radical break with conventional neutrality than this Lend-Lease Act. The President was authorized, under any terms he thought proper, to lend, lease, sell, or barter arms, ammunition, food or any "defense article" or any "defense information" to "the government of any country whose defense the President deems vital to the defense of the United States." Secretary Hull helped explain the new plan to the nation. He said that the United States had to take this step lest the control of the seas pass into hostile hands. Should such a catastrophe occur, he warned that the New World would no longer be immune from attack. Here was the gist of the controversy between the administration and America First: Was the defense of Great Britain vital to the security of the United States?

Congress debated the issue hotly for two months, for the isolationists realized that the fate of their cause hinged upon the outcome of the vote. They had opposed the *sale* of munitions to either side, and now the President proposed to *give* weapons to one set of belligerents. Senator Taft, who in 1939 had voted in favor of repealing the arms embargo, placed his great talents on the side of the opposition to lend-lease. He quipped that lending war goods was like lending chewing gum —it was something that you did not want returned. Taft's logical mind led him to conclude that if one granted the President's premise that American security warranted the spending of huge sums of money to defend Britain, we were then morally obliged to start shooting, for we had accepted the contention that it was our war. There was a good deal to be said for this point of view, but Roosevelt was interested in immediate results and refused to debate fundamental concepts. According to Senator Wheeler, lend-lease was the New Deal's "Triple-A foreign policy to plow under every fourth American boy." The President made a point of allowing the press to quote him directly as saying that the Montana Senator's remark was "the most untruthful . . . dastardly . . . rottenest thing said in public life in my generation."[27] Tempers flared dangerously on both sides.

The congressional debates reveal that lend-lease was op-

282

posed by two different groups for somewhat divergent reasons. The outright isolationists argued that the passage of the bill would lead to war with Germany, and, while the conflict was pending, it would milk the United States of resources needed for its own defense. A more moderate group wanted to extend further help to Britain, but was distinctly unwilling to invest the President with the power to help any country whose defense he happened to think vital to the United States. Some men, even then, envisaged a death struggle between Nazi and Soviet totalitarianism and were reluctant to entrust Roosevelt with the power to put the resources of the United States at the disposal of Stalin.

The country at large echoed the voices heard in Congress. To the Chicago *Tribune,* Roosevelt was clearly out to "destroy the Republic." On the local front the issue was debated between branches of America First and units of the White Committee. In Buffalo, the former group said that the bill's true purpose was to help England achieve its sole war aim—the preservation of the British Empire. A Protestant minister said that Hitlerism was only a symptom of an international disease that produced the same effects in Germany, England, and all the "pluto-democracies." A former congressman warned that if Congress gave such far-reaching power to the President, they would never be returned to the legislative branch of the government. If Roosevelt had built up the manpower of the nation instead of having wasted money on raking leaves, said one newspaper correspondent, then the country would be strong enough to defend itself regardless of what happened to Britain.

The President's supporters quoted Herr Hitler himself to refute these arguments. "Two worlds are in conflict, two philosophies of life," *Der Führer* had announced, "one of these two worlds must break asunder."[28] The Niagara Frontier Committee for the Defense of America stated that "the time has come for Congress and the people to prove that they mean what they say when they agree that our security demands that the aggressors be defeated."[29] Both this committee and the local branch of America First urged their respective supporters to make their views known to members of Congress.

When the votes were tallied, the administration won a clear victory in both houses. The count, however (260 to 165 in the House, 60 to 31 in the Senate), connoted a strong minority dissent. This and the recriminatory nature of the debates were clear signals to Roosevelt that still bolder proposals might turn the tide against him. Eric F. Goldman has pointed out that isolationism of a liberal kidney had all but vanished when F.D.R. signed the Lend-Lease Act, March 11, 1941. With a few notable exceptions, the men who opposed the President's foreign policy were conservative anti-New Dealers. The majority in Congress had endorsed the President's new brand of "neutrality"—all help, short of shooting war, to insure a British victory.

The isolationists were depressed by their defeat, but were determined to fight on. The extent of their dismay can be measured by the words that Senator Vandenberg recorded in his diary:

> We have tossed Washington's Farewell Address into the discard. We have thrown ourselves squarely into the power politics and the power wars of Europe, Asia and Africa. We have taken the first step upon a course from which we can never hereafter retreat.[30]

But the Senator did not know all that had been done. While Congress was still debating, the American and British Chiefs of Staff anticipated its approval by agreeing on how to make lend-lease effective and by laying plans for future cooperation if and when the United States became an active partner in the war. In order to avoid any clear commitment, Roosevelt decided not to initial this "ABC-1 staff agreement," but that was a technicality.[31]

A little over three months after the success of the Lend-Lease Act deflated the hopes of the isolationists, their cause gained new logic and strength when Hitler's panzer divisions drove across the Soviet border. Now the cry was heard in the land: "Let the dictators fight it out among themselves." The tough and unexpected Russian resistance made Americans breathe easier than they had since the French surrender. Hitler had turned his back on Britain and the Atlantic and was spending his strength against another unscrupulous dictator. The situation promised relief from the anxiety over an attack on America based on the western Atlantic springboard. Fifteen top Republican leaders, including Herbert Hoover, former Vice-President Dawes, Alfred M. Landon, and former Governor Frank O. Lowden of Illinois, issued a joint statement declaring that Churchill's decision to ally his country with Russia had turned the struggle into one of power politics with no bearing upon the future of liberty and democracy. The Buffalo branch of America First challenged their opponents to a "Referendum Day" in order to determine whether or not the people of the United States wanted to grasp the hands of the Communists as brothers-in-arms. Charles A. Lindbergh went a step further and said that he preferred an alliance with Germany, "or even England" to Roosevelt's prompt extension of lend-lease aid to Russia. "Mr. Democrat" himself, then Senator Harry S. Truman of Missouri, remarked:

> If we see that Germany is winning, we ought to help Russia, and if Russia is winning we ought to help Germany and that way let them kill as many as possible, although I don't want to see Hitler victorious under any circumstances. Neither of them think anything of their pledged word.[32]

To such contentions the Niagara Frontier Committee for the Defense of America replied that Hitler was a "Brown Bolshevist" whose strength would become overpowering if he were allowed to add fertile Russia to his other conquered resources. The Committee therefore heartily approved extending lend-lease assistance to Stalin, for as the old Arab saying had it, "the enemy of my enemy is my friend." "When there are rats to be exterminated," explained the chairman, "one does not examine the social credentials of the rat catcher."

The Russo-German war, nevertheless, gave a temporary fillip to congressional isolationist voting power. A plague-on-both-their-houses feeling threatened to sweep the country. The administration, partly as a result of its own insistence that the country was not going to be involved in war, almost failed to secure passage of a bill in Congress providing that the term of service of peace time draftees be extended beyond one year, and that they be allowed to be dispatched beyond the confines of the western hemisphere. In one of the tensest moments of the long tug of war with the isolationists, Roosevelt's proposal carried in the House, August 12, 1941, by the breathtaking margin of 203 yeas to 202 nays. The Old Guard mind relished the thought that the Red and Brown terrors would destroy each other in mortal combat. Shouldn't America sit back on the sidelines and watch these unworthy gladiators fight to the finish?

As everyone knows today, the Russian victory, made possible by American help, substituted one totalitarian peril for another. Some recall Senator Taft's warning that Stalin was potentially more dangerous to civilization than Hitler. It has even been suggested that, had Roosevelt been a true statesman, he would have alternately helped both sides until the rival furies were equally spent.

Such a misanthropic policy, defensible only in the light of hindsight, was neither possible nor wise at the time. It was not possible because gross Machiavellian schemes cannot be undertaken in a popular democracy where cardinal decisions must run the gamut of Congress, a free press and radio, and the public forum. Nor would it have been wise to have taken any chances on so callous a plan that might well have boomeranged in the form of a Hitlerian victory. Foster Rhea Dulles has reminded us that if the defeat of the Axis left us with the Russian colossus on our hands, this fact does not in any way minimize the Nazi peril of 1941. Roosevelt could either have helped the Soviets as he did, or else could have left that country to its fate at the hands of a stronger adversary. The probabilities are that Hitler would have prevailed, and his megalomaniac mind would not have allowed him to be satisfied with the subjugation of half the world. It might not have happened, but it was a risk that no responsible American statesman could have taken.

While Hitler's armies were driving deep wedges into the Russian heartland, the question of delivering the lend-lease goods became acute. There was no sense, as the isolationists had predicted during the course of the debates in Congress, in converting the country's factories to military production, and then in allowing German U-boats to send these so called "defense articles" to Davy Jones' locker. Roosevelt, preferring to fight the isolationists in installment fashion, carefully evaded the problem of patrolling the seas or helping the British convoy duty. He allowed pressure to mount in the country urging him to insure the delivery of our goods to the fighting front.

In the spring of 1941, the administration prepared the way for the safe carriage of war goods by extending American control over the North Atlantic islands guarding the approach to the New World. While the isolationists were hemispheric-minded, they were severely limiting the boundaries of the continents in a globe contracted by air-power. F.D.R. resolved the question by taking an over-generous view of the limits of western hemispheric defense. On April 9, 1941, the administration made an agreement with the anti-Nazi Danish minister in Washington that allowed for American occupation of Greenland where the Germans had already set up weather stations. Three months later American soldiers landed in Iceland, after coming to terms with both the local authorities and the British government which had already stationed troops on the island.

The next step was to find a way to relieve the hard-pressed

Royal Navy, which, in addition to keeping the home waters open, after June, 1941 had to protect the sea route around the northern tip of Norway in order to land supplies at the Russian *entrepôt* of Murmansk. Roosevelt was equal to the occasion. He decided to extend the New World neutrality patrol-belt (agreed upon by a 1939 Conference of American Foreign Ministers in Panama but subsequently violated by both belligerent powers) to North Atlantic waters west of Iceland and to "publish the position of possible aggressor ships or planes when located in the American patrol area."[33] This meant that the American Navy would scout these waters for Nazi submarines and warn the British convoys of their position.

Hitler was determined to to give Roosevelt a *casus belli* through naval provocation, but there was a limit beyond which the Germans could not go without serious injury to their own war effort. On September 4, 1941, the destroyer *Greer* was attacked by a Nazi submarine. The President found it expedient not to tell the public that the *Greer* had been signaling the U-boat's whereabouts to a nearby British plane. Instead, in a fireside chat of September 11, he denounced the attack as "piracy" and warned that he had ordered the navy to "shoot on sight" German or Italian war vessels that prowled the "American" part of the North Atlantic. The Niagara Frontier Committee for the Defense of America said that Germany had made war on us and demanded that our navy "clear the oceans of such piratical raiders and make the seas safe for our legitimate commerce." The local America Firsters replied that the President had courted Nazi retaliation by repairing British battleships in our ports, by arming Hitler's foes, and by projecting American troops and ships far beyond our legitimate lines of defense.

The isolationists spoke more accurately than their critics, but they were wrong in impugning the ultimate motives of the President as well as the means he chose to get the country to allow him to achieve them. Probably historians will never agree in assessing Roosevelt's handling of the situation, for the amount of charity one is apt to use in judging his case depends upon the way one replies to two moot questions: Would a Hitlerian victory have spelled eventual disaster for the United States? Does the end, however praiseworthy, ever justify the means? The answers to these questions must necessarily be based on value judgments rather than historical evidence. As far as the latter is concerned, there is no question that the President made the most of the naval incidents which arose as we tried to secure the convoy route to Reykjavik where the

Royal Navy assumed complete responsibility for the "defense articles." After the destroyer *Kearny* was hit by a torpedo with the loss of eleven American lives, Roosevelt told the country: "We have wished to avoid shooting. But the shooting has started. And history has recorded who fired the first shot." Four days after he spoke, the *Reuben James* went down with 96 casualties. The undeclared naval war with Germany was in full swing.

The last stand of the pre-Pearl Harbor isolationists came in November, 1941, when they tried to defeat Roosevelt's request that Congress repeal that part of the Neutrality Law forbidding the arming of merchantmen. There was a stiff fight, and the isolationist voting power held up well, but still they lost this last round. Actually Congress gave the President more than he requested, for virtually all of the neutrality legislation was wiped off the statute books. Henceforth armed American merchant ships, laden with any type of cargo, were free to set sail for belligerent ports. At Roosevelt's behest, Congress decided to go back to the older American principle of defending the "freedom of the seas" without any neutrality safeguards. With an informal naval war with Germany already under way, future collisions between the two powers were made all the more inevitable by allowing American vessels to sail into the most fiercely contested combat zones.

Could the tension have continued indefinitely without a formal declaration of war by one side or the other? It is not necessary to answer this question for, eight days after President Roosevelt signed the new law, the Japanese naval task force, under the command of Admiral Chuichi Nagumo, lifted anchor off the Kurile Islands for its surprise visit to Hawaii. What if there had been no Pearl Harbor to bring on a two-front declared war? Roosevelt, Robert E. Sherwood later remarked, had completely exhausted his bag of "short of war" tricks. It is possible that we would have drifted into war with Germany in the winter of 1941-1942. Without a Japanese attack to fuse American public opinion, however, the likelihood is that the President would have had to contend with the kind of partisan dissent that handicapped Madison in 1812 against England, and Polk in 1846 against Mexico. The bombs over Pearl Harbor were lethal, but some of Roosevelt's most perplexing problems vanished with the smoke that they created.

Curiously enough, neither America First nor the interventionists expected that all-out war would result from the Japanese complication. European, not Asiatic crises had been the traditional isolationist bugbear. Part of the popular failure to recognize the gravity of the Far Eastern situation came from the American tendency to belittle the prowess of non-Caucasian races. The Japanese were written off, in popular estimation, as jackals who waited in hiding to pick up stray pieces of territory pried loose during a major encounter of white nations. The isolationists, moreover, were so absorbed with the question of checkmating Roosevelt's anti-German moves, that they paid little attention to the steadily mounting Japanese crisis. Some of them, Senator Wheeler in particular, strongly backed the President's policy of aiding Chiang Kai-shek in resisting Japanese aggression. On the whole, they were much more willing to give Roosevelt a free hand in Asia than in Europe. Little complaint was heard as steps were taken that led up to the impasse that preceded Pearl Harbor—the 1939 abrogation of our commercial treaty with Japan, the supplying of goods to embattled China, and the drastic 1941 step of banning all exports to Nippon.[34] As that shrewd English observer of American politics, Dennis W. Brogan, has noted, public opinion went along with Roosevelt "when he put Japan in the position of having to put up or shut up." Thus the crisis of November, 1941 caught almost everyone off guard. Before the isolationists could rouse themselves to meet the new danger, the war had begun. The fact that they had been asleep at the switch explains why, in self-vindication, they were later so predisposed to accept the dubious theory that F.D.R. kept them busy guarding the front door to war, while he beckoned to Mars that the back entrance was unlatched.

Thus the Pearl Harbor disaster was destined to become the keynote of the post-1945 isolationist medley. A whole genre of literature has sprung up concerning the events of the fateful months and days that preceded December 7, 1941. A detailed examination of the morass of conflicting evidence is beyond the scope of the present work, but in view of the later importance of the problem, an epitome of the most reliable findings on this complicated problem is in order. A plexus of circumstances, torn out of their full context, has convinced some investigators, that, until proven innocent, the President must be presumed guilty of provoking Japan to war. There is no question that Roosevelt wanted the country to go to war with Germany and the Japanese attack pulled him off the horns of a nasty dilemma. In handling the Japanese crisis, the American statesmen did not explore every possible opportunity for compromise settlement. When the diplomatic situation got out of control and war was clearly in the offing, neither the Washington Chiefs of Staff nor the Hawaiian naval and military field commanders made the proper use of intelligence information about Japanese war plans. Had they done so, the Pearl Harbor disaster might have been averted, or at least mitigated.

That much having been said, it would be a *non sequitur* to deduce, as some historians have, that Roosevelt incited Japan to the attack in order to involve the United States in the European war, and that he deliberately exposed the fleet at Pearl Harbor so as to shock the American people into united support for the war. The evidence points clearly to error in judgment about the possibility of a compromise with Japan, bad guesses as to where the blow would strike, and culpable negligence in not making proper use of the intelligence information garnered from decoded Japanese dispatches. Viewing Pearl Harbor as the ultimate result of illegal Japanese aggressions, Professor Pratt states correctly that "to say that the United States, or President Roosevelt, provoked Japan to attack is equivalent to saying that the victim who defends himself or his neighbor provokes the robber to violence." This same authority points out, moreover, that Roosevelt could not possibly have known for certain that Germany would honor her defensive alliance with Japan in such a way as to draw the United States into the European war. Tokyo, we now know, received no absolute assurance from Berlin until long after the President's "diabolical" orders were supposed to have gone out. It certainly must have been something other than a sense of honor that led Hitler to keep his word with Japan and declare war on the United States instead of remaining neutral and letting the American public cry "on to Tokyo" while Germany conquered Europe.

To accept the conspiracy theory of Pearl Harbor, as some well-known investigators have, one must not only ignore the bulk of direct and circumstantial evidence, but one must also assume that Roosevelt and his accomplices were statesmen in the fullest Machiavellian sense of the term. Despite Pratt's verdict, shared by practically all responsible professional authorities, there is just enough inexplicable military blundering left in connection with Pearl Harbor to permit a semi-plausible case for those prepared to believe the worst about Franklin D. Roosevelt.[35] Thus, in the flames that covered Pearl Harbor on that Sunday in December, the old isolationism was consumed and a new variety was fashioned.

Chapter 13

The Repudiation of a Tradition: Pearl Harbor to Tokyo Bay

THE JAPANESE sneak attack on Pearl Harbor was eventually to become an isolationist saga, but its immediate effect shattered the inter-war isolationist front. The America First spirit was so badly broken that, in later years, it could be revived only in splinter forms. Monolithic American isolationism was destroyed between December, 1941 and September, 1945. The ideological movements generated from its ruins were hydra-headed variants, nourished by a somewhat different type of soil, and consequently derived their rationale from different root causes.

The flaming torch of war temporarily cauterized the ugly wounds created by the great debate over foreign policy. The sudden descent of unlimited war from the December skies provided an answer to many of the questions that had perplexed Americans since the Wilson Era. A European-Asiatic Axis had attacked the Hawaiian Islands which President John Tyler and Secretary of State Daniel Webster had declared within the American orbit. The same territory had been annexed in 1898 for the purpose of guarding the western approaches to the United States.

This was a far different situation from 1917 when *we* declared war on Germany for reasons so far removed from the every-day concern of Americans that President Wilson found it convenient to tell the people that they were fighting for the preservation of democracy. In 1941, the Japanese onslaught was promptly followed by a declaration of war against *us* by the other Axis partners. Roosevelt wasted few words in explaining why we were at war. It was self-evident that the United States was waging, as the President said, a "War for Survival." The way in which the war began precluded a repetition of the 1919 variety of popular recoil.

The grim events that followed Pearl Harbor taught us a tragic and expensive lesson on the geographical unity of the modern world. Pajama-clad Americans tuned in on morning world news broadcasts and, at the end of a long day, sleepily turned off the radio voices recounting General Douglas Mac-

Arthur's island-ladder crawl toward Tokyo, the seesaw tank warfare on African deserts, the hunting down of German battleships in icy seas, the Russian stand along the Dneiper, or the American round-the-clock bombing of the more familiar European landmarks.

The United States, in 1941, became a world power in every sense of the term when two American forces appeared in the Middle East. Men and women in the nation's service penetrated almost all regions of the earth. They were stationed from the Arctic Circle to the bulge of Brazil, from New Zealand to Iceland, and from New Guinea to Morocco. America's soldiers roved strange lands, her sailors ventured above or below unfamiliar seas, while her air pilots fought in the most distant skies. As Wendell Willkie put it in 1942, there were no more remote places left in the world.

Space had all but disappeared. The news came that giant bombers had crossed the Atlantic in six hours—as long as it took a crack New York Central train to make the run from Grand Central Station to Syracuse. Late in the war, the Germans used guided missiles against Britain and popular speculation began as to how long it would be before the inter-continental distances would fall within range of these remote-controlled wonder-weapons. The explosion of the first atomic bomb, originally developed and used by the United States, shocked public opinion. Man, so it seemed, had perfected the technology of destruction to a point where it bade fair to put an end to civilization unless modern warfare was held in check by an international organization efficient enough to keep the peace.

The economic interdependence of the industrialized nations, long appreciated by geologists and geographers, was now brought home to ordinary Americans in many ways. The Nazi cult of geopolitics, fostered by General Karl Haushofer, attracted increased attention. To Haushofer, the state was a growing organism that must feed upon new territory and natural resources secured, if necessary, by the force of military might. Although Americans generally did not accept the amoral premises of Haushofer's theory, they used some of its teachings to plan military strategy. Geopolitical jargon helped them realize that uncontrolled expansive forces let loose in a science-shrunken world, had destroyed their geographical insulation and menaced the supply of raw materials that produced the wonders of their mechanized civilization. War demonstrated that the isolationists had greatly overestimated American self-sufficiency.

More accurate knowledge of the distribution of the world's resources was shocking to the many naive Americans who formerly thought of essential imports in terms of Havana cigars, Brazilian coffee, and Scoteh whiskey. Their eyes were opened when the Japanese sledgehammer brought the riches of the East Indies under Tokyo's control, and Nazi submarines impeded the importation of vital materials. There was a shortage of rubber, iron ore, manganese, chromium, and many other materials that the United States could produce only in part or not at all. To win, we had to imitate the Nazi device of stockpiling strategic materials, and it became evident that many of these sinews of war lay outside our own continent. Moreover, we had to plan our war strategy in such a way as to prevent our enemies from utilizing their sources of raw materials.

To those Americans who listened carefully to their radios, or who digested what they read, our military strategy highlighted the economic interdependence of the world. Various moves of Allied forces, often involving the deployment of our own troops, were made to achieve our purpose of economic strangulation. This was particularly true of the military and naval maneuvers designed to cut Germany off from her supply of essential steel alloys—the manganese of India and the Russian Caucasian region, the tungsten of Spain, and the chromium of Turkey. Similarly, one of the chief objectives of the New Caledonia campaign was to deprive Japan of that island's nickel and other resources. Americans became cognizant of a fact that was to play a great part in the future shaping of their foreign policy—more than half of the world's proved oil reserves lay beneath the surface of the troubled Middle East. There was not enough petroleum in the United States to power the engines of our civilization—certainly not enough for adequate long-run planning.

Not all of these geographical, geological, and economic implications reached the public in understandable form, and such items as did, the ordinary reader heeded less than the dramatic announcements of victories and defeats. Nevertheless, Americans learned a great deal about physical and economic geography from their wartime experience. The geographical postulate of the old isolationism and its economic corollaries had been proven false. If a new isolationism was to appeal to any group but the uninformed, it would have to find other justifications.

For the first time since the War of 1812, the American masses realized that events beyond the seas were intimately related to their own future peace and security. The old isolation-ist assumption that America had a destiny all its own was com-pletely refuted as it became apparent that our own survival was linked with that of all of the nations that formed the Grand Alliance against the Axis. As Hitler had said, one of the two worlds struggling against each other in mortal combat must break asunder. In the dreary spring of 1942, as Axis armies, pushing forward in northern Africa, eastern Europe, and southeastern Asia, threatened to converge at the vital Suez crossroad, men realized that Wilson had been right. We had failed to heed his warning that peace was impossible in the modern world unless predatory forces were held in check by an organized collective effort. It was only natural, amidst the unlimited sacrifices of total war, to recall how much more sensible it would have been to have taken timely preventive action. Thus, the ghost of Woodrow Wilson began to haunt the land.

Fortunately, neither the war hysteria nor the abridgment of civil liberties, that so afflicted the home front of 1917-1918, accompanied that apparition. There was far less marching to fife and drum, people did not over-react to the excitement, and mob psychology did not lead to a house-hunt for fascist witches. On the whole, the American behavior was mature, self-collected, and unemotional. Japanese-Americans on the West Coast were uprooted and sequestered, but this unneces-sary violation of the democratic spirit proved to be an isolated instance of the kind of prejudice so often engendered by the war mind.

There are many reasons why the prediction of America First that war would "leave the corpse of Liberty swinging grotesquely in the air" was not fulfilled.[1] The country accepted the conflict as a grim task that would be rendered more diffi-cult by heroics and bombast. Twenty years of anti-war propa-ganda had kept the memories of the sordid side of battle fresh in the American mind. There was no ebullition of the martial spirit as there had been in 1898 or 1917, when the popular image of warfare had been glorified by distorted and dimmed recollections of Civil War exploits.

Because there was no effective domestic dissent to over-come, Roosevelt was not tempted to use strong-arm methods. German- and Italian-Americans, with the exception of a hand-ful of pro-fascist traitors, caused little trouble. In distinct con-trast to 1917-1918, Socialists and Communists aided rather than hindered the war effort. Thus Roosevelt, unlike Wilson, did not fight the war in such a way as to alienate the zealous liberal guardians of civil liberties. Whereas Wilson went into the war as the champion of the liberals and subsequently estranged them, Roosevelt regained most of his genuinely liberal backers who had temporarily deserted him during the quarrel over neutrality. The balance of the independents, after 1940, supported Wendell Willkie's campaign to liberalize and internationalize the Republican party.

The general satisfaction of the liberals with the conduct and aims of the war had two far-reaching effects upon the future of isolationism. It demolished another staple of the old isolationist line: that an American war against fascism in its course would destroy the values that it sought to preserve. It meant, too, that unlike 1919, there would be few liberals disillusioned enough to join the reactionaries in a new isolationist coalition. Thus the war disproved the favorite nationalist argument of geographical invulnerability, and the liberal contention that armed intervention would once more eclipse the sun of domestic freedom.

There is another striking contrast between the two major wars of our century. Historians deal largely with tangible evidence and are understandably hesitant to dabble with subconcious motivation. Nevertheless, it seems safe to conjecture that the American people were secretly much more gratified by the wartime restoration of prosperity than the written records will ever reveal. The earlier war interrupted a period of model normality and economic equipoise, while the latter conflict put an end to a wearisome cycle of deflation, unemployment, make-work relief programs, and hard-scrabble existence. For the nine-tenths of the population not in uniform the war was the open sesame to prosperity. The life of the civilian masses was revolutionized by new opportunities, higher pay, and a new standard of living. One is certainly not justified in concluding that there was a large-scale conscious wish for war, but it is reasonable to suppose that war fulfilled many pleasant civilian dreams.

The war of 1917 had also lifted the underprivileged masses by their bootstraps. But the boom, like the war that created it, was of short duration and the sharp panic of 1921-1922 demonstrated the transient nature of the prosperity. Men longed for the return of the leisurely, pleasant, and more stable "good old days." Isolationism was one of the manifestations of this epidemic of acute nostalgia. But who, in 1945, wanted to go back to the dismal 1930s? This time, because of the pent-up demand for the consumer goods and the new military build-up against Russia, the boom phase of the business cycle seemed to possess lasting vitality. Probably the Pied Piper of war would some day have to be paid in the coin of depression, but the settlement was too far off to cause much concern. The net result of this delayed reaction was to deprive isolationism of the economic disillusionment and longing for past days that had rejuvenated it after the First World War. Many of its economic and psychological props had crumbled.

Nevertheless, it was quite apparent, even amidst the turmoil of war, that a hard core of ultra-nationalists would keep their camp fires burning until fate would provide them with new fuel to lighten the skies. War, Winston Churchill had said, is a "catalogue of blunders," and the isolationists were gratuitously furnished with many mistakes.

Some of these errors seem, in the lucid light of perspective, to have been avoidable. Many of them were made because of the inherent handicaps under which a popular government must operate. Men and women in a free society grow restive from bearing the yoke of war and they create almost irresistible pressure for short-cut methods to end the fighting. Even though they may relish the prosperity that accompanies successful warfare, they long for complete enjoyment of their new status with their boys back once more. As the popular Civil War song phrased it, "We'll all be gay when Johnny comes marching home again."

During the Second World War, Americans were, as yet, only in the chrysalis stage of adjustment to their nerve-racked age. They still regarded war as an aberrant unpleasantness that would terminate suddenly with the unconditional surrender of their foes. So long had the United States been shielded from a harsh struggle for national existence that its people had grown impervious to two facts: First, that there is a continuum to strife, or as Clausewitz observed, "war is a mere continuation of policy by other means"; second, that when a country allies itself with one totalitarian power in order to defeat another, such a victory can be expected to yield only palliative relief.

Our wartime alliance with Russia was destined to evoke a new disillusionment and islationism, although other factors were to stunt the growth of these twin reactions. The 1941 isolationists, preponderantly conservative in attitude, found our wartime association with the Reds peculiarly distasteful. This dislike was to be justified by subsequent events. They were to use the Communist threat, at home and abroad, as an entrenching tool to clear away the ruins of their old ramparts and dig a new embankment.

One does not have to probe deeply to discover why the Roosevelt administration, supported by majority opinion, explained away or underestimated the fathomless chasm between the war aims of the United States and those of the U.S.S.R. Statesmen, like ordinary mortals, are more prone to use expediency in meeting a present danger than to speculate about a future peril. Hitler and the Japanese warlords were so malignant that it seemed reasonable to believe that after they had been consigned to Gehenna, a war-weary and anaemic Russia would want nothing so much as peace. The primary step in securing Communist postwar cooperation, so the many reasoned, was to remove Stalin's doubts about our good intentions. Our record must be spotless enough, it was argued, so that the most obdurate Communist in the Kremlin would be convinced of his error in assuming that Marxist Russia would not be safe in a capitalistic world.

Some grounds existed for the erroneous belief that the Communists were slowly freeing themselves from their hidebound tenets. Had not Stalin liquidated the old Bolshevists who remained firm to the dogma that Socialists and free enterprise nations could not co-exist? Had not the Third International been dissolved? Was not the Trotskyite heresy of non-coexistence the worst of all Soviet crimes? On paper, the Soviet constitution of 1936 read like a glorified version of our own Bill of Rights. To be sure, the subsequent Moscow blood purges had belied these fine promises, but then Americans had been generously endowed by Providence with the will to believe. Many of them were in a mood to explain away Stalin's 1939 deal with Hitler, his share in the cynical partition of Poland, his absorption of his other neighbors, and his attack on the little Finland that was in the process of paying her American debt in full.

Walter Lippmann has pointed out the tendency of democratic states to paint their wartime allies and enemies in snow-white and lamp-black colors. The Second World War, men said, was either a crusade to make the world safe for Roosevelt's Four Freedoms, or it was a crime against civilization. The American mind of 1941-1945 was still strongly influenced by the vestigial strains of nineteenth-century optimism. It could not, as yet, perceive the predominant gray shade of all international relations.

The roseate disposition of most Americans led them to think of the Russian soldiers as noble crusaders holding back the Nazi infidel hordes. In 1941, Joseph E. Davies, lawyer, diplomat, and Democratic politician, wrote his Soviet apologetic,

Mission to Moscow. Its message reached the masses when the book was turned into a Hollywood feature presentation. The new cordiality toward Russia was by no means limited to Democrats or New Dealers. The anti-Roosevelt magazines published by Henry R. Luce (husband of Republican Representative Clare Boothe Luce) explained that the Soviet secret police, like the F.B.I., had to use strong methods in "tracking down traitors." The aristocracy of smug, conservative Philadelphia crowded into a local music hall to hear the Philadelphia Orchestra introduce the new Russian anthem, "Hymn to the Soviet Union."[2] At a Freedom Rally held in Buffalo shortly after Pearl Harbor, staid conservatives sat cheek by jowl besides well-known citizens of distinctly radical persuasion while the Red Flag of Bolshevism decorated the stage along with the colors of the other anti-Axis nations. The myth that only Communists, fellow travelers, and New Dealers blessed this wartime collaboration with Stalin is a product of a later disillusionment. There were dissenters, but they formed a negligible minority.

The Russo-American alliance was a marriage of convenience and, until 1943, the Moscow partner made it difficult to establish even temporary bonds of affection. Washington's patience toward its difficult ally can be explained, in part, by the temper of the American people. The very nature of our democratic government demands a close apposition between the rulers and the ruled. There was strong pressure to wage the war with minimum loss of life. This laudable desire to conserve manpower led to the selection of policies that would end the war in the shortest possible order rather than to a strategy that would leave us in a strong bargaining position with Russia when hostilities would cease. Americans, Walter Lippmann writes, in time of peace convince themselves either that war is an outmoded institution or else that it can be abolished. When, nevertheless, foreigners go to war, their first inclination is to shield themselves from the strife by neutrality and enhanced isolationism. If this plan fails, as it did in 1917 and 1941, American public opinion then insists that the enemy be brought to his knees by the swiftest means at hand.[3] During the Second World War, this demand meant full utilization of Russian help. Such a course was bound to jeopardize our position when the short-run military aims of war would be replaced by long-haul diplomatic designs calculated to preserve the gains won on the battlefield.

The decision to acquire immediate benefits by mortgaging the future resulted in policies that would soon replenish the dried-up wellsprings of isolationism. The wide and awful gap that existed between one people devoted to the enlightened principles incorporated in the Declaration of Independence and another steeped in the doctrines of Marxism, was bridged by a flimsy structure. An obvious fact was overlooked: nations that do not share the same basic mores can neither agree upon first principles, nor can they successfuly compromise their differences to create a workable world police system.

So much for the intellectual milieu in which the President fashioned his Russian policies. But could not a master leader of men, with a lifetime of realistic political and international experience behind him, be expected to be more prescient than the short-sighted public? Ought he not to have resisted wishful thinking about Communist willingness to yield to a burgeois pattern of international organization? The answers to these questions lie in F.D.R.'s interpretation of the opportunities that fate had seemingly placed in his hands.

Roosevelt, all too familiar with Wilson's mistakes, did not repeat the error of heralding the war as the precursor of a democratic millennium. He tried to prevent the inflation of another balloon filled with the volatile gas of exaggerated idealism. The President did not want to create once more a bag of false hopes, vulnerable to puncture, and certain to lead to another deflation of the American internationalist spirit. But if Roosevelt avoided some of Wilson's blunders, he made same of his own that were to descredit him and the objectives that he sought to achieve. His greatest mistake was a failure to grasp the workings of the crustaceous Marxist mind.

This cardinal error, which F.D.R. perceived in the very last days of his life, was based upon an overestimation of his own powers of personal conciliation, and an underestimation of Stalin's Marxist fundamentalism. Accustomed to working with domestic opponents who knew that political compromises must be kept, Roosevelt placed undue importance on his own personal magnetism and agility in making these bargains. An invincible optimist, he seems to have taken for granted that he would always be on the scene and in a position of authority which would allow him to reason with the Russians. He apparently had little insight into the difficulties involved in dealing with bigoted Communists through ordinary diplomatic give-and-take-methods. He shared the widespread liberal fallacy that there was an essential difference between the totalitarianism of Berlin and that of Moscow. The Nazis, so the argument went, were utterly devoid of any moral scruples. Communists, on the other hand, pursued bad methods but their ultimate aims for mankind were not too far removed from the utopian goals of the democratic reformers. Somehow these common ambitions must be used to bridge the gap between the democracies and their Russian ally. Such reasoning says the theologian-philosopher Reinhold Niebuhr, obscured the fact that "the most terrible cruelties could be generated by these (Soviet) utopian illusions."

In Roosevelt's defense, it should be recognized that his personal contacts with Stalin came at a time when sheer necessity made that dynast somewhat amenable to persuasion. Although Churchill viewed the Muscovites with a more realistic eye, he, too, was convinced that no means should be spared to establish permanent accord with them. Both men understandably shrank from facing the dread realization that the war's end might leave a world still cloven into two hostile ideological camps.

Stalin cleverly exploited a serious difference of opinion between Roosevelt and Churchill as to the future of British and French colonialism. The President and the Prime Minister could not agree on this question and F.D.R. indulged in the thought that Russia and America would stand together against the reactionary imperialists. As Winston Churchill later remarked in his classic narrative of the war, F.D.R. reasoned that even as the thirteen American colonies had benefited from the revolt against King George III, self-determination for India, Ceylon, Burma, French Indochina, and the Netherland Indies would be a boon to those subject peoples and to world peace. The United States, during Roosevelt's long tenure of office, had completed the liquidation of its Caribbean empire and had made every preparation to withdraw from the Philippines. Why could not England and France follow our example and remove the stain of imperialism from the democratic free world? It is interesting to note that Dwight D. Eisenhower shared this conviction, for the General told Congress, shortly after the war, that the United States had nothing to fear from Russia for the two countries both disliked colonialism.[4]

President Roosevelt did not foresee the danger involved in playing the Communist game of stirring up colonial unrest. The disintegration of the American Empire did not create any power lacunae, for no nation dared invade our Caribbean threshold, and the Phillippines were isolated enough to prevent immediate penetration. But after the war, the collapse of the ancient European imperialisms created tempting vacuums that removed road blocks to the Communist advance. When the props of Asiatic and African imperialism collapsed (after Roosevelt had at least helped to pry them loose), some of these lands fell to the Communists, others became dangerous arenas of ideological civil war, while other fledgling nations were to pursue a tantalizing neutrality in the power contest of our time. At the same time, British outposts—Egypt in particular—were to threaten the peace by opening doors to Communist influence. The colonial upsurge generated by the war was to plague American foreign policy and to provide many additional arrows with which to replenish the isolationist quiver.

In summation, during the years when isolationism declined to the nadir of its influence, certain of Roosevelt's decisions helped it to rise again. His policies toward both the European and Far Eastern crises, prior to Pearl Harbor, were replete with historical source material for a new and stinging revisionism. The American people were not psychologically prepared for the kind of abrupt volte-face so typical of Marxist zigzag diplomacy. Roosevelt, like Wilson, failed to insure the postwar conduct of our allies at a time when our power position would have allowed us to seize the initiative. In all charity to Roosevelt, one must concede that a dictatorial stand might not have stopped the Russians and, had it failed, he would now be indicted by historians for having broken faith. At least, as it turned out, he left the American record clean enough to show up Stalin's deeds for what they were. But, unlike Churchill, Roosevelt did not realize that wartime diplomatic and military strategy had to be geared to long-run national interests. F.D.R. chose the shortest route to the unconditional surrender of the Axis and to the creation, on parchment, of a new peace mechanism. But he badly underestimated the potential menace of Communist totalitarianism. When the time was ripe, his isolationist opponents would capitalize upon his mistakes.

While the Second World War was sowing the seeds of a new isolationism, it also provided the internationalists with a chance to harvest their crop of ideas. During the war the majority of Americans embraced once more the concept of collective security. The intellectual revolution that overthrew the regnant pre-war isolationism was already under way before Hitler's legions goose-stepped into Poland. Its course was accelerated by the sense of crisis created by the 1940 Axis victories, the shock of Pearl Harbor, and the alarm over the perilous Allied military situation in the dreary spring of 1942. Americans reacted to these dangers in a natural manner by seeking to unify all nations willing to stand with them against their foes.

Roosevelt handled the enthusiastic internationalists gingerly for, prior to December 7, 1941, he did not want to complicate his task of helping Britain by letting America Firsters charge that he was prepared to barter away the sovereignty of the United States. He was still skeptical about long-range plans for world peace when, in August, 1941, he conferred with Churchill in a secret meeting at Argentia, Newfoundland. The most celebrated result of this colloquy was the Atlantic Charter. The President, head of a government which was technically non-belligerent, was cautious in making future advance commitments. At the moment, the Nazis were driving toward Moscow and the Japanese were encroaching southward, with greedy eyes fixed on Singapore. Putting first things first, Roosevelt's prime consideration was help for Hitler's enemies—a blueprint for a new world order would have to await a more propitious occasion. Hence the Atlantic Charter merely stated that the aggressors would be disarmed, pending the establishment of a lasting organization for general security. F.D.R. hesitated to commit himself to any specific peace program. He had to be persuaded by Churchill, and his own personal confidant, Harry L. Hopkins, to agree to even the innocuous collective security language of the Atlantic Charter.

Four months later, the United States was up to the hilt in total war, and for some time the administration's energies were entirely absorbed in the military effort. Nevertheless, the Declaration by United Nations (January 1, 1942) which created the Grand Alliance, repeated the promise of the Charter that, ultimately, "some wider and permanent system of general security" would be established. The popular acclaim with which this Declaration by the United Nations was received illustrates the effect of Pearl Harbor upon American thinking. Roosevelt, without consulting Congress, had repudiated the entire tradition of isolationism by making what was tantamount to a formal alliance with twenty-five other belligerent nations. Unlike 1917, when we had insisted on describing ourselves as an "associated power," we became, in 1942, one of the Allies. And yet, as Dexter Perkins has noted, hardly a word was muttered in protest in a country where isolationist sentiment had so recently been predominant. The eggs of the new internationalism hatched rapidly in the warm incubator of total war.

The next concrete step in planning for a new world order was not taken until the fall of 1943, when the chief Allied foreign ministers met at Moscow. By that time, popular pressure was so strong that Roosevelt and Hull would have had to recognize it, even if they themselves had not already been convinced that out of war must come a surety for peace. Let us look more closely, then, into these mounting pressures.

There are many reasons for this triumph of the internationalist spirit. Once again the lingering memories of the First World War influenced the reaction of men to the later conflict. For a while, America relived the neutrality years of 1914-1917 until these recollections gave way, in parallel chronological sequence, to the old League spirit of 1917-1918. The phantom of the wartime Wilson, at the summit of his glory, made its appearance on Pearl Harbor Day. Thus, from the beginning, the American people lapsed back into the habit of associating military victory with the triumph of collective security.

The roots of the new internationalism were also grounded in realistic soil. Until 1939, a majority of Americans had looked to non-entanglement and neutrality to keep the country out of foreign wars. Twice within one generation these policies had failed to produce the desired results. Men, therefore, demanded the erection of more reliable diplomatic defenses to preserve the peace that would come with victory. It was now generally conceded that the peace of America depended upon the peace of the world. The question thus resolved into a discussion over which possible method would best achieve this larger aim. Circumstances seemed to rule out several alternate plans to mutual security. If the United States decided to police the world singlehandedly, it would mean an expensive and inconvenient perpetual mobilization. It was a course that appealed only to ambitious militarists and rabid nationalists.

There was talk of a permanent alliance of the victor powers to prevent the renewal of aggression. This plan, however, ran counter to the current surge of idealism. In the light of hindsight, it would have been unrealistic, for a peacetime alliance with Russia could hardly hold in check Communist expansionism, and any combine that would exclude the Soviet Union was unthinkable in the war years.

Another possibility was to balance the power in traditional European fashion, and some realists favored this course. But, while the American public had been prepared by propaganda to accept collective security, both isolationists and internationalists had inveighed for a generation against power politics.

Alternating blasts of Russian hot and cold war would eventually make realism the core of American policy, but in 1945 the country was not ready to abandon its ancient prejudices. The goal of international organization, it was argued, was peace, whereas alliances and power politics would inevitably lead to war. Collective security, in the Wilsonian sense, appeared to wartime America as the only feasible substitute for isolationism. Joining a revamped League of Nations would mean a sharp break with tradition, but it would entail less of a deviation from the past than any other non-isolationist plan. Collective security had been argued long enough to have been partially consecrated as an American tradition and it had a hagiolatry all of its own. It would, moreover, preserve the idealistic strain in American foreign policy, whereas *Realpolitik* would scrap idealism along with isolationism. The creation of a new international organization, composed of absolutely sovereign states, was the one alternative to isolationism least calculated to divide Americans. It was in the logic of history that it be tried.

Historiography, always a delicate seismograph of prevailing intellectual ferment, soon recorded the shift of thought in regard to foreign affairs. Professor Thomas J. Pressly has demonstrated that the retreat from isolationism had reverberations even on the never-ending controversy over the Civil War. During the 1930s the interpretations prevailed of those historians who thought the war needless. A heady group of northern and southern extremists, so this school argued, had forced a repressible conflict upon an unwilling people. But, after the fall of France, the tone of many historians began to change. They were no longer quite so certain that all past wars had been senseless, for they knew too well what would happen if the Axis were to win. Some began to re-examine the part that irreconcilable ideologists had played in the war between the Blue and the Gray. Could the scourge of human slavery, some of the bolder writers asked, have ever been extirpated without surgery by the sword? The decision lost by the Confederates at Appomattox and reversed in many history books was again in danger of reversal. This change of opinion was naturally more marked in the historiography of the First World War. One of the leaders of the anti-revisionists was Edward Meade Earle of Princeton's Institute for Advanced Study. Wilson, said Earle, went to war against Emperor William II on the irreproachable ground that a German victory would be inimical to the welfare of the United States.

As the French lines reeled before the Nazi onslaught, the

poet Archibald MacLeish (then Librarian of Congress) broadened the base of the attack. He labeled the disillusionist genre of novelists "The Irresponsibles" and indicted them for sapping the fighting spirit of the democracies.[5] The erroneous belief that past wars had been fought without cause, said MacLeish, had precipitated a moral apathy that paralyzed the free countries and made them defenseless against their assailants. Unless the people of the United States, he warned, shed their indifference to the moral issue raised by Hitler, then the thing that had strangled the Allies would also strangle us. Here was a direct refutation of the philosophy summed up in novelist John Dos Passos's aphorism that "repudiation of Europe is, after all, America's main excuse for being."

MacLeish's words drove a wedge between the liberal intellectuals and the narrow isolationists. It was Walter Lippmann, however, who refuted the munitions-banker thesis of World War I on a more popular level. Throughout a long and unique career as a philosophically oriented commentator on human affairs, Lippmann had changed his mind several times. He now returned to his original contention that we had fought, in 1917, because our historic destiny was interwoven with the fate of other countries on the Atlantic littoral. All other reasons for American intervention, he said, would not have overcome the peace pressures of the day unless "a majority of the American people had not recognized intuitively, and if some Americans had not seen clearly, what the threatened German victory could mean to the United States."

Lippmann cited no new evidence to bolster his conclusions, but his writings were widely read by the intellectually curious. In his own clear, forceful, and persuasive style he hammered home the current implications of his "Atlantic Community" thesis. The outward thrust of Nazidom, by uncovering the European flank of the Atlantic defense system, had dramatically revealed the way in which our own security was emeshed with that of the western democracies. In 1776, Lippmann explained, the United States had severed its political ties with England, but had found it geographically impossible to withdraw from the "strategic security" circle of the other Atlantic nations. This was equivalent to saying that American isolation had always existed in fancy rather than in fact. Hence, we were discarding a dangerous delusion rather than an outmoded policy. The United States, Lippmann warned, in 1943, was the vital center of western civilization, and unless it accepted the mantle of world leadership that had been thrust on its shoulders, the Atlantic Community would become a decaying fringe around the expanding Soviet Union and the emergent peoples of Asia.[6]

The United States had lost the 1919 peace because its people had failed to remember why they had gone to war. This reminder of Lippmann's was perhaps a gentle hint that it was time to rewrite the story of the Treaty of Versailles and its American aftermath. The historians, however, needed no prodding to complete the vindication of Woodrow Wilson. Heroes and villains of the 1919-1920 League of Nations drama now reversed positions, and the Irreconcilables became once more the "evil men" and "obstructionists" who, as Wilson had said, wanted to break the heart of the world. Gerald W. Johnson, a popularizer of history, wrote a series of articles for *Look* which were gathered together in an attractive pictorial narrative with a title that epitomized the spirit of the day: *Woodrow Wilson: The Unforgettable Figure Who Has Returned To Haunt Us.* "The word 'Wilson,'" Johnson explained, "now has a new definition. It means peace."[7] In the heyday of the Nye Committee, less than a decade before, "Wilson" had been almost a synonym for "war"!

Like other prominent success stories, the Wilson epic was filmed in Hollywood. Produced by 20th Century-Fox in 1944, it reached the first-run theaters just in time to propagandize the San Francisco Conference that adopted the United Nations' Charter. The movie "Wilson" was a hit and critics declared it the best feature presentation of 1945. This new tendency to accent the positive accomplishments of wars, so different from the disillusionment emphasized during the depression years, was manifested by Samuel Eliot Morison in 1950, in his presidential address to the American Historical Association. Historians, said Morison, instead of decrying wars, should teach that "war does accomplish something, that war is better than servitude, that war has been an inescapable aspect of the human story."

Some observations are in order concerning the new collective security impulse. A public opinion poll, taken before the movement reached full bloom, revealed that 73 percent of those interviewed favored active American participation in a new world association. Significantly, a breakdown of these findings discloses that the midwest was only 1 percent under other regions in the percentage of favorable replies.[8] The ethnic, economic, and geographical bulwarks of mid-western isolationism had been loosened—if only temporarily.

By V.J. Day one seldom heard the old bromide that wars were made by greedy munitions-makers and international bankers. Instead, it had become commonplace to say that after wars were won by millions of valiant soldiers, they were lost in the Senate Chamber by a handful of blackguard reactionaries. The American people who had so long magnified the difficulties of collective security in a relatively stable world, now underestimated the task of organizing a world rent asunder by two conflicting ways of life.

The wartime popularity of the collective security ideal posed a serious problem for the Republicans. By 1941, the G.O.P. leaders were frustrated and almost desperate, for they had lost three successive elections to Roosevelt and, in all probability, he would try for a fourth term. Were they to bear the now discredited tag of "isolationist" along with the other names that F.D.R. had already fastened upon them? Pondering the situation, the party leaders derived cold comfort from their voting record. Approximately 85 percent of Republican members of the House of Representatives had gone on record as opposing the Lend-Lease Bill and the extension of Selective Service in the crucial year of 1941. After Pearl Harbor, to be sure, these congressional isolationists shouted their support of the war effort from the housetops. However, the question still remained: Would or could the minority party reverse its long-standing opposition to American participation in a world police organization? The Old Guard mentality was still dominant in party caucuses on Capitol Hill, and it was habitually insensible to shifting currents of mass opinion. The G.O.P. would have to become more flexible if the United States was to lead in the formation of a new international organization, for such a move could be thwarted by 32 senators. As Wilson had discovered to his sorrow, a radical about-face in foreign policy required bipartisan support.

Fortunately for Roosevelt and Hull, the titular leader of the Republican party was Wendell Willkie. This recent convert to Republicanism set out upon an evangelical crusade to internationalize the party that had nominated him for President. But Willkie was suspected, hated, and feared by the G.O.P. congressional conservatives and many professional politicians. The right-wingers had more to fear from victory under Willkie's banner than from defeat by the Democrats for, as President, Willkie would transform the party and wrest control of it from their hands. The standpatters determined to prevent a 1944 Willkie comeback.

In order to checkmate this ambitious newcomer, the orthodox Republicans began to reconsider their discredited isolationism. But Willkie's influence far transcended the bounds of the Republican party. He circled the war-stricken globe, and came home in the autumn of 1942 to write *One World,* the most persuasive internationalist book of the decade. The sale of two million copies gave the collective security movement a welcome fillip. Willkie told the country that inasmuch as Soviet Russia was our ally, we had no choice but to accept her Communist government, and work with her leaders to secure lasting peace. Science, he said, had brought all nations into intimate association, so that henceforth "our thinking must be world-wide." The future of peace, he warned, depended upon the ability of the anti-Axis powers to reconcile their ideological differences so that they could work together in a new international organization.

By 1943, the anti-Willkie Republican captains realized that the party would have to change its thinking on foreign policy. In August of that year, the G.O.P. high command drew up the so-called Mackinac Charter. This compromise resolution tried to placate the nationalists by declaring against any form of world government, but it did favor the "responsible participation by the United States in postwar cooperative organization among sovereign nations to prevent military aggression and to attain permanent peace with organized justice in a free world."[9]

The new departure had electric effects. Governor John W. Bricker, an antediluvian isolationist, spoke, for the moment, like Woodrow Wilson. "Instead of accepting, with intelligent self-interest, a degree of responsibility for world events commensurate with our rank," he admitted, "we have allowed events to control us." The wartime tack of Bricker's fellow-Ohioan, the much more brilliant and understanding conservative, Senator Taft, was equally surprising. After Pearl Harbor silenced the debate on isolationism, Taft's name and utterances seldom made the front page. The general public, recalling the Senator's isolationism, learned of his 1944 speeches with amazement. Taft, who as a young man had sympathized with his sire's work for the League of Nations, announced that, in the future, the United States must rely upon a system of collective security as a means of obtaining the ultimate aim of national safety. But the Senator allowed himself plenty of room for retreat, for he insisted that a new international body must rest upon the firm foundation of "fair" postwar territorial settlement and economic arrangements among the powers.[10] For the nonce, however, Taft stood on record as a convert to internationalism.

In the meantime, the Democratic strategists eased the embarrassment of the Republicans in repudiating their former policies and helped the G.O.P. internationalists defeat the die-hards. Roosevelt's generosity arose not from political altruism, but rather from a determination to avoid two of Wilson's worst errors. Hence, the administration watched public opinion with careful eyes, kept the people informed on the progress of its plans for international organization, and cautiously shied away from any radical "one-world" program that would outrun the possibilities of general support. Secretary Hull, with the President's approval, assiduously tried to keep collective security from becoming a political football. He took leading Republicans into his confidence in order to insure bi-partisan approval of the administration's plans. Roosevelt and Hull made collective security an all-American proposition, so that it would not again come before the Senate as a prize plank of the Democratic party.

By the fall of 1943, this patient planning began to show results. Congress indicated to the world that it favored the creation of a successor to the League of Nations. The House Fulbright and the Senate Connally Resolutions (both passed by large majorities) declared that the United States, acting "through its constitutional processes," should join the other nations in setting up adequate international machinery to prevent further aggression and to maintain world peace.[11] Congressional action placed a marker upon the grave of the older form of isolationism. The domestic road ahead had been cleared, but the Russian stumbling block had yet to be removed.

Stalin had not proven an agreeable ally, even at a time when the resistance of his hard-pressed armies depended upon American largesse. In 1940, with virtually its last gasp, the League of Nations had expelled Russia for the unprovoked attack on Finland. Collective security had left a bad taste in the marshal's mouth. Was he now willing to mortgage his future liberty to expand at will by creating still another world tribunal? To settle this, and other annoying problems arising from Soviet perverseness, Secretary Hull, in October, 1943, braved hostile skies to fly to Moscow. A twelve-day conference of the chief allied foreign ministers yielded the Declaration of Four Nations on General Security. (At Hull's urging, China had been invited to join the United States, Russia, and Great Britain in the formal statement.) Here was the first concrete promise that the moribund League would be supplanted by a new organization. The four powers pledged to continue their wartime unity in the interest of peace, and in order to achieve this purpose, they would, at the earliest possible moment, establish a permanent association.

The gaunt and aging Hull returned from his adventurous flight in high spirits. Like the men who were to succeed to his high office, he learned slowly that Communists are for more generous with promises than deeds. Relying upon a cooperation that was never to be realized, the Secretary told a joint session of Congress:

> As the provisions of the Four-Nation Declaration are carried into effect, there will no longer be need for spheres of influence, for alliances, for balance of power, or any other of the special arrangements through which, in the unhappy past, the nations strove to safeguard their security or to promote their interests.[12]

During the latter part of the war some optimism about Russia was justified, for the Moscow Conference had temporarily cleared the air. Later in 1943 Roosevelt, Churchill, and Stalin conferred at Teheran, the capital city of Iran. In addition to many immediate military and future territorial decisions, the powers agreed to use international force for the preservation of order. To Roosevelt, collective security had come to mean that the United States, Britain, Russia, and China as the Four Policemen, would bear the burden of protecting international life and property. The success of the President's program thus hinged upon turning Stalin into a trustworthy guardian of law and order. This world police force, it soon developed, could be kept intact only by appeasing a bribe-hungry precinct captain with an insatiable desire for other people's territory.

On June 6, 1944, the long-awaited "D-Day," General Dwight D. Eisenhower invaded "Fortress Europa." Thus began the *Götterdammerung* for the Third Reich. As victory over Hitler loomed close on the horizon, the time came to lay down the keel of the new international ship of state. The blueprint for the new vessel had been sketched by enthusiastic architects. Apparently, all the major problems that had delayed the dry-dock construction had been overcome. Congress and the Republican party had sponsored the project, and Stalin had agreed to serve as co-captain of the great ship that would free the international seas of piratical adventurers.

In this atmosphere of hope and confidence, the United States invited the major powers to meet at the Dumbarton Oaks estate (in Washington, D.C.) to draw up a tentative charter for the United Nations. The Dumbarton Oaks Proposals (published October 9, 1944) revealed the contours of the new organization. Agreement was reached upon the salient details of the General Assembly, the Security Council, the Secretariat, the Economic and Social Council, and the International Court of Justice. Julius W. Pratt has thus summarized the Dumbarton Oaks Plan which, with some alterations, evolved into the Charter of the United Nations:

> It was the hope of the architects . . . that the General Assembly and the Economic and Social Council would remove or alleviate causes of friction, the International Court would settle peaceably any disputes susceptible of judicial determination, and the Security Council would assist in the peaceful settlement of disputes and suppress any acts of aggression or breaches of the peace that might unfortunately occur.[13]

When the meeting adjourned, certain weighty questions remained that could only be answered at another conference "at the summit." A date and place had to be agreed upon where all the peace-loving nations could act upon the Dumbarton Oaks proposals. Which nations were to be invited to this constituent assembly? Were the sixteen republics of the Soviet Union to be entitled to separate membership in the United Nations as their common master, Marshall Stalin, had suggested? The most perplexing problem of all concerned the veto power of permanent members of the Security Council over the proceedings of that body. In addition to these general questions, the United States had some national interests that it sought to protect. Top military authorities (backed by important Republican and Democratic senators) were unwilling to surrender unequivocally to a United Nations agency control over such Japanese strategic island outposts that might be in our possession at the end of the war. Some formula, moreover, had to be agreed upon to distribute power in the new organization among the major and lesser member nations. In order to settle these and other pressing matters, the Big Three decided to meet again—this time in the former Czarist Black Sea resort town of Yalta.

Two events, occurring during the four-month interval between Dumbarton Oaks and Yalta, brought the wave of collective security enthusiasm in the United States to flood tide. The *first* of these happenings was the 1944 presidential election. The Republicans nominated Governor Thomas E. Dewey of New York on a platform that repeated the internationalist promise of the Mackinac Charter. Dewey, with a quasi-isolationist handicap to overcome, fought an energetic campaign in which he tried to put his party squarely on record for a world organization. But domestic issues aroused a good deal of bitterness, and F.D.R. tried to draw off Dewey's fire by reopening the isolationist issue. When the Republican candidate evaded a direct answer as to how much power ought to be given to the American representative on the proposed Security Council, the President clarified his own position. "To my simple mind it is clear," he declared, "that, if the world organization is to have any reality at all, our American representative must be endowed in advance by the people themselves, by constitutional means through their representatives in Congress, with authority to act."[14] This minor exchange of blows, however, and some other skirmishes on the foreign relations front, did not obscure the fact that, for the first time in American history, both major parties pledged themselves to promote the country's entry into a general security organization. Only eight short years before, Republican and Democratic platforms and candidates alike had promised to maintain unimpaired the policy of non-entanglement.

The 1944 elections dealt another mortal blow to the old isolationism. This was not because of Roosevelt's safe but relatively narrow margin of victory, for Dewey's defeat had no direct bearing on isolationism. But when the politicians analyzed the outcome of the congressional elections, they perceived that Dewey ran much stronger than the isolationist Republicans who clung to his coattails. In both the primaries and the general elections the voters markedly rebuked the isolationists. Representatives Hamilton Fish of New York (in Congress since 1921) and Stephen Day of Illinois (who had written a book called *We Must Save the Republic*) went down to defeat along with such die-hards as Senators Gerald P. Nye and Bennett Champ Clark (Missouri). In Ohio, the senatorial statesman, Robert A. Taft, just managed to squeeze through to victory, running against an almost unknown Democrat. Thus the 1944 elections flashed a yellow light of caution to those congressional isolationists who retained their seats. The country was in no mood to see the melodrama of 1919-1920 re-enacted. Wendell Willkie, who had worn himself out trying to wrest control of the party from the Old Guard Republicans, died before the election. His passing helped the moderate G.O.P. internationalists, for Willkie had become a symbol of hate to the ultraists. They were now willing, for the nonce, to call a truce.

The *second* incidental factor that smoothed the way for senatorial accepance of the United Nations was Senator Arthur H. Vandenberg's dramatic about-face. His senate speech of January 10, 1945, publicly announcing his new views, was to have far-reaching effects upon the future of American foreign policy. Made on the eve of the Yalta Conference, Vandenberg's confession of faith merits detailed analysis, for his conversion to internationalism is highly revealing of the trend of the time.

Vandenberg's story illustrates the impact of world turmoil on the thinking of an unmistakable mid-westerner who was made more sensitive to changing conditions because of his position as a ranking leader of the Senate Foreign Relations Committee. A lifelong resident of Grand Rapids, Michigan, Vandenberg's higher education had been limited to one year of a pre-law course at the University of Michigan. He switched, however, to journalism and edited the Grand Rapids *Herald* for a number of years before entering the Senate, in 1928. As a young and enterprising Republican newspaperman, he had been a League reservationist, and had also followed the moderate wing of his party in supporting America's entry into the World Court. However, like so many lukewarm internationalists of his day, Vandenberg reverted to profound isolationism.

Editing the *Herald* did not consume all the Senator's glowing energy, and he found time to write short stories, lyrics, two cumbrous, verbose books on his favorite American hero, Alexander Hamilton, and one on his pet tradition, isolationism. He made the latter subject his crotchet, and, in 1926, analyzed it in a jumbled and ponderous volume entitled *The Trail of a Tradition*. The title page of the book proclaimed that "Nationalism—not 'Internationalism'—is the indispensable bulwark of American independence." Vandenberg seemed to have been almost obsessed by the fear that "alien contagions," spread by the internationalists, would destroy the American spirit. The tradition of isolationism, he explained, was one of rigid independence rather than of social or economic aloofness. In order to remain true to the teachings of the Founding Fathers, he advised no political connections with the war-breeding League of Nations, for such a course would make the United States "a perpetual recruit to Mars."

This book, and Vandenberg's other effusions, reveal little basic insight or keenness of mind. Any competent reviewer of the day would have been unable to predict that their author

313

would, in time, become a senatorial statesman of world renown.

Vandenberg, however, was intellectually curious, interested in self-improvement, and capable of broadening his perspective. One of his favorite men of history was St. Paul. The Senator, who weighed the possibility of writing a biography of the great apostle, perhaps thought of himself as another Saul on the road to Damascus who had unexpectedly seen a sudden flash of light. Actually, there was nothing breathtaking about Vandenberg's repudiation of his old beliefs. On the contrary, it took years of soul-searching before he gradually concluded that the fortunes of his country had become so irreversibly linked to those of the rest of mankind that an enlightened self-interest demanded that isolationism be replaced by a system of general security. Without doubt, his nephew, General Hoyt S. Vandenberg, who was high in the command circles of the Army Air Force, helped convince him that the oceans could not bar an air attack on the New World.[15]

In March, 1941, Arthur Vandenberg was a generalissimo of the senatorial coalition that opposed the Lend-Lease Bill. Within the next two years he moved to a position where he tried to reconcile "enlightened selfishness" with "general idealism" in foreign affairs. "I am hunting," he wrote in his diary for August 4, 1943, "for the middle ground between those extremists . . . who would cheerfully give America away and those extremists . . . who would attempt a total isolation which has come to be an impossibility." A few months later, he told a critic that if he was an internationalist, then black was white, but that no choice was left to the United States save that of cooperating with all like-minded nations in the interest of world peace.

Vandenberg's influence over his Republican colleagues was all the greater because he changed his opinion without abandoning his stout nationalism. He constantly insisted that the President protect the primary interests of the United States abroad, and preserve the full vigor of constitutional government at home. Congress, the Senator declared, must make the final decision as to where American troops were to be used to quell world disorder, and if they were to be so used. As one of the eight senators with whom Secretary Hull consulted to plan for the United Nations, Vandenberg influenced the administration's thinking. He approved the giving of a veto power over actions of the Security Council to each country with a permanent seat. This, he thought, would not only insure the Senate's consent to the Charter, but would also be a safeguard against the possibility of the United States being forced into a coercive action that it did not sanction.[16]

Vandenberg's public profession of faith (January 10, 1945) came after careful deliberation. He consulted with old friends of the newspaper world, and used their suggestions as he labored over a dozen drafts of his contemplated speech. Undoubtedly, he had mixed motives but, in later years, he said that he was primarily interested in creating a United Nations strong enough to give the Kremlin leaders pause in the event they contemplated the expansion of Communism by force. If that were indeed his aim, he failed to achieve it, but his words were destined to have other noteworthy results.

The Senator began by saying that he did not relish, more than any other American, the thought of weighing down his country with heavy global burdens. But, he declared, conditions left us no choice, since our geographical insulation was gone, and we had to find some way of controlling the all-enveloping octopus of modern warfare. "If World War III ever unhappily arrives," he warned, "it will open new laboratories of death too horrible to contemplate. I propose to do everything in my power to keep these laboratories closed for keeps." An adequate system of general security, he added, was the only possible way of averting such a new catastrophe. He pointed out that Russia would gain immeasurably from such a plan, for the Soviets would be much better off in a stable world than they would be ringed by a group of uneasy states, whose people were suppressed by the Red Army.

Had Vandenberg stopped at this point, the speech would have been important, but it would not have been an eye-opener. He went one step further, however, and proposed "a hard-and-fast treaty" between the victorious Allies to prevent any possible resurgence of the Axis powers. This from a man who had been the favorite presidential candidate of the G.O.P. isolationists in 1940! The Office of War Information thought Vandenberg's statements so important that it broadcast a transcription of the speech to all American forces, then scattered over the four corners of the earth.

Senator Vandenberg had exploded a bombshell. His remarks drew instant fire from the inflexible isolationists, which makes it possible for the historian to identify the location and to measure the strength of these resistors. The Chicago *Tribune* called the Senator "Judas" and "Benedict Arnold." Its sister papers of the McCormick-Patterson family alliance, the New York *Daily News* and the Washington *Times-Herald*, joined in hinting that the time had come for all patriots to form a truly nationalist third party. The suggestion, however, was not pressed, and the ultraists laid low, awaiting a more favorable moment for a counterattack. Their opportunity would come shortly, perhaps more quickly than they themselves anticipated, for the dictator of the Kremlin would soon cool the enthusiasm of the American people for collective security.

The favorable response to Vandenberg's startling reversal was more surprising than the hostility it aroused. James Reston of the New York *Times*, a canny Scot soon to be awarded the Pulitzer Prize for national correspondence, thought that the greatest significance of the Michigan Senator's proposal of an alliance was the acclaim with which it was received. Walter Lippmann hoped that Vandenberg's speech would encourage American diplomats to seize the initiative in planning the postwar settlement.[17]

We know today that Vandenberg neither halted Russian expansionism nor healed permanently the G.O.P. schism over foreign policy. His words did not assure the ultimate success of the United Nations experiment, nor did they prod the administration to insist upon the stabilization of fluid boundary lines. The speech, nonetheless, had many important and unexpected results. First of all, it helped Senator Vandenberg to achieve an eminence seldom granted by circumstances to American legislators. He was now in a position to use his constellation of talents for the good cause of peace—a remarkable sense of timing, an instinctive grasp of the crucial issues of world politics, and an unusual measure of legislative skill. Vandenberg's natural caution and tendency to restrain unwarranted enthusiasm stood him in good stead in handling those Republicans and Democrats who were still unwilling to accept America's new World role. More than any other person, Vandenberg prevented a Republican relapse into isolationism in the frustrating years after 1945. Patient and understanding, he allowed his opponents to talk themselves out, until it became apparent to all but an obdurate minority that the national interest demanded bi-partisan cooperation in foreign affairs. This procedure, so largely Vandenberg's handiwork, was the prime factor in preserving the new Republican internationalism from destruction at the hands of the resurgent right-wingers.

Less than a month after Vandenberg's epoch-making address, the Big Three met at Yalta, February 4-11, 1945. Here Roosevelt made a number of decisions that were destined to supplement isolationist arguments already fashioned from

F.D.R.'s pre-Pearl Harbor record. One of the most unsparing critics of Roosevelt's diplomacy, the much-traveled writer, William Henry Chamberlin, has summed up the verdict of his school by calling Yalta a crime, a blunder, "a heartbreak and a disgrace."

In view of the persisting influence of the Yalta compact upon American thinking, some comment upon the details of the conference is in order. The President's decisions can only be understood correctly and fairly by evaluating them in the frame of reference that prevailed in 1945. Roosevelt believed, and his conviction was shared by a majority of his fellow countrymen, that the interests of peace demanded that the wartime coalition of first-class powers be kept intact. In order to get the calculating Stalin to give wholehearted cooperation to the ultimate war aims of the West, he thought that some concessions were wise and necessary. For good or evil, the success of collective security had been predicated upon the assumption that the major victors had no designs against the peace, and could therefore act as the trusted policemen of the world. It had been obvious in 1944 at Dumbarton Oaks that the Charter would work only if all the key nations had honorable intentions, for coercive action taken against any great country by the Security Council would mean another war. Hence it seemed essential to insure Russia's good behavior by making her a willing partner in the new venture.

It is also necessary to understand that Roosevelt's scope of vision for world peace was limited to collective security. Trained in the school of Woodrow Wilson, he thought it his duty to improve the work of the master by guaranteeing that the United Nations would not be crippled by Russia's defection as the League had been by that of the United States. This calamity he sought to avert by yielding somewhat to Stalin's demands prior to the formal launching of the United Nations. Roosevelt had made his position clear in his last State of the Union message on January 6, 1945. Herein, he linked perfectionism with isolationism and power politics as obstacles to peace, and called for the fulfillment of our responsibilities "in an admittedly imperfect world." Though his words were larded with realistic insights, he still did not think of the Russians as men of parts—bad parts.

Probably F.D.R. never fully comprehended the nature of the Soviet mendacity. Neither did he seem to realize that he was dealing with men who would not keep their word on territorial compromises because they considered it their mission to push Communism into the soft spots created by the prostration of Germany, Italy and Japan. But it is only fair to add that Roosevelt's hardest critics have not taken into consideration all the factors that existed in February, 1945. We know now that during the Yalta Conference the non-Marxist Polish Government in exile warned Roosevelt of Stalin's intentions, stating that "if peace in Europe is to be durable, it must be based on principles of justice, on respect of law, on good neighborly relations as well as honesty in international life."[18] By that time, however, there was little that either Roosevelt or Churchill could do to keep Stalin from making a cruel jest of his promises to agree to a new provisional government in Poland and to abide by the results of "free elections" in the other newly liberated countries of eastern Europe. Russian troops were on the spot, for, as General Nathan Bedford Forest would have put it, Stalin had got there "fustest with the mostest men." The Red Army had crossed the Oder River and stood forty miles east of Berlin. General Eisenhower, in the west, had not yet crossed the Rhine.

On January 21, 1945, before the Conference began, Averell Harriman, United States Ambassador at Moscow, informed the President that the Russians were talking of taking two or three million Germans eastward for a ten-year period of slave labor as part of a war reparations scheme.[19] While there was no formal agreement to this morally reprehensible plan to enthrall the Germans, one must recall that it was broached just when an outraged humanity learned the full extent of Hitler's genocide. Because of these shocking revelations, right-thinking men could hardly object to the publicized Yalta decision which quartered the Reich into four occupied zones. What American could prophesy, in 1945, that the United States would so soon rehabilitate a barbarous enemy to balance the power against its Russian ally?

The most vulnerable part of the Yalta bargain was the delivery to Stalin of certain Far Eastern territories in return for a Russian war declaration on Japan. The simplest explanation here is that the President, with the atomic bomb project still in the experimental stage, thought that Soviet help would save the many American lives which would be sacrificed in bringing the Far Eastern war to a rapid conclusion. Japan still occupied Manchuria, Korea, the Chinese coastline, all of Southeast Asia, and Indonesia. American and British military opinion held that the Allies must plan for at least eighteen months of intensive fighting before the Nippon would be forced to submit. Had Roosevelt decided against any such strategic measures, says Walter Lippmann, public opinion would have charged him with betraying "the vital interest of the American people in saving the lives of their sons."

In making this decision, F.D.R. acted on the counsel of his trusted Chief of Staff, General George C. Marshall. If securing Russian aid against Japan was, indeed, Roosevelt's and Marshall's principal consideration, the concessions were made in vain. Somehow the latest military intelligence report from the Far East, which showed Japan far nearer exhaustion than previously reported, had never filtered up from the Pentagon to the Chief of Staff! It has been suggested, however, that Roosevelt had more than military reasons for wanting Russia in the Pacific war. According to this theory, he felt that Stalin shared his own views about Asiatic imperialism and, as a fighting partner, "Uncle Joe" would strengthen the American stand for colonial self-determination against the imperial-minded Churchill.[20]

Regardless of his motives, Roosevelt should not have paid Russia with Chinese land. To make certain that Stalin would keep his word and pounce upon Japan within two or three months after the collapse of Nazi resistance, Russia was promised the southern half of Sakhalin Island (ceded by the Czar to Japan in 1905) and the Japanese Kurile Islands. In addition, the Soviets were to enjoy joint control over China's Manchurian railroads, and, in fulfillment of the old Romanov imperialist dream, they were to have special privileges in the important seaports of Dairen and Port Arthur. The position of our ally, Chiang Kai-shek, was weakened by giving Communists, incapable of sharing power, partial control over vital Chinese industrial areas.

However, the most bitter fruits of Yalta were not tasted until 1949, when Mao Tse-tung defeated Chiang and Roosevelt's detractors blamed the disaster on the 1945 concessions. But it is doubtful, even had the President acted as his critics have suggested, that the ultimate result would have been very different. In all probability, Russia would have attacked Japan anyway and taken what she wanted of the Nipponese Empire. It has even been suggested that Yalta prolonged rather than shortened Chiang's rule over the mainland, for, in the absence of any written agreement, the powerful Red Army might have taken much more Chinese territory.[21] Actually, Stalin technically fulfilled his 1945 pledge and made a treaty of friendship and alliance with Chiang, an agreement soon to be relegated to the overflowing wastebasket filled with written Soviet promises.

Had Roosevelt not compromised the principle of self-determination at Yalta, his record would have read much better in history books, but it is unlikely that a firm stand would have halted the Red march eastward. What is more to be regretted than any particular item of the Yalta deal is Roosevelt's (and perhaps Churchill's) unjustifiable trust that once having been bought, Stalin would be honest enough to stay bought. It was the failure of Russia to abide by her pledges, and not these concessions in themselves, that made of Yalta a major catastrophe.

The Crimean compromises on the establishment of the United Nations are less controversial than those concerning territorial settlements. At Yalta, the Big Three agreed that the constituent assembly would be held at San Francisco, to begin on April 25, 1945. Those countries already cooperating in the Grand Alliance's war effort would be invited to send delegates; also there would be representatives from any nations which would declare war on the Axis before the first of March. Stalin pared down his demands for separate membership for his 16 U.S.S.R. republics and agreed to accept individual status for only the Ukraine and White Russia. It looked like a promising beginning.

Because the Soviet Union has so long abused its veto power in such a way as to hamstring the Security Council, the compromise on this question has been severely censured. Originally, our own State Department opposed this absolute veto of the great powers. By February, 1945, however, it was apparent that if the Charter made no such provision, neither Russia nor the United States Senate would find it acceptable. Roosevelt yielded for obvious reasons; he wanted neither a 1919-1920 League encore, nor a Russian secession. Thus the compromise made at Yalta (given formal endorsement by the San Francisco Conference) awarded the United States, Great Britain, Russia, China, and France permanent seats on the Security Council with the right to veto a motion holding any country (including their own) guilty of aggression, or to veto any motion to level sanctions against themselves or any other nation—in other words, on all substantive measures. Vesting Soviet Russia with the power to veto crucial decisions of the Security Council all but destroyed the peace-preserving functions of that body. Without this provision, however, the United Nations could not have been established. The new undertaking was born with the heel of Achilles, for it could work only if all first-class powers, including the U.S.S.R., intended to keep the spirit and the letter of the Charter.

By the time the nations foregathered at San Francisco,

Harry S. Truman had succeeded to the presidency. It is not necessary, for the purpose at hand, to reconstruct the details of this two-month Donnybrook of forty-six nations that completed the Charter of the United Nations. A few pertinent observations will suffice to indicate the prevailing winds of opinion.

The American delegation, a handpicked bi-partisan group headed by the handsome platinum-haired Secretary of State, Edward R. Stettinius, Jr., hoped to form an association of sovereign states which they assumed would operate in a free world where each national group would enjoy as much self-determination as circumstances would allow. The Washington authorities brought leading educators, prominent men of letters, and other leaders of civic thought to San Francisco to witness the birth of a new world order. A wave of United Nations evangelism swept the land, creating an unjustified optimism for the success of international partnerships. Two weeks after the Conference started, the war in Europe ended and the air was filled with the elation of victory and bright hopes for a peaceful future. All too few radio commentators and newspaper columnists were willing to face the unpleasant fact that the surliness of the Russian delegates, who took their cues from Molotov, boded ill for the new enterprise.

Senator Vandenberg was a delegate to San Francisco. Although he dreamed of the United Nations' General Assembly as "to-morrow's Town Meeting of the World," his suspicions of Russia were heightened by Molotov's blunderbuss language. The Senator began to wonder "whether this is Frisco or Munich." He had become an internationalist because he believed that his country's interests would be best served by a system of general security. But, in the course of his conversion, he may well have pondered Theodore Roosevelt's parting suggestion that the major powers assume regional responsibility for world order. At San Francisco this idea cropped up once more, for it offered a way of safeguarding the Monroe Doctrine within the framework of the Charter. Vandenberg, along with John Foster Dulles, Assistant Secretary of State Nelson A. Rockefeller, and certain Latin Americans were concerned lest some future Soviet veto on the Security Council block action against an aggressor with designs on the New World. Their anxiety bore a fortunate result, for the American delegation was able to secure the addition of the invaluable Article 51 to the Charter. (Dulles wrote in 1950 that he drafted this article, consulting with Vandenberg and Rockefeller.) [22] Under its broad terms, member states reserved, in event of aggression, "the inherent right of individual or collective self-defense" until such time as the Security Council would be able to handle the crisis.

Adopted over the strong protests of Russia, this article proved to be the safety valve of the Charter. Without it, it is extremely doubtful that the United States could have long remained in one world organization with the U.S.S.R. Without violating the letter of the Charter, we were subsequently able to strengthen our defense ties with other New World nations and to negotiate mutual security agreements with most countries of western Europe, and with strategically located non-Communist states in the region of the western Pacific.

The spadework necessary to assure Senate approval of the Charter had been carefully and thoroughly done. Thus the United States which had spurned membership in the League of Nations joined its successor with alacrity, enthusiasm, and a remarkable display of unanimity. The Senate consented to the Charter by a vote of 89 to 2—the nays voiced by a pair of old-time progressive-isolationists, William Langer of North Dakota and Henrik Shipstead of Minnesota. Fate prevented Senator Hiram Johnson, who lay on his deathbed at the Naval Hospital, from taking a final stand for what he had so long called the preservation of "pure Americanism." By a vote of 60 to 2, the Senate agreed to adhere to the Statute of the new International Court of Justice, accepting even compulsory jurisdiction in certain categories of cases. In 1945, the cycle begun in 1917 came to full turn, and the spirits of Woodrow Wilson and Franklin D. Roosevelt had reason to rejoice.

The men and women at San Francisco, however, still held to the collective security axioms of the pre-Atomic Age, for the work on the epoch-making bomb was so secret that even Vice-President Truman was not told of it until after he was sworn in as Chief Executive. The delegates, with the possible exception of the very highest ranking American officials, had no inkling that the speed and effectiveness of offensive warfare was about to be revolutionized. The Charter, then, that they adopted was not designed to cope with two new conditions that developed in the fateful year of 1945. The Soviet decision to push Communism into the fluid areas of war-racked Europe and Asia demolished the foundations of an edifice erected upon the proposition that all the great nations desired a stabilized world. The second change came even more unexpectedly when the first atomic bomb was dropped only six weeks after the San Francisco Conference adjourned.

President Truman's decision to use atomic warfare to speed

up the surrender of a Japan whose collapse was imminent poses another great might-have-been of history. It is difficult to say, in the light of our present knowledge, what part, if any, the A-bomb played in influencing or impelling Stalin's decision to hamstring the United Nations. Certain it is, however, that this drastic change in the methods of warfare further complicated an already ominous international situation.

The first A-bomb shook that concept of world order upon which the United Nations had been founded. Collective security posited that middle or small-sized states, lying in the path of an aggressor power, could at best hold the foe until the associated nations sent reinforcements, or, at worst, be occupied until they could be liberated by joint action. Now, however, such nations were faced with instant mass destruction on a scale that defied the human imagination. They could hardly put their trust in promises of eventual aid, for not only would such help be useless, but anticipated reliance upon it might even invite annihilation. The margin of reserve power, upon which collective security rested, had vanished. Henceforth nations not able to defend themselves from an aggressor armed with super-weapons would tend to yield to threats of force, or if out of the immediate course of the aggressor's path they would veer toward neutrality in the contest between rival power factions within the United Nations. If they were to be kept within the orbit of the peace-loving bloc they would have to be made secure by permanent alliances and strengthened by immediate military help. Whether or not the United Nations would be able to deter aggression depended originally upon the good intentions of the major powers, including Russia. This was in itself a most serious defect. But the A-bomb made even more certain that collective security would not work. The ancillary agencies of the United Nations, like those of the League before it, were to advance the cause of humanitarianism. But, if this progress were to have any lasting benefits, peace would have to be maintained by other ways, in addition to the efforts of that new debating society called the Security Council.

The American people, having reconciled themselves to substituting collective security for isolationism as the touchstone of their foreign policy, had not made a final adjustment in their thinking. The implications of nuclear power quickly forced them out of their new complacency, for it destroyed the very last vestiges of geographical security. As Charles A. Lindbergh said, until 1945 it could be argued that while transoceanic bombing was possible, no nation was apt to try it, for its cost would be out of proportion to any damage inflicted. But the wartime developments of guided missiles and nuclear energy, said Lindbergh in 1947, made it evident that "no earthly distance is adequate defense against the latest weapons of science."[23]

This development destroyed another favorite postulate of Woodrow Wilson and Franklin D. Roosevelt. Both men had assumed that military intervention against a dangerous aggressor would keep the havoc of war from American soil. Hence both men looked to a mutual security organization as the most feasible method of preventing foreign wars that might imperil our security. But the atom bomb and its more lethal hydrogen successor, so swiftly to be duplicated by the Soviet scientists, changed the entire situation. The only choice left to the United States was to prevent the most probable enemy from building superior stockpiles of these wonder-weapons. If this could not be done by the United Nations, then, to keep nuclear order, we would have to resort to alliances, balances of power, and all those other European diplomatic devices long abhorred by both isolationists and internationalists.

Because the United Nations Charter was to be so speedily trammeled, it is regrettable that the San Francisco Conference was over-advertised to the people. The implications of the A-bomb were hardly foreseeable at the time, for the first successful trial explosion did not take place until July 16, 1945, three weeks after the Conference adjourned. Harry S. Truman relates in his *Memoirs* that when he first learned of the project, his personal Chief of Staff, Admiral William D. Leahy, assured him that the bomb would never go off. But rapidly mounting evidence of Soviet recalcitrance should have kept the government from whetting popular enthusiasm. Averell Harriman, Ambassador to Moscow, warned Washington bluntly in April, 1945, that Communist expansionism might well lead to a new ideological warfare "as vigorous and dangerous as Fascism." While the delegates were still arguing at San Francisco, Acting Secretary of State Joseph C. Grew, a realist with twenty-one years of first-hand diplomatic experience, noted that the war had transferred "totalitarian dictatorship and power from Germany and Japan to Soviet Russia which will constitute in [the] future as grave a danger to us as did the Axis."[24]

Such realism, however, was largely confined to certain members of the administration's inner circle, and little of it penetrated to government propaganda agencies or private radio and press commentators. Once more, as in the pro-League propaganda of a previous generation, the case for collective security had been overstated.

Only a fortnight and two days after the Senate approved the Charter, Japan surrendered. Americans were sated with forced military service, high taxes, incessant international crises, rationing, and other interruptions to the normal pursuits of business and pleasure. The prevailing mood was to forget the nightmare of war and to make up for the lost years with all possible haste. No one who lived through those exciting August days of 1945 can ever forget the joyful relaxation of the masses. The boys would soon come home, khaki uniforms would be relegated to Memorial Day parades, and the world would live happily in peace ever after.

When the Communists quickly and rudely awoke a dreaming America, another great let-down seemed in the making. Many of the factors that led to the disenchantment of the 1920s were again present. With wartime secrecy lifted, historians and autobiographical writers were free to delve into the accumulated pile of rich source material to make some startling revelations about our entry into the war and the compromises subsequently made in the name of building up a peacetime coalition of the great powers. Such books, articles, and newspaper editorials, some of which were written as diatribes and others as Rooseveltian eulogies, were to confound the public's understanding of the basic reasons for the war.

Postwar events appeared to justify the accusations of the extreme revisionists, for our sacrifices had ended one totalitarian threat only to confront us with another. Russian expansionism gave logic to the old isolationist adage that all wars create more problems than they solve. Faced with new perils, a war-weary America was prone to forget that the Allied statesmen of 1939-1945 had to deal with the acute situation presented by the Axis thrust and had to take their chances upon future Soviet complications. When the immediate danger was passed, the physicians were promptly indicted for not having been more circumspect about the use of the powerful Soviet counter-irritant that they had prescribed.

With far greater urgency and shock than had been present in 1920, the Americans of 1945 had to replace their wartime idealism with sobering realism. They had to dispel quickly the illusions that Russia would keep the peace. The calculated risk, upon which all the concessions had been made, had proved foolhardy.

The chances for a profound disillusionment and a new isolationism were peculiarly great because of the domestic political situation. Never before in American history had the Republican party suffered so long a period of successive reverses. The isolationist right-wingers could taunt the G.O.P. internationalists with the fact that acquiescence to Roosevelt's foreign policy had only played into the hands of the Democrats. Like every other major party too long denied the power to govern, the Republicans had lost the habit of responsibility. Although the internationalists were destined to maintain a precarious control over major party decisions, the Old Guard, so strongly entrenched in Congress, were to sound a clarion call to return to Republican orthodoxy. They were to raise a question that was to be agitated by the postwar disclosures of domestic Communist espionage and infiltration into government circles. The Red Scare was to be the elixir of the new isolationism.

Despite these advantages, the isolationists of the postwar decade were destined to regain only a fraction of their old influence. They would indeed resume the great debate that was interrupted by Pearl Harbor, but they were to lose the count on every major issue both in Congress and in the high councils of the Republican party. Their ingenious words and changed poses could not overcome stubborn reality. Communist expansionism was a fact. That this new outward totalitarian challenge had to be either contained or reversed was accepted as a fact by reasonable men. This the United States would have to do singlehandedly, or else collectively with the aid of allies. The latter policy, which seemed to make much more sense, was the antithesis of non-entanglement. It was this grim realization, shared by controlling elements in both major parties, that guaranteed that in the foreseeable future there would not be a successful reaction against the Rooseveltian repudiation of isolationism.

Chapter 14

Fission and Fusion in World Politics

IN THE electric autumn of 1945, the American spirit ran high. The war was over on both fronts, G.I.'s were returning to civilian ranks, and headlines blazoned forth once more the news of domestic altercations. On Tuesday, October 24, the United Nations was officially proclaimed and to many this seemed to have sounded the death-knell of isolationism. The United States, it was generally assumed, would henceforth place full trust in the new system of collective security. There were, to be sure, some isolationist dissenters, but they seemed incapable of perpetuating the tradition. No one apparently foresaw that within a decade the classic isolationist-internationalist cleavage on foreign affairs would again appear in a new alignment. The fact is, however, that while the United States was not destined to relapse into isolationism, its postwar policies did not conform to the 1945 international blueprint. New cataclysms were to play as much havoc with the plans of Franklin D. Roosevelt as the Axis onslaught had with the designs of William E. Borah. Curiously enough, as the United States became more and more entangled in world politics, the United Nations became less and less significant in the eyes of the American people. We had accepted collective security too late, and the limited sacrifices that the Charter envisaged were not enough to keep the peace.

America's dream of world stability was shattered by a series of inter-related catastrophes, caused by Stalin's decision to spread Communism by force.

Many explanations have been offered for war-torn Russia's refusal to give the bleeding world a chance for peaceful recovery. Some writers assume that so obdurate a Communist as Stalin could conceive of no other course except to complete the world revolution plotted by Marx and instigated by Lenin. Others concluded, in 1946, what the Kremlin did not admit until ten years later—that Comrade Joseph V. Stalin was an unscrupulous paranoiac who lacked even bad principles. Some western observers early argued that Stalin reasoned that the friendship of the free world was more dangerous to his one-man tyranny than was its enmity, for Russian soldiers, penetrating into the outside world during the war years, had found it quite different from the description with which they had been indoctrinated. If Stalin had, in 1945, continued to co-operate with the non-Marxist powers, he would have been forced to open the intellectual windows of Russia which would have let in a gust of western air. This, he may well have feared, might blow away the party-line cobwebs.

Some authorities point out that the Stalin regime misunderstood Truman's precipitate ending of lend-lease and resented the cavalier way in which Washington rejected its request for a reconstruction loan. These rebuffs, coming at a time when our development of the A-bomb upset the balance of power, reinforced orthodox Marxist thinking on the nature of foreign relations. According to Communist dogma, long-run diplomatic moves must reflect the economic basis of the policy-making nations. The Kremlin regarded the wartime friendly overtures of their allies as tactical maneuvers that would be followed by a western attempt to fill with capitalist forces the power vacuums created by the collapse of the Axis. To the Russian mind, therefore, it seemed necessary to compensate for the A-bomb by occupying fluid areas before the western powers could complete their slower moving program of penetration. It is entirely possible that Stalin was as shocked by the western assumption that peaceful co-existence would continue after the war as Truman was by the Marshal's decision to extend Communism by force.

Professor Foster Rhea Dulles, taking a more charitable view of Russian hostility, has suggested that Stalin's course was originally dictated by an inbred fear of the capitalist world, and only later evolved into a dynamic imperialism. Possibly all of these factors influenced the generalissimo's thinking. We do not yet know exactly why the Soviet bulldozer began to roll over neighboring territory in 1945, but the effects of its movements are readily apparent.

By 1946 it was clear that the war had brought no surcease from totalitarian aggression. The revised Russian pattern of behavior began to make itself manifest in all the ways that have since become commonplace. The Communists now openly spoke their inverted language—peace is war, lies are facts, and nations who protest against the enslavement of Russia's victims are imperialistic warmongers. By cleverly alternating hot with cold war, and frowns with disarming smiles, the Communists were able at will to raise or depress the spirits of the peace-hungry democracies. Russia could locate and percuss every soft spot in a badly disarranged world.

Where there was little or no resistance the Soviets used their armies to insure Communist domination; while in Asia where there was serious fighting to be done, they incited the downtrodden masses to take the offensive. The United States, the recognized leader of the free world, was impaled on the horns of an ugly dilemma. It could either stop these dangerous incursions by using its precious manpower and material resources, or allow the new totalitarian snowball to roll on unchecked.

Because Russia intervened in the series of local crises that formed the backwash of world war, the United States was forced to counter the Communist thrust by a worldwide system of entangling alliances. While American statesmen patiently explored the possibilities of compromise in order to prevent a new major clash, the Kremlin followed a theory of non-coexistence. Evidently Russia wished to wear us out by repeated exasperation. Had Stalin really understood the American mood of 1945, he would have allowed sufficient breathing space in his timetable of conquest. This might well have led to an American withdrawal from the tiring game of power politics. Instead, the blatant Communist threat to the balance of power made a return to isolationism too perilous to contemplate.

The United Nations had hardly passed its first birthday when Ely Culbertson, lecturer, expert on contract bridge, and chief promoter of a plan to federalize all governments into one world union, quipped that collective security had proved to be neither collective nor secure. Lake Success, where the U.N. met, pending construction of its imposing headquarters in the heart of New York City, was commonly referred to as "Lake Failure." Every intelligent schoolboy knew why the U.N. had been rendered impotent. Its Charter had not been designed to control the actions of a stubbornly defiant Russia. Roosevelt and Churchill had lost their gamble on Stalin's good intentions. A fair-minded critic could find much to praise in the U.N.'s social, economic, and humanitarian work. Such auxiliary bodies as UNESCO and the Commission on Human Rights did yeoman service by ameliorating some conditions that had formerly bred international strife or had lowered the resistance of underdeveloped regions to the Communist infection. The free world, however, knew only too well from the bitter experience of the League of Nations that these laborious efforts could be wiped out overnight by the scourge of war. The touchstone of the U.N. was general security, and this it had failed to bring. The nations could not agree to implement the Charter by setting up a Military Staff Committee, nor did they halt the ominous stockpiling of nuclear weapons. The U.N. helped settle problems in Syria, Lebanon, and Indonesia, but it fumbled badly in handling such tasks as straightening out the Greek frontier line and choosing for Trieste a temporary governor acceptable to both Italy and Jugoslavia. Its record on settling minor crises was worse than that of the League's, for Communist agitators tried to fan each smoldering stump into a forest conflagration.

Under these circumstances popular enthusiasm for the United Nations steadily declined. Public opinion, stimulated by wartime idealism, had naively believed that the provisions of the U.N. Charter would automatically go into successful operation if accepted by America. Once more, as in the 1920s, the immediate object of preserving peace was confused with the long-range goal of creating a world order whose foundations rested upon the fine principles of international law and elementary justice. In 1950 the United States secured the adoption of the "Uniting for Peace" resolution which sought to place more peace-preserving power in the hands of the veto-free General Assembly. But this plan, too, proved disappointing. As the United Nations admitted more member states, its General Assembly (where every country had one vote) promised to fall under the control of an antiwestern Afro-Asian-Soviet bloc. Moreover, the General Assembly had power only to voice, but not to enforce, what was euphemistically called "the conscience of mankind." A people accustomed to quick dividends from speculative ventures tired rapidly of a peace association whose aims were lost in a thicket of international polemics.

The prestige of the United Nations was injured by still other factors. Some of the more ardent internationalists, disgusted with the creaking machinery of collective security, formed groups that pressed for world government or for closer integration of the experienced democracies. The first of these organizations was Clarence K. Streit's The Federal Union Inc., which dated from 1943. As League of Nations correspondent for the New York *Times* in the 1930s, Streit had seen the helpless League founder on the shoals of totalitarian aggression. Convinced that only effective world organization could checkmate the evil forces of our time, he wrote *Union Now* in 1939. Encouraged by the sale of over 300,000 copies of his book, Streit planned The Federal Union in the critical period of the war. He called for federalization of the governments of the allied democracies which, he hoped, would gradually unite all nations. Thus, from the beginning, Streit and his associates thought the Charter of the United Nations too feeble an instrument to preserve world order.

The immolation of the United Nations by Soviet Russia gave rise to many other plans for effective world unity. Cord Meyer, Jr., a veteran of World War II, organized The United World Federalists in 1947. Drawing up a blueprint with visionary overtones, this group demanded that the United Nations be converted into a federalized form of world government. Robert M. Hutchins, long-time head of the University of Chicago, chaired a committee that drew up a preliminary Draft of a World Constitution. Considerable attention was attracted by Ely Culbertson's Citizens Committee for U.N. Reform. This group narrowed down its proposals to an "ABC" formula: A—Abolish the UN veto; B—Ban the armament race; C—Create a world armed force to maintain peace.

A more modest and less doctrinaire step toward international organization was advocated in 1949 with the organization of the Atlantic Union Committee. Founded by former Supreme Court Justice Owen J. Roberts, promoted by the public opinion analyst Elmo Roper, former Secretary of War Robert P. Patterson, and Under Secretary of State William L. Clayton, the committee worked for an exploratory convention of delegates from certain "civil liberty democracies." It was the hope of this group that such a convention would plan for the eventual military, political, and economic union of a limited number of democratic nations within the larger framework of the UN and NATO.

Although supported by some of the country's most distinguished statesmen, academicians, and industrialists, the Atlantic Union Committee was often confused with more extremist groups that demanded a world government. Characteristically, the nationalist-isolationists tarred all such organizations with the same brush, accusing them of promoting a secret United Nations' plan to undermine the sovereignty of the United States.

These utopian plans for world government provided much fuel for the isolationists. But more than anything else, the super-nationalists capitalized upon two developments which dampened American enthusiasm for the United Nations. Collective security presupposed that, in the event of aggression, all of the peace-minded member states would combine forces to maintain the status quo. The post-1945 aggressions, however, came at a time when the old European and Asiatic balances of power were no longer operative. For the first time in the century, power became localized at two major poles, Washington and Moscow. Inasmuch as the United States and the U.S.S.R. were almost never aligned on the same sides in any crisis, effective police action to allay aggression was tantamount to inviting war. The Korean debacle of 1950-1953 proved the unworkability of collective security in a world torn by ideological conflict. Put to a test, the experiment of maintaining peace by collective action left the United States with the unpleasant choice of halting the fighting short of victory, or of enlarging the police action to the point where it might conceivably foment another world war. Thus the United Nations was reduced to a debating forum where the rival power blocs could do little but vent their respective spleens.

Russian obstructionism helped destroy American faith in collective security in still another way. By hamstringing the Security Council, the Communists prevented it from easing the war-breeding tensions produced by the revolt of the colonial peoples. The failure of the United Nations to negotiate differences between restive subject peoples and their European rulers further undermined American faith in collective security.

Until 1945 there was large-scale agreement in the United States that it was high time for Europe to follow our own example in the Caribbean and the Philippines by granting independence, or at least dominion status, to their subject peoples. The strains and tensions of war ignited the fuse of colonial unrest all over the world.

The worldwide penetration of troops equipped with the apparatus of modern science accelerated the demand for rapid westernization. In addition, the underprivileged colonial populations demanded national self-determination and the end of feudal land-holding systems. The situation would have been serious even without Communist intervention. Russia, however, brought the crisis to a head by promising the colonials independence, land reform, and a plan of industrialization to be achieved by collectivization rather than through foreign aid for capital investments. No matter how specious these promises were to westerners who understood the Russian game, they had magnetic appeal for the landless masses of Asia and Africa.

The nationalist aspirations of the colonial peoples could not be suppressed by their war-enfeebled masters in London, Paris, and The Hague. Britain relinquished all significant control in India, Ceylon, Pakistan, Egypt, and the Anglo-Egyptian Sudan. So it was that by 1956, the Tory government of Sir Anthony Eden was holding on desperately to strategic Cyprus where the overwhelming majority wanted union with nearby Greece. France was forced to fight an eight-year war in Indo-China only to make peace in 1954 at the price of considerable concessions to the Communist-inspired rebels. This contagious nationalism spread to the one hundred million dependent peoples of Africa. The ancient French holdings in the Dark Continent seethed with colonial unrest. Meanwhile, the formal establishment of the United States of Indonesia (1949) left Holland with only a vestige of her vast East Indian empire. European imperialisms collapsed far more precipitously than effusive Americans had expected, and their prostration created many vexing problems.

Had these colonial uprisings not been exploited by the Kremlin, the United States could have either applauded or remained indifferent to the outcome. They created, however, dangerous power vacuums that were promptly filled by Red propagandists or soldiers. It was a galling situation, for while Rusisan leaders blandly told some 600,000,000 newly freed colonials that imperialism was "a disgrace for present-day mankind, "the Kremlin enslaved Estonia, Latvia, Lithuania, Hungary, Bulgaria, Czechoslovakia, Poland, Albania, and East Germany, as well as holding in thralldom the non-Russian areas of Soviet Asia. Russia presented the United States with a devil's choice of either upholding decaying European imperialisms or being forced to outbid the Communists in order to keep these fledgling nations within the orbit of the free world. Americans argued the question heatedly, for some were convinced that only a strengthened imperial control could prevent these peoples from falling eventually into Communist hands; while others maintained that we had to offer one-third of the world's population (thus far uncommitted in the power duel) something much more substantial than rearmament and preparation for a defensive war against the Sino-Soviet alliance.[1]

A pertinent example illustrates the nature of the American dilemma. By 1954, the United States was subsidizing 70 percent of the costly French war effort against the Viet Minh Communist leader, Ho Chi Minh. Making a virtue of necessity, we had indirectly allied ourselves with the unsavory native ruler of Vietnam, Emperor Bao-Dai. But the sacrifice of our dollars and our moral principles was in vain, for France was ready to come to terms with Ho, and we were unwilling to commit American troops in an all-out effort to crush the

333

Viet Minhese Communists. Thus, in 1954, we gave silent assent to a compromise which divided Vietnam between the Marxist and non-Marxist natives. Once more, as in Korea, we learned that limited wars fought in a world in which no conflict could be localized were costly, frustrating, and futile. Circumstances forced us to jettison the prime postulate of collective security—that preventive police action, by deterring aggression, could preserve world peace.

London, unlike Paris, preferred in the 1940s to withdraw rather than to use its army against recalcitrant subject peoples. Nonetheless, the gradual liquidation of the British Empire posed many unlooked-for problems. When the laudable principle of self-determination freed Pakistan and India of English direction, their leaders pursued a tantalizing neutrality between east and west that gave Washington many anxious moments. Or, for another instance, in the Ceylonese parliamentary elections of 1956, the People's United Front ousted the pro-western, anti-Communist United Nationalists who had held office for a quarter of a century. The new government, riding to power on a wave of xenophobia, promptly demanded that Britain evacuate her bases on the island. In spite of the fact that Ceylon needed the revenue derived from these key links in the Commonwealth's chain of Asiatic outposts, and was in no position to defend herself against invasion, the People's United Front was more concerned with selling the country's surplus rubber to Russia and Red China than with holding back Communist penetration. The Ceylonese elections clearly revealed the wide gap that existed in former colonial countries between the prosperous minority who looked westward for protection against Communism, and the poverty-stricken masses who felt that they had nothing to lose by flirting with Red devils. Ceylon, moreover, illustrated to the world that hyper-nationalism could oust a pro-western party in a political arena virtually free of Communist propagandists.[2]

The unsettled conditions resulting from the collapse of imperialism created a political vortex that threatened to draw the United States into its swirl. Forced out of the Suez bastion by the Egyptian nationalists, Britain compensated for the loss by building a naval base on Episkopi Bay in Cyprus. When it became apparent that this strategic island could be held only by the subjection of the pro-Greek nativist majority, London explained that it resorted to brass-knuckle tactics against the Cypriots in order to hold the southern underpin of a European defense system vital to the security of the United States. Moreover, with the Arab-Israeli volcano threatening momentary eruption, the British contended that a Middle Eastern fire station was necessary should the western powers decide upon prompt intervention. The British point of view was highlighted to America when, in 1956, President Nasser of Egypt nationalized the vital Suez waterway twelve years ahead of schedule.

There was, however, strong dissent. General James Van Fleet, who under Truman's directive had helped Greece to bolster its defenses against Communist aggression, pointed out that any base was worthless if it formed but an island in the midst of a sea of hostile Cypriots. America, said Van Fleet, was perplexed by recurrent colonial uprisings because we had defended Anglo-French imperialisms "instead of taking an independent, clear-cut road, consistent with our statements and principles."[3] Evidently the General wanted the United States to court rather than to alienate the good will of the restive colonials. But this would involve increased foreign aid to underdeveloped regions, would entail even more direct intervention in foreign colonial problems, and would undoubtedly jeopardize relations with our ancient western European allies.

Van Fleet's suggestion highlighted the new American alignment on colonialism. In the 1920s, isolationist anti-imperialists wished to limit severely our overseas commitments, while Anglophiles and Francophiles were usually ardent advocates of the League of Nations. The post-1945 emergence of the colonial nations reversed these positions. The old pro-British group, and to a lesser degree their pro-French equivalents, deplored the liquidation of Afro-Asiatic imperialism, and their arguments, sometimes, had isolationist overtones. Thus they contended that if Laos, Cambodia, Thailand, Burma, India, Vietnam, and Indonesia insisted upon self-determination, the United States was under no moral or economic obligation to help them maintain their independence. This group joined some conservative non-isolationists in demanding that the remote colonial nations be written off as expendable. They emphasized the benefits of European imperialism, and held that its collapse in Asia and Africa had led to corruption, civil war, Communist subversion, unbridled religious and racial fanaticism, and exploitation of the masses. Discounting the possibility of turning these fledgling nations into dependable allies, they favored letting them wallow in their own home-grown, poverty-stricken despotism. Some Americans demanded that the United States reassess its antagonism to imperialism before a thousand primitive African tribes rose in rebellion.[4] A decade after V.J. Day many erstwhile League of

Nations enthusiasts were trying to set bounds and limits to the American sphere of influence.

On the other hand, many old-time liberal isolationists counseled an opposite course. They tried to educate the American people to some of the predicaments that faced subject peoples who rightfully demanded national freedom and a better standard of living than that known to their ancestors. The post-1945 liberals pointed out that these nascent countries faced one of three choices: they could retain their colonial status, which would provide them with the imperialist variety of capital at the expense of continued subservience to Europe; they could hearken to their Communist-minded leaders who promised them national self-determination and a swift modernization of their backward agrarian economies by imitating Russian collectivization; or they could avoid the harshness of Communism by revolutionizing their economies with the aid of long-term loans for capital development.[5] The neo-liberals held that, in its own self-interest, the United States must make the colonial peoples see the wisdom of this third choice. This meant, of course, that Washington must add sufficient funds for capital improvement to its grants of technical assistance and military defense. Such a substantial increase in American largesse, it was argued, was necessary to keep millions of peasants, workers, and small businessmen from falling into the Communist trap. The legatees of the liberal tradition supported a program that might well mean a ten-fold increase in the American economic stake in backward and remote areas. It was a doctrine that would have astounded their anti-imperialist forbears.

Even before the question of large-scale American funds for capital development grew acute, the colonial upsurge had already drawn the United States into many unexpected involvements. Simultaneously, the anti-imperialist revolt increased the task of the United Nations, for, in addition to creating many crises, it led to endless bickering. The Dutch quarreled with the Indonesians over Western New Guinea, Yemen challenged British control of Aden, and the French walked out of the U.N.'s General Assembly when that body agreed to consider Algerian demands. The cumulative effect of this agitation was to deepen American distrust of collective security.

Because the U.N. did not replace western European imperialism as a roadblock in the path of the Communist bandwagon, the United States was forced to buttress collective security with a series of mutual defense agreements. Within a short span of years we contracted alliances with 42 countries that committed us to action in virtually every corner of the earth. Hence in 1951, the United States signed one security treaty with the Republic of the Philippines and a joint one with Australia and New Zealand. Three years later the French made a treaty with Ho Chi Minh that seemed an opening wedge for the communization of all of southeast Asia. Unless preventive steps were taken, it looked as if the 17th parallel that divided Vietnam would be as vulnerable as the 38th parallel had been in Korea. To abort this danger, we negotiated SEATO—still another regional security arrangement that provided for collective action in the event of Red aggression. The collapse of imperialism had led to surprising American entanglements that far exceeded our 1945 expectations.

Russia's decision against peaceful co-existence touched off a chain of actions and reactions. It compelled the United States to expand the commitments made in the Charter of the United Nations by the contraction of alliances, by the delineation of spheres of influence, and by the creation of a new balance of power. We were faced suddenly with something entirely alien to our national experience—the necessity of dealing with allies on a long-haul peacetime basis. Such relationships were bound to be different from our wartime associations where the military situation and mutual interdependence had served to lessen friction. Few countries were ever more poorly prepared for the give-and-take of coalition diplomacy. The strains and stresses it generated help explain the mid-century mood of the American people.

Certain ingrained prejudices made it difficult for us to accept allies on an equal basis, or to understand the peculiar problems that shaped foreign diplomacy. The idea of European inferiority, so long and so intimately related to historic isolationism, was difficult to eradicate. This condescension was particularly marked in our attitude toward non-Caucasian nations. Americans seemed unable to comprehend that their own land had been peculiarly blessed by Providence with material bounty and geographical advantages. It had long ago been summed up by Goethe when he remarked, *"Amerika, du hast es besser."* We seemed purblind to some elementary facts: our abundance had trickled down to the masses in sufficient measure to moderate class conflicts; our general well-being had created a unified national community; and our economic success had made us notable enthusiasts of the system of free enterprise.

Americans were all too prone to take the measure of other

peoples by their own yardstick. There was little confidence in the intelligence and good intentions of foreigners, and the belief was widespread that other nations would do well to regard us as the mentor for mankind. Throughout the period of the great nineteenth-century folk migrations, the highest compliment that could be paid to an immigrant was that he had become "Americanized." By the postwar decade the third and fourth generations of these uprooted had achieved comfortable middle-class status. Many of them experienced an inward gratification from vaunting their Americanism by deriding foreign nations. Hence the prevailing attitude toward the foibles of our free-world partners was not a tolerant one. The situation was especially difficult because the United States had to grubstake the proud nations of western Europe before they could become helpful allies. There was bound to be a patronizing attitude on our part, and a resentment and seeming ingratitude on the part of peoples who partook of our bounty. Meanwhile, the ubiquitous Russians were always on hand to exploit every inter-alliance squabble.

In turn, our allies and the non-Caucasian neutral peoples complained that Uncle Sam preached human equality abroad and practiced Jim Crow at home. Europeans also noted that Americans distrusted Old World sanitary conditions, and that they often carried with them food-kits "sterilized like the mask of a surgeon." The Asiatics were less sensitive in such matters, but they disliked westerners in general and Americans in particular, for they were the richest of the white peoples. Therefore, said a French journalist, Americans are detested in spite of the fact that in ten years Washington gave a sum to foreign nations that would have provided every American bride of the postwar decade with a $2,500 dowry.[6]

Our attempt to build up a power coalition was rendered even more difficult by political and economic factors. Americans were startled when, even before the Japanese surrender, the British electorate replaced the masterful Churchill with the colorless Attlee. This election coincided with an American conservative rebound. Many industrialists and small businessmen, with unpleasant memories of New Deal reforms, tended to regard British Labour Socialism as a more immediate menace to free enterprise than Russian Communism. Because our powerful labor leaders were not associated with foreign workers in the bond of Socialism, the cult of individualism permeated all ranks of American society. Attlee's blueprint for the nationalization of England's basic industries and the intemperate remarks of his more radical colleagues led to a new

338

wave of American Anglophobia. On the other hand, the decimated progressive ranks cheered the British experiment. Once more, as in the case of imperialism, American business tycoons and social reformers had exchanged positions.

French and Italian politics were even more incomprehensible to Americans. The political self-immolation of France made her a vacillating ally. Americans had long taken for granted the French habit of dismissing premiers more often than Broadway showmen changed their billboards. What they could not tolerate, however, was the 4,900,000 Communist votes in the French election of 1951 and the 5,400,000 Communists ballots cast five years later. Shrewd observers of the French scene explained this away by calling it a protest against the economic status quo rather than an approval of Marxism. But Americans characteristically looked at cold figures, and these disconcertingly revealed that one out of four members of the new National Assembly now belonged to the Communist party. To this number *Newsweek* added the neo-fascist Poujadists and concluded that one-third of the new legislature constituted a disloyal anti-democratic opposition. "The depressing fact," said this widely quoted *Newsweek* editorial, "is that an assembly, hamstrung between Communists and neo-Fascists, whose center parties are torn by personal feuds, is an accurate image of France as she really is." This journal of opinion felt that France must be demoted from the position of a major power to that of a great civilization, and that America must look to West Germany as her most important continental ally.[7]

The Bonn Republic eventually became the fifteenth member of the Atlantic alliance, but the Germans showed little enthusiasm for becoming human shock absorbers to break the impact of a Russian onslaught. A year after West Germany regained its sovereignty with a pledge to NATO of a 500,000-man army for mutual defense purposes, less than 10,000 Germans were in uniform and Chancellor Konrad Adenauer's bill to re-establish conscription had not yet been approved by the Bundestag. When the United States presented Bonn with arms worth a billion dollars, the Germans complained that the equipment was obsolete. While Reich industrialists called for tax reductions and market outlets behind the Iron Curtain, Finance Minister Fritz Schäffer asked Washington for another outright gift of two billion dollars in defense equipment. It seemed to casual observers that our pro-Bonn policy had diminished Paris enthusiasm for collective European defense, without securing compensatory help from the Germans.

Moreover, said French cynics, America, by failing to support their foundering North African imperialism, had lost their good will without gaining the friendship of the restless Arabs.[8]

The case of Italy was even more perplexing because of her intimate relationship with the world's greatest anti-Communist moral force, the Holy See of Rome. Generally speaking, Americans failed to grasp the root causes of Italian discontent. They understood little of the unequal distribution of land or of the age-old Italian problem of improving the condition of the depressed southland. By 1956, the Italians had doubled their pre-war industrial output, developed their steel plants, partially solved the housing situation, and were in the act of trying to ameliorate southern conditions. Nevertheless, large-scale unemployment still harassed the country, and accounted, in part, for a bloc of some six million Communist votes. There seemed little hope that this strong minority would decrease in power especially since the Nenni Socialists had reached a working agreement with the Communists which jeopardized the control of the non-Marxist coalition.[9]

In the light of these circumstances, Americans looked upon the future of France and Italy with doubt and apprehension. Men and women who, in the popular idiom of the day, "had never had it so good," did not understand that large groups of Frenchmen and Italians had been alienated from the national community. Politics in both countries were so chaotic that only the Communist platform seemed to hold out any promise of change for the better. In view of these strong Marxist minorities, how trustworthy an ally would either country make in event of war against the Soviet Union? To Americans this was the all-important question.

The non-Communist peoples of Europe and Asia tended to be less alarmed about Moscow and Peiping than their American counterparts. Owing to this difference of opinion, there were recurrent arguments among the free world powers as to which policies would best checkmate Communist expansionism. Because they were much closer to arenas of ideological and physical warfare, Europeans and Asiatics based their estimate of the situation on experience rather than upon anti-Communist propaganda. Asiatics, for instance, had taken the measure of Generalissimo Chiang Kai-shek, and Europeans that of Dictator Francisco Franco. Countries laid waste by the Nazi and Japanese furies feared a revival of anti-Communist totalitarianism. Meanwhile, G.I.s stationed in occupied Germany felt at home among its well-scrubbed, industrious burghers and rosy-cheeked *fräuleins*. Americans tended to equate civilization with cleanliness and progress with technological efficiency. Europeans and Asiatics, on the other hand, were understandably reluctant to accept our assumption that the Communist devil must be fought with any kind of fire.

Moreover, many foreign thinkers dissented from the American appraisal of the Communist threat. Comprehending from first-hand experience the grass roots nature of local radicalism, they refused to admit that Communist uprisings throughout the world were planned in the Kremlin. This school insisted that the sporadic revolts of the postwar decade could be explained in terms of both internal and external causes. Hence they charged Washington with mistaking local social and economic revolutionary forces for a grand plot to destroy the United States. Russia, therefore, was deemed less blameworthy for world unrest than most Americans realized. In fact, foreigners frequently argued that domestic reform would blunt the cutting edge of the Communist scythe. They asserted that if war could be avoided long enough, the proletarian revolution would lose its momentum and Moscow and Peiping could be induced to negotiate a durable peace. This line of reasoning led many non-Marxist foreigners to decry the popular American belief that any understanding with Russia or Red China would be appeasement à la Munich. One striking incident points up this reversal in American and European reasoning. When, in 1946, Winston Churchill delivered his celebrated Iron Curtain speech in Fulton, Missouri, he shocked an American opinion still laboring under the spell of a One World idealism. Eight years later, Sir Winston paid a special visit to President Eisenhower to urge upon him a more conciliatory policy toward Russia.

These combined factors made it difficult to keep the free world alliance in balance. Isolationism had proven an impossible policy and had given way to collective security. When international organization failed to deter aggression, the United States supplemented general security with regional alliances, but only to find that power politics had their own vexations. We did not understand the western European Communist minorities, and our allies were bewildered by the illogic of our ultra-nationalists. "America," said the French purveyor of existentialism, Jean-Paul Sartre, "has the rabies." Frenchmen, replied critical Americans, cannot govern themselves; consequently, they should realize they are unfit to rule over their subject peoples.

Europeans turned apprehensive eyes upon the Russo-American race for superiority in nuclear weapons. They feared that in the event of war they would be annihilated because American policy was based, as Secretary of State John Foster Dulles said in 1953, upon "massive retaliation." Eventual liberation in the pattern of 1918 or 1945 would effect no good if there were no countries left to liberate. Hence the new type of warfare cast its shadow over power politics just as it had helped destroy collective security. It made our European allies demand advance and adequate protection from Soviet hydrogen bombs and guided missiles. We, on the other hand, with stockpiles of these super-weapons, and situated at a relatively safer distance from Soviet military bases, took a different attitude toward this protection. We frequently accused our allies of being selfishly isolationist. And Europe, in return, often discounted American pretensions, and predicted that we would risk total war only to protect our own immediate interests.

Such prolonged tensions, augmented by the mounting expenses of world guardianship, profoundly influenced American thinking. Every time an acute difference arose among the democratic allies, there were dark mutterings against "globaloney politics," "give-away diplomacy," "handouts to beggars," and "do-good statesmanship." An ever-increasing number of Americans wondered whether our generosity had bought world friends or had created allies whom we could depend upon in an hour of need.

In summary, four extremely significant developments revolutionized American thinking on foreign affairs in the postwar decade. The *first*, and most fundamental of these events, was Stalin's decision to extend Communism by force and subversion. This, in turn, led to the *second* change—disillusionment with collective security. The *third* was Communist immobilization of the Security Council, which turned the collapse of imperialism from an anticipated blessing to a dangerous nuisance. The *fourth* development, a logical outgrowth of the preceding events, was the frustrations and disturbances resulting from our new power position. Ten years of dizzy reversals, during the course of which allies became enemies, and enemies were transformed into friends, led to bewilderment and confusion. Allied with Russia, we defeated Germany; allied with China, we defeated Japan. But our victories were Pyrrhic since we subsequently had to build up a truncated Reich to help us against the Muscovites, and to woo Nippon so that she would hold Peiping in check. No wonder that the naval historian, Captain William D. Puleston, remarked that the United States reminded him of a "cat chasing its own tail."[10] In 1937 we were devoted isolationists. In 1945 we were ardent one-worlders. This in turn was replaced by a mood that sanctioned isolationism, power politics, collective security, or any combination of these policies that best served the national interest. The same America that hailed the liberal internationalism of Franklin D. Roosevelt found itself, shortly after his death, flirting and consorting with the world's choicest reactionaries—Syngman Rhee in Korea, Emperor Bao-Dai in Vietnam, Franco in Spain, and Chiang in Formosa. And to demonstrate to the world that we would not spurn a leftist totalitarian, we embraced the anti-Moscow Communist, Marshal Tito of Jugoslavia!

While some Americans grumbled that the State Department made a fetish of upholding decadent and corrupt authoritarian regimes others complained that Washington was using foreign aid funds to make the world safe for socialism. Thrust into a position of world leadership from which there was no escape, the United States became entangled in alliances that would have shocked the most heady 1945 advocate of international unity. Step by step we became involved in world politics to the point where Franco-German rivalry threatened our European defense system, where Republican Italy's quarrel with Communist Jugoslavia jeopardized our plans for the Balkan Peninsula, where border warfare between Egypt and Israel promised to draw us into a Middle Eastern conflict, and where Ceylonese indifference to our overtures was a matter of serious concern. Americans were as confused by ERP, SHAPE, NATO, and SEATO as they had once been by the countless New Deal alphabetical agencies. The more cynical among them quipped that both sets of acrostics amounted to the same thing—I.O.U.

Perhaps never before in American history had so few years provided so many reasons for disillusion. Only five years after our rash demobilization, President Truman proclaimed another national emergency (December 16, 1950) and once more we assembled men and reconverted our industries to fight the inconclusive Korean War. Meanwhile, we poured manpower and dollars into western Europe only to discover that our allies were unable either to defend themselves or to produce the engines of modern warfare. Seven months after the Armistice of 1918, the Treaty of Versailles had stabilized national boundary lines, while eleven years after V.J. Day, Germany was still cloven in two. The intense desire of the emergent nations of Asia for national freedom and economic progress resulted in human exploitation that often made the old imperialism shine by contrast. Moreover, Africa stood on the brink of revolt against its European masters, and there was little reason for expecting the world to gain if the natives succeeded in overthrowing their colonial governments. In America it became trite to say that the engines of civilization had been thrown into reverse gear.

Nevertheless, history failed to repeat itself and the new wave of disillusionment took a different form from the reaction of the 1920s. It was impossible for men to turn their backs on a disorderly world at a time when every crisis, no matter how remote, threatened to reignite the faggots of world war. There was no wholesale return to isolationism, for too many reasoning Americans knew that another Armageddon would jeopardize the lives of their families, compel them to evacuate their comfortable homes, and force every able-bodied man and woman into the national service. There was no escape from the reality of this situation. In the 1920s a conjectural threat of war had evoked fanciful thinking which took the form of an exaggerated reliance on either isolationism or the League of Nations. Coolidge's America breathed an air of confidence because all assumed that, at the very worst, any possible foreign menace could be obliterated by the timely intervention of the United States. Thus the debate was an academic one, revolving around the question of whether or not we ought to pay an insurance premium against future disorders by joining a world protective association. Faced, in Truman's day, with the possibility of the destruction of our cities in the first hours of a new war, Americans demanded that our policy be purged of idealistic and sentimental overtones. Samuel Lubell has noted that while the old isolationism was marked by an indifference to foreign affairs, the new assumed that America had been ensnared by the course of world events. Now a trapped people put a premium on the use of force which might liberate them. Americans discovered an elementary fact long obscured by extraordinary conditions, *i.e.*, that power is the fulcrum of a successful diplomacy.

By 1950 the United States had returned not to the isolationism of Warren Harding, but rather to the *Realpolitik* of Theodore Roosevelt. For the discerning majority, the problem was no longer to choose between isolationism or internationalism, but rather to blend parts of both traditions into a policy that would prevent nuclear warfare. Nevertheless, differences of opinion over a new formula evoked even more heat than the spirited debates of the 1920s, for it was evident that the future of the country lay at the mercy of a competent diplomacy. In an era where any policy involved a calculated risk, Americans found it impossible to avoid bitter polemics, unreasoned prejudices, and a good deal of irrational behavior. Irresponsible politicians engaged in a frantic hunt for scapegoats upon whom to pin the blame for our lost security. Adlai E. Stevenson diagnosed the situation correctly when he said that our perturbation was caused by "the frustrations and agonies of this troubled age."

While overseas the international tempest raged, Americans reveled in an exceptional domestic prosperity. Their natural inclination was to fasten doors and windows tightly so as to shut out the angry elements. The wonder, therefore, is not that the spirit of isolationism revived; it is, rather, that isolationism failed to regain its former potency under conditions which were more than favorable for a vigorous regrowth. Men who optimistically pronounced isolationism dead with the creation of the United Nations found that it was to have a long funeral procession, and the corpse was to quicken before the cortege reached the cemetery.

Many basic factors explain this persisting vitality of the isolationist tradition. It had, to begin with, deeply imbedded emotional roots that had not been destroyed by the unrelenting forces of modern history. To be sure, when the Russians dropped the Iron Curtain in 1946, central Europe rather than the Atlantic Ocean became the dividing line between two antagonistic ways of life.[11] But the attitudes that had given rise to the American mood of aloofness persisted. Decades rather than months or years were needed to dispel the ingrained prejudice against what Herbert Hoover called "the eternal malign forces of Europe." The historian, Dixon Ryan Fox, once noted that "the cast-off garments of the intellectuals of one age are found, albeit soiled and ragged, on the backs of the ignorant many in the next." Fox's observation is pertinent, for the isolationist pattern of mind was a carry-over from a time when the policy had been the creed of the informed. Although the tradition had been long disavowed by men acquainted with the facts of international life, the masses still retained the tendency to regard non-involvement as the sovereign remedy for all foreign ills. The folk instinct, British observers of the American scene noted, was still for isolationism.[12] When world conditions made the policy in its original form ridiculous, its adherents camouflaged it in a new form.

There is a tendency in human nature to escape from unpleasant reality by regressing in thought to a period when these disagreeable problems did not exist. Many Americans disliked the world convulsions that thrust revolutionary nations, backward races, and suppressed classes into a position of importance. Their distaste for these changes became acute when they realized that these power shifts had created world tensions which increased their taxes, endangered their personal security, and put their sons in military service. A wave of nostalgia for the old order swept the country, finding outlets in period novels and movies, square dancing, the Davy Crockett craze, the hoop skirt fad among women, and a bicycle-era fashion in men's apparel. All this partially reflected a deep yearning to withdraw from the strange postwar world and crawl back into the comfortable shell of an isolated America.

The philosopher-theologian, Reinhold Niebuhr, has made a penetrating analysis of the contemporary cleavage in American and western European thought patterns. He feels that our economic well-being and military prowess has led us to cling far longer than the other peoples to the roseate optimism of the late nineteenth century. Unlike Europe and Asia, he remarks, our countryside escaped the physical devastation of war. To the majority of Americans, the hardships of the Second World War had been confined to a mild rationing of food, to a struggle to obtain cigarettes and nylon stockings, to keeping the old automobiles in condition, and to the petty annoyance of air-raid drills. American soldiers returned from the war to find their wives and sweethearts untouched by invading conquerors or liberators. After 1945, the contrast between the New and Old Worlds was sharply focused. On this side of the ocean there was a paradise of abundance and domestic security; on the other, there was a hell of poverty, hunger, and anarchy.[13] To men inclined toward snap judgments, isolationism still seemed to make good sense.

Certain other factors accelerated the reaction against the wartime foreign involvements. By and large, Americans are monolingual, with little penchant for alien languages and cultures. Paradoxically, the war against the Axis aroused enthusiasm for international organization but simultaneously fanned the flames of world nationalism. The fire was catching, and spreading to America; it helped the cause of the national-isolationists. Americans who were uninformed or insensitive to changing world conditions placed the blame for the inconclusive wars of our time upon the statesmen who had waged them. If our leaders had taken into consideration only primary American interests, so the common argument went, the results would have been different.

Inasmuch as the average mind in not analytical, it was difficult for many Americans to grasp the complexity of the situation which faced their policy-makers. The United States had been catapulted into a position of world leadership with insufficient preparation and little zest for its task. Its people, long accustomed to speedy results and to the quick abandoning of unsuccessful efforts, grew weary of the tedium involved in keeping order in a thermonuclear age. The old idea, that all the world had to do to become good was to follow our bright example, died hard.

The political situation of postwar America helped preserve the after-image of isolationism. Unlike England, where the basic aims of foreign policy are seldom altered by party revolutions, American diplomacy has been relatively unstable and therefore more prone to be tossed about by the winds of domestic politics. A brace of factors made it especially difficult to maintain a water-tight bi-partisan foreign policy. In a country where politics and patronage are two sides of the same coin, a minority party will be reluctant to hand the majority an advantage by agreeing with its conduct of diplomacy. "Any stick to beat a dog" is an old byword of politicos, and isolationism was a particularly tempting rod for the office-famished Republicans. A strong faction within the G.O.P. remembered vividly how the party had won with isolationism in the 1920s, and how they had used this issue in the following decade as a wedge to split the liberal Democratic front. Moreover, after 1945, the United States was faced with only bad diplomatic choices. Hence there was bound to be disagreement over the choice of the lesser evil. In a decade of G.O.P. ascendancy, the isolationists would once more gain the upper hand unless the world-minded Republicans retained their precarious control over the party.

The Republicans were as dangerously divided over foreign policy as were the Democrats on the Negro question. The G.O.P. international cooperationists had gained dominance during the war. This group struggled to maintain its leadership, arguing that isolationism was obsolete, that the United States needed European allies, and that such associations would help promote foreign trade and investments.

However, the resistant forces within the G.O.P. were frequently strong enough to make the party appear schizoid. The isolationists were strongly intrenched in rural areas where people were habitually indifferent to outside affairs and entertained no philosophical speculations about the brotherhood of man. The draft, continued in order to maintain our military position, bore especially hard on farmers already suffering from a labor shortage. West of the Alleghanies, the businessmen were much more concerned with reducing taxes than with building up foreign markets. The isolationist issue offered almost irresistible temptations to a party with many wealthy members who paid so great a share of the taxes needed to provide funds for an "international W.P.A." Republicans who wanted to give priority to national interests demanded economy, lower taxes, loyalty to the party tradition of a high tariff, and a balanced budget. The majority of American voters had, since 1932, repeatedly protested against this conservative approach. Some G.O.P. leaders wanted to disguise an unattractive economic platform by capitalizing upon widespread disillusion over entanglements.

By chance, the Republicans had been out of office before, during, and immediately after both world wars. Why not exploit the failure of the Democrats to keep the country out of these wars as well as the way in which they waged them? Through over-simplification and by snatching facts and figures out of context, it was possible to reach the following specious calculations:

28 years of Democratic rule (Wilson, F. D. Roosevelt, and Truman) yielded 1,628,480 war casualties.

24 years of Republican rule (Theodore Roosevelt, Taft, Harding, Coolidge, and Hoover) yielded 0 war casualties.[14]

Circumstances prevented the Republican isolationists from making full use of these bizarre figures. The G.O.P. won control of both houses of Congress in November, 1946. This victory, coming after sixteen years of political reverses, dispelled some of the accumulated frustration and revived the party's sense of national responsibility. For it was the Republican Eightieth Congress, inspired by Senator Vandenberg, that cooperated with President Truman to meet the Russian challenge. Confident of complete victory in the coming presidential bout of 1948, the Republicans were not tempted to exploit the foreign issue. But the spirit of the G.O.P. slumped badly in that year when their candidate, Governor Dewey, managed "to snatch defeat from the jaws of victory." On the heels of this unexpected set-back came the Communist conquest of the Chinese mainland. This was followed by the Korean War with the net result that the Republican intransigents again almost recaptured control. Fate, however, intervened once more and the availability of General Eisenhower meant that the Republican Restoration of 1953 was a party rather than a diplomatic revolution. Thus 1920 was not repeated when the outs returned to power carrying the torch of isolationism.

We have so far probed the emotional and political roots of contemporary isolationism. The postwar years, however, revealed that the tradition was even more solidly imbedded in American economic thinking. It has been often noted that the United States abandoned political non-involvement with much greater alacrity than it forsook the economic theories that supported the policy. This lag has persisted in spite of the fact that in ten years the United States spent over 50 billion dollars to buttress the economies and defense systems of foreign countries that remained out of the Soviet web.

The iron grip of economic isolationism was strengthened by a resurgence of domestic conservatism. Popular attention, in the years immediately following the war, was absorbed by demobilization, the reconversion of industry, recurrent inflationary cycles, and an acute shortage in housing and automobiles. Avid businessmen strove to make up for the lost decade of the depression. Generally speaking, the most important industrial leaders were reconciled to the limited commitments envisaged by the Charter of the United Nations, but their eyes watched other foreign expenditures warily. Businessmen hoped to relax the New Deal controls over private enterprise, to scale down taxes, and to keep the federal government from increasing its sway over local matters. If America shouldered additional responsibilities for world peace, it was obvious that the government could not contract its war-swollen budget or relinquish its newly granted powers. Moreover, there was a genuine fear among businessmen that they might be paying for the liquidation of world capitalism, for outside aid could be used to socialize the economics of western Europe. In addition, increased foreign aid might increase corporation and income taxes to the point where private initiative in the United States would be stifled. William Porter Witherow, one-time president of the National Association of Manufacturers, summed up this attitude when he stated his oft-quoted wartime warning: "I am not making guns or tanks to win a people's revolution. I am not fighting for a quart of milk for every Hottentot, or for a T.V.A. on the Danube." After V.J. Day there was a concerted effort to keep the liberal internationalists from creating what their conservative opponents termed a globalized welfare state. An excellent case could be made for stringent economy in government, until Soviet aggressions recalled to mind of F.D.R.'s observation that national survival was more important than the national debt.

Even after the Communist expansionism loosened the federal pursestrings, vestigial economic isolationism outlived the principle of political non-involvement. The Senate, for instance, blocked American entry into an International Trade Organization. The New Deal policy of reducing tariff rates by reciprocal agreements with other countries was retained, but the Republican Eightieth Congress impeded the program by adding a "peril point" feature to the law. Under this new provision, the President was compelled to explain to Congress any reduction in rates that the Tariff Commission thought injurious to domestic trade. Significantly, a Democratic Congress removed the "peril point" amendment only to restore it several years later.[15] The bi-partisan nature of current economic nationalism was vividly illustrated in 1956 when a Democratic Congress stood ready to pare down a Republican President's request for foreign aid. Senator Richard B. Russell of Georgia, chairman of the Senate Armed Services Committee, announced his opposition to any increase in foreign grants unless they were earmarked for a military build-up against the Communists. His colleague, the venerable Walter F. George, who had sat in the Senate since 1923, gave up his fight for re-election rather than face Governor Herman Talmadge in the Democratic primary. Talmadge, who combined the white supremacy issue with isolationism, accused Senator George of voting to give away to foreigners American dollars that could have been better spent in Georgia. An increasing number of Democrats, especially in the South, accused President Eisenhower of trying to play Santa Claus with the Federal Treasury. Samuel Lubell has noted that southern leaders in both parties showed a strong distaste for the economic implications of power politics. Thus, while in 1952 only 19 percent of the southern bloc in Congress voted against foreign aid, by 1955 the percentage had doubled.[16] It is only fair to add, however, that even in the latter year more Republicans than Democrats voted against these subsidies.

But congressional politicians in both parties were reluctant to accept an economic policy liberal enough to satisfy the demands of our free world allies and the neutralist states. During his 1952 campaign, Eisenhower had promised to taper off and eventually to end foreign subsidies. Circumstances forced the Republicans to discard this pledge, but the Eisenhower administration refused to advise economic aid for countries unwilling to pledge us their military support. Hence suggestions that the United States compete with Bulganin's Russia by extending aid to countries that wished to remain unentangled came from outside of government circles. Adlai E. Stevenson, campaigning for the 1956 Democratic nomination, voiced the demand of our NATO allies that economic aid be channeled to needy countries through the United Nations. As the titular leader of the minority party, Stevenson criticized Dulles's insistence on drawing up "rubber-check military pacts which will bounce as soon as we try to cash them."[17] Paul G. Hoffman, former administrator of the European Recovery Program, felt that the United States ought to counteract Soviet moves by spending $25 billion in an economic campaign to "wage peace." The Eisenhower administration, however, continued to insist that our money be spent only on countries that were willing to "stand up and be counted" in the anti-Communist ranks. The President was understandably skeptical of Russian promises of aid to countries that insisted upon neutrality. In reply to demands that the United States aid uncommitted countries in a measure sufficient to allow them to make capital improvements, Eisenhower agreed to appoint a commission to re-evaluate our program of foreign spending. But the Republican party was badly divided on the issue. Secretary of the Treasury George M. Humphrey, speaking for the conservatives, strongly opposed help that would allow Indonesia to develop its government-owned industry. Eisenhower, a devotee of free enterprise at home, was reported to have told Humphrey that an underdeveloped country such as Indonesia was forced to turn to collectivization because it lacked domestic capital and could not borrow from more advanced nations.

Despite the President's rather belated comprehension of the problem, it seemed improbable that he could convince the tax-conscious politicans on Capitol Hill to liberalize our foreign aid program. The White House's 1956 request for foreign aid appropriation was slashed in the House of Representatives, with many Republicans joining the Democratic majority to vote against the President. Representative George S. Long (a Louisiana Democrat) voiced the growing conviction of many members of both parties when he called our foreign aid program "the greatest fraud since money became a medium of exchange."[18]

Despite the demands of the liberal internationalists for increased foreign aid for neutralist areas, the country at large did not equate prudence in dispensing federal largesse with a return to isolationism. Opponents of augmented foreign spending were by no means always isolationists, for many conservative Republicans and Democrats approved the commitments

351

already made although they doubted the value of indefinite and indiscriminate pump-priming in remote regions of the world. Foreign aid, observed William S. White of the New York *Times's* Washington staff, had come to be regarded, like taxes, as a necessary nuisance. Thus, commented White, while most congressmen had no real thought of abandoning the "inescapable routine burden" of overseas help, they were not at all certain that Eisenhower's program was attuned to the world of Bulganin and Khrushchev. Moreover, many internationalists on Capitol Hill reasoned that a political settlement with the Kremlin, designed to lessen the drain on the Federal Treasury, was in order.[19]

Politicians in both parties, however, were reluctant to recognize the relationship between our coalition diplomacy and the perennial domestic farm question. Rigid support for falling farm prices, the bugbear of contemporary American politics, created a vicious cycle that hampered the exchange of goods between the free nations. Our farm subsidies encouraged the overproduction of staples, thus closing the American market to foreign argricultural products. "While we struggle for export markets to absorb our manufacturers," notes one foreign affairs analyst, "our agricultural surpluses overhang the economies of our best customers."[20] But neither party could afford to rework its antiquated conception of the national interest, for the all-important farm vote hung in the balance.

Thus it is self-evident that America was more willing to give up political than economic isolationism. The failure to coordinate diplomatic commitments with economic policy made it difficult to keep our free world coalition in proper balance. While we demanded that our allies raise their economic sights to a supra-national level, we kept our own eyes focused on politics designed to prosper America first. By not relaxing our tariff barriers to the point where Britain and Japan could dispose of their surpluses here, we tempted them to ship goods behind the Iron Curtain. Commenting on the hold that the narrow nationalistic school had on matters of immigration restriction, tariff protection, and race supremacy, Dean McGeorge Bundy of Harvard University concludes that "in every one of these great problems the status quo is surrounded by heavily armed batteries of defenders." These economic and social residues of yesterday bid fair to become the great issues of tomorrow. There was good reason to believe, on the tenth anniversary of the Japanese surrender, that the heirs of Stalin had decided to try to conquer the world by means short of thermonuclear war. The new Russian plan, disarmingly suave, threatened to dissolve the free world bloc. The power contest of the second postwar decade seemed likely to be fought with economic rather than with military weapons.

To recapitulate, the psychological, political, and economic seeds of isolationism had not been destroyed with the withering of the above-surface foliage. These seeds had been well sown and they sprouted anew with each change in the diplomatic weather. The demand for a return to political isolation was particularly marked among older men and women whose ideas had crystallized in a bygone age. Such an about-face also appealed to those younger people who demanded a quick solution to a complex situation that defied simple analysis. However, the Axis nightmare had sifted the more informed and the more sensitive ones from the isolationist ranks. The Russian menace continued this separating process, leaving the inflexible isolationists with few men of intellectual stature. Hence, despite the vitality of the old tradition, it could not recover its former strength. The American instinct was still for isolationism, but this natural inclination was held in check by the dictates of national interest. Despite the presence of some disillusioning factors, until 1950 there was general agreement on foreign policy, and it was the mid-century Asiatic reverses that for a season threatened to inundate the country with a new tidal wave of isolationism. Before evaluating the effects of the Far Eastern upset, it is necessary to consider the basic factors counterweighing the contemporary isolationist impulse.

The postwar isolationists have been repeatedly thwarted because the achievement of their aims would have delighted the Russians. Admiral Ellis M. Zacharias, who based his opinion on intimate contact with Soviet bigwigs, has said that the Kremlin's real goal is not the military subjugation of the United States nor its communization; it is, rather, to force it into an exasperated withdrawal back to its "Monroe area." Then, says Zacharias, Russia will plant Communist time-bombs in selected Latin-American spots underneath the United States, thus keeping it "from ever breaking out of its degrading, decaying, impotent isolation."[21] While the validity of this theory is debatable, there is no question that the isolationists faced the unpleasant fact that Communists, domestic and foreign, cheered their efforts.

The obvious Soviet desire to force America out of Europe and Asia placed the isolationists on the defensive. Although they were venomously anti-Russian, they found themselves unwittingly opposing measures designed to halt the spread of Communism. It was self-evident that Communists, provided

353

with all their apparatus for infiltration, were prepared to exploit an American withdrawal. Each time the isolationists demanded the contraction of our sphere of influence, the domestic radicals cried "Hear! hear!" To discourage this embarassing applause, the isolationists concentrated their attention on home-grown Marxists. They resorted to red-baiting in a manner so indiscriminate and vindictive that it incurred the wrath of both moderate and liberal-minded men.

After 1945, it was difficult to champion a return to a policy of non-involvement, for the Communists detonated all local mines of unrest. At some point Moscow and Peiping had to be stopped, or else the explosions would destroy our potential allies. The choice faced by the United States was no longer between isolationism and collective security; it was rather whether we could best protect our interests by a unilateral or a multilateral diplomacy.

The old-line isolationists still preferred to go it alone. Their defense of this position was vulnerable, for the country's best minds were agreed that without allies America possessed neither sufficient manpower nor natural resources to outmatch the Communist combination. We needed our allies almost as much as they needed us, and the Soviets seldom relaxed the international tension long enough to let us forget it. During the first postwar decade, Great Britain and France fought shooting wars against the Asiatic Communists, and the United States was virtually compelled to support their efforts. Only Moscow and Peiping would have been the gainers had the isolationists won the day.

Dorothy Fosdick, formerly of the State Department's Planning Commission, has observed that while the alternatives faced by American statesmen were all bad, the isolationists made the choice of the greatest peril. If coalition diplomacy often taxed Washington's patience, such chronic vexation was preferable to burdening ourselves with the sole task of saving western civilization. It seems safe to say that if the United States had spurned the captaincy of the anti-Communist forces, a large segment of western Europe and possibly all of Asia would have fallen prey to the Soviet menace. Now it was Americans who feared the spread of a mood of non-entanglement among Europeans and Asiatics. The isolationist shoe was on the other foot.

For a season, the Communist thrust obliterated remaining traces of the inter-war isolationist coalition. After V.J. Day, a liberal rump sought to revive the wartime amity with Russia by opposing Truman's stiffened anti-Communist policy. Its last important stand, however, came in 1948 when Henry A. Wallace's short-lived Progressive party denounced both Republicans and Democrats as warmongers. Significantly, Wallace himself soon recanted and in the 1950's the erstwhile ultra-New Dealer supported President Eisenhower.

Revolutionary events had destroyed all the remaining liberal arguments for isolationism. The ancient prejudice against colonialism was rendered obsolete by the ruin of the European empires. Communist and Socialist power blocs within the United Nations made it impossible to label this organization another League of Nations working for Wall Street. By 1956 commentators on the national scene noted that control of both major parties was in the hands of moderates who walked the narrow ridge between the chasms of conservatism and liberalism. Social reform had lost its appeal to an America in which erstwhile underprivileged groups were now enthusiastic junior partners in the free enterprise venture. The legatees of liberalism, calling themselves the ADA (Americans for Democratic Action) emphasized personal rights, racial equality, and the dignity of man, rather than economic oppression. As champions of civil rights, these neo-liberals favored close cooperation with other democratic nations, and internationalism was as endemic in their circle as isolationism had been in that of their predecessors of the 1920s. Progressively minded Americans had moved out of the isolationist camp. This defection clearly identified the remaining isolationists with the forces of reaction.[22]

Simultaneously there was a relative decline in the kind of isolationism evoked by ethnic considerations. The absolute independence of Ireland cooled the passions of American sons of Erin, so long opposed to any partnership with Britain. The fangs of nativist and hyphenate Anglophobes were blunted when England relinquished effective control over her most important colonial possessions. The Prime Ministers of the British Commonwealth of Nations met occasionally to discuss common problems, but India and Pakistan accepted the Crown only as a symbol and gave no allegiance to the Queen. Moreover, Commonwealth members were often at cross purposes in foreign policy, for while Britain was a member of SEATO, India bitterly opposed this mutual defense pact. Speaking frankly, the London *Economist* called the Commonwealth "a gentle let-down" created to help England adjust to her loss of status.[23] From time to time, anti-British Americans still accused London of colonial exploitation, but such shopworn epithets sounded as stale as jokes about the NRA.

Vengeful memories of two world wars lingered among German-Americans, but their effectiveness was lessened by new circumstances. In 1949 the United States not only sponsored the establishment of the Federal Republic of West Germany, but also bade the new government welcome into the concert of free nations. Many German-Americans remained staunch isolationists, but as bitter opponents of Communism, they were often embarrassed for arguments with which to attack the Truman-Eisenhower policy of building up Bonn as the western outpost against Moscow.

Nor were the isolationists able to find new ethnic allies to compensate for the loss of hyphenate support. Russian and Chinese minorities were negligible, and the Communist issue estranged the former nationals of Iron Curtain countries from effective homeland influence. The post-Versailles isolationists had successfully capitalized upon two conditions that proved ephemeral. The great folk migrations of the nineteenth century had left large national blocs not yet assimilated into the bloodstream of American thought. Thus isolationists of the Borah-La Follette stripe were able to play upon the emotions of these groups by portraying the League of Nations as an Anglo-French conspiracy to dominate Germany, Italy, Austria, and Hungary. In the 1950s, however, the doors to America had been shut for a full generation, and time had decimated the hyphenate ranks. Moreover, many surviving first-generation immigrants recognized that a resurgent isolationism would be inimical to the welfare of their European kinsmen. In order to attract such hyphenate sentiment as remained, American super-nationalists became perversely isolationst and recklessly pledged the speedy liberation of enslaved satellite countries from Soviet bondage. Such large-scale interventionism, however, was hardly calculated to attract widespread popular support among Americans who abhorred the thought of another war.

In whichever direction the perplexed isolationists moved, they stubbed their toes on the Communist stumbling block. Popular interest in world politics was greater than ever, for as Vera Micheles Dean has so aptly put it, foreign affairs are no longer foreign. The government used the mass public communications systems to explain that the best hope of halting the Communist steamroller was to convert the people who lay in its path into staunch American allies. This policy was frequently irksome and always expensive, but no responsible statesman seemed to have a better alternative.

The revolution in warfare made coalition diplomacy all the

more necessary. Probably the United States could win a hydrogen duel with Russia, but it was taken for granted that before we blotted out the enemy, many of our own cities would be radioactive rubble. Attempts to coordinate civilian air-raid defense were lackadaisical because there was no place to hide. Hence the surest protection against wholesale desruction lay in deterring the aggressors by threats of immediate retaliation. But in order to insure the SAC (American Strategic Air Command) sufficient long-range striking power to give the Kremlin pause, we needed overseas allies to furnish us with a ring of air bases near the Soviet borders. Peace-by-deterrence seemed the best promise of security against thermonuclear destruction, yet the scheme could work only if supported by a tight military alliance with European countries who were willing to have their lands turned into springboards for an air assault against Russia. A return to isolationism in the traditional meaning of the word would surely jeopardize these plans for military security.

In a sense, isolationism had become antithetical to national survival. The 1946 test explosions on the North Pacific atoll of Bikini revealed the effects of deadly radioactive particles on fish. By 1949 there was no doubt that Soviet scientists had constructed and exploded an atomic bomb. On January 31, 1950, President Truman directed that work should proceed on a hydrogen bomb, and this undertaking was soon paralleled by the Russians. The implications of these developments on the possible future of the human race may be seen in the following comparison: one hydrogen bomb was said to be twenty times as lethal as the two million tons of explosives dropped from the skies during the Second World War. But even this contrast understates the case for, by 1955, super H-bombs had been developed. Atomic Energy Commissioner Thomas E. Murray bluntly warned of the new dangers that these weapons posed. Among other threats which he described was the possibility that the nation's food supply would be jeopardized by a "fall-out of radioactive strontium from thermonuclear explosions."[24] War, it has been noted, was no longer an instrument of self-defense; it had been turned overnight into a means of self-destruction.

Based upon these latest developments, a group of responsible American experts predicted: if war came before 1960, it would be fought with heavy bombers flying the North Pole short-cut between America and Russia, each plane prepared to deliver 20 to 50 megaton explosions (the equivalent of 20 to 50 million tons of old-fashioned T.N.T.). In addition, inter-

357

mediate range guided missiles would be launched from submarine carriers that would prowl coastal waters. In 1955, it was said that the Soviets already had a guided rocket that could travel 1,500 miles, and Marshal Bulganin stopped smiling long enough to boast that his country would soon produce the ultimate weapon, capable of crossing the oceans faster than the speed of sound. Thus American scientists reckoned that in a war fought in the 1960s, guided rockets with nuclear warheads, capable of obliterating a great city without warning, would be hurled through the stratosphere. This gloomy prediction accompanied a warning that the enemy would use chemical and biological warfare to demoralize and destroy the homeless survivors of the preliminary attacks.[25] Ten years of debate in the United Nations had advanced neither the art of world government nor suggested a workable international control of atomic energy. Instead, the events of the decade had demonstrated that man had learned how to put an end to his own history.

The implications of these cataclysmic changes were staggering. The very words "national defense" lost their meaning, because no major war could be fought to victory without the annihilation of large segments of our urban population. Sir Winston Churchill, in his own incomparable way, said that peace was at the mercy of a "balance of terror." American Pollyannas argued that war might be eliminated because it had become a game of Russian roulette with all chambers loaded against participants. Possibly these optimists were correct, but there was little in the story of mankind to warrant such a cheerful conclusion. Certainly no responsible statesman could rely upon mere conjecture. Policy-makers would have to act with the dread possibility in mind that the flames of World War III would consume the free and totalitarian worlds together. Perhaps Albert Einstein was not over-stating the case when he predicted that the *Fourth* World War would be fought with bows and arrows!

These considerations made any return to a foreign policy of non-involvement both dangerous and absurd. The most localized foreign crisis was given high priority in the State Department, for the Communist fished in all troubled waters, threatening to create a tempest in every teapot. The United States found it hazardous to neglect security arrangements with friendly nations great or small. Under existing circumstances, the only feasible choice left was to negotiate a chain of entangling alliances designed to offset the Sino-Soviet Axis. International altruism played but a small part in the search for trustworthy allies. American diplomats were generally agreed that the surest way of deterring the Kremlin from taking an irrevocable step was to make it manifest that aggression would be met by instant reprisal. Therefore, pending some future date when our giant bombers could deliver sledgehammer blows from New World springboards, our 150 European air bases were of prime necessity. This was especially true since the Communists had the advantage of bases from Prague to Peiping. Such a handicap could only be overcome by stationing our planes on the territory of our allies. For purposes of defense, such foreign outposts had to be regarded, for the time being, as part of our expanded coastline. In the postwar years, the geographical case for isolationism was reduced to an absurdity. To make any kind of a case for their proposal, the isolationists were compelled to advance a fresh set of arguments.

While, as we have seen, the isolationist impulse remained strong, the emotions it aroused were restrained by international pressures. The Russian army stood poised to fill vacuums created by an American retreat. Moreover, radical changes in warfare made unashamed power politics the only middle way between a dangerous acquiescence to the land-hungry Communists and an equally perilous attempt to halt the Red march by unilateral action. Most important of all, perhaps, an isolationist resurgence was frustrated because American statesmen proved themselves sensitive to changing conditions and adjusted their policies to meet shifting conditions. Had the Truman administration stubbornly insisted on unmodified collective security, western Europe as well as the Asiatic mainland might well have fallen to the Communists. In that case, the United States would have had to choose between a war of liberation or an isolationism of disgust. It is quite probable that public opinion would have insisted upon withdrawal.

The greatest turning point in postwar American foreign policy came in the early months of 1947. Truman's earlier actions indicate that he overestimated the restraining power of the United Nations and underestimated the force of Communist expansionism. The President bowed to the popular will by sharply curtailing military expenditures and by reducing the armed forces, within a period of two years, from 12 to 1½ million men. The other free world victors also disarmed in unilateral fashion, at a price, said the New York *Times*, "of catastrophe for some nations and an almost suicidal peril to themselves."[26] Such action demonstrated a sincere desire for peace, but, unhappily, the Kremlin saw the move as a green light for the prowling Red Bear. Several years elapsed before Truman and his advisers realized that the Russians turned deaf ears to protests voiced by any nation carrying a whittled-down stick.

The reasons for the two-year period of American vacillation are complex. As Vice-President, Truman had not been privy to the innermost secrets of state, and it took him time to get his bearings. Like so many of his countrymen, the President was loath to accept American foreign commitments over and beyond the stipulations of the Charter of the United Nations. During the period immediately following the Japanese surrender, it seemed possible to retrieve part of our pre-war advantages. Thus, lend-lease was abruptly terminated, and UNRRA ended as of January 1, 1947. Only gradually did the administration come to realize that in order to prevent the social festering that invites Communist encroachment, the United States would have to rebuild the economics of both our former friends and enemies.

Superficially viewed, our military situation appeared sound. During the war we had mobilized the most efficient striking force in the world, and men took it for granted that any new challenge to our security would allow us time for another mobilization. As long as we held a monopoly on the production of A-bombs, this supposition seemed reasonable. The old militia spirit, a part of the isolationist tradition, took a long time to die.

Gradually, however, the grim revolutionary forces of our time spurred the American leaders into action. They recognized that their U.N. blueprint for international organization was unworkable in its present form, and that totalitarianism was again on the rampage. Once more we were faced with the same choice that confronted Roosevelt in 1940: whether to allow an aggressor to force an antagonistic way of life upon our natural allies, or to use American power to prevent the catastrophe. In many ways the 1947 policy of containing Russian expansionism resembled F.D.R.'s moves to check the Nazis by measures short of shooting war.[27] For example, we re-armed and lent economic and defense assistance to countries willing to resist Communist intrusion. Each step in Truman's program was opposed by hard-bitten isolationists who, in the manner of 1939-1941, waged lengthy debates only to lose every congressional battle. Robert Waitham has suggested that these isolationist dissenters served a salutary purpose, for in answering their protests, the majority convinced the wavering country that American help for western Europe was the lesser evil. The great debate of 1939-1941, temporarily halted by the war, was resumed.

On Wednesday, March 12, 1947, the President stepped jauntily to the Speaker's rostrum in the House of Representatives, and presented to a joint session of Congress a key proposal that has come to be known as the Truman Doctrine. With its major corollaries, adopted by Congress in piecemeal fashion, this policy marked a more emphatic repudiation of non-entaglement than any plan ever envisaged by either Woodrow Wilson or Franklin D. Roosevelt. The Truman Doctrine was the first step in a diplomatic démarche that offered American financial aid, defense equipment, and, in some instances, military assistance to any nation threatened with internal or external Communist aggression. Enacted in time of peace, the legislation of 1947-1949 eventually resulted in a chain of military alliances which bound our fortunes to those of nations situated on five continents. The links were double-riveted, for they were originally proposed by a Democratic President and approved by a Republican Congress. This fact helps explain their durability. With Truman, a new era in American foreign policy had begun.

Both deep-seated and immediate causes played their parts in dictating Truman's historic departure. The Russian obstructionist tactics of 1945 were followed by hostile actions in northern Iran, an attempt to blackmail Turkey into surrendering two provinces, and the incitement of guerilla warfare against Greece. Previous to these new aggressions, Truman had met Stalin at Potsdam—an experience that taught him that the Bolshevists begin negotiations by demanding impossible concessions. The President also learned that, once he had compromised with Stalin in the name of world peace, the generalissimo was able to trump up reasons for not keeping his bargain almost before the ink was dry on the agreement.

For seventeen months after Potsdam the President and Secretary of State James F. Byrnes tried to reason with Stalin, but to no avail. American statesmen flitted across the Atlantic to parley with the Russians, but found it impossible to reach a mutual understanding with men whose ultimate aim was to prevent just that. In a desperate attempt to allay Stalin's "fears," Byrnes revived Senator Vandenberg's proposal of a four-power pact to insure Russia's boundaries, but he was coldly rebuffed. In similar fashion, our 1946 Baruch plan for international atomic control was derided, spurned, and eventually vetoed by Moscow. By the fall of 1946 the South Carolinian was no longer willing to coddle the snarling Russian bear. Byrnes spoke out at Stuttgart and in Paris in language designed for Russian ears. He bluntly warned that the United States would not allow Germany to remain as a pawn to be pushed around the European chessboard, nor would exasperation by the Kremlin force us back into our "Monroe area." Experience, said the Secretary, had taught us that we could not stay out of Europe's wars, and hence we had no choice but to pursue policies designed to prevent their outbreak.[28] This was tantamount to saying that we intended to retain our foothold in western Europe.

In 1939, other powers took the lead in trying to halt Hitler, but by 1946 no other nation was left besides the United States who cherished the existence of a free world area and who, at the same time, had the power to keep it intact. We had half of the world's gold supply, over half of all the shipping, and our industrial capacity outmatched that of all other countries combined.[29] Either this democratic colossus had to meet the challenge, or only an act of God would halt a Red march to the English Channel. Thus Washington became the capital of the non-Marxist world. Having accepted the task that was thrust upon their shoulders, our statesmen naturally wished to muster the forces of all like-minded countries. The economic situation in Europe was so bad, however, that, as Dean Acheson has said, we had to create efficient allies before we could negotiate an effective alliance. Since the 1945 Nazi collapse, America has poured $11 billion into Europe in the form of loans and gifts, UNRRA supplies, and help from private philanthropic organizations. But even this sum was piddling in view of the wholesale devastation wrought by the war.[30] The situation could only be salvaged by our government's promoting foreign recovery on a scale unprecedented in peacetime history.

Truman's over-all aim was to prevent any further Soviet contraction of remaining free regions. To this end he coupled the economic rehabilitation of Europe with active efforts to prevent any forward movement of the Iron Curtain. The chief architect of this containment plan was George F. Kennan, a scholarly and sure-footed diplomat who had analyzed the Communist mind while serving as counsellor to the American Embassy in Moscow. In an anonymous article published in *Foreign Affairs* (July, 1947), Kennan drafted a blueprint designed to shut the floodgates on Communist poisoned waters. It should be our purpose, he declared, to face the Russians "with unalterable counter-force at every point where they show signs of encroaching upon the interest of a peaceful and stable world." The men around Truman regarded containment as an escape from the nightmarish choices of letting the Communist juggernaut go unhalted, or else going to war to stop it. Like all compromise policies, containment was open to attack from hotheads who wanted to do more and soreheads who wanted to do less.

Two pressing complications led the President to make his landmark decision. He acted while the foreign ministers were deadlocked in Moscow over the question of German unification and at a time when American patience was entirely exhausted by Russian obstructionism. "Moscow," experts writing for the Council on Foreign Relations have observed, "really marked the end of the road which began at Teheran and Yalta."[31] Even more important than the impasse over the German question was the rapidly deteriorating Balkan situation. London had informed Washington that it could no longer afford to uphold the Greek monarchy against the Communist-minded rebels who sought to destroy it. If Greece fell, as it surely would unless the United States acted promptly, then Turkey would be ringed by Soviet power. With Greece and Turkey turned into Russian satrapies, Moscow would have the Middle East in lead strings. The United States had to choose between intervention or acquiescence to a further shrinkage of the free world area. Harry S. Truman has thus stated his reactions to this 1947 perplexity:

> If we were to turn our back on the world, areas such as Greece, weakened and divided as a result of the war, would fall into the Soviet orbit without much effort on the part of the Russians. The success of Russia in such areas and our avowed lack of interest would lead to the growth of domestic Communist parties in . . . France and Italy . . . Inaction, withdrawal, 'Fortress America' nations could only result in handing to the Russians vast areas of the globe now denied to them.[32]

There was more, however, to the new American policy than a mere attempt to checkmate Moscow's political power. The popularity of the free enterprise system, thanks to the war-made prosperity, was at an all-time high. The American people did not wish, nor could they afford, to be left as capitalistic hermits in a collectivized world. To prevent this, we found it expedient to support the institutional and ideological status quo in foundering non-Marxist countries. We accomplished this by giving them the arms to protect their freedom and by priming their economic pumps with American dollars. The theory that underlay our actions held that if foreign free enterprise were made workable, a widely spread prosperity would discourage the trend toward radicalism. Mr. Truman recalls that when he explained the Balkan crisis to a bi-partisan group of congressional leaders at the White House conference of February 27, 1947, no voice was raised in dissent.

The Truman Doctrine, incorporated in the President's speech to Congress of March 12, 1947, declared "that it must be the policy of the United States to support free peoples who are resisting attempted subjugation by armed minorities or by outside pressures." This broad statement of principle was accompanied by a request for an appropriation of $400,000,000 for economic and military aid to be sent to Greece and Turkey. This relatively modest request launched a long-range program during the course of which America underwrote the economic rehabilitation and the military defense of western Europe. The first legislative step came on May 22, 1947, when Truman wrote into law a measure which approved the monetary appropriation and authorized the President to send military and civilian advisers to Greece and Turkey. This act produced the desired effects, and the Russian lunge toward the Dardanelles was parried.

New requests to Congress followed in swift order. As early as May 8, 1947, Under Secretary of State Dean Acheson suggested large-scale economic help for friendly European powers. This wider-scope operation, destined to go down in history as the Marshall Plan, was outlined by Secretary of State George C. Marshall in his Harvard Commencement Address of 1947. The Secretary reasoned that the United States must open its coffers in sufficient measure to put western Europe back on its economic feet. Our action, declared Marshall, was not motivated by hostility toward any nation, but it was designed rather to make war against "hunger, poverty, desperation, and chaos." (This generous offer, which included help for Communist-ruled countries, was denounced by the Kremlin as "American imperialism" and was subsequently spurned by Russia, its helpless satellites, and Finland and Czechoslovakia who chose not to defy the Soviet edict.) It was accepted by sixteen European nations, excluding Franco's Spain to which no offer was made, and occupied Germany which, at the time, had no government of its own. A Committee of European Economic Cooperation, consisting of delegates from the sixteen willing nations, reported in

September, 1947, with comprehensive plans for the restoration of European self-sufficiency. The President modified these proposals and, in December, 1947, asked Congress for $17 billion to be spent over a period of some eleven years.

The relative ease with which Truman got the substance of this European Recovery Program (E.R.P.) through an economy-minded Republican Congress can be easily explained. The administration had done unusually careful and thorough spadework. Sensing the conservative temper of the country, it made business leaders partners in the venture. The success of E.R.P. in Congress was assured when the three most powerful national pressure groups were persuaded that their constituents, as well as the United States, stood to gain from the proposal. The business group (represented by the National Association of Manufacturers) hesitated to bolster the socialist economies among the sixteen nations. The N.A.M. realized, however, that European recovery would foster American foreign trade and might possibly uproot the seed-beds of Communism in France and Italy. Moreover, Truman's liaison officers promised that E.R.P. would be run according to "sound business principles," and that it would help counteract the trend toward socialism. True to his word, the President called upon the business elite to help administer the new program. E.R.P. was headed by the president of the Studebaker Corporation, Paul G. Hoffman, who pleased the industrial bigwigs by advertising abroad the merits of the American system of free enterprise.

The all-important agricultural associations were also enthused by the prospect of increased foreign outlets for farm products, as were the A.F.L. and C.I.O. who, well acquainted with the techniques of Communist infiltrators, hoped to keep foreign unions from falling into radical hands. Veteran and patriotic organizations were likewise attracted by the administration's argument that E.R.P. would save western Europe from Communism. The support of the country's most influential lobbies was secured before Congres began its debates.[33]

Senator Vandenberg, in a 9,000 word speech, proposed the establishment of the Economic Cooperation Administration which would set the Marshall Plan in operation. With characteristic caution, the Republican leader reviewed the international scene, examined possible alternative policies, and declared "the pending program . . . . the best of these risks." Opposition was confined to some ultra-conservatives who insisted upon a return to "little government," and to some legislators who let their desire for immediate tax reductions outweigh all other considerations. Any doubt that the bill would pass by overwhelming majorities was dispelled when the Russians engineered a Communist *coup* (February, 1948) in long-suffering Czechoslovakia. Once more the shortsightedness of the Kremlin leaders and their poor sense of timing helped convince Americans that it was more dangerous to withdraw from Europe than to remain there. Congress pared down Truman's requests, but it established E.C.A. for a period of three years during the course of which the United States spent $10½ billion on the project. Western Europe showed prompt signs of recovery, and the success of E.C.A. led to a broadened program of economic help for non-Marxist countries in other regions.

The next step was outlined by President Truman in his inaugural address of January 20, 1949. The Chief Executive reasoned that the policy of containment would be futile if it only deflected the Red advance from western Europe to other continents. Inasmuch as collectivism had an unusual appeal to the teeming millions of the former colonial nations, its attraction would have to be offset by American aid to such countries. Forced industrialization, precipitated by mass coercion, was very tempting to people who neither understood nor practiced democracy. Such men looked to Russia as a shining example of an agrarian country that, by squeezing the necessary capital out of her people, had pioneered a short cut to modernization. Unless the United States provided a convenient way of obtaining capital and technical assistance, India, Indonesia, and even some Latin American states might enroll as pupils of the Soviet Union. During the course of their tutelage in the art of collectivization, they would naturally gravitate toward the Moscow pole of the divided world.

To avert this peril, Truman suggested his famous Point Four program, declaring that the program would make "the benefits of our scientific advances and industrial progress available for the improvement and growth of underdeveloped areas." The Point Four program was launched in 1950. By the end of the first postwar decade (June 30, 1955) the United States had spent approximately $14⅔ billion for military assistance to friendly countries, and $36⅔ billion to rehabilitate foreign economies, to render technical assistance, and to put our mutual security pacts into effective operation. In round numbers, $33.5 billion went to western Europe, $10 billion to Asia and outlying Pacific nations, $4.3 billion to the Middle East and Africa, and $1.2 billion to our slighted friends in the New World.[34]

Time, however, proved that even these astronomic figures did not solve the basic problem. Little money went for permanent capital improvements and we had merely whetted the appetite of backward peoples for capital loans. The situation grew acute when, in the middle 1950s, Stalin's business-minded successors packed their sample cases and peddled a Sovietized Marshall Plan in Asia and Africa. American opinion was badly divided as to whether the United States should write off the uncommitted nations as expendable, or else outbid the Kremlin for their support.

To return once more to the enactment of Truman's 1947 program, the United States soon perceived the folly of merely fattening the western European goose for the Russians to pluck. Franklin D. Roosevelt, who originally tried to stop Hitler by cold warfare, soon discovered that lend-lease aid was valueless unless the United States made sure that the goods would reach its overseas destination. In like manner, Truman was quick to realize that economic aid was useless unless the recipients were made strong enough to protect their rehabilitated countries against Soviet intrusion. Mulling this problem, American statesmen conceded that the U.N. was incapable of preventing aggression; yet they hesitated to deal the organization a heavy blow by building a defense system that ignored the Charter. Senator Vandenberg, working closely with his fellow Republican, Under Secretary of State Robert A. Lovett, discovered a way out of the dilemma. He found the solution to their problem in Article 51 of the Charter which permitted regional defense arrangements among members of the United Nations. Such agreements, of course, could be negotiated and operated without running afoul of a Soviet veto in the Security Council. The Vandenberg Resolution of 1948, approved by the Senate with only six dissenting votes, advised the President to insure the safety of the free world by arranging mutual defense agreements within the general framework of the United Nations. Carefully worded, the Vandenberg Resolution stipulated that these treaties must be negotiated by the usual constitutional process.[35] Moreover, the Michigan Senator replaced the emotion-packed word "alliance" with the euphemism "mutual aid."

The United States already had invoked Article 51 in negotiating the Pact of Rio de Janeiro which united the western hemisphere for joint defense. After the passage of the Vandenberg Resolution, Robert A. Lovett began preliminary work on a collective security arrangement with the countries of western Europe. The new Secretary of State, Dean Acheson, took counsel with the Senate Foreign Relations Committee, thus easing the way for approval of the proposed North Atlantic Treaty Organization. Subsequently, the Senate watered down the administration's proposal by making military support subject to due constitutional procedure. The heart of the treaty was Article 5 which declared that an attack on one signatory power would be construed as an attack against all members. Each power pledged itself to take "such action as it deems necessary, including the use of armed force." Hence, even with the modifications inserted by the Senate, the United States was bound by the strongest kind of moral commitment to defend against attack any of the other eleven states with whom it had entered into the most entangling kind of alliance. One era in American history came to an end on July 21, 1949, when the Senate consented to NATO. Senator Taft, who had voted for the Marshall Plan, was now leading the opposition, but he was able to muster only 13 nays against 82 votes to approve the treaty.

The military headquarters of NATO (SHAPE) was set up near Paris in 1951 with General Dwight D. Eisenhower in command. From the very beginning the NATO authorities did not intend to build up a land force capable of resisting a full-scale Russian plunge westward. Rather was it the purpose of SHAPE to make the Kremlin think twice before making such a move. If, on the other hand, the Russians could not be deterred from making war on the West, NATO's forces would serve the free world by fighting a holding action against the invaders until the Strategic Air Command could reduce the Soviet military depots to rubble. Because France feared that a united continental army would stimulate a revival of German militarism, Paris did not join the European Defense Community until 1954. Later, member nations of the Western European Union found that their original military plan had been rendered obsolete when the Soviets perfected both a hydrogen bomb and an intermediate ballistic rocket that might make it impossible for American bombers to launch retaliatory blows from European bases. By 1956, competent observers stated that either the United States would have to prevent war by reaching an understanding with Bulganin, Khrushchev and Co., or else modernize and reinforce its European line of defense.

In treating certain aspects of postwar developments it has been necessary to touch upon events occurring after 1949. The main theme of the present chapter, however, has been the four restless years that followed V.J. Day. They were characterized, of course, by Soviet aggression and its consequent unpleasantness. Nevertheless, an isolationist flood tide, for reasons previously mentioned, had little chance of sweeping the American nation. Instead, our foreign policy became realistically oriented to the new order. Thus came the American diplomatic revolution of 1947 with the Truman Doctrine and its logical extension, a series of regional security pacts.

Collective security had given way to *Realpolitik,* and the immediate postwar disillusionment had not been intense enough to revive isolationism. But the American people found that war is like a major operation in that complications often develop long after the surgery has been completed. They had yet to learn that the treatment of these complications almost invariably involves new and unpleasant therapy. At midcentury, a series of delayed war reactions threatened them with a relapse into isolationism. These unlooked-for disasters brought to the surface an inner longing for the old order and crystallized the isolationist tradition into its various current forms.

Chapter 15

The Mid-Century Upheaval

THE MEMBERS of the Eighty-first Congress fled from Washington on October 19, 1949, after the longest peacetime session in twenty-seven years. On that autumn day, there were many reasons for believing isolationism moribund. Since V.J. Day, the major parties had been in essential agreement on foreign policy. In the surprising Democratic upsurge of 1948, the liberal internationalist, Paul H. Douglas, defeated the Chicago *Tribune* isolationist, Senator Wayland Brooks. On July 28, 1949, the Senate approved the NATO treaty which capped the collective defense program designed to halt the Soviet advance in Europe. While seven mid-western senators opposed the treaty, interested observers noted that seventeen voted with the majority. The isolationists had had their day in court, but their opponents had won a clear-cut victory. Even the bitter-enders in Congress must have believed their cause hopeless as they packed their bags for a short vacation from law-making.

Until the fall of 1949, President Truman's foreign policy seemed to be working well in Europe. He had stood firm for over a year while Stalin tried to squeeze the West out of Berlin by closing its corridor to free territory. The Anglo-American air-lift was a proven success for, in May, 1949, the Russians ended the blockade. This welcome news came at a time when the European skies were brightening. The Soviet satellites watched enviously as the Marshall Plan rebuilt the war-torn economies of their western neighbors. There were, as yet, no signs of the friction that would arise over the implementation of NATO's defense blueprint. Western Europe breathed easily for the moment, but fear of Russian vengeance returned when, in September, 1949, President Truman revealed that the Soviets had broken the American monopoly on the A-bomb.

Meanwhile, the Far Eastern situation was rapidly deteriorating. In the summer of 1949 the Chinese Nationalist army was heavily pummeled by Mao Tse-tung's soldiers, but Americans were slow to realize the implications of a Communist victory on the Asiatic mainland. With some notable exceptions, prior to 1949, public opinion commended Truman's decision to let the Chinese fight it out among themselves. American complacency was fostered by improved home conditions. The acute postwar commodity shortage was over, the labor front was relatively quiescent, and the inflationary spiral seemed to have run its course. The calm that prevailed in the early autum of 1949 resembled the mood of self-satisfaction on the eve of the Great Depression. In 1929, economic collapse destroyed the international equipoise by creating a spirit of intensified nationalism. Twenty years later, a series of diplomatic reverses destroyed the American truce on foreign policy. The Chinese tragedy was the detonating agent which set off a chain of new explosions, destined to disrupt the unity of the free world.

The victory of the Chinese Communists, highlighted by Chiang Kai-shek's flight to Formosa (December, 1949), profoundly shocked America. Stalin had already blighted the fruits of our victory in Europe, and now the substitution of an aggressive China for a rapacious Japan did the same for our war in the Pacific. The Far Eastern reverse was ironic; for Americans had long considered the Chinese their special wards. In addition, China's loss to the free world was particularly disturbing since so much of our energy, both physical and emotional, had been spent in the Far Eastern fighting. It would be difficult to conceive of a greater disillusion than the realization that, by defeating Japan, we had removed the roadblock to the eastward roll of Communism. In human fashion, Americans began a frantic search for scapegoats, living and dead, whom they could blame for this misfortune.

The immediate origins of the Chinese tangle go back to 1943 when, at the Cairo Conference, Chiang Kai-shek's storm-tossed China had been admitted to the inner circle of the Grand Alliance. "President Roosevelt," Harry S. Truman later declared, "had built up the idea that China was a great power because he looked to the future and wanted to encourage the Chinese people."[1] To the amazement of Churchill, F.D.R. assumed that Chiang could compromise with his Communist critics, make his country strong enough to act as one of the world's four guardians, and, at the same time, keep Stalin from irritating China's internal wounds. All of these assumptions proved groundless.

In the fall of 1945, the irascible Patrick J. Hurley resigned his post as United States Ambassador to China. Hurley had failed to bring Chiang and Mao to terms and, to prevent all-out civil war between the two rivals, President Truman dispatched George C. Marshall to the scene. The General was instructed to get a cease-fire agreement between the two factions and to act as midwife in the birth of a united Chinese government.

The failure of Marshall's 1946 mission is familiar history. His task was peculiarly difficult, for the Chinese Communists constituted something more than a militant minority party. Mao Tse-tung headed a rival government that controlled territory and ruled one-fourth of China's teeming masses. Moreover, the Russians had overrun nearby Manchuria and, despite his promises, Stalin had no intention of letting Chiang subdue his enemies or even of allowing the civil war to end in compromise.

President Truman and General Marshall were guided by some basic considerations. Both men thought it futile to send large-scale military assistance to Chiang unless he demonstrated that he could unite his people. Before Marshall left the United States, we had stopped UNRRA shipments to China because our goods found their way into the black market. A segment of American public opinion, hitherto friendly to Chiang, showed signs of impatience with wholesale corruption and inefficiency. Hence the President and his emissary were persuaded that the United States should not dictate terms of peace in China nor do anything more than to place our good offices at Chiang's disposal. Viewing the situation at first hand, Marshall concluded that the remaining American troops ought to be promptly withdrawn from the Chinese theater, so as to leave Stalin no possible excuse for military intervention. A military realist, the General grasped the weakness of Chiang's position, and warned him against following the advice of his most rash commanders.[2]

When the Russians withdrew from Manchuria, Mao's soldiers occupied strategic points in that province. Truman bluntly warned Chiang that unless he held a tight rein on his trigger-happy militarists and corruption-ridden reactionaries, the United States would be forced to revise its Chinese policy. However, the generalissimo heeded the advice of his propagandists in Washington, and made no real efforts to clean house. Instead, Chiang held the Communists responsible for all of China's woes, and said that his Nationalists would not lay down arms until Mao agreed to a satisfactory political settlement. Meanwhile, the Communists preached peace when it suited their convenience, and waged war when it appeared profitable to do so. After a year of futile parleying, Marshall asked to be recalled, December 28, 1946. The following year, his appointment as Secretary of State was widely acclaimed, and no senator voted against confirmation. At the time,

Americans felt that the General had been given an impossible assignment in China and should not be blamed for having failed to reconcile the irreconcilable.

In the summer of 1947, Truman directed General Albert C. Wedemeyer, a wartime commander in the China theater, to reappraise the situation. On his return to Washington, Wedemeyer advised large-scale "moral, advisory, and material support" for the Nationalists, provided (at least implicitly) Chiang would agree to economic and political reforms. To save Manchuria from the Chinese Soviets, the General suggested that it be placed under a five-power "guardianship," the occupation conforming to the Charter of the United Nations. (Wedemeyer's report was kept secret until 1949, and its full text was not released until 1951.)

Truman has been severely criticized for disregarding the Wedemeyer program, and for deciding to stand pat until the "dust settled" in China. The motives behind the President's watchful inaction are fairly clear. He felt that in order to save Chiang, such a large-scale intervention was necessary that there was danger of our army bogging down in the Chinese quagmire. Moreover, Wedemeyer had stressed the corrupt and repressive rule of the Kuomintang, and Washington had no assurance that the generalissimo would or could make the necessary drastic changes.[3] Had Truman proceeded as his critics have so often suggested, he might have invited World War III, for Stalin might have tried to save Mao, or might have marched westward while our army was fighting for Chiang. The President thought these grave risks unjustified for the sake of upholding a bribe-hungry warlord government which lacked popular support. From the vantage of today Truman may have been guilty of error, but his decision must be judged by the way the Chinese puzzle appeared to him in 1947.

Chiang's fall was hastened by the poor military judgment and venality of his commanders. Instead of making the destruction of the enemy forces their prime objective, some of his generals shut up their armies in walled cities, allowing the Communists to sever their railroad supply lines. Other of his followers deserted to the Reds, carrying with them American military equipment. When it became apparent that a considerable amount of our material was falling into Mao's hands, Truman cut off all help to the Nationalists.

In retrospect, it seems probable that nothing short of a major American expedition could have prevented the Red Chinese victory in 1949. As disastrous as Chiang's defeat proved to be to the free world, it is doubtful if American public opinion would have tolerated intervention in the civil war. Nor is it certain that such action would have been wise, for the lesson of the Korean War should give pause to those Monday morning quarterbacks who assume that we could have defeated Mao with relative ease and with conventional armaments.

Confronted with only bad choices in China, Truman decided not to risk a new war. It can, of course, be argued that he lacked foresight, but his most palpable mistake was in failing to share his perplexity with Congress and the people. In sharp contrast to his European decisions of 1947-1949, taken only after deliberate counsel with spokesmen for many diverse interests. Truman formulated his Chinese policy in secrecy. Perhaps the President feared to air an issue which badly divided his own official family. Hence public opinion was not prepared for the loss of China, despite the fact that General Marshall had long foreseen Mao's triumph. The American people might have been, in the long run, much more understanding if, as in the case of Europe, they had been told the brutal facts.

Opposition to Truman's Far Eastern policy mounted slowly and gradually. It was not an important issue in the presidential election of 1948. Senator Vandenberg admitted, in that year, that it was impossible "to know the quantity and type of aid necessary for the restoration of a stable and independent China."[4] The wholesale reaction began in December, 1948, when Alfred M. Landon rose from his political grave to blame the portending Asiatic catastrophe upon our bi-partisan foreign policy. Landon's call was echoed by other Republicans, smarting over the loss of a presidential victory that they had prematurely celebrated. The G.O.P. right wing revolted against "me-tooism" in foreign policy which, they now could claim, had failed the party in three successive presidential elections. Truman's opponents made nasty politics out of the Chinese mishap.[5] The issue became more tempting after Chiang was driven from the mainland and Sino-Soviet teamplay upset the balance of power in the Far East. Republicans charged, with considerable plausibility, that Truman had closed the door to the Communists in western Europe only to open it to them in the Far East. This mistake played right into the hands of the isolationists for it gave them an opportunity to freshen their stale program by passing it off as unilateralism. Single-handed diplomacy was more logical in the Far East than in Europe, for other western powers were unable to give us much help in Asia, and there were no friendly Pacific countries interested enough to demand treatment as equal partners. The isolationists, traditionally sympathetic to a spirited diplomacy in the Far East, found natural allies among groups already pressing Washington to bail Chiang out of Formosa.

The most important of these pressure groups was the China Lobby which began in 1940 when T.V. Soong arrived in the United States to get increased assistance for his brother-in-law, Chiang Kai-shek. Soong and Ludwig Rajchman, a Polish cosmopolite who later joined the Communist faction in his own country, cultivated influential newspaper men and magazine editors. The Chinese plight had a special appeal to American emotions, for the Kuomintang was trying to throw off the yoke of the Japanese. The stage was thus set for portraying Chiang as the apostle of liberty. The efforts of the China Lobby were rewarded by generous loans to the Kuomintang and by the admittance of China as a senior partner in the Grand Alliance.

After V.J. Day, Soong broke with the China enthusiasts of the New Deal and cast his fortunes with business-minded conservatives. Sensing the postwar resurgence of congressional authority and the growing anti-Russian feeling on Capitol Hill, the China Lobby turned its attention to the anti-Truman right-wingers. Soong secured concessions for American business men interested in China. In 1948 he helped General Claire L. Chennault (who had served Chiang as commander of the Flying Tigers and who later activated the U.S. 14th Air Force) and Whiting Willauer to obtain control of a valuable Chinese air line. Significantly, Chennault advised sending 20,000 American troops to China in 1948, urged Congress to send Chiang more aid, and later admitted sharing his views with 85 senators. In addition, he lent his signature to many ghost-written articles which pleaded the Nationalist cause.

With fabulous funds at their disposal, Lobby agents entertained lavishly. Although the Republican Eightieth Congress pared down the Truman request for a one-year grant to Nationalist China of $463 million, Soong's closest congressional associates were Republican right-wingers and Democratic anti-Fair Dealers. In spite of the fact that Governor Dewey gave the Chiang enthusiasts little encouragement in his 1948 campaign, the Lobby was bitterly disappointed when he lost. This let-down came in the same month that Chiang's demoralized troops were routed out of Mukden. The only hope left for the Kuomintang lay in a political upset in the United States which would put Chiang's G.O.P. supporters in control.

The Lobby became desperate and allied itself with red-baiting demagogues to foster the illusion that our China policy was proof positive that the State Department was honeycombed with Communists.

The China Lobby's stepped-up anti-Communist campaign was begun by Alfred Kohlberg, an importer of Chinese embroideries, who had made many visits to the Far East. Kohlberg began by accusing the Institute of Pacific Relations in New York City of Communist affiliation. In his short-lived magazine, *Plain Talk,* Kohlberg published the "confession" of one Emmanuel S. Larsen, a weird story of a "highly organized campaign to switch American policy in the Far East . . . to the Soviet line." Larsen subsequently repudiated his statement before a congressional committee, but Kohlberg's propaganda sheet had planted seeds of doubt concerning the loyalty of General Marshall, General Joseph W. Stilwell, and former Vice-President Henry A. Wallace.

Meanwhile, Madame Chiang Kai-shek came to the United States to reinforce the Lobby's efforts, setting up headquarters in the comfortable New York suburban home of her brother-in-law, H. H. Kung. The Lobby began a concentrated attack on Secretary of State Acheson, who, it charged, was dominated by Chiang's "archenemy," General Marshall. When Madame Chiang returned to Formosa in 1950, she left more than one million dollars in cash for the Lobby's use. Of this sum and other funds available to the lobbyists (reckoned by some to run into eight-figure numbers) the commentator Philip Horton has written: "In a massive stream it flowed from the United States to China. It has returned to the United States via numberless channels to create more millions, more propaganda [and] more aid."

By mid-century, the Lobby was full grown. It consisted of a weird coalition of honest believers in Chiang, disillusioned Communists, obsessed men and women who believed that the Reds had taken Washington by infiltration, professional hate-mongers, unscrupulous polticians trying to make headlines, and veteran anti-New Dealers. In February, 1950, Senator McCarthy opened fire on the State Department, with Alfred Kohlberg supplying ammunition. Later the same year, the outbreak of the Korean War temporarily boosted Chiang's fortunes in the United States. In the long run, however, the China Lobby fell victim to its own machinations. It helped whip up enthusiasm for clearing the Communists out of Washington, but it failed to arouse Americans to the point where they were ready to sacrifice their soldiers to restore Chiang to power in Asia major.[6]

Spurred on by the China Lobby, isolationists began to popularize their theory that State Department subversives had delivered China into the hands of the Soviets. This bizarre accusation was accepted by the uncritical because some Communists were found and convicted. Had President Truman been more responsive to some deserved criticism for laxity, he might have drawn the fangs of his more unscrupulous accusers. By brushing off all legitimate criticism of existing security regulations as political claptrap, Truman unwittingly helped the extremists.

The more circumspect isolationists blamed the loss of China on a group of non-Communist State Department men who had been influenced by the party line solution to Asia's woes. Until 1950, John T. Flynn, a former chairman of New York's America First Committee, had largely neglected the Far East in his polemical books on Franklin D. Roosevelt. In 1952, however, he published *While You Slept: Our Tragedy in Asia and Who Made It,* a book marked by heavy China Lobby overtones. Although Flynn conceded that Secretary Marshall was not a Communist, he said that the General's ignorance of world politics had made him an unintential dupe of Moscow. Surrounded by misled fellow-travelers, said Flynn, Marshall had put the country "at the mercy of men who had become enamoured of values and forms of life alien to our nature."[7]

The Chinese debacle was also exploited by certain non-islationist Republicans who, prior to 1952, wanted to restore the G.O.P. to power and thereafter to retain Republican control. An outstanding example of this group was T.V. Soong's friend, Henry Luce, whose wife, Claire Booth Luce, had served as president of the pro-Chiang America-China Policy Association. Luce's magazines, *Time* and *Life,* reflected the views of the world-minded eastern industrialists. Such men were in essential agreement with Truman's European policy, but, as staunch Republicans, they found the President's Asiatic mistakes a convenient avenue of attack. In contrast to the reckless fulminations of the isolationist die-hards, the Luce magazines charged the Democrats with mistaken judgment on the Far East rather than with wholesale disloyalty. The 1946 Marshall mission to China, *Life* explained, was the "archfailure" that led to all subsequent errors. Truman's administration was indicted on three counts: 1 - It failed to take Asiatic communism "seriously enough soon enough"; 2 - The President and his advisers, underestimating the importance of holding the Far East at all costs, fell victim to a foolish and paralyzing attitude of defeatism in regard to Asia; 3 - The Democratic policymakers allowed their personal dislike of Chiang to keep them from supporting "the tragic hero of history's Asian tale."[8]

All that was said and written about Truman's failure to keep the Kuomintang in control of China helped undermine the faith of the American people in the policy of containment. Inevitably, reaction against multilaterism redounded to the benefit of the isolationists who advocated a contrary policy. Nevertheless, the loss of China was only an underlying cause of the isolationist recoil. The reaction was set off by the outbreak of war in Korea.

On Sunday, June 25, 1950, the cold war against Communism became suddenly hot when the North Korean Communists crossed the 38th parallel that separated their territory from the non-Marxist South Korean republic. President Truman, recalling vividly how the failure to halt unabashed aggression had destroyed the League of Nations, promptly determined to preserve the principle of collective security. Failure to act, would in all probability, have been construed as a green light for further violations, and the timing and locale of the next thrust might make collective resistance impossible.

Meeting at Truman's behest on the very day of the invasion, the Security Council denounced North Korea as an aggressor, and called upon all members of the United Nations "to render every assistance" in military action designed to hold back the outlaw forces. The President at first ordered American air and naval forces to cover the retreating South Korean army. Three days later, he dispatched ground troops, and also directed the Seventh Fleet to shield Chiang's Formosa from invasion by the Chinese Communists. Acting under U.N. authorization, on July 7 he directed General Douglas MacArthur to go from Japan to Korea to head the international army fighting under the blue and white banner. It was the first command of its kind in history, bestowed, ironically enough, upon a man who was to become the symbol of red-blooded American nationalism.

President Truman, acting in his capacity as Commander-in-Chief, chose not to imperil the military situation while Congress debated the necessity of American intervention. He rode the crest of a wave of popularity as long as it seemed that General MacArthur would make good his celebrated promise to have the fighting over by Christmas. As everyone recalls, when MacArthur carried the war (under a rather vague U.N. authorization and under a directive for which Truman bears the ultimate responsibility) to the Manchurian border, he was hurled back by Red Chinese "volunteers." Retreating in the sub-zero northern Asiatic weather, the general saved his army from complete disaster and stabilized a front south of the 38th parallel. The agonizing and prolonged stalemate that ensued tried the patience of Americans who knew little of limited and undeclared war. From the first, influential Washington circles feared that an all-out campaign to crush the Communist forces involved a serious risk of a showdown with the Soviet Union.

Coincidental factors also led to a widespread denunciation of Truman's foreign policy. When the Korean War proved vexatious and unfruitful, the Republicans promptly charged that Secretary of State Dean Acheson had invited aggression on January 12, 1950, by publicly excluding South Korea and Formosa from our "defense perimeter" in the Pacific. In the same speech Acheson had indicated that countries lying outside of our limited defense circle would have to look to the United Nations for protection. Although fair-minded critics did not accuse the Secretary of inciting the Communists to action, it was argued that North Korea (or Russia) might have been deterred had Acheson not publicly indicated a line marking the limits of our vital interest in the Far East, in which Korea was conspicuously excluded. The isolationists had accused the Roosevelt administration of starting war by baiting Japan; they charged its successor with inviting hostilities by loose statements, with waging war in defiance of the Constitution, and with failure to follow through its illegal course to victory.

That keen political analyst, Samuel Lubell, has shown how domestic factors aggravated the discontent of the early 1950s. The Korean War was fought at a time when the national debt had been tremendously swollen by twenty years of deficit spending to alleviate a depression, to subdue the Axis, and to rehabilitate foreign economies. Taxes were already eating up one-third of the national income, and people had no stomach for new foreign adventures that promised to add to their burdens. Veterans' memories of combat were too fresh for them to desire more action in a war ostensibly fought to help a remote oriental country regain its independence. Business men wanted neither another whirl of the inflationary cycle, nor the stringent government controls that might hold it in check. Korea, says Lubell, came at a time when it was peculiarly difficult "to balance the interests of business, farmers, and workers with one another and with those of the unorganized public."[9]

Politics, it has been well observed, "is the art of the possible." Truman, therefore, had little choice but to yield to the popular demand that business go on with as little interruption as possible. As a result of this political expediency, the sacrifices of war were unequally distributed. A million American soldiers saw service in the Land of the Morning Calm, but it became necessary to maintain their flagging morale by rotating front-line assignments. It was the most unattractive kind of warfare imaginable, with no clarion call of unconditional surrender to spur the soldiers on to victory.

Truce negotiations with thick-skinned Communist envoys, trained to bewilder and exasperate the men who faced them at the council table, lagged on for over two harrowing years. Long before the cease-fire agreement of July 27, 1953, men had dubbed the whole affair "Mr. Truman's war." The setting formed a superb catapult from which to hurl isolationist missiles.

The most dangerous of these isolationist harpoons were aimed at America's allies, for they threatened to destroy the very principle of collective defense that Truman was trying to preserve. The spotty response of the U.N. countries to the Security Council's call (only 16 of the 60 member states sent fighting contingents to Korea) gave isolationism a fresh fillip. Our strongest allies, England and France, had good reasons for their token efforts, for they were fighting the Communists on fronts in Malaya and Indo-China. But Americans, bearing a disprorortionate cost of the common war effort in blood and dollars cared little for such excuses. The Korean War provided a graphic demonstration of the difficulties inherent in waging a collective war and maintaining a coalition diplomacy. In 1945, most Americans had taken it for granted that timely preventive action would have made the Second World War unnecessary. When, however, police action was tried in 1950, it led to many unexpected complications. Uncle Sam had to bear the brunt of restraining the aggressor and, at the same time, had to pull his punches lest he lose his apprehensive European partners. Many people were persuaded that while our allies were always ready to talk in time of crisis they were only willing "to fight to the last American."

Any chance that the Korean War would not be fully exploited by the isolationists was dispelled when, on April 11, 1951, President Truman summarily removed the five-starred General MacArthur from all his Far Eastern commands. Fate now presented the hero-starved nationalists with the leader of their dreams—a man who had become a legend in his own lifetime. Here was a martyr to the cause of unspoiled Americanism, a Republican with strong party convictions, and an extraordinarily effective orator. Thus a group of isolationists who had been hysterically calling for a halt to the bloodshed in Korea now defied the man who wanted to carry the war into Manchuria. This paradox of paradoxes is a pointed commentary on how desperation twisted the logic of isolationism.

The *cause célèbre* between the President and the Supreme Commander had reached a climax after many months of bickering. MacArthur was anxious to rehabilitate his military reputation by a large-scale offensive against the Peiping Communists. He thus urged a naval blockade of China, the use of Chiang's troops as a diversionary tactic, and the bombing of the enemy's supply depots in Manchuria. These proposals, so widely advertised by MacArthur himself, alarmed Washington, for such a policy was the antithesis of that devised by the administration. Truman and his advisers regarded Russia as the principal foe and they did not wish to weaken our European defenses by pouring our strength down the Chinese drain. Outright war with China, they reasoned, might tempt Stalin to honor his 1950 mutual aid pact with Mao. Moreover, all the U.N. countries with fighting contingents in Korea considered MacArthur's tactics highly dangerous, for an American-Chinese war would weaken the defense of western Europe and open the way for Communist internal or external aggression in that area. It would also thrust this nation into an ugly civil conflict in China. General Omar N. Bradley of the Joint Chiefs of Staff summed up the administration's thinking when he said that an attempt to pound China into submission would be "the wrong war, at the wrong place, at the wrong time, and with the wrong enemy."

On the other hand, General MacArthur felt that Washington was wrong in yielding to allied pressure, because Russian atomic stockpiles were not sufficiently completed to permit the Kremlin the choice of war with the United States. Moreover, the general believed that the main Communist push was directed toward the east, and that it was there that the Red march must be halted. When MacArthur tried to change Truman's policy by presenting his views to the Republican minority leader, Representative Joseph W. Martin, Jr., the President lost patience.

Relieved of command, the General returned to the United States after an absence of fourteen years. He was promptly hailed as a Brobdingnagian Republican warrior who had been martyred by a Lilliputian Democratic President. The isolationists had their long-awaited field day when the General addressed Congress and later testified at a joint hearing before two senatorial committes. MacArthur, prior to his recall, had been at cross-purposes with the old-line isolationists on many scores. He had approved military assistance to western Europe, and, concurring with Truman's Point Four program, had justified American economic help to the former colonial nations. Nor did his soldierly attitude permit him to join the extremists in impugning the motives of the Joint Chiefs of Staff. But, above all, MacArthur was an unwavering Republican of a conservative stripe, and a common political philosophy bound him to such G.O.P. stalwarts as Herbert Hoover, Joseph W. Martin, Kenneth S. Wherry, and Robert A. Taft. When the General was dismissed by Truman, he fell quite naturally into the welcoming arms of the Republican right-wingers.

MacArthur had begun by attacking Truman's handling of the Pacific crisis; he ended by indicting the administration's entire foreign policy. While still in Korea he had argued that Europe would be won on the battlefields of Asia; after his return he discounted the value of Uncle Sam's allies. During the course of the congressional hearings he used the catch phrase "go it alone," and his stentorian voice repeated the words—"alone, if necessary." Although he had received his Korean command at the behest of the United Nations, he did not mention that organization in his remarks to Congress and slighted it thereafter in other speeches. MacArthur now intimated that the policy of containment was wrong because there could be no compromise with "atheistic communism."[10]

As a Republican whose expansive nationalism resembled that of Theodore Roosevelt, the General wanted the United States to play the leading role on the stage of global politics. This aim seemed in conflict with the cardinal isolationist postulate of a self-imposed withdrawal from world leadersihp. But the contradiction was more superficial than real for the reservations that MacArthur attached to his original premise were congenial to the spirit of the old tradition. Intervene to settle dangerous foreign quarrels we must, said MacArthur, but let us not dissipate our energies by appeasing European allies or by squandering our material resources upon them. This spirit of unilateralism was the modern expression of the ancient isolationist belief in American self-sufficiency. There was, moreover, another bond of union between the MacArthur nationalists and the old-line isolationists. America had always been more reticent about European involvements than about entanglements in the affairs of other continents. It was Mac-Arthur himself who had proclaimed the Pacific the ocean of the future. When the General pointed to Asia as the pathway to American glory, he called to mind that the Stars and Stripes, under Republican aegis, had been planted on Hawaii and the Philippines. "With MacArthur," it has been said, "American isolationism received its classical mid-century formulation."[11]

Thus it was that the Korean War, with the MacArthur episode, threatened to replace the Democratic multilateral approach with a refurbished Republican unilateralism. The postwar bi-partisanship on foreign affairs, shaken by the victory of the Red Chinese, was broken by the Korean reverse. The G.O.P. international cooperationists, who had dominated the party since 1940, fell back in retreat before a powerful isolationist counterattack. For a season, Republican congressional policy was formulated by a conservative coalition, determined to "wipe the dust off isolationism." But for certain factors then present, the right-wingers might have regained complete control of the G.O.P. In 1952, to mention one, the Republican non-isolationists were able to present a candidate with the irresistible appeal of Dwight D. Eisenhower, and they won a narrow victory in the national convention. But despite General Eisenhower's multilateralist convictions, the isolationist resurgence actually helped produce the landslide that swept him into the White House. For twenty years the G.O.P. had labored under the blame for the Great Depression; now they evened the score by tagging the war label on their opponents. Korea was the ultimate argument that convinced the masses that it was time for a change.

When, after 1953, the Eisenhower Republicans were at the helm, the Republican ship had to ride the waves of the isolationist storm. An influential G.O.P. segment in Congress demanded that the new administration scotch the Democratic foreign policy of collective self-defense. Korea thus began a political cycle that lasted four years. It started in November, 1950, when the Chinese Soviets drove General MacArthur from the banks of the Yalu; it ended in November, 1954, when the election of a Democratic Congress permitted General Eisenhower to hurl back the Republican extremists along the banks of the Potomac.

The Chinese debacle and the Korean deadlock, primary causes of the mid-century reaction against the Democratic diplomacy, are historic events with dramatic and measurable results. The cumulative effects of a decade of polemical historical writing, however, are by their very nature more intangible. Nevertheless, the proliferation of books and articles about the Second World War and its bitter aftermath helped create the popular recoil against internationalism. These revisionist interpretations reached flood tide at a period when events lent seeming plausibility to the argument that the American people were the innocent victims of their sometimes unscrupulous and always imprudent statesmen.

A fair evaluation of the modern revisionists must rest upon certain premises. The shedding of new light on the origins and conduct of any war is both inevitable and salutary. It is certain to happen because governments cannot and do not immediately reveal the full facts surrounding cardinal decisions on foreign policy; it is beneficial because citizens in a free country are entitled to know the facts as soon as it it safe to reveal them. Furthermore, the passage of time alone can give historians the necessary perspective for a penetrating interpretation of the past. However, it is essential to differentiate between a rational rewriting of history by men who try to be objective and the effusions of biased amateurs or purblind professionals who make an improper use of hindsight. Like the surgeon's scalpel, the historian's pen can be wielded cautiously or recklessly.

A good deal, but by no means all, of the revisionist output since 1941 has been markedly biased. During Franklin D. Roosevelt's protracted presidency, his domestic liberalism enraged the conservatives, and his foreign policy antagonized the isolationists. These avid anti-New Dealers were incensed by F.D.R.'s lasting influence on the course of domestic and foreign policy. They became all the more bitter because the sluice-gates of liberalism, opened by the Squire of Hyde Park, unloosed a flood that threatened to inundate the Republicans. A small minority of the bitter-enders wrote history in self-vindication; the large majority confirmed their prejudices by reading bizarre accounts of "plots," "betrayals," and "conspiracies." When the Second World War brought no surcease from totalitarian aggression, it was natural for erstwhile America Firsters to nod knowingly and say "I told you so." The isolationists used the revisionist writings as a smokescreen to hide the elementary fact that, although Franklin D. Roosevelt made mistakes in implementing his decisions, his basic premise that the United States could not afford to let the Axis win was sound.

The pioneer revisionist of the World War II genre was the

master craftsman Charles A. Beard. Although Beard had illuminated the pages of American history with many original and acute interpretations, in his last years he fell victim to a tendency that he had once denounced—the habit of oversimplifying the causes of a world upheaval in such a way as to portray American interventionism as a conspiracy hatched by a handful of diabolical statesmen. A steadfast liberal who clung to the theory that America could shape its destiny regardless of wholesale commotion overseas, Beard held Roosevelt responsible for luring the country into war. The veteran historian kept a watchful eye on the 1944-1946 congressional inquest into the causes of Pearl Harbor, and prepared a memorandum that helped the Republicans present a Minority Report which refused to exonerate the President. By 1946, Beard had selectively marshalled the available evidence, and was ready to share his findings with the general public.

Before death interrupted his labors, Beard wrote two seminal works: *American Foreign Policy in the Making, 1932-1940* and *President Roosevelt and the Coming of the War, 1941*. The latter book, published in 1948, was as tightly constructed as a lawyer's brief. Beard primarily wished to establish two points: 1 - That Roosevelt had made a moral commitment to keep the country out of war and had broken his promise by pursuing policies that made war inevitable; 2 - That Roosevelt mendaciously evaded the constitutional safeguards surrounding the conduct of foreign policy, thus blazing the trail for a future dictator.

Generally speaking, the facts accumulated by Beard's patient research are sound. Like the less meticulous revisionists who followed in his footsteps, however, he described Roosevelt's behavior out of the context of the world catastrophe of the day. Frankness on the President's part would have established his reputation for personal integrity, but it seems clear that such rectitude might have risked an Axis triumph. Beard and his successors have insisted that Roosevelt's actions were as politically futile as they were morally reprehensible, for the war solved no basic problems. To this contention, Professor Charles C. Griffin has replied: "We may have moved from the frying pan into the fire, or vice versa, since 1940, but to condemn the policy which led to Pearl Harbor on that account it would be necessary to show what our situation might be today had Hitler won the European war and the United States had remained aloof."[12]

George E. Morgenstern, World War II veteran and member of the editorial board of the Chicago *Tribune,* had published a strongly revisionist account of Pearl Harbor even before Beard's last book came off the press. While the anti-Roosevelt school of writers was inspired by Beard's basic approach, its ultimate conclusions on the immediate origins of the Japanese war owe more to Morgenstern's conjectures. It was the Chicago writer who charged that Roosevelt provoked Tokyo to the attack by a well-laid "monstrous, unbelievable conspiracy" to which his highest military and naval advisers were accessories. While Morgenstern buttressed his more incontrovertible statements with stout documentation, his major conclusions were predicated on inadequate circumstantial evidence.[13]

In 1950, William Henry Chamberlin widened the front of the revisionist attack by examining both the European and Asiatic root causes of the war. Chamberlin utilized the published memoirs and papers of leading participants to call attention to the wide gap between the professed war aims of the United States and the end results of our intervention. He concluded that the war bore only bitter fruits because it was fought to victory by men who acted under the spell of six major illusions, the last and most perilous of which was F.D.R.'s fancy "that a combination of appeasement and personal charm could melt away designs of conquest and domination which were deeply rooted in Russian history and Communist philosophy."[14] Although the book vindicated many contentions of the pre-Pearl Harbor isolationists, Chamberlin was too strongly anti-Communist to advocate a new American withdrawal in the face of Red expansionism. Instead, he suggested that America rectify its previous mistakes by converting Germany and Japan into stout bastions of defense against the aggressive Muscovites. As time went on, Chamberlin became a leading exponent of the China Lobby's proposal that Chiang be given enough American aid to invade the Chinese mainland.

While American soldiers were fighting the seesaw war in Korea, book dealers advertised Charles Callan Tansill's *Back Door to War: The Roosevelt Foreign Policy, 1933-1941*. Written by a recognized expert in the field of diplomatic history, and freighted with formidable scholarly apparatus, this book argued that the Soviet Union had instigated both the European and Far Eastern wars. Roosevelt, said Professor Tansill, should have seen through these Machiavellian tactics but, instead, played into Stalin's hands by urging Britain to go to war to prevent the German conquest of Poland. Two years later, said Tansill, Roosevelt added to this initial error by needling the Japanese into striking Hawaii so that he could get the United States into the shooting war through the Pacific "back door." Tansill showed his usual erudition and skill in weaving together a story based upon hitherto unexploited primary sources. If one accepts his basic premise that a double-barreled Axis victory would not have been inimical to American security, then it is difficult to refute him. However, his faith in the sincerity of some isolated Japanese peace-feelers before Pearl Harbor, convinced few experts that Tokyo was ready to follow words with deeds which would have led to a satisfactory diplomatic settlement with the United States. On balance, Tansill left the Pearl Harbor story pretty much as he found it, with the Roosevelt-haters believing the President guilty of criminal stupidity and the overwhelming majority of historians still accepting the more tenable conclusion that the disaster of December 7, 1941 was due to collective blundering on the part of the White House, the chiefs of staff, and the commanding officers in Hawaii.[15]

In the early 1850s a group of southern fire-eaters had collaborated to produce that bulky compendium entitled *The Pro-Slavery Argument*. One hundred years later, Harry Elmer Barnes edited an anthology of revisionist findings called *Perpetual War for Perpetual Peace*. No man in the country was better equipped for the task, for Barnes had been popularizing revisionism for thirty years. After 1945, Barnes turned his attention to the fertile possibilities of America's second war of the century, beginning with the private publication of brochures carrying such titles as *The Court Historians versus Revisionism*, and *The Struggle Against the Historical Blackout*. According to Barnes, revisionists were denied access to vital source material, a conspiracy of publishers made it difficult for them to purvey their findings, and an "American Smearbund" stood ready to rebut their conclusions as soon as they appeared in print. In 1953, Barnes gathered salient selections from leading revisionist writers and published them in a volume, writing the introduction and conclusion himself. The most striking thing about Barnes's summation is his assertion that isolationism has become "a smear term." He explained that the Founding Fathers were not isolationists in the ordinary meaning of the word, for "they were vigorous advocates of international intercourse and understanding." As in most of his writings, Barnes welcomed "the vision of world government at some distant date when it becomes feasible." But pending that far-off day, he insisted that "isolation from selfish foreign quarrels" was "even more essential to our national salvation and security today than it was a century and a half ago."[16] It is difficult indeed to follow a line of reasoning that decries the use of the word isolationism, waters down its meaning, and then advocates a foreign policy that must be construed as isolationist in the accepted sense of the term.

Current revisionism of the extreme variety is more accusatory and complex than the disillusionist works of the inter-war period. At worst, Woodrow Wilson and his coterie were accused of being dupes, and their most carping critics never questioned their personal motives. The most recent revisionists, however, have intimated that the Roosevelt circle fomented war to cover up failures in domestic policy and to create conditions favorable to the perpetuation of the New Deal regime.[17] Some have even gone so far as to suggest that F.D.R. deliberately paved the way for the expansion of Communism. Such extravagant charges have particularly marked the expositions on Yalta which, along with Pearl Harbor, became an ace card in the isolationist suit. Yalta commanded the public attention as did no other contemporary international conference. Its very name became an American synonym for failure. Because of the voting strength of Polish and cognate ethnic groups, Yalta became a staple political argument. This was especially true following the publication of papers that revealed Roosevelt's concern for the Slavic vote prior to his 1944 re-election. His subsequent yielding to Stalin at Yalta, in return for empty promises of free elections and coalition interim governments in eastern Europe, was denounced as chimerical, craven, and shameful.

In 1949, when Americans realized that the Peiping Communists had nullified our Pacific victory, all postwar reverses were traced to Roosevelt's failure at Yalta to protect the anti-Marxist governments in Europe and China. In the heat of the argument, international and military conditions that underlay F.D.R.'s 1945 "surrenders" were commonly overlooked. Moreover, uncritical readers refused to concede that the tragedies that stemmed from Yalta came not from compromises made at the conference, but from Stalin's callous disregard of his bargain. In the uproar that raged with each new publication of papers, memoirs, and interpretive writings, it was difficult to hear the retort that the Kremlin would, in all probability, have pursued the same course even if Roosevelt had never made his fateful journey to the Crimea.

This spate of revisionist writings coincided with the unhappy years of the Korean War. A vicious cycle was inaugurated when writers, influenced by the pervading disillusionment, expounded their beliefs only to deepen popular distrust in recent American diplomacy. Eventually, some irresponsibles summed up the whole indictment as "twenty years of treason." It was a charge that in the past had seldom been voiced in political diatribes, to say nothing of appearing in print in the pages of books that passed for history.

Revisionist accounts of the First World War had appealed to anti-Wilson liberals, pacifists, isolationists, and ethnic minorities who deplored an intervention that had resulted in an Allied victory. Such groups assumed that the 1914 war had been none of our business and that the true American interest had demanded an impartial neutrality. Current revisionism, however, defies such simple analysis. Some writers contend that Roosevelt was justified in preventing a Hitlerian triumph, but accuse him of a short-sighted wartime diplomacy. This point of view is popular among Anglophiles who feel that F.D.R. should have heeded Churchill's advice, checkmated Stalin's seizure of eastern Europe, and should have fostered the retention of British control over restive colonial peoples.

Perhaps the earlier revisionists were less vindictive because they began their work in the roseate years of the 1920s. A quarter of a century later, when their successors reviewed the Second World War, the United States was burdened with the bitter legacies of both conflicts. In an age when the lives, fortunes, and personal welfare of some 168,000,000 Americans hinged on every major turn in foreign policy, historians showed little charity for mistaken judgments. This tendency was even more marked among their readers who demanded clairvoyance on the part of their diplomats. Men forgot that national leaders must make decisions in the light of information at hand. Hence they are seldom able to pursue policies devoid of risk, and measured gambles are often lost by imponderable and uncontrollable factors. But Americans are prone to judge actions by their results, and the revisionist case was strengthened by the commonplace observation that the wars waged by Wilson, Roosevelt, and Truman had failed to pacify the world. People now demanded a reappraisal of American foreign policy and the isolationists gained from the reaction against internationalism.

Another important factor in this nationalist rebound was the call for a more realistic approach to foreign policy. The realists were practical men who blamed our postwar perplexities upon the inclination of Wilson and the second Roosevelt to confuse realistic aims with visionary ideals. The fruitless sacrifices of two world wars, followed in each case by a futile attempt for effective world organization, evoked a skeptical attitude toward these wars and the panaceas that they had failed to bring. The post-1945 wave of chauvinism, which whipped up the nationalist emotions of the suppressed colonial nations, spilled over upon the vanquished and victorious peoples alike.

This intensification of American nationalism accompanied the disenchantment with international idealism. Americans, living in a world of nations made all the more selfish by the havoc of one war and the dread of another, felt that it was high time to espouse openly and frankly the principle of self-interest. With the United Nations helpless to prevent another major war, Washington sought to improve our position by building up a power bloc, by delineating spheres of influence, and by old-fashioned diplomatic horse-trading with Russia. Our postwar diplomacy thus bore a closer resemblance to the statecraft of Princes Metternich and Bismarck than to the doctrines of Presidents Wilson and F. D. Roosevelt. The new emphasis was on flexibility in foreign policy, for reasons of state might in the future make it necessary to forsake our ideological scruples and to settle our differences with the Kremlin. Such negotiation would be easier if morality and idealism were divorced from foreign policy. The unromantic philosophy of the realists, calling for a severely practical diplomacy, conformed to postwar circumstances.

The realists sprang from both the old isolationist and internationalist ranks. In 1946, the veteran isolationist, Edwin M. Borchard, dressed up his old arguments in garments bearing the new look. Viewing the United Nations with a skeptical eye, the Yale professor observed that nations never judge each other in a courtroom atmosphere, but rather regard the actions of their sister powers "in the light of their interests, their alliances, and their prior commitments."[18] If one narrowly defines self-interest, and considers all peacetime alliances to be antithetical to the national interest, as did Borchard and his intellectual heirs, then isolationism becames the *summum bonum* of realism.

For the most part, however, the old concept of self-interest was revived and popularized by men of broader outlook. One of the earliest of this school was Reinhold Niebuhr—theologian, professor, philosopher, and acute observer of passing events. Originally a liberal in religion, Niebuhr later championed the neo-orthodox Protestant point of view. He was strongly influenced by the Swiss religious thinker, Karl Barth, and rekindled in America an interest in original sin.

Niebuhr held that man was driven to evil because of an

inherent feeling of psychological inferiority which derived from the tragedy of his existence in a universe lacking bounds and limits. He influenced a considerable body of opinion for, despite his rejection of the old liberal postulate of unilinear progress, he combatted all forms of totalitarianism, and stoutly defended democracy. The Axis triumphs of the early war years led Niebuhr to denounce modern Christian and secular perfectionism which he believed had placed a dangerous premium upon pacifism and non-resistance. The liberal democracies, he argued, had weakly surrendered to the evil aggressors because their devotion to perfectionism had made them deficient in understanding "the tragic sense of life."

After the war, Niebuhr focused his attention upon the all-absorbing question of national security from the Bolshevist threat. He expanded upon his earlier thesis by stating that only the proper use of force by law-abiding nations could counter-act the striking power of the new war-makers. The Communists, exploiting modern technology for bad purposes, would soon have the free world at their mercy, unless the advantage was seized and held by the right-minded nations. Niebuhr, however, was unwilling to have the United States fritter away its resources recklessly. Power, he insisted, must be used only to achieve well-defined and obtainable objectives, for he had no faith in causes that transcended the understanding of the people and were thus unlikely to evoke sustained effort. This was a sharp reprimand to the chimerical internationalists who he believed had set impossible goals for the country. We must not, he warned, wear ourselves out in a futile attempt to push history forward.[19]

No one did more to popularize the new realism than Walter Lippmann whose bi-weekly column in the New York *Herald Tribune* was syndicated in leading newspapers throughout the land. In addition, with clock-like regularity, the columnist published trenchant articles and thought-provoking books. Thus Lippmann was avidly followed by both the makers of foreign policy and the intellectually curious laymen who molded opinion in their own communities.

In the crucial years of the Hitlerian war, Lippmann redirected his thinking on foreign policy. He prefaced his 1943 book (*United States Foreign Policy: Shield of the Republic*) with an apology for using hindsight to criticize others "for holding views which at the time I myself may have shared." Persuaded that the isolationist reactionaries and internationalist dreamers had alike failed to fashion a suitable diplomacy, Lippmann called for a foreign policy that would bring into proper balance "the nation's commitments and the nation's power." He declared that our statesmen must determine those essential foreign commitments the American people would support and then they must create a stable balance of power in the light of this limiting factor. To succeed in this aim, Lippmann counseled, we must forget utopian schemes, accept the world for what it is, and be guided only by a "fully enlightened" evaluation of "the true American national interest." However, in 1943, he expressed his doubts that Americans could overcome "the abiding illusions of more than a century of inexperience in the realities of foreign policy."[20]

By 1947, Lippmann was completely disillusioned. He was convinced that our statesmen were incapable of preventing foreign wars, of staying out of them, of preparing the country to settle them with minimum efforts, or of capping costly victories with a durable peace. Reflecting upon these repeated failures, he concluded in 1955 that liberal democratic governments were unable to formulate stable foreign policies because their statesmen were at the mercy of a capricious mass opinion. Like other realists, Lippmann looked nostalgically upon the pre-Jacksonian years when a "public philosophy" rather than political expediency was the lodestar of statesmen.

Certain top-echelon State Department advisers shared this conviction that the national interest alone must dictate the course of our diplomacy. This attitude was particularly strong in the Policy Planning Staff, established in 1947 to keep the department abreast of long-range international developments. This brains trust, consisting in the main of seasoned diplomats with advanced educational training, formed a well-head of realistic thought. As its members, for political or other reasons, left the government service, they frequently put their ideas into print. These highly influential writings clashed sharply with the views of academic authorities who, more often than not, still retained the liberal internationalist outlook.

The founder of the contemporary school of literary diplomats was George Frost Kennan. Mr. Kennan's impressive erudition, his experience as a key man in Truman's Washington, and his first-hand acquaintance with Stalin's Moscow gave his observations penetration and authority. Kennan was already famous as the chief architect of the policy of containment, and as such his admonitions commanded public attention.

In *American Diplomacy*, 1900-1950, Kennan weighed the results of a half century of conflicting foreign policy aims. He concluded that two major wars failed to achieve the ends for which they were fought because we had refused to accept "power realities," had followed a legalistic-moralistic approach, and had failed to recognize that "our own national interest is all we are really capable of knowing and understanding." Kennan argued that we dare not gamble our manpower and material resources upon achieving impossible ends, but must instead limit our policy to actions designed to promote an enlightened self-interest.[21]

Kennan's fundamental thesis was reiterated by Charles Burton Marshall and Dorothy Fosdick, who also drew upon their experiences on the Policy Planning Staff. In her delightful *Common Sense and World Affairs* (1955), Miss Fosdick apologized for devotion to *Realpolitik* by explaining that our own national interests, properly viewed, happily coincided with the best welfare of humanity.

It was, however, a professor rather than a career diplomat who carried the case for realism to its utmost conclusions. Hans J. Morgenthau was born and educated in Germany, where even non-fascist scholars were frequently uncompromising nationalists. Morgenthau, as director of the University of Chicago's Center for the Study of American Foreign Policy, applied German *Realpolitik* to delineate our diplomatic aims. His influence partially explains the current popularity of Bismarckian concepts in the United States. To Morgenthau, international politics was a jungle through which he tried to chart an American path. His stimulating but controversial book, *In Defense Of The National Interest,* was published in 1951. The Korean War had soured the American taste for idealistic ventures and Morgenthau struck a responsive chord.

In sharp contrast to Kennan, the apostle of containment, Morgenthau had little faith in the policy. He believed that if Americans would stop weighing foreign policy decisions on the scales of morality, we could avoid war by arriving at an understanding with the Communists. Such a course, he argued, would conform into the realistic statecraft of the Founding Fathers. He attacked the provincial isolationists with the same vigor that he used against the internationalist utopians. Members of both schools of thought, said Morgenthau, failed to accept the grim facts of world politics. He even charged Woodrow Wilson with having been a subconscious isolationist, since the President had naively assumed that the United States had no *material* interests outside of the western hemisphere.

Concurring with many other realists, the Chicago professor agreed that Roosevelt's intervention against the Axis was necessary. But he added, once the acute danger of the national interest had subsided, F.D.R. fell into Wilson's error of believing that the complete defeat of the present enemy would bring lasting peace. This folly, said Morgenthau, led to our postwar dilemma. He held that legitimate negotiations with any nation, however debased, are not the equivalent of cowardly appeasement. Hence our problem could be solved by a mutually advantageous agreement with the Communists, always provided that the end goal of our diplomacy be the national interests.[22]

While the realists certainly did not wish to revive isolationism, it seems clear that their writings were often mistaken for tirades against international commitments. The desperate isolationists had been fighting the Wilsonians so long that they were willing to embrace any new movement that castigated their ancient enemies. Furthermore, the realists engenderd a new enthusiasm for early American diplomacy. Although they repeatedly pointed out that the Founding Fathers were flexible statesmen and not hidebound isolationists, this important distinction failed to dispel popular illusions about the Farewell Address. Moreover, the isolationists liked the term "national interest" and managed to reduce its scope to conform with their own limited ideas. The isolationists preferred to call themselves nationalists and this created another tenuous tie with extreme realists, even though the latter usually warned that a return to nineteenth-century isolationism would be the height of folly.

It has been cogently observed that the progressive-isolationists of the Beardian school were at least moralists in a limited sense, for they looked hopefully to progress on this side of the water, while the realists appear to have no goal over and beyond an effective power politics. A careful analysis, however, of Beard's 1939 writings reveals the ideological kinship between the old isolationists and the new realists. Beard pointed out that in her own national interest, Britain paid Prussians to fight Frenchmen and later used France to balance power against Germany. Genuine isolationists, said Beard, did not advocate that America withdraw from the world, but regarded the international scramble with cold detachment and preferred to deal with it "in terms of national interest and security on this continent."[23]

The rise of realism and the postwar resurgence of isolationism both derived from recent American diplomatic failures. Although the major premises of both movements were, for the most part, diametrically opposed, they bore a superficial affinity that accounts for the mistaken identity. The situation was confused in the popular mind because men who clung to the venerable American tradition of promoting freedom and democracy throughout the world indicted all critics of collective security on the same counts. The liberal internationalists pointed out that while the isolationists refused to accept the existence of the United Nations, the realists derided its accomplishments and sought to make it a tool of our own diplomacy. In addition, the steadfast believers in collective security charged both groups with faulty reasoning. Thus the internationalists argued that while the isolationists failed to grasp the unity of a world whose spaces had been shrunken by science, the realists mistakenly believed that the power politics diplomacy of authoritarian regimes could serve the purposes of a popular democracy.

The revolt against Truman's policies, launched in full force during the Korean impasse, gained impetus because of certain ephemeral conditions. In the congressional elections of 1950, the victory-hungry Republicans failed to regain control of either house. Nevertheless, Senator Taft won a smashing victory in Ohio, and Senator McCarthy barnstormed Maryland to help John M. Butler defeat Millard E. Tydings for a fifth senatorial term.[24] Based on these and other local results, G.O.P. right-wingers demanded a frontal assault on the administration's foreign policy. The call for such action came while the Red Chinese blocked MacArthur in Korea, and at a time when Senator Vandenberg's failing health prevented him from rallying the non-isolationist Republicans. With the disruption of the Vandenberg-Taft diarchy (the Michigan Senator died on April 18, 1951), Republican congressional leadership passed into the hands of the survivor. Taft, anxious to gain support in the 1952 national convention, reached an informal understanding with the extreme right wing of his party. The main objective of this coalition was to wrest party control from the hands of the Dewey faction. To accomplish this end, an all-out assault on the international cooperationists was indispensable.

The time was ripe for a triple-pronged attack—against an unpopular war that had been ignited by blunder and waged with stupidity; against a "give-away" program of foreign aid that had failed to create "fighting" allies; and against a lackadaisical government that had only half-heartedly ferreted the subversives out of the State Department. The Republican assailants capitalized upon the Asiatic crisis to press their case. How much, they asked, could the United States afford to squander upon foreign countries without resorting to a confiscatory taxation that would dry up the wells of our own prosperity? How long, they demanded to know, would the country tolerate Truman's failure to end shooting in Korea and treason in Washington? Around Christmas, 1950, these questions swelled into an angry chorus of voices, for the season brought no peace on earth and little good will toward the men who were running the country.

The drive to cut back foreign aid had important military implications. NATO's defense plan for western Europe had been devised before it was certain that the Soviets had exploded an A-bomb. When our atomic monopoly was broken, in 1949, the original NATO defense blueprint became obsolete. The United States had to make one of three unpleasant choices: it could continue to depend on an ineffective ground-force protection of the Atlantic fringe of Europe; it could spend additional millions to try to make the NATO line secure from thermonuclear attack; or it could drastically contract our ring of overseas bases. Economy-minded right-wingers wanted to pursue the third course, arguing that a shortened defense line would both lessen the drain on the Federal Treasury and enhance our own security. Proponents of this plan assumed that, in the event of total war, we had a stockpile of A-bombs sufficient to protect the western hemisphere by reducing Russia and Red China to rubble. They therefore suggested that we curtail our perimeter of defense and, by relying on super-weapons and naval superiority to protect our own interests, avoid an annoying peacetime conscription and a burdensome increase in tax rates. This plan appealed to the isolationists, for such sacrifices as it entailed would be made for America first. It could, moreover, be implemented without consulting troublesome allies. For the first time since 1940 the isolationists had a plausible case, as well as one endowed with political appeal.

The whole question boiled down to the oft-debated choice between paying less for immediate security, or of spending more now in order to avoid a costly future war.[25] Secretary of State Dean Acheson upheld the latter position. Backed, of course, by President Truman, Acheson insisted that the expenses of the Korean War should not be allowed to interfere with foreign aid to Europe, or with the implementation of the Point Four program. The Secretary stood his ground, firmly maintaining that only a "total diplomacy" would weld a globe-wide alliance, strong enough to withstand the Communist push. Was the United States, however, rich enough and powerful enough to afford this type of blanket security, or ought our strength be concentrated in holding a more limited area? This was the issue that began the great congressional debate of 1951.

To implement his program of foreign aid, Acheson had to persuade a balky Congress to appropriate many additional billions for world wide defense. The Secretary's genteel background, appearance, and patrician poise so incensed the provincial isolationists that they singled him out as a prize target. It is a striking comment on the unreason of the period that Secretary Acheson, so closely identified with the business elite, was branded as the "Red Dean" of Washington, while President Truman, who did so much to hold back the Sino-Soviet aggressions, was popularly believed to be "soft on Communism." These weird contradictions are partially understandable if one makes allowance for the heat of political campaigning. But more than that, it was the bitter atmosphere in which the Korean War was fought that permitted such reckless use of language. The isolationists staged their comeback during singularly intolerant years.

As noted before, the postwar isolationist rebound started in earnest when Chiang Kai-shek's flight to Formosa, December 8, 1949, highlighted the loss of the Chinese mainland. A month before, Governor Adlai E. Stevenson had noted the mad hunt for a "cut-rate security" and the growing unwillingness of the American people to bear the tax burdens of world leadership. Displaying an acute receptiveness to this trend, Stevenson said that current happenings abroad provided provincial pianists with a brand new keyboard upon which to sound their tunes. With remarkable prescience, the Illinois governor predicted the coming heyday for isolationist demagogues. Eastern Republican internationalists were similarly alarmed, and, in 1950, Governor Thomas E. Dewey also spoke out against "the ominously rising trend toward isolationism."[26]

Dewey's warning came six weeks before the North Korean Communists crashed across the 38th parallel (June 25, 1950). Truman's prompt action temporarily revived enthusiasm for collective defense, but this fervor rapidly waned with the military reverses of November, 1950. The immediate cause of the isolationist revolt was MacArthur's retreat in Korea. It was former President Hoover who gave the signal for the broadside.

Hoover had made his political return from Elba some time

previously. Ignored for twelve years by F.D.R., he was treated cordially by Truman and was given an important assignment. Hoover's stature grew as a new mood of conservatism, growing out of the fabulous postwar prosperity, replaced the reformist spirit of the depression decade.

As the ex-President's popularity steadily mounted, he began to pay increasing attention to foreign affairs. Long before events set the stage for another act in the isolationist drama, Hoover had prepared a new set of cues for the cast. In 1946, he had demanded that Uncle Sam stop playing Santa Claus, and act the part of a business man who confines his charity to the indigent, but is ever on the alert to engage in profitable trade with potential customers.

As became his Quaker upbringing, Hoover abhorred the thought of subduing Russia by force of arms. He was convinced that if the United States would spar for time, the Soviet ramshackle empire would eventually collapse from internal corrosion. Pending that happy day, Hoover wanted to maintain American security by making West Germany and Japan strong enough to hold the Iron Curtain in place. The ex-President repeatedly denied that he was an isolationist, but insisted that the western nations must all share the burden of upholding an enlightened and free civilization. In 1947 he had suggested that Communism could be contained less expensively, if we confined our help to vital areas whose people were anxious to perpetuate the values of a free society. Hoover reasoned that both the security and economic welfare of the country would be enhanced if the United States contracted its lines of power, and concentrated upon the defense of a more centralized foreign area. In time, the conservative Republicans adopted this proposition as an alternative to the Democratic demand for globe-wide defense outposts.

In 1948, Hoover had approved the Marshall Plan with pointed caveats. He wanted Europe to make more extended use of American private capital in promoting recovery, and demanded that economic and military governmental assistance be frugally given. Furthermore, he insisted that the recipients of our aid make every effort to become self-supporting as soon as possible.

By 1950, the former President was convinced that our allies had not learned a much-needed lesson. "In persistence to an old habit," he remarked in reference to the cost of NATO, "we are taking up the check."[27] Hoover became increasingly critical of the United Nations for he thought that it provided a convenient smokescreen for Communist imperialism similar to the way in which the League of Nations had formerly disguised Anglo-French colonialism. The United States, said Hoover at the outset of the Korean War, must either purge the United Nations of its Marxist marplots, or else give up the idea of collective defense and guard only those foreign areas essential to its own security.[28]

During the fall of 1950 Hoover sharply criticized our NATO allies for their indifference to the Asiatic war and, on December 20, 1950, he made the most important and controversial suggestions of his post-presidential career. This speech (which coincided with an isolationist blast by former Ambassador Joseph P. Kennedy), initiated a dispute on foreign policy that rocked the country.

Hoover proposed a Republican substitute for Secretary Acheson's "total diplomacy." America, said the ex-President, must recognize that its limited manpower made it impossible for us to retain a firm foothold on the European and Asiatic mainlands. We must, therefore, make "this Western Hemisphere the Gibraltar of Western Civilization." By protecting the island nations that lay on the far side of the Atlantic and the Pacific, our oceans could still serve defense purposes. Hoover reasoned that if we kept our troops off the continents, the New World and the approaches to it could be guarded by naval and air force units. While he admitted the desirability of protecting all of western Europe from Communist invasion, he argued against reinforcing NATO until our allies proved willing to share the burden of their defense. Turning his attention to the Far East, Hoover cheerily predicted that Communism would wear itself out on the barren steppes of Asia. He felt that to tighten and strengthen our defense rings in such fashion was not isolationism, but rather prudence and common sense.[29]

Hoover's bombshell exploded with repercussions heard all over the world. *Pravda* reported the speech, and, faithfully echoing the master's voice, complained that the ex-President did not carry his isolationism far enough.[30] Press opinion in the free world reiterated the fear that the American eagle, tired of flapping his wings abroad, would withdraw once more to his New World eyrie.

The far-reaching implications of Hoover's plan were not lost upon American observers. They took the speech for what it really was—a bold attempt to salvage a good part of the isolationist tradition. "What would we do," asked Governor Dewey, "an island of freedom in a Communist world, outnumbered 14 to 1, with oceans which would no longer be our protecting moat but a broad highway to our front door?"[31] The publicist, Elmer Davis, remarked that Hoover had recklessly invited "his fellow countrymen to crawl under the bed, shut their eyes, plug their ears, and hope for the best." Sumner Welles, veteran protagonist of a global diplomacy, called attention to Hoover's incurable short-sightedness. If we followed his advice, said Welles, the free world alliance would be gone and the Communists could mop up everything save our self-delineated Gibraltar.[32] Nor did Hoover arouse the enthusiasm of tough-minded realists, for they did not share his optimistic assumption that Communism would die of auto-intoxication. This skepticism was vindicated when, in the 1950s, the Soviet economy was apparently able to increase its output of both military and consumer goods. By 1956, informed observers feared that a Russian version of the Marshall Plan, designed to undermine American influence in neutralist areas, might ultimately prove more dangerous than the Soviet stockpile of wonder-weapons. In retrospect, it seems clear that Hoover's propositions were even more perilous than his most severe 1951 critics realized.

As a Republican elder statesman, Hoover could only sound the bugle for battle against the Democrats. The leadership of the campaign had to be taken over by the party's right-wingers, under the general command of Robert A. Taft. The Ohio Senator seized the opportunity to unite the Republicans behind him by presenting his views to the country. Although he failed to heal the breach in his own party, Taft succeeded in marshalling a large group of enthusiastic supporters.

The pitched congressional battle of 1951 began when the administration insisted that the defense of Europe be implemented despite the hot war in Asia. Truman had named General Eisenhower as Supreme Commander of the NATO forces and, acting on his own constitutional authority, increased American ground forces in Germany and Austria from two to six divisions. Senator Taft sounded off for the opposition on January 5, 1951, by declaring that "the principal purpose of the foreign policy of the United States is to maintain the liberty of our people." Three days later, Kenneth Spicer Wherry, of Nebraska, clarified the issue by introducing the following Senate resolution:

> Resolved, that it is the sense of the Senate that no ground
> forces of the United States should be assigned to duty in
> the European area for the purposes of the North Atlantic

Treaty pending the formulation of a policy with respect thereto by the Senate.

The pros and cons of this resolution, often called the Second Great Debate, lasted four months. The arguments revolved primarily around the President's peacetime authority to dispatch American troops to foreign areas without the prior consent of Congress. This technical issue broadened into a general re-evaluation of Truman's diplomacy, in raising these crucial questions: Should our perimeter of defense be cut down to Hoover's specifications? Would a total defeat of the Red Chinese parry the main outward thrust of Communism? How much military and economic assistance ought we to send abroad? In which countries would our help best serve our own national goals? Was the Point Four program for helping underdeveloped countries a military necessity or an expensive luxury?

In answering these questions, the Republican right-wingers demanded a revision of our entire postwar diplomacy, while Acheson caustically remarked that the Taft "re-examinationists" reminded him of a farmer who pulled up his crops each morning to assure himself that they were growing.[33] Ultimately, the constitutional question was left in abeyance, for the Senate approved the reinforcements to NATO with the advice attached that no more troops be sent to Europe without congressional consent. Although the protracted debate settled no fundamental issues, it had important consequences: First, it helped regenerate the isolationist spirit by raising many old doubts and misgivings; second, out of the crucible of controversy came a new isolationist mood which, for several years, seriously embarrassed our multilateral diplomacy; and, finally, the congressional debate of 1951 crystallized the current brands of isolationism.

The most moderate variety was the Hoover approach, embellished and systematized by Senator Taft. Like Hoover, whom he admired and respected, Taft was a pre-Pearl Harbor isolationist who wished to preserve the tradition by modifying its form. In contrast to the G.O.P. extremists, the Ohio Senator tempered emotion with reason, attributing the mistakes of the Democratic majority to bad judgment rather than to disloyalty to American interests. Roosevelt and Truman, said Taft, overestimating the material resources of the country, had thus outrun the limits of national power. Taft wanted to re-direct the aims of our diplomacy so that they would serve once more their true purpose—"the peace and liberty of the United States."

Emulating the responsible leaders of the America First coalition of 1940-1941, Taft declared that there was a wide common ground upon which all foes of totalitarianism could stand. His motives in framing a platform designed to attract as many supporters as possible were complex. At sixty-three, the Senator realized that 1952 was his fourth and last chance to achieve his most coveted goal—a Taft Restoration in the White House. To gain the nomination, he had to hold the G.O.P. right flank, and, at the same time, avoid alienating moderate segments of the party. He tried desperately to convince the G.O.P. international cooperationists that isolationism was no longer an issue. "How can we be isolationists," he asked, "when we are involved in wars and treaties and every kind of international relationships? It cannot be more than a question of degree of participation in world politics and certainly not of principle." To this he added that anyone who called anyone else an isolationist was an idiot.[34]

Senator Taft conceded that the United States had no choice but to accept the moral leadership of the free world. However, as a rock-ribbed domestic conservative, he viewed with alarm a national debt comprehensible only in astronomical figures and he deplored the rapid exhaustion of our national resources. What, he asked in 1951, were the measurable results of our profligacy? He answered this rhetorical question by pointing to the war in Korea, the threatening Communist minorities in France and Italy, and to our subsidized NATO allies who proved to be anything but foul-weather friends. To Taft it seemed self-evident that it was time to clutch every dollar that Truman and Acheson wanted to pour into this bottomless international pit.

In the domestic field, Taft had a well-thought-out philosophy, and his foreign policy ideas derived from his economic and political conservatism. He feared, for example, that unless national expenditures were drastically curtailed, ever-increasing tax rates would cripple free enterprise and the country would drift into socialism. In the modern conservative fashion, he believed that Congress must exert maximum influence to protect business against unlawful encroachments by the President. He carried this fear of White House dictatorship over into the field of foreign affairs, reasoning now, as in 1940, that only a tight check-rein on the Chief Executive would safeguard the country from dangerous overseas adventures.

Taft's emphasis upon congressional authority endeared him

to the G.O.P. ultra-conservatives who entertained hopes of turning the clock on Capitol Hill back to 1932. The extreme isolationists nodded approval when Taft accepted MacArthur as "a comrade of convenience." While they undoubtedly felt that the Senator made too many concessions to the internationalists, they were satisfied that he remained "in the tradition of Americans who wished the rest of the world did not exist."[35] Although Taft must have often deplored the dangerous overstatements and the rude manners of the ultraists, a contemporary observer noted that the Senator treated the irrationals with a "carefully studied attitude of public indifference and private approval that a nineteenth-century gentleman might have displayed toward the village Jezebel."[36]

Taft found it more difficult to placate the G.O.P. non-isolationists in his effort to make himself an acceptable presidential candidate. He, therefore, outlined a middle-of-the-road program in his 1951 book, *A Foreign Policy for Americans*. The basic assumptions of this platform drew heavily upon the premises of the 1919 Republican League reservationists. This resemblance was more than an artificial one, for Robert A. Taft, like his illustrious father, had been a Republican proponent of the League of Nations. Nevertheless, the Senator's 1951 draft owed more to the nationalist philosophy of old Henry Cabot Lodge than to the international orientation of William Howard Taft. Senator Lodge had wanted to accept fewer American foreign responsibilities than President Wilson had proposed and, in similar fashion, Senator Taft wanted to reduce President Truman's commitments. Like the elder Lodge, Taft insisted on no advance pledges of American military help, and complete liberty of action in event of a future breach of the peace. In addition, the Ohioan believed, in the best Coolidge tradition, that America's primary duty to the world was to set a moral example for the rest of mankind. Nor did Taft share the Wilsonian conviction that the collective action of the peace-minded nations could prevent the ou break of major wars. His attitude toward the United Natic was quixotic, for, while he distrusted it, he admitted that looked forward to the eventual triumph of a collective sec organization grounded on the principles of law and ju Like so many other older Americans, Senator Taft ofte got that Queen Victoria was dead. He confused the sh problem of keeping peace in a highly volatile world wi run plans for the universal acceptance of the princip ternational law and justice.[37]

In contrast to the more inflexible isolationists

403

Taft realized that the day of complete withdrawal from world politics had passed beyond recall. Hence he thought it imperative to mold our foreign policy to conform with changed circumstances. The Senator delineated a larger perimeter of defense than Hoover's "Western Hemisphere Gibraltar," but he insisted, along with the former President, that all diplomatic moves be determined by consideration of their effects on the national security and the drain they imposed upon our material resources. Thus he proposed a bargain variety of containment, based upon the following major principles: 1 - Reliance on air power rather than on ground forces to parry any Soviet blows against American security; 2 - Temporary military assistance to foreign countries, until such time as West Germany would be strong enough to defend Europe and Japan able to hold at bay the Far Eastern Communists; 3 - The United States should contemplate no offensive war to destroy Communism, but undermine instead the Sino-Soviet alliance by a vigorous overseas propaganda effort that would keep the Communists occupied in crushing revolts among their satellites; 4 - Abandonment of the expensive and ineffectual Point Four program of help to poverty-stricken underdeveloped countries; 5 - Make full use of private American capital in order to rehabilitate the economies of countries whose economic recovery would aid the cause of freedom.[38]

Taft hoped that his formula would unite the splintered Republicans. The Senator left himself open to many charges of inconsistency, for he had straddled vital issues in a vain attempt to build a compromise platform on foreign policy. He had attempted the impossible, for a maximum Communist challenge could not be met by a minimum tax on the American economy.

Nevertheless, the Ohio Senator's active leadership of the ...ssional bloc opposed to Truman and Acheson had far-
...results. First of all, it precipitated a moderate isola-
...eprint, designed to attract the support of lukewarm
...ernationalists. This program of "cut-rate security"
... appeal to some Republican ladies who discussed
...cy in study groups, and to their conservative hus-
...nulled over the same question in countless service
...ns. Second, it seems clear that Taft's concessions
...ma ultimate purpose, for, although he appeased the
Sena he spelled out a semi-isolationist policy that
denbe vulnerable a presidential candidate. Had the
...n with the isolationists, as did Arthur H. Van-
...homas E. Dewey, it is possible that he might

have won the closely contested 1952 nomination. Third, while Taft and his congressional lieutenants failed to make major changes in our foreign policy, they forced the State Department to give careful consideration to the effects of its actions upon the domestic economy. In the few short months of life left to him after the 1953 Republican Restoration, Senator Taft directed the legislative program of his party in Congress and, after his death, a G.O.P. cult tried to perpetuate his principles. Although the Eisenhower administration was captained by international cooperationists, staunch Taft men held key Cabinet positions where they could voice their opinions and make them felt. The diplomacy of Eisenhower and Dulles often bore subtle traces of the enduring Taft influence on Republican thinking.

In the critical spring of 1951, while Taft was arguing for a thrifty security, the recall of MacArthur precipitated another form of isolationism. The long congressional debate over the implementation of NATO highlighted the belief that the United States was not strong enough to smash Communism in Asia and still insure the safety of western Europe. The return of MacArthur brought these issues to a head: Should the United States, against the advice of its western allies and the desire of the uncommitted peoples of Asia, subdue the Red Chinese, thus possibly inviting a Russian attack against the thin NATO line? Or ought we to limit the Korean War to a face-saving action to uphold the principle of collective security, husbanding our strength for some future direct Russian move against the Atlantic Alliance? MacArthur's followers, who placed the strategic importance of the Far East ahead of the task of saving Western Europe, were called Asia Firsters. It was a loose term, applied by journalists to the motley coalition that backed the General.

MacArthur's declaration that there is "no substitute for victory" was hailed by the old national-imperialists who could not reconcile themselves to fighting a war short of unconditional surrender of the enemy. There was certainly something to be said for the General's insistence that America's real enemy was international Communism rather than the USSR. Hence, MacArthur contended that we must fight it out in Asia, where, he declared, the Communists had elected to make their main thrust. "If we lose the war to Communism in Asia," MacArthur had informed Representative Joseph W. Martin, Jr., "the fall of Europe is inevitable; win it and Europe most probably would avoid war and yet preserve freedom."[39] MacArthur assumed that the Kremlin's master plan was to bypass Europe, making only enough feints in a westwardly direction to hold down American forces while it pushed Communism forward by flank movements southward and eastward. If this assumption were correct, we would have to hold Asia at all costs, and it would be wise to utilize Chiang's 5,000,000 soldiers on Formosa to harass Peiping from the south, while American forces wiped out the enemy's "privileged sanctuary" in Manchuria. To charges that such a bold course would invite Russian intervention, MacArthur replied: First, that he did not think Stalin would fight unless the Soviet Union were invaded; second, that Truman should have known before he made his initial decision to save South Korea that such a course involved a calculated risk of total war; and third, that Red China was already exerting maximum military strength against us and that nothing that we would do in retaliation could augment the striking power of an enemy already fighting to the limit of its endurance.[40] Many Far Eastern experts believe that it would have been relatively easy and strategically prudent to have destroyed or crippled Mao in the Korean War rather than to have allowed Peiping to remain as an oriental bastion of Communist power; others argue that such a course would have fitted in perfectly with Stalin's desire to force us into an all-out war with China that would have exhausted our strength and split NATO asunder. It is impossible either to prove or refute the validity of MacArthur's military suggestions.

Curiously enough, the General's bold tactics appealed to isolationists of all varieties. Throughout World War II, a militant remnant of the America First coalition refused to accept Roosevelt's and Churchill's decision to make Germany the primary target of attack. The war against Japan was the favorite front of the isolationists, for here we could fight without overt help or counsel from Britain, and the Pacific war was, for all intents and purposes, over before the Soviet Union came to our aid. Thus MacArthur became a symbol for those Americans who bore lingering resentments against our 1917 and 1941 European allies. It had long been fashionable in isolationist circles to regard MacArthur as a wartime victim of the Europe-first internationalists.

MacArthur, the isolationist hero, returned home at a time of bitter resentment against collective security. When the Asia First bandwagon began to roll, many opportunistic isolationists scrambled aboard, paying little heed to logical consistency. Reinhold Niebuhr has explained the reasoning of the ingrained isolationists in championing the cause of a general who wanted to turn a small foreign war into a big one. According to Niebuhr, there are two ways of denying one's responsibility to fellow creatures—by paying no attention to their difficulties, or by intervening in their affairs in domineering fashion. Thus, Niebuhr argued, extremists who felt that it was no longer possible for America to withdraw from world politics embraced the reverse fallacy and held that it was her mission to run the universe. The isolationists were torn by mixed feelings of superiority and inferiority toward other peoples. MacArthur's program allowed them to indulge both of these attitudes, for he assumed that the United States was good enough and strong enough to checkmate the Communists without help from other quarters. This confident mood prevailed in 1951, because our prosperity was overflowing, our economy booming, and our armed forces were backed potentially by a stockpile of A-bombs. In Asia we could flex our muscles without help or advice from poverty-stricken allies, for there our leadership could not be challenged (in the foreseeable future) by any non-Communist power willing to go our way. If, on the other hand, we continued to place the defense of Europe ahead of victory in Asia, we would still be plagued with allies who would insist upon mutual consultation and action in the campaign against Communism. Senator Kenneth S. Wherry best expressed this feeling of national superiority when he said in 1940: "With God's help, we will lift Shanghai up and up, until it is just like Kansas City."[41] Although General MacArthur had shown deep understanding of and concern for alien oriental cultures, his isolationist followers failed to grasp that, even if the main battle against Communism were waged on Asiatic soil, we would have to pay deference to the people of that area to keep them in our power orbit.

Probably many G.O.P. right-wingers who sprang to MacArthur's defense in the common struggle against Truman gave only lip service to the General's military strategy. These Republican politicians were much more interested in recapturing control of their own party and in ejecting the Democrats from Washington than in enlarging the war in Asia. Hence, there was often an alliance of expediency between the Hoover-Taft conservatives who wanted a smaller defense budget and the avid Asia Firsters whose military aims would inevitably increase federal expenditures. Some of MacArthur's supporters were in dead earnest about crushing the Red Chinese, while others were far more interested in defeating their political enemies, whether Republicans or Democrats.

Because of these inner conflicts, the Asia Firsters were never able to resolve the glaring inconsistencies in their program. This coalition of right-wingers demanded, simultaneously, tax reductions and an increase in America's military might. They wanted to do business with foreign customers who would borrow our capital on stringent terms, but they were strongly opposed to the tariff reductions necessary to give other nations the dollars with which to pay back their obligations. Inspired by the writings of the extreme revisionists, many MacArthurites assumed that Franklin D. Roosevelt's refusal to negotiate with the Axis had involved the country in war; yet they now denounced all suggestions of diplomatic compromise with the Communists as craven appeasement. They demanded close cooperation with Franco and Chiang, but thought the Atlantic Alliance with the western nations unnecessary and dangerous.

Islationism of all varieties suffered a set-back in 1952 when Eisenhower defeated Taft for the nomination, and ended the 20-year G.O.P. exile from the White House. At long last, the G.O.P. liberal internationalists had proved that their candidate could win in the voting booths as well as on the floors of the party's national conventions. President Eisenhower headed a political party that had to decide whether Communism should be contained by alliance in Europe or exterminated by fire in Asia. Only the Korean truce of July 27, 1953, tabled the question for the time being.

Following this Korean compromise peace, popular enthusiasm for Syngman Rhee and Chiang Kai-shek waned. Americans, including their soldier-President, wanted everything booming but the guns, while neither Rhee nor Chiang would accept the status quo in the Far East. In 1954, the South Korean President alienated many erstwhile admirers when he beat the war drums while addressing a joint session of Congress. He became even more unpopular when he presented the United Nations with an exorbitant bill, which, if honored, would have fallen in large measure upon Washington. The tactless Rhee itemized $471,700 for rent of land used by the U.N. armies that had saved his country. In addition, he demanded a large sum for transportation and public utility services rendered the U.N. forces. *Time,* which had once hailed Rhee as the knight-errant of freedom, now caustically reminded him that the U.N. had rehabilitated South Korea's rickety transportation system, and had shot electricity into his dimly-lighted country from huge generating barges moored offshore. What, asked *Time* pointedly, had become of the two billions that the United States had sunk into Rhee's mismanaged economy since 1953?[42]

Chiang retained more of his American supporters, for the China Lobby had done unusually thorough work. Nevertheless, it was quite clear that he had strong personal reasons for wanting more gunplay in Asia. This led to a strange line-up in America, with right-wing isolationists demanding bold action in the Far East, and the internationalists patiently awaiting the proper opportunity to iron out differences with Peiping. When, in 1955, the Red Chinese tried to steal the island bases guarding the home plate on Formosa, President Eisenhower used the utmost caution in forestalling their play. The popular applause that greeted the President's restraint reflected the American distaste for any further Far Eastern adventures. By 1955, it was the Asia First isolationists who had to answer to charges of warmongering, while the so-called "United Nations worshipers" had become the appeasers.

Although the Asia First movement lost rather than gained momentum under Republican rule, the issues it raised have not been definitely settled. Wiliam F. Knowland, who succeeded to the G.O.P. Senate leadership upon Taft's death, holds to a brand of Republicanism that is certainly more Asia First than Europe First.[43] The Knowland point of view, reflected in some widely read newspapers and magazines, tenaciously clings to the theory that MacArthur's recall was but one link in a chain of related Far Eastern tragedies: the enfeeblement of South Korea, the consolidation of Red control over China, the dangerous division of South Vietnam, the loss of Tibet, the closing of the Communist ring around Formosa, and a perilous diminution of American prestige in non-Communist Asia. These "Asialationists," as they have been called, contend that if America abandons Chiang as an expendable diplomatic pawn, the American defense ring circling around Nationalist China, Japan, Okinawa, and the Philippines will be broken. According to this reasoning, the Red Chinese will eventually push through the opening to pocket the oil of Indonesia, the rice of Thailand, and the rubber of Malaya. In the event of such a calamity the United States would be caught between the jaws of a vise, which could be manipulated at will by the uncrupulous men in Moscow and Pieping.[44]

Because no one can accurately predict the oscillating course of Communist policy, it is difficult to speculate whether or not Asia Firstism will revive its 1951 strength. Wholesale aggressions from Peiping, launched with or without Moscow's assent, could change the picture overnight. If Mao or one of his successors decided to throw down the gauntlet, General Eisenhower's diplomacy of compromise might give way to the sledgehammer military tactics advocated by General MacArthur. How the United States would meet a new formidable threat in the Far East would depend, as it did in 1952, upon the outcome of an internal G.O.P. convulsion and upon the results of the unceasing struggle for power between the two major parties. Pending a new major Communist push in Asia, however, the dominant Eisenhower Republicans and practically all Democrats prefer the status quo in the Far East to another round of fighting which would break the 1953 draw decision on Korea.

So far we have been talking of isolationists who were amenable to compromise, or those who said that if we must play at world politics, let us play the game single-handed. Some rugged old-line isolationists, however, steadfastly maintained that a return to hemispherism (or even continentalism) was the only was out of our unhappy predicament. This school, in the timeless manner of all powerless minorities, teamed up with the more flexible isolationists in the grand assault on Truman. The smoke of politics often obscured the fundamental differences that divided the isolationists of the 1950s.

The unchangeables believed that a complete return to non-entanglement and neutrality would shield America, now as always, from a bellicose world. Hence, in principle, they opposed both MacArthur's militancy and Taft's plan to delineate our world-defense area. Yet in practice they usually gave vigorous support to any organized attack on our existing foreign policy.

Thus a united isolationist front sponsored the proposed Bricker Amendment to the Constitution. In the first year of Eisenhower's presidency they almost had their way in Congress. This amendment sought to limit the President's power by making executive agreements as well as treaties subject to legislative approval. In addition, it attempted to curtail the treaty-making power of the Chief Executive by forbidding the negotiation of an agreement encompassing any power not delegated to the Federal government by the Constitution. Although Senator Bricker's amendment and all substitute proposals were defeated by the Senate in 1954, the debates revealed how far the isolationists were willing to go in order to get rid of the "curse of diplomacy."[45] Had the amendment passed Congress in its original form and been ratified by three-quarters of the states, the President's hands would have been fettered at a time when national survival depended upon a flexible diplomacy.

The isolationists had been checkmated for the time being, but in 1956 Senator Everett M. Dirksen of Illinois reported a new amendment out of the Judiciary Committee. This time the isolationists proposed to forbid the negotiation of any international agreement whose provisions were in conflict with the Federal Constitution. During the hearings on the matter it was manifest that the authors sought to ban even an executive agreement that modified or superseded a congressional or state law. Congress failed to accept this thinly veiled design to accomplish Bricker's purpose, but it seemed unlikely that the isolationists would abandon the fight. The movement to curb diplomatic freedom of action, noted the Washington *Post* and *Times Herald,* "stands as a grave threat to the solidarity of the free world . . . it is a camouflaged maneuver designed to undermine American leadership in international affairs."[46]

While Truman's most formidable enemies shouted from the rooftops that they were not isolationists, the die-hards proudly waved their banners. Unless Americans once more chose to be unabashed isolationists, said the Chicago *Tribune,* they would either dissipate their wealth in a futile attempt to stay Communism in Europe, or else use up their precious manpower on remote Asiatic battlefields. The *Tribune,* as the staunchest champion of old-fashioned isolationism, opposed Truman's 1950 intervention in Korea and, in 1955, argued against fighting Red China in order to protect Formosa. Inasmuch as the paper had so often praised McArthur in the intervening years, its editorial page explained that an uncompromising refusal to make a diplomatic deal with Peiping did not make isolationists Asiatic imperialists any more than President Eisenhower's stern opposition to Moscow made him a European imperialist.[47] It further declared that loyal isolationists are not "Asia Firsters," "Europe Firsters," or "global salvationists," but patriotic Americans who firmly believe that all our international difficulties stem from an imprudent meddling in the affairs of other nations. "Every traitor," said Colonel Robert R. McCormick, "calls a patriot an isolationist."[48]

The *Tribune* was splendidly equipped for its isolationist role for, unlike most metropolitan papers, it maintained a private staff of high-calibre foreign correspondents. This made the *Tribune* virtually independent of the wire services of the Associated Press, the United Press, the International News Service, and Reuters of London. Thus, boasted its editors, their judgments on foreign policy were based on fresh information rather than on pre-digested syndicated releases.[49]

Characteristically quixotic, the *Tribune's* editorial page often lauded Hoover, Taft, and MacArthur. Nevertheless, Colonel McCormick and his successors championed a brazen isolationism that was not watered down by proposals for a bargain-rate internationalism or for a militant unilateralism in Asia. Death on foreign battlefields or stagnation in Siberian prison camps, it declared, was not worth "whatever World War III can produce by way of human happiness in England and France." The *Tribune,* in the best Borah fashion, still thought of Europe as an evil Svengali leading a hypnotized American Trilby into dangerous corners of the earth.

Curiously enough, Colonel McCormick, who had breathed fire and brimstone in the placid twenties, a generation later sponsored editorials that sounded like pacifist propaganda. Thus, in 1953, the *Tribune* called the Joint Chiefs of Staff megalomaniacs who thought only of augmenting their own power and of providing additional brass for shoulder-straps.

The Irreconcilables of the 1950s insisted that everything used to be all right until Wilson began the pernicious habit of minding the business of other peoples. They argued that before 1914 the Americans were in intimate and peaceful contact with all countries, for they enjoyed innumerable trade and cultural contacts. Prudently, our government clung to the time-proved policies of promoting peace by diplomatic negotiation, treaties of arbitration and conciliation, and it cautiously abstained from passing moral judgment upon foreign belligerents as long as these wars did not impinge upon our own immediate interests. This splendid and privileged position, so the argument went, was bartered away piecemeal by starry-eyed dreamers who told Americans that it was their bounden duty to save the world from perdition. Refusing to concede for a moment that inexorable change rather than misguided diplomacy had destroyed the idyllic world of the 1880s, the *Tribune* charged that an "America Last" crowd had undermined the country's security. Do we not take pride in being blessed with an uncommon amount of common sense? If so, why not abandon a profligate foreign policy that has brought nothing but trouble, and return to a diplomacy that gave the country a century of peace, security, happiness, and true "freedom from fear?"

The old-line isolationists delighted in pointing out that as the United States abandoned non-entanglement, other nations adopted the policy and used it to splendid advantage. The

412

canny Swedes and the shrewd Swiss, it was observed, stayed out of both World Wars and reaped the rewards of their good judgments. The *Tribune* even expressed a sneaking admiration for Jawaharlal Nehru who took our hand-outs but made it clear that India would be strictly neutral in event of war with Russia.

According to the inflexible isolationists, the billions that the give-away diplomats spent abroad had not bought friends or trustworthy allies for America. Nor would these die-hards accept even the pared-down foreign aid budgets suggested by Hoover and Taft. While Taft approved the collective security principle and said that he hoped for its ultimate triumph, the neo-Irreconcilables contended that world organization poisons the relations of nations with one another. The United Nations, they said, tied the hands of American diplomats who sought to obey the spirit of the Charter while other member states stubbornly refused to restrict their sovereignty or limit their complete freedom of action. While Taft would have retreated to the half-hearted internationalism of the 1919 Republican League reservationists, the more obdurate isolationists wanted to turn the clock back to 1914. This refusal to accept the burdens of national maturity was most marked among midwesterners, conservative businessmen whose prosperity was not dependent upon foreign trade, certain old-stock Americans who resented the wartime upsurge of the newer immigrants at home and the non-white peoples abroad, and some individuals whose economic status was adversely affected by the inflationary spiral.[50]

Other special groups particularly disliked large armed forces, continuous high taxes, and the mounting cost of production. Smaller manufacturers and tradesmen whose goods were not purchased by government agencies resented a rearmament that prospered their neighbors while making it difficult for them to stay in business. In some quarters the large-scale manufacturing and business mergers of the postwar period revived the old Populist-Progressive fears of over-concentration of wealth. Although the sharply accelerated tendency toward business consolidation was the result of many factors, men who produced primarily for the home market blamed their plight upon swollen government expenses that necessitated high taxes and raised labor costs. This dangerous trend, argued many lesser capitalists, could be halted only by a return to continentalism. This attitude explains why the Republicans failed to agree on foreign policy, for they drew their voting strength from both big and small business circles.

Naturally enough, older strains in the population generally retained faith in the isolationism that had prevailed in their youth. Retired military and naval officers, for example, often reflected views of their days of service. Captain William D. Puleston, USN Ret., historian and commentator on current affairs, wrote in the best naval tradition of the 1920s. He demanded that the United States recoup strategic areas over which we had surrendered partial control, and then defend only the New World, the West Atlantic, and "most of the Pacific." According to Captain Puleston, if we withdrew behind these barriers, "it would be a desperate nation that risked war with us." He outlined a revamped foreign policy for the State Department, but warned that there was no possibility of avoiding all wars. Such conflicts that we must fight, he said, should be followed by a moderate peace, unencumbered by a plan to unite the world.[51]

The isolationist flood of the early 1950s was thus fed by many different wellsprings. A strong current of irrational thought wound its way through these waters. While sometimes this gulfstream of unreason formed a separate whirlpool, it often mingled with the more moderate currents to cap them with an angry foam. This commotion had disturbed legitimate isolationist thought since the days of Woodrow Wilson, but its violence increased suddenly at mid-century.

A complex of inter-related factors explains the paroxysm of unreason that shook the country during the Korean War. The American psyche was discomposed by the accumulated tensions of twenty years of depression, total war, and recurrent international frustrations. By 1950 the United States was impaled on the horns of a dilemma from which it could not escape by the time-honored means of withdrawing from the world turmoil or of waging full-scale war to destroy the foreign devils.

Professor Talcott Parsons, a Harvard sociologist familiar with the mechanism of mass reactions, has used a social-psychological approach to investigate our transient mood of intolerance. According to Parsons, it is axiomatic that neither individuals nor societies undergo major structural changes without evincing some degree of irrational behavior. Hence a temporary national psychosis was evoked by an accumulation of deep stresses and strains that reach the breaking point during the Korean War. The historian accepts this explanation, but adds that a peculiar combination of circumstances, existing in 1950, precipitated the phenomenon called McCarthyism. Reinhold Niebuhr observes that "a squalid demagogue's name was used in fact to characterize the mood of the hysterical era, although he only exploited and did not create the fears that dominated the consciousness of the public."[52]

The Wisconsin Senator emerged from obscurity at a time when the ultra-conservatives were willing to grasp at any straw to reverse the course of American history. These extremists felt that even the moderate conservatives had betrayed them, for middle-of-the-road Republicans had accepted the cardinal New Deal domestic reforms and were trying to increase their usefulness. Moreover, the overwhelming majority no longer questioned the necessity of international cooperation, but asked instead how much we ought to spend in foreign lands and in which countries our money would best promote American security.

A hard-core minority, however, rebelled against the verdict of the majority. It was apparent that neither party could arrest certain deeply rooted economic, social, and diplomatic trends without inviting political disaster. The extremists refused to accept the permanent changes wrought in the American pattern of life by two wars and the Great Depression. Some colonial stock Americans and some descendants of pre-Civil War immigrant groups resented the rapid decline of the old social taboos and the steady lowering of racial barriers. By 1950 it had become apparent that laborers, newly arrived ethnic groups, and Negroes had gained more from the New Deal reforms and the postwar inflation than some other classes. Hence families who had fared better under a different social order became hypernostalgic for the good old days.

All of this feeling was related to isolationism in several ways. First of all, an emotional attachment to non-entanglement formed part of the ordinary conservative outlook. Besides, many Americans who had been well-to-do before 1914 felt that they were impoverished by high taxes that the government spent on foreign aid. They became all the more bitter in 1953 when the victorious Republicans retained the essential parts of the foreign and domestic policies of their Democratic predecessors. Any hope of change through the usual channels seemed lost, and the malcontents hailed the demagogues who brushed aside the conventional rules of political fair practice.

The patriotism whipped up by the struggle against world Communism could not spend itself in total war against the new enemy. Some of this pent-up aggression found an outlet in the Asia First fervor, but much of it was turned inwardly against the "Communist traitors in Washington." Men who kept their sense of balance found it difficult to quiet the hysteria evoked by this Second Red Scare, for while people over-reacted to the danger, there was no question that some grounds existed for the excitement.

While we were allied with Stalin against Hitler, says a competent investigator, "Communist and fellow travellers had entered the government in droves . . . [and] in the Office of Strategic Services, it was common knowledge that the employment of pro-Communists was approved at very high levels provided they were suited for specific jobs."[53] In 1945, this carelessness bore bad fruit when a raid on the offices of *Amerasia* (a pro-Red journal that sought to influence our Far Eastern policy) unearthed important military and diplomatic documents. The very next year a Canadian Royal Commission discovered that several Soviet spy rings had forwarded secret atomic information and samples of fissionable uranium to Mossow. Following these exposures, President Truman ordered a full investigation of all federal employees. The F.B.I. tracked down some 14,000 suspected cases, after which more than 2,000 civil servants chose to resign their jobs, and 212 persons were dismissed because their loyalty was suspected. After the outbreak of the Korean War, Truman signed into law a bill that permitted specified government departments and agencies to dismiss employees whose disloyalty could not be proven, but who nevertheless seemed dangerous security risks.[54]

Despite these precautions, a spate of sensational trials and confessions at mid-century fanned the leaping flames of suspicion and intolerance. Truman, regarding these exposures as a personal affront, made some unwise political remarks which were promptly exploited by his political enemies. The most celebrated case was that of Alger Hiss which began in 1948 when Whittaker Chambers, a repentant Communist, told his story to the House Un-American Activities Committee. Hiss, who had resigned a responsible government position to head the Carnegie Endowment for International Peace, brought suit for libel. Chambers produced documentary evidence and, after one trial ended in a hung jury, a federal court convicted Hiss for perjury, January 21, 1951.

The Hiss decision increased public concern about internal security, for in 1948 President Truman was reported to have called the House committee's investigations a "red herring," and subsequently an imposing roster of Americans had vouched their belief in the personal integrity of the accused man. Moreover, during the three years when the Hiss affair was front-line news, the story broke that Soviet agents in London and Washington had forwarded vital atomic secrets to the Kremlin. Inasmuch as our government revealed in 1949 that the Russians had developed a successful A-bomb, many people concluded that Washington's laxity was responsible for putting this dangerous weapon in Communist hands. A justifiable dread of annihilation, a partly understandable fear of wholesale subversion, and the Korean military reverses of 1950, had racked American nerves. The day of the demagogue had arrived.

A group of irresponsible politicians and journalists tried to use isolationism as an axe to fell the New Deal tree with all its branches. They cleverly identified the Communists as intruders who had sown unwanted seeds of liberal reform and international cooperation in the American forest. By insisting that the primary danger to the United States was domestic subversion rather than foreign aggression, they could denounce the policy of containment without leaving themselves open to the charge that their isolationism mirrored Kremlin propaganda. At the same time, the extremists could magnify the impact of Soviet thinking on the New Deal and Fair Deal reformers.

The extreme charges of the irrational right-wingers appealed to groups of gullible Americans who were looking for an easy and swift way out of an international situation that defied single analysis or quick solution. "Driving the rats out of Washington," as the saying went, attracted simple-minded souls who disliked the tedium and costliness of collective defense, or who had little stomach for a Red dragon hunt in Asia. The naive assumption that national well-being could be restored by purging the State Department of Communists was welcomed by those Americans who Eric Goldman has said crave "a foreign policy which has the supreme virtue of getting rid of the need for a foreign policy."[55]

McCarthy, with tar and brush in hand, pushed his way to the center of the political stage while the audience was stunned by the Far Eastern upset. There was enough truth in his whole story to make it sound plausible and to embarrass the men who sought to refute the more extravagant charges.

The junior Senator from Wisconsin, whose name was to acquire household familiarity, was a forty-year old bachelor lawyer. Starting out in politics as a Democrat, he turned Republican during the G.O.P. upsurge of 1938. At the time, however, the Republicans ordinarily ran behind the Democrats and the La Follette Progressives in Wisconsin elections. McCarthy had spent his entire life in a state where the German-American vote counted for much. The La Follette dynasty had thrived for many years on the votes of men who believed that United States foreign policy had long been bedeviled by pro-ally Anglophiles. If McCarthy could switch this allegiance to himself, he could undermine the La Follette machine. Just when this thought occurred to McCarthy is not certain, for his political career was interrupted by wartime service in the Marine Air Force Intelligence where he rose to the rank of captain.

Political dopesters were surprised when "the fighting marine" defeated the distinguished Senator Robert M. La Follette, Jr., for the 1946 Republican senatorial nomination and when the G.O.P. sweep of that year carried him to Washington. In 1946, however, McCarthy's foreign policy convictions had not yet become fixed for, in campaigning against La Follette, he charged that the Senator's isolationist votes made him an unwitting tool of Moscow. This fact lends plausibility to Samuel Lubell's observation that McCarthy and many of his camp-followers did not really believe isolationism feasible, but recognized its political usefulness in eliciting support in areas filled with voters who still bear resentments against our intervention in both world wars.

Once in Washington, however, McCarthy promptly cast his lot with the ultra-isolationists, voting against the Marshall Plan and NATO. It soon became apparent that the fledgling Senator was a brazen, ruthless, and callous politician who did not hesitate to violate the accepted rules of the game. He was cynical to the point where he admitted motives that less hardened men would conceal. With eyes always fixed on his fortunes, he cared little for the future of the party. The Senator soon developed the techniques that were to bring him notoriety. Always on the offensive, he timed his blows carefully, and tried to keep in the headlines at all costs. He reverted to the political law of the jungle, constantly assuming that the memory of the general public is proverbially short-lived and that what his constituents did not forget they would forgive when he came home and shook their hands.[56]

In 1950, Senator McCarthy's political fortunes were ebbing, and he set out to restore his popularity by launching a reckless crusade against the "Communist-ridden" Truman regime. The phenomenal publicity that he got in the following four years came because he understood and maliciously exploited the mass unrest of the period. The Wisconsin Senator, says Max Ascoli, gave Americans a "chance to escape the rigors of world civil war against international Communism by fighting their own private civil war against the McCarthy-made Com-

418

munists at home." Here was a demagogue who, from the privileged sanctuary of the Senate floor, abandoned principles of good taste and integrity. He dealt his opponents blows beneath the belt, he defied the responsible leaders of his party, and he became expert in the passing of sly innuendos and in the use of accusatory language. With characteristic irresponsibility, he spread the dangerous doctrine of guilt by association.

McCarthy started his anti-Communist campaign in Wheeling, West Virginia, February 9, 1950. In this, and in subsequent speeches, he said that he could name 205, or 57, or 81 Reds (the numbers usually varied with each harangue) in the State Department. When he was unable to substantiate these charges by naming one Communist survivor of the Truman purge, he pointed out Owen Lattimore, Far Eastern specialist at Johns Hopkins University, as head of "the espionage ring in the State Department." Under the chairmanship of Senator Tydings, a committee investigated Lattimore and exonerated him.[57]

Infuriated by this set-back, McCarthy opened fire on some better known public servants, charging that Professor Philip C. Jessup, American representative in the General Assembly of the United Nations, associated with Communists. He tried to besmirch the reputation of General George C. Marshall, and, on June 14, 1951, he declared that General Dwight D. Eisenhower's dilatory military tactics had made possible Stalin's drive for world dominion.[58] In the congressional elections of 1950, McCarthy took his anti-Red circus on the road, and his political stock soared when Maryland voters denied Tydings a fifth senatorial term. Some victory-famished Republican politicians, ordinarily more scrupulous than the Wisconsin Senator, began to ape his brass-knuckle methods.

During the presidential campaign of 1952, there was a strained truce between Eisenhower and McCarthy, Unfortunately for the Republicans, however, the strength of the Eisenhower current helped carry McCarthy back to Washington for another term. When the G.O.P. organized the Senate in 1953, McCarthy succeeded to the chairmanship of the Permanent Sub-Committee on Investigations. He used his position to pry into the security situation at the Army Signal Center, in Ft. Monmouth, New Jersey. This started a new chain of speeches and hearings. Thanks to the modern media of mass communications, this congressional inquest was followed by millions of television fans. In the spring of 1954, the rabble-rouser from Wisconsin seemed invincible. Professor Arthur S. Link asserts that McCarthy, more than any other man of his time, confused public opinion at home and tarnished the name of his country abroad.

Contributing factors made the Senator's tirades all the more dangerous. Senator Taft died in 1953, leaving the legitimate rightists without a leader strong enough to bridle the G.O.P. mavericks. The Republicans, determined to avoid an open party rupture during Eisenhower's political honeymoon, tried to appease the McCarthy faction. But the G.O.P. irresponsibles refused to listen to reason and, for a short time, the President was perplexed enough to toy with the idea of forming a separate middle-of-the-road party.[59]

McCarthy's most vociferous supporters in the country at large came from the hate-groups that had once formed the lunatic fringe of America First. Quiescent for a decade, the crackpot leaders rebuilt their pressure groups, exploiting the tensions of the Cold War in the same way that they had once capitalized upon the social pathology and exaggerated isolationism of the depression decade. These hate-mongers used the smoke created by McCarthy's broadsides to screen a rightist variety of totalitarian subversion.

To the super-patriots and nativist fanatics the marriage with McCarthy was one of convenience. Inasmuch as their organizations were usually militantly Protestant, their leaders regarded the senator's Catholicism with some apprehension. Moreover, professional rabble-rousers who called the United Nations a "Jew-Communist plot" and the Korean mishap the "Third Zionist War," found it difficult to accept Roy M. Cohn as a senior partner in the McCarthy brains trust. In the hope, however, that McCarthy would evoke a new spell of bigotry, the irrationals hitched themselves to the Senator's kite. McCarthy neither rapped their knuckles nor extended a welcoming hand.

During the 1940s the number of fanatical isolationist organizations declined to about 100 active groups. An examination of the platforms of the hate-societies that survived the war reveals a striking similarity. Almost all savagely attacked "Communist internationalism," Negro, Jewish (or Zionist) "rule," and movements whose aim it was to preserve domestic civil liberties. The isolationism of these extremists was contradictory, for they embraced any and all programs that promised to free the country from the alleged one-worldism of Truman and Eisenhower. Generally speaking, however, these hypernationalists argued that Communism was an internal and not an external danger. Old-fashioned isolationism, they assumed, had once insulated the United States from dangerous foreign ideologies. Thus they held with McCarthy that the Marxist boil must be lanced in Washington, and the national windows hermetically sealed to prevent further infection of the body politic. The Wisconsin Senator himself remarked: "I do not think we need fear too much about the Communists dropping bombs on Washington. They would kill too many of their friends that way."[60] Many rabid isolationist leaders were ready to resort to the use of such familiar fascist tools—"big lie" propaganda and strong arm methods to subdue the opposition.

Unlike the Bundists and Christian Fronters of 1940, their mid-century successors staged public rallies only on important occasions, and seldom engaged in street brawls. They imitated instead the techniques of the despised Communists, and infiltrated and tried to dominate legitimate right-wing organizations. Compiling a select mailing-list of persons apt to read their propaganda, they sent out news letters, intelligence reports, and slick-style magazines well larded with literary gimmicks. The money for this propaganda evidently came from some wealthy patrons whose generosity allowed the fanatics to compensate for poor coverage in the national press and little or no time on the country-wide broadcasting systems.

The more rabid nationalists stemmed largely from splinter religious denominations and ethnic minorities with vengeful memories of foreign wars. Fundamentalist Protestant sects, composed in large measure of rural nativists, provided the leadership. In 1947, Gerald L. K. Smith, an evangelist formerly allied with Father Coughlin, launched a new political party called the Christian Nationalist Crusade. Without MacArthur's permission, Smith ran the General on a minor party ticket in 1952. Then Smith tried to form a new San Francisco conference to abolish the United Nations. When this, too, proved abortive, he openly cast his lot with McCarthy.

The spirit of ultra-nationalism was strong enough to attract some support from religious and racial minorities. McCarthy's hands were upheld by Rabbi Benjamin Schultz who led a front organization called the American Jewish League Against Communism. Leonard A. Feeney, an unfrocked and excommunicated Boston Jesuit, compounded anti-Communism with anti-Semitism in an attempt to form a Catholic sect which was declared heretical by Church authorities. Although, like the majority of the minority groups, the Negroes perceived the danger of the spread of bigotry, a small faction formed a militant anti-white society called the Nation of Islam.[61]

The public mind, however, regained its sense of balance more quickly than might have been expected. The clouds of unreason began to recede in the autumn of 1954. Through a strange quirk of politics, a Democratic congressional victory freed a Republican President from the McCarthy stranglehold. The Wisconsin Senator lost his key chairmanship and was publicly censured by his colleagues for past sins. The 1954 elections revealed the dependence of the Republicans upon Eisenhower's personal popularity, and, thereafter, few G.O.P. right-wingers were willing to forego the opportunity of future rides to victory behind the President's magic coattails. The administration reached a bi-partisan foreign policy agreement with the victorious Democrats, for there was no serious difference in this area between the moderate leadership in both parties. This new arrangement was less vulnerable to attack than the working agreement of Truman's day, for no sane man could be persuaded that either Eisenhower or the eminently conservative southern Democrats who dominated their party in Congress were "soft on Communism." Moreover, unlike Truman, President Eisenhower had the backing of big business, most of the influential newspapers, and many important press and radio commentators.

Tolerance is a luxury of abundance, and the incredible prosperity of the mid-1950s played its part in creating a softer atmosphere. Americans dreamed once more, as in the 1920s, of the twin blessings of peace and plenty. A flourishing national income fulfilled part of the dream, while slowly brightening foreign skies gave some hope of realizing the entire reverie. The Republicans negotiated a cease-fire in Korea and, although this was not a national victory, it was a highly popular face-saving compromise. Furthermore, to the profound satisfaction of the great majority of Americans, the Eisenhower administration preferred discretion to valor and settled the dangerous Asiatic crisis that followed the Korean War without again unsheathing the sword.

Meanwhile, the Russian horizon brightened, leaving Americans completely bewildered. Stalin died in 1953, and the West breathed easier as the Marshal's eager heirs quarreled over the succession. By 1955, however, the free world could only guess as to whether the great Moscow upheaval promised peace or a more subtle and dangerous program of Communist expansion. Stalin's immediate successor, Georgi Malenkov, was deposed in January, 1955. Although few Americans considered the ex-Premier a good insurance risk, Malenkov was demoted rather than liquidated, and was soon traveling about the world as an ambassador of Soviet good will. Optimists pointed to the rise of a Russian group of bureaucrats, engineers, and technicians, cheerily predicting that this new middle class would temper authoritarian rule even as the bourgeoisie, two hundred years before, had ended royal tyranny in western Europe. This belief gained credence in 1956 when, at the twentieth Soviet Congress, Khrushchev denounced Stalin's "cult of the individual" and throughout the Communist world statues of the Marshal toppled from their pedestals. Usually reliable intelligence reports insisted that Russia's new dictators, who had barely escaped Stalin's wholesale purges, would never again allow power to be consolidated in the hands of one man. But what did this collective dictatorship portend for world peace? Was the denigration of Stalin a "carefully stage-managed optical illusion," or did it mean that the unleashed forces of Russian liberalism would eventually erode the Iron Curtain barrier that divided the world into two hostile camps? Would the end of Moscow's reign of terror stir up so much revolt among its satellite peoples that the Kremlin would promptly resume its time-honored methods of dealing with opponents, or would the Red empire evolve into a federation of self-governing nations? The tragic events of the Fall of 1956 left the picture still clouded.

While Americans were anxiously awaiting the answers to these questions, Bulganin and Khrushchev were trying to win the Cold War by means short of a hydrogen-bomb duel. Russia's expanding economy allowed her to increase economic aid and to extend long-term credits to India, Indonesia, the Middle East, and even to Argentina. The Soviets could implement their Marshall Plan without consulting a budget-conscious Congress or without any immediate fear that their largesse would provide ammunition for political opponents. Notoriously generous with promises, the Russians told isolationist-minded countries in Asia and Africa that Communist help for their underdeveloped countries did not hinge upon making military pact with Moscow or Peiping. Thus India contracted for a huge steel mill, Egypt was promised an atomic reactor, and other countries were similarly baited. Inasmuch as none of these areas could modernize without technical assistance, Russian engineers and other trained personnel poured into any land that accepted the Kremlin's outstretched arm. Only the naive could hope that the education of these Communists had been limited to technology and that they were not also skilled propagandists and fifth columnists.

As the new Communist pattern of economic and social penetration into neutralist areas took definite form, Americans were faced with a terrific challenge. By 1956, it was apparent that American influence in Asia and Africa was being steadily undermined. President Sukarno of Indonesia came to Washington and bluntly admitted that his country would accept aid from either the free or Marxist world provided that no military strings were attached to the agreement.

Nor was Indonesia an individual case, for all the former colonial nations felt pretty much the same way. Their peoples, said the New York *Times,* demanded absolute self-determination, equal treatment for non-Caucasian races, and swift and immediate help for their ill-fed, ill-housed, and ill-clothed millions. The Russian démarche called into question the Truman-Eisenhower policy of help for only those nations willing to stand up and be counted in the ranks of the free world. Economic competition between democracy and communism became acute in the uncommitted areas.

Both domestic and foreign difficulties perplexed the Eisenhower administration. Washington had to decide whether to enter into economic competition with Russia, or to reconcile itself to loss of the neutralist nations. If we decided to outbid Russia, as most forward-looking men thought we must, ought we frankly to abandon our policy of favoring our military allies and discriminating against peoples who insisted upon non-entanglement? In revamping our foreign policy, should we continue to make overseas aid an essentially American program, or should such help be channeled through an international program in which the Russians would be invited to participate? Eisenhower and Dulles were faced with a devil's choice, for to stand pat was dangerous abroad, and to abandon their oft-repeated avowals of no deals with Communists would invite attack at home. Furthermore, the demand for a drastic overhauling of our foreign aid program was most loudly voiced by liberal Democrats, and politicians find it embarrassing to acknowledge the validity of their opponents' arguments. Nor was the Democratic congressional majority, under the leadership of conservative southern Bourbons, apt to agree to a new foreign policy that necessitated a relaxation of tariff barriers, economic collaboration, and a disarmament agreement with the Soviets. An anonymous official in Washington thus stated the Republican dilemma: "How do you treat a fellow who sticks out one chubby hand with a big smile on his face and says 'Let's be friends,' while you know that in his other hand, behind his back, he holds the strings to a military machine capable of clobbering you any moment?[62]

The situation was further complicated by our NATO allies who, with the exception of Adenauer's Germany, assumed that the balance of hydrogen terror ruled out the possibility of a big war. Western Europe was impressed as Bulganin and Khrushchev softened their tyranny at home, apologized to Tito in Belgrade, and toured Europe and Asia trying to look innocent as visiting delegates to a Chamber of Commerce convention. By banishing European fears of immediate war, "B and K," as the British press called them had weakened NATO. Led by the Canadians, a group of nations insisted that in order to conform to new conditions, NATO must be strengthened. They suggested activating Article II of the alliance, designed to promote close economic and political cooperation among the signatory powers. Sensing this unrest, Secretary of State Dulles agreed that it was time to implement the "totality of NATO." At their May, 1956, meeting in Paris the NATO foreign ministers designated a sub-committee of three members to explore the possibilities of broadening the base of the alliance. Supporting Dulles's stand, President Eisenhower cautiously spoke of an Atlantic Alliance Cabinet that might execute the broadened program.[63] Meanwhile, however, there were many misgivings, for member powers were defaulting in their defense obligations. This was the situation in October, 1956, when the outbreak of the Suez War shook the NATO alliance to its foundations and made closer Western cooperation more improbable than ever.

Possibly the mellow Russian plan to spread Communism with the ruble would prove more dangerous to American security than Stalin's iron-fisted lunges. For the time being, however, the thaw in the Cold War helped melt away the McCarthy bloc of isolationists. Events rendered two planks in the Senator's platform utterly absurd. If Moscow was challenging the United States to a game of "competitive co-existence," there was all the more reason for Washington to increase its program of foreign aid in order to keep our avowed allies and the uncommitted nations from falling into the velvet-lined Communist trap. In addition, Eisenhower and Dulles could not afford to defy the West by a stubborn refusal to explore the possibilities of reaching a peace settlement with Russia. Thus cries of "appeasement" and "no compromise with atheistic Communism" fell on the deaf ears of the peace-hungry American majority. In the spring of 1954, the Army-

McCarthy hearings brought the flood of unreason to its high-water mark. A year later, the tide had receded to the point where McCarthy could muster only four dissenting votes when the Senate approved an agreement that made it possible for President Eisenhower to sit down with the Soviet bigwigs at a Geneva council table.

Senator McCarthy unquestionably had given isolationism its biggest boost since the 1940 formation of America First. In the long run, however, he did the movement incalculable harm. First of all, his unprincipled methods alienated the support of many isolationists who cherished the traditional American fair play. It is quite possible that but for McCarthy's recklessness, moderate and right-wing G.O.P. elements might have joined some conservative Democrats in forming a stable congressional coalition. McCarthy made this impossible by insisting that the Democratic foreign policy was fashioned by traitors rather than by short-sighted Presidents. Furthermore, when McCarthy challenged the American tradition of civil liberties, he cut the last tie between the conservative and liberal isolationists. The cords had been snapping since 1939, but, until the Korean War days, there was still a vocal group of progressives who frowned upon a foreign policy which buttressed reactionary regimes all over the world and studiously tried to revive a martial spirit in Bonn and Tokyo. McCarthy's fulminations strengthened the moderate control in both parties, and this leadership was, on the whole, more internationally-minded than isolationist.

To sum up, the inverse isolationism of the Asia Firsters seems to possess greater vitality than any other segment of the splintered America First monolith. The Hoover-Taft program is hamstrung by the Russian challenge to economic war, the isolationist purists seem moribund, and the irrationalists have suffered an almost fatal setback. In desperation, remaining rabid isolationist groups seem ready to scrap their differences and to acknowledge the leadership of Douglas MacArthur. As a father-image for all isolationists, the General became the leading evangelist for the hoary tradition of unadulterated American nationalism.

Unilateralism is the cohesive of the Irreconcilables of our time. Some want to "go it alone" in an aggressive campaign to wipe out Communism in Asia, some want the United States to free itself of all overseas obligations, and some oscillate with pendulum-like precision between these antitheses. By and large, these men and women want a drastic reduction of federal spending abroad and governmental power at home; they

426

look at the future of free enterprise through narrow-rimmed spectacles; they tend toward chauvinism; and they either overvalue or undervalue the use of force in settling the ideological controversy that plagues the world. At times, they have been supported by spirited ethnic groups, determined that if America cannot liberate their kinsmen from the thrall of Communism it should make no diplimatic agreement with Russia that would freeze the status quo.

In Congress the leading isolationist spokesmen are bitter right Republicans who have not become reconciled to President Eisenhower. Typical of this group is Senator William E. Jenner of Indiana who, according to *Time*, has been transformed "from a reactionary into a fossil." In a 1956 Chicago speech, Jenner called Eisenhower's foreign policy "nauseating," and charged that Secretary Dulles "talks anti-Communism but silently, secretly carries on a planned retreat before the Communist advance." It was Jenner, rather than McCarthy, who had once labeled General Marshall a "front man for traitors."[64]

On Washington's Birthday, 1956, the extremists staged a rally in New York's Carnegie Hall. Sponsored by a new national organization, For America, this mass meeting was called to unite all isolationists under the banner of Douglas MacArthur. Senator McCarthy, sensing the decline of his own fortunes, seemed ready to abdicate in favor of the General. Thus he hailed MacArthur as the "contemporary George Washington," and inveighed against the "reigning liberal bipartisan regime" that brought upon the United States "the bitter disgrace of Korea" and the shameful and bootless appeasement of the Geneva parley of 1955. General Washington, said McCarthy, would have blessed General MacArthur's insistence that the United States fight only American wars, and would have scorned the U.N. foreigners who made us abandon our tradition of forcing our enemies to their knees. "We have," Senator Jenner told the audience, "quit our ground to stand upon foreign ground."[65]

Press reporters related that it was impossible to keep the isolationist hate-groups from infiltrating into the ranks of the new formed coalition. Pickets marched before the entrance to Carnegie Hall with placards reading "Communism is Bad—Zionism is Worse." These signs boded no good for future isolationist success, for all too often had fanatics shamed a once honorable tradition.

Chapter 16

The Climatical Lag

AT THE outset of this historical analysis, that complex mass of
sentiment and policy known as American isolationism was
likened to the glacier that eons ago covered the northern part
of our continent. Geologically speaking, this ice sheet resulted
from abnormal weather, for ordinarily the earth's climate is
not conducive to persisting large-scale glaciation. Similarly,
American isolationism was the product of extraordinary conditions that prevailed in the world for four hundred years after
Columbus.

Glaciers begin to recede as the weather reverts to its
normal pattern; in like fashion, monolithic isolationism visibly
began to crack in the late nineteenth century when the international climate no longer fostered its existence. In the manner of glaciers, isolationism slowly thawed. Twentieth-century
world politics proved much warmer than expected and the
fires of war accelerated the process. By 1945, authentic isolationism was all but gone, albeit its retreat left a terrain rough
in spots and littered with debris.

After an ice glacier has ridden over the countryside, there
commences a relatively long period of geological adjustment.
As the ice melts and the weight is lifted, the surface of the
earth rises. The greatest compensatory rise occurs where the
ice has been thickest. The magnitude of difference in readjustment among portions of the glacial pavement frequently
leads to earthquakes which testify to the prior existence of
the ice mass.

Analogously, the disintegration of isolationism required a
more severe readjustment among certain portions of the population than among others. The magnitude of difference in this
process of acclimatization to modern world conditions produced recurrent shocks which jolted our diplomacy. Some
short-sighted politicians failed to understand the ephemeral
nature of these effects and hopefully regarded the upheavals
as signs that the isolationist glacier had reversed its course.
The international climate, as unpredictable as the long-range
weather pattern of the earth, might some time in the future
create another period of isolationist glaciation. For the time

being, however, the rumblings that disturb our foreign relations are reverberations of by-gone days rather than portents of another ice age.

American thinkers, miscalculating the length of the period of readjustment to our new world position, often prematurely hailed the passing of the policy of non-entanglement. Thus, in 1919, Professor John H. Latané called his textbook on diplomatic history *From Isolationism to Leadership*. This tendency grew most rapidly after 1945. It even became fashionable to assume that the American people had made their final choice.

Much can be said in support of this widespread conviction that American isolationism has been relegated to the museum of outworn traditions. Significantly, although the aftermath of World War II justified profound disillusionment and frustration, there was no wholesale revival of the spirit of isolationism. Moreover, it seems reasonable to assume that America's passion for free enterprise will offset the deep-seated provincialism of its people. The world is filled with newborn nations determined to pursue the quickest means to modernization and industrialization. Unless these underdeveloped economies are bolstered by an ever freer flow of American capital than before, their leaders could conceivably espouse Soviet techniques. If the erstwhile colonial nations are rebuffed by the United States, they are not likely to consider the cost in human suffering and self-degradation, of collectivized economies.

The southern Democrats who, by virtue of seniority, play a key role in congressional decisions, have been more tardy in facing the Russian economic challenge than the Eisenhower Republicans. There is a predisposition among certain factions in both parties to risk the loss of the neutralist countries. Such men reason, says James Reston, that "after a long tradition of isolation followed by a generation of internationalism, the time has come to review the whole story and take from each of these two eras the best politics and procedures." Some members of Congress argue that we ought to let Nasser, Nehru, Sukarno, and even King Saud glut themselves on the repast of Bolshevist economic assistance, on the assumption that they will retch not from surfeit but from dearth. At that point, it has been predicted, they will turn back to the United States for help, and we can grant it upon our own terms. If, on the other hand, Russia should prove foolish enough to fritter away her resources upon the backward nations, then her satellite leeches may bleed her from a healthy red to an anemic pink.

To prevent the Communists from upsetting our balance of power, however, we will have to continue to afford aid to our avowed allies and, by enhanced economic assistance, insure the good will of the uncommitted peoples. Such a program, which, despite the popular demand for curtailment of federal spending, has the support of the moderate leaders of both major parties, is the very antithesis of isolationism.

Skeptics may counter, with considerable justification, that our present concern for the peace and prosperity of remote nations is but a passing response to the Communist threat. Nevertheless, even if, on one hand, the present war clouds should burst into violent storm, or on the other, vanish into thin air, it is unlikely that the United States could repudiate its foreign commitments. Our State Department would still have to contend with the new power vacuums created by a possible collapse of the major Communist partners, with a resurgent Germany or Japan, and with the fecund peoples of Asia and Africa. It is now taken for granted that middle-sized and perhaps even small nations will soon produce nuclear weapons, whereupon any one of them would be as dangerous as a boy with a loaded pistol. The peace will still have to be maintained by collective security alone or by using an international organization to balance power. Barring the unlikely event that the behavior of man will ameliorate, a victorious western coalition would still have to stand watch over a volatile world. The task may then be somewhat easier and more congenial than it is now, but we would still have to decide whether we desire to do all the policing ourselves or prefer to share the task with kindred peoples.

However, the twentieth-century international climate is so fickle that a prolonged spell of foul weather might evoke another mood of withdrawal. For example, should the present stalemate be prolonged indefinitely, it is entirely possible that American patience could be exhausted. Should this weariness coincide with some convincing acts of good faith on the part of the Communist leaders, we might be tempted to withdraw entirely from Europe and Asia in return for a Russian promise to neutralize the satellite countries and a re-united Germany. Excluding the possibility of a *rapprochment* with Moscow and Peiping, a sharp curtailment of the national income, especially if accompanied by large-scale unemployment, could readily force an "agonizing re-appraisal" of our present policy. Thus far the Cold War against Communism has cost American taxpayers some $350 billion without creating a balance of power either strong enough to prevent a hydrogen-bomb war, or sufficiently stable to assure us of adequate foreign support in the event of a showdown. Should we, despite the built-in stabilizers, designed to balance the economy, be confronted with a "hair-curling" depression, the results on foreign policy would be unpredictable. The collapse of prosperity might, as it did in the 1890s, lead to an orgy of jingoism and expansionism. Or it might, as in the 1930s, create an overriding demand for a withdrawal from the costly game of world politics.

The situation is peculiarly difficult to appraise because we have not yet found an adequate substitute for isolationism. After one-third of a century of sporadic efforts, the collective security ideal is still in the blueprint stage. Nor does the Truman-Eisenhower policy of creating a free power bloc within the structure of the United Nations seem capable of withstanding internal strains and stresses. It is difficult to maintain enthusiasm for so negative a policy as containment; like all compromise proposals, it is vulnerable to attack from the international cooperationists who would do more, and the obdurate isolationists who would do less. The first step in Truman's 1947 démarche, the economic rehabilitation of western Europe, was a brilliant success. Logically, the economic recovery of this area had to be allowed by a tight Atlantic Alliance, lest the Communists push in from the east and reap the benefits of our financial investment. At this point, the plan disclosed its weaknesses, for neither America nor Europe proved sufficiently willing to sacrifice short-run national aspirations in order to build up a foolproof military coalition.

The Luce publications, ordinarily hearty supporters of President Eisenhower, admitted, in 1956, the failure of his administration "to develop a coherent, long-term foreign economic policy which will command general assent at home and understanding abroad."[1] Nor could the Republicans agree among themselves how to treat the neutralist nations. Senator Knowland, voicing the opinions of the G.O.P. conservatives, wants to deny aid to any country that will not ally itself with the United States. President Eisenhower, on the other hand, has persistently shown more understanding of these non-joiners and even appears willing to tolerate their desire to remain unentangled. The situation became even more confused when Secretary Dulles publicly called neutrality obsolete, only to beat a hasty retreat when his words annoyed certain isolationist-minded Asiatic leaders.[2]

Actually, it seems that the international situation is even more precarious today than when the frosty gales from Moscow instituted the Cold War. Recent Russian economic expansionism has posed a new challenge that will tax American ingenuity to the fullest. While Russia was using subversion and violence to advance Communism, we were able to count on Soviet errors to arouse the suspicion and hostility of the uncommitteed peoples. But despite the tragedy of Budapest, Moscow seems to have become more sensitive to outside criticism of strong-arm methods in treating her subject peoples. Should the 1956 Soviet dulcet approach prove permanent rather than ephemeral, it could tilt the economic balance of power in Russia's favor. Thus far, the United States has failed to fashion a policy that will hold in our orbit those countries unwilling to subscribe to our own conservative economic philosophy. Sooner or later Washington will have to decide whether to take the calculated risk of losing the uncommitted peoples, or to outbid Russia for their friendship. It is impossible to know what the eventual choice will be, for while President Eisenhower seems willing to match the Russian offer of aid without entanglement, Congress appears far less generous. And what after Eisenhower? There is no absolute indication that, bereft of their popular leader, the Republican moderates could keep the party from falling into the hands of a new coalition of rational Old Guardists and irrational bitter-enders. If the isolationists could recapture control of the G.O.P., they could rejuvenate the insular tradition with the help of the provincial Dixiecrats and other Democrats willing to make political capital of the foreign aid issue.

In addition to an economic or political upheaval in the United States, any number of possible foreign calamities could once more render isolationism a feasible and even an attractive policy. Suppose, for instance, the Communist minorities in western Europe, with or without assistance from Moscow, should become the majority. The Atlantic Ocean would then replace the Iron Curtain as the dividing line between two antagonistic ways of life. Should this happen, says Professor Samuel F. Bemis, we might be forced to fall back upon the New World as our second line of defense, or we might even have to concentrate our forces once more upon the North American continent.[3] It is not likely, but it could happen.

One might also imagine a situation where our present allies, without changing their forms of government, might put themselves under leadership groups that would align their countries with a tamed, but anti-American, Russia. The pages of history books are replete with instances where poorer and weaker nations coalesced against the richest and strongest world power. It has even been suggested that our present policy might lead to such a diplomatic revolution. Faced with a solid European and Asiatic opposition, the United States would become involuntarily re-isolated. "History," Reinhold Niebuhr observes, "is full of surprising contingencies which no one can foresee or forecast."[4]

It is far more likely that, if the United States and Russia maintain nuclear parity, the desire for self-preservation will force a Pax-Atomica. Dr. Vannevar Bush, the gifted scientist who did so much to usher in the nuclear era, has stated that a Third World War would be so mutually destructive that its very prospect will prevent its outbreak. Should Bush's conjecture prove correct, such wars as might be fought would be limited conflicts decided by the use of conventional weapons. In such a case, the spirit and outlook of the Victorian Age, so salutary to isolationist reasoning, might return. Or, if the United States should some day find itself engaged in another local war similar to the Korean holding action, and should our NATO or SEATO allies prove lackadaisical or recalcitrant, the balance might well swing in favor of American unilateralism. Any number of international possibilities could reverse the present long-run trend toward increasing international cooperation.

A new era began when the dogs of war were unleashed at Sarajevo. Ever since, Americans have been torn between a desire to use their national power to stabilize the world, and a conflicting urge to remain aloof from overseas turmoil. Probably there will be no irreversible decision in this never-ending debate over foreign policy. Only in times of acute foreign or domestic crisis has one desire or the other dominated public opinion. The rest of the time the internationalists and the isolationists have fought each other with varying fortunes. Present signs point to a decision rather than a knock-out victory for the internationalists. But any new sharp turn of the wheel of fortune could put the isolationists in position to demand a rematch. The ultimate outcome is imponderable, for, as it has been said, the only certain thing about the future is its uncertainty.

BIBLIOGRAPHY

Bibliography

I. MANUSCRIPT SOURCES

Carl L. Becker MSS, Cornell University

Edward Price Bell MSS, Newberry Library, Chicago, Ill.

Albert J. Beveridge MSS, Library of Congress*

William E. Borah MSS, L.C.

George Lincoln Burr MSS, Cornell University

Calvin Coolidge MSS, L.C.

William E. Dodd MSS, L.C.

Emma Goldman MSS, New York Public Library

Charles E. Hughes MSS, L.C.

David Fulton Karsner MSS, New York Public Library

Victor Fremont Lawson MSS, Newberry Library

George W. Norris MSS, L.C.

Rand School Papers, New York Public Library

Franklin D. Roosevelt MSS, F.D. Roosevelt Library, Hyde Park, N.Y.

Gustav Scholer MSS, New York Public Library

Jacob Gould Schurman MSS, Cornell University

Lincoln Steffens MSS, Columbia University

Henry L. Stimson MSS, Yale University

Oswald Garrison Villard MSS, Harvard University

Frank P. Walsh MSS, New York Public Library

Thomas J. Walsh MSS, L.C.

William Allen White, MSS, L.C.

II. OFFICIAL UNITED STATES PUBLICATIONS

Congressional Record: 56 Cong., 1 sess.; 61 Cong., 1 sess.; 65 Cong., 1 sess.; 65 Cong., 3 sess.; 66 Cong., 1 sess.; 66 Cong.,

*Hereafter L.C.

2 sess.; 67 Cong., 1 sess.; 67 Cong., 2 sess.; 67 Cong., 3 sess.; 67 Cong., 4 sess.; 68 Cong., 1 sess.; 68 Cong., 2 sess.; 69 Cong., 1 sess.; 70 Cong., 2 sess.; 74 Cong., 2 sess.; 75 Cong., 1 sess.; 75 Cong., 3 sess.; 76 Cong., 1 sess.; 77 Cong., 1 sess.; 82 Cong., 1 sess.

Hull, Cordell, *Peace and War: United States Foreign Policy, 1931-1941* (Washington, 1942).

Moore, John Bassett, *A Digest of International Law,* 8 vols. (Washington, 1906).

Papers Relating to the Foreign Relations of the United States, 1922, I, Washington, 1938. 1925, I, Washington, 1940.

Richardson, James D. (editor), *A Compilation of the Messages and Papers of the Presidents,* 10 vols. (Washington, 1904).

Senate Report No. 1716, 84 Cong., 2 sess., Calendar No. 1649. *Constitutional Amendment Relative to Treaties and Executive Agreements* (Washington, 1956).

United States Senate, 70 Cong., 2 sess., *Hearings before the Committee on Foreign Relations on the General Pact for the Renunciation of War* (Washington, 1928), I.

III. UNOFFICIAL DOCUMENTARY COLLECTIONS

Adams, Charles F. (editor), *The Works of John Adams,* 10 vols. (Boston: Little, Brown & Company, 1850-1856).

Baker, George E. (editor), *The Works of William H. Seward,* 3 vols. (New York: Redfield, 1853).

Baker, Ray Stannard and Dodd, William E. (editors), *The Public Papers of Woodrow Wilson: War and Peace,* 2 vols. (New York: Harper & Brothers, 1927).

[Hearst, William Randolph] *Selections from the Writings and Speeches of William Randolph Hearst* (San Francisco: Publication private, 1948).

Hoover, Herbert, *Addresses Upon the American Road, 1948-1950* (Stanford: Stanford University Press, 1951).

——————*Addresses Upon the American Road, 1950-1955* (Stanford: Stanford University Press, 1955).

Hughes, Charles E., *The Pathway of Peace* (New York: Harper & Brothers, 1925).

Latané, John H. (editor), *Development of the League of Nations Idea: Documents and Correspondence of Theodore Marburg,* 2 vols. (New York: The Macmillan Company, 1932).

Millis, Walter (editor), *The Forrestal Diaries* (New York: Viking Press, 1951).

Morison, Elting E. (editor), *The Letters of Theodore Roosevelt,* 8 vols. (Cambridge: Harvard University Press, 1951-1954).

Nevins, Allan (editor), *American Press Opinion, Washington to Coolidge* (Boston: D. C. Heath & Company, 1928).

Root, Elihu, *Men and Policies,* addresses collected and edited by Robert Bacon and James Brown Scott (Cambridge: Harvard University Press, 1926).

Rosenman, Samuel I. (editor), *The Public Papers and Addresses of Franklin D. Roosevelt,* 13 vols. (New York: Harper & Brothers, 1938-1950).

[Sumner, Charles] *Charles Sumner: His Complete Works,* 20 vols. (Boston: Lee & Shepard, 1900).

Vandenberg, Arthur H., Jr., and Morris, Joe E. (editors), *The Private Papers of Senator Vandenberg* (Boston: Houghton Mifflin Co., 1952).

IV. PAMPHLETS

Becker, Carl L., compiler, *America's War Aims and Peace Program* (Washington: The Committee on Public Information, 1918). [*War Information Series, No. 21*]

———————"German Attempts to Divide Belgium," in *World Peace Foundation Pamphlets*, I, No. 6 (August, 1918), pp. 307-340.

Bittleman, Alexander, *Parties and Issues in the Election Campaign* (Chicago: Workers' Party of America, 1924).

The Facts: *LaFollette-Wheeler Campaign Text Book* (Chicago: Publication private, 1924).

Hobbs, William H., *Would President Wilson's Covenant of the League of Nations Prevent War?* (Ann Arbor: League for the Preservation of American Independence, 1920).

Kellogg, Paul U., *Ten Years of the Foreign Policy Association* [N.p.], 1929.

Lippmann, Walter, *The Basic Problem of Democracy* (Boston: Atlantic Monthly Press, 1919).

Nearing, Scott, *Europe and the Next War* (New York: Rand Book Store, 1920).

O'Brien, Michael J., *Irish First in American History* (Chicago: Illinois chapter, Irish Historical Society, 1917).

Perkins, Dexter, *The Story of U.S. Foreign Policy* (New York: Foreign Policy Association, 1951), [*Headline Series No. 90*]

The Platform of the Class Struggle (New York: Workers' Library Publishers, 1928).

Report of the First Annual State Convention of the American Association for the Recognition of the Irish Republic (Butte: Montana State Directorate of the American Association for the Recognition of the Irish Republic, 1921).

Steele, Jack, *Peddlers of Hate*, [N.p.; N.d.]

Warburg, James P., *Turning Point Toward Peace* (New York: Current Affairs Press, 1955).

V. MISCELLANEOUS UNPUBLISHED MATERIAL

Beale, Howard K., Letter to author, December 5, 1954 with pertinent information on Professor Beale's opinion concerning Theodore Roosevelt's views on foreign affairs.

Blum, John M., "Nativism, Anti-Radicalism, and the Foreign Scare, 1917-1920." Ms. of a paper read by Professor Blum before the Boston meeting of the American Historical Association, 1949.

Burbank, Lyman B., "Internationalism in American Thought: 1919-1929." (Doctoral dissertation, New York University, June, 1950).

Freeman, Lorraine L., "Isolationist Carry-Over, 1933-1937." (M.A. thesis, University of Buffalo, June, 1955).

Freidel, Frank, "Franklin D. Roosevelt, Molder of an Opposition Foreign Policy." Ms. of a paper read by Professor Freidel before the Lexington meeting of the Mississippi Valley Historical Association, 1953).

Grande, Joseph A., "Republican Wartime Politics, 1941-1945." (M.A. thesis, University of Buffalo, June, 1955).

Horton, John T., "Imperialism Reconsidered." Ms. of a speech delivered to the student body of the University of Buffalo summer session, 1954.

——————Scrapbook, 1939-1941, containing letters and clippings relating to Professor Horton's work on various local committees in behalf of the allied cause.

Link, Arthur S., "The Middle West and the Coming of the First World War." Ms. of a paper read by Professor Link before the Chicago meeting of the Mississippi Valley Historical Association, 1952.

Marcus, Jacob R., photostat of notes made by Professor Marcus of Hebrew Union College of a conversation with Senator Gerald P. Nye at Cincinnati, September 18, 1941.

Randazzo, Sarah, Ms. of a speech delivered by Miss Randazzo in December, 1937, as member of the debate team of Grover Cleveland High School, Buffalo, arguing against the Neutrality Act of May 1, 1937.

Weaver, Norman, "The Effect of the Knights of the Ku Klux Klan on the Foreign Policy of the United States." Ms. of term paper written by Mr. Weaver in the course of his graduate studies at the University of Wisconsin.

VI. NEWSPAPERS

California
  Long Beach *Sun*, October 31, 1925.
  San Francisco *Call and Post*, March 4, 1923.

District of Columbia
  Washington *Post*, August 2, 1923; May 7, 1956.
  Washington *Star*, August 10, 1924.

Illinois
  [Chicago] *British American*, April 2, 1921.
  Chicago *Evening Post*, February 21, 1921.
  Chicago *Tribune*, 1918; 1922-1929; 1947-1955.

Indiana
  Fort Wayne *Journal-Gazette*, June 7, 1918.
  Indianapolis *Star*, May 31, 1918.

Massachusetts
  Boston *Herald*, July 22, 1921.
  [Boston] *Christian Science Monitor*, January 12, 1925.

Missouri
  Kansas City *Star*, 1919-1928.

New Jersey
  Newark *Evening News*, April 27, 1931.

New York
  Buffalo *Courier-Express*, 1940-1941; 1955-September 1, 1956.
  Buffalo *Evening News*, 1926-1927; 1941; 1953; 1955-September 1, 1956.
  [Ithaca] *Cornell Daily Sun*, January 6, 1920.
  New York *American*, June 4, 1927.
  New York *Evening Post*, November 3, 1920; February 21, 1921; January 7, 1924.
  New York *Herald Tribune*, 1928; 1933; 1952; 1955-August 1, 1956.
  New York *Sun*, 1919; 1924; 1925-1926.
  New York *Times*, 1920-1929; 1935; 1939; 1941; 1945; 1947; 1949; 1955-August 15, 1956.
  New York *World*, 1919-1921; 1925.

Ohio
  Cincinnati *Enquirer*, September 19, 1941.

Pennsylvania
  Philadelphia *North American*, May 30, 1918.

South Carolina
  Greenville *Piedmont*, September 23, 1924.

Wisconsin
  [Madison] *Wisconsin State Journal*, August 7, 1927.

VII. GENERAL LITERATURE

A. BIOGRAPHIES AND MEMOIRS

Baker, Ray Stannard, *Woodrow Wilson, Life and Letters,* 8 vols. (New York: Doubleday, Doran & Company, 1927-1939).

Blum, John M., *The Republican Roosevelt* (Cambridge: Harvard University Press, 1954).

Butler, Nicholas Murray, *Across the Busy Years,* 2 vols. (New York: Charles Scribner's Sons, 1939-1940).

Byrnes, James F., *Speaking Frankly* (New York: Harper & Brothers, 1947).

Carlson, Oliver, *Brisbane: A Candid Biography* (New York: Stackpole Sons, 1937).

Current, Richard N., *Secretary Stimson: A Study in Statecraft* (New Brunswick: Rutgers University Press, 1954).

Dawes, Charles G., *Notes As Vice President: 1928-1929* (Boston: Little, Brown & Company, 1935).

Dennett, Tyler, *John Hay* (New York: Dodd, Mead & Company, 1933).

Dennis, Charles H., *Victor Lawson: His Time and His Work* (Chicago: University of Chicago Press, 1935).

Freidel, Frank, *Franklin D. Roosevelt: The Ordeal* (Boston: Little, Brown and Company, 1954).

Garraty, John A., *Henry Cabot Lodge, A Biography* (New York: Alfred A. Knopf, 1953).

Grew, Joseph A., *Turbulent Era* [edited by Walter Johnson], 2 vols. (Boston: Houghton Mifflin Company, 1952).

Harrod, Roy F., *The Life of John Maynard Keynes* (London: The Macmillan Company, 1951).

Harvey, George, *Henry Clay Frick* (New York: Charles Scribner's Sons, 1928).

Hoover, Herbert, *The Memoirs of Herbert Hoover* [I]: *Years of Adventure, 1874-1920* (New York: The Macmillan Company, 1951).

——————*The Memoirs of Herbert Hoover* [II]: *The Cabinet and the Presidency, 1920-1933* (New York: The Macmillan Company, 1952).

Hull, Cordell, *The Memoirs of Cordell Hull,* 2 vols. (New York: The Macmillan Company, 1948).

Hunt, Frazier, *The Untold Story of Douglas MacArthur* (New York: Devin-Adair Company, 1954).

James, Henry, *Charles W. Eliot*, 2 vols. (Boston: Houghton Mifflin Company, 1930).

Jessup, Philip C., *Elihu Root*, 2 vols. (New York: Dodd, Mead & Company, 1938).

Johnson, Claudius O., *Borah of Idaho* (New York: Longmans, Green & Company, 1936).

Johnson, Walter, *William Allen White's America* (New York: Henry Holt & Company, 1947).

Johnson, Willis F., *George Harvey* (Boston: Houghton Mifflin Company, 1929).

Kerney, James, *The Political Education of Woodrow Wilson* (New York: The Century Company, 1926).

Lawrence, William, *Henry Cabot Lodge: A Biographical Sketch* (Boston: Houghton Mifflin Company, 1925).

Leopold, Richard W., *Elihu Root and the Conservative Tradition* (Boston: Little, Brown and Company, 1954).

Longworth, Alice R., *Crowded Hours* (New York: Charles Scribner's Sons, 1933).

Lovett, Robert M., *All Our Years* (New York: Viking Press, 1948).

Nevins, Allan, *Henry White* (New York: Harper & Brothers, 1930).

Osborn, George C., *John Sharp Williams: Planter Statesman of the Deep South* (University Station, Baton Rouge: Louisiana State University Press, 1943).

Pusey, Merle J., *Charles Evans Hughes*, 2 vols. (New York: The Macmillan Company, 1951).

Sherwood, Robert E., *Roosevelt and Hopkins: An Intimate History* (New York: Harper & Brothers, 1948).

Stimson, Henry L., and Bundy, McGeorge, *On Active Service in Peace and War* (New York: Harper & Brothers, 1948).

Truman, Harry S., *Memoirs by Harry S. Truman* [I]: *Year of Decisions* (Garden City: Doubleday & Company, 1955).

—————*Memoirs by Harry S. Truman* [II]: *Years of Trial and Hope* (Garden City: Doubleday & Company, 1956).

Watson, James E., *As I Knew Them* (Indianapolis: The Bobbs-Merrill Company, 1936).

White, William Allen, *Woodrow Wilson, the Man, His Times, and His Task* (Boston: Houghton Mifflin Company, 1924).

Willoughby, Charles A., and Chamberlain, John, *MacArthur: 1941-1951* (New York: McGraw-Hill Book Company, 1954).

B. General Works

Adams, George B., *The British Empire and a League of Nations* (New York: G. P. Putnam's Sons, 1919).

Adams, Henry, *The Degradation of the Democratic Dogma* [with an introduction by Brooks Adams] (New York: The Macmillan Company, 1920).

Adams, Randolph G., *History of the Foreign Policy of the United States* (New York: The Macmillan Company, 1924).

Allen, Frederick L., *Since Yesterday* (New York: Harper & Brothers, 1939).

——————*The Big Change* (New York: Harper & Brothers, 1952).

Almond, Gabriel A., *The American People and Foreign Policy* (New York: Harcourt, Brace & Company, 1950).

Altschul, Charles, *The American Revolution in our School Text Books* (New York: George H. Doran Company, 1917).

Bailey, Thomas A., *A Diplomatic History of the American People* (New York: Appleton-Century-Crofts Inc. [5th ed.], 1955).

——————*The Man in the Street* (New York: The Macmillan Company, 1948).

——————*Woodrow Wilson and the Great Betrayal* (New York: The Macmillan Company, 1945).

——————*Woodrow Wilson and the Lost Peace* (New York: The Macmillan Company, 1944).

Baker, Ray Stannard, *What Wilson Did at Paris* (Garden City: Doubleday, Page & Company, 1919).

Barck, Oscar T., and Blake, Nelson M., *Since 1900* (New York: The Macmillan Company [rev. ed.], 1952).

Barnes, Harry Elmer (editor), *Perpetual War for Perpetual Peace* (Caldwell, Idaho: Caxton Printers, 1953).

Bartlett, Ruhl J., *The League to Enforce Peace* (Chapel Hill: University of North Carolina Press, 1944).

Bassett, John S., *The League of Nations* (New York: Longmans, Green & Company, 1928).

Bass, John F., *The Peace Tangle* (New York: The Macmillan Company, 1920).

Bass, John F., and Moulton, Harold G., *America and the Balance Sheet of Europe* (New York: The Ronald Press Company, 1921).

Beard, Charles A., and Beard, Mary R., *America in Midpassage* (New York: The Macmillan Company, 1939).

——————*The Rise of American Civilization*, 2 vols. (New York: The Macmillan Company, 1927).

Beard, Charles A., *American Foreign Policy in the Making, 1932-1940* (New Haven: Yale University Press, 1946).

——————*President Roosevelt and the Coming of the War, 1941* (New Haven: Yale University Press, 1948).

——————*The Devil Theory of War* (New York: Vanguard Press, 1936).

——————*The Open Door at Home* [with the collaboration of G.H.E. Smith] (New York: The Macmillan Company, 1934).

Beard, Charles A. (editor), *Whither Mankind* (New York: Longmans, Green & Company, 1928).

Belmont, Perry, *National Isolation an Illusion* (New York: G. P. Putnam's Sons, 1925).

Bemis, Samuel F., *A Diplomatic History of the United States* (New York: Henry Holt and Company [3rd ed.], 1950).

Blakeslee, George H., *The Recent Foreign Policy of the United States* (New York: Abingdon Press, 1925).

Boeckel, Florence B., *Between Peace and War: A Handbook for Peace Workers* (New York: The Macmillan Company, 1928).

Borchard, Edwin M., *American Foreign Policy* (Indianapolis: National Foundation Press, 1946).

Borchard, Edwin M., and Lage, William P., *Neutrality for the United States* (New Haven: Yale University Press [2nd ed.], 1940).

Brinton, Crane, *United States and Britain* (Cambridge: Harvard University Press, 1945).

Buehrig, Edward H., *Woodrow Wilson and the Balance of Power* (Bloomington: Indiana University Press, 1955).

Buell, Raymond Leslie, *Isolated American* (New York: Alfred A. Knopf, 1940).

Bundy, McGeorge (editor), *The Pattern of Responsibility* (Boston: Houghton Mifflin Company, 1952).

Butler, Nicholas Murray, *The Path to Peace* (New York: Charles Scribner's Sons, 1930).

Carter, John F., *Conquest: America's Painless Imperialism* (New York: Harcourt, Brace and Company, 1928).

Chafee, Zechariah Jr., *Freedom of Speech* (New York: Harcourt, Brace & Company, 1920).

Chamberlin, William H., *America's Second Crusade* (Chicago: Henry Regnery Company, 1950).

Churchill, Winston S., *Their Finest Hour* (*The Second World War*, Vol. II, Boston: Houghton Mifflin Company, 1949).

——————*The Grand Alliance* (*The Second World War*, Vol. III, Boston: Houghton Mifflin Company, 1950).

Colcord, Samuel, *The Great Deception* (New York: Boni & Liveright, 1921).

Cole, Wayne S., *American First* (Madison: University of Wisconsin Press, 1953).

Commager, Henry S. (editor), *Living Ideas in America* (New York: Harper & Brothers, 1951).

Cook, Thomas I., and Moos, Malcolm, *Power Through Purpose: The Realism of Idealism as a Basis for Foreign Policy* (Baltimore: Johns Hopkins Press, 1954).

Croly, Herbert, *The Promise of American Life* (New York: The Macmillan Company, 1909).

Culbertson, William S., *International Economic Policies: A Survey of the Economics of Diplomacy* (New York: D. Appleton & Company, 1925).

Curti, Merle, *Peace or War: The American Struggle, 1636-1936* (W. W. Norton & Company, 1936).

Davies, Joseph E., *Mission to Moscow* (New York: Simon & Schuster, 1941).

Davis, George T., *A Navy Second to None* (New York: Harcourt, Brace & Company, 1940).

Davis, Jerome, *Contemporary Social Movements* (New York: The Century Company, 1930).

Dealey, James Q., *Foreign Policies of the United States* (Boston: Ginn & Co., 1926).

Dennett, Tyler, *A Better World* (New York: George H. Doran Company, 1920).

Donovan, Robert J., *Eisenhower: The Inside Story* (New York: Harper & Brothers, 1956).

Drummond, Donald F., *The Passing of American Neutrality* (Ann Arbor: University of Michigan Press, 1955).

Dulles, Foster Rhea, *America's Rise to World Power, 1898-1954* (New York: Harper & Brothers, 1954).

Dulles, John Foster, *War or Peace* (New York: The Macmillan Company, 1950).

Engelbrecht, Helmuth C., and Hanighen, F. C., *Merchants of Death* (New York: Dodd, Mead & Company, 1934).

Feis, Herbert, *The Diplomacy of the Dollar: First Era, 1919-1932* (Baltimore: Johns Hopkins Press, 1950).

Ferrell, Robert H., *Peace in Their Time: The Origins of the Kellogg-Briand Pact* (New Haven: Yale University Press, 1952).

Fish, Carl R., *American Diplomacy* (New York: Henry Holt & Company [4th ed.], 1923).

—————(compiler), *Foundations of American Neutrality* (Madison, 1922), [University of Wisconsin History reprint No. 1].

Fisher, Charles, *The Columnists* (New York: Howell, Soskin & Company, 1944).

Fleming, Denna F., *The United States and the World Court* (Garden City: Doubleday, Doran & Company, 1945).

—————*The United States and World Organization, 1920-1933* (New York: Columbia University Press, 1938).

Flynn, John T., *While You Slept: Our Tragedy in Asia and Who Made It* (New York: Devin-Adair Company, 1951).

Fosdick, Dorothy, *Common Sense and World Affairs* (New York: Harcourt, Brace and Company, 1955).

Foster, John W., *A Century of American Diplomacy* (Boston: Houghton Mifflin Company, 1900).

Frank, Waldo R., *The Re-discovery of America* (New York: Charles Scribner's Sons, 1929).

Garner, James W., *American Foreign Policies* (New York: New York University Press, 1928).

Gibson, Hugh, *The Road to Foreign Policy* (Garden City: Doubleday, Doran and Company, 1944).

Goldman, Eric F., *Rendezvous with Destiny* (New York: Alfred A. Knopf, 1952).

Grattan, C. Hartley, *The Deadly Parallel* (New York: Stackpole Sons, 1939).

—————*Why We Fought* (New York: Vanguard Press, 1929).

Guthrie, William D., *The League of Nations and Miscellaneous Addresses* (New York: Columbia University Press, 1923).

Haas, Ernst B., and Whiting, Allen S., *Dynamics of International Relations* (New York: McGraw-Hill Book Company, 1956).

Halle, Louis J., *Civilization and Foreign Policy* (New York: Harper and Brothers, 1955).

Harriman, Edward A., *The Constitution of the Crossroads* (New York: George H. Doran Company, 1925).

Herzog, Siegfried, *The Future of German Industrial Exports* [with an introduction by Herbert Hoover, Vernon Kellogg, and Frederic C. Walcott] (Garden City: Doubleday, Page & Company, 1918).

Hill, David J., *American World Policies* (New York: George H. Doran Company, 1920).

——————*Present Problems in Foreign Policy* (New York: D. Appleton & Company, 1919).

——————*The Problem of a World Court: the Story of an Unrealized American Idea* (New York: Longmans, Green & Company, 1927).

Holcombe, Arthur N., *The Political Parties of Today* (New York: Harper & Brothers, 1924).

Hoover, Herbert, *American Individualism* (Garden City: Doubleday, Page & Company, 1922).

Howland, Charles P., *Survey of American Foreign Relations, 1928* (New Haven: Yale University Press, 1928).

Hughes, Charles E., *Our Relations to the Nations of the Western Hemisphere* (Princeton: Princeton University Press, 1928).

Johnson, Gerald W., *Incredible Tale* (New York: Harper & Brothers, 1950).

——————*Woodrow Wilson* [with the collaboration of the editors of *Look* Magazine] (New York: Harper & Brothers, 1944).

Johnson, Walter, *The Battle Against Isolationism* (Chicago: University of Chicago Press, 1944).

Jordan, David S., *Democracy and World Relations* (Yonkers: World Book Company, 1918).

Kallen, Horace M., *The Structure of Lasting Peace* (Boston: Marshall Jones Company, 1918).

Kennan, George F., *American Diplomacy, 1900-1950* (Chicago: University of Chicago Press, 1951).

——————*Realities of American Foreign Policy* (Princeton: Princeton University Press, 1954).

Kent, Frank R., *The Democratic Party: A History* (New York: The Century Company, 1928).

Keynes, John Maynard, *The Economic Consequences of the Peace* (New York: Harcourt, Brace & Company, 1920).

Langer, William L., and Gleason, S. Everett, *The Challenge to Isolation* (New York: Harper & Brothers, 1952).

——————*The Undeclared War, 1940-1941* (New York: Harper & Brothers, 1953).

Lape, Esther E. (editor), *Ways to Peace* (New York: Charles Scribner's Sons, 1924).

Latané, John H., *From Isolation to Leadership* (Garden City: Doubleday, Page & Company, 1918).

Latourette, Kenneth S., *The Christian Basis of World Democracy* (New York: Association Press, 1919).

Lewis, Sinclair, *Babbitt* (New York: Harcourt, Brace & Company, 1922).

Link, Arthur S., *American Epoch: A History of the United States Since the 1890's* (New York: Alfred A. Knopf, 1955).

——————*Woodrow Wilson and the Progressive Era* (New York: Harper & Brothers, 1954).

Lippmann, Walter, *Essays in the Public Philosophy* (Boston: Little, Brown & Company, 1955).

——————*Isolation and Alliances: An American Speaks to the British* (Boston: Little, Brown & Company, 1952).

——————*The Political Scene: An Essay on the Victory of 1918* (New York: Henry Holt & Company, 1919).

——————*Public Opinion* (New York: Harcourt, Brace & Company, 1922).

——————*U. S. Foreign Policy: Shield of the Republic* (Boston: Little, Brown & Company, 1943).

——————*U. S. War Aims* (Boston: Little, Brown & Company, 1944).

Lodge, Henry C., *The Senate and the League of Nations* (New York: Charles Scribner's Sons, 1925).

Lubell, Samuel, *The Future of American Politics* (New York: Harper & Brothers, 1952).

Luthin, Reinhard H., *American Demagogues: Twentieth Century* (Boston: Beacon Press, 1954).

Lydgate, William A., *What Our People Think* (New York: Thomas Y. Crowell Company, 1944).

McCartan, Patrick, *With De Valera in Amercia* (New York: Bretano, 1932).

McElroy, Robert M., *The Pathway of Peace: An Interpretation of Some British-American Crises* (New York: The Macmillan Company, 1927).

McKay, Donald C., *The United States and France* (Cambridge: Harvard University Press, 1951).

McKay, Kenneth C., *The Progressive Movement of 1924* (New York: Columbia University Press, 1947).

McLaughlin, Andrew C., *Steps in the Development of American Democracy* (New York: Abingdon Press, 1920).

Madariaga, Salvador de, *Disarmament* (New York: Coward-McCann, Inc., 1929).

Marshall, Charles B., *The Limits of Foreign Policy* (New York: Henry Holt & Company, 1954).

May, Arthur J., *Europe and Two World Wars* (New York: Charles Scribner's Sons, 1947).

Miller, Charles Grant, *The Poisoned Loving-cup: United States Histories Falsified through pro-British Propaganda in Sweet Name of Amity* (Chicago: National Historical Society, 1928).

—————*Treason to American Tradition* (N.p., 1921?).

Miller, David Hunter, *The Peace Pact of Paris* (New York: G. P. Putnam's Sons, 1928).

Millis, Walter, *Road to War: America 1914-1917* (Boston: Houghton Mifflin Company, 1935).

Moore, John Bassett, *American Diplomacy: its Spirit and Achievements* (New York: Harper & Brothers, 1905).

Morgenstern, George, *Pearl Harbor: The Story of the Secret War* (New York: Devin-Adair Company, 1947).

Morgenthau, Hans J., *In Defense of the National Interest* (New York: Alfred A. Knopf, 1951).

Morrison, Charles C., *The Outlawry of War: A Constructive Policy for World Peace* (Chicago: Willett, Clark & Colby, 1927).

Mott, T. Bentley, *Myron T. Herrick, Friend of France* (Garden City: Doubleday, Doran & Company, 1929).

Mowrer, Edgar A., *Challenge and Decision* (McGraw-Hill Book Company, 1950).

—————*The Nightmare of American Foreign Policy* (New York: Alfred A. Knopf, 1948).

—————*This American World* (New York: J. H. Sears Company, Inc., 1928).

Mowrer, Paul S., *Our Foreign Affairs* (New York: E. P. Dutton & Company, 1924).

Murray, Robert K., *Red Scare: A Study in National Hysteria, 1919-1920* (Minneapolis: University of Minnesota Press, 1955).

Myers, William S., *The Foreign Policies of Herbert Hoover, 1929-1933* (New York: Charles Scribner's Sons, 1940).

Nearing, Scott, *Labor and the League of Nations* (New York: Rand Book Store, 1919).

—————*The American Empire* (New York: Rand Book Store, 1921).

Nevins, Allan, *The New Deal and World Affairs* (New Haven: Yale University Press, 1950). [Chronicles of America Series, Vol. LXVI]

Nevins, Allan, and Hacker, Louis M., *The United States and its Place in World Affairs, 1918-1943* (Boston: D. C. Heath and Company, 1943).

Niebuhr, Reinhold, *Christianity and Power Politics* (New York: Charles Scribner's Sons, 1946 ed.).

——————*The Irony of American History* (New York: Charles Scribner's Sons, 1952).

Nock, Albert J., *The Myth of a Guilty Nation* (New York: Viking Press, 1922).

O'Brien, Michael J., *A Hidden Phase of American History* (New York: Devin-Adair Company, 1919).

Ogg, Frederic A., and Beard, Charles A., *National Governments and the World War* (New York: The Macmillan Company, 1919).

Osgood, Robert E., *Ideals and Self-Interest in America's Foreign Relations* (Chicago: University of Chicago Press, 1953).

Page, Kirby, *Dollars and World Peace* (New York: George H. Doran Company, 1927).

——————(editor), *Recent Gains in American Civilization* (New York: Harcourt, Brace & Company, 1928).

Paxson, Frederic L., *American Democracy and the World War*, 3 vols. (Boston: Houghton Mifflin Company, 1936-1948).

Pearson, Drew and Brown, Constantine, *The American Diplomatic Game* (Garden City: Doubleday, Doran & Company, 1935).

Pease, Theodore C., *The United States* (New York: Harcourt, Brace & Company, 1927).

Perkins, Dexter, *Hands Off* (Boston: Little, Brown & Company, 1941).

——————*The Evolution of American Foreign Policy* (New York: Oxford University Press, 1948).

——————*The Evolution of America Foreign Policy* (New York: Oxford University Press, 1948).

Phillips, W. Alison, *The Revolution in Ireland, 1906-1923* (London: Longmans, Green & Company, 1923).

Pierce, Bessie L., *Public Opinion and the Teaching of History in the United States* (New York: Alfred A. Knopf, 1926).

Pillsbury, Walter B., *The Psychology of Nationalism and Internationalism* (New York: D. Appleton & Company, 1919).

Pratt, Julius W., *A History of United States Foreign Policy* (New York: Prentice-Hall Inc., 1955).

Pringle, Henry F., *The Life and Times of William Howard Taft*, 2 vols. (New York: Farrar & Rinehart, 1939).

Rappard, William E., *International Relations as Viewed from Geneva* (New Haven: Yale University Press, 1925).

Reinsch, Paul S., *Secret Diplomacy* (New York: Harcourt, Brace & Company, 1922).

Rogers, Will, *Letters of a Self-Made Diplomat to His President* (New York: Boni & Liveright, 1926).

Roosevelt, Franklin D., *Whither Bound?* [Lectures at Milton Academy, May, 1926] (Boston: Houghton Mifflin Company, 1926).

Ross, Edward A., *What Is America?* (New York: The Century Company, 1919).

Rovere, Richard H., and Schlesinger, Arthur M., Jr., *The General and The President* (New York: Farrar, Strauss & Young, 1951).

Santayana, George, *Character and Opinion in the United States* (New York: Charles Scribner's Sons, 1920).

Saveth, Edward N., *Understanding the American Past* (Boston: Little, Brown & Company, 1954).

Scott, James B., *James Madison's Notes of Debates in the Federal Convention of 1787 and their Relation to a More Perfect Society of Nations* (New York: Oxford University Press, 1918).

Seymour, Charles, *American Diplomacy During the World War* (Baltimore: Johns Hopkins Press, 1934).

—————*American Neutrality, 1914-1917* (New Haven: Yale University Press, 1935).

Simonds, Frank H., *American Foreign Policy in the Post-War Years* (Baltimore: Johns Hopkins Press, 1935).

—————*Can America Stay at Home?* (New York: Harper & Brothers, 1932).

—————*Can Europe Keep the Peace?* (New York: Harper & Brothers, 1931).

—————*How Europe Made Peace Without America* (New York: Doubleday, Doran & Company, 1927).

Slosson, Preston W., *The Great Crusade and After, 1914-1928* (New York: The Macmillan Company, 1931). [History of American Life, Vol. XII]

Smith, Henry N., *Virgin Land: The American West as Symbol and Myth* (Cambridge: Harvard University Press, 1950).

Snow, Alpheus H., *The American Philosophy of Government* (New York: G. P. Putnam's Sons, 1921).

Stearns, Harold E., *Liberalism In America* (New York: Boni & Liveright, 1919).

Stoner, John E., *S. O. Levinson and the Pact of Paris* (Chicago: University of Chicago Press, 1942).

Storey, Moorfield, *Problems of To-Day* (Boston: Houghton Mifflin Company, 1920).

Straight, Michael W., *Make This the Last War* (New York: Harcourt, Brace & Company, 1943).

Taft, Robert A., *A Foreign Policy for Americans* (Garden City: Doubleday & Company, 1951).

Tansill, Charles C., *America Goes to War* (Boston: Little, Brown & Company, 1938).

——————*Back Door to War: The Roosevelt Foreign Policy* (Chicago: Henry Regnery Company, 1952).

Tardieu, André, *France and America* (Boston: Houghton Mifflin Company, 1927).

Thayer, William Roscoe, *Democracy: Discipline: Peace* (Boston: Houghton Mifflin Company, 1919).

Turner, John Kenneth, *Hands Off Mexico* (New York: Rand Book Store, 1920).

The United States in World Affairs, 1947-1948 (New York: Published for Council on Foreign Relations by Harper & Brothers, 1948).

Van Alstyne, Richard W., *American Crisis Diplomacy* (Stanford: Stanford University Press, 1952).

——————*American Diplomacy in Action: A Series of Case Studies* (Stanford: Stanford University Press, 1944).

Vandenberg, Arthur H., *The Trail of a Tradition* (New York: G. P. Putnam's Sons, 1926).

Warburg, James P., *The United States in a Changing World* (New York: G. P. Putnam's Sons, 1954).

Welles, Sumner, *Seven Decisions that Shaped History* (New York: Harper & Brothers, 1950).

Weyl, Nathaniel, *The Battle Against Disloyalty* (New York: Thomas Y. Crowell Company, 1951).

White, Morton G., *Social Thought In America* (New York: Viking Press, 1949).

Whitney, Edson L., *The American Peace Society: a Centennial History* (Washington: The American Peace Society, 1928).

Wilbur, William H., *Guideposts to the Future: A New American Foreign Policy* (Chicago: Henry Regnery Company, 1954).

Williams, Benjamin H., *The Economic Foreign Policy of the United States* (New York: McGraw-Hill Book Company, 1929).

Willkie, Wendell L., *One World* (New York: Simon & Schuster, 1943).

Wilmot, Chester, *The Struggle for Europe* (New York: Harper & Brothers, 1952).

Winter, Ella, *Red Virtue* (New York: Harcourt, Brace & Company, 1953).

Wisconsin, University, *War Book of the University of Wisconsin.* Papers on the Causes and issues of the war by members of the faculty (Madison, 1918).

Wister, Owen, *Straight Deal: or the Ancient Grudge* (New York: The Macmillan Company, 1920).

Young, Ernest W., *The Wilson Administration and the Great War* (Boston: R. G. Badger, 1922).

Zacharias, Ellis M., *Behind Closed Doors: The Secret History of the Cold War* (New York: G. P. Putnam's Sons, 1950).

VIII. ARTICLES

"A Golden A.E.F. to Save Europe Again," *Literary Digest*, LXXV, 5-7 (December 30, 1922).

Acheson, Dean, "The Parties and Foreign Policy," *Harper's*, CCXI, 29-34 (November, 1955).

Adams, Brooks, "The Spanish War and the Equilibrium of the World," *Forum*, XXV, 641-651 (August, 1898).

Adams, James T., "History and the Lower Criticism," *Atlantic*, CXXXII, 308-317 (September, 1923).

Addams, Jane, "What I Saw in Europe," *LaFollette's Magazine*, 20-21 (February, 1922).

Adler, Selig, "Isolationism Since 1914," *American Scholar*, XXI, 335-344 (Summer, 1952).

————"The Congressional Election of 1918," *South Atlantic Quarterly*, XXXVI, 447-465 (October, 1937).

————"The War-Guilt Question and American Disillusionment, 1918-1928," *Journal of Modern History*, XXIII, 1-28 (March, 1951).

"African Troops on the Rhine," *New Republic*, XXVI, 29-30 (March 9, 1921).

"America's Refusal to Go to Geneva," *Literary Digest*, LXXIII, 18-19 (April 15, 1922).

"An Open Letter to Woodrow Wilson," *Current Opinion,* LXXII, 433-434 (April, 1922).

"Arms and Men," *Fortune,* IX, 53-57ff. (March, 1934).

Armstrong, Hamilton Fish, "Last Time," *Foreign Affairs,* XXIII, 349-377 (April, 1945).

——————"On an Anniversary," *ibid.,* XXVI, 1-4 (October, 1947).

Armstrong, John P., "The Enigma of Senator Taft and Foreign Policy," *Review of Politics,* XVII, 206-231 (April, 1955).

Ascoli, Max, Horton, Philip, and Wertenbaker, Charles, "The China Lobby," *Reporter,* IV, 2-24 (April 15, 1952); 4-24 (April 29, 1952).

"Backsliding to Isolationism?" *Catholic World,* CLXIII, 297 (July, 1946).

Baker, Newton D., review article, *American Historical Review,* XXXIV, 842-844 (July, 1929).

Barnes, Harry Elmer, "Woodrow Wilson," *American Mercury,* I, 479-490 (April, 1924).

Barton, Bruce, "Are We Biting Off More Than We Can Chew?" *Reader's Digest,* LIII, 45-48 (December, 1948).

Bartlett, Ruhl J., review article, *Mississippi Valley Historical Review,* XXXIX, 580-581 (December, 1952).

Beard, Charles A., "Giddy Minds and Foreign Quarrels," *Harper's,* CLXXIX, 337-351 (September, 1939).

——————"Heroes and Villains of the World War," *Current History,* XXIV, 730-735 (August, 1926).

——————"Prospects for Peace," *Harper's,* CLVIII, 320-330 (February, 1929).

Becker, Carl L., "A Chronicle of Facts," *New Republic,* XXV, 382-383 (February 23, 1921).

——————"Europe Through the Eyes of the Middle West," *New Europe,* XV, 98-104 (May 13, 1920).

——————"Jacob Gould Schurman," in *Yearbook of the American Philosophical Society, 1942,* 378-381.

——————"Tender and Tough Minded Historians," *Dial,* LXV, 106-109 (August 15, 1918).

——————"The New Map of Europe," *New Republic,* XX, 26 (November 26, 1919).

——————"The Shaking World," *Nation,* CXV, 552-553 (November 22, 1922).

——————unsigned review articles in *ibid.,* CVIII, 328-329 (March 1, 1919); CIX, 225-227 (August 16, 1919).

Beloff, Max, "Historians in a Revolutionary Age," *Foreign Affairs,* XXIX, 248-262 (January, 1929).

——————"The Foundations of American Policy—II," *Spectator,* CXCIV, 247-249.

Bemis, Samuel F., "A Clarifying Foreign Policy," *Yale Review,* XXV, 221-240 (December, 1935).

——————"The Background of Washington's Foreign Policy," *ibid.,* XVI, 316-336 (January, 1927).

——————"The Shifting Strategy of American Defense and Diplomacy," *Virginia Quarterly Review,* XXIV, 321-335 (Summer, 1948).

——————"Washington's Farewell Address: A Foreign Policy of Independence," *American Historical Review,* XXXIX, 250-268 (January, 1934).

Bent, Silas, "International Window-Smashing," *Harper's,* CLVII, 421-428 (September, 1928).

Beveridge, Albert J., "What to do About Mexico," *Collier's,* LIX, p. 5 ff. (May 19, 1917).

——————"Pitfalls of a 'League of Nations'," *North American Review,* CCIX, 305-314 (March, 1919).

Billington, Ray A., "The Origins of Middle Western Isolationism," *Political Science Quarterly,* LX, 44-64 (March, 1945).

Binkley, Robert C., "Ten Years of Peace Conference History," *Journal of Modern History,* I, 607-629 (December, 1929).

Bittelman, Alexander, "Kellogg in Paris—Johnson in the Senate," *Workers' Monthly,* 201-203 (March, 1923).

"Blackening a Black Record," *Labor Herald,* II, 28 (May, 1923).

Blakeslee, George H., "The Foreign Policy of the United States," in Quincy Wright (editor), *Interpretations of American Foreign Policy* (Chicago: University of Chicago Press, 1930), 3-35.

——————"Will Democracy Alone Make the World Safe?" *Proceedings of the American Antiquarian Society,* XXVII, new series, 358-374 (October, 1917).

Bliven, Bruce, "This is Where I Came In," *New Republic,* XCIII, 245-246 (January 5, 1938).

Bolles, Blair, "How Will MacArthur Debate Affect U.S. Policy?" *Foreign Policy Bulletin,* XXX, 1-2, (May 11, 1951).

Boorstin, Daniel J., "Selling the President to the People," *Commentary,* XX, 421-427 (November, 1955).

Borah, William E., "The Embargo and European Power Politics," *Vital Speeches,* VI, 21-23 (October 15, 1939).

——————"Washington's Foreign Policy," *Daughters of the American Revolution Magazine,* LIII, 187-191 (April, 1919).

Borchard, Edwin M., "Common Sense in Foreign Relations," *Journal of International Relations*, XI, 27-44 (July, 1920).

——————"League of Nations A Menace," *La Follette's Magazine*, 65-66 (April, 1919).

——————"Limitations on the Functions of International Courts," *The Annals of the American Academy of Political and Social Science*,* XCVI, 132-137 (July, 1921).

——————"Our Foreign Policy," *Yale Review*, X, 511-530 (April, 1921).

——————"United States Foreign Policy," *American Journal of International Law*, XLIII, 333-335 (April, 1949).

Bourne, Randolph, "The War and the Intellectuals," *Seven Arts*, II, 133-146 (June, 1917).

Brock, Henry I., "Chronicle and Comment," *Unpartizan Review*, XV, 205-221 (January-March, 1921).

Brogan, Dennis W., "The American Enigma," *Spectator*, CXCV, 257-258 (August 19, 1955).

Browder, Earl W., "Rear Admirals and Russian Recognition," *Workers' Monthly*, p. 243ff. (April 1, 1925).

Brown, Philip M., "American Aloofness," *Weekly Review*, III, 312-313 (October 13, 1920).

Buck, Philo M., Jr., "Pacifism in the Middle West," *Nation*, CIV, 595-597 (May 17, 1917).

Bullard, Robert Lee, "The Possibility of Disarmament by International Agreement," *The Annals*, XCVI, 49-52 (July, 1921).

Burt, Struthers, "Furor Britannicus," *Saturday Evening Post*, CC, Part I, p. 6ff. (August 20, 1927).

Butler, Nicholas Murray, "The Development of the International Mind," *International Conciliation*, No. 192, 775-785 (November, 1923).

"Calvin Coolidge," *Fortnightly Review*, CXIV, 849-863 (December 1, 1923).

Capper, Arthur, "The American Farmer and Foreign Policy," *Foreign Affairs*, I, 127-135 (June 15, 1923).

Carleton, William G., "A New Era in World Politics?" *Virginia Quarterly Review*, XXXI, 353-372 (Summer, 1955).

——————"Isolationism and the Middle West," *Mississippi Valley Historical Review*, XXXIII, 377-390 (December, 1946).

——————"There is Still a Middle Way," *Virginia Quarterly Review*, XXVII, 352-366 (Summer, 1951).

* Hereafter *The Annals*

Cartier, Raymond, "Pourquoi les Américains sont-ils détestés," Paris *Match,* March 24, 1956, p. 20ff.

Castle, William R., Jr., "America and the League," New York *Herald Tribune,* October 8, 1933.

Chamberlin, William H., "Five Delusions of Appeasement," *American Mercury,* LXXXI, 51-56 (September, 1955).

"Clues to the Coolidge Foreign Policy," *Literary Digest,* LXXVIII, 9-11 (September 1, 1923).

Clarke, John H., "The Evolution of a Substitute for War, and How America Can Share in it without Becoming Entangled in European Political Affairs," *Proceedings of the Sixty-Fifth Annual Meeting of the National Education Association* [Seattle, Washington, July 3-8, 1927] LXV, 718-729 (1927).

—————"The Relation of the United States to the Permanent Court of International Justice," *The Annals,* CXX, 115-124 (July, 1925).

—————"What I Am Trying to Do." *World's Work,* XLVI, 581-584 (October, 1923).

Corwin, Edward S., "Wilson and the Senate," *The Review,* I, 228-229 (July 26, 1919).

Cruikshank, R. J., "The Dear Dead Days of Coolidge's Isolation," *United Nations World,* II, 24-26 (December, 1948).

"Cyprus: Too Much Death," *Time,* LXVII, 25-26 (January 9, 1956).

Dangerfield, Royden J., "The Senatorial Diplomats," *American Mercury,* XXXVII, 359-362 (March, 1936).

Davis, John W., "The Permanent Bases of American Foreign Policy," *Foreign Affairs,* X, 1-12 (October, 1931).

Dean, Vera M., "U. S. Role in U. N. Basic Issue in 'Greater Debate'," *Foreign Policy Bulletin,* XXX, 1-2 (May 4, 1951).

—————"Would 'New United Front' Lead to New Isolationism?" *ibid.,* XXIX, 1-2 (May 5, 1950).

Dennett, Tyler, " 'Blessed Chaos' in Spain," *New Republic,* XIX, 86-87 (May 17, 1919).

Dennis, Alfred L. P., "Foreign Policy and Party Conventions," *North America Review,* CCXIX, 746-757 (June, 1924).

Dewey, John, "Ethics and International Relations," *Foreign Affairs,* I, 85-95 (March 15, 1923).

—————"If War Were Outlawed," *New Republic,* XXXIV, 234-235 (April 25, 1923).

—————"Our National Dilemma," *ibid.,* XXII, 117-118 (March 24, 1920).

——————"Shall We Join the League?" *ibid.,* XXXIV, 36-37 (March 7, 1923).

——————"The Discrediting of Idealism," *ibid.,* XX, 285-287 (October 8, 1919).

Dewey, Thomas E., "Dewey Opposes Trend Toward Isolationism," *Foreign Policy Bulletin,* XXIX, 1-2 (May 12, 1950).

——————"Enlarge North Atlantic Treaty," *Vital Speeches,* XVII, 290-293 (March 1, 1951).

Diamond William, "'American Sectionalism and World Organization' by Frederick Jackson Turner," *American Historical Review,* XLVII, 545-551 (April, 1942).

Dickinson, Edwin D., "The United States and World Organization," *American Political Science Review,* XVI, 183-193 (May, 1922).

"Diplomacy: The Morality of Give and Take," *Time,* LXVIII, 23 (July 23, 1956).

Dodd, William E., "The Converging Democracies," *Yale Review,* VIII, 449-465 (April, 1919).

——————"The End of Europe As A Leader of Mankind," *World's Work,* XXXVIII, 254-257 (July, 1919).

Donovan, John C., "Congressional Isolationists and the Roosevelt Foreign Policy," *World Politics,* III, 299-316 (April, 1951).

Drexel, Constance, "The Foreign Correspondent," *New Republic,* XXXVII, 252-254 (January 30, 1924).

Dulles, Foster Rhea, "Wellsprings of American Policy," *Saturday Review,* XXXV, 22-23 (October 11, 1952).

Earle, Edward Mead, "A Hhalf Century of American Foreign Policy: Our Stake In Europe, 1898-1948," *Political Science Quarterly,* LXIV, 168-188 (June, 1949).

Eliot, Charles W., "The Next American Contribution to Civilization," *Foreign Affairs,* I, 49-65 (September 15, 1922).

Eulaw, Heinz, "Mover and Shaker: Walter Lippmann as a Young Man," *Antioch Review,* XI, 291-312 (September, 1951).

Evans, Hiram W., "The Klan's Fight For Americanism," *North American Review,* CCXXIII, 33-63 (March-May, 1926).

Flanders, Dwight P., "Geopolitics and American Post-war Policy," *Political Science Quarterly,* LX, 578-585 (December, 1945).

Fosdick, Raymond B., "The League as an Instrument of Liberalism," *Atlantic,* CXXVI, 553-563 (October, 1920).

——————"The State Department and the League of Nations," *Review of Reviews,* LXIX, 378-382 (April, 1924).

France, Joseph I., "The Concert of Nations," *The Annals,* XCVI, 141-146 (July, 1921).

Frankfurter, Felix, "French Policy and Peace in Europe," *New Republic*, XXIV, 138-140 (October 6, 1920).

Gannett, Lewis S., "Williamstown," *Nation*, CXV, 247-248 (September 13, 1922).

"Germany 1914; France 1923," *New Republic*, XXXIV, 54-55 (March 14, 1923).

Gibbons, Herbert A., "The Evolution of the Foreign Policy of the United States Since the Spanish-American War," *New World*, I, 119-139 (May, 1919).

——————"Wanted: An American Foreign Policy," *Century*, C, 474-481 (August, 1920).

Glazer, Nathan, "The American People and the Cold War Policy," *Commentary*, XVII, 461-465 (May, 1954).

Goldman, Eric F., "What Is Prosperity Doing to Our Political Parties?" *Saturday Review*, XXXVIII, p. 9ff. (October 8, 1955).

Goodrich, Nathaniel H., "Anti-Semitic Propaganda," *Contemporary Jewish Record*, II, 20-26 (November-December, 1939).

——————"Nazi Interference in American Affairs," *ibid*, III, 370-380 (July-August, 1940).

——————"Politics and Prejudices," *ibid.*, 624-626 (November-December, 1940).

Graham, James M., "American History A La Mode," *Catholic World*, CXVII, 182-195 (May, 1923).

Grantham, Dewey W., Jr., "The Southern Senators and the League of Nations," *North Carolina Historical Review*, XXVI, 187-205 (April, 1949).

Griffin, Charles C., review article, *American Historical Review*, LIV, 382-386 (January, 1949).

Hackett, Francis, "The Impasse in Ireland," *New Republic*, XXIV, 160-163 (October 13, 1920).

Handlin, Oscar, "How U.S. Anti-Semitism Really Began," *Commentary*, XI, 541-548 (June, 1951).

——————"The Immigration Fight Has Only Begun," *ibid.*, XIV, 1-7 (July, 1952).

Hard, William, "The New World Court," *Nation*, CXXII, 6-7 (January 6, 1926); 30-31 (January 13, 1926); 58-60 (January 20, 1926).

"Harding," *New Republic*, XXIII, 99-100 (June 23, 1920).

Harley, Lewis R., "A New Treatment of American History," *Education*, XL, 15-25 (September, 1919).

Hart, Albert B., "Treasonable Textbooks and True Patriotism," *Current History*, XXVII, 630-632 (February, 1928).

Harvey, George, "A Forlorn Continent," *North American Review*, CCXXI, 577-581 (June-August, 1925).

——————"The Great Lesson of the Elections," *ibid.*, CCXX, 193-195 (December, 1924).

——————"The Independence of America," *ibid.*, CCIX, 433-445 (April, 1919).

——————"The Plight of England," *ibid.*, CCXXII, 193-208 (December, 1925-February, 1926).

——————"Uncle Shylock Looks Abroad," *ibid.*, CCXXIII, 385-399 (September-November, 1926).

Hayes, Carlton, J. H., "The American Frontier — Frontier of What?" *American Historical Review*, LI, 199-216 (January, 1946).

Hicks, Granville, "The Liberals Who Haven't Learned," *Commentary*, XI, 319-329 (April, 1951).

Hill, David J., "American Cooperation for World Peace," *International Conciliation*, No. 194, 23-49 (January, 1924).

——————"Americanizing the Treaty," *North American Review*, CCX, 155-171 (August, 1919).

——————"The Betrayal of the Monroe Doctrine," *ibid.*, CCXII, 577-593 (November, 1920).

——————"The League of Nations," *Saturday Evening Post*, CXCVI, Part I, p. 8ff. (August 11, 1923).

"Hiram Johnson's Opening Gun," *Literarfiy Digest*, LXXVIII, 16 (August 4, 1923).

Hodder, Frank H., "Propaganda as a Source of American History," *Mississippi Valley Historical Review*, IX, 3-18 (June, 1922).

Holmes, John Haynes, "Onward, Christian Soldiers," *Nation*, CXV, 435-436 (October 25, 1925).

Holt, Hamilton, "The League of Nations Effective," *The Annals*, XCVI, 1-10 (July, 1921).

Hook, Charles R., "A Business Man's Comments on the Ruhr Episode," *Review of Reviews*, LXVII, 380-382 (April, 1923).

Houston, David F., "An Answer to Pessimists," *Harper's*, CXLIX, 1-9 (June, 1924).

House, Edward M., "America in World Affairs: A Democratic View," *Foreign Affairs*, II, 540-551 (June 15, 1924).

Hoving, John, "My Friend McCarthy," *Reporter*, II, 28-31 (April 25, 1950).

Hudson, Manley O., "The Effect of the Present Attitude of the United States Toward the League of Nations," *The Annals,* CXX, 112-114 (July, 1925).

Hughes, Charles E., "Some Observations on the Conduct of our Foreign Relations," *American Journal of International Law,* XVI, 365-374 (July, 1922).

—————"The Centenary of the Monroe Doctrine," *International Conciliation,* No. 194, 3-22 (January, 1924).

—————"The Foreign Policy of the United States," *Current History,* XVII, 837-845 (February, 1923); XIX, 575-583 January, 1924).

Hull, William I, "The Permanent Court of International Justice as an American Proposition," *The Annals,* CXIV, 147-149 (July, 1924).

Hyde, Charles Cheney, "Charles Evans Hughes," in Samuel F. Bemis (editor), *The American Secretaries of State and Their Diplomacy,* 10 vols. (New York: Alfred A. Knopf, 1927-1929), X, 221-401.

"Isolation is Out, But Realism May Get Respectable," *Saturday Evening Post,* CCXXIII, Part II, 10 (December 16, 1950).

Jenner, William E., "Let Us Safeguard America First," *American Mercury,* LXXX, 39-44 (January, 1955).

Johnson, Hiram W., "Why 'Irreconcilables' Keep Out of Europe," New York *Times,* January 14, 1923.

Kallen, Horace M., "The Covenant of the League of Nations, American Foreign Policy and the Washington Conference," *Journal of International Relations,* XII, 266-279 (October, 1921).

Kay, Hubert, "Boss Isolationist: Burton K. Wheeler," *Life,* X, 110-119 (May 19, 1941).

Keynes, John Maynard, "British Policy in Europe," *New Republic,* XXXIV, 337-338 (May 23, 1923).

Lawrence, D. H., "America, Listen to Your Own," *ibid.,* XXV, 68-70 (December 15, 1920).

La Follette, Belle C., "Substitute for War," *La Follette's Magazine,* 166-167 (November, 1922).

La Follette, Robert M., Jr., "Great Powers Dominate World Court," *ibid.,* p. 22ff. (February, 1926).

Langer, William L., "Isolation, Diplomatic," in E. R. A. Seligman (editor), *Encyclopaedia of Social Sciences,* 15 vols. (New York: The Macmillan Company, 1930-1935), VIII, 352-355.

—————"When German Dreams Come True," *Yale Review,* XXVII, 678-698 (June, 1938).

Lasch, Robert, "The Vanishing Isolationist," *Reporter*, I, 22-23 (November 8, 1949).

Latané, John H., "America's Foreign Policy," *World's Work*, XLI, 505-511 (March, 1921); 619-624 (April, 1921).

——————"Friendship of a Hundred Years," *ibid.*, XLII, 628-632 (October, 1921).

——————"The League of Nations and the Monroe Doctrine," *ibid.*, XXXVII, 441-444 (February, 1919).

Leighton, Etta V., "Patriotism Through Education," *Popular Educator*, XXXVI, 248-249 (January, 1919).

Leighton, George R., "Beard and Foreign Policy," in Howard K. Beale (editor), *Charles A. Beard: An Appraisal* (Lexington: University of Kentucky Press, 1954), 161-184.

Leland, Waldo G., "The Anglo-American Historical Conference," *Historical Outlook*, XIV, 280-281 (October, 1923).

Leopold, Richard W., "The Mississippi Valley and American Foreign Policy, 1890-1941: An Assessment and an Appeal," *Mississippi Valley Historical Review*, XXXVII, 625-641 (March, 1951).

——————"The Problem of American Intervention, 1917: An Historical Retrospect," *World Politics*, II, 405-425 (April, 1950).

Lerner, Max, "The Chances of War—I," New York *Post*, January 23, 1956.

"Let Us Alone," *New Republic*, XXVIII, 121 (September 28, 1921).

Levermore, Charles H., "Anglo-American Diplomatic Relations During the Last Half-Century," *Historical Outlook*, X, 436-446 (November, 1919).

"Lindbergh, Charles A.," in *Current Biography*, II, 42-46 (July, 1941).

"Lindbergh Still Solos in Anonymity," *Newsweek*, XXXIV, 23-25 (December 5, 1949).

Lippmann, Walter, "A Reply to Mr. Hard," *Nation*, CXXII, 60-61 (January 20, 1926).

——————"Assuming We Join," *New Republic*, XX, 145-146 (September 3, 1919).

——————"Mr. Dulles and the Black Cat," Buffalo *Courier-Express* (July 19, 1956).

——————"Notes for a Biography," *New Republic*, LXIII, 250-252 (July 16, 1930).

——————"Philosophy and United States Foreign Policy," *Vital Speeches*, XIV, 242-244 (February 1, 1948).

Livermore, Seward W., "The Sectional Issue in the 1918 Congressional Elections," *Mississippi Valley Historical Review*, XXXV, 29-60 (June, 1948).

Lodge, Henry Cabot, "Foreign Relations of the United States, 1921-1924," *Foreign Affairs*, II, 525-539 (June 15, 1924).

Lovestone, Jay, "America Facing Europe," *Communist*, 7-16 (March, 1927).

—————"The Big Stick Gets Bigger," *Workers' Monthly*, 79-81 (December, 1924).

Lowry, Edward G., "Waiting for Europe to Jell," *New Republic*, XXVI, 314-315 (May 11, 1921).

—————"With the Original Cast," *ibid.*, XXIII, 143-145 (June 30, 1920).

Lubell, Samuel, "Is America Going Isolationist Again?" *Saturday Evening Post*, CCXXIV, Part IV, p. 19ff. (June 7, 1952).

—————"The Politics of Revenge," *Harper's*, CCXII, 29-35 (April, 1956).

—————"Who Votes Isolationist and Why," *ibid.*, CCII, 29-36 (April, 1951).

MacArthur, Douglas, "General MacArthur Makes His Reply," *Life*, XL, 95-108 (February 13, 1956).

McCamant, Wallace, "The American Text-book Controversy," *Landmark*, VI, 83-88 (February, 1924).

McCormick, Medill, "Political Panaceas or Economic Remedies for Europe," *Saturday Evening Post*, CXCV, Part III, p. 22ff. (February 17, 1923).

MacDonald, William, "And Peace Proclaims," *Nation*, CXXVI, 160-161 (February 8, 1928).

McElroy, Robert M., "British-American Diplomacy," *Quarterly Review*, CCXLVII, 203-230 (October, 1926).

MacLeish, Archibald, "The Irresponsibles," *Nation*, CL, 618-623 (May 18, 1940).

McMahon, Patrick, "Uncle Sam, the World's Prize Sucker," *American Mercury*, LXXVIII, 57-62 (February, 1954).

Malin, James C., "United States Foreign Policy Since the World War," *Historical Outlook*, XIX, 13-22 (January, 1928); 61-70 (February, 1928).

Manly, Marie B., "Second Conference on Cure of War," *La Follette's Magazine*, 12-13 (January, 1927).

Mann, Golo, "How Not to Learn from History," *Yale Review*, XLI, 380-390 (Spring, 1952).

Martin, Charles E., "1778 French Treaty an Influence on American Aloofness," *Current History*, XXVII, 645-650 (February, 1928).

May, Henry F., "The Twenties: Normalcy and Revolution," in Richard W. Leopold and Arthur S. Link (editors), *Problems in American History* (New York: Prentice-Hall, Inc., 1952), 788-836

Mencken, Henry L., "Notes on a Moral War," unidentified clipping in William E. Borah MSS, L.C.

Mendelsohn, Maurice, "Uncle Shylock," *Workers' Monthly*, 531-535 (October, 1926).

Mervis, Leonard J., "The Social Justice Movement and the American Rabbi," *American Jewish Archives*, VII, 171-230 (June, 1955).

Miller, David Hunter, "European Insecurity and American Policy," *The Annals*, CXX, 129-133 (July, 1925).

Millis, Walter, "1939 Is Not 1914," *Life*, VII, p. 69ff. (November 6, 1939).

Moore, John Bassett, "An Appeal to Reason," *Foreign Affairs*, XI, 547-588 (July, 1933).

——————"The Monroe Doctrine," *The Annals*, XCVI, 31-33 (July, 1921).

Morgenthau, Hans J., "Policy of the U. S. A.," *Political Quarterly*, XXII, 43-56 (January-March, 1951).

——————"The Primacy of the National Interest," *American Scholar*, XVIII, 207-212 (Spring, 1949).

"Mr. Adams' Oration," *Niles' Weekly Register*, XX, 326-332 (July 21, 1821).

"Mr. Roosevelt's Imaginary League," *New Republic*, XXIII, 348-349 (August 25, 1920).

Niebuhr, Reinhold, "The Cause and Cure of the American Psychosis," *American Scholar*, XXV, 11-20 (Winter, 1955-1956).

Noble, David W., "The New Republic and the Idea of Progress, 1914-1920," *Mississippi Valley Historical Review*, XXXVIII, 387-402 (December, 1951).

Noble, George B., "The Voice of Egypt," *Nation*, CX, 861-862 (January 3, 1920).

"Old Treatment for New Treaties," *Literary Digest*, LXXII, 11-12 (March 11, 1922).

Olgin, M. J., "Locarno-Geneva-Moscow," *Workers' Monthly*, 297-305 (May, 1926).

"Opinion: Mr. Republican's Book," *Time*, LVIII, 23-24 (November 26, 1951).

"Our Isolationists," *Commonweal,* LIII, 315 (January 5, 1951).

"Our Worst Errors in Foreign Policy Catch Up With Us," *Saturday Evening Post,* CCXXII, Part III, 10 (February 11, 1950).

Palmer, Herriott Clare, "How the War Should Affect the Teaching of History," *Proceedings of the Mississippi Valley Historical Association,* X, 304-312 (1918-1921).

Parker, Sir Gilbert, "The United States and the War," *Harper's,* CXXXVI, 521-531 (March, 1918).

Parsons, Talcott, "McCarthyism and American Social Tensions: a Sociologist's Views," *Yale Review,* XLIV, 226-245 (December, 1954).

Paxson, Frederic L., "The Great Demobilization," *American Historical Review,* XLIV, 237-251 (January, 1939).

Perkins, Dexter, "Seeking the Touchstone," *Saturday Review, Diplomats: 1919-1939* (Princeton: Princeton University Press, XXXIV, 19-20 (July 14, 1951).

——————"The Department of State and American Public Opinion," in Gordon A. Craig and Felix Gilbert (editors), *The* 1953), 282-308.

Perry, Ralph Barton, "A Communication," *New Republic,* XXXIV, 96-97 (March 21, 1923).

"Pity the Poor Historian," *Weekly Review,* IV, 484 (May 21, 1921).

Poe, Elisabeth E., "The Peace Treaties of the United States," *Daughters of the American Revolution Magazine,* LIII, 10-17 (January, 1919); 91-96 (February, 1919).

Pratt, Julius W., review article, *American Historical Review,* LVIII, 150-152 (October, 1952).

——————review article, *Mississippi Valley Historical Review,* XLII, 110-111 (June, 1955).

"Public Opinion and the Washington Conference," *New Republic,* XXVIII, 309-310 (November 9, 1921).

Puleston, William D., "How Long Can U.S. Trust Allies?" *U.S. News and World Report,* XXXIX, 102-105 (July 22, 1955).

Reed, Edward B., "Common Sense and the League," *Yale Review,* XIII, 276-288 (January, 1924).

Repplier, Agnes, "On a Certain Condescension in Americans," *Atlantic,* CXXXVII, 577-584 (May, 1926).

Reston, James S., "Why We Irritate Our Allies," *Harper's,* CCII, 29-34 (May, 1951).

Rippy, J. Fred, and Debo, Angie, "The Historical Background of the American Policy of Isolation," in *Smith College Studies in History,* IX, Numbers 3 & 4, 71-165 (April-July, 1924).

Robins, Raymond, "The Outlawry of War—The Next Step in Civilization," *The Annals*, CXX, 154-156 (July, 1925).

Rodgers, William L., "Can Courts and Tribunals Maintain World Peace?" *ibid.*, 69-76

Rogers, Lindsay, "American Politics in 1920," *Contemporary Review*, CXVII, 184-191 (February, 1920).

Roosevelt, Franklin D., "Our Foreign Policy: A Democratic View," *Foreign Affairs*, VI, 573-586 (July 1928).

Root, Elihu, "A Requisite for the Success of Popular Diplomacy," *ibid.*, I, 3-10 (September 15, 1922).

Ruggiero, Guido de, "Liberalism," in *Encyclopaedia of the Social Sciences*, IX, 435-441.

Ruthenberg, C. E., "What is the Election About?" *Workers' Monthly*, 578-579 (November, 1926).

Sands, Theodore, "Do We Need Another 'Great Debate'," *Antioch Review*, XV, 233-245 (Summer, 1955).

Savelle, Max H., "Colonial Origins of American Diplomatic Principles," *Pacific Historical Review*, III, 334-350 (September, 1934).

Schafer, Joseph, "Popular Censorship of History Texts," *Wisconsin Magazine of History*, VI, 450-461 (June, 1923).

Schlesinger, Arthur M., "Points of View in Historical Writing," *Publishers' Weekly*, CXIII, 145-158 (January 14, 1928).

Schlesinger, Arthur M., Jr., "Roosevelt and His Detractors," *Harper's*, CC, 62-68 (June, 1950).

————"The New Isolationism," *Atlantic*, CLXXXIX, 34-38 May, 1952).

Schrader, Frederick F., "The Genesis of the Steuben Society of America," *The Progressive*, 205-208 (February 15, 1927).

Schuman, Frederick L., "Formulas for Foreign Policy," *Nation*, CLXXX, 241-242 (March 19, 1955).

Schuyler, Robert L., "Standing History on its Head," *Bookman*, XLVIII, 570-574 (January, 1919).

Scott, James B., "President Harding's Foreign Policy," *American Journal of International Law*, XV, 409-411 (July, 1921).

————"The Foreign Policy of the United States," *ibid.*, 232-234 (April, 1921).

Sears, Louis M., "The Place of American Diplomatic History in the Curriculum," *Education*, XLVI, 313-318 (January, 1926).

"Senator France," *New Republic*, XXII, 173-175 (April 7, 1920).

"Senator Knowland Answers Twenty Questions on Foreign Policy," *American Mercury*, LXXXI, 5-11 (October, 1955).

Seymour, Charles, "The League of Nations," *Yale Review*, IX, 28-43 (October, 1919).

"Shall Uncle Sam Help Break the Ruhr Deadlock?" *Literary Digest*, LXXVIII, 5-7 (July 28, 1923).

Shotwell, James T., "A Formula for the Briand Treaty," New York *Herald Tribune*, March 20, 1928.

——————"Ten Years After the Armistice—I," *Current History*, XXIX, 175-180 (November, 1928).

Simonds, Frank H., "The Fifteenth Anniversary," *Review of Reviews*, LXXX, 57-65 (August, 1929).

Slosson, Edwin E., "Freezing Out Uncle Sam," *Independent*, CIV, 360-361 (December 11, 1920).

Smuckler, Ralph H., "The Region of Isolationism," *American Political Science Review*, XLIV, 386-401 (June, 1953).

Soule, George H., "Herbert Croly's Liberalism," *New Republic*, LXIII, 253-257 (July 16, 1930).

"South Korea: Account Rendered," *Time*, LXVII, 22 (January 2, 1956).

Sparks, Fred, "The Facts About Formosa," *Reader's Digest*, LXVII, 83-88 (July, 1955).

Stephenson, George M., "The Attitude of Swedish Americans Toward the World War," *Proceedings of the Mississippi Valley Historical Association*, X, 79-94 (1918-1921).

Stevenson, Adlai E., "The Challenge of a New Isolationism," New York *Times*, November 6, 1949.

Strachey, John, "From Isolation to Empire," *Forum*, XCI, 46-49 (January, 1934).

"Striving to Perpetuate the Ancient Grudge," *Spectator*, CXXXI, 278-279 (September 1, 1923).

"Struggling for Peace," *New Republic*, LIX, 193-194 (July 10, 1929).

"Substitute for the League," *ibid.*, XXIV, 58-59 (September 15, 1920).

Taft, Robert A., "Post-war Peace Organization of Nations," *Vital Speeches*, X, 492-495 (June 1, 1944).

Ten Eyck, Andrew, "Are We Out of Europe?" *New Republic*, XXV, 364-366 (February 23, 1921).

"The American and the World," *Round Table*, XLV, 107-117 (March, 1955).

"The Atlantic Report on Washington," *Atlantic*, CXCVIII, 8-10 (July, 1956).

"The Atom: Biggest Show on Earth," *Time*, LXVI, 17-18 (November 28, 1955).

"The Democratic Party and the Liberal Vote," *New Republic*, XXIV, 82-83 (September 22, 1920).

"The Dilemma of France," *Newsweek*, XLVII, 29-35 (January 16, 1956).

"The End of American Isolationism," *New Republic*, I, 9-10 (November 7, 1914).

"The Growing Revolt Against the Treaty," *Nation*, CVIII, 856 (May 31, 1919).

"The Hughes Way to Peace," *Literary Digest*, LXXVIII, 13 (September 22, 1923).

"The K. of C. Historical Commission," *Fortnightly Review*, XXX, 457-458 (December 1, 1923).

"The New Revolt of the Irreconcilables," *Literary Digest*, LXXXIV, 5-7 (January 31, 1925).

"The President and Foreign Aid," *Life*, XL, 30 (July 9, 1956).

"The Presidency of Woodrow Wilson—A Symposium," *Pacific Review*, I, 562-595 (March, 1921).

"The Threat from the Axis," *New Republic*, CIII, 466-467 (October 7, 1940).

"The Verdict on the League," *ibid.*, XXIV, 254-255 (November 10, 1920).

Thompson, William H., "Shall We Shatter the Nation's Idols in School Histories?" *Current History*, XXVII, 619-625 (February, 1928).

"Three Presidents on the League to Enforce Peace," *Independent*, LXXXVI, 264 (May 22, 1916).

"Truman, China, and History," *Life*, XL, 40 (January 23, 1956).

Turner, Frederick J., "Since the Foundation of Clark University, 1889-1924," *Historical Outlook*, XV, 335-342 (November, 1924).

Turner, John Kenneth, "Peace League or War League," *Nation*, CIX, 140-141 (August, 1919).

———————"Standing Behind the President—An Impossibility," *ibid.*, CXI, 370-372 (October 6, 1920).

Turner, Raymond, "Are American School Histories Now Too Pro-British?" *Landmark*, IV, 250-255 (April, 1922).

"Two Years of American Foreign Policy," *Foreign Affairs*, I, 1-24 (March 15, 1923).

Usher, Roland G., "Our Foreign Policy and Peace Problems," *Forum*, LX, 677-686 (December, 1918).

Villard, Oswald Garrison, "Frank A. Munsey: Dealer in Dailies," *Nation*, CXVI, 713-715 (June 20, 1923).

——————"Germany, 1922," *ibid.*, CXV, 116-118 (August 2, 1922).

——————"Henry Cabot Lodge—A Scholar in Politics," *ibid.*, CXIX, 539-541 (November 19, 1924).

——————"The Kansas City Star—A Waning Luminary," *ibid.*, CXV, 684-686 (December 20, 1922).

——————"The Public Ledger: A Muffled Opportunity," *ibid.*, CXVI, 61-64 (January 17, 1923).

——————"The World's Greatest Newspaper," *ibid.*, CXIV, 116-118 (February 1, 1922).

——————"What of the League?" *ibid.*, CXVII, 455-456 (October 24, 1923).

——————"William Randolph Hearst and His Moral Press," *ibid.*, CXVI, 357-361 (March 28, 1923).

Vinson, J. Chal, "The Parchment Peace: The Senatorial Defense of the Four-Power Treaty of the Washington Conference," *Mississippi Valley Historical Review*, XXXIX, 303-314 (September, 1952).

Waithman, Robert, "The American Argument: How Isolationists Help," *Spectator*, CLXXXV, 753-754 (December 29, 1950).

"War is in the Air!" *Workers' Monthly*, 15-16 (November, 1924).

Weinberg, Albert K., "Washington's 'Great Rule' in its Historical Evolution," in Eric F. Goldman (editor), *Historiography and Urbanization: Essays in American History in Honor of W. Stull Holt* (Baltimore: Johns Hopkins Press, 1941), 109-138.

West, George P., "Hiram Johnson After Twelve Years," *Nation*, CXV, 142-144 (August 9, 1922).

West, W. Reed, "Senator Taft's Foreign Policy," *Atlantic*, CLXXXIX, 50-52 (June, 1952).

"West Germany: Year of Disappointment," *Time*, LXVII, 36-37 (May 21, 1956).

Weyl, Walter, "Prophet and Politician," *New Republic*, XIX, 173-178 (July 7, 1919).

"What Europe Wants of America," *Freeman*, VIII, 100-101 (October 10, 1923).

"What Johnson Would Do As President," *Literary Digest*, LXXIX, 8-9 (December 22, 1923).

"What Liberalism May Do," *Nation*, CVII, 692 (December 7, 1918).

"What the Arms Parley Accomplished," *Literary Digest*, LXXII, 7-10 (February 18, 1922).

Whelpley, James D., "An American Political Year," *Fortnightly Review*, CXIV, 969-979 (December, 1923).

"White Man's Burden," *Barron's*, XXXV, 1 (October 10, 1955).

White, William S., "What Bill Knowland Stands For," *New Republic*, CXXXIV, 7-10 (February 27, 1956).

Wickersham, George W., "The Senate and Our Foreign Relations," *Foreign Affairs*, II, 177-192 (December 15, 1923).

Williams, David C., "Does America Have a Policy?" *Twentieth Century*, CLVI, 104-112 (August, 1954).

Wittke, Carl, "Mr. Justice Clarke—A Supreme Court Judge in Retirement," *Mississippi Valley Historical Review*, XXXVI, 27-50 (June, 1944).

Wood, Junius B., "Our Isolationism: Fact or Fiction?" *Nation's Business*, XXXIII, p. 62ff. (October, 1945).

Woodward, C. Vann, review article, *American Historical Review*, LIII, 188 (October, 1947).

Woolsey, Lester H., "The Personal Diplomacy of Colonel House," *American Journal of International Law*, XXI, 706-715 (October, 1927).

"World Without Friends," *Time*, LVI, 9 (December 25, 1950).

Wriston, Henry M., "Washington and the Foundations of American Foreign Policy," *Minnesota History*, VIII, 3-26 (March, (1927).

NOTES

Notes

CHAPTER I

1. Max H. Savelle, "Colonial Origins of American Diplomatic Principels," *Pacific Historical Review,* III (September, 1934), 334-350.

2. Charles F. Adams (ed.), *The Works of John Adams* (10 vols., Boston, 1856), II, 505.

3. Foster Rhea Dulles, *America's Rise to World Power, 1898-1954* (New York, 1954), 6.

4. *Niles' Weekly Register,* XX (July 21, 1821), p. 326ff., quoted in *ibid.,* 6-7.

5. Webster's reaction is described, and his words are quoted in Julius W. Pratt, *A History of United States Foreign Policy* (New York, 1955), 280. For Clay's statement, see John Bassett Moore, *American Diplomacy* (New York, 1905), 139.

6. Dulles, *America's Rise to World Power,* 20. In developing this concept, Professor Dulles relied upon the spade work of Henry Nash Smith, in his *Virgin Land: The American West as Symbol and Myth* (Cambridge, Mass., 1950).

7. James D. Richardson (ed.), *A Compilation of the Messages and Papers of the Presidents, 1789-1902* (10 vols., Washington, 1904), VIII, 301, quoted in Dulles, *America's Rise to World Power,* 20.

8. Dulles, *America's Rise to World Power,* 60.

9. *Ibid.,* 28.

10. George E. Baker (ed.), *The Works of William H. Seward* (3 vols., New York, 1853), I, 250. The passage is quoted in Dulles, *America's Rise to World Power,* 16.

11. *Congressional Record,* 56 Cong., 1 sess., 704.

12. Hay to Roosevelt, August 2, 1903, quoted in Tyler Dennett, *John Hay* (New York, 1934), 406. Professor Dulles stresses the point in his *America's Rise to World Power,* 60.

13. Dulles, *America's Rise to World Power,* 33.

14. *Congressional Record,* 61 Cong., 2 sess., *Appendix,* 119.

15. John M. Blum, *The Republican Roosevelt* (Cambridge, Mass., 1954), p. 125ff. Professor Howard K. Beale to author, December 5, 1954.

16. Roosevelt to Joseph Hodges Choat. Elting E. Morison (ed.), *The Letters of Theodore Roosevelt* (8 vols., Cambridge, Mass., 1951-1954), IV, 1302.

17. Chicago *Tribune*, November 13, 1950.

18. Sumner's remarks are analyzed in Dulles, *America's Rise to World Power*, 13. The speech itself can be found in *Charles Sumner: His Complete Works* (20 vols., Boston, 1900), III, 178-179. Seward is quoted in John Bassett Moore, *A Digest of International Law* (8 vols., Washington, 1906), VI, 23.

19. The statement was made by Harry Elmer Barnes in his composite book, *Perpetual War for Perpetual Peace* (Caldwell, Idaho, 1953), 34.

20. Brooks Adams, "The Spanish War and the Equilibrium of the World," *Forum*, XXV (August, 1898) 641-651.
Professor Dulles discusses Adams's view in his *American Rise to World Power*, 61-62.

CHAPTER II

1. Anonymous soldier to Thomas J. Walsh, n.d. Walsh MSS., Library of Congress.

2. Siegfried Herzog, *The Future of German Industrial Exports* (with an introduction by Herbert Hoover, Vernor Kellogg and Frederic C. Wolcott [Garden City, 1918], introduction.

3. Becker to George Lincoln Burr, August 13, 1918. Burr MSS., Cornell University.

4. Charles P. Howland, *Survey of American Foreign Relations, 1928* (New Haven, 1928), 326.

5. Tarkington to Albert J. Beveridge, June 3, 1918. Beveridge MSS., Library of Congress.

6. Frederic A. Ogg and Charles A. Beard, *National Governments and the World War* (New York, 1919), 589.

7. Walter B. Pillsbury, *The Psychology of Nationality and Internationalism* (New York, 1919), 305-307.

8. "What to do About Mexico," *Collier's*, LIX (May 19, 1917), p. 5ff.

9. Beveridge to C. J. Sharp, October 10, 1917. Beveridge MSS.

10. Louis A. Coolidge to Beveridge, June 11, 1918. Beveridge MSS.

11. Turner spelled out these checks in a paper written in November 1918, and sent apparently to President Wilson shortly thereafter. Turner argued for the creation of international political parties on the ground that sectionalism and especially nationalism would thereby be lessened in the proposed league. See "American Sectionalism and World Organization," *American Historical Review,* XLVII (April, 1942), 545-551.

12. Beveridge to Ernest Bross, October 5, 1918; Beveridge to L. A. Coolidge, October 14, 1918. Beveridge MSS.

13. Lodge to Beveridge, December 3, 1918. Beveridge MSS.

14. Roosevelt to Beveridge, October 31, 1918. Beveridge MSS.

15. *Democracy: Discipline: Peace* (Boston, 1919). 112.

16. Clipping from the Philadelphia *North American,* May 30, 1918 in George W. Norris MSS., Library of Congress.

CHAPTER III

1. Unsigned review in *Nation,* CIX (August 16, 1919), 225-227. Authorship determined by use of copy in Becker MSS., Cornell University.

2. Villard to William E. Dodd, October 6, 1916. Villard MSS., Harvard University.

3. *Nation,* CVIII (February 8, 1919), 193-195.

4. Villard to LaFollette, August 5, 1919. Villard MSS.

5. Walter Lippmann, *The Political Scene* (New York, 1919), 81. The introduction to this book is dated March 23, 1919.

6. Unidentified letter of Lincoln Steffens, dated August 18, 1920. Steffens MSS., Columbia University.

7. Robert K. Murray, *Red Scare: A Study in National Hysteria, 1919-1920.* (Minneapolis, 1955), 53.

8. April 26, 1919. Borah MSS., Library of Congress.

9. Colcord to Villard, December 31, 1919. Villard MSS.

10. "The Growing Revolt Against the Treaty," CVIII (May 31, 1919), 856.

11. George H. Soule, "Herbert Croly's Liberalism, 1920-28," *New Republic*, LXIII (July 16, 1930), 253-257.

12. Roy F. Harrod, *The Life of John Maynard Keynes* (New York, 1951), p. 263ff.

13. Charles A. Beard, "Heroes and Villians of the World War," *Current History*, XXIV (August, 1926), 730-735.

14. Hamilton Fish Armstrong, "Last Time," *Foreign Affairs*, XXIII (April, 1945), 349-377.

15. Villard to R. S. Baker, April 17, 1929. Villard MSS.

CHAPTER IV

1. *Democracy: Discipline: Peace* (Boston, 1919), 112.

2. "The United States and the War." *Harper's*, CXXXVI (March, 1918), 521-531.

3. Beveridge to Mark Sullivan, December 16, 1918; Beveridge to Clarence W. Alvord, July 2, 1921. Beveridge MSS., Library of Congress.

4. *With De Valera in America* (New York, 1932), 120.

5. Borah to Thomas Mannix, n.d. Borah MSS., Library of Congress.

6. Andrew C. Smith to Borah, June 4, 1919. Borah MSS. The case in point refers to Oregon, but Borah's correspondence is studded with similar letters.

7. Frederic L. Paxson, *Postwar Years, Normalcy, 1918-1923* (Berkeley, 1948), 217.

8. "Myth of Egyptian Independence—A British Propaganda," Ms., dated 1920, in the Frank P. Walsh MSS., New York Public Library. Indian leaders of this period frequently wrote in terms suggesting that they closely followed the Soviet line. Nevertheless, The Friends of Freedom for India had Irish names on its executive board, including besides Frank P. Walsh, John Fitzpatrick.

9. Ghose to Walsh, May 17, 1920. Frank P. Walsh MSS.

10. Alice R. Longworth, *Crowded Hours* (New York, 1933), 285.

11. Thomas J. Walsh to John P. Spiridulois, August 27, 1919. Walsh MSS., Library of Congress.

12. Quoted in Arthur M. Schlesinger, "Points of View in Historical Writing," *Publishers' Weekly*, CXIII (January 14, 1928), 145-158.

CHAPTER V

1. William G. Jordan, "What Every American Should Know About the League of Nations," reprinted in *Congressional Record*, 66 Cong., 1 sess., 3670-3680.

2. Quoted in *La Follette's Magazine*, May, 1920, 79.

3. Quoted in *Atlantic Monthly*, CXXXVII (May, 1926), 579.

4. Edward M. House to William E. Dodd, January 8, 1919. Dodd MSS., Library of Congress.

5. Paul S. Conwell to Senator Sheldon P. Spencer, June 8, 1919. Borah MSS., Library of Congress.

6. Captain O. D. Platt to Borah, March 22, 1919. Borah MSS.

7. Beveridge to Borah, January 31, 1919. Borah MSS.

8. Borah to Williams, May 6, 1919. Borah MSS.

9. John M. Blum, "Nativism, Anti-Radicalism, and the Foreign Scare, 1917-1920," Ms. of a paper read before the Boston meeting of the American Historical Association, 1949.

10. Harding to White, August 21, 1920. White MSS., Library of Congress. This letter is very revealing about Harding's character. It is a long defense against White's complaints concerning his platitudes and "school book" phraseology. "I think I know the worst of you," Harding wrote, "and that you do not know the best of me."

11. Harding to Schurman, September 21, 1920. Schurman MSS., Cornell University.

12. The importance of the hyphenate vote is well argued in Samuel Lubell, *The Future of American Politics* (New York, 1951), 135, 147, 170. For a contrary opinion, see Frank Freidel, *Franklin D. Roosevelt: The Ordeal* (Boston, 1954), 88.

13. "Substitutes for the League," *New Republic*, XXIV (September 15, 1920), 58-59.

CHAPTER VI

1. "A Requisite for the Success of Popular Democracy," *Foreign Affairs,* I (September 15, 1922), 3-10.

2. Vandenberg, *The Trail of a Tradition* (New York, 1926), Foreword, VII.

3. Ms. of a speech delivered at Hotel Astor, New York City, November 10, 1925. Hughes MSS., Library of Congress.

4. Emma Wold told William E. Borah of the new organization in a telegram, October 13, 1919. Borah MSS., Library of Congress.

5. Samuel F. McConnell to F. D. R., December 18, 1924. Roosevelt MSS., Group 11. Franklin D. Roosevelt Library, Hyde Park.

6. Ray G. Farrington to F. D. R., December 18, 1924. F. D. Roosevelt MSS.

7. Editorial in New York *Sun,* March 17, 1919.

8. White to Guy T. Viskniskki, September 9, 1921. White MSS., Library of Congress.

9. Oswald G. Villard, "The World's Greatest Newspaper," *Nation,* CXIV (February 1, 1922), 116-118.

10. Constance Drexel, "The Foreign Correspondent," *New Republic,* XXXVII (January 30, 1924), 252-254.

11. Paul U. Kellogg, *Ten Years of the Foreign Policy Association* (n.p., 1929), 14.

12. Robert H. Ferrell, *Peace in Their Time* (New Haven, 1952), 21.

13. Putnam to Villard, January 27, 1928. Villard MSS., Harvard University.

14. A convenient list of the peace societies of the 1920s is in Ferrell, *Peace in their Time,* 13-30.

15. Lyman B. Burbank, "Internationalism in American Thought: 1919-1929" (Ms. doctoral dissertation, New York University, June, 1950), p. 58ff.

16. Ferrell, *Peace in their Time,* 29.

CHAPTER VII

1. Paul Scott Mowrer, *Our Foreign Affairs* (New York, 1924), 340.

2. Quoted in *ibid.,* 21.

3. Address before the American Legion, Kansas City, Missouri. Printed in *Congressional Record,* 67 Cong., 1 sess., 7387-7390

4. *The Memoirs of Herbert Hoover: The Cabinet and the Presidency* (New York, 1952), 27.
   See also Hoover's *American Individualism* (New York, 1922).

5. White to Harding, August 8, 1921; White to Bishop William F. Anderson, August 6, 1921. White MSS., Library of Congress.

6. Quoted in George W. Wickersham, "The Senate and Our Foreign Relations," *Foreign Affairs,* II (December 23, 1923), 177-192.

7. There is a full discussion of the matter in Merlo J. Pusey, *Charles Evans Hughes* (2 vols., New York, 1951), II, 436. For a less generous judgment on Hughes' action, see John Spencer Bassett, *The League of Nations* (New York, 1928), 338-340.

8. Hughes to George W. Wickersham, March 28, 1923. Hughes MSS., Library of Congress.

9. "Our National Dilemma," *New Republic,* XXII (March 24, 1920), 117-118.

10. *Congressional Record,* 67 Cong., 4 sess., 2935.

11. *Letters of a Self-Made Diplomat to His President* (New York, 1926), 180, 254.

12. William E. Dodd to Daniel C. Roper, June 26, 1924. Dodd MSS., Library of Congress.

13. Young, E. Allison to William E. Borah, July 30, 1919. Borah MSS., Library of Congress.

14. Ms. of a speech delivered in Boston Symphony Hall, October 30, 1922. Hughes MSS.

15. Brandegee to Beveridge, October 26, 1921. Beveridge MSS., Library of Congress.

16. *Papers Relating to the Foreign Relations of the United States, 1922* (Washington, 1938), I, 302.

17. *America and the Balance Sheet of Europe* (New York, 1921), 332.

1. Henry F. Pringle, *The Life and Times of William Howard Taft* (2 vols., New York, 1939), II, 926.

2. George H. Blakeslee, "The Foreign Policy of the United States," in Quincy Wright (ed.), *Interpretations of American Foreign Policy* (Chicago, 1930), 3-35.

3. Alexander Bittelman, *Parties and Issues in the Election Campaign* (pamphlet published by the Workers' Party of America. Chicago, 1924).

4. *Loc. cit.*

5. Darcy to Steffens, 1934. Steffens MSS., Columbia University. In 1933 Ella Winter wrote *Red Virtue* which was published in New York.

6. Unmarked and undated newspaper clipping, quoting Steffens, and preserved in the Steffens MSS.

7. George Santayana, *Character and Opinion in the United States* (London, 1920), 219.

8. *New Republic*, XXXIV (March 28, 1923), 139-140.

9. Based on an interview between Eric F. Goldman and Beard. Goldman, *Rendezvous with Destiny* (New York, 1952), 283.

10. Pound to Steffens, n.d. Steffens MSS.

11. This study was made by William G. Rice, Jr., Professor of International Law at the University of Wisconsin. His report on investigations undertaken in Wisconsin and Michigan in the summer of 1925 is in the Calvin Coolidge MSS., Library of Congress.

12. Arthur S. Link, *Woodrow Wilson and the Progressive Era: 1910-1917* (New York, 1954), 180.

13. *Congressional Record*, 68 Cong., 2 sess., 2986.

14. Herbert Feis, *The Diplomacy of the Dollar: First Era, 1919-1932* (Baltimore, 1950), 40-43.

15. Julius W. Pratt, *A History of United States Foreign Policy* (New York, 1955), 564.

16. Ms. of speech delivered November 1, 1928. Schurman MSS., Cornell University.

17. *Congressional Record*, 69 Cong., 1 sess., 2303-2304.

18. "The Great Lesson of the Elections," *North American Review*, CCXX (December, 1924), 193-195.

CHAPTER IX

1. See Frank Freidel, *Franklin D. Roosevelt: The Ordeal* (Boston, 1954), 137.

2. *Wither Bound?* (Lectures at Milton Academy, May, 1926 [Boston, 1926]), 28.

3. *Congressional Record,* 67 Cong., 1 sess., 863-864.

4. J. R. Bolling to Walsh, October 27, 1921. Thomas J. Walsh MSS., Library of Congress.

5. Morison to Albert J. Beveridge, September 28, 1923. Beveridge MSS., Library of Congress.

6. Ms. of a speech, 1923, in the Edward Price Bell MSS., Newberry Library, Chicago, Ill.

7. New York *Times,* October 19, 1924.

8. Statement of Bok in Esther E. Lape (ed.), *Ways to Peace* (New York, 1924), Preface, XI.

9. There is a note in the Roosevelt MSS. to this effect, dictated and signed by the President, September 15, 1944. Franklin D. Roosevelt Library, Hyde Park.

10. Quoted in Frank Freidel, "Franklin D. Roosevelt, Molder of an Opposition Foreign Policy, 1921-1928," ms. of a paper read before the Lexington meeting of the Mississippi Valley Historical Association, 1953.

11. Albert J. Beveridge to George H. Moses, January 31, 1924. Moses to Beveridge, February 2, 1924. Beveridge MSS.

12. Henry James, *Charles W. Eliot* (2 vols., Boston, 1930), II, 288-289.

13. *Congressional Record,* 67 Cong., 4 sess., 4498-4500.

14. *Ibid.,* 68 Cong., 1 sess., 5075.

15. George A. Mahan to Roosevelt, December 15, 1924. All replies to the circular letter of December 4, 1924 are preserved in Group 11 of the Roosevelt MSS.

16. Freidel, "Franklin D. Roosevelt, Molder of an Opposition Foreign Policy."

CHAPTER X

1. "The Will to Peace," address before the League of Nations Non-Partisan Association, January 10, 1927, in Butler, *The Path to Peace* (New York, 1930), 55-68.

2. "Cooperation Through Existing Machinery of the League of Nations," in Esther E. Lape (ed.), *Ways to Peace* (New York, 1924), 277-298.

3. Philip C. Jessup, *Elihu Root* (2 vols., New York, 1938), II, 430.

4. "The Opportunity of the American People," Address before the Foreign Policy Association of Chicago, December 31, 1927, in Butler, *The Path to Peace*, 115-130.

5. Charles A. Beard (ed.), *Whither Mankind* (New York, 1928), 407-408.

6. "Prospects for Peace," *Harper's*, CLVIII (February, 1929), 320-330.

7. Borchard, "International Arbitration and the 'World Court'," printed in Jerome Davis, *Contemporary Social Movements* (New York, 1930), 813-831.

8. *The Memoirs of Herbert Hoover: The Cabinet and the Presidency, 1921-1933* (New York, 1952), 330-332; 337.

9. "The Background of Washington's Foreign Policy," *Yale Review*, XVI (January, 1927), 316-336.

10. Review article in the *Nation*, CXXVI (February 8, 1928), 160-161.

11. Robert H. Ferrell, *Peace in Their Time* (New Haven, 1952), 34; 36.

12. "If War Were Outlawed," *New Republic*, XXXIV (April 25, 1923), 234-235.

13. Quoted in Drew Pearson and Constantine Brown, *The American Diplomatic Game* (Garden City, 1935), 28.

14. *Congressional Record*, 70 Cong., 2 sess., 21.

15. Kellogg to Borah, August 10, 1928. William E. Borah MSS., Library of Congress.

16. *Dollars and World Peace* (New York, 1927), 48.

17. Washington *Post*, January 9, 1929, quoted in Ferrell, *Peace in Their Time*, 247. For McKellar's denial of this statement and an evaluation of his protestation, see *ibid.*, p. 247, fn. 26.

18. U.S. Senate, 70 Cong., 2 sess., *Hearings before the Committee on Foreign Relations, on the General Pact for the Renunciation of War* (Washington, 1928), I, 14.

19. *Congressional Record*, 70 Cong., 2 sess., 1728.

20. Arthur S. Link, *American Epoch: A History of the United States Since the 1890's* (New York, 1955), 290.

CHAPTER XI

1. Julius W. Pratt, *A History of United States Foreign Policy* (New York, 1955), 564.

2. *Ibid.*, 579.

3. Quoted in Arthur J. May, *Europe and Two World Wars* (New York, 1947), 479.

4. Foster Rhea Dulles, *America's Rise to World Power, 1898-1954* (New York, 1954), 163-164.

5. Pratt, *A History of United States Foreign Policy*, 585.

6. P. F. O'Gara to Norris, April 8, 1932. George W. Norris MSS., Library of Congress.

7. John Bassett Moore, "An Appeal to Reason," *Foreign Affairs*, XI (July, 1933), 547-588.

8. Quoted in Arthur M. Schlesinger, Jr., "Roosevelt and His Detractors," *Harper's*, CC (June, 1950), 62-68.

9. *Congressional Record*, 77 Cong., 1 sess., 1677.

10. Speech delivered by Miss Sarah Randazzo of Grover Cleveland High School. Ms. in possession of the present writer.

11. Roosevelt to House, October 19, 1937. Franklin D. Roosevelt MSS. Quoted in Lorraine L. Freeman, "Isolationist Carry-Over, 1933-1937" (M. A. thesis, University of Buffalo, June, 1955), 119.

12. Leonard J. Mervis, "The Social Justice Movement and the American Rabbi," *American Jewish Archives*, VII (June, 1955), 171-230.

13. Address of the Secretary of State, Cordell Hull, at Washington, March 17, 1938. *Peace and War: United States Foreign Policy, 1931-1941* (Washington, 1942), 54-55.

14. Arthur S. Link, *American Epoch: A History of the United States Since the 1890's* (New York, 1955), 474.

CHAPTER XII

1. Speech at Indianapolis, Indiana. Ray Stannard Baker and William E. Dodd (eds.), *The Public Papers of Woodrow Wilson: War and Peace* (2 vols., New York, 1927), I, 606-620.

2. Daniel J. Boorstin, "Selling the President to the People," *Commentary*, XX (November, 1955), 421-427.

3. William A. Lydgate, *What Our People Think* (New York, 1944), 35.

4. *Vital Speeches*, VI (October 15, 1939), 21-23.

5. Winston S. Churchill, *The Second World War: Their Finest Hour* (Boston, 1949), 225-226.

6. Foster Rhea Dulles, *America's Rise to World Power, 1898-1954* (New York, 1954), 191.

7. Samuel I. Rosenman (ed.), *The Public Papers and Addresses of Franklin D. Roosevelt* (13 vols., New York, 1938-1950), 1940 vol., 259-264.

8. My colleague, Professor John T. Horton, chairman of the Department of History and Government at The University of Buffalo, has placed at my disposal his scrapbook for the years 1939-1941, and my information concerning the intimate details of the Buffalo situation in this period is derived from his collection of sources.

9. Frank Delano to John T. Horton, April 12, 1941. Horton Scrapbook.

10. Nathaniel H. Goodrich, "Anti-Semitic Propaganda," *Contemporary Jewish Record*, II (Nov.-Dec., 1939), 20-26; "Nazi Interference in American Affairs," *ibid.*, III (July-August, 1940), 370-380; "Politics and Prejudices," *ibid.* (Nov.-Dec., 1940), 624-626.
See also the factual reports in the *Contemporary Jewish Record*, III (Jan.-Feb., 1940), 55; III (March-April, 1940), 167-169; III (May-June, 1940), 286-287; III (July-August, 1940), 411-412; III (Sept.-Oct., 1940), 530-531; III (Nov.-Dec., 1940), 624-626; IV (Feb., 1941), 56.

11. *Congressional Record*, 77 Cong., 1 sess., 4726.

12. See William L. Langer and S. Everett Gleason, *The Undeclared War, 1940-1941* (New York, 1953), 733.

13. Eric F. Goldman, *Rendezvous With Destiny* (New York, 1952), 378.

14. *Loc. cit.*
For a penetrating discussion of the dilemma of the liberals, see Robert E. Osgood, *Ideals and Self-Interest in America's Foreign Relations* (Chicago, 1953), p. 369ff.

15. "This Is Where I Came In," *New Republic*, XCIII (January 5, 1938), 245-246.

16. Charles A. and Mary R. Beard, *America in Midpassage* (New York, 1939), 452-453.

17. "The Threat from the Axis," *New Republic*, CIII (October 7, 1940), 466-467.

18. Buffalo *Courier-Express*, January 9, 1941.

19. Wayne S. Cole, *America First* (Madison, Wisconsin, 1953), 15-16.

20. Buffalo *Courier-Express*, June 9, 1941.

21. Richard W. Van Alstyne, *American Diplomacy in Action: A Series of Case Studies* (Stanford, California, 1944), 397.

22. For light upon Lindbergh's course of action, see New York *Times*, Sept. 16, 1939, April 24, 1941; *Current Biography*, II (July, 1941), 42-46; "Lindbergh Still Solos in Anonymity," *Newsweek*, XXXIV (December 5, 1949), 23-25. For Lindbergh's 1947 reversal of opinion see New York *Times*, April 14, 1947.

23. New York *Times*, April 24, 1941.

24. *Ibid.*, September 12, 1941.

25. Contemporary notation of a conversation between Nye and Professor Jacob R. Marcus of the Hebrew Union College, spokesman for the Cincinnati Jewish leaders, September 18, 1941. I am grateful to Professor Marcus for sending me a photostatic copy of the notes he jotted down immediately after the meeting with the senator. See also Cincinnati *Enquirer*, September 19, 1941.

26. For an explanation of the origin of this promise, and Robert E. Sherwood's part in persuading the President to make it, see Sherwood's *Roosevelt and Hopkins* (New York, 1948), 191; 201.

27. *Life*, X (May 19, 1941), 118.

28. Quoted in Buffalo *Courier-Express*, March 23, 1941.

29. *Loc. cit.*

30. Arthur H. Vandenberg, Jr., and Joe E. Morris (eds.), *The Private Papers of Senator Vandenberg* (Boston, 1952), 10.

31. Langer and Gleason, *The Undeclared War*, 285-289.

32. Quoted in James P. Warburg, *Turning Point Toward Peace* (pamphlet, New York, 1955), 40.

33. Winston S. Churchill, *The Second World War: The Grand Alliance* (Boston, 1950), 140.

34. Dulles, *America's Rise to World Power*, 198-199.

35. My judgment of the nettled problem of Pearl Harbor has been strongly influenced by the penetrating analysis of Julius W. Pratt in his *A History of United States Foreign Policy* (New York, 1955), 659-662.

CHAPTER XIII

1. Buffalo *Courier-Express,* September 4, 1941.

2. Eric F. Goldman, "What Is Prosperity Doing to Our Political Parties?" *Saturday Review,* XXXVIII (October 8, 1955), p. 9ff.

3. "Philosophy and United States Foreign Policy," *Vital Speeches,* XIV (February 1, 1948), 242-244.
   See also Lippmann's *Essays in The Public Philosophy* (Boston, 1955), 22-24.

4. "The Cause and Cure of the American Psychosis," *American Scholar,* XXV (Winter, 1955-56), 11-20.

5. "The Irresponsibles," *Nation,* CL (May 18, 1940), 618-623.

6. *United States War Aims* (Boston, 1944), 73-95; 208-209.

7. P. 291.

8. William A. Lydgate, *What Our People Think* (New York, 1944), 47.

9. Quoted in Foster Rhea Dulles, *America's Rise to World Power, 1898-1954* (New York, 1954), 211.

10. "A Post-War Peace Organization of Nations," speech delivered at Cleveland, Ohio, May 6, 1944. *Vital Speeches,* X (June 1, 1944), 492-495.
    John P. Armstrong, "The Enigma of Senator Taft and Foreign Policy," *Review of Politics,* XVII (April, 1955), 206-231.

11. Julius W. Pratt, *A History of United States Foreign Policy* (New York, 1955), 695.

12. *The Memoirs of Cordell Hull* (2 vols., New York, 1948), II, 1314-1315.

13. Pratt, *A History of United States Foreign Policy,* 696.

14. Quoted in Dulles, *America's Rise to World Power,* 215.

15. Arthur H. Vandenberg, Jr., and Joe A. Morris (eds.), *The Private Papers of Senator Vandenberg* (Boston, 1952), Preface, XIX.

16. *Ibid.,* 200.

17. *Ibid.,* 138; 141.

18. Buffalo *Evening News,* December 30, 1955.

19. *Loc. cit.*

20. Chester Wilmot, *The Struggle for Europe* (London, 1952), 652.

21. Pratt, *A History of United States Foreign Policy,* p. 690, fn. 18.

22. *War or Peace* (New York, 1950), 89-91.

23. New York *Times,* April 14, 1947.

24. See Walter Millis (ed.), *The Forrestal Diaries* (New York, 1951), 47.
Joseph C. Grew, *Turbulent Era* (2 vols., Boston, 1952), II, 1445.

CHAPTER XIV

1. James P. Warburg, *Turning Point Toward Peace* (pamphlet, New York, 1955), 53-54.

2. See New York *Times,* May 6, 1956.

3. *Time,* LXVII (January 9, 1956), 26.

4. *Barron's,* XXXV (October 10, 1955), 1.

5. William G. Carleton, "A New Era in World Politics?" *Virginia Quarterly Review,* XXXI (Summer, 1955), 353-372.

6. Raymond Cartier, "Pourquoi les Américains sont-ils détestés," Paris *Match,* March 24, 1956, p. 20ff.

7. *Newsweek,* XLVII (January 16, 1956), 29.

8. Cartier, "Pourquoi les Américains sont-ils détestés." *Time,* LXVII (May 21, 1956), 35-36.

9. Peter Cottrell in New York *Herald Tribune,* January 23, 1956.

10. "How Long Can United States Trust Allies?" *U. S. News and World Report,* XXXIX (July 22, 1955), 102-105.

11. Julius W. Pratt, review article in *Mississippi Valley Historical Review,* XLII (June, 1955), 110-111.

12. See Dennis W. Brogan, "The American Enigma," *Spectator,* CXCV (August 19, 1955), 257-258, Max Beloff, "The Foundations of American Policy—II," *ibid.,* CXCIV (March 4, 1955), 247-249.

13. Reinhold Niebuhr, "The Cause and Cure of the American Psychosis," *American Scholar,* XXV (Winter, 1955-56), 11-20.

14. Summarized from tables listed in Harry E. Barnes (ed.), *Perpetual War for Perpetual Peace* (Caldwell, Idaho, 1953), 35.

15. Julius W. Pratt, *A History of United States Foreign Policy* (New York, 1955), 574.

16. Samuel Lubell, "The Politics of Revenge," *Harper's,* CCXII (April, 1956), 29-35.

17. Quoted in New York *Times,* May 6, 1956.

18. Buffalo *Courier-Express,* June 8, 1956.

19. New York *Times,* June 10, 1956.

20. Warburg, *Turning Point Toward Peace,* 15.

21. *Behind Closed Doors—The Secret History of the Cold War* (New York, 1950), 12-13.

22. Eric F. Goldman, "What Is Prosperity Doing to Our Political Parties?" *Saturday Review,* XXXVIII (October 8, 1955), p. 9ff.

23. Quoted in New York *Times,* May 6, 1956.

24. *Time,* LXVI (November 28, 1955), 17.

25. Nat S. Finney in Buffalo *Evening News,* January 5, 1956.

26. Editorial in New York *Times,* May 6, 1956.

27. Samuel F. Bemis, *A Diplomatic History of the United States* (rev. ed., New York, 1950), 921.

28. James F. Byrnes, *Speaking Frankly* (New York, 1947), 188-191.

29. Thomas A. Bailey, *The Man in the Street* (New York, 1948), 255.

30. Foster Rhea Dulles, *America's Rise to World Power, 1898-1954* (New York, 1954), 234.

31. *The United States in World Affairs, 1947-1948* (New York, 1948), 78.

32. *Memoirs by Harry S. Truman: Years of Trial and Hope* (Garden City, 1956), 102.

33. Ernest B. Haas and Allen S. Whiting, *Dynamics of International Relations* (New York, 1956), 258; 289.

34. Elie Abel in New York *Times,* May 6, 1956.

35. Arthur H. Vandenberg, Jr., and Joe A. Morris (eds.), *The Private Papers of Senator Vandenberg* (Boston, 1952), p. 406ff.

1. *Memoirs by Harry S. Truman: Years of Trial and Hope* (Garden City, 1956), II, 61-62.

2. *Ibid.*, 67-80.

3. New York *Times*, August 6, 1949. See also Richard H. Rovere and Arthur M. Schlesinger, Jr., *The General and the President* (New York, 1951), 211.

4. Arthur H. Vandenberg, Jr., and Joe A. Morris (eds.), *The Private Papers of Senator Vandenberg* (Boston, 1952), 525.

5. Dorothy Fosdick, *Common Sense and World Affairs* (New York, 1955), p. 11ff.

6. In assessing the influence of the China Lobby, I have drawn heavily on the detailed investigations of Max Ascoli, Philip Horton, and Charles Wertenbaker in their articles, "The China Lobby," *Reporter,* VI (April 15, 1952), 2-24; (April 29, 1952), 4-24.

7. *While You Slept* (New York, 1951), 176-177; 184.

8. "Truman, China and History," *Life*, XL (January 23, 1956), 40.

9. "Is America Going Isolationist Again?" *Saturday Evening Post*, CCXXIV, pt. 4 (June 7, 1952), p. 19ff.

10. Rovere and Schlesinger, *The General and the President*, 226.

11. *Ibid.*, 235.

12. Review article, *American Historical Review*, LIV (January, 1949), 382-386.

13. *Pearl Harbor: The Story of the Secret War* (New York, 1947), 329-330. C. Vann Woodward in *American Historical Review*, LIII (October, 1947), 188.

14. *America's Second Crusade* (Chicago, 1950), 353.

15. See review articles by Ruhl Bartlett in *Mississippi Valley Historical Review*, XXXIX (December, 1952), 580-581; and Julius W. Pratt in *American Historical Review*, LVIII (October, 1952), 150-152.

16. Harry E. Barnes (ed.), *Perpetual War for Perpetual Peace* (Caldwell, Idaho, 1953), 659.

17. Arthur M. Schlesinger, Jr., "Roosevelt and his Detractors," *Harper's* CC (June, 1950), 62-68.

18. *American Foreign Policy* (Indianapolis, 1946), 56.

19. See Niebuhr's *Christianity and Power Politics* (New York, 1946 ed.), Preface, IX-X; *The Irony of American History* (New York, 1952), 2; 22; "The Cause and Cure of the Ameri-

can Psychosis," *American Scholar,* XXV (Winter, 1955-56), 11-20.
For a penetrating evaluation of Niebuhr's influence, see Robert E. Osgood, *Ideals and Self-Interest in America's Foreign Relations* (Chicago, 1953), 381-383.

20. *U.S. Foreign Policy: Shield of the Republic* (Boston, 1943), 46.

21. *American Diplomacy, 1900-1950* (Chicago, 1951), 99; 102-103. Kennan enlarged upon his thesis in his *Realities of American Foreign Policy* (Princeton, 1954). Unlike some of the more extreme realists, Kennan understood that the pressure of public opinion, always playing upon policy-makers, frequently forced departures from realistic diplomacy. But, he queries, can we afford too many failures simply because our democratic process is at the root of them?

22. See Morgenthau's *In Defense of the National Interest* (New York, 1951), 28-29; 31; 100; 241-242; his "Policy of the U. S. A.," *Political Quarterly,* XXII (January, 1951), 43-56; and his "The Primacy of the National Interest," *American Scholar,* XVIII (Spring, 1949), 207-212. For the relationship between the realists and the isolationists, see *Catholic World,* CLXIII (July, 1946), 297; Foster Rhea Dulles, "Wellsprings of American Policy," *Saturday Review,* XXXV (October 11, 1952), 22-23; George A. Lundberg, "American Foreign Policy in the Light of the National Interest at the Mid-Century," in Barnes (ed.), *Perpetual War for Perpetual Peace,* 557-623; and Harry E. Barnes in *ibid.,* 658-659.

23. "Giddy Minds and Foreign Quarrels," *Harper's,* CLXXIX (September, 1939), 337-351.

24. Arthur S. Link, *American Epoch: A History of the United States Since the 1890's* (New York, 1955), 646.

25. Fosdick, *Common Sense and World Affairs,* 42.

26. Adlai E. Stevenson, "The Challenge of a New Isolationism," New York *Times,* November 6, 1949.
Foreign Policy Bulletin, XXIX (May 12, 1950), 1.

27. Quoted in *Foreign Policy Bulletin,* XXIX (May 5, 1950), 1.

28. Broadcast from New York City, October 19, 1950, in Herbert Hoover, *Addresses upon the American Road,* 1948-1950 (Stanford, 1951), 91-99.

29. Broadcast from New York City, December 20, 1950, in Herbert Hoover, *Addresses Upon the American Road, 1950-1955* (Stanford, 1955), 3-10.

30. *Nation,* CLXXI (December 30, 1950), 688.

31. *Vital Speeches,* XVII (March 1, 1951), 260.

32. Sumner Welles, *Seven Decisions That Shaped History* (New York, 1950), 223-224.

33. Foster Rhea Dulles, *America's Rise to World Power, 1898-1954* (New York, 1954), 263.

34. Chicago *Tribune*, December 28, 1950.

35. McGeorge Bundy in *Reporter*, V (December 11, 1951), 37-38.

36. Douglass Cater in *ibid.* (September 18, 1951), 26.

37. John P. Armstrong, "The Enigma of Senator Taft and American Foreign Policy," *Review of Politics*, XVII (April, 1955), 206-231.

38. Robert A. Taft, *A Foreign Policy for Americans* (Garden City, 1951), *passim*.
    Senator Taft summarized his basic points on p. 66.
    See also Arthur M. Schlesinger, Jr., "The New Isolationism," *Atlantic*, CLXXXIX (May, 1952), 34-38.

39. Quoted in Charles A. Willoughby and John Chamberlain, *MacArthur, 1941-1951* (New York, 1954), 421-422.

40. Douglas MacArthur, "General MacArthur Makes His Reply," *Life*, XL (February 13, 1956), 95-108.

41. Quoted in Eric F. Goldman, "What is Prosperity Doing to our Political Parties?" *Saturday Review*, XXXVIII (October 8, 1955), p. 9ff.

42. LXVIII (January 2, 1956), 22.

43. William S. White, "What Bill Knowland Stands For," *New Republic*, CXXXIV (February 27, 1956), 7-10.

44. Fred Sparks, "The Facts About Formosa," *Reader's Digest*, LXVII (July, 1955), 83-88.

45. Charles B. Marshall, *Limits of Foreign Policy* (New York, 1954), 122-123.

46. Quoted in *Senate Report* No. 1716, 84 Cong., 2 sess., Calendar No. 1649, 31.

47. Chicago *Tribune*, May 25, 1955.

48. Quoted in *ibid.*, November 2, 1950.

49. *Ibid.*, May 6, 1947.

50. Goldman, "What is Prosperity Doing to our Political Parties?"

51. "How Long Can U.S. Trust Allies?" *U.S. News and World Report*, XXXIX (July 22, 1955), 102-105.

52. Niebuhr, "The Cause and Cure of the American Psychosis."

53. Nathaniel Weyl, *The Battle Against Disloyalty* (New York, 1951), 180.

54. Link, *American Epoch: A History of the United States Since the 1890's*, 644.

55. Goldman, "What is Prosperity Doing to our Political Parties?"

56. John Hoving, "My Friend McCarthy," *Reporter*, II (April 25, 1950), 28-31.

57. Link, *American Epoch: A History of the United States Since the 1890's*, 646.

58. *Congressional Record*, 82 Cong., 1 sess., p. 6561ff.

59. Robert J. Donovan, *Eisenhower: The Inside Story* (New York, 1956), 151-153.

60. *Congressional Record*, 82 Cong., 1 sess., 6557.

61. My information on these splinter groups has been drawn largely from the exposures of Jack Steele, Scripps-Howard staff writer, whose articles written for the New York *World-Telegram* have been reprinted in a pamphlet, "Peddlers of Hate," n.p.; n.d.

62. *Atlantic*, CXCVIII (July, 1956), 10.

63. Washington *Post*, May 7, 1956.
    New York *Times*, May 6, 1956.

64. *Time*, LXVII (February 27, 1956), 27.

65. New York *Times*, February 23, 1956; accounts of eye witnesses to the meeting interviewed by the writer.

CHAPTER XVI

1. "The President and Foreign Aid," *Life*, XL (July 9, 1956), 30. See also *Time*, LXVIII (July 9, 1956), 12-13.

2. Walter Lippmann, "Mr. Dulles and the Black Cat," in Buffalo *Courier-Express*, July 19, 1956.

3. "The Shifting Strategy of American Defense and Diplomacy," *Virginia Quarterly Review*, XXIV (Summer, 1948), 321-335. See also review article by Julius W. Pratt in *Mississippi Valley Historical Review*, XLII (June, 1955), 110-111.

4. "The Cause and Cure of the American Psychosis," *American Scholar*, XXV (Winter, 1955-56), 11-20.

INDEX

Index

497